Exploring Advances in Interdisciplinary Data Mining and Analytics:

New Trends

David Taniar
Monash University, Australia

Lukman Hakim Iwan
RMIT University, Australia

Information Science
REFERENCE

Managing Director:	Lindsay Johnston
Senior Editorial Director:	Heather Probst
Book Production Manager:	Sean Woznicki
Development Manager:	Joel Gamon
Development Editor:	Myla Harty
Acquisitions Editor:	Erika Gallagher
Typesetters:	Adrienne Freeland, Chris Shearer
Print Coordinator:	Jamie Snavely
Cover Design:	Nick Newcomer, Greg Snader

Published in the United States of America by
Information Science Reference (an imprint of IGI Global)
701 E. Chocolate Avenue
Hershey PA 17033
Tel: 717-533-8845
Fax: 717-533-8661
E-mail: cust@igi-global.com
Web site: http://www.igi-global.com

Copyright © 2012 by IGI Global. All rights reserved. No part of this publication may be reproduced, stored or distributed in any form or by any means, electronic or mechanical, including photocopying, without written permission from the publisher. Product or company names used in this set are for identification purposes only. Inclusion of the names of the products or companies does not indicate a claim of ownership by IGI Global of the trademark or registered trademark.

Library of Congress Cataloging-in-Publication Data

Exploring advances in interdisciplinary data mining and analytics : new trends
/ David Taniar and Lukman Hakim Iwan, editors.
    p. cm.
Includes bibliographical references and index.
Summary: "This book is an updated look at the state of technology in the
field of data mining and analytics offering the latest technological,
analytical, ethical, and commercial perspectives on topics in data mining"--
Provided by publisher.
  ISBN 978-1-61350-474-1 (hbk.) -- ISBN 978-1-61350-475-8 (ebook) -- ISBN 978-
1-61350-476-5 (print & perpetual access) 1. Data mining. 2. Web usage
mining. I. Taniar, David. II. Iwan, Lukman Hakim, 1976-
  QA76.9.D343E997 2012
  006.3'12--dc23
                          2011043675

British Cataloguing in Publication Data
A Cataloguing in Publication record for this book is available from the British Library.

All work contributed to this book is new, previously-unpublished material. The views expressed in this book are those of the authors, but not necessarily of the publisher.

Table of Contents

Detailed Table of Contents

Social networks and collaborative tagging systems are rapidly gaining popularity as a primary means for storing and sharing data among friends, family, colleagues, or perfect strangers as long as they have common interests. del.icio.us3 is a social network where people store and share their personal bookmarks. Most importantly, users tag their bookmarks for ease of information dissemination and later look up. However, it is the friendship links, that make del.icio.us a social network. They exist independently of the set of bookmarks that belong to the users and have no relation to the tags typically assigned to the bookmarks. To study the interaction among users, the strength of the existing links and their hidden meaning, we introduce implicit links in the network. These links connect only highly "similar" users. Here, similarity can reflect different aspects of the user's profile that makes her similar to any other user, such as number of shared bookmarks, or similarity of their tags clouds. The authors investigate the question whether friends have common interests, they gain additional insights on the strategies that users use to assign tags to their bookmarks, and they demonstrate that the graphs formed by implicit links have unique properties differing from binomial random graphs or random graphs with an expected power-law degree distribution.

Chapter 2

Social Bookmarking Systems (SBS) have been widely adopted in the last years, and thus they have had a significant impact on the way that online content is accessed, read and rated. Until recently, the decision on what content to display in a publisher's web pages was made by one or at most few authorities. In contrast, modern SBS-based applications permit their users to submit their preferred content, to comment on and to rate the content of other users and establish social relations with each other. In that way, the vision of the social media is realized, i.e. the online users collectively decide upon the interestingness of the available bookmarked content. This paper attempts to provide insights into the dynamics emerging from the process of content rating by the user community. To this end, the paper proposes a framework for the study of the statistical properties of an SBS, the evolution of bookmarked content popularity and user activity in time, as well as the impact of online social networks on the content consumption behavior of individuals. The proposed analysis framework is applied to a large dataset collected from digg, a popular social media application.

The authors present and evaluate an approach to trend detection in social bookmarking systems using a probabilistic generative model in combination with smoothing techniques. Social bookmarking systems are gaining major interest among researchers in the areas of data mining and Web intelligence, since they provide a large amount of user-generated annotations and reflect the interest of millions of people. Based on a vast corpus of approximately 150 million bookmarks found at del.icio.us, the authors analyze bookmarking and tagging patterns and discuss evidence that social bookmarking systems are vulnerable to spamming. They present a method to limit the impact of spam on a trend detector and provide conclusions as well as directions for future research.

The Web is a continuously evolving environment, since its content is updated on a regular basis. As a result, the traditional usage-based approach to generate recommendations that takes as input the navigation paths recorded on the Web page level, is not as effective. Moreover, most of the content available online is either explicitly or implicitly characterized by a set of categories organized in a taxonomy, allowing the page-level navigation patterns to be generalized to a higher, aggregate level. In this direction, the authors present the Frequent Generalized Pattern (FGP) algorithm. FGP takes as input the transaction data and a hierarchy of categories and produces generalized association rules that contain transaction items and/or item categories. The results can be used to generate association rules and subsequently recommendations for the users. The algorithm can be applied to the log files of a typical Web site; however, it can be more helpful in a Web 2.0 application, such as a feed aggregator or a digital library mediator, where content is semantically annotated and the taxonomic nature is more complex, requiring us to extend FGP in a version called FGP+. The authors experimentally evaluate both algorithms using Web log data collected from a newspaper Web site.

In this paper the authors present a novel method for finding optimal split points for discretization of continuous attributes. Such a method can be used in many data mining techniques for large databases. The method consists of two major steps. In the first step search space is pruned using a bisecting region method that partitions the search space and returns the point with the highest information gain based on its search. The second step consists of a hill climbing algorithm that starts with the point returned by the first step and greedily searches for an optimal point. The methods were tested using fifteen attributes from two data sets. The results show that the method reduces the number of searches drastically while identifying the optimal or near-optimal split points. On average, there was a 98% reduction in the number of information gain calculations with only 4% reduction in information gain.

Chapter 6

Amit Saxena, G G University, India
John Wang, Montclair State University, USA

This paper presents a two-phase scheme to select reduced number of features from a dataset using Genetic Algorithm (GA) and testing the classification accuracy (CA) of the dataset with the reduced feature set. In the first phase of the proposed work, an unsupervised approach to select a subset of features is applied. GA is used to select stochastically reduced number of features with Sammon Error as the fitness function. Different subsets of features are obtained. In the second phase, each of the reduced features set is applied to test the CA of the dataset. The CA of a data set is validated using supervised k-nearest neighbor (k-nn) algorithm. The novelty of the proposed scheme is that each reduced feature set obtained in the first phase is investigated for CA using the k-nn classification with different Minkowski metric i.e. non-Euclidean norms instead of conventional Euclidean norm (L2). Final results are presented in the paper with extensive simulations on seven real and one synthetic, data sets. It is revealed from the proposed investigation that taking different norms produces better CA and hence a scope for better feature subset selection.

Chapter 7

Jing Lu, Southampton Solent University, UK
Weiru Chen, Shenyang Institute of Chemical Technology, China
Malcolm Keech, University of Bedfordshire, UK

Structural relation patterns have been introduced recently to extend the search for complex patterns often hidden behind large sequences of data. This has motivated a novel approach to sequential patterns post-processing and a corresponding data mining method was proposed for Concurrent Sequential Patterns (ConSP). This article refines the approach in the context of ConSP modelling, where a companion graph-based model is devised as an extension of previous work. Two new modelling methods are presented here together with a construction algorithm, to complete the transformation of concurrent sequential patterns to a ConSP-Graph representation. Customer orders data is used to demonstrate the effectiveness of ConSP mining while synthetic sample data highlights the strength of the modelling technique, illuminating the theories developed.

    Yanwu Yang, Chinese Academy of Sciences, China
    Christophe Claramunt, Naval Academy Research Institute, France
    Marie-Aude Aufaure, Ecole Centrale Paris, France
    Wensheng Zhang, Chinese Academy of Sciences, China

Spatial personalization can be defined as a novel way to fulfill user information needs when accessing spatial information services either on the web or in mobile environments. The research presented in this paper introduces a conceptual approach that models the spatial information offered to a given user into a user-centered conceptual map, and spatial proximity and similarity measures that considers her/his location, interests and preferences. This approach is based on the concepts of similarity in the semantic domain, and proximity in the spatial domain, but taking into account user's personal information. Accordingly, these spatial proximity and similarity measures could directly support derivation of personalization services and refinement of the way spatial information is accessible to the user in spatially related applications. These modeling approaches are illustrated by some experimental case studies.

    Shichao Zhang, Zhejiang Normal University and Zhongshan University, China

In this paper, the author designs an efficient method for imputing iteratively missing target values with semi-parametric kernel regression imputation, known as the semi-parametric iterative imputation algorithm (SIIA). While there is little prior knowledge on the datasets, the proposed iterative imputation method, which impute each missing value several times until the algorithms converges in each model, utilize a substantially useful amount of information. Additionally, this information includes occurrences involving missing values as well as capturing the real dataset distribution easier than the parametric or nonparametric imputation techniques. Experimental results show that the author's imputation methods outperform the existing methods in terms of imputation accuracy, in particular in the situation with high missing ratio.

    Zhengzheng Xing, Simon Fraser University, Canada
    Jian Pei, Simon Fraser University, Canada

Finding associations among different diseases is an important task in medical data mining. The NHANES data is a valuable source in exploring disease associations. However, existing studies analyzing the NHANES data focus on using statistical techniques to test a small number of hypotheses. This NHANES data has not been systematically explored for mining disease association patterns. In this regard, this paper proposes a direct disease pattern mining method and an interactive disease pattern mining method to explore the NHANES data. The results on the latest NHANES data demonstrate that these methods can mine meaningful disease associations consistent with the existing knowledge and literatures. Furthermore, this study provides summarization of the data set via a disease influence graph and a disease hierarchical tree.

This paper presents a new approach using data mining techniques, and in particular a two-stage architecture, for classification of Peer-to-Peer (P2P) traffic in IP networks where in the first stage the traffic is filtered using standard port numbers and layer 4 port matching to label well-known P2P and NonP2P traffic. The labeled traffic produced in the first stage is used to train a Fast Decision Tree (FDT) classifier with high accuracy. The Unknown traffic is then applied to the FDT model which classifies the traffic into P2P and NonP2P with high accuracy. The two-stage architecture not only classifies well-known P2P applications, but also classifies applications that use random or non-standard port numbers and cannot be classified otherwise. The authors captured the internet traffic at a gateway router, performed pre-processing on the data, selected the most significant attributes, and prepared a training data set to which the new algorithm was applied. Finally, the authors built several models using a combination of various attribute sets for different ratios of P2P to NonP2P traffic in the training data.

Chapter 12

In multidimensional database mining, constrained multidimensional patterns differ from the well-known frequent patterns from both conceptual and logical points of view because of a common structure and the ability to support various types of constraints. Classical data mining techniques are based on the power set lattice of binary attribute values and, even adapted, are not suitable when addressing the discovery of constrained multidimensional patterns. In this chapter, the authors propose a foundation for various multidimensional database mining problems by introducing a new algebraic structure called cube lattice, which characterizes the search space to be explored. This chapter takes into consideration monotone and/or anti-monotone constraints enforced when mining multidimensional patterns. The authors propose condensed representations of the constrained cube lattice, which is a convex space, and present a generalized levelwise algorithm for computing them. Additionally, the authors consider the formalization of existing data cubes, and the discovery of frequent multidimensional patterns, while introducing a perfect concise representation from which any solution provided with its conjunction, disjunction and negation frequencies. Finally, emphasis on advantages of the cube lattice when compared to the power set lattice of binary attributes in multidimensional database mining are placed.

Chapter 13

Special clustering algorithms are attractive for the task of grouping an arbitrary shaped database into several proper classes. Until now, a wide variety of clustering algorithms for this task have been proposed, although the majority of these algorithms are density-based. In this chapter, the authors extend the dissimilarity measure to compatible measure and propose a new algorithm (ASCCN) based on the results. ASCCN is an unambiguous partition method that groups objects to compatible nucleoids, and merges these nucleoids into different clusters. The application of cluster grids significantly reduces the computational cost of ASCCN, and experiments show that ASCCN can efficiently and effectively group arbitrary shaped data points into meaningful clusters.

In many data mining applications, both classification and clustering algorithms require a distance/similarity measure. The central problem in similarity based clustering/classification comprising sequential data is deciding an appropriate similarity metric. The existing metrics like Euclidean, Jaccard, Cosine, and so forth do not exploit the sequential nature of data explicitly. In this chapter, the authors propose a similarity preserving function called Sequence and Set Similarity Measure (S3M) that captures both the order of occurrence of items in sequences and the constituent items of sequences. The authors demonstrate the usefulness of the proposed measure for classification and clustering tasks. Experiments were conducted on benchmark datasets, that is, DARPA'98 and msnbc, for classification task in intrusion detection and clustering task in web mining domains. Results show the usefulness of the proposed measure.

Introducing spatial data into multidimensional models leads to the concept of Spatial OLAP (SOLAP). Existing SOLAP models do not completely integrate the semantic component of geographic information (alphanumeric attributes and relationships) or the flexibility of spatial analysis into multidimensional analysis. In this chapter, the authors propose the GeoCube model and its associated operators to overcome these limitations. GeoCube enriches the SOLAP concepts of spatial measure and spatial dimension and take into account the semantic component of geographic information. The authors define geographic measures and dimensions as geographic and/or complex objects belonging to hierarchy schemas. GeoCube's algebra extends SOLAP operators with five new operators, i.e., Classify, Specialize, Permute, OLAP-Buffer and OLAP-Overlay. In addition to classical drill-and-slice OLAP operators, GeoCube provides two operators for navigating the hierarchy of the measures, and two spatial analysis operators that dynamically modify the structure of the geographic hypercube. Finally, to exploit the symmetrical representation of dimensions and measures, GeoCube provides an operator capable of permuting dimension and measure. In this chapter, GeoCube is presented using environmental data on the pollution of the Venetian Lagoon.

Yongsong Qin, Guangxi Normal University, China
Shichao Zhang, Zhejiang Normal University, China & University of Technology, Australia
Chengqi Zhang, University of Technology, Australia

The k-nearest neighbor (kNN) imputation, as one of the most important research topics in incomplete data discovery, has been developed with great successes on industrial data. However, it is difficult to obtain a mathematical valid and simple procedure to construct confidence intervals for evaluating the imputed data. This chapter studies a new estimation for missing (or incomplete) data that is a combination of the kNN imputation and bootstrap calibrated EL (Empirical Likelihood). The combination not only releases the burden of seeking a mathematical valid asymptotic theory for the kNN imputation, but also inherits the advantages of the EL method compared to the normal approximation method. Simulation results demonstrate that the bootstrap calibrated EL method performs quite well in estimating confidence intervals for the imputed data with kNN imputation method.

Preface

INTRODUCTION

With rapid progress of mobile device technology, a huge amount of moving objects data can be geathed easily. This data can be collected from cell phones, GPS embedded in cars or telemetry attached on animals. Location of mobile phone user can be collected by locating the cell connected with their mobile phone. In addition, The GPS-equiped vehicle can be tracked.

Useful knowledge can be discovered automatically from moving objects data. For example mobile phone logs can be extracted to form a pattern of mobile user movement. This pattern can be used to improve services of network providers. In addition, GPS-equipped vehicle position data can also be extracted to discover frequent routes of vehicle movements. This pattern can be used for traffic management.

Moving object data containd spatial and temporal elements. Spatial data is related with geographic aspects, whereas temporal data related with the time properties. Unlike the traditional relational databases, relation among spatial objects is more complex. Ester, Kriegel and Sander (2001) state three basic types of spatial relations, namely: topological, distance, and direction relations (as illustrated in Figure 1). The first type is based on the positions of two objects. The position of these objects could be classified as inside, disjoint or overlaps. For example: *x* disjoints *y*, *x* overlaps *y*. Distance relation type is based on the distance between two objects. The distance between two objects can be compared with a defined number. As a result the distance between two objects can be classified as equal, lower than or greater than the specified number. Finally, Direction relation of spatial data is based on the directions of the two objects. In order to do that, one of the two objects is defined as the source object. The direction between two objects depends on the source object. For example: *z* north *x* means that object *z*, as a source object, is located north of object *x*.

Figure 1. Spatial relations

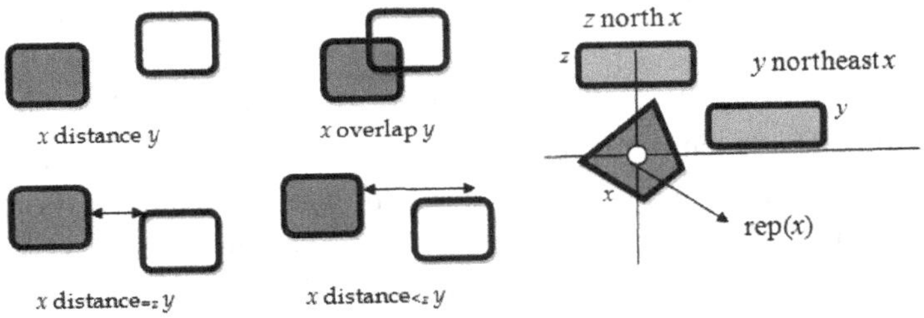

The characteristics of spatial data is unique compared to the other databases. In relation to data mining field, Buttenfiled et al. (2000) argued three characteristic of spatial data, namely: huge data, collected cyclically & data foundation. Most of spatial data is obtained automatically by the system rather than input manually, which is retrieved cyclically. The problem of cycled data is that the time information may not be mentioned. Thus, the first challenge before the mining process begins is to mine the cycle pattern of the data. The last characteristic is that spatial data mostly contains raw data.

Mining pattern from spatio-temporal databases is more challenging than on numerical data. Because of the spatio-temporal data complexity, primitive data mining techniques cannot be applied straightforward as those for numerical data. In this section, we highlight data mining techniques for discovering usefull knowledge from spatio-temporal data including: movement pattern, trajectory pattern, relative motion pattern, location prediction and trajectory clustering.

MOVEMENT PATTERN MINING

Mobile user movement data is the data, which can be obtained from users or cars, which carry or embed geographic track devices, such as, mobile phone and GPS. Based on this data, patterns can be discovered, including most people are likely to move from A to B, or the group of people who have same trajectory route on daily movement. Basically, there are two types of pattern, namely: location-based and user-based movement pattern.

Location-Based Movement Pattern

In location-based pattern mining, we are interested on the object or location, rather than the mobile user who visited the location. An example of pattern that we can discover is: Location A will be visited after Location B. It means that most mobile users visit location B and then Location A.

Three related works on location-based pattern mining are: 2-step walking pattern, Location Link Pattern and Periodic Pattern. First, Goh & Taniar (2006) proposed a 2-step walking pattern mining method. This pattern is taken from a mobile user database, which contains the x- and y-coordinates indicating the location of the user at a particular time. The knowledge derived from this pattern is that with the 2-given steps, the mobile user walks from one point to another point. The points represent the location of interest.

The process of 2-step walking pattern mining works as follows: Initially, the user movement data set and the location of interest become a data source for this process. Next, the coordinate location in the user movement data set is converted to a relevant location of interest, with regard to the user-defined minimum duration value. The result of this conversion is shown in Table 1. Then, using the user defined minimum weight value, the user location database is analyzed to generate user location summary database. Finally, the user location summary database is posted to the Walking-Matrix or Walking-Graph algorithm to generate the pattern.

The following walk-through illustrates the working of the 2-step walking pattern mining using the Walking-Matrix algorithm. This example is taken from Goh and Taniar (2006) experiments. Firstly, the user location database in Table 1 is generated from a user movement database. For example, user movement database of u_1 is converted to l_1 and l_2 at $time$ 1. It implies that user u_1 stayed in both location l_1 and l_2 at $time$ 1. Let the $min\_dur = 3$ and $min\_weight = 0.5$. Next, using the min_weight value, the user location database is analyzed to form a user location summary database (see Table 2). The user move-

Table 1. User location database

T	u_1	u_2	u_3	u_4	u_5	u_6
1	l_1, l_2	l_5	l_1, l_2	l_1, l_2	l_2	l_2
2	l_1, l_2	l_5	l_1, l_2	l_1, l_2	l_2	l_2
3	l_1, l_2	l_5	l_1, l_2	l_1, l_2	l_2	l_2
4	l_2	l_2, l_4	l_2	l_2	l_2, l_4	l_3
5	l_2	l_2, l_4	l_2	l_2	l_2, l_4	l_3
6	l_2	l_2, l_4	l_2	l_2	l_2, l_4	l_3
7	l_2, l_4	l_3	l_2, l_4	l_3	l_5	l_6, l_3
8	l_2, l_4	l_3	l_2, l_4	l_3	l_5	l_6, l_3
9	l_2, l_4	l_3	l_2, l_4	l_3	l_5	l_6, l_3
10	l_2	l_6, l_3	l_3	l_6, l_3	l_1, l_2	l_1, l_2
11	l_2	l_6, l_3	l_3	l_6, l_3	l_1, l_2	l_1, l_2
12	l_2	l_6, l_3	l_3	l_6, l_3	l_1, l_2	l_1, l_2
13	l_3	l_2	l_6, l_3	l_2	l_2	l_2
14	l_3	l_2	l_6, l_3	l_2	l_2	l_2
15	l_3	l_2	l_6, l_3	l_2	l_2	l_2
16	l_5	l_3	l_2	l_2, l_4	l_3	l_2, l_4
17	l_5	l_3	l_2	l_2, l_4	l_3	l_2, l_4
18	l_5	l_3	l_2	l_2, l_4	l_3	l_2, l_4
19	l_2, l_4	l_6, l_3	l_2, l_4	l_1, l_2	l_6, l_3	l_6, l_3
20	l_2, l_4	l_6, l_3	l_2, l_4	l_1, l_2	l_6, l_3	l_6, l_3
21	l_2, l_4	l_6, l_3	l_2, l_4	l_1, l_2	l_6, l_3	l_6, l_3

ment $l_x \rightarrow l_y$ implies that user moves from l_x to l_y. However, if $x=y$ the user movement is removed because there is no significant movement of that user. Lastly, the Walking-Matrix algorithm is used for mining 2-step walking pattern from the user location summary database. Walking-Matrix is shown in Table 3. The weight of each 2-step walking pattern is counted. If the *weight* is greater than *min_weight*, these patterns are valid, otherwise pruned.

Next, location-based pattern mining is Location Link Pattern (Iwan & Safar, 2009). The pattern consists of location sequences, which have a link. For example, as we can see from Figure 2 that all mobile users (u_1, u_2, u_3, u_4, u_5) visit childcare before go to school. From that fact, it is possible to summarize that childcare and school have a strong relationship. In other word, there is a link between school and childcare. Iwan & Safar (2009) proposed an algorithm for mining location link pattern from mobile user movement data. This algorithm discovers location link pattern from daily user movement pattern. The well-known Apriori algorithm (Agrawal et al., 1993) is used to generate the patterns. The algorithm for mining location link patterns consists of 2 steps: generating 1-location links and mining location link patterns. The 1-location link pattern mining algorithm uses the daily mobile user movement pattern from all users (instead of a single user) in the mobile user movement database.

The location link pattern algorithm is the main process for mining location link patterns. This algorithm requires the location set 1-LLP, the set of daily mobile movement pattern *DMP*, and the *min_user* threshold as inputs. Initially, 1-LLP is stored to a valid user movement 1 variable, VUM_1. After that, *k-*

Table 2. The result from analysis of a User location summary database

u_1	u_2	u_3	u_4	u_5	u_6
$l_1 \to l_2$ $l_2 \to l_2$ $l_2 \to l_2$ $l_2 \to l_4$ $l_2 \to l_2$ $l_4 \to l_2$ $l_2 \to l_3$ $l_3 \to l_5$ $l_5 \to l_2$ $l_5 \to l_4$	$l_5 \to l_2$ $l_5 \to l_4$ $l_2 \to l_3$ $l_4 \to l_3$ $l_3 \to l_6$ $l_3 \to l_3$ $l_6 \to l_2$ $l_3 \to l_2$ $l_2 \to l_3$ $l_3 \to l_6$ $l_3 \to l_3$	$l_1 \to l_2$ $l_2 \to l_2$ $l_2 \to l_2$ $l_2 \to l_4$ $l_3 \to l_3$ $l_4 \to l_3$ $l_3 \to l_6$ $l_3 \to l_3$ $l_6 \to l_2$ $l_3 \to l_2$ $l_2 \to l_2$ $l_2 \to l_4$	$l_1 \to l_2$ $l_2 \to l_2$ $l_2 \to l_3$ $l_3 \to l_6$ $l_3 \to l_3$ $l_6 \to l_2$ $l_3 \to l_2$ $l_2 \to l_2$ $l_2 \to l_4$ $l_2 \to l_1$ $l_2 \to l_2$ $l_4 \to l_1$ $l_4 \to l_2$	$l_2 \to l_2$ $l_2 \to l_4$ $l_2 \to l_5$ $l_4 \to l_5$ $l_5 \to l_1$ $l_5 \to l_2$ $l_1 \to l_2$ $l_2 \to l_2$ $l_2 \to l_3$ $l_3 \to l_6$ $l_3 \to l_3$	$l_2 \to l_3$ $l_3 \to l_6$ $l_3 \to l_3$ $l_6 \to l_1$ $l_6 \to l_2$ $l_3 \to l_1$ $l_3 \to l_2$ $l_1 \to l_2$ $l_2 \to l_2$ $l_2 \to l_2$ $l_2 \to l_4$ $l_2 \to l_6$ $l_2 \to l_3$ $l_4 \to l_6$ $l_4 \to l_3$

Table 3. A walking-matrix

	l_1	l_2	l_3	l_4	l_5	l_6
l_1	*	5				
l_2	1	*	6	7	1	1
l_3	1	4	*		1	6
l_4	1	2	3	*		1
l_5	1	4		2	*	
l_6	1	4				*

Figure 2. An example of a mobile user movement

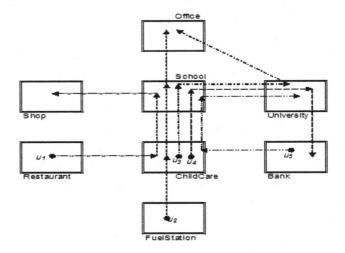

valid user movement candidate VUC_k is generated by self joining each member of VUM_{k-1}. Because daily mobile user movement patterns are classified as sequential data, the joining step is similar to that of the sequential-pattern mining algorithm (Srikant and Agrawal, 1996). Next, if the member of VUC_k is one of the *DMP* subsets, then the number of users is counted. After that, if the number of users is greater than or equal to the *min_user* threshold, then this candidate is considered to be a valid user movement. This process runs recursively until no more valid user movements can be generated. The output of this algorithm is a set of location link patterns.

Another movement pattern based on location is the Periodic Pattern. Mamoulis et al. (2004) proposed a periodic pattern mining method from spatio-temporal data. Spatio-temporal data in this pattern is daily routes over a regular time interval. For example, people are using similar routes from home to office everyday. The routes may not be exactly the same. The route consists of a set of location points. The location points are close to each other if they have the same cluster. The periodic mining {*AB*C*} means that people move to *B* from *A*. After that, they do not move to any other location point. Finally, they move to *C*.

The process of mining the periodic patterns consists of two stages: discovering frequent 1-patterns and discovering a longer pattern. In the first stage, the user movement data is clustered for each time-stamp. Traditional clustering technique such as DBSCAN (Ester et al., 1996) can be used. The frequent 1-pattern is generated by checking the number of points in the cluster. The frequent 1-pattern is valid if the number of points of that cluster is greater than the minimum support threshold, *min_sup*.

In the second stage of mining the periodic pattern, the frequent longer patterns are discovered. Mamoulis et al. (2004) proposed two methods for generating frequent longer pattern: bottom-up and top-down approaches. While the bottom-up approach called STPMine1, which is based on the *Apriori-TID* algorithm (Agrawal and Srikant, 1994), the top-down approach is called SPTMine2 Algorithm. The frequent 1-pattern is the input for both algorithms. In the bottom-up approach, candidate $\underline{k}$ pattern is generated by joining segment ID of pairs ($k-1$) pattern. After that, each candidate pattern is checked to determine whether or not its number of segments is greater than *min_sup*. Finally, in order to make sure that the region of that candidate is still clustered, the pattern is validated.

User-Based Movement Pattern

Unlike location-based pattern mining, user-based movement patterns are interested in the movement itself. One existing pattern mining algorithm based on user movement is group pattern mining. Group pattern is a relatively new in the data mining research area. Initially, Wang et al. (2003) and Wang et al. (2006) proposed two group pattern mining algorithms: AGP and VG-Growth algorithms. Subsequently, using a spherical location summarization method, Wang et al. (2004) improved the efficiency of the group pattern mining algorithm on a large number of users and lengthy logging duration in order to reduce the processing time required to mine 2-valid groups. Subsequently, Wang et al. (2008) revised the AGP and VG-Growth algorithms in order to mine max-valid groups. The revised algorithms are called: AMG and VGMax algorithms.

A group pattern can be extracted from mobile user movement dataset. A user movement dataset is a set of time series of locations for each user. The locations are defined as a set of *x*- and *y*-coordinates, while a time series is defined as the time when the user moved to that location. Each record of this dataset contains a triple set of fields: *t*, *x*, and *y* denoting *x*- and *y*- coordinates is the location of the user at time *t*. An example of a user movement data set is shown in Figure 3.

Figure 3. User movement dataset

U_1				U_2				U_3				U_4				U_5		
t	x	y		t	x	y		t	x	y		t	x	y		t	x	y
0	6	14		0	24	40		0	2	21		0	54	97		0	22	97
1	57	18		1	5	16		1	54	45		1	19	40		1	66	2
2	31	59		2	51	14		2	66	61		2	62	73		2	27	30
3	41	56		3	82	17		3	34	21		3	49	75		3	53	53
4	49	20		4	59	48		4	71	94		4	37	7		4	93	84
5	61	28		5	38	58		5	7	48		5	96	76		5	17	62
6	33	11		6	55	72		6	44	24		6	95	55		6	44	8
7	7	71		7	60	22		7	10	89		7	64	25		7	88	13
8	67	3		8	82	72		8	88	94		8	0	75		8	48	41
9	16	4		9	63	25		9	63	38		9	88	24		9	1	17

A group pattern is defined as a group of users whose distance is less than the maximum distance between them and the duration of time for which they remain together is greater than, or equal to, the minimum duration. Both maximum distance and minimum duration are the user-defined thresholds.

The distance between users is calculated using Euclidean distance whose formulation is shown:

$$d\left(\left(x_1, y_1\right),\left(x_2, y_2\right)\right) = \sqrt{\left(\left(x_1 - x_2\right)^2 + \left(y_1 - y_2\right)^2\right)}$$

For example, the distance between u_1 and u_2 at time 1 denoted by $d(u_1, u_2) = 52$.

In addition, the validity of the group pattern is determined by its *weight* value. The *Weight* of group pattern P is defined as:

$$weight\left(P\right) = \frac{\sum_{i=1}^{n}\left|S_i\right|}{N}$$

where:

- P = group pattern
- S_i = Valid segment of i
- n = number of valid segment
- N = number of time points in database

A group pattern is called a valid group if the weight of the group pattern is greater than the *min_weight* user-defined threshold.

Consider the following user movement dataset in Table 4. The problem to be solved in this example is to find a group of users which remained together for a period of time. Let the maximum distance, *max_dis* = 3, the minimum duration, *min_dur* = 3 and the minimum weight, *min_wei* = 6. As we can see from Table 4, the distance between users u_1 and u_2 from time 1 to time 3 and from time 7 to time 10 is less then *max_dis*. Therefore, u_1 and u_2 fulfill the distance requirements of group pattern. The other requirement is the duration. The durations of u_1 and u_2 from time 1 to time 3 and time 7 to time 10 are 3 and 4 respectively. Therefore, u_1 and u_2 have a duration that is greater than or equal to *min_dur*. The last requirement is weight. The total number of weights of u_1 and u_2 being closed to each other is 7 which is greater than *min_wei*. Therefore, u_1 and u_2 are classified as one group because both users satisfied all of the requirements of group pattern.

The generation of 2-valid group patterns using the AGP algorithm above is inefficient. The number of 2-valid groups is huge, especially when there are a large number of users. In order to solve this problem, Wang et al. (2004) proposed an efficient method for generating 2-valid group patterns which uses a spherical location summarization approach. In Wang et al. (2004) experiments, the execution time of the AGP algorithm using the SLS method is less than that using the AGP algorithm without the SLS method.

A maximal valid group is a set of valid groups without redundancy. Although the AGP algorithm above mines a complete a set of valid groups from user movement dataset, the AGP algorithm produces some redundant valid groups. In order to resolve the redundancy valid group problem, Wang et al. (2008) proposed a maximal valid group mining algorithm for discovering group patterns without redundant valid groups.

Another work of user-based pattern mining is User Link Pattern (Iwan & Safar, 2009). As we can see from Table 4 that mobile user u_3, u_4 and u_5 have the same daily movement. They go to school before going to campus and go to childcare before going to school. Based on this fact, it is possible to conclude that u_3, u_4 and u_5 may have a strong relationship.

The user link pattern mining algorithm consists of two procedures. The first procedure generates user link candidates. With this procedure, a $(n-1)$-valid user link is joined to obtain an n-user link candidate. The join process is based on the prefix join method. Two or more users are joinable if they have the same prefix user link set. Otherwise, these users are not joinable.

The second procedure in the mining step is the user link candidate validation algorithm. This procedure validates whether or not the size of location movement intersection between them is greater than or equal to *min_loc*. This procedure consists of two steps: location intersection base generation and intersection step. In the first step, the first user in user link candidate set becomes the location base intersection. Specifically, each subset of the first user location segment where has size greater than equal to *min_loc*, is used as a location intersection process. In the second step, each member of location intersection base set intersects with the other user location segments in user link candidate. If the size of location movement intersection result is greater than or equal to *min_loc*, than this user link candidate is valid.

Table 4. User movement dataset example

Time	u_1	u_2	$d(u_1,u_2)$
1	(4, 7)	(4, 6)	1
2	(4, 8)	(4, 8)	0
3	(4, 7)	(4, 6)	1
4	(70, 50)	(90,50)	20
5	(70, 51)	(90, 53)	20
6	(70,52)	(90,52)	20
7	(74, 57)	(74, 56)	1
8	(74, 58)	(74, 58)	0
9	(74, 57)	(74, 56)	1
10	(74, 58)	(74, 58)	0

TRAJECTORY PATTERN MINING

Trajectories are sequences that consist of spatial and temporal data about movements. Giannotti et al. (2007) defined trajectory as spatio-temporal sequences (ST-sequence): $<(x_0,y_0,t_0),....,(x_n,y_n,t_n)>$. x_i and y_i are the position coordinate relative to the orgin whereas t_i is the time stamp for the position information. The example of trajectory data $<(x_0,y_0,t_0), (x_1,y_1,t_1), (x_2,y_2,t_2), (x_3,y_3,t_3), (x_4,y_4,t_4), (x_5,y_5,t_5)>$ can be illustrated in Figure 4.

In order to obtain a usefull knowledge from movement data above, Giannotti et al. (2007) proposed an algorithm for mining spatio-temporal pattern called a Trajectory Pattern (T-Pattern). T-pattern is formed by examining a set of each trajectories data which has visited almost the same point of interest on similiar times. T-Pattern is defined as a couple (s,a), where:

$$s = \left\langle \left(x_0, y_0\right),...,\left(x_n, y_n\right)\right\rangle$$

is a sequence of $n+1$ locations

$$a = \left\langle \alpha_1,...,\alpha_n\right\rangle$$

are the transision times such that

$$\alpha_1 = \Delta t_i = t_i - t_{i-1}.$$

$$T = S_0 \xrightarrow{\alpha_1} S_1 \xrightarrow{\alpha_2} ... \xrightarrow{\alpha_n} S_n$$

A T-pattern T will be discovered in a subseqeunce S if it matches the following two conditions:

- Each (x_i, y_i) in T, matches a point $(x_i^{,}, y_i^{,})$ in S
- The transition times in T are similar to those in S.

Figure 4. Trajectory data illustration

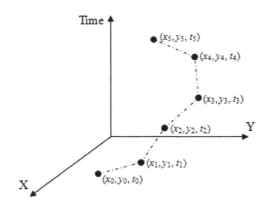

In fact, it is hard to find exact the same spatial location (x, y) and transition times occurs often on trajectory data. However, the same area is often represented by close location coordinate and the same behavior is often indicated by the close times of trajectory data.

This problem can be tackled by the notion of spatial neigborhood and temporal tolerance (Giannotti et al., 2007). Spatial neigborhood is used for defining the location area whereas temporal tolerance is used for defining transisiton times. The two pints will be defined as one area if one and another point falls within a spatial neigborhood and. The two transition times will be defined as one time if the diferences between the two is less than or equal to T.

Furthermore, as generating all T-patterns is too computational intensive, the concept of regions of interest is used (Giannotti et al., 2007). Region of interest is used for defining similar point of interest. The region is built from set of point which have same neighbors. Otherwise, the point is not region if they do not have a neighbors. Furthermore, Giannotti et al. (2007) used density-based algorithm for finding regions of interest.

With region of interest approach, Giannotti et al. (2007) proposed algorithm for mining T-pattern with pre-defined region interest and dynamic region of interest (*RoI*). Pre-defined *RoI* technique is used if the region interest is given whereas dynamic *RoI* technique is used if the region of interest is unknown.

RELATIVE MOTION PATTERN

Motion pattern can be formed based on the relative motion (REMO) concept proposed by Laube et al. (2004). There are three basic REMO concept, namely: constance, concurrence, and trend-setter. First, pattern forms constance when sequence moving point object (MPOs) moves on the same motion attribute for given period of time. Next, concurrence can be formed when the number of MPOs have the same motion attributes on the given period of time. The last concept is trend-setter. This pattern is formed when one MPO encourages of other MPOs moving to the same direction.

The basic REMO concept disregards the information space. In fact, information space is important to detect patterns. For example, trend-setter of one MPO in location A influences other MPOs in location B. However, if location A has diferent information space with location B, we cannot say that MPO in location A is trend-setter the MPOs in location B. Therefore, information space is essensial for detecting a pattern.

In order to solve the above problem, Laube et al. (2004) extended the basic REMO concept for mining spatially constrained REMO patterns, namely: track, flock, and leadership. First, constance pattern with spatial constraint is defined as track. Next, concurence pattern with spatial pattern forms a flock. Lastly, leadership can be build by combining trend-setter and spatial constraints. The extended of basic REMO concept is illustrated in Figure 5.

Furthermore, Laube et al. (2004) proposed spatial REMO pattern convergence. This concept is to detect groups of MPOs aggregating in space and time. Convergence is built when groups of MPOs from any location move to the same circular region of the given radius. The convergence pattern is illustrated in Figure 6. A convergence pattern is discovered from 4 MPOs for p_2, p_3, p_5, and p_6.

In order to detect aggreration pattern, Laube proposed a spatial data mining approach. Aggreration pattern including flocking behaviour and convergence in spatial-temporal data. The apporach is based on object motion properties and spatial constraint.

Figure 5. An extended basic REMO concept: track, flock, leadership

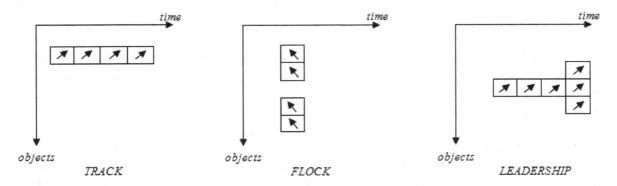

Figure 6. Convergence pattern

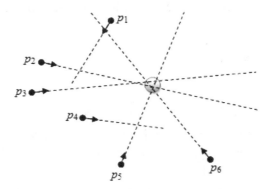

LOCATION PREDICTION

Location prediction for moving object can be classified as based on one moving object and based on all moving objects' trajectories. Based on one moving object, location prediction is defined as a prediction of the next location on a defined timestamp. This location prediction is based on the past movement history. Consider Figure 7 taken from Tao et al. (2004) as an example. Assume we want to predict the location at the next time 4 timestamp based on 2 past movements history at time 1 and time 2. The white dots in Figure 7 illustrate the location prediction at the next 4 timestamp at time 1 and time 2 respectively.

However in reality most of movements are not linear. As illustrated in Figure 7, object *o* is moving not linear showed in the black dots. In order to predict location from non-linear movement, Tao et al. (2004) proposed algorithm for predicting location from non-linear movement patterns. Specifically, Tao et al. proposed three contributions to solve the problems on location prediction, namely: system architecture, the recursive motion function and the STP Tree (spatio-temporal prediction tree).

The first, Tao et al. (2004) assumed the system architecture is client-server (refer to Figure 8). The client maintains the location path history and calculates its single motion function continuously whereas the server receives information from all clients, stores the path history and delivers location prediction based on user query.

Figure 7. Location prediction

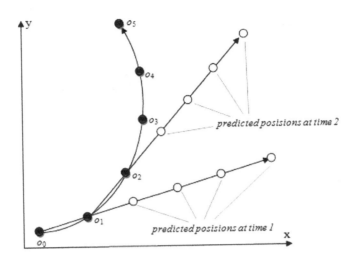

Location prediction is based on both pattern and path history. Therefore it can predict location in the future, even the current time is longer than the requested time. It is focused on time when the prediction requested. Similar with Tao et al. (2004), Jeung et al. (2008) concerned on non-linear moving objects which can predict the longest time.

One of techniques for predicting location based on all moving object's trajectories is WhereNext (Monreale et al., 2009). WhereNext predicts locations using frequent trajectory pattern of other moving objects. The moving object is likely to follow a pattern where most moving objects formed a pattern.

In order to predict locations, WhereNext has four main steps, namely: data selection, trajectory pattern (T-pattern) mining, T-pattern Tree building, and prediction. In the data selection step, a location area and a time period are selected. The purpose of this step is for taking only the moving object that passing the location area in some period of time. After that the selected data is extracted for mining the frequent movement pattern. The process of extracting data is using trajectory patterns algorithm called T-patterns. In the third step, T-pattern Tree is constructed by combining T-patterns in a prefix tree. Finally, the future location of moving object can be predicted by using T-pattern Tree. An example of T-pattern Tree of Table 4's T-Pattern is shown in Figure 9 which is taken from Moonreale et al. (2009).

Figure 8. System architecture on location prediction

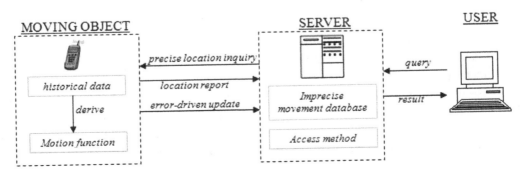

Table 4. T-pattern

<(), C> <(15,20), B)> *supp*:20	<(), C> <(10,12), D> *supp*:35
<(), A> <(4,20), A)> *supp*: 26	<(), C> <(70,90), C> *supp*:21
<(), A> <(9,12), C)> <(10,12), D> *supp*:21	<(), F> <(2,51), D> *supp*:37
<(), A> <(9,12), B)> <(10,56), E> *supp*:21	<(), A> <(9,15), B> *supp*:31
<(), A> <(9,12), C)> <(15,20), B> *supp*:10	<(), B> <(8,70), E> *supp*:28

Figure 9. T-pattern tree construction

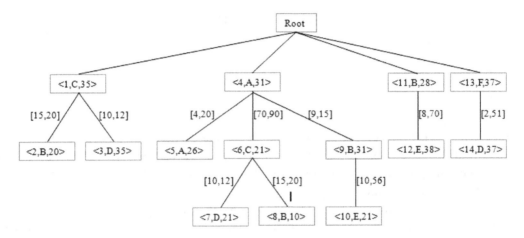

The T-Pattern: $<(), loc_1> <(t_{min}, t_{max}), loc_2>$ sup:n
Where:

- loc_1 = *the source location*
- loc_2 = *the destination location*
- t_{min} = *the minimum time interval from source to destination location*
- t_{max} = *the maximum time interval from source to destination location*
- n = *the support value of this pattern*

TRAJECTORY CLUSTERING

There are two types of clustering spatio-temporal data, namely: distance-based and shape-based clustering. Distance-based clustering aims to discover a group of objects moving together whereas shape-based clustering aims to discover similar shape trajectories.

Unlike existing algorithms where cluster trajectories as a whole, Lee et al. (2007) proposed a partition and group framework for clustering trajectories. Clustering trajectories as a whole may lead to miss essential information. In particular, common behavior may not be discovered because all trajectories can move in different directions. An example of this problem can be seen in Figure 10. As a whole

Figure 10. An example of a common trajectory

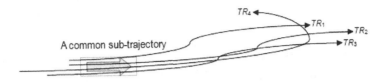

trajectory, all trajectories (TR_1, TR_2, TR_3, and TR_4) move to totally different directions. As a result, the cluster is not discovered. However, the cluster will be discovered when we partition the trajectories into sub-trajectories. As can be seen, the dotted rectangle is a common sub-trajectories which form a cluster.

In order to tackle the problem above, Lee et al. (2007) proposed a trajectory clustering algorithms, TRACLUS, based on partition-and-group framework. According to this framework, TRACLUS discovers the common sub-trajectories in two steps, namely: partitioning and grouping. In the partitioning step, the characteristic points are identified by using the minimum description length (MDL) technique. The characteristic point classified a point where the behavior of trajectory changes dramatically. After that a trajectory partition is formed at every characteristic point. In the grouping step, the clusters are discovered by applying density-based clustering, DBSCAN. After that, overall movement of the trajectory partitions is described. This common sub-trajectory forms a cluster.

CONCLUSION

The purpose of this preface was to highlight data mining techniques for spatio-temporal data. We show that the usefull knowledge can be discovered by extracting spatio-temporal data. This knowlege including: movement pattern, trajectory pattern, relative motion pattern, location prediction and trajectory clustering.

David Taniar
Monash University, Australia

Lukman Hakim Iwan
RMIT University, Australia

REFERENCES

Agrawal, R., Imielinski, T., & Swami, A. (1993). Mining association rules between sets of items in large databases. In the *Proceedings of the 1993 ACM SIGMOD International Conference on Management of Data*. pp. 207-216. Washington, D.C., United States. ACM.

Agrawal, R., & Srikant, R. (1994). Fast Algorithms for Mining Association Rules in Large Databases. *Proceedings of the 20th International Conference on Very Large Data Bases*. pp 487-499. Santiago, Chile. Morgan Kaufmann Publishers Inc.

Buttenfield, B., Gahegan, M., Miller, H., & Yuan, M. (2000). Geospatial Data Mining and Knowledge Discovery. Technical report, University Consorsium for Geographic Information Science Research White Paper. Washington, D.C. Available online at http://www.ucgis.org/priorities/research/research_white/2000%20Papers/emerging/gkd.pdf.

Ester, M., Kriegel, H., & Sander, J. (2001). *Algorithms and Applications for Spatial Data Mining. Geographic Data Mining and Knowledge Discovery, Research Monograph in GIS.* Taylor and Francis.

Ester, M., Kriegel, H.-P., Sander, J. & XU, X. (1996). A density-based algorithm for discovering clusters in large spatial databases with noise, *Second International Conference on Knowledge and Data Mining.* pp 226-231. Portland, Oregon. AAAI Press.

Giannotti, F., Nanni, M., Pinelli, F., & Pedreschi, D. (2007). Trajectory pattern mining. *Proceedings of the 13th ACM SIGKDD international conference on Knowledge discovery and data mining.* pp 330-339. San Jose, California, USA. ACM.

Goh, J., & Taniar, D. (2006). *On Mining 2 Step Walking Pattern from Mobile Users. Computational Science and Its Applications - ICCSA 2006* (pp. 1090–1099). Glasgow, UK: Springer.

Iwan, L.H. and Safar, M. (2009). Pattern mining from movement of mobile users, *Journal Ambient Intelligence and Humanized Computing, 1- 4(2010)*, pp. 295-308.

Jeung, H., Liu, Q., Shen, H. T., & Zhou, X. (2008). A Hybrid Prediction Model for Moving Objects. *In Proceedings of the 24th International Conference on Data Engineering (ICDE '08).* pp 70-79. Cancun, Mexico. IEEE.

Laube, P., Kreveld, M., & Imfeld, S. (2004). Finding REMO — Detecting Relative Motion Patterns in Geospatial Lifelines. *Developments in Spatial Data Handling: Proceddings of the 11th International Symposium on Spatial Data Handling.* pp. 201-214.

Lee, J., Han, J., & Whang, J. (2007). Trajectory clustering: a partition-and-group framework. In *Proceedings of the ACM SIGMOD International Conference on Management of data* (SIGMOD '07). pp 593-604. Beijing, China, ACM.

Mamoulis, N., Cao, H., Kollios, G., Hadjieleftheriou, M., Tao, Y., & Cheung, D. W. (2004). Mining, indexing, and querying historical spatiotemporal data. *Proceedings of the 10th ACM SIGKDD International Conference on Knowledge Discovery and Data Mining.* pp. 236-245. Seattle, WA, USA. ACM.

Monreale, A., Pinelli, F., Trasarti, R., & Giannotti, F. (2009). WhereNext: a location predictor on trajectory pattern mining. *Proceedings of the 15th ACM SIGKDD international conference on Knowledge discovery and data mining* (KDD '09). pp 637-646. Paris, France, ACM.

Srikant, R., & Agrawal, R. (1996). Mining sequential patterns: Generalizations and performance improvements. *Proceedings of the 5th International Conference on Extending Database Technology: Advances in Database Technology.* pp. 3-17. Avignon, France. Springer.

Tao, Y., Faloutsos, C., Papadias, D., & Liu, B. (2004). Prediction and indexing of moving objects with unknown motion patterns. In *Proceedings of the 2004 ACM SIGMOD international conference on Management of data* (SIGMOD '04). pp. 611-622. Paris, France. ACM.

Wang, Y., Lim, E.-P., & Hwang, S.-Y. (2003). On mining group patterns of mobile users. *The 14th International Conference on Database and Expert Systems Applications - DEXA 2003.* pp. 287-296. Prague, Czech Republic. Springer.

Wang, Y., Lim, E.-P., & Hwang, S.-Y. (2004). Efficient group pattern mining using data summarization. *The 9th International Conference on Database Systems for Advanced Applications - DASFAA 2004.* pp. 895-907. Jeju Island, Korea. Springer.

Wang, Y., Lim, E.-P., & Hwang, S.-Y. (2006). Efficient mining of group patterns from user movement data. *Data & Knowledge Engineering, 57,* 240–282. doi:10.1016/j.datak.2005.04.006

Wang, Y., Lim, E.-P., & Hwang, S.-Y. (2008). Efficient algorithms for mining maximal valid groups. *The International Journal on Very Large Data Bases - . The VLDB Journal, 17,* 515–535. doi:10.1007/s00778-006-0019-9

Chapter 1
Investigating the Properties of a Social Bookmarking and Tagging Network

Ralitsa Angelova
Max Planck Institut für Informatik, Germany

Marek Lipczak
Dalhousie University, Canada

Evangelos Milios
Dalhousie University, Canada

Paweł Pralat
Dalhousie University, Canada

ABSTRACT

Social networks and collaborative tagging systems are rapidly gaining popularity as a primary means for storing and sharing data among friends, family, colleagues, or perfect strangers as long as they have common interests. del.icio.us[3] is a social network where people store and share their personal bookmarks. Most importantly, users tag their bookmarks for ease of information dissemination and later look up. However, it is the friendship links, that make del.icio.us a social network. They exist independently of the set of bookmarks that belong to the users and have no relation to the tags typically assigned to the bookmarks. To study the interaction among users, the strength of the existing links and their hidden meaning, we introduce implicit links in the network. These links connect only highly "similar" users. Here, similarity can reflect different aspects of the user's profile that makes her similar to any other user, such as number of shared bookmarks, or similarity of their tags clouds. The authors investigate the question whether friends have common interests, they gain additional insights on the strategies that users use to assign tags to their bookmarks, and they demonstrate that the graphs formed by implicit links have unique properties differing from binomial random graphs or random graphs with an expected power-law degree distribution.

DOI: 10.4018/978-1-61350-474-1.ch001

Copyright © 2012, IGI Global. Copying or distributing in print or electronic forms without written permission of IGI Global is prohibited.

INTRODUCTION

Social bookmarking and collaborative tagging services lead to the formation of a new type of organically grown network structure. In such networks, users are linked to other users through social connections (e.g. directed friendship links) and to network specific online resources (e.g. bookmarks, photos, books, etc.) by either explicitly linking to them, tagging them with appropriate terms, or commenting on them. Clustering users in this context is a challenging problem, as it involves accounting for multiple types of social linkage among users and diversity of content ranging from personal photos (flickr.com) or bookmarks (del.icio.us) to whole libraries of read books throughout the user's lifetime (The Personal Library, librarything.com). The complexity of the clustering problem raises dramatically if we look at the overall electronic fingerprint of these users after connecting all their profiles from the various social networks they actively contribute to (Moser et al., 2007). Not only is clustering itself challenging but evaluation of the clustering solution is also very hard as reference class assignments are typically missing or very expensive to manually gather. These class assignments (also known as ground truth) are ignored in the clustering process. They are used exclusively in the evaluation phase to compare the groups produced by the clustering technique to the known classes it comprises. Modelling social bookmarking and tagging services is a way to generate synthetic data sets that mimic the behaviour of such social networks. Moreover, the synthetic data generative model also provides the corresponding ground truth for performance evaluation and comparison. A requirement for the design of useful models is an in-depth understanding of the properties of real-life data sets obtained from on-line social networks such as del.icio.us.

A collaborative tagging system like del.icio.us can be visualized as a tripartite structure (Halpin et al., 2007), where links (edges) are established between users, tags and bookmarks. Additionally, the social dimension introduces "friendship" links between users. Several research questions about the structure of the social network and its implications arise:

- What is the role of friendship in relation to interest sharing as reflected in the bookmarks and tags of users. Do friends appear to have more common interests than non-friends?
- Do "highly social" users share more topics of interest with others than the "less social" users?
- What are the structural properties of the friendship graph and the graphs induced by the implicit similarity-based links among users? Is their degree distribution indicative of power-law graphs? What are their connectivity and local density properties, measured by the clustering coefficient, as a function of in their -core analysis (Healy et al., 2008)? How do they compare with binomial random graphs (Janson et al., 2000) and random graphs with an expected power-law degree distribution (Chung and Lu, 2004)?
- What are the common properties of the friendship, bookmark-based and tag-based links? In particular, how do the three types of links correlate for individual users?

We are not the first to analyze social collaboration on the Web. Evolution models of two online social networks - Flickr and Yahoo! 360 are examined in (Kumar et al., 2006). In the experiments performed in (Negoescu, 2007) on the photo sharing network Flickr, after taking a random subset of photos and their owners or users, it is demonstrated that Flickr exhibits the characteristics of small-world and scale-free networks described earlier by (Barabasi, 2002, Cohen et al., 2003). Search and ranking techniques applied to social networks are discussed in (Hotho et al., 2006).

A detailed analysis of three other online social networks is presented in (Ahn et al., 2007). Tagging distributions in del.icio.us are shown to stabilize into power law distribution with a limited number of stable tags and a much larger "long-tail" of more idiosyncratic tags. Similar results are noted in (Golder and Huberman, 2005). Both results give strong evidence that collaborative tagging systems (like del.icio.us) can be exploited for reliable automatic creation of taxonomies. More recently, a study of a tag co-occurrence network was carried out (Schmitz et al., 2007). The nodes of this network are tags, and tags are linked when the two tags occur together in the set of tags assigned to a specific bookmark by a user (the post). A weight is given to a link that depends on the number of posts in which the two tags co-occur. The tag co-occurrence network was shown to reveal spamming behaviour.

DEFINITIONS OF GRAPHS AND ASSOCIATED METRICS

To answer the questions above, we study various graphs on the data provided by the social bookmarking network del.icio.us. For all graphs, vertices correspond to users. The edges are defined differently for each graph as follows.

The Friendship Graph

Edges correspond to directed friendship links between users. In this paper, as discussed in Sec. 3, we ignore the direction of friendship links and obtain an undirected friendship graph. Bidirectional edges (i.e. representing mutual friendship) are included only once.

Common Entity Graphs

In this type of implicit graph two vertices are connected by an undirected weighted edge, if the corresponding users have sufficient entities (tags or bookmarks) in common. The edge weight reflects the number of entities that the connected users have in common. A drawback of the common entity method is that it does not take into consideration the number of terms in both sets - having three common terms has the same meaning, no matter if the total number of user's terms is ten, or fifty. This similarity metric is symmetric, and its range is from 0 to the maximum number of entities. The two subtypes of graph under the common entity type are the following:

- **The common bookmark graph:** where the set of entities of a user is the set of bookmarks of that user.
- **The common tag graph:** where the set of entities of a user is the set of tags the user assigned to all her bookmarks.

Similarity Graphs

In this type of implicit graph, two vertices are connected by an undirected weighted edge. The edge weight reflects the cosine similarity between the entity vectors of the connected users. In these similarity graphs, entities can be either bookmarks or tags. The user entity vector belongs to a vector space defined on the entire data set, but captures only the individual entities belonging to the specific user.

The definition of a user entity vector is analogous to that of a document vector in information retrieval, where users are the equivalent of documents and entities (bookmarks or tags) the equivalent of terms.

Based on the discussion in Sec. 3, neither bookmarks nor tags contain the equivalent of stop words. Therefore, we include the most frequent bookmarks and tags in computing user similarity metrics. To reduce noise, we remove low frequency entities while defining the dimensions in our vector space model. That is, bookmarks used by less than 2 users and tags used by less than 3 users are removed.

The two subtypes of similarity graph that we study are derived as follows:

- **The bookmark similarity graph:** is derived by considering bookmarks as entities. The weight of a bookmark in any user vector is binary.
- **The tag similarity graph:** The tag similarity graph is derived by considering tags as entities. The weight of a tag in any user vector is the tf-idf score for this tag. The term frequency factor (tf) is the number of times a user used a given tag. The inverted document frequency factor (idf) is the inverse of the natural logarithm of the number of users that used a given tag plus one.

The cosine similarity between entity vectors, Eq. 1, is used to define the distance between users, where U_i is the vector of user i, and $w_{i,j}$ is its j-th coordinate. The cosine distance has the advantage that it is normalized with respect to the length of vectors. Cosine similarity is symmetric, and its range is from 0 to 1.

$$\cos\_sim(U_1, U_2) = \frac{\sum_{j=1}^{n} w_{1,j} * w_{2,j}}{\sqrt{(\sum_{j=1}^{n} w_{1,j}^2) * (\sum_{j=1}^{n} w_{2,j}^2)}}$$

$$(1)$$

Unweighted Graph Versions

Many interesting graph properties are defined for unweighted graphs, such as clustering coefficient and diameter. To measure these properties, we transform the weighted common entity and similarity graphs into unweighted versions. A set of thresholds is selected for each graph such that, after removing connections with weight lower than the threshold, a specified fraction of edges remains. The number of edges for each thresholded

graph is presented in Table 1. Table 2 presents real threshold values that select the expected fraction of strongest connection edges. This approach allows us to compare different graphs at similar density levels.

Clustering Coefficient

A quantity of interest in measuring the local density properties of the various graphs is the *clustering coefficient* (Ahn et al., 2007). Given an undirected graph $G=(V,E)$, the clustering coefficient of vertex $i \in V$ is defined as:

$$c_i = |\{(v,w)| (i,v),(i.w),(v,w) \in E|/\binom{k_i}{2}$$

where k_i is the degree of vertex i. The clustering coefficient is not defined for vertices of degree at most 1. The clustering coefficient of a graph G is the average over all vertices (of degree at least 2) in the graph, that is,

$$C(G) = \sum_{i \in V, \deg(v) \geq 2} C_i / |\{v \in V : \deg(v) \geq 2\}|$$

Its values always lie between 0 and 1. The clustering coefficient is asymptotically almost surely $(1 + o(1)) |E|/\binom{|V|}{2}$ for a binomial random graph. For real-world networks it is usually much larger.

K-cores

A k-core of a graph is a maximal induced subgraph of minimum degree at least k. If no subgraph has this property, then we say that the k-core is empty. It is possible to show (Batagelj and Zaveršnik, 2002) that the degree core is unique for a given graph and a given k, and can be obtained by recursively removing all vertices with degree less than

Table 1. Number of edges in thresholded graph, for each threshold value

	0.1%	0.05%	0.02%	0.0125%	0.01%	0.005%
k-common bookmarks	99994	47929	18602	11668	9206	4608
bookmarks cosine similarity	92179	45991	18466	11661	9158	4663
k-common tags	91992	45699	18360	11505	9199	4586
tags cosine similarity	91427	45726	18274	11424	9142	4567

Table 2. The set of threshold values that produces binary graph with a specific percentage of strongest connections

	0.1%	0.05%	0.02%	0.0125%	0.01%	0.005%
k-common bookmarks	22	30	44	53	58	75
bookmarks cosine similarity	0.08	0.10	0.14	0.16	0.17	0.21
k-common tags	471	551	668	736	769	880
tags cosine similarity	0.55	0.60	0.65	0.68	0.69	0.72

k. The k-cores of a graph can consist of multiple components. The difference between the k-core and simply filtering out all vertices with degree less than k is best illustrated by comparing their effects on a simple tree. In the case of a tree, the filtering of all degree-one vertices results in the pruning of all of a tree's leaves, whereas the degree core with $k=2$ would prune back the leaves of a tree at each recursion, thus destroying the tree completely. Cores were first introduced in studying social networks in (Seidman, 1983) and popularized in (Wasserman and Faust, 1994). In (Batagelj and Zaveršnik, 2002) Seidman's work was generalized beyond simple degree to include any monotone function p. The same authors go on to define the core number of a vertex to be the highest order of a core that contains this vertex.

In this paper, we perform degree-based k-core analysis of the friendship, common entity and similarity graphs, by repeatedly increasing k by one until the k-core is reduced to empty. We then plot various properties of the k-core sequence of graphs, including the diameter, size, average distance and average clustering coefficient of the vertices between vertices of the largest component, and the number of components.

Note that the k-core analysis can become prohibitively expensive as the input graphs get dense. We control density by the use of thresholds on similarity measures.

EXPLORING THE DATA SET

We perform our experiments on a data set obtained by an automated Web crawl on the social community platform del.icio.us. The subset of del.icio.us we have at hand consists of 13,514 users, 4,574,587 bookmarks, and 47,807 friendship connections, 6,876 of which are mutual (bidirectional) connections. Most users (13,238) have at least one bookmark. Most users (13,439) also point to at least one friend. The total number of tags used in our subset is 643,889.

The crawl on del.icio.us is a Breadth First Search (BFS) of the friendship graph, starting with the user with the highest number of friends as a seed node. This resembles the so called *snowball sampling* technique which is argued to be the only feasible sampling method for crawling such networks (Ahn et al., 2007).

The Friendship Graph

It is a straightforward representation of the directional connections between users. We observe that this graph is quite sparse, with 40,931 unidirectional edges, and 6,876 bi-directional edges corresponding to mutual friendships. Only 14% of friendships are mutual, due to the fact that by design friendships do not have to be confirmed in the online system supporting del.icio.us.

Bookmark Distributions and Properties

Intuitively two users are connected when they point to similar sets of bookmarks. We investigate the hypothesis that bookmarks can be treated as terms in the standard Information Retrieval sense, where each user is viewed as a document, and the user's bookmarks are viewed as terms. The proportion of bookmark urls used only once over the total number of unique bookmark urls is 78%, where the proportion of unique words in Wikipedia used only once over the total number of unique words is 52% (second and fifth column of Table 4).

We further examine whether the distribution of bookmark urls follows Zipf's law. The log-log plot of the url frequency against rank of urls sorted by decreasing order of frequency, has the following characteristics (a) a slowly declining part for the top 1000 urls, (b) a fairly straight part up to rank of about 10^6, and (c) a horizontal part at frequency equal to 1 up to rank of about 0.25×10^7 corresponding to a large number of bookmarks

appearing only once (Figure 1). Inspecting the frequencies of the ten most frequently bookmarked urls shows that their frequency differences are small, which confirms the shape of Figure 1. Surprisingly, bookmarks to general use sites (e.g., google.com) are not among the ten most frequent bookmarks. We would expect such sites to be analogous to stop words in standard text repositories. One possible explanation is that users avoid adding these stop-word-like urls to their bookmarks to keep the bookmark list smaller. The addresses of general purpose websites are easy to remember and do not have to be stored in del.icio.us. (Table 3). If we prune urls keeping only their domain, the frequency-against-rank plot shows that the domains of bookmarks do match Zipf's law (Figure 2). The proportion of bookmark url domains used only once over the total number of unique bookmark url domains is 56%, a very close match to the proportion of unique words in Wikipedia used only once over the total number of unique words, which is 52% (third column of Table 4). Furthermore, the list of ten most frequently bookmarked domain addresses contains indeed the most popular websites. Despite a better fit to Zipf's law, we do not think that the list of pruned bookmarks is useful for finding real connections between users, as domains are usually too general to capture users' interests.

Tag Distributions and Properties

Shared tags between two users may be interpreted as showing their overlapping interests. Although tags are mostly nouns and adjectives, and they do not form grammatically correct sentences, we conjecture that they match the characteristics of terms in text repositories. The proportion of tags used only once with respect to the total number of unique tags is 53%, matching very closely the proportion of unique words in Wikipedia used only once with respect to the total number of unique words of 52% (fourth column of Table 4). Similarly to bookmarks, tag frequency is not

Table 3. List of the ten most frequently bookmarked websites. None of the websites is present in the dataset more than 2000 times, and they also look very specific. Comparing the results to the real frequencies in the complete del.icio.us dataset, we see that our crawl is only a very rough approximation of the latter, judging by the relative frequencies. Real frequency data was gathered using www.xinureturns.com 28-Jan-08

Rank	Frequency	Real frequency	Url
1	1815	27359	script.aculo.us/
2	1745	10157	pechere.blogspot.com/2005/02/absolutely-delicious-complete-tool.html
3	1725	37346	www.pandora.com/
4	1421	29433	www.netvibes.com/
5	1371	21592	www.alvit.de/handbook/
6	1342	24830	www.last.fm/
7	1247	17335	typetester.maratz.com/
8	1207	19069	www.instructables.com/
9	1206	40314	www.flickr.com/
10	1202	6542	johnvey.com/features/deliciousdirector/

Figure 1. Frequency distribution of bookmark urls (top), and tags (bottom)

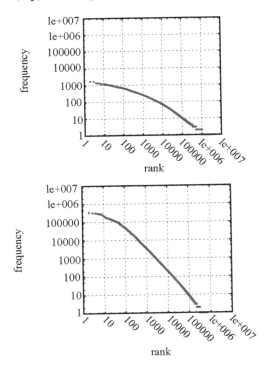

Figure 2. Frequency distribution of domain portion of bookmarked urls. The domains reveal the importance of general purpose websites. Users' bookmarks link to some specific information contained in them. The frequency against rank plot shows that the domains of bookmarks match Zipf's law.

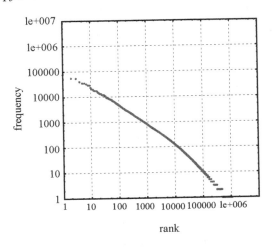

Table 4. Counts (in thousands) of bookmark urls and tags, treating bookmarks and tags as "terms", the user as the "document", and the set of all users as the corpus. The same counts are shown for the Wikipedia text corpus. We see that the proportion of terms used only once is much higher in the bookmark url corpus than either the tag or the Wikipedia corpus.

Counts (in K)	Urls	url domains	Tags	Wikipedia words
Total number of unique terms	4,575	1106	644	4,098
Termes used more than once	1,017	483	303	1,978
Terms used only one	3,558	623	341	2,120

Table 5. Average strength of the connection between friends (column 2) and non-friends (column 3). We observe that friends have significantly stronger connections than non-friends based on the bookmark similarity metrics, whereas this is not true for the tag-based similarity metrics.

	Friend pair average	Non-friend pair average
k-common bookmarks	1.931	0.372
bookmark cosine sim	0.011	0.004
k-common tags	54.157	41.816
tag cosine sim	0.081	0.085

Figure 3. Frequency vs. rank distribution of tags for two individual users. We notice the most frequently used tags, which are likely the ones recommended by del.icio.us, and the tail of infrequently used tags, which are likely the individualized tags, specific to the user's organization of her bookmarks. A significant fraction of the tags is used only once.

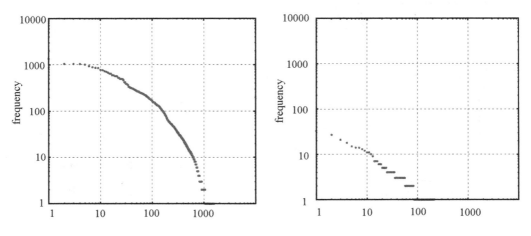

Figure 4. Zipf distribution of tags associated with the url flickr.com by all users in our crawled data set. The flat part of the curve corresponds to the most frequent tags, which are likely the ones proposed by del.icio.us. Similar curves were obtained for urls del.icio.us, pandora.com and youtube.com.

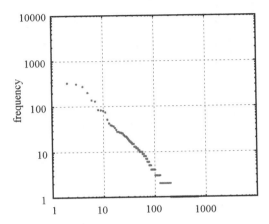

distributed according to Zipf's law for the highest ranks, indicating that there are no stop-word-like tags (Figure 1). The most frequently used tags correspond to general categories, therefore they still convey content information.

Interestingly, in (Sigurbjörnsson and van Zwol, 2008) it is shown that tags in the popular photography sharing social network flickr.com follow a power law distribution much closer than what the observed one in the bookmarking social network del.icio.us.

RELATING FRIENDSHIP WITH BOOKMARK AND TAG SIMILARITY

We now study the question whether friends have more similar bookmarks or tags than non-friends. We calculate the average connection strengths (according to the previously defined user similarity metrics) over pairs of friends and pairs of

Figure 5. Scatter plot of tag similarity versus bookmark similarity for 10,000 randomly sampled pairs of the bookmark similarity graph, showing no correlation between bookmarks and tags.

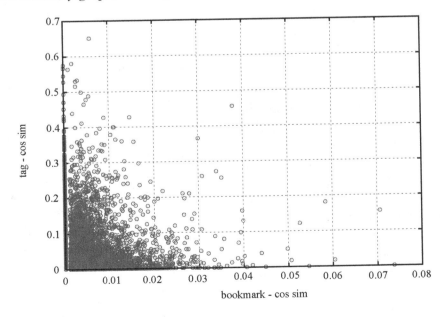

Figure 6. This plot focuses on the largest component of the common bookmark graph, and it depicts its average distance between nodes (top) and its size (bottom) as a function of k in the k-core analysis. This behaviour is typical of the other common entity and entity similarity graphs.

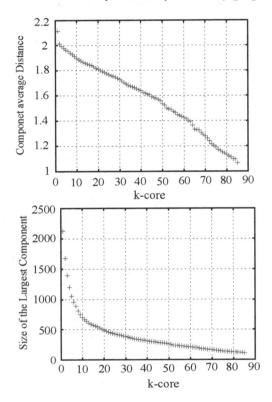

Figure 7. This plot focusses on the largest component of the friendship graph, and it depicts its average distance between nodes (top) and its size (bottom) as a function of k in the k-core analysis

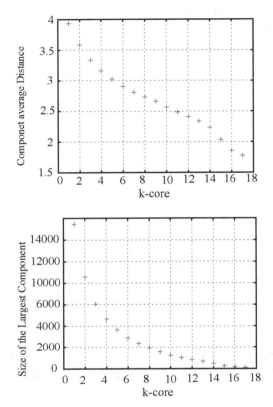

non-friends, shown in Table 5. We observe that friends have significantly stronger connections than non-friends based on the bookmark similarity metrics, whereas this is not true for the tag based similarity metrics. We conjecture that the reason for this is that the majority of the tags are individualized, dependent on the individual user's way of organizing their bookmarks and their background in the corresponding areas. The number of tags that capture the generic meaning of a bookmarked page is a small fraction of the total number of tags associated with that page. In other words, friends who share bookmarks choose mostly different tags for them. To further explore this conjecture, we

inspect the Zipf distribution of tags for individual users, Figure 3, and bookmarked web sites. Figure 4. In the plots for individual users, we notice the most frequently used tags, which are likely to be the ones recommended by del.icio.us, followed by the tail of infrequently used tags, which are likely to be individualized tags, specific to the user's organization of her bookmarks. A significant fraction of the tags of a user is used only once. In the plots for individual bookmarked web sites, we also notice a small number of most frequently used tags, followed by a large number of user-specific tags, used only once.

This can be easily explained with the difference of user backgrounds and their depth. People, who are more knowledgable in a particular area are highly likely to use very specific tags while describing a bookmark. On the other hand, if the same URL is bookmarked by a less knowledgable person, he or she will highly likely associate very generic tags to ease search for the same URL later. Take as an example the URL http://www.birds.cornell.edu/AllAboutBirds/BirdGuide/Red-winged_Blackbird.html. Suppose a person, whose hobby is birdwatching, visits this URL and wants to store it in his bookmarks collection. He would highly likely use a tag 'red-wing blackbird' for describing the page. Contrary to that, if a person who is not knowledgable in birds visits that URL and wants to save it, he would highly likely just tag it as 'wild birds', which is a very generic description of the page. Therefore, though both users bookmarked the same page, their tags differ significantly.

Finally, we investigate the correlation between the similarity metrics of two users based on tags and bookmarks, using a scatter plot constructed as follows. An edge is sampled randomly from a bookmark similarity graph. The bookmark similarity of the edge is the x-coordinate of the point corresponding to the edge in the scatter plot. For the same edge, the tag similarity is computed, serving as the y-coordinate of the point in the scatter plot. The scatter plot shows practically no correlation between bookmark similarity and tag similarity between two users (Figure 5).

DENSITY PROPERTIES OF THE FRIENDSHIP GRAPH AND THE CONTENT-BASED SOCIAL GRAPHS

We now apply the concept of k-core introduced in Sec. 2 to discover the density properties of the friendship graph and our content-based social graphs (common bookmark/tag, and bookmark/tag similarity graphs), and compare them with the properties of binomial random graphs (Janson et al., 2000) and random graphs with power-law de-

Figure 8. The average distance between nodes and the size of the largest component in the k-core analysis of binomial and power-law random graphs

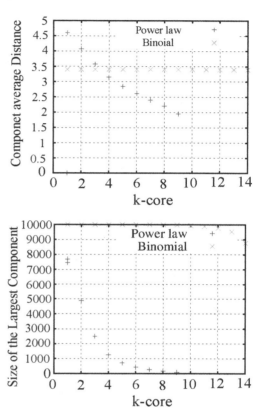

gree distribution (Chung and Lu, 2004). We focus on plots of properties of the graphs as a function of increasing k in the k-core computation. For fairly small k the smaller components disappear and we are left with a single component, which becomes progressively denser with increasing k, and eventually disappears. The properties of interest are: the number of components, and, for the largest component, its size (number of vertices), its average distance between vertex pairs, and its diameter. We furthermore generate scatter plots of the clustering coefficients versus degree for the graphs' vertices, and the average clustering coefficient of the vertices of the largest component.

Figure 9. The average clustering coefficient over the vertices of a given degree as a function of degree (left). The average clustering coefficient over all vertices of the largest component in the k-core analysis, as a function of k (right). We observe that less "social" individuals tend to have a closely knit set of neighbours, who are likely to be connected to each other, because of their very specialized interests.

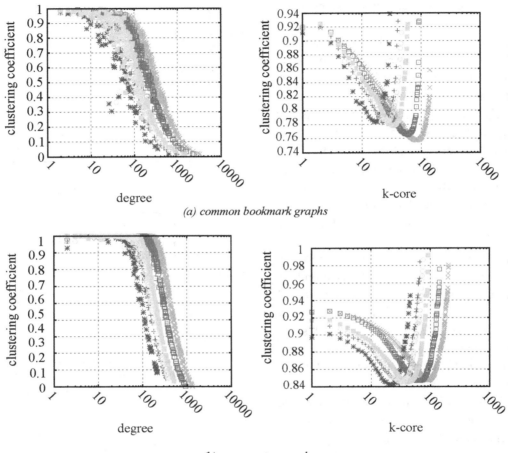

(a) common bookmark graphs

(b) common tag graphs

Basic k-Core Properties of the Content-Based Social Graphs

The average distance between pairs of points of the largest component in the k-core analysis of common bookmark graphs is shown in Figure 6. The linear nature of the curves is also worth noting.

The diameter of the largest component in the k-core analysis of common bookmark graphs is lower than 7.

The number of components in the k-core analysis of common bookmark graphs drops very quickly to one, as k increases in the k-core analysis. Having a single component is similar to binomial random graph behaviour.

It is worth noting that this behaviour is unlike the behaviours observed in (Healy et al., 2008) for the majority of the social graphs examined there, including the.gov web graph, patent citation graph and the DBLP co-authorship graph. It is only similar to that of an organizational email communication graph.

The size of the largest component (number of vertices) in the k-core analysis of common

Figure 10. The average clustering coefficient over the vertices of a given degree as a function of degree (left). The average clustering coefficient over all vertices of the largest component in the k-core analysis, as a function of k (right).

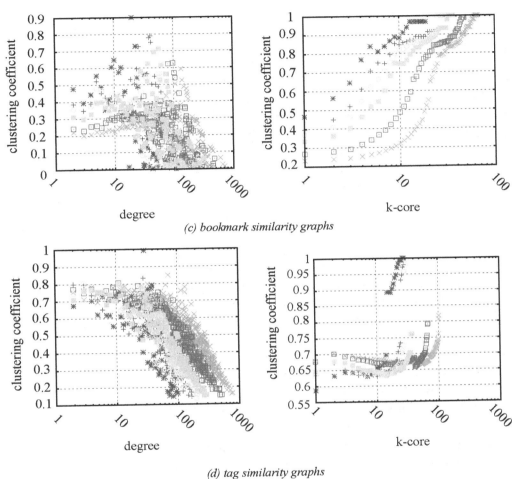

(c) bookmark similarity graphs

(d) tag similarity graphs

bookmark graphs is shown in Figure 6. The size of the last non-trivial k-core is very close to k, and the average distance between nodes is close to 1, so these vertices form an induced subgraph that is close to a clique. This behaviour is very different from binomial random graphs, as shown in Figure 8. It is also different from power-law graphs, because the last non-trivial k-core is not as dense. The average distance between nodes and graph size as a function of k for the friendship graph are shown in Figure 7. We note that the friendship graph behaves very similarly to the power law graph.

Clustering Coefficient of k-Cores

In this subsection we examine the clustering coefficient and its relation to the degree of the graph vertices. A plot of the average clustering coefficient for vertices of a given degree is shown as a function of degree in the left column of Figure 9 and 10. For a binomial random graph and random graph with expected power law degree distribution, the corresponding theoretical curve would be horizontal, since the fact that two vertices are friends of a third vertex does not affect the probability of them being linked.

Figure 11. The average clustering coefficient over the vertices of a given degree as a function of degree (left) for the friendship graph. The average clustering coefficient over all vertices of the largest component in the k-core analysis, as a function of k (right), for the friendship graph.

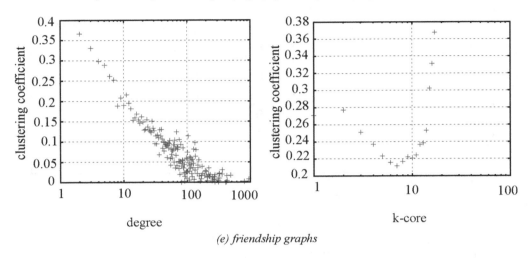

(e) friendship graphs

The average clustering coefficient over all vertices as a function of k in the k-core analysis is shown in the right column of Figure 9 and 10. These plots are consistent with the plots in the left column, considering that the low-degree vertices are dropped first as k increases in the k-core analysis. For low values of k, low degree vertices are lost. When such vertices have high clustering coefficient, we see a drop in the average clustering coefficient, down to a minimum for a value of k. As k increases past that minimum, the densification process prevails and we see the expected monotonic increase in the average clustering coefficient. In the friendship graph, shown in Figure 11, we observe the same trend of low degree vertices having high clustering coefficients, with the average monotonically decreasing with increasing degree. This implies that friends of users (represented by vertices) with low degrees, or equivalently, few friends, tend to be friends themselves, while friends of users with large degrees are not necessarily connected.

For comparison, the clustering coefficient as a function of degree, and the average clustering coefficient as a function of k in the k-core analy-

sis are shown in Figure 12. Here we note that the behaviour of the binomial random graph is very different. The power law graph shows an average clustering coefficient that increases monotonically as a function of k.

DISCUSSION

In this paper, we closely examined the properties of a typical social bookmarking and tagging data set, to obtain insights for facilitating creation of models for such data. We summarize our observations as follows:

• Friendship correlates well with common bookmarks or similar bookmark vectors of users, but not well with common tags or similar tag vectors. This implies that the majority of tags that users assign to bookmarks are user-specific tags, and only a small fraction of the tags capture the generic meaning of the bookmarked web page.

• Tags behave more like words in text, while bookmarks less so, in the sense that a much

Figure 12. The average clustering coefficient over the vertices of a given degree as a function of degree (left) for binomial and power-law random graphs. The average clustering coefficient over all vertices of the largest component in the k-core analysis, as a function of k (right), for binomial and power-law random graphs.

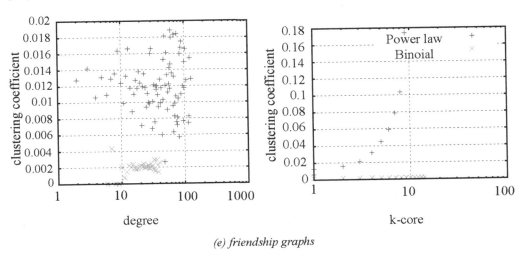

(e) friendship graphs

higher proportion of bookmarks are used only once compared to the proportion of tags and words in the Wikipedia corpus that are used only once.

- There are no tags or bookmarks behaving like stop words in text. Even the highest frequency tags or bookmarks do not appear that frequently to deserve the characterization of stop words.

- The clustering coefficient as function of k in the k-core analysis displays a U-shaped curve. This is not consistent with binomial random graphs or random graphs with a power law degree distribution.

ACKNOWLEDGMENT

We are grateful for the financial support of the Natural Sciences and Engineering Research Council of Canada, the MITACS Network of Centres of Excellence, and Genieknows.com. Tom Crecelius, and Mouna Kacimi of the Databases and Information Systems Department, Max Planck Institut für Informatik directed by Prof. Gerhard Weikum, kindly provided the del.icio.us data set for this project. Jacek Wolkowicz gave us the Wikipedia statistics. The computations required for the k-core results would not be possible without access to the Atlantic Computational Excellence Network ACEnet and the Shared Hierarchical Academic Research Computing Network SHARCNET computing clusters.

REFERENCES

Ahn, Y.-Y., Han, S., Kwak, H., Moon, S., & Jeong, H. (2007). Analysis of topological characteristics of huge online social networking services. In *World Wide Web (WWW) Conference* (pp. 835–844), Banff, Alberta.

Angelova, R., Lipczak, M., Milios, E., & Pralat, P. (2008). Characterizing a social bookmarking and tagging network. In A. Nanopoulos & G. Tsoumakas (Eds.), *Mining Social Data (MSoDa), a Workshop of the 18th European Conference on Artificial Intelligence (ECAI 2008)*, University of Patras, Greece.

Barabasi, A.-L. (2002). *Linked: The New Science of Networks*. Cambridge, MA: Perseus.

Batagelj, C., & Zaveršnik, M. (2002). Generalized Cores. *ArXiv Computer Science e-prints*.

Chung, F., & Lu, L. (2004). *Complex graphs and networks*. American Mathematical Society, U.S.A.

Cohen, R., Avraham, D., & Havlin, S. (2003). Structural properties of scale free networks. In S. Bornholdt & H. G. Schuster (Eds.), *Handbook of graphs and networks*. Wiley-VCH.

Golder, S., & Huberman, B. (2005). *The structure of collaborative tagging systems*. Technical report, Information Dynamics Lab, HP Labs.

Halpin, H., Robu, V., & Shepherd, H. (2007). The complex dynamics of collaborative tagging. In *World Wide Web (WWW) Conference* (pp. 211–220), Banff, Alberta.

Healy, J., Janssen, J., Milios, E., & Aiello, W. (2008). Characterization of graphs using degree cores. In *Algorithms and Models for the Web-Graph: Fourth International Workshop, WAW 2006*, volume LNCS-4936 of *Lecture Notes in Computer Science*, Banff, Canada: Springer Verlag.

Hotho, A., Jaeschke, R., Schmitz, C., & Stumme, G. (2006). Information retrieval in folksonomies: Search and ranking. In *Proceedings of the 3rd European Semantic Web Conference*, Lecture Notes in Computer Science. Springer.

Janson, S., Łuczak, T., & Ruciński, A. (2000). *Random Graphs*. New York: Wiley.

Kumar, R., Novak, J., & Tomkins, A. (2006). Structure and evolution of online social networks. In *Knowledge Discovery in Databases (KDD) Conference* (pp. 611–617), Philadelphia, PA: ACM.

Moser, F., Ge, R., & Ester, M. (2007). Joint cluster analysis of attribute and relationship data without a-priori specification of the number of clusters. In *Knowledge Discovery in Databases (KDD) Conference* (pp. 510–519), San Jose, CA: ACM.

Negoescu, R. (2007). An analysis of the social network of flickr. Technical report, Laboratory of nonlinear systems - LANOS, School of Computer and Communication Sciences, École Polytechnique Fédérale de Lausanne, Switzerland.

Schmitz, C., Grahl, M., Hotho, A., Stumme, G., Cattuto, C., Baldassarri, A., et al. (2007). Network properties of folksonomies. In *World Wide Web Conference (WWW)*, Banff, Canada.

Seidman, S. B. (1983). Network structure and minimum degree. *Social Networks*, 269–287. doi:10.1016/0378-8733(83)90028-X

Sigurbjörnsson, B., & van Zwol, R. (2008). Flickr tag recommendation based on collective knowledge. In *WWW '08: Proc. the 17th international conference on World Wide Web* (pp. 327–336). ACM.

Wasserman, S., & Faust, K. (1994). *Social network analysis: Methods and applications*. Cambridge: Cambridge University Press.

ENDNOTES

1. Authors listed in alphabetical order
2. This article is an expanded version of (Angelova, Lipczak, Milios, and Pralat 2008)
3. http://del.icio.us

This work was previously published in International Journal of Data Warehousing and Mining, Volume 6, Issue 1, edited by David Taniar, pp. 1-19, copyright 2010 by IGI Publishing (an imprint of IGI Global).

Chapter 2
The Dynamics of Content Popularity in Social Media

Symeon Papadopoulos
Aristotle University of Thessaloniki, Greece & Informatics & Telematics Institute, Greece

Athena Vakali
Aristotle University of Thessaloniki, Greece

Ioannis Kompatsiaris
Informatics & Telematics Institute, Greece

ABSTRACT

Social Bookmarking Systems (SBS) have been widely adopted in the last years, and thus they have had a significant impact on the way that online content is accessed, read and rated. Until recently, the decision on what content to display in a publisher's web pages was made by one or at most few authorities. In contrast, modern SBS-based applications permit their users to submit their preferred content, to comment on and to rate the content of other users and establish social relations with each other. In that way, the vision of the social media is realized, i.e. the online users collectively decide upon the interestingness of the available bookmarked content. This paper attempts to provide insights into the dynamics emerging from the process of content rating by the user community. To this end, the paper proposes a framework for the study of the statistical properties of an SBS, the evolution of bookmarked content popularity and user activity in time, as well as the impact of online social networks on the content consumption behavior of individuals. The proposed analysis framework is applied to a large dataset collected from digg, a popular social media application.

INTRODUCTION

The startling success of Web 2.0 applications during the last years has reshaped our views on how information is generated and distributed to the masses. While traditionally the content items that appeared in the web pages of online publishers (e.g. news sites) were selected by a single authority or a small committee of experts, the advent of Web 2.0 applications, such as the Social Bookmarking Systems (SBS), has allowed mass participation in the content selection process.

DOI: 10.4018/978-1-61350-474-1.ch002

Copyright © 2012, IGI Global. Copying or distributing in print or electronic forms without written permission of IGI Global is prohibited.

In an SBS, users upload and save links to web pages (bookmarks) that they deem interesting. These bookmarks are usually public: Once they are submitted by a user, the rest of the community is able to view them and if they consider them interesting, they may give a 'thumbs up', i.e. rate them. Thus, applications of this kind, originally meant to provide a convenient tool to organize one's bookmarks, have evolved to act as a content popularity (or 'interesting-ness') ranking mechanism. Examples of such systems are digg[1], propeller[2] and newsvine[3]. The proliferation and success of such applications has created online communities where the bookmarked content items undergo a perpetual rating process by the community. Typically, the most popular content items coming out of this process are displayed in a prominent place at the application's site. In that way, the vision of *social media* is realized.

The work presented in this paper has been mainly motivated by the fact that the content rating processes, such as the ones taking place within social media applications, have not been sufficiently studied so far from the temporal and social point of view. For this reason, we established a framework for the study of such social media aspects and applied it for analyzing the content rating dynamics emerging in the digg application. More specifically, through the work described in this paper, we make the following contributions:

- Introduce the *Diggsonomy* framework, inspired by the *Folksonomy* framework of (Mika, 2005) and (Hotho et al., 2006a), to enable the study of online content popularity;
- Collect and analyze the statistical properties of an extensive data set from digg;
- Provide insights to the temporal evolution of popularity and to the role of the social relations on the content rating process.

We consider the work presented here to be of significance for the following applications:

- **Administration of SBS and social media applications.** Since the operation of such a service involves a large investment in server and network equipment, better understanding of page popularity and thus request patterns could contribute to smoother service provision and/or reduced infrastructure costs by means of efficient data partitioning and page caching schemes.
- **Recommender system development.** Understanding of the temporal and social dynamics of content popularity can be exploited to improve the precision and relevance of recommendations for systems where these aspects are of particular significance (e.g. news articles, advertisements).

The rest of this paper is structured as follows. Section 2 provides a short overview of existing work in the fields of mining web 2.0 data and analysis of related temporal and social phenomena. In Section 3 the proposed social media analysis and modeling framework is introduced. Further, the data collection and the associated experimentation as well as a discussion of the findings are provided in Section 4. Finally, Section 5 concludes the paper.

RELATED WORK

The recent emergence of Web 2.0 applications and the vast amounts of data resulting from the online activities of users has spawned a new wave of research, focused on the analysis of users' behavior within a web application and the semantics emerging from this. First, the advent of Social Tagging Systems (STS), i.e. systems where users organize their bookmarked or uploaded content items by attaching tags to them, motivated researchers to formalize the notion of a Folksonomy (Mika, 2005). Within the Folksonomy framework, novel information retrieval paradigms were proposed (Hotho et al., 2006a) and established data mining methods were applied to gain better insights to the so-called *Social Web* data (Giannakidou et al., 2008). Such works have mostly focused on the semantic aspects of this data, with a primary focus on the tagging patterns of users; however, they do not address the evolution of such patterns in time.

The temporal aspect of Social Web data has also attracted significant interest from the research community in the last years. The studies in (Falkowski & Spiliopoulou, 2007; Golder & Huberman, 2006; Halpin et al., 2007; Hotho et al., 2006b) deal with the temporal aspects of tags and user communities. Some large-scale experimental work was presented in (Cha et al., 2007), where the phenomenon of popularity evolution in *User Generated Content* systems, such as YouTube[4] and Daum[5], is partly studied. Two comprehensive studies of the temporal aspects of web resource popularity were presented by Kaltenbrunner et al. (2007a; 2007b); there, the evolution of comment activity in Slashdot is analyzed. The aforementioned studies, however, disregard the influence of the social factor on the evolution of popularity.

The study of social influence and cascading behavior in social networks had already attracted the interest of marketing academics as early as the 1960s (Bass, 1969), but has recently been revived thanks to the emergence of large online communities. In (Kempe et al., 2003), the authors study the problem of identifying the most influential nodes of a social network in order to maximize the impact of marketing strategies. Similarly, the work in (Song et al., 2007) addresses the problem of information flow through a social network and incorporates the rates of information diffusion through the network to rank influential users. Recently, an investigation based on statistical tests was carried out to unveil the nature of social correlations, i.e. whether they stem from homophily, confounding or influence (Anagnostopoulos et al., 2008).

Finally, some interesting work on the analysis of data collected from user activity in digg has recently been published. A first study of *collective attention* in digg was presented in (Wu & Huberman, 2007), where the distributions of user votes to content items and their evolution in time is studied. Subsequently, the author of (Lerman, 2007) introduced a mathematical model to describe the influence of several visibility factors on digg content popularity. Finally, the work in (Papadopoulos et al., 2008), which initiated the work presented here, introduced the Diggsonomy framework to facilitate the empirical study of social media applications.

The study presented in this paper which considers popularity evolution within a social media application is unique in that it discusses both the temporal and the social aspects of the phenomenon. Our contributions, i.e. the extension of the well-established Folksonomy framework with a temporal component, the confirmation of the heavy tail nature of popularity, the temporal analysis of content popularity and the quantification of the social influence on it, hopefully provide new insights to the dynamic phenomena that appear in the context of such systems.

POPULARITY ANALYSIS FRAMEWORK

This section establishes a framework to facilitate the analysis of popularity within social media systems. Note that although the framework was formed in order to study the phenomena arising from the usage of digg, it can be applied in a multitude of similar applications, e.g. propeller and newsvine. The section also presents a series of indispensable tools for the analysis and understanding of the data produced within an SBS, namely the power law model for skewed distributions, the temporal normalization for aggregating time series, and two measures of social influence on content popularity. Before proceeding with the presentation of the aforementioned framework and tools, we first briefly review the basics of digg in order to exemplify the principles of social media applications.

The motivation behind digg is the empowerment of simple users with the means to collectively decide upon the significance (or interesting-ness) of web items (mostly news items, images and videos; for convenience, these will be referred to as 'stories' in the rest of the paper). This is achieved by providing registered users, called *diggers*, with two basic rights: (a) submitting stories that they deem interesting, (b) voting on previously submitted links. Votes can be either positive (i.e. the user 'diggs the story') or negative (i.e. the user 'buries the story'), but only the positive ones, namely the 'Diggs', are available for public view. A user may vote in favor or against a particular story only once.

An additional possibility offered to diggers, similarly to the users of other Web 2.0 applications, is the possibility to form social networks with the intention of keeping track of other diggers, whose submissions they find interesting. Since digg offers two kinds of relations between users, namely 'has-friend' and 'is-fan-of', the resulting network has the form of a directed graph. One would expect that the *digging* behavior of users is partly influenced by the digging activity of users belonging to their social network.

Diggsonomy, A Time-Aware Folksonomy

In an SBS such as digg, we consider the finite sets U, R, T, S, and D denoting the set of users, stories, timestamps (i.e. T is an ordered set), social relations and user Diggs respectively. In addition, the notation π_X denotes the projection of a Cartesian product of sets to set X.

- **Definition 1 (Diggsonomy):** Given an SBS, its derived Diggsonomy B is defined as the tuple $B = (U, R, T, S, D)$, where $S \subseteq U \times U$ is the social network of the SBS users, and $D \subseteq U \times R \times T$ is the users' voting set, modeled as a triadic relation between U, R, and T.
- **Definition 2 (Personomy):** The Personomy P_u of a given user $u \in U$ is the restriction of B to u, i.e. $P_u = (R_u, S_u, D_u)$ with $D_u = \{(r, t) \in R \times T \mid (u, r, t) \in D\}$, $S_u = \pi_U(S) \subseteq U$, $R_u = \pi_R(D_u) \subseteq R$ and $\pi_T(D_u) \subseteq T$.
- **Definition 3 (Vote-history):** The Vote-history for a particular resource (story) r, denoted as Hr is defined as the projection of the Diggsonomy D on $U \times T$ restricted on r, i.e. $H_r = \pi_{U \times T}(D \mid r) \subseteq U \times T$. The user u_0 for whom the statements $(u_0, t_0) \in H_r$ and $\forall\, t \in \pi_T(H_r) \subseteq T, t_0 < t$ hold is called the submitter of the story.

This formalism is similar to the Folksonomy definitions appearing in (Mika, 2005) and (Hotho et al., 2006a). The major difference is that the Diggsonomy formalism provides an additional focus on the temporal aspect of popularity; therefore it incorporates the ordered set T of timestamps in the definitions. Also, the set of tags which was part of the Folksonomy formalism does not appear here.

The Heavy Tails of Popularity

In order to gain an overview of the nature of content popularity as well as of other variables observed in the context of an SBS, one needs first to study their distributional properties. It is common practice to approximate such distributions by means of statistical models. Frequently, distributions arising in natural and social phenomena are of skewed form, e.g. they may follow a power law, a widely researched and empirically supported model. A comprehensive review of the power law properties and their application in modeling real distributions are provided by Newman (2005).

According to this model, the probability density function of the skewed variable under study should be described by the following law:

$$p(x) = Cx^{-a}$$

In Equation 1, α is called the exponent of the power law (the constant C is part of the model in order to satisfy the requirement that the distribution $p(x)$ sums to 1). A straightforward way to empirically identify a power-law in a measured quantity is to plot its histogram. However, this might be tricky in practice since the tail of the distribution would appear very noisy (due to the regular histogram binning which is not appropriate for functions following the power-law). A potential solution to this problem would be to employ logarithmic binning; however, a more elegant way to deal with the problem is to calculate and plot the Cumulative Distribution Function (CDF) *P(x)*. Based on Equation 1, we get:

$$P(x) = \int_0^\infty p(x')dx' = C\int_0^\infty x'^{-a}\,dx' = \frac{C}{a-1}x^{-(a-1)}$$

Thus, the cumulative distribution function *P(x)* in Equation 2 also follows a power law, but with a different exponent (α-1). Since *P(x)* is derived by integrating over $p(x)$, the resulting curve has a much smoother tail (integration acts as a low-pass filter), thus rendering clear the power-law nature of the distribution. Recent research on social web data has confirmed the power-law nature of a series of Web 2.0 originating distributions, e.g. tag usage in delicious (Halpin et al., 2007; Hotho et al., 2006a), number of votes to questions/answers in the Yahoo! Answers system (Agichtein et al., 2008), video popularity in YouTube and Daum (Cha et al., 2007) and story popularity in digg (Papadopoulos et al., 2008).

The value for the exponent α of the power law can be reliably estimated by use of the fitting method introduced by (Clauset et al., 2007). The proposed method employs an approximation to the Maximum Likelihood Estimator (MLE) for the scaling parameter of the power law:

$$\hat{a} \cong 1 + n\left[\sum_{i=1}^{n} \ln \frac{x_i}{x_{min} - \frac{1}{2}}\right]^{-1}$$

This estimator assumes that the value x_{min} above which the power law holds is known. In order to estimate this value, the authors recommend the use of the Kolmogorov-Smirnov (KS) statistic as a measure of goodness-of-fit of the model with parameters (α, x_{min}) with the observed data. The KS statistic is defined as the maximum distance between the CDF of the data *S(x)* and the fitted model *P(x)*:

$$D = \max_{x \geq x_{min}} |S(x) - P(x)|$$

where *S(x)* is the CDF of the data for the observations with value at least x_{min}, and *P(x)* is the CDF for the power-law model that best fits the data in the region $x \geq x_{min}$. Obviously, multiple tests are carried out in order to explore the parameter space (α, x_{min}) and identify the optimal model.

Temporal Evolution of Content Rating

Most research related to time series analysis has focused on the assumption of stationarity for the time series under study (Box & Jenkins, 1994). Furthermore, these series usually span long intervals, so it is possible to derive stable statistics about their temporal behavior. Contrary to these assumptions, digital content popularity and online user activity are highly non-stationary and have a transient temporal nature. This is recognized by (Kaltenbrunner et al., 2007b), where the user reaction time to a discussion-thread is modeled by means of a log-normal distribution.

The temporal data appearing within an SBS are usually generated by means of recording event timestamps; specifically, the set of instances when a story collects votes from users constitute the popularity timeline of the particular story (cf. $\pi_T(H_r)$ of Definition 3) and the instances when a user gives votes to stories form his/her activity timeline (cf. $\pi_T(D_u)$ of Definition 2). For convenience, we will denote the raw timestamp set comprising the event instances of object x (where x can either denote a story or a user) in an ordered fashion as $T_x = \{t_0, t_1, \dots t_N\}$. The first step in analyzing such data is to select a small but sufficiently representative subset of stories or users and then to inspect their timestamp sets on an individual basis.

However, these timestamp sets are not time series in a typical sense, i.e. they are not the result of measuring the value of a variable at regular intervals. Thus, in order to visually convey the information contained in them in a meaningful way, we consider two kinds of time series based on these raw timestamp sets: (a) the time series of the aggregate count of events at time t, and (b) the time series of the count of events falling in the interval *[t-Δt, t+Δt]*. For ease of reference, we shall denote the aforementioned time series as *N(t)* and *n(t)* respectively. Figure 1 illustrates the characteristics of such time series for a small sample of digg story popularity time series.

In the proposed temporal analysis process, one proceeds further by studying at a mass level the temporal evolution of content rating. This can only take place by aggregating over multiple popularity curves; however, the time series of interest (story popularities, user activities) are defined in different time intervals, i.e. they have a different starting point and a different duration; to this end, a kind of time series normalization is required. Therefore, we consider the following transformation of T_x:

$$T_x = \frac{T_x - \min(T_x)}{\max(T_x) - \min(T_x)}$$

Application of the transformation of Equation 5 makes it possible to perform a set of operations between time series, e.g. addition, subtraction, averaging and so on. This possibility is of significance since we are particularly interested in deriving an "average" time series which is representative of hundreds or even thousands of time series. Figure 2 depicts the effect of the transformation on the set of time series of Figure 1 (under the representation *n(t)*, i.e. number of events per time interval). One should note that while the transformation removes the notion of temporal scale from the individual time series, it preserves their structural characteristics.

Finally, it is possible to apply the transformation of Equation 5 to a subsequence of a given time series and in that way to map a particular "phase" of a time series to the *[0, 1]* interval with the purpose of comparing the evolution of the phenomenon within this phase to its evolution within the full lifetime of the time series. Comparison between time series phases provides additional insights to the understanding of temporal phenomena, especially in cases where there is prior knowledge that a phenomenon takes place in more than one phases, e.g. the popularity of a digg story may grow in two phases as will be discussed below, in the Experiments section.

Social Network Influence on Content Rating

After studying the statistical properties and the temporal characteristics of the Diggsonomy entities, we further study the impact that the social

Figure 1. Two alternatives for inspecting event-based time series: (a) cumulative number of Diggs, (b) number of Diggs per hour. Here, three sample digg story popularity curves are shown.

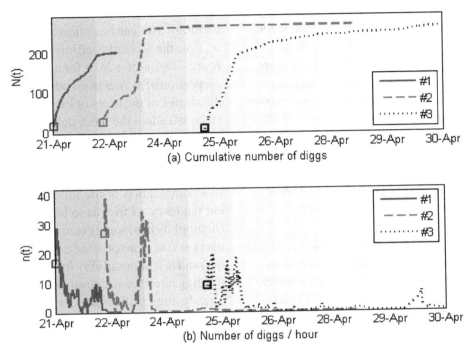

Figure 2. The effect of the proposed time series normalization

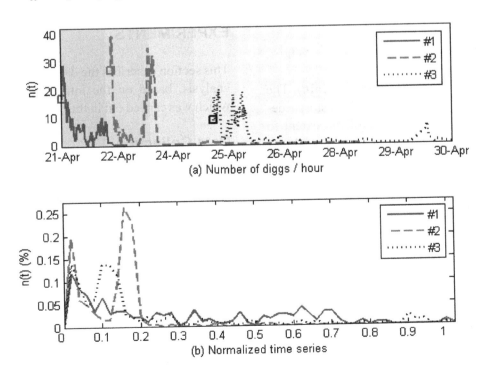

networks of SBS users have on the content rating process. Understanding and identifying patterns of influence in online communities is increasingly attracting research and industrial interest, since managing social influence can be beneficial for a series of applications, e.g. implementing more effective online advertising campaigns (Richardson & Domingos, 2002) or identifying experts in online knowledge sharing communities (Zhang et al., 2007). Therefore, we introduce here two measures in order to quantify the social influence on the content rating process. We name these two measures, the u*ser Social Susceptibility* (SS) I_u, and the *story Social Influence Gain* (SIG) I_r.

- **Definition 4 (Social Susceptibility):** The social susceptibility of a given user u denoted by I_u quantifies the extent to which his/her voting behavior follows the behavior of his/her friends' voting behavior.

$$I_u = \frac{|D_u'|}{|D_u|}, \text{ where}$$

$$D_u' = \{(r_u, t_u) \in D_u \mid \exists f \in S_U, (r_u, t_f) \in D_f, t_f < t_u\}$$

- **Definition 5 (Social Influence Gain):** The social influence gain for a given story r denoted by I_r is a measure of the extent to which r has benefited from the social network of the story submitter.

$$I_r = \frac{|H_r'|}{|H_r|}, \text{ where}$$

$$H_r' = \{(u, t_k) \in H_r \mid \exists (u_0, t_0) \in H_r, u_0 \in S_U, t_0 < t_k\}$$

and u_0 is the submitter of the story as defined in Definition 3.

SS and SIG are similar in nature to the concept of *Social Correlation* as discussed in (Anagnostopoulos et al., 2008). Social Correlation (SC) within an SBS can be defined either for two users, u_1, u_2 as the Jaccard coefficient of the sets R_{u1} and R_{u2} (cf. Definition 2) or for a single user u as the proportion of his/her stories that are common with the stories of the users of his/her social network. Here, we adopt the latter definition since it is directly comparable with the SS of a user, i.e. it can be derived by removing the temporal constraint from Equation 6. Note that SC may be attributed to a combination of the following: (a) an inherent tendency of friends to have similar interests (homophily), (b) some external factor causing two users to vote in favor of the same story (confounding) and (c) the possibility for users to see through the digg interface which stories their friends have already dugg (influence). By imposing temporal constraints in Equations 6 and 7, we attempt to isolate the effect of (a) and (b) in order to use SS and SIG as measures of social influence rather than measures of generic SC.

EXPERIMENTS

This section describes the data collection and the analysis, based on the introduced framework, which was carried out in the context of this work.

Data Collection

We collected a large dataset from digg by means of the public API which has been made available from the service. During the week between 24 and 30 April 2008, the stories appearing in the 'Upcoming' section of the site were downloaded, locally stored and monitored for the two following weeks. A total of 109,360 stories appeared in the site during this period, which indicates an average story submission rate of over 15,000 stories per day (or 650 stories per hour). Out of this initial story set, 105,108 stories were retained, since 3.88%

of the initially collected story set vanished from digg very soon. We will refer to this dataset as the *core* dataset and denote it by D_0. Table 1 provides a summary of the statistics of D_0 per story topic.

Subsequently, we downloaded the friends of the users contained in D_0 and the friends of their friends, i.e. the union of the two-hop neighborhoods of the nodes belonging to the original social network of core-digg-data. This collection phase resulted in a total of 358,143 users. Finally, for each of those users, we downloaded his/her full Personomy (cf. Definition 2). This dataset will be referred to as *extended* dataset and denoted by D_1.

The story popularity tracking of the first data collection phase was carried out by querying the API at predetermined intervals for potential new Diggs for each of the initially stored stories. As the stories grew older these intervals were increased since, as will be observed in the following, the majority of Diggs for a given story are received on average during the first 10% of the story lifetime. In this way, redundant calls to the service were kept to a minimum.

Data Analysis

As a first step in our analysis, we examine the heavy-tail nature of four variables of interest arising through the mass usage of digg. The following distributions are examined:

- Diggs collected by stories.
- Comments collected by stories.
- Diggs given by users.
- Friends in the digg social networks of users.

Figure 3 contains logarithmic plots of the aforementioned distributions. The figure renders clear the heavy-tail nature of the depicted distributions, by overlaying on top of the observed distributions their power-law fits according to the fitting method presented in (Clauset et al., 2007) and formalized in Equations 3 and 4 of the previous section. Apparently, the plain power-law model is not sufficient for accurately fitting all of the observed distributions. For instance, the shape of the distribution of Diggs per user in Figure 3(c) indicates that a truncated log-normal distribution would be a better fit for the observed variable. Further, by inspection of the number of friends per user, a few conspicuous outliers can

Table 1. Summary of dataset D_0

Topic	# Stories	# Domains	# Users	Avg. Diggs	Max Diggs	Avg. Story Life (hours)
			Statistics			
Technology	16,257	6,999	7,604	17.31	6,886	29.93
World & Business	25,897	8,048	9,786	14.19	4,964	29.05
Science	4,504	2,094	2,573	28.69	2,991	37.96
Gaming	6,182	2,071	2,712	18.43	5,442	26.99
Lifestyle	18,070	7,811	7,966	8.47	4,419	22.79
Entertainment	15,088	4,775	6,073	9.28	7,842	21.31
Sports	5,604	2,052	2,382	9.11	3,236	26.29
Offbeat	13,509	5,260	7,251	22.12	8,517	27.53
TOTAL	105,108	30,944	34,593	14.60	8,517	26.92

Figure 3. Four distributions arising within digg

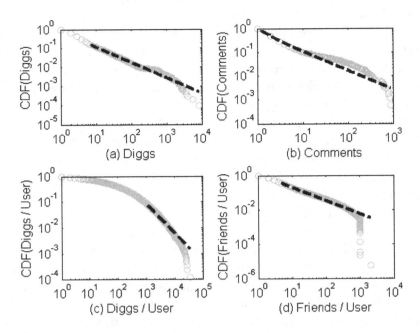

Figure 4. Two possible popularity evolution patterns. Note the two different phases in the popularity evolution for stories that are selected for the 'Popular' section of the site

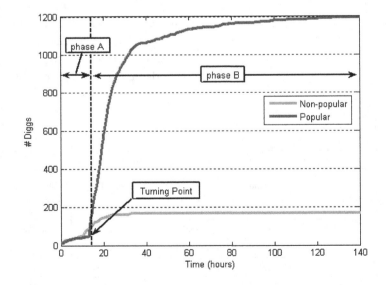

Figure 5. Digg arrival time distributions of popular vs. non-popular stories

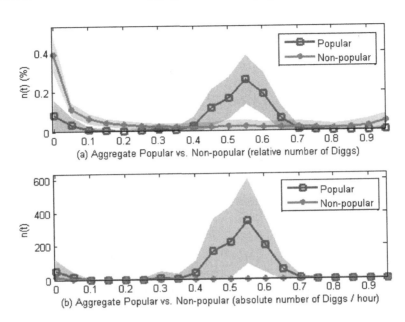

be identified that deviate significantly from the fitted power-law. Nevertheless, the plain power law model is still useful for approximating the shape of the distributions.

Subsequently, we carry out the temporal study of story popularity curves according to the methodology presented in the previous section. A first noteworthy observation about the popularity of submitted stories in digg is that they typically evolve in two ways: (a) they reach a plateau of popularity while in the 'Upcoming' section of the site and remain there until they are completely removed in case they do not receive any Diggs for a long time, (b) they attain the 'Popular' status after some time and they are moved to the 'Popular' section, where they undergo a second phase of popularity growth at a much higher intensity. Figure 4 depicts the cumulative number of diggs, $N(t)$, collected by a sample popular and a sample non-popular story during their lifetime. For convenience, we denote the set of stories of the first type as R_U and the set of popular stories as R_P.[6]

After establishing by inspection the difference of temporal evolution between popular and non-popular stories, we then proceed with comparing the distributions of their Digg arrival times. To this end, the time series, $n(t)$, of 5,468 non-popular and 852 popular stories, which were normalized by means of the transformation of Equation 5, were aggregated[7]. This resulted in the distributions of Figure 5. Together with the distributions we present the areas of confidence for their values; more specifically, around each instance $n(t)$, we draw the interval $[n(t)-\sigma_n/3, n(t)+\sigma_n/3]$. In 5(a), the time series of the number of Diggs $n(t)$ is normalized with respect to the total number of Diggs throughout the whole lifetime of each story. In that way, it is possible to directly compare the local temporal structures of popular stories to the ones of the non-popular stories. In Figure 5(b), we present the absolute number of Diggs per hour in order to provide a complete picture of the comparison between the popular and the non-popular stories.

Figure 6. Aggregate user digging behavior

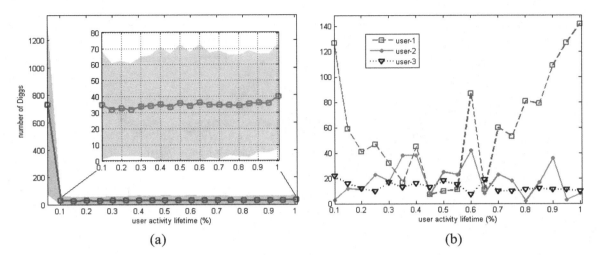

(a)   (b)

Figure 7. (a) Scatter plot of social correlation vs. social susceptibility, (b) Social susceptibility distributions for frequent vs. circumstantial users

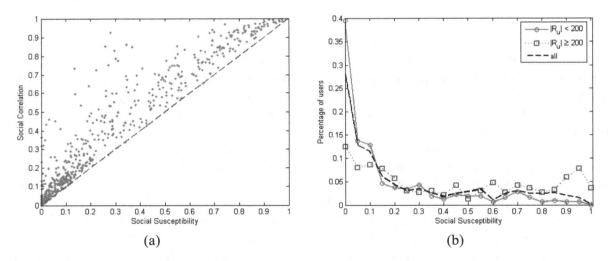

(a)   (b)

Figure 5 clearly illustrates the fact that while the non-popular stories gather the majority of their Diggs during the very first moments of their lifetime (first two bins in the histogram), the popular ones are characterized by two growth stages: (a) a first growth stage which is similar to the full lifetime of the non-popular stories, i.e. it is characterized by a monotonically decreasing trend, (b) a second growth stage, which takes place once a story is moved to the 'Popular' section of the site and is characterized by a steep increase in the number of votes that a story receives.

The intensity of popularity growth for the stories that become members of R_p can be attributed to the high exposure that these stories get for a few minutes after they are moved to the 'Popular' section (which happens to be the front page of

Figure 8. Distribution of story Social Influence Gain (SIG) for popular and non-popular stories

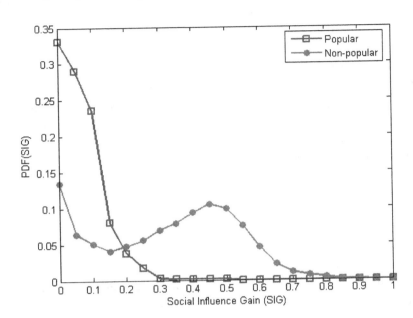

digg). Also, one should note that big search engines continuously index and rank favorably the most popular stories of digg (and stories coming from other SBS and social media applications) and thus they act as a secondary source of exposure for these stories, which contributes to sustain their popularity growth for some time.

After analyzing the temporal evolution of story popularity, we apply a similar analysis on the user digging behavior. For such a study, we investigate the structure of the time series that are formed from counting the number of Diggs given by users to stories that fall within the interval $[t-\Delta t, t+\Delta t]$. Figure 6(a) presents the result of aggregating the user activity over 539 users drawn randomly from the set of users belonging to D_0^8. Inspection of the outer diagram reveals that digg users are intensively active during the very first period after subscription to the service (note the extremely high number of diggs occurring in the first 5-10% of the users' lifetime). This is not particularly surprising since users are more

enthusiastic and eager to explore the service once they discover it. As time goes by, their enthusiasm wears off resulting in more stable usage patterns (as one can deduce by studying the inner diagram of Figure 6).

A further noteworthy observation can be made by comparing the aggregate user activity time of Figure 6(a) series with the three sample activity time series of Figure 6(b) which come from three individual users. It appears that the individual activity time series do not present any distinct pattern. On the other hand, the aggregate activity is quite stable (though the high variance indicated by the magnitude of the shaded area in 6(a) implies the instability of the individual time series). Thus, it appears that a set of independent behavior patterns of individuals leads to a stable mass behavior when aggregated.

The last part of the experimental work involved the estimation of the distributions for the social influence measures of Definitions 4 and 5, namely the SS of digg users, as well as the story

SIG values. These estimations were based on a subset of users and stories randomly selected[9] from the core dataset. From Equations 6 and 7, it is clear that these computations require data that fall outside the core data set (e.g. the Personomies of the users' friends); it was for this reason that the extended dataset D_I was collected.

The estimation of the SS distribution was based on a random sample of 672 users, of whom the SC and SS values were computed. Inspection of the scatter plot of the SC versus the SS of these users, cf. Figure 7(a), reveals that social susceptibility closely follows social correlation. That means that in most cases, when a story has been dugg by both a user and one or more of his/her friends, it is likely that the one or more of the user's friends dugg the story before the user. Few users deviate from this behavior and can thus be considered as the *opinion leaders* of the system (the more a point in Figure 7(a) deviates from the unitary straight line the more the user represented by this point can be considered an opinion leader).

Furthermore, a look into the user SS distributions as presented in Figure 7(b) indicates that the majority of circumstantial digg users (these users that have dugg a story less than 200 times) present low social susceptibility. In contrast, digg users with more intense activity tend to be influenced by their social network at a higher frequency. This may indicate that the more users are active within the system the more they rely on their online friends as a source of potentially interesting content.

Finally, insights into the mechanism of story promotion employed by digg are provided through a study of the story SIG patterns. Figure 8 clearly depicts the difference in the SIG distributions between the popular and the non-popular stories. These distributions were estimated by sampling 830 popular and 5076 non-popular stories and computing their respective SIG values. The histograms indicate that the event of a story with $I_r >$ *0.35* becoming popular is highly unlikely while in contrast it is very common for non-popular stories

to take SIG values in the interval *[0.2, 0.7]*. This could support the hypothesis that high SIG for a story implies low probability of becoming popular; however, instead of the above conclusion, we would rather speculate that digg employs filters based on social measures similar to I_r to prevent groups of 'friends' from gaining control over which stories appear in the 'Popular' section[10].

CONCLUSION

We presented a study of online content popularity in the context of SBS applications, such as digg, which act as social media applications. The study was based on the Diggsonomy formalism which endows the well-established Folksonomy model with a temporal aspect, and thus facilitates the unified analysis of social bookmarking activity of users from three aspects: statistical, temporal and social.

The statistical analysis of the collected data confirmed the heavy tail nature of popularity and indicated that the plain power law model can be used as a rough approximation of the real distributions. Furthermore, examination of the temporal characteristics of content popularity revealed the transient nature of popularity and the effects of high content exposure to its popularity. In addition, by studying the evolution of individual and aggregate user activity in time, we observed how a mass of users acting with no consistent pattern can result in a stable aggregate behavior. Finally, two measures were defined to quantify the social influence on content popularity in an SBS: the social susceptibility of a user and the social information gain of a story. The relation of social susceptibility with generic social correlation was considered as a means of identifying opinion leaders in an SBS, and evidence was provided that SBS administrators probably employ measures of social influence as a means to prevent artificial popularity boosts by communities of users.

In the future, we plan to extend the depth of our study and to investigate the feasibility of predicting web content popularity (in an SBS context) by taking into account different features of SBS content items, namely temporal, semantic, and social, in order to pose popularity prediction as a standard machine learning problem. Furthermore, we intend to expand the scope of our studies to data sets of larger amounts and of different origin (e.g. del.icio.us, flickr) as a means of testing the generality of the observations established here.

ACKNOWLEDGMENT

This work was supported by the MESH and WeKnowIt projects, partially funded by the European Commission, under contract numbers FP6-027685 and FP7-215453 respectively. Furthermore, improvements to this paper were possible thanks to the valuable comments of the reviewers.

REFERENCES

Agichtein, E., Castillo, C., Donato, D., Gionis, A., & Mishne, G. (2008, February 11-12). Finding high-quality content in social media. In *Proceedings of the international Conference on Web Search and Web Data Mining*, Palo Alto, California, USA, WSDM '08 (pp. 183-194). New York: ACM.

Anagnostopoulos, A., Kumar, R., & Mahdian, M. (2008, August 24-27). Influence and Correlation in Social Networks. In *Proceedings of the 14th ACM SIGKDD international Conference on Knowledge Discovery and Data Mining*, Las Vegas, Nevada, USA (KDD '08) (pp. 7 – 15). New York: ACM.

Barabási, A.-L., & Albert, R. (1999). Emergence of Scaling in Random Networks. [AAAS.]. *Science, 286*(5439), 509–512. doi:10.1126/science.286.5439.509

Bass, F. (1969). A new product growth model for consumer durables. *Management Science, 15,* 215–227. doi:10.1287/mnsc.15.5.215

Box, G. E. P., & Jenkins, G. M. (1994). *Time Series Analysis: Forecasting and Control.* New York: Prentice Hall PTR.

Cha, M., Kwak, H., Rodriguez, P., Ahn, Y., & Moon, S. (2007, October 24-26). I Tube, You Tube, Everybody Tubes: Analyzing the World's Largest User Generated Content Video System. In *Proceedings of the 7th ACM SIGCOMM Conference on internet Measurement*, San Diego, California, USA (IMC '07) (pp. 1-14). New York, NY: ACM.

Clauset, A., Shalizi, C. R., & Newman, M. E. J. (2007). *Power-law distributions in empirical data.*

Falkowski, T., & Spiliopoulou, M. (2007). Users in volatile communities: Studying active participation and community evolution. *User Modeling, 2007,* 47–56. doi:10.1007/978-3-540-73078-1_8

Giannakidou, E., Koutsonikola, V., Vakali, A., & Kompatsiaris, I. (2008). *Co-clustering tags and social data sources.* Paper presented at the 9th International Conference on Web-Age Information Management (WAIM 2008), Beijing, China.

Golder, S., & Huberman, B. A. (2006). The Structure of Collaborative Tagging Systems. [Sage Publications, Inc.]. *Journal of Information Science, 32*(2), 198–208. doi:10.1177/0165551506062337

Halpin, H., Robu, V., & Shepherd, H. (2007, May 8-12). The complex dynamics of collaborative tagging. In *Proceedings of the 16th international Conference on World Wide Web*, Banff, Alberta, Canada (WWW '07) (pp. 211-220). New York: ACM.

Hotho, A., Jäschke, R., Schmitz, C., & Stumme, G. (2006). Information Retrieval in Folksonomies: Search and Ranking. In Y. Sure & J. Domingue (Eds.), *The Semantic Web: Research and Applications* (pp. 411-426). Springer.

Hotho, A., Jäschke, R., Schmitz, C., & Stumme, G. (2006). Trend Detection in Folksonomies. In *Lecture Notes in Computer Science 4306/2006, 56-70.* Springer Berlin / Heidelberg.

Kaltenbrunner, A., Gómez, V., & López, V. (2007). *Description and Prediction of Slashdot Activity.* Paper presented at the LA-WEB 2007 5th Latin American Web Congress, Santiago, Chile.

Kaltenbrunner, A., Gómez, V., Moghnieh, A., Meza, R., Blat, J., & López, V. (2007). *Homogeneous temporal activity patterns in a large online communication space.* Paper presented at the 10th Int. Conf. on Business Information Systems. Workshop on Social Aspects of the Web (SAW 2007), Poznan, Poland.

Kempe, D., Kleinberg, J., & Tardos, É. (2003). Maximizing the Spread of Influence through a Social Network. In *Proceedings of the 9th ACM SIGKDD international conference on Knowledge Discovery and Data Mining* (KDD '03), (pp. 137-146). New York: ACM.

Lerman, K. (2007). Social Information Processing in News Aggregation. In *IEEE Internet Computing special issue on Social Search 11*(6), 16-28. IEEE.

Mika, P. (2005). Ontologies are us: A unified model of social networks and semantics. In *The Semantic Web* (ISWC 2005) (pp. 522-536). Springer Berlin / Heidelberg.

Newman, M. E. J. (2005). Power laws, Pareto distributions and Zipf's law. *Contemporary Physics, 46,* 323–351. doi:10.1080/00107510500052444

Papadopoulos, S., Vakali, A., & Kompatsiaris, I. (July, 2008). *Digg it Up! Analyzing Popularity Evolution in a Web 2.0 Setting.* Paper presented at MSoDa08 (Mining Social Data). *A satellite Workshop of the 18th European Conference on Artificial Intelligence,* Patras, Greece.

Richardson, M., & Domingos, P. (2002). Mining knowledge-sharing sites for viral marketing. In *Proceedings of the 14th ACM SIGKDD International Conference on Knowledge Discovery and Data Mining* (KDD '02), (pp. 61-70), Las Vegas, USA: ACM.

Song, X., Chi, Y., Hino, K., & Tseng, B. L. (2007, May 08-12). Information flow modeling based on diffusion rate for prediction and ranking. In *Proceedings of the 16th international Conference on World Wide Web,* Banff, Alberta, Canada (WWW '07) (pp. 191-200). New York, NY: ACM.

Wu, F., & Huberman, B. A. (2007). Novelty and collective attention. [PNAS.]. *Proceedings of the National Academy of Sciences of the United States of America, 104*(45), 17599–17601. doi:10.1073/pnas.0704916104

Zhang, J., Ackerman, M. S., & Adamic, L. (2007, May 8-12). Expertise networks in online communities: structure and algorithms. In *Proceedings of the 16th international Conference on World Wide Web,* Banff, Alberta, Canada (WWW '07) (pp. 221-230). New York: ACM.

ENDNOTES

[1] http://digg.com

[2] http://www.propeller.com

[3] http://www.newsvine.com

[4] http://www.youtube.com

[5] http://ucc.daum.net

[6] Whether a story jumps to the 'Popular' section or not does not solely depend on the number of Diggs it receives (although it is certainly taken into account). The digg administrators make this decision on the basis of a set of proprietary criteria and heuristics, which they keep secret since sharing such knowledge would render the system prone

to malicious attacks (e.g. to artificially boost the popularity of a story).

[7] Only stories with $|H_r| > 20$ were studied to prevent the 'noisy' time series from distorting the resulting aggregate time series of the non-popular stories.

[8] Users with $|R_u| < 20$ were not considered in the sample selection in order to prevent users with sparse (and therefore noisy) activity to affect the aggregate activity time series.

[9] The filtering rules of $|R_u| > 20$ and $|H_r| > 20$ were applied here too.

[10] The post in http://blog.digg.com/?p=106 reinforces this speculation.

This work was previously published in International Journal of Data Warehousing and Mining, Volume 6, Issue 1, edited by David Taniar, pp. 20-37, copyright 2010 by IGI Publishing (an imprint of IGI Global).

Chapter 3
Detecting Trends in Social Bookmarking Systems:
A del.icio.us Endeavor

Robert Wetzker
Technische Universität Berlin, Germany

Carsten Zimmermann
University of San Diego, USA

Christian Bauckhage
University of Bonn and Fraunhofer IAIS, Germany

ABSTRACT

The authors present and evaluate an approach to trend detection in social bookmarking systems using a probabilistic generative model in combination with smoothing techniques. Social bookmarking systems are gaining major interest among researchers in the areas of data mining and Web intelligence, since they provide a large amount of user-generated annotations and reflect the interest of millions of people. Based on a vast corpus of approximately 150 million bookmarks found at del.icio.us, the authors analyze bookmarking and tagging patterns and discuss evidence that social bookmarking systems are vulnerable to spamming. They present a method to limit the impact of spam on a trend detector and provide conclusions as well as directions for future research.

INTRODUCTION

Social bookmarking systems, such as del.icio. us, *StumbleUpon* or *CiteULike*, have been very successful in the recent past. Their success originated from members' ability to centrally store bookmarks on the web. However, with the coming of age of these services, the perceived value of social bookmarking systems shifted towards the underlying social aspects, such as trend indication, advanced web search or recommendation functionality. These services are an invaluable source of information, since they provide a vast amount of user-generated annotations, such as

DOI: 10.4018/978-1-61350-474-1.ch003

Copyright © 2012, IGI Global. Copying or distributing in print or electronic forms without written permission of IGI Global is prohibited.

tags, and reflect the interests of millions of users. One *social* aspect of these systems derives from the fact that resources, in general web pages, are tagged by the community and not by the creator of content alone, as in other services like Flickr or YouTube (Marlow, Naaman, Boyd, & Davis, 2006). This characteristic, called collaborative tagging, was shown to provide relevant metadata (Heymann, Koutrika, & Garcia-Molina, 2008) and is expected to boost the semantic quality of labels (Surowiecki, 2004).

One of the first and most popular social bookmarking systems is del.icio.us. Because of its early acceptance in the market, the vast growth over the past five years and easy data accessibility, del.icio.us represents a suitable case for analyzing the characteristics of social bookmarking communities. Figure 1 shows the del.icio.us main page that lists the currently popular bookmarks and tags. Though this article mainly examines del.icio.us,

we conjecture that the results presented here also apply for other social bookmarking services and collaborative tagging systems in general.

As shown by Heymann, Koutrika, and Garcia-Molina (2008), trends within the del.icio.us tagging and bookmarking behavior strongly correlate with real world events. This characteristic makes bookmarking services a valuable source for trend detection and creates new opportunities in areas such as product tracking or marketing. We will investigate the nature of trends within social bookmarking services and present a probabilistic method for the automated detection of trends within the del.icio.us community. In order to succeed in the trend detection task, we further present a method which limits the influence of spam users as their frequent appearance in the data and their anomalous behavior would, otherwise, strongly interfere with any trend patterns.

Figure 1. The del.icio.us main page (September 2008)

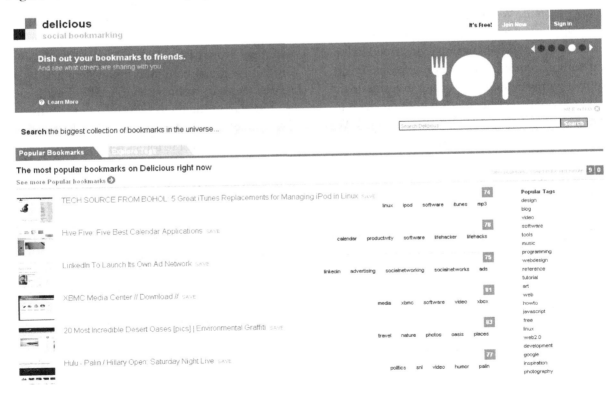

The purpose of this work is threefold: First, we investigate the underlying bookmarking and tagging dynamics of social bookmarking systems using the example of del.icio.us. Second, we discuss evidence that social bookmarking systems are highly vulnerable to spam and hence need to be preprocessed before any sophisticated analysis can take place. Finally, we show that trends within the bookmarking community can be successfully detected using a probabilistic generative model combined with smoothing techniques where trends are considered statistical anomalies. For a comprehensive study, we collected a corpus of 142,341,551 del.icio.us bookmarks, which - to the best of our knowledge - is the biggest dataset of its kind analyzed to date.

The paper is structured as follows: We start with an introduction into the specifics of social bookmarking systems using the example of del. icio.us. We then present our method of data mining and analyze the bookmarking and tagging patterns within the retrieved corpus. We also show that bookmarking systems are vulnerable to different forms of spam. We present behavioral patterns that help characterizing spam users and propose a method that limits their impact on trend detection without requiring high computational effort. Applying this method, we further investigate the possibility of detecting trends within the del.icio. us community using probabilistic measures. We present the results of our trend detector and conclude by discussing our findings and directions for future research.

THE DEL.ICIO.US BOOKMARKING SERVICE

As shown in Figures 2(a) - 2(d), del.icio.us is a fast growing on-line community. Users can centrally collect and share their bookmarks that may refer to web resources of any type as long as these resources can be identified by a URL. These bookmarks can then be organized by assigning freely chosen tags which simplifies later retrieval. del.icio.us also allows users to forward new bookmarks to friends and a user can easily find out what his friends or other community members are currently interested in.

When posting a bookmark, users can provide a description, by default the title of the web site, an extended description and a collection of tags they consider related. In order to simplify the bookmarking process and to support convergence, del.icio.us suggests tags that were assigned frequently to the bookmarked resource or by the user before. A bookmark can be marked as *private* so that it remains hidden from the community. A user can post a bookmark by going to the del.icio.us web site or, more conveniently, by using one of the many browser plug-ins that make bookmarking with a social bookmarking system and later retrieval as easy as browser-based bookmarking.

Three main channels of information diffusion exist in del.icio.us. Users can subscribe to other users' bookmarks or to topics represented by tags using Really Simple Syndication (RSS) web feeds. This way, they receive updates about developments

Figure 2. The monthly growth of del.icio.us between 2004 and 2008 by posted bookmarks (a), new users (b), new URLs (c) and new tags (d)

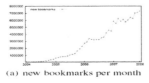 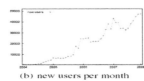  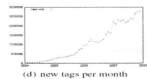

(a) new bookmarks per month   (b) new users per month   (c) new URLs per month   (d) new tags per month

in their friends or colleagues interests or about new URLs appearing in a certain domain in real-time. The second channel is the del.icio.us main page. Once a resource reaches a popularity threshold, it will appear in the list of popular resources on this page and will attract the attention of other users. The main page, too, can be subscribed via RSS. Finally, users can create networks with friends, colleagues or other members of interest and forward bookmarks, which emphasizes the social aspect of bookmarking services.

del.icio.us went on-line in September 2003 and its community of users and their corresponding bookmark collections have been growing ever since. According to our dataset, there were at least 7,305,559 newly added bookmarks and 47,429 newly appearing del.icio.us users in December 2007.

Model

According to Hotho, Jäschke, Schmitz, and Stumme (2006), a social bookmarking system can be described as a tripartite graph whose vertex set is partitioned into three disjoint sets

$$U = \{u_1,...,u_k\}$$

$$T = \{t_1,...,t_l\}$$

$$R = \{r_1,...,r_m\}$$

These sets correspond to the sets of users, tags and resources (URLs), respectively. The authors also define relations $Y \subseteq U \times T \times R$, so that the tripartite hypergraph is given by $G = (V,E)$, where $V = I \cup T \cup R$ and $E = \{\{u,t,r\}|(u,t,r) \in Y\}$. We follow the approach by Mika (2005) and simplify this structure to three bipartite graphs G_{UR}, G_{UT} and G_{RT} which model the link structure between each pair of sets separately.

Crawling and Dataset

There exists no perfect strategy for crawling del.icio.us. One of the most straightforward approaches, applied for instance by Golder and Huberman (2006) or Heymann, Koutrika, and Garcia-Molina (2008), is the monitoring of the del.icio.us recent or popular pages that list the most recent bookmarks or currently popular URLs. Despite its simplicity, this crawling method is rather time consuming and does not allow for crawling old posts. Furthermore, we find that the recent feed only contains a small percentage of the entire posted content and it remains unclear what kind of filtering criteria apply. This crawling method therefore hardly results in representative data sets. However, it may produce a set of graph nodes as seed for further crawling.

Another crawling approach follows the links within the user to user network (Angelova, Lipczak, & Pralat, 2008). This approach is expected to limit the percentage of spam in the resulting data as spam users are unlikely to be marked as friends by other users. Despite of this advantage, the method will result in a data bias towards inter-connected users, whereas users without connections within the friendship graph will not appear. Furthermore, we did not want to discard spam users as we were particularly interested in their impact on the service.

The most common method to crawl del.icio.us or similar services is to follow the links of the tripartite hypergraph G (Heymann, Koutrika, & Garcia-Molina, 2008; Hotho, Jäschke, Schmitz, & Stumme, 2006; Mika, 2005). As a starting point we downloaded all bookmarks related to the tag "web2.0". From the resulting set of bookmarks, we extracted all related tags and recursively used these for further queries. The crawler thus followed the links within the sub graph of G whose vertices only consist of tags. As a result of this process we obtained 45 million unique bookmarks. During our retrieval process, we found that the del.icio.us service limits the number of returned bookmarks when queried tag-wise which lead to an incomplete representation of frequent tags within the initial corpus. The limitation in query results seems to occur only for the tag-wise retrieval while user-wise or item-wise queries are not affected. We therefore additionally downloaded the bookmarks of the most active users within the initial corpus.

For the analysis presented here, we only consider the bookmarks obtained by the user based retrieval. This dataset consists of 142 million del. icio.us bookmarks downloaded between September 19, 2007 and January 22, 2008. By the time of our analysis, we obtained an overall corpus of 142,341,551 bookmarks from 978,979 users which - to the best of our knowledge - is the biggest data set of this kind analyzed to date. Global statistics of the corpus are shown in Table 1.

The result of a random crawler that follows the hypergraph links tends to be biased versus frequent items. Furthermore, as our initial, tag-wise crawl was biased towards recent items, we expect this bias to reappear in the second corpus. Finally, since we only downloaded the most active users from the initial data set, users with a low participation rate are underrepresented. We will consider these limitations of our data set when discussing our findings.

BOOKMARKING PATTERNS

Table 2 lists the most popular URLs in our corpus. The list is thematically split into sites related to social resource or knowledge sharing (entries 1, 2, 5, 6, 7 and 8) and web development related sites (entries 4, 9 and 10).

Not surprisingly, the del.icio.us community is biased towards web community and web technology related content. However, as most web portals use a deep linking structure for content access, the aggregation over URLs does not provide the

Table 1. Corpus details

item	count
users	978,979
bookmarks	142,341,551
assignments	450,113,886
URLs	54,401,067
domains	8,828,058
tags	6,933,179

full picture. We therefore list the Top 10 domains in Table 3. Here, we find news providers and enterprise portals among the Top 10 items, where articles or other content are identified by deep links. Table 3 also underlines the fact that enterprise domains tend to have a lower bookmarks per user rate than domains with highly dynamic content, such as news sites where users follow the news feeds and bookmark articles of interest to them.

In accordance with findings by Heymann, Koutrika, and Garcia-Molina (2008) and Hotho, Jäschke, et al. (2006), we find the user activity to follow a power law distribution with few users being responsible for a high number of posts as shown in Figure 3(a). The Top 1% of users proliferates 22% of all bookmarks, the Top 10% contributes 62%. Note that these values are above the values reported by Heymann, Koutrika, and Garcia-Molina (2008). We assume that this difference is due to an increase in spam posts within the recent months. This effect is complemented by the shortcomings of our crawling method which incompletely represents users with low participation rate. The bias of our dataset also explains the missing power law compliance of Figure 3(a) for users with less than 10 bookmarks.

Another power law dependency can be found for the occurrence frequencies of URLs. Here, 39% of all bookmarks link to the Top 1% of URLs and 61% to the Top 10% (Figure 3(b)). Furthermore, we find that 80% of all URLs appear only once in the corpus. Frequent URLs seem less

Table 2. Top 10 most frequent URLs in the corpus

	URL	bookmarks
1.	http://www.flickr.com	33,222
2.	http://www.pandora.com	32,634
3.	http://www.netvibes.com	26,743
4.	http://script.aculo.us	26,082
5.	http://slashdot.org	25,272
6.	http://en.wikipedia.org/wiki/Main_Page	23,983
7.	http://www.youtube.com	23,530
8.	http://www.last.fm	22,757
9.	http://oswd.org	20,430
10.	http://www.alvit.de/handbook	20,230

Table 3. Top 10 most frequent domains in the copus

	domain	bookmarks	users
1.	http://en.wikipedia.org	919,465	205,639
2.	http://www.youtube.com	915,789	186,326
3.	http://www.flickr.com	535,176	162,363
4.	http://www.nytimes.com	503,776	101,375
5.	http://www.google.com	392,360	156,990
6.	http://lifehacker.com	368,078	90,628
7.	http://www.amazon.com	314,414	91,073
8.	http://news.bbc.co.uk	317,978	75,610
9.	http://www.microsoft.com	290,501	101,947
10	http://community.livejournal.com	280,020	29,655

polluted by spam as users can bookmark a URL only a single time. Golder and Huberman (2006) observe that the del.icio.us community pays attention to new URLs only for a very short period of time. As a result, these URLs receive most of their posts very quickly and disappear shortly afterwards. Figure 4 shows the popularity of the most popular URLs in June 2006 that were unknown the month before. As can be seen, each URL peaks within very few days before the number of posts drastically decreases. According to Golder and Huberman (2006), this burst in popularity is likely to be caused by the appearance of an URL on the del.icio.us main page triggered by external reasons, such as the appearance of a URL on a widely read blog. Another cause of an initial popularity increase could be the spread of interest within the network of del.icio.us users itself.

TAGGING PATTERNS

On average, we find each bookmark to be labeled with 3.16 tags. However, according to our data set, this number is not constant over time and strongly varies among users. Figure 5 shows a rise in the average number of tags per bookmark from the start of del.icio.us until December 2007.

Figure 3. Some node degree distributions found on del.ico.us

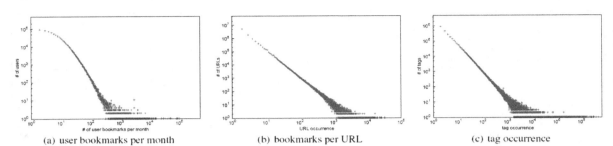

    (a) user bookmarks per month   (b) bookmarks per URL   (c) tag occurrence

This effect is partly caused by the augmentation of spam users that use a large number of tags to make their posts visible. However, we also find a higher tagging rate for non-spam users. We believe this can be explained by the constant growth of del.icio.us and the resulting need for more tags in order to categorize and retrieve bookmarks. In the beginning of the service, users could distinguish their bookmarks using only a limited number of common tags. However, with growing bookmark collections more tags were needed for structure and transparency. Further-

more, we assume that in 2003, when del.icio.us went on-line, most users were not yet familiar with tagging at all. Thus, the increase in tag assignments over time also represents the adoption of the concept of tagging itself. This fact is emphasized by the results shown in Figure 6. Here, we initially find a constant decrease in the percentage of bookmarks without any tag assignment. Whereas, in the beginning of del.icio.us, approximately 18% of all bookmarks were untagged this number changed to approximately 5% only one year later when tagging became popular with

Figure 4. Popularity of 5 sample URLs as percentage of overall bookmarks in June/July 2007. Most upcoming URLs disappear after peaking

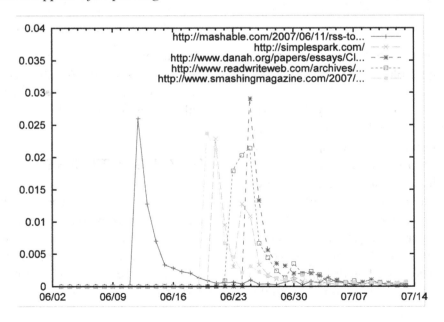

Figure 5. Average number of tags assigned to a bookmark over time. The dotted line represents the average when months are weighted by the number of bookmarks.

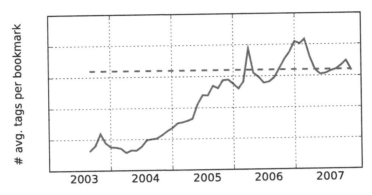

the success of Web 2.0 services. The rise in un-tagged posts in recent years is very likely caused by spammers that post large numbers of untagged content. This culminates in December 2007 when the bulk upload of untagged posts by a single spammer causes an increase in the portion of non-tagged elements by 10%.

The number of tags per bookmark also strongly depends on the user. Figure 7 plots the number of average tag assignments per user compared to the number of bookmarks a user has. It can be seen that some extreme "users" assign more than hundred tags on average, which further highlights the impact of spam.

Golder and Huberman (2006) note that tags assigned to a bookmark can perform different functions. The authors identify seven tagging purposes, such as describing the topic or the type of the bookmarked resource. Our analysis underlines these findings as can be seen from Table 4 that lists the 20 most frequent tags within our corpus. Complementary to the results of Golder and Huberman (2006), we find that users often assign tags in order to organize their bookmarks and ease later retrieval. The importance of the retrieval aspect is also highlighted by the fact that 15% of all users in the data set structure their tags by aggregating them manually into *tag bundles*.

Figure 6. Percentage of bookmarks without any tag assignment. The dotted line represents the overall average when months are weighted by the number of bookmarks. The peak in the last month is caused by spam.

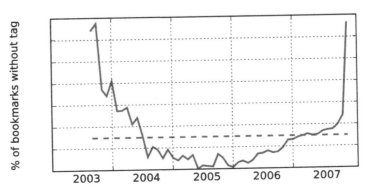

Figure 7. The number of user bookmarks compared to the average number of tags assigned by the user

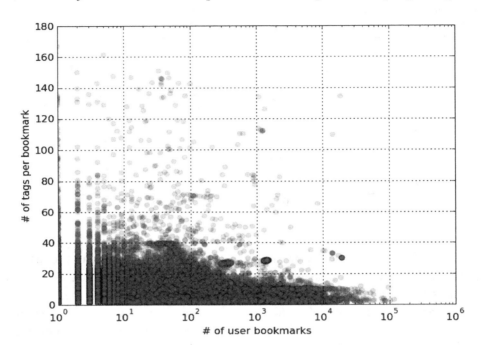

Tag bundles are a functionality offered by del.icio.us where users can define categories (bundles) and list the tags which should fall into each category. The created *tag bundles* then behave like (meta-)tags and can act as filters during the search process identically to standard tags. The need for organization only occurs once a user reaches a certain number of bookmarks. This intention may, therefore, have been less present in the beginning of del.icio.us, when Golder and Huberman (2006) performed their analysis. Table 4 again highlights that del.icio.us is biased towards web and web development related topics.

The vocabulary of del.icio.us users is highly standardized. Although, there exist around seven million tags in our corpus, less than 700 account for 50% of all assignments. This convergence is likely to be aided by the tag recommendation mechanisms provided by del.icio.us. The users' interests in a standardized vocabulary for easier retrieval of own bookmarks likely further support

this trend. 55% of all tags were found to appear only once in the data. Figure 3(c) plots the power law distribution of tags.

The distribution of tags within del.icio.us is not constant but changes over time and often significantly correlates with external events. Figure 8 presents the dynamics of 5 sample tags in 2007. As can be seen from the time series, the tagging trends reflect both the upcoming of new technologies, such as Google's 'Android' which was announced in early November 2007, and periodic events, such as 'Christmas'. The delay between an external event and its echo on del.icio.us is generally marginal, which was also reported by Heymann, Koutrika, and Garcia-Molina (2008). Social bookmarking services can therefore provide a valuable and cheap resource for the detection, monitoring and even prediction of real world trends. We will present a method for trend detection in this environment in the final section of this article.

Table 4. Top 20 most frequent tags in the corpus (* in millions)

	tag	count*			tag	count*
1.	design	4.93		11.	free	2.50
2.	blog	4.02		12.	web2.0	2.42
3.	software	3.95		13.	art	2.30
4.	web	3.27		14.	linux	2.25
5.	tools	3.23		15.	css	2.21
6.	reference	3.15		16.	howto	2.17
7.	programming	3.08		17.	tutorial	1.98
8.	music	2.99		18.	news	1.96
9.	video	2.60		19.	photography	1.76
10.	webdesign	2.54		20.	business	1.71

SOCIAL BOOKMARKING AND SPAM

An initial analysis of our corpus reveals a frequent occurrence of bookmarks, which presumably are spam and were posted by automated mechanisms. As with applications such as email, the impact of spam is severe for social bookmarking. An analysis of the Top 20 most active del.icio.us users uncovered 19 users of apparently non human origin posting tens of thousands of URLs pointing to only few domains. These 19 "users" alone account for 1,321,316 bookmarks or approximately 1% of the corpus. Unfortunately, this result comes to no surprise since del.icio.us offers an interface for remote postings and URLs that appear on del.icio.us have the potential of reaching thousands of users. Additionally, spammers may hope to augment the search engine ranking of their sites

Figure 8. Occurrence of 5 sample tags in 2007 as percentage of overall assignments

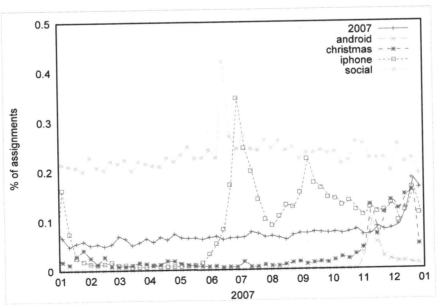

when their URLs appear on as many del.icio.us pages as possible.

del.icio.us is not the only bookmarking service vulnerable to spam. Krause, Hotho, and Stumme (2008) report, that among the 20,000 users of the BibSonomy bookmarking service (http://www.bibsonomy.org) they manually identified 18,500 as spammers. These spammers accounted for 90% of all posts.

The behavior and thus the impact of the spam creators differs. For example, we found one user who labeled all of his 7,780 bookmarks with the exact same six tags. All these bookmarks refer to the same blog site. Another spammer added over 10,000 posts linking to only few web portals and labeled each bookmark with more than 100 tags, presumably in order to make the related sources more visible to del.icio.us users and search engines alike. Furthermore, we encounter bulk uploads, a phenomenon also reported for Flickr by Dubinko et al. (2006), where users upload thousands of

bookmarks within minutes and rarely actively contribute thereafter. We also found spammers with multiple user accounts. The most prolific spammer posted at least 538,045 bookmarks to only 5 domains using more than 10 accounts.

Generally, we find spammers to exhibit one or more of the following characteristics:

- **Very high activity:** Automated posting routines may reach much higher participation rates than human users.
- **Few domains:** The URLs posted by spam users are likely to belong to a very small set of domains. Figure 9 plots the number of posts going to a domain versus the number of users bookmarking this domain. Many domains receive a very high number of postings coming from only a few users.
- **High tagging rate:** Some spam users tend to label their bookmarks with an exorbitant

Figure 9. The number of bookmarks compared to the number of users linking to a domain

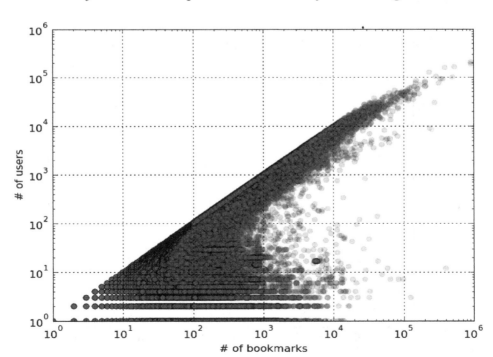

number of tags in order to increase their visibility.

- **Very low tagging rate:** Other spam users do not tag at all, but constantly upload bookmarks without any tags.
- **Bulk posts:** Bulk uploads generally imply automated postings. However, bulk uploads are not always spam. Instead, automated postings may also appear for human users, e.g. if a user synchronizes his local bookmarks or bookmarks from another bookmarking service with del.icio.us using existing software tools.
- **No tag bundles:** Spammers are only interested in distributing their content in the community but do not need to access it later. Spammers therefore have no motivation to structure their tags into groups using the del.icio.us tag bundle functionality. The missing retrieval intention is also likely to result in anomalous tag distributions for spam users, such as a very low tag entropy for spammers that always assign the same tags or an above average entropy for spammers that assign tags randomly.
- **Combinations of the above:** In most cases, we find a combination of the above characteristics. Figure 7, for example, shows the correlation between the number of bookmarks a user has and the average number of tags she assigns to each bookmark. As can be seen from the figure, some users tend to have very high values in both dimension and can thus easily be identified as spammers.

The presence of spam may result in highly misleading results when bookmarking systems are considered in areas such as trend detection or ontology creation based on tag patterns. In these cases, spam filtering should precede any sophisticated analysis. However, in some cases, detecting spam may be computationally expensive or ambiguous. We therefore propose a new concept which we call *diffusion of attention* that helps to reduce the influence of spam on the distribution of tags without the actual need of filtering. We define the attention a tag attracts in a certain period of time as the number of users using the tag in this period. The diffusion for a tag is then given as the number of users that assign this tag for the first time. This way, we measure the importance of an item by its capability to attract new users. Every user's influence is limited and a trend can only be created by groups of users. Figure 10 shows the effect of the concept of *diffusion of attention* on the tags we already plotted in Figure 8. A comparison of both figures reveals that the diffusion of attention concept reflects all major trends also obtained by an occurrence based measurement. We find that the measure is able to reflect both seasonal and newly popular tags. The only 'trend' not appearing within the new plot is the peak of the 'social' tag in June 2007. An analysis showed this peak to be caused by the activity of one single user posting 5,666 bookmarks all tagged 'social' within the relevant week. All of these bookmarks link to the same domain. This spam trend does not appear using our *diffusion of attention* measure as it weights all users equally.

Retaining only combinations of users and tags that appear for the first time in our corpus reduces the number of total tag assignments from 450 million to 102 million.

TREND DETECTION

We want to discover trends within a social bookmarking service at different points in time. Due to symmetry and without loss of generality, we restrict our discussion to the detection of trends within the tag distribution and therefore base our analysis on the graph $G_{UT} = (V_{UT}, E_{UT})$ where

$$V_{UT} = U \cup T$$

$$E_{UT} = \{\{u,t\} | (u,t) \in U \times T\}$$

Figure 10. Diffusion of attention for the 5 sample tags of Figure 8. The plot shows the number of users assigning a tag for the first time as percentage of the overall first assignments.

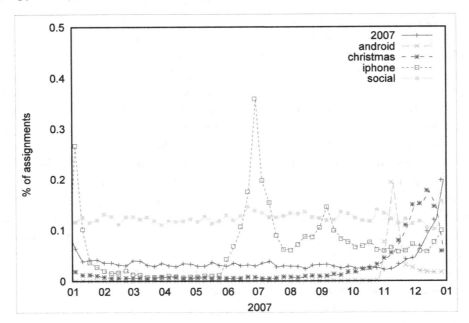

We apply the *diffusion of attention* concept presented in the previous section and determine the impact of a tag in a given interval by counting the users assigning this tag for the first time. This count equals the number of new edges E_{UT} in that period. We then consider an item, i.e. a tag, to signify a trend, if it attracts significantly more new users in a monitored period of time than it did in the previous period. Since we consider trends as statistical anomalies, we measure their significance using a probabilistic generative model. For this purpose, we compare the item distributions D_0 and D_1 resulting from the counts over two consecutive periods t_0 and t_1 and assume that all items in D_1 were generated independently at random from D_0. If the probability of an item i at time t_0 is assumed to be $p_0(i)$, the probability of observing item i at a frequency of $f_1(i)$ in the period t_1 is given by

$$p(f_1(i)) = \binom{n_1}{f_1(i)} p_0(i)^{f_1(i)} (1 - p_0(i))^{n_1 - f_1(i)} \qquad (1)$$

where n_1 denotes the number of all observations in t_1. In order to avoid problems related to zero counts, i.e. items that did not occur in t_0 but do occur in t_1, we choose a beta distribution

$$F(p_0; \alpha, \beta) = \frac{\Gamma(\alpha + \beta)}{\Gamma(\alpha)\Gamma(\beta)} p_0^{\alpha-1} (1 - p_0)^{\beta-1} \qquad (2)$$

as a prior, where $\alpha = \varepsilon$ and $\beta = (Z-1)\varepsilon$. Here, Z denotes the number of existing items and ε the assumed prior frequency of each item. Combining the prior and the observations at t_0, the $p_0(i)$ in equation (1) becomes

$$p_0(i) = \frac{f_0(i) + \varepsilon}{n_0 + \varepsilon Z}. \qquad (3)$$

Using the prior thus has the same effect as the *additive smoothing* well known from language modeling (e.g. Chen and Goodman (1996)). Moreover, the additive parameter ε allows for controlling the influence of the prior distribution with respect to the observations at t_0 and thus for controlling the degree of smoothing. As the resulting bias toward rare items may be interpreted as a trend itself, we also apply smoothing to D_1 in order to neutralize this effect.

Finally, we calculate a score for all items for which $p_1(i) > p_0(i)$. It is given by

$$score(i) = -\log(p(f_1(i))) \qquad (4)$$

We then consider the items with the highest score to be most significant.

As the exact calculation of $p(f_1(i))$ is computational expensive, we estimate the binomial probability mass function by a Gaussian of the type $N(n_1 p0(i), n_1 p_0(i)(1 - p_0(i)))$. In our experimental evaluation, we generate monthly snapshots of the del.icio.us corpus. For each snapshot, we determine the number of new edges per tag in G_{UT}. We then measure the evolution of a tag from one month to the next by calculating its score us-

ing equation (4). Table 5 presents the Top 5 tag trends for different months in 2007 and different values of ε.

The presented results show that our measure can detect new events, such as the announcement of Google's "Android" or of Apple's "Mac OS X Leopard", and, at the same time, seasonal events, such as "Christmas" and "Halloween". Furthermore, we observe that the parameter ε gives us control over the importance of the relative versus the absolute development of an item. Choosing larger values for ε favors popular items which are already well spread throughout the bookmarking system. On the other hand, upcoming, often short-living, tags benefit from a small ε.

RELATED WORK

Social web communities including social bookmarking systems have received increasing research popularity in recent years. As one of

Table 5. Top 5 tag trends for different months and different values of ε (see also Figure 10)

		$\varepsilon = 0.2$		$\varepsilon = 1$		$\varepsilon = 100$	
		tag	score(f_0/f_1)	tag	score(f_0/f_1)	tag	score(f_0/f_1)
Oct'07	1	inrainbows	51747 (0/148)	leopard	65453 (102/3203)	leopard	44647 (102/3203)
	2	leopard	44284 (102/3203)	radiohead	12617 (81/1231)	radiohead	7483 (81/1231)
	3	bit200f07	42420 (0/134)	opensocial	11477 (5/422)	halloween	7168 (476/2380)
	4	twine	31743 (1/285)	twine	9750 (1/285)	imap	5596 (207/1459)
	5	decenturl	23626 (0/100)	prism	9307 (27/663)	prism	3425 (27/663)
Nov'07	1	android	290314 (22/3556)	android	360132 (22/3556)	android	102030 (22/3556)
	2	kindle	130602 (3/930)	kindle	78912 (3/903)	opensocial	18865 (42/3366)
	3	gos	78083 (2/579)	gos	37159 (2/579)	kindle	8470 (3/903)
	4	gracenote	47711 (0/136)	opensocial	17378 (422/3366)	thanksgiving	5300 (158/1223)
	5	dalvik	20434 (0/89)	quicklook	9113 (14/480)	vector	4945 (1818/4030)
Dez'07	1	simpledb	1955161 (0/826)	simpledb	117574 (0/826)	simpledb	8127 (0/826)
	2	knol	937602 (0/572)	knol	56484 (0/572)	christmas	6180 (2219/4648)
	3	remastersys	39233 (0/117)	alphabetize	5078 (2/203)	2007	5314 (1030/2803)
	4	blazeds	20708 (0/85)	alphabetizer	4404 (2/189)	wii	4376 (993/2531)
	5	diso	19745 (0/83)	christmas	4353 (2219/4648)	knol	4080 (0/572)

the first publications in this area, Golder and Huberman (2006) provide an overview about the structure of collaborative tagging systems. Based on a small subset of the del.icio.us corpus, they investigate the motivation of tagging and tagging habits. Marlow et al. (2006) present a taxonomy for the classification of tagging systems based on the design choices such as the tagging rights (who can tag what?) or the type of underlying resources (what can be tagged?). The authors also suggest classifying a tagging system according to the incentives of its users.

Mika (2005) argues that social tagging systems can be described as tripartite graphs, involving users, tags and resources, and extending the traditional bipartite ontology model by the user dimension. Based on the tripartite model, the authors show that semantically related tags can be clustered in order to discover emerging ontologies. The integration of collaborative tagging systems with the semantic web concept is also the goal of Specia and Motta (2007). The authors combine filter and cluster techniques to extract the semantics emerging from the tag space. Both, Mika (2005) and Specia and Motta (2007), base parts of their analysis on del.icio.us data but only consider data sets with less than 100,000 bookmarks. The most complete analysis of the del.icio.us bookmarking system is provided by Heymann, Koutrika, and Garcia-Molina (2008). The authors investigate the potential of collaborative bookmarking to enhance web search. Among other results, the authors show that there exists a reasonably high overlap between search query terms and tags found in del.icio.us. Furthermore, they report that social bookmarking systems reflect changes within the underlying web structure, such as newly appearing or recently modified web pages, earlier than search engines or directory services, such as the Open Directory (http://www.dmoz.org). Cattuto et al. (2007) expand this investigation by looking at the network properties of del.icio.us and other bookmarking services. They observe a high interconnectivity between the entities in the tripartite community hypergraph. Furthermore, the authors find that social bookmarking services feature small world properties. During their analysis, the authors also noticed the distortion of their data by spam.

The effect of spam on the quality of social bookmarking data has been mainly ignored in the past. A recent study on the detection and prevention of spam in tagging systems is presented by Koutrika, Effendi, Gyöngyi, Heymann & Garcia-Molina (2007). Also, Krause et al. (2008) describe their first results on the construction of a spam detection framework for the BibSonomy bookmarking system. The authors test standard machine learning approaches in order to identify the features that characterize social spam. Furthermore, in 2008 the European Conference on Machine Learning and Principles and Practice of Knowledge Discovery in Databases (ECML PKDD) hosted a track on spam detection in social bookmarking systems, where participants had to identify spam users within the real world BibSonomy corpus. The best teams reached a detection accuracy of above 97% applying classification techniques well known from text categorization. Their method detects spammers based on the tags they assigned or the key terms within their posted URLs (Gkanogiannis & Kalamboukis, 2008).

Social bookmarking systems also provide a promising source for the detection of trends. Hotho, A., Jäschke, R., Schmitz, C., & Stumme, G. (2006) apply the tripartite community model and a diffusion technique similar to Google's PageRank algorithm in order to detect trends in social resource sharing communities. Their algorithm enables the authors to rank items (users, tags, URLs) with respect to a given topic preference vector. The model then detects trends by comparing the popularity, i.e. the rank, of items at different points in time. The proposed method is evaluated on a data set of 7.7 million del.icio.us posts. Dubinko et al. (2006) visualize tag trends over time for Flickr. They propose an *interestingness* measure defined as $int(i,t) = f_t(i)/(C + f(i))$, where $f(i)$ is the overall occurrence of an item, $f_t(i)$ its occurrence in interval t and C is a regularization constant that increases robustness against scarce observations.

Apart from trend detection, tagging systems have been studied for their applicability to search quality improvement (Heymann, Koutrika, & Garcia-Molina, 2008) and search personalization (Xu, Bao, Fei, Su, & Yu, 2008). The problem of predicting and recommending tags in such systems was discussed in Jäschke, Marinho, Hotho, Schmidt-Thieme & Stumme (2007), Heymann, Ramage, & Garcia-Molina (2008), Sigurbjörnsson & Zwol (2008), Tatu, Srikanth and D'Silva (2008), Lipczak (2008) as well as in Katakis, Tsoumakas & Vlahavas (2008).

CONCLUSION AND FUTURE WORK

We investigated the bookmarking and tagging behavior within the del.icio.us community and find a classical long-tail distribution in the participation rate and the interest levels. Our results highlight that users had to become accustomed to the concept of tagging over time and that the tagging rate increased once a certain amount of bookmarks had been posted.

Social bookmarking provides a valuable source for information retrieval and social data examination. However, in the case of del.icio.us spam highly distorts any analysis. This, despite of being a burden to the users, also reduces the success of potential applications for ontology learning or trend detection. For future work, we therefore plan to investigate how the identified spam characteristics can help in the automated spam detection and filtering process. In this context, we also plan to apply existing spam detection methods known from other domains, such as emails or blogs (e.g. Kolari, Finin, and Joshi (2006)).

Social bookmarking has the potential of playing an important role in areas such as trend detection, product tracking or viral marketing. We find that many real world events echo within the tagging and bookmarking behavior of the del.icio.us community with no or little delay. We have proposed a method for the early detection of trends within the community based on a probabilistic generative model. The smoothing of the item distributions not only makes it possible to cope with formerly unknown items but also allows to control the trade-off between the absolute versus the relative popularity change. Future work could be directed towards the identification of user preferences and the topic-aware detection of trends.

REFERENCES

Angelova, R., Lipczak, M., Milios, E., & Pralat, P. (2008). Characterizing a social bookmarking and tagging network. *European conference on artificial intelligence (ECAI): mining social data (msoda) workshop proceedings* (pp. 21-25).

Cattuto, C., Schmitz, C., Baldassarri, A., Servedio, V. D. P., Loreto, V., & Hotho, A. (2007). Network properties of folksonomies. *AI Communications Special Issue on Network Analysis in Natural Sciences and Engineering, 20*, 245–262. IOS Press.

Chen, S. F., & Goodman, J. (1996). An empirical study of smoothing techniques for language modeling. In *Proceedings of the 34th annual meeting on association for computational linguistics* (pp. 310–318). Morristown, NJ, USA: Association for Computational Linguistics.

Dubinko, M., Kumar, R., Magnani, J., Novak, J., Raghavan, P., & Tomkins, A. (2006). Visualizing tags over time. In *Proceedings of the 15th international conference on World Wide Web* (pp. 193-202). New York: ACM.

Gkanogiannis, A., & Kalamboukis, T. (2008). A novel supervised learning algorithm and its use for spam detection in social bookmarking systems. In *ECML PKDD discovery challenge 2008*.

Golder, S. A., & Huberman, B. A. (2006). Usage patterns of collaborative tagging systems. *Journal of Information Science, 32*(2), 198–208. doi:10.1177/0165551506062337

Heymann, P., Koutrika, G., & Garcia-Molina, H. (2008). Can social bookmarking improve web search? In *Wsdm '08: Proceedings of the international conference on web search and web data mining* (pp. 195–206). New York: ACM.

Heymann, P., Ramage, D., & Garcia-Molina, H. (2008). Social tag prediction. *In Sigir '08: Proceedings of the 31st annual international acm sigir conference on research and development in information retrieval* (pp. 531–538). New York: ACM.

Hotho, A., Jäschke, R., Schmitz, C., & Stumme, G. (2006). Information retrieval in folksonomies: Search and ranking. In *Lecture Notes in Computer Science: The Semantic Web: Research and Applications* (Vol. 4011) (pp. 411-426). Springer.

Hotho, A., Jäschke, R., Schmitz, C., & Stumme, G. (2006). Trend detection in folksonomies. *In Lecture Notes in Computer Science* []. Springer.]. *Semantic Multimedia, 4306,* 56–70. doi:10.1007/11930334_5

Jäschke, R., Marinho, L., Hotho, A., Schmidt-Thieme, L., & Stumme, G. (2007). Tag recommendations in folksonomies. In *Proceedings of the 11th European conference on Principles and Practice of Knowledge Discovery in Databases* (pp. 506-514). Springer.

Katakis, I., Tsoumakas, G., & Vlahavas, I. Multilabel Text Classification for Automated Tag Suggestion. *In ECML PKDD discovery challenge2008.*

Kolari, P., Finin, T., & Joshi, A. (2006). SVMs for the Blogosphere: Blog Identification and Splog Detection. *In AAAI spring symposium on computational approaches to analysing weblogs.* University of Maryland, Baltimore County.

Koutrika, G. E_endi, F. A., Gy¨ongyi, Z., Heymann, P., & Garcia-Molina, H. (2007). Combating spam in tagging systems. In *Airweb '07: Proceedings of the 3rd int. workshop on adversarial information retrieval on the web* (pp. 57–64). New York: ACM.

Krause, B., Hotho, A., & Stumme, G. (2008). The anti-social tagger - detecting spam in social bookmarking systems. In *Airweb '08: Proceedings of the 4th int. workshop on adversarial information retrieval on the web* (pp. 61-68). New York: ACM.

Lipczak, M. Tag Recommendation for Folksonomies Oriented towards Individual Users. In *ECML PKDD discovery challenge2008.*

Marlow, C., Naaman, M., Boyd, D., & Davis, M. (2006). Ht06, tagging paper, taxonomy, flickr, academic article, to read. In *Hypertext '06: Proceedings of the seventeenth conference on Hypertext and hypermedia* (pp. 31-40). New York: ACM.

Mika, P. (2005). Ontologies are us: A unified model of social networks and semantics. In *Lecture Notes in Computer Science: The Semantic Web – ISWC 2005* (pp. 522–536). Springer.

Sigurbjörnsson, B., & van Zwol, R. (2008). Flickr tag recommendation based on collective knowledge. In *WWW '08: Proceeding of the 17th international conference on world wide web* (pp. 327–336). New York: ACM.

Specia, L., & Motta, E. (2007). Integrating folksonomies with the semantic web. In *Lecture Notes in Computer Science: The Semantic Web: Research and Applications* (Vol. 4519) (pp. 624-639). Springer.

Surowiecki, J. (2004). The *wisdom of crowds: Why the many are smarter than the few and how collective wisdom shapes business, economies, societies and nations.* Doubleday.

Tatu, M., Srikanth, M., & D'Silva, T. RSDC'08: Tag Recommendations using Bookmark Content. In *ECML PKDD discovery challenge 2008*.

Xu, S., Bao, S., Fei, B., Su, Z., & Yu, Y. (2008). Exploring folksonomy for personalized search. In *SIGIR'08: Proceedings of the 31st annual international ACM SIGIR conference on Research and development in information retrieval* (pp. 155-162). New York: ACM.

This work was previously published in International Journal of Data Warehousing and Mining, Volume 6, Issue 1, edited by David Taniar, pp. 38-57, copyright 2010 by IGI Publishing (an imprint of IGI Global).

Chapter 4
Mining Frequent Generalized Patterns for Web Personalization in the Presence of Taxonomies

Panagiotis Giannikopoulos
University of Peloponnese, Greece

Iraklis Varlamis
Harokopio University of Athens, Greece

Magdalini Eirinaki
San Jose State University, USA

ABSTRACT

The Web is a continuously evolving environment, since its content is updated on a regular basis. As a result, the traditional usage-based approach to generate recommendations that takes as input the navigation paths recorded on the Web page level, is not as effective. Moreover, most of the content available online is either explicitly or implicitly characterized by a set of categories organized in a taxonomy, allowing the page-level navigation patterns to be generalized to a higher, aggregate level. In this direction, the authors present the Frequent Generalized Pattern (FGP) algorithm. FGP takes as input the transaction data and a hierarchy of categories and produces generalized association rules that contain transaction items and/or item categories. The results can be used to generate association rules and subsequently recommendations for the users. The algorithm can be applied to the log files of a typical Web site; however, it can be more helpful in a Web 2.0 application, such as a feed aggregator or a digital library mediator, where content is semantically annotated and the taxonomic nature is more complex, requiring us to extend FGP in a version called FGP+. The authors experimentally evaluate both algorithms using Web log data collected from a newspaper Web site.

DOI: 10.4018/978-1-61350-474-1.ch004

Copyright © 2012, IGI Global. Copying or distributing in print or electronic forms without written permission of IGI Global is prohibited.

INTRODUCTION

The role of recommendations is very important in everyday transactions. When buying a product, or reading a newspaper article, one would like to have recommendations on related items. To achieve this, recommendation engines first build a predictive model, by discovering itemsets or item sequences with high support among users. Recommendations are subsequently generated by matching new transaction patterns to the predictive model. Most current approaches in Web personalization consider that a Web site consists of a finite number of Web pages and build their predictive models based on this assumption (Mobasher, 2007). The Web, however, is a continuously evolving environment and this assumption does no longer hold. News portals are typical examples of this situation since they update their content on a regular basis. As a result, the traditional usage-based approach that takes as input the navigation paths recorded on the Web page level is not as effective. Since most predictive models are based on frequent itemsets, the more recent a page is, the more difficult it is to become part of the recommendation set; at the same time, such pages are more likely to be of interest for the average user. This problem can be addressed by generalizing the page-level navigation patterns to a higher, aggregate level (Eirinaki et. al. 2003; Mobasher, 2007).

In this work, we present the FGP algorithm, to address the aforementioned problem. The FGP algorithm is in essence the result of the modification and combination of two algorithms that have been proposed in different contexts. The first one, FP-Growth (Han et. al. 2004), is given a database of user transactions that comprise one or more unordered items (itemsets) and a minimum support threshold. The algorithm processes the transaction database and mines the complete set of frequent itemsets (whose frequency surpasses the threshold). FP-Growth considers the support of each item in the set to be equal to one. In this work, we extend the algorithm so that it assigns different weights to every item in the set depending on its importance in the transaction. We should note that the FP-Growth algorithm does not consider any relation between items in the database. This, however, is not the case in the Web, where items in a Web site are (conceptually) hierarchically organized. This intrinsic characteristic of the Web can be tackled by the second algorithm, GP-Close (Jiang and Tan, 2006; Jiang et. al., 2007). GP-Close considers a hierarchical organization of all items in the transaction database and uses this information to produce generalized patterns. The two algorithms are very efficient and solve many of the problems of pattern mining, such as the costly generation of candidate sets and the over-generalization of rules.

The FGP algorithm works efficiently in the case of Web sites that have a well-defined underlying hierarchy of topics, such as news portals. Many Web 2.0 sites, however, present a more complex underlying structure. For instance, feed aggregators summarize and present content that is collected from multiple sources. In such sites, the content is not necessarily classified into pre-defined categories (Inform 2007), being described by user-defined tags instead. This collaborative tagging process results into folksonomies (Voss 2007; P. Heymann and H. Garcia-Molina 2006) that differentiate from the traditional top-down taxonomies. The more complex structure of folksonomies, the use of plurals, the synonym polysemy and specificity of tagging raise new issues for the recommendation engines. In this context, we propose an extension of the FGP algorithm, named FGP+ that takes a more composite topic hierarchy as input, and supports multiple category assignments per topic.

In brief, the contributions of our work are outlined in what follows:

- We modify and combine the forces of FP-Growth and GP-Close in one efficient generalized pattern mining algorithm, named FGP which:

○ extends the frequent-pattern tree, the main structure of the FP-Growth algorithm, to include weight information about items, thus producing a weighted FP-Tree (*WFP-Tree*)

○ addresses the problem of continuously updated content by using the WFP-Tree and the taxonomic information related to the Web site's content as input to GP-Close, and generates generalized recommendations

• We present an extension of FGP, named FGP+ that supports an extended taxonomy of topic categories and/or multiple category assignments per item. The extended algorithm directly addresses the special characteristics of social networking applications.

• We experimentally evaluate our approach using data collected from a newspaper Web site.

The paper is organized as follows. First, we provide an overview of the related research in the area of pattern and association rule mining, as well as in the area of personalizing news sites. Furthermore, we briefly describe the fundamentals of the FP-Growth and GP-Close algorithms, and we present the details of the FGP algorithm. Moreover, we motivate the need for an extension of the basic algorithm, and convey our solution, as well as the experimental results. We conclude with our plans for future work.

RELATED WORK

There exist numerous approaches that address the problem of personalizing a Web site. An extensive overview can be found in (Mobasher, 2007). In this paper, we overview those that are more similar to ours with regards to: a) the personalization of news sites and b) the abstraction of the generated patterns using a hierarchy.

Both research projects (Antonellis et. al., 2006; Banos et. al., 2006; Katakis et. al. 2008, Gabrilovich et. al., 2004) and commercial sites, such as Spotback (http://spotback.com) and Topix (http://www.topix.net), have attempted to address the need of personalizing the content of a news site according to users' preferences. Most of those approaches, however, are based on the preference information explicitly provided by the users. However, users' interests change from time to time. In the existence of this concept-drift issue (Tsymbal, 2004; Katakis et. al., 2008), either Web users should continuously update their preferences, or the system will eventually fail to present useful, personalized recommendations. We can see that this is a situation analogous to the cold-start problem, which appears when a system should make predictions in the absence of any transaction history. The cold-start problem has been addressed mainly in the context of collaborative filtering systems (Lam et. al., 2008; Schein et. al., 2002), by creating hybrid recommender systems that take into account both the content of the site and the user ratings or profiles. When there is not adequate user-based information, similarities between the content can be used to make predictions.

The idea of integrating the content in the recommendation process has also been addressed by generalizing the page-level navigation patterns to a higher, aggregate level, with the aid of a topic hierarchy. In a previous work, we have proposed the mapping of all user sessions to the topics of a hierarchy (Eirinaki et. al., 2003). These generalized sessions were then used as input to the Apriori algorithm (Agrawal and Srikant, 1994), in order to generate category-based recommendations. Oberle et. al. (2003) proposed a similar framework for semantic Web sites, where the content was annotated using an ontology. This framework focused on Web mining instead of personalization tasks. In (Middleton et. al., 2004) an approach focusing on recommending academic research papers was proposed. The authors mapped the user profiles as well as the research papers to ontology terms, and used these data as input to a collaborative filtering recommender.

Considering several shortcomings of collaborative filtering, such as data sparsity and lack of scalability (Mobasher, 2007), we opted for an association rule mining algorithm as the core of the personalization process. Compared to Apriori or its extensions, namely, AprioriTid and AprioriHybrid (Agrawal and Srikant, 1994), the FP-Growth algorithm is more efficient in that it does not generate candidate itemsets, but adopts a pattern-fragment growth method instead. Moreover, we use the topic hierarchy as an inherent component of our algorithm, and adapt the GP-Close mechanism in order to produce generalized recommendations taking as input hierarchical, as well as complex taxonomies. In contrast to existing techniques that recommend either pages or categories, FGP and its extension generate frequent itemsets consisting of both of them. Thus, it supports the generation of recommendations that include a combination of pages and page categories.

FP-GROWTH AND GP-CLOSE

The FP-Growth Algorithm

The details of the FP-Growth algorithm can be found in the related bibliography (Han et. al. 2004). In what follows we present an overview of the algorithm using a running example. This same example is employed in order to demonstrate the differences between FP-Growth and our algorithm, FGP.

In the first step, FP-Growth scans the transaction database, finds all frequent items (minimum support is 3 in our example) and orders them in descending frequency order. In a second database scan, the FP-Tree is constructed. Each transaction is mapped to a path in the FP-Tree. For the items already in the tree, the count of the respective nodes in the path is updated, whereas new nodes

are added for the remaining items. For items belonging to more than one frequent itemsets, all their appearances in the tree are linked. An index table containing all frequent items sorted in descending global frequency order, points to the first appearance of each item in the FP-Tree. The FP-Tree resulting from the transaction database of Table 1 is shown in Figure 1.

As proven by Han et al. (2004), the FP-Tree is adequate for mining frequent patterns and can replace the transaction database. In order to compute the support of a k-itemset, FP-Growth scans the tree in order to find the less frequent items in the set. The items in the path from the root to the item under examination form the *conditional pattern base* of the item and their support equals the support of the item under examination (count adjustment). Table 2 contains the conditional pattern base for the FP-Tree of Figure 1.

The GP-Close Algorithm

The GP-Close algorithm takes as input a transaction database *DB* and a taxonomy *T*, containing all items of *DB*. Using a minimum support threshold, it generates a tree called *closure enumeration tree* (CET) that contains all the frequent generalized itemsets. The children of a node in the CET expand their parent itemset by adding one item.

The first step of the algorithm is to locate all frequent 1-itemsets and generate all their frequent generalizations by looking up to *T*. After sorting them in a support increasing manner, it gradually

Table 1. A sample transaction database

TID	Itemset	Ordered frequent items (min freq=3)
100	f, a, c, a, d, g, i, a, m, c, p	f, c, a, m, p
200	a, b, c, f, c, l, a, m, o	f, c, a, b, m
300	b, f, h, j, o, f	f, b
400	b, c, k, s, p, c, b	c, b, p
500	a, c, f, c, e, l, f, p, m, n, a	f, c, a, m, p

Figure 1. The steps of constructing an FP-Tree

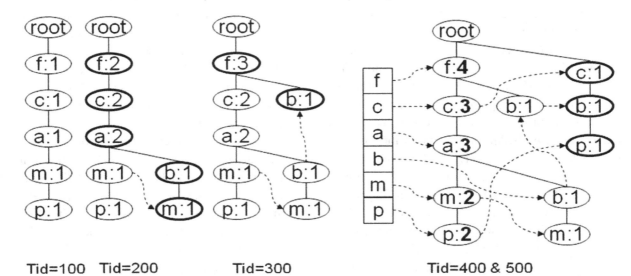

Tid=100   Tid=200   Tid=300   Tid=400 & 500

expands them to *n*-itemsets, by combining smaller sets and updating support count. Two pruning techniques prevent from exploring unnecessary combinations: the Subtree pruning and the Child-Closure pruning. The details of the algorithm and an explanation of the pruning techniques are available in (Jiang and Tan, 2006).

THE FGP ALGORITHM

In order to demonstrate how the FGP algorithm functions we use the running example introduced in the previous principal Section. Consider that

Table 2. The conditional pattern base and FP-Tree

Item	Conditional pattern base	Conditional FP-Tree
p	{fcam:2, cb:1}	{c:3}|p
m	{fca:2, fcab:1}	{f:3, c:3, a:3}|m
b	{fca:1, f:1, c:1}	{}
a	{fc:3}	{f:3, c:3}|a
c	{f:3}	{f:3}|c
f	{}	{}

all items in the transaction database of Table 1 are articles in a news site and that the taxonomy of topics depicted in Figure 2 exists for this site (numbers correspond to topic ids, and letters to article ids). Without loss of generality we assume that each article belongs to a single topic. We show how the algorithm is extended to handle multiple category assignments in the following main Section.

Pre- Processing: Item Weighting

We should point out that the information we store in the FP-Tree differs from that of the original implementation. In the original paper (Han et al. 2004), each transaction identifier (TID) stores only one occurrence for each node. However, in the case of Web log files, a user might visit a Web page more than once during a session. Repetitiveness signifies the importance of a page for a specific user, thus the input format is modified to include *<pageID, weight, support>* triplets, instead of merely pageID information.

Although the importance of a page in a session depends on the number of repetitive visits,

Figure 2. The taxonomy of items

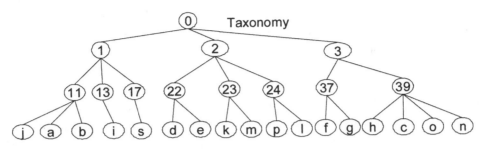

its importance in the database is related to the number of distinct sessions it appears in. Thus, analogously to term weighting in document collections (i.e. tf*idf), we consider the weight of a page in a session to be the number of its appearances in the session divided by the total number of page hits in the session (page frequency) and the support of a page to be the number of sessions that contain this page (inverse session frequency).

The FGP Algorithm

The FGP algorithm takes as input a transaction database (as in Table 3) and a taxonomy (as in Figure 2) and constructs a set of generalized association rules as follows:

1. Scan the transaction database and construct the WFP-Tree
2. Find frequent 1-itemsets using the WFP-Tree
3. Create frequent generalized 1-itemsets using the hierarchy

a. Sort 1-itemsets in increasing support order
b. **Prune Children:** While creating the generalization tree prune 1-item generalizations that have support equal to a frequent 1-itemset already in the tree
4. Combine 1-itemsets to generate the complete generalized itemsets tree
a. **Prune subtrees:** If a n-itemset A can be subsumed by an identified k-itemset B already in the tree with n ⊂ k and support(A)=support(B) then A and its corresponding subtree is pruned.

In what follows, we demonstrate the implementation of the FGP algorithm on the WFP-Tree and put light on the details of support counting, tree generation and pruning, using the running example introduced before.

Table 3. The Web log entries grouped by session

TID	Session items (PID, hits)	Total hits/session
100	(a,3), (c,2), (f,1), (d,1), (g,1), (i,1), (m,1), (p,1)	11
200	(a,2), (c,2), (b,1), (f,1), (l,1), (m,1), (o,1)	9
300	(f,2), (b,1), (h,1), (j,1), (o,1)	6
400	(b,2), (c,2), (k,1), (s,1), (p,1)	7
500	(a,2), (f,2), (c,2), (e,1), (l,1), (p,1), (m,1), (n,1)	11

The result of this processing for Table 1 is depicted in Table 3, which is consequently mapped to the WFP-Tree.

Construction of the WFP-Tree

In order to construct the *WFP-Tree*, the transaction database is parsed and the support and weight for each individual page in a transaction is calculated. The algorithm then aggregates the weights of the remaining page ids and stores a reference to the header table. The transactions are stored in decreasing weight order. The final result for the database in Table 3 is depicted in Figure 3. The *WFP-Tree* can replace the original transaction database in the remaining steps of the algorithm.

Discovering Frequent 1-Itemsets and their Generalizations

The header table, which accompanies the *WFP-Tree*, contains a reference to every page in the tree. This table, along with the taxonomy, is used as input in order to find *frequent 1-itemsets* and produce the corresponding *frequent generalized 1-itemsets*. These itemsets are, in essence, the frequently visited categories in the database.

Since categories correspond to more than one page, in order to find the total weight for each category (internal node in the taxonomy tree), FGP finds all the corresponding pages (leaf nodes) in the taxonomy tree. It subsequently processes the index file, from bottom to top, in order to locate all the appearances of the leaf nodes in the WFP-Tree and sum their weights.

For computing the support of a topic (i.e. the number of transactions that contain at least one page from this topic), FGP examines all appearances of the corresponding pages in the WFP-Tree. The transactions that contain many pages from the same topic are counted only once in the support of the latter.

For example, the support for category 11 is computed based on pages j, b and a. First, the

Figure 3. The Weighted FP-Tree

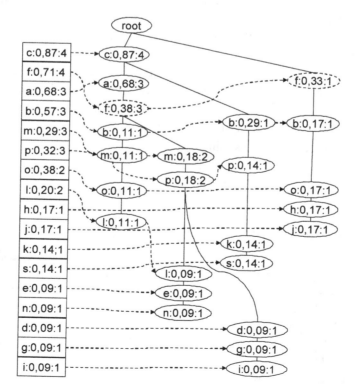

algorithm aggregates the appearances of j (1), which is lower in the header table, then of b (1+1 + 1-1, due to j) and consequently those of a (3-1 since b has been added). The total support for category 11 is consequently 5, which corresponds to the number of transactions that contain at least one of {j, b, a}. The weight of 11 is 1.42, which is the sum of the weights of j, b and a.

Pruning 1-Itemset Generalizations

In this step all 1-itemsets and their generalizations that do not have high support (e.g. support < 3 in our example) are being pruned.

Furthermore, in order to avoid the combinatorial explosion of GP-Close when it searches for all frequent *n*-itemsets, FGP also prunes those frequent 1-item generalizations that have the same support as one of their specializations. For example, the support of category 37, comprising pages f and g, is 4, which is equal to the support of f. As a result, the generalization of 37 is pruned from the final tree and so do all the combinations of 37.

In order to prune the frequent 1-item generalizations the algorithm sorts all frequent 1-itemsets in increasing support order. If a generalization has the same support as one of its specializations, then it is pruned from the closure enumeration tree. The first level of the tree containing the frequent generalized 1-itemsets is shown in Figure 4.

Discovering Frequent K-Itemsets

FGP incrementally combines the frequent 1-itemsets to generate larger sets. After computing their support and weight, the sets that do not meet the minimum support requirements are pruned. The support for the itemset K is computed over the WFP-Tree as follows:

Suppose that L_z is the set of all leaf nodes for item z. If z is a page then $L_z = \{z\}$.

1. Construct $LS = \{L_z\}: \forall z \in K$ support$_K$=0
2. For $L_1 \in LS$, the first set of pages in LS
3. $\forall i \in L_1$ find i_{ALL}: all appearances of i in WFP-Tree
4. $\forall i_x \in iA_{LL}$ if contain(subnodes(ix$_j$, LS-L1$_)$

then support$_K$=support$_K$+supportlast where the method contain() parses the list of subnodes of i_x until at least a page from all the sets in $(LS-L_1)$ is found, and supportlast is the support of the last page checked. If the end of a subnodes list has been reached without finding a page for every set then supportlast=0.

To provide an example, we calculate the support of $K=\{f, 24\}$. We first construct $LS=\{\{f\},\{p,l\}\}$. We check all appearances of f and search for either p or l in the sub-node lists. The support for K is 1 (the support of left shaded l in Figure 3) + 2 (the support of the leftmost occurrence of p in the WFP-tree) + 0 (the rightmost f does not contain p or l in its node list). A support of 3 is above the minimum threshold in our example, so {f,24} is a frequent 2-itemset. The weight of this itemset is the aggregate of the weights of all WFP-Tree nodes involved in the support counting, which means f and l in the leftmost branch (0.38+0.11) and p and l (0.18+0.09) in the second leftmost sub-branch (which shares f as an ancestor). The total weight for K is 0.76.

Pruning Redundant Subtrees

It is obvious that certain combinations will be pruned due to insufficient support. For example, a scan in the WFP-Tree of Figure 3 gives to {m,p} a support of 2, which is below the specified threshold. Thus, {m,p} and its subtree are directly pruned. All the 2-itemsets generated from {m} are listed in Figure 5.

A second pruning strategy is applied in this step. According to this, when a *k*-itemset has equal

Figure 4. Frequent generalized 1-itemsets

Figure 5. Creating the 2-itemsets for the first 1-itemset

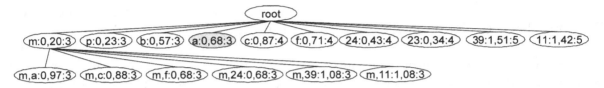

support to a *(k+1)*-itemset and is a subset of this itemset then it is a subsumed one and can be pruned. For example, the shaded node a in Figure 5 is pruned. This strategy further reduces the possible combinations that need to be checked in the next expansion step.

The complete expansion of the first *1*-itemset results in pruning most of the *n*-itemsets created (*n*>1). Figure 6 illustrates the result of this expan-

sion, where all shaded nodes are pruned. Expansion continues with the remaining *1*-itemsets.

When the tree of sets cannot be further expanded, each node in the tree is exported as a *frequent k-itemset,* which can be used to generate recommendations. For example, similarly to association rules-based recommendations, the recommender system can find the *k-itemset* that is more similar to the current user's navigation, by comparing the *k-1* items (pages or categories)

Figure 6. Expansion of the first 1-itemset and subtree pruning

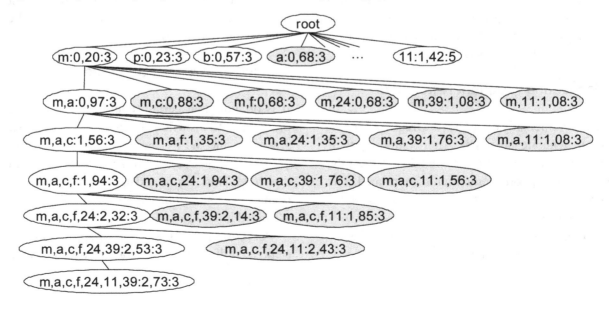

to the current visit. The system can then recommend the *k*-th item, if it is a page (e.g. a news article), or the most popular/recent pages belonging to the *k*-th item, if it is a category.

THE FGP+ ALGORITHM

The FGP algorithm can be used for generating recommendations in sites where the categories are organized in a hierarchy and each page is characterized by a single category. However, in the case of feed aggregators or digital library mediators, the underlying connectivity of categories is more complex (i.e. taxonomies are enhanced with "related category" links and categories have multiple direct ancestors) and pages (or items in general) are assigned to multiple categories. In what follows, we propose FGP+, which is an extension of the FGP algorithm that addresses the aforementioned issues.

Major Differences between a Newspaper Site and an Aggregator

In the newspaper world, things are quite simple: there is a collection of articles, each one belonging to a single category only, and a hierarchy of categories, strictly defined by the administrator, so that every node has one parent at most. Never-

theless, this is not the case in Web 2.0 sites where both the content and the category "tagging" is user-controlled. Even when the users select from a list of predefined tags to assign to their articles (e.g. blog posts), they may choose more than one per item. Moreover, those tags may belong to inner categories of the taxonomy (e.g. page i in Figure 7, which is assigned to categories 2 and 13).

In several cases the tags assigned to items are different but share similar meaning. Such related or synonym categories can be shown in the taxonomy with horizontal relations (e.g. the relation between categories 3 and 17 in Figure 7). This implies that we need a method to map words to their synonyms in the taxonomy.

Principal Extensions to the FGP Algorithm

The modifications in the taxonomy do not affect the original transaction database and the structure of the WFP-Tree. The taxonomy tree, however, has to be enhanced with additional relations allowing each node to have more than one parent. Thus a *taxonomy graph* should be created, which will maintain its directed acyclic nature. Additionally, each category can have a set of synonyms associated with it, in order for the mining algorithm to address cases where different users describe the same content using different category tags.

Figure 7. The modified taxonomy of Figure 2, in which it is allowed for a node to have more than one parents

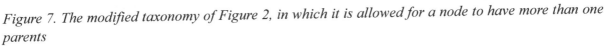
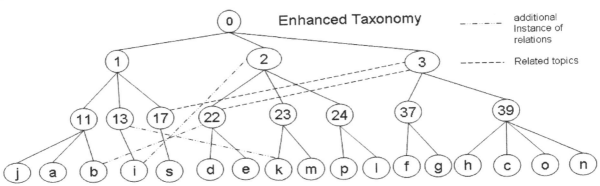

The construction of the extended tree structure and especially the computation of support and weight for a composite itemset, comprising both pages and categories, is not a straightforward task. In fact, even in case we consider no "related topic" edges for the taxonomy graph, the latter should be constructed very cautiously so as to take into account multiple parent assignments for the same internal or leaf node.

Moreover, when we further extend our data structure, allowing each node to contain a list of synonyms associated with it, things become really challenging. For example, Figure 8 presents a taxonomy enhanced with synonymous/related categories information. Furthermore, both leaf and inner categories have instances (pages, denoted with letters).

In what follows, we discuss the different situations that need to be handled during the construction of the extended closure enumeration tree and the actions that are taken for the support and weight computation (the relations between nodes are depicted in the taxonomy graph of Figure 8):

- **Compute the support and weight of categories containing items that have a parent/child relationship** (e.g. {18, 182} in Figure 8). In this case we can either, a) ignore the subclass relation in the creation of the closure enumeration tree, i.e. regard the two categories as unrelated, or b) consider that either the parent or the child is support-ed when an instance of the child category is found (e.g. k). In our implementation, we follow the first alternative and ignore the existence of the child nodes, as far as the parent one is concerned, when computing the support and weight. For example, the support and weight computation for the pair {18, 182} of the closure enumeration tree of Figure 8 occurs independently for the two nodes, taking the sessions containing p and m, or p and k but not those that contain m and k but not p, into account.

- **Handle nodes having descendant/ancestor relationships** (e.g. {1, 111} in Figure 8), which is in essence a generalization of the parent/child relationship. Thus, we follow the same solution as before. For example, we will not take into consideration the items tagged with 111 during the support and weight computation of category 1.

- **Handle synonym/related relationships** (e.g. nodes {1} and {2} in Figure 8). The corresponding values for support and weight should be aggregated over all items belonging to synonym categories. For example, the values of support and weight for any of the two categories {1} and {2} should be the aggregate of the corresponding values of instances j and f.

- **Handle synonyms in descendant/ancestor relations** (e.g. {2, 182} in Figure 8). We are currently facing the problem of

Figure 8. The taxonomy graph now supports a list of synonyms for each node, whereas the instances (words from actual tags) do not necessarily belong to the same level

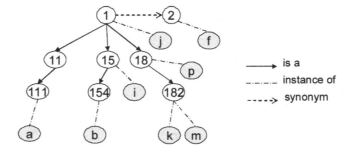

support and weight computation for nodes, which, despite seeming irrelevant, possess an ancestor/descendant relationship indeed. In order to identify such relations, we must first replace each instance of a synonym by its principal term. For example, node {2} should be replaced by {1} which is easily identified as an ancestor of 182.

In order to deal with the utilization of synonym tags by the users (e.g. in blog posts), we can keep a list of synonyms associated with each principal category (for example in Figure 8, {1} is a principal category, whereas {2} corresponds to a synonymous one). This list should be used in order to replace all synonyms by their principal categories, prior to applying FGP+. In this way, the articles belonging to the synonymous category will be considered as members of the principal one, too.

EXPERIMENTAL EVALUATION

Performance Testing

In order to evaluate the performance of the FGP and FGP+ algorithms we use the Web log files of a news site (www.reporter.gr) collected over a 31 days' period (during August 2006). The log files were cleaned, preprocessed, and sessionized, based on the assumption that the Web pages viewed by a user within half an hour belong to the same session. The log files were transformed into a transaction database as the one shown in Table 3. Each page in the Web site belongs to a topic and the hierarchy of topics was used as input to our algorithm. Table 4 shows the statistics of our log file set.

When no pruning is used, the time needed for the creation of the Closure Enumeration Tree (CET) is 21.04 seconds and the tree contains 1707 rules on average, against only 17.2 seconds and 281 rules obtained by applying the two pruning

Table 4. Log files processing statistics

Total number of files	31
Avg num of hits per day	8708
Avg num of sessions per day	882
Avg session length (in page hits)	8.5
Avg num of k-item sets per day (FP-Growth)	7
Avg num of generalized k-item sets per day	56

techniques (Child-Closure pruning and Subtree pruning) to FGP. This shows that the two pruning strategies avoid redundancies and accelerate the tree creation.

In order to evaluate FGP+, we use the same set of log files, but this time we take into account the tag information assigned by the site owners. Although in this data set the tag information is centrally controlled by the administrators, it has some useful features that allow us to test the extension of the FGP algorithm, since a) multiple tags are assigned per article, and b) the tags correspond to topics in the aforementioned hierarchy, in which it is allowed for a node to have more than one parents. As a result, we are able to use FGP+ and find frequent generalized itemsets comprising both articles and tags.

Validity of Results of the FGP Algorithm

The output of the FGP algorithm is a set of frequent k-itemsets, each one associated with a weight and a support score. A recommendation engine can use these frequent k-itemsets against Web usage patterns: when a user's pattern matches the $(k-1)$ items in the set, then the k-th item is suggested to the user, as a recommended hyperlink. The recommendation is considered successful if the user clicks on the hyperlink. Furthermore, if this element corresponds to a category, the n most recent articles belonging to it are recommended, thus providing a solution to the cold-start problem (Lam et. al., 2008; Schein et. al., 2002). We

Figure 9. Session coverage (24 hours)

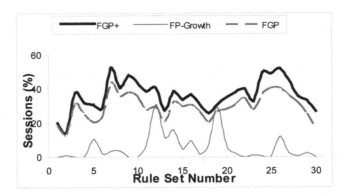

could even propose the (k-r) items in the pattern, provided that the user has requested the rest r, where r is a system parameter.

We measure the accuracy of the recommendations generated by FGP as follows: we produce frequent *k*-itemsets by applying FGP to the log file of a certain day and evaluate the rules against the Web log file of the following day. We repeat the same process for every pair of consecutive days and find the average values, performing in essence a 30-fold cross-validation. We validate the itemsets produced from a day's logs only against the logs of the subsequent day, since the life of article ids in the logs is short and rules containing solely article ids will have limited support. In our experiments, we do not make use of the support and weight information of itemsets when counting for sessions matching a set of elements.

We define the *session coverage* (SC) of a set of rules (frequent *k*-itemsets) measured against a set of sessions as the number of sessions that match at least one rule in the set divided by the total number of sessions, as shown in formula (1):

$$SC = \frac{validSessions}{allSessions} \qquad (1)$$

The results of our experiments are depicted in Figure 9. The horizontal axis corresponds to the day used for generating the frequent *k*-itemsets, whereas the vertical axis shows the percentage of sessions that match at least one rule (session coverage). The results in Figure 9 show that the coverage of the generalized itemsets is larger than that of the page-level ones. The average coverage

Figure 10. Valid itemsets per session (24 hours)

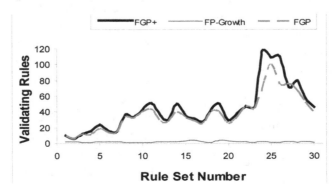

Figure 11. Session coverage (12 hours)

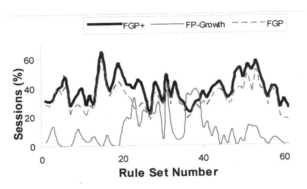

Figure 12. Valid itemsets per session (12 hours)

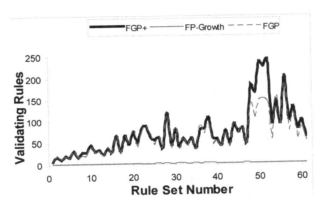

for the generalized itemsets produced by FGP is almost 29% (dashed line in Figure 9), and it lowers into 5.4% when page-level itemsets are only used (thin line in Figure 9).

In a second set of experiments, we count the total number of rules being matched, for those sessions that satisfy at least one rule for both FGP and FP-Growth. The average values per day are shown in Figure 10 (dashed and thin line for FGP and FP-Growth respectively). We should point out that the number of matching rules is strongly related to the size of the recommendation set, since the more rules that are matched, the more recommendations will be provided to the end-users. As shown in Figure 10, the average number of rules, produced by FGP, that match a session

for the complete dataset is approximately 37, while the value for FP-Growth is almost 2.

After the initial evaluation, we proceeded in evaluating our algorithm by utilizing the half-day (i.e. 12 hours) log as a training set (i.e. for rule generation) and the next half as a test set (i.e. for evaluation). This approach makes sense in continuously updated sites, such as news sites, where new articles are published every few hours and visitors tend to read the most recent of them. The results, shown in Figures 11 and 12, prove this necessity. This is also an indication that in a recommendation engine, the rule database should be constantly refreshed to capture the readers' shift of interest.

Table 5. Summary of average values for the three algorithms

Average values		FP-Growth	FPG	FPG+
24 hours	Coverage (%)	5.48	29.18	36.30
	Rules per session	1.82	37.70	44.02
12 hours	Coverage (%)	10.48	32.29	39.02
	Rules per session	1.92	62.82	73.88

More specifically, as depicted in Figure 11, the average coverage for the generalized itemsets produced by FGP increases to almost 32,3% (dashed line in the graph), while when page-level itemsets are only used (thin line) the coverage raises but is still smaller (hardly reaches an average of 10.5%). Similarly, as shown in Figure 12, the average number of rules produced by FGP that match at least one session for the complete dataset almost doubles (raises to 63), whereas the value for FP-Growth remains 2.

Working with Enhanced Hierarchies

In order to test the ability of FGP+ to work with more complex taxonomies, we used the tag information and repeated the same set of experiments using the 24 and 12 hour log files. The results of FGP+ are illustrated with a thick line in Figures 9 to 12.

Table 5 summarizes the average values for the three techniques. According to these results, the average coverage for the generalized itemsets produced by FGP+ raises to 36.3% when full day logs are used and to 39% when we use half day logs.

CONCLUSION AND FUTURE WORK

In this paper, we presented the FGP algorithm, which takes as input a database of transactions consisting of items that are organized in a taxonomy, as well as the taxonomy itself, and produces a set of frequent k-itemsets comprising items and/or categories from the hierarchy. The set consists of all itemsets above a minimum support threshold and their generalizations but omits redundant generalizations. In the current implementation we modified and combined two state-of-the-art algorithms: FP-Growth for frequent itemset creation and GP-Close for itemset generalization and pruning of redundancies. The proposed algorithm, as well as its extension named FGP+, is capable to deal with taxonomies of various levels of complexity, ranging from simple ones (i.e. taxonomy tree of a newspaper site) to more complicated ones (i.e. taxonomy graph of a feed aggregator), allowing each node to have more than one parents. FGP+ also handles multiple category assignment and a list of synonyms for each concept. The performance evaluation of FGP and FGP+ has shown that they produce many useful itemsets, while avoiding redundancies.

An extensive evaluation of FGP+ against more Web log data sets is in our next plans. We also plan to perform a user-based evaluation by implementing a recommendation engine on top of the FGP algorithm and use it on a news feed aggregator.

REFERENCES

Agrawal, R., & Srikant, R. (1994). Fast Algorithms for Mining Association Rules in Large Databases. In J. B. Bocca, M. Jarke, & C. Zaniolo (Eds), *Proceedings of the 20th International Conference on Very Large Data Bases*. San Francisco, CA: Morgan Kaufmann Publishers.

Antonellis, I., Bouras, C., & Poulopoulos, V. (2006). Personalized News Categorization Through Scalable Text Classification. In *Proceedings of the 8th Asia-Pacific Web Conference-Frontiers of WWW Research and Development, Lecture Notes in Computer Science: Vol. 3841*. New York: Springer-Verlag.

Banos, E., Katakis, I., Bassiliades, N., Tsoumakas, G., & Vlahavas, I. (2006). *PersoNews: A Personalized News Reader Enhanced by Machine Learning and Semantic Filtering*. Paper presented at the 5th International Conference on Ontologies, DataBases, and Applications of Semantics (ODBASE 2006), Montpellier, France.

Eirinaki, M., Vazirgiannis, M., & Varlamis, I. (2003). SEWeP: using site semantics and a taxonomy to enhance the Web personalization process. In *Proceedings of the 9th ACM SIG-KDD International Conference on Knowledge Discovery and Data Mining* (pp. 99-108). New York: ACM Press.

Gabrilovich, E., Dumais, S., & Horvitz, E. (2004). Newsjunkie: providing personalized newsfeeds via analysis of information novelty. In *Proceedings of the 13th International Conference on World Wide Web* (pp. 482-490). New York: ACM Press.

Han, J., Pei, J., Yin, Y., & Mao, R. (2004). Mining Frequent Patterns without Candidate Generation: A Frequent-Pattern Tree Approach. *Data Mining and Knowledge Discovery, 8*, 53–87. doi:10.1023/B:DAMI.0000005258.31418.83

Heymann, P., & Garcia-Molina, H. (2006). *Collaborative creation of communal hierarchical taxonomies in social tagging systems* (Preliminary Technical Report). InfoLab, Stanford, 2006. Retrieved September, 26, 2008, from: http://heymann.stanford.edu/taghierarchy.html.

Inform Inc. (2008), *Inform's Essential Technology Platform*. Retrieved September, 26, 2008, from: http://www.inform.com/contents/pdf/inform-whitepaper.pdf

Jiang, T., & Tan, A. H. (2006). Mining RDF Metadata for Generalized Association Rules: Knowledge Discovery in the Semantic Web era. In *Proceedings of the 15th International Conference on World Wide Web* (pp. 951-952). New York: ACM Press.

Jiang, T., & Wang, K. (2007). Mining Generalized Associations of Semantic Relations from Textual Web Content. *IEEE Transactions on Knowledge and Data Engineering, 19*(2), 164–179. doi:10.1109/TKDE.2007.36

Katakis, I., Tsoumakas, G., Banos, E., Bassiliades, N., & Vlahavas, I. (2008). An adaptive personalized news dissemination system. *Journal of Intelligent Information Systems*. Springer. DOI - 10.1007/s10844-008-0053-8

Katakis, I., Tsoumakas, G., & Vlahavas, I. (2008). An Ensemble of Classifiers for coping with Recurring Contexts in Data Streams. In M. Ghallab, C. Spyropoulos, N. Fakotakis, & N. Avouris (Eds.), *Proceedings of the 18th Europeen Conference on Artificial Intelligence* (pp.763-764), Amsterdam: IOS Press.

Lam, X., Vu, T., Le, T., & Duong, A. (2008). *Addressing cold-start problem in recommendation systems*. In *Proceedings of the 2nd international Conference on Ubiquitous Information Management and Communication* (pp. 208-211). New York: ACM Press.

Middleton, S., Shadbolt, N., & De Roure, D. (2004). Ontological User Profiling in Recommender Systems. *ACM Transactions on Information Systems, 22*(1), 54–88. doi:10.1145/963770.963773

Mobasher, B. (2007). Data Mining for Personalization. In P. Brusilovsky, A. Kobsa, & W. Nejdl, (Eds.), *Lecture Notes in Computer Science: Vol. 4321. The Adaptive Web: Methods and Strategies of Web Personalization* (pp. 90-135). Berlin-Heidelberg: Springer.

Oberle, D., Berendt, B., Hotho, A., & Gonzalez, J. (2003). Conceptual User Tracking. In *Proceedings of the Atlantic Web Intelligence Conference, Lecture Notes in Computer Science: Vol. 2663.* Springer.

Schein, A., Popescul, A., & Lyle, H. (2002). Methods and Metric for Cold-Start Recommendations. In *Proceedings of the 25th Annual International ACM SIGIR Conference on Research and Development in Information Retrieval* (pp. 253-260). ACM.

Tsatsaronis, G., Varlamis, I., & Vazirgiannis, M. (2008). Word Sense Disambiguation with Semantic Networks. In *Proceedings of the 11th International Conference on Text, Speech and Dialogue*, Brno, Czech Republic.

Tsymbal, A. (2004). *The problem of concept drift: definitions and related work* (Technical Report). University of Dublin. Retrieved September 26, 2008, from https://www.cs.tcd.ie/publications/tech-reports/reports.04/TCD-CS-2004-15.pdf.

Voss, J. (2007). *Tagging, Folksonomy & Co - Renaissance of Manual Indexing?* In *Proceedings of the International Symposium of Information Science* (pp. 234–254).

This work was previously published in International Journal of Data Warehousing and Mining, Volume 6, Issue 1, edited by David Taniar, pp. 58-76, copyright 2010 by IGI Publishing (an imprint of IGI Global).

Chapter 5
An Efficient Method for Discretizing Continuous Attributes

Kelley M. Engle
University of Maryland Baltimore County, USA

Aryya Gangopadhyay
University of Maryland Baltimore County, USA

ABSTRACT

In this paper the authors present a novel method for finding optimal split points for discretization of continuous attributes. Such a method can be used in many data mining techniques for large databases. The method consists of two major steps. In the first step search space is pruned using a bisecting region method that partitions the search space and returns the point with the highest information gain based on its search. The second step consists of a hill climbing algorithm that starts with the point returned by the first step and greedily searches for an optimal point. The methods were tested using fifteen attributes from two data sets. The results show that the method reduces the number of searches drastically while identifying the optimal or near-optimal split points. On average, there was a 98% reduction in the number of information gain calculations with only 4% reduction in information gain.

INTRODUCTION

Data mining is an active area of research that has found wide usage for knowledge discovery in databases in application areas ranging from assessment of loan applications to screening satellite images (e.g., Bagui, 2006; Han & Kamber, 2006; Hand et al., 2001; Tzanis et al., 2007; Witten & Frank, 2005). Many data mining algorithms, including decision trees and classification rules, require discretization when predictor attributes are continuous. Discretization refers to the process of

DOI: 10.4018/978-1-61350-474-1.ch005

Copyright © 2012, IGI Global. Copying or distributing in print or electronic forms without written permission of IGI Global is prohibited.

converting the values of a continuous variable in two or more bins, the boundaries of which are referred to as split points. While there are many ways that this binning can be performed, the quality of binning can have a significant impact of the performance of the algorithm.

Discretization can be either static or dynamic. In static discretization all continuous variables are discretized at the outset of the learning algorithm after which the discretized continuous variable is treated like a discrete variable. In dynamic discretization a continuous variable is discretized while the model is being built. Hence, the discretization process may be repeated several times for each continuous attribute over the model building process. Many decision tree-based learning systems such as ID3 (Quinlan, 1986) C4.5 (Quinlan, 1993) and CART (Breiman & Friedman et al., 1998) are based on dynamic discretization. The most commonly used method for discretization (Holte, 1993) is to compare a measure such as information gain for every possible value of a predictor attribute, which we refer to as "brute force" and is clearly not feasible in large data sets. While a number of approaches for discretization of continuous attributes have been developed in the literature, most of them require a significant amount of time for the discretization process or result in loss of predictive accuracy. The only definitive study in this area shows that the optimal split points (referred to as cut points in Fayyad & Irani (1992)) occur at the boundaries where the values of the target or class attribute changes value. However, in very large datasets, the number of such boundary points can also be quite large, which does not solve the problem of having to apply a "brute force" method to the boundary points in trying to find the optimal split point for a continuous attribute

There are many examples of very large datasets in today's world where large volumes of routinely collected data require efficient methods for analysis. One such example is the astronomical data in the Sloan Digital Sky Survey (2008)

that consists of 9TB of images and 3.6 TB of data collected in an effort to map a quarter of the entire sky. Another example is the Baruch Options Data Warehouse (2008) at the Subotnik Financial Services Center that contains trades, quotes, open interest, and end of day volumes for all options series on US equities and indexes with a total data size of 60TB as of March 2008. Current data mining algorithms need to be scalable to handle such large volumes of data.

In this paper we propose a novel approach for finding optimal split points for discretizing continuous attributes. The method is based on univariate parameter optimization and uses a combination of golden section search method (Press et al., 2007) and gradient descent based on Newton-Raphson method (Hand et al., 2001). The predictive accuracy is measured in terms of information gain. We have shown through empirical tests using a number of datasets of varying sizes that the method would identify the optimal or near optimal solutions and has an extremely high degree of computational efficiency by a drastic reduction in the number of points for which information gain is computed and compared. The rest of the paper is organized as follows. We briefly present the related work in the next section, followed by the methodology, experimental results, and conclusions.

RELATED WORK

There are a number of different methods of discretization for continuous attributes. Dougherty et al. (1995) present three ways of classifying discretization: (1) global vs. local; (2) supervised vs. unsupervised and; (3) static vs. dynamic. Alternatively, Liu et al. (2002), present a hierarchical framework to describe the various discretization methods. Their framework decomposes the methods first by merging vs. splitting and then each of those categories is further broken down into supervised vs. unsupervised.

Table 1. Summary of discretization methods

	Global	Local
Supervised	1RD (Holte 1993) Entropy-based discretization (Fayyad and Irani 1992; Fayyad and Irani 1993; Ting 1994) Hierarchical discretization (Chiu, Cheung et al. 1990) D-2 (Catlett 1991) Entropy with MDL (Pfahringer 1995) Predicative Value Maximization (Weiss, Galen et al. 1990) ChiMerge (Kerber 1992) StatDisc (Richeldi and Rossotto 1995) Zeta (Ho and Scott 1997)	C4.5 (Quinlan 1993) Vector Quantization (Kohonen 1989) Entropy-based discretization (Fayyad and Irani 1992; Fayyad and Irani 1993)
Unsupervised	Equal Width Equal Frequency Gaussian Approximation/Uniform/K-tile (Chickering, Meek et al. 2001) Self-Organizing Maps (Vannucci and Colla 2004)	k-means clustering
Hybrid	Adaptive Quantizers (Chan, Batur et al. 1991) Maximal Marginal Entropy (Wong and Chiu 1987) MCC (Van de Merckt 1993)	

*Adapted from Table 1 in Dougherty, Kohavi et al. (1995), p. 3.

Global discretization refers to the process by which split points are determined prior to applying a machine learning algorithm. Local discretization is a discretization method that is embedded in an algorithm such as a decision tree and will reiterate numerous times for each attribute (at each level of the decision tree). Table 1 summarizes all the discretization methods discussed in this section by global/local and supervised, unsupervised and hybrid. This table is adapted from Table 1 in Dougherty and Kohavi et al. (1995) – it differs in that we have added an additional category for hybrid methods.

Supervised discretization involves any discretization process that uses the class label as part of the partitioning logic. Unsupervised discretization does not use the class label – these methods such as equal width/equal binning simply partition the predictor attribute into k number of bins as specified by the user. The supervised and unsupervised discretization methods, as described in literature, will be discussed in more detail in subsequent sections.

Static discretization methods "perform one discretization pass of the data for each feature and determine the value of k for each feature independent of other features (Dougherty & Kohavi et al., 1995, p. 2)." Alternatively, dynamic discretization methods "conduct a search through the space of possible k values for all features simultaneously, thereby capturing interdependencies in feature discretization (Dougherty & Kohavi et al., 1995, p. 2)."

There are also a number of discretization methods that could be described as hybrids. They combine both unsupervised and supervised partitioning in determining split points. These methods will be discussed in more detail in a later section.

Supervised Discretization

Entropy-based discretization can be found in a number of papers including those by Fayyad and Irani (1993), Ting (1994) and Pfahringer (1995). This discretization process uses the entropy and information gain calculations to determine the optimal split point for each continuous attribute. There have been a number of papers that have worked to improve the efficiency of entropy-based discretization, including proving that the optimal split point for a continuous attribute will also be at the class label boundary (Fayyad & Irani, 1992) and will further reduce the number of calculations by utilizing the MDL (Minimal Description Length) (Friedman & Goldszmidt, 1996). Some other examples of entropy-based methods include hierarchical discretization, which seeks to maximize the Shannon entropy (Chiu & Cheung et al.,1990), as well as a method by Pfahringer (1995), which uses entropy to initially identify split points and then uses a MDL (Minimum Description Length) heuristic to determine the best discretization. The D-2 algorithm by Catlett in 1991 utilizes a number of different stopping criterion to discover the best split. These stopping criterion include: (1) minimum number of samples in a partition; (2) a maximum number of partitions and; (3) a minimum information gain. Entropy-based discretization can be used locally or globally.

Zeta, as presented by Ho and Scott (1997), is a measure of association that is utilized in discretization. It is based upon the *lambda* measurement which measures the strength of association between nominal variables and specifically "measures the proportionate reduction in prediction error that would be obtained by using one variable to predict another, using a modal value prediction strategy in all cases (Ho & Scott, 1997, p. 4)." The *zeta* measure was developed to address deficiencies in the lamba measure due to conditions where two variables may have modal values of zero. This was accomplished by pairing each value of the independent variable with the value of the class label (Ho & Scott, 1997).

1RD is a simple supervised method in which it creates a 1-level stump and is bundled with the 1R algorithm by Holte (1993). The Predicative Value Maximization is an algorithm that seeks split points that are most likely to make correct classification decisions (Weiss & Galen et al., 1990). Both 1RD and the Predicative Value Maximization are considered global methods.

Some examples of local supervised methods include: (1) C4.5 (Quinlan, 1993), (2) Vector Quantization (Kohonen, 1989) and, (3) Some entropy-based methods (Fayyad & Irani, 1993). C4.5 is a decision-tree algorithm, which includes discretization of a continuous attribute at each level of the decision tree (Quinlan, 1993) (Quinlan, 1996). Vector Quantization attempts to "partition an N-dimensional space into a *Voronoi Tessellation* and then represent the set of points in each region by the region into which it falls (Dougherty & Kohavi et al., 1995, p. 4)." Because this method creates local regions, it is considered a local method. Entropy-based methods, as described previously, can also be utilized as a local discretization method.

There are also some statistical methods that can be used to discretize continuous attributes. ChiMerge, by Kerber, can be described as bottom-up approach where the data is initially partitioned and then the method will perform a X^2 test to determine where bins should be merged (Kerber, 1992). Similarly, Stat Disc, by Richeldi and Rossotto (1995), employs a comparable method in that it will initially partition the attribute, but then will apply the Φ measure to merge the bins.

Unsupervised Discretization

Equal width and equal frequency are two of the simplest unsupervised discretization methods. Equal width binning partitions the data into k number of bins as defined by the user – then the minimum and maximum data value are added together and divided by k. Equal frequency binning will consider the total number of data points in the continuous attribute and divide it by k. This method ensures that the bins will have an even number of data points within each partition. The one major limitation to equal frequency binning is that the range can become skewed by outliers (Catlett, 1991).

There have been a number of extensions to the equal width and equal frequency methods. For instance, there are three methods, presented by Chickering and Meek et al. (2001) that utilize the concept of quantile binning: (1) Gaussian approximation, (2) Uniform approximation and, (3) K-tile method. The Gaussian approximation method utilizes an assumed standard distribution and applies the mean and standard deviation to partition the attribute. Likewise, uniform approximation, assumes the continuous attribute is distributed evenly between its minimum and maximum value. The k-tile method is also a quantile approach but uses the empirical distribution function.

Clustering is another method used for unsupervised discretization. An example of clustering was presented by Vannucci and Colla (2004) for application in association rule mining. The continuous attributes are discretized using a SOM (self-organizing map). This method addresses the weaknesses in equal width/equal frequency including: (1) discretization should account for the original distribution of the attribute; (2) the discretized attributes should not hide patterns and; (3) the intervals should be meaningful to the user (Dougherty & Kohavi et al., 1995).

Hybrid Discretization

Hybrid discretization refers to those methods that combine supervised and unsupervised methods. For example, adaptive quantizer combines binary equal width partitioning with classification rule measures (Chan & Batur et al., 1991). The method begins by performing a binary equal width split – it then proceeds to run a classification algorithm to collect the predictive accuracies of the splits. The partition with the lowest accuracy is then split again by the binary equal width method. This process will be performed until some minimum predictive accuracy is obtained.

Another hybrid method, called maximal marginal entropy, initially employs the unsupervised method, equal frequency, but then will make modifications to the boundaries based on the entropy calculations. The purpose of these modifications is to decrease the entropy for the final split (Wong & Chiu, 1987).

The last hybrid method to be discussed is the Monothetic Contrast Criterions (MCC), which is a combination of two methods, clustering and entropy-based discretization (Van de Merckt, 1993). The first method utilizes a clustering algorithm and is therefore unsupervised. The second method employs the (supervised) entropy calculation to divide the previously partitioned data.

In this article we propose to extend the current state of the art by describing a method for dynamic discretization in large data sets.

Scalability Issues in Decision Tree Induction

There is an abundance of research in the area of scalability for various data mining algorithms including association rules (Zaki, 2000), clustering (Ng & Han, 2002), classification (Kamber et al., 1997), decision trees (Catlett, 1991; Gehrke et al., 1999; Gehrke et al., 2000; Li, 2005) and neural nets (Charles, 2004). However, for the purposes of our research, we are most concerned with scalability approaches for decision tree induction since our method is designed to alleviate the problem of discretizing continuous attributes. The issue of scalability has long been associated with decision tree induction since it is considered an NP-complete problem (Hyafil & Rivest, 1976; Quinlan, 1993). In particular, discretizing continuous attributes at each level of the decision tree makes the building operation quite expensive. In this section we will delve more deeply into the research as it relates directly to decision trees.

The need for scalability in data mining algorithms lies in the theory that working with larger datasets is preferable since the accuracy of any data mining task (including classification) will be improved by using large datasets. This theory has been studied and corroborated by a number of researchers including Catlett (1991) and Chan and Stolfo (1993a, 1993b). Scalability is defined by Ganti and Gehrke et al. (1999) as "given a fixed amount of main memory, its runtime increases linearly with the number of records in the input database" (p. 38).

There have been a number of approaches proposed to address the issue of scalability in data mining algorithms. Some of these methods, such as SLIQ (Mehta & Agrawal et al., 1996),

SPRINT (Shafer & Agrawal et al., 1996), Rainforest (Gehrke& Ramakrishnan et al., 2000) and PUBLIC (Rastogi & Shim, 2000), attempt to address scalability issues by directly tackling the problem of main memory issues. Decision tree algorithms operate on the premise that a dataset must be able to fit into main memory. For large datasets, this is often not possible and so the methods mentioned previously address this deficiency.

For instance, SLIQ (Mehta & Agrawal et al., 1996) allows for both continuous and categorical data in its algorithm and uses a pre-sorting approach on disk resident data to address the main memory deficiency issue. As a result this method only sorts once instead of sorting data at each node. One criticism of the SLIQ method is that the performance will suffer if the class list cannot fit into main memory. SPRINT (Shafer & Agrawal et al., 1996), however, removes all main memory issues through the use of hash trees. However, this process may become expensive as the dataset grows due to the complex joins in the tree.

Rainforest (Gehrke & Ramakrishnan et al., 2000) uses AVC (attribute-value-count) sets which will list the counts for attributes into main memory. These AVC lists either be at the group (node) level (from here on called *AVC-group*) or at the individual attribute level (from here on called *individual AVC-sets*). Table 2 gives an example of an AVC-Group node table taken from Gehrke and Ramakrishnan et al. (2000). Gehrke and Ramakrishnan et al. (2000) describes three scenarios based on the amount of main memory: (1) The *AVC-Group* of the root in its entirety will fit into main memory; (2) An *individual AVC-set* can fit into main memory but not the *AVC-group*

Table 2. Example of AVC-Group

Age	Buys PC	
	YES	NO
Youth	2	3
Middle-aged	4	0
Senior	3	2

and; (3) none of the *AVC-Group* or *individual AVC-sets* of the root fit in main memory. A number of algorithms were developed to address the first two scenarios – the combination of which are summarily called Rainforest. For the last scenario the authors propose, in theory, a hybrid version of their work combined with the SPRINT algorithm.

Sampling methods are another avenue for addressing the scalability issues in the induction of decision trees. The basic premise of these methods is that a smaller sample of the original dataset is used to construct the decision tree. Although none of these methods (including our own) are optimal, they are still practical methods when dealing with very large datasets such as the astronomy data described earlier which is now in the range of 15+ terabytes. As championed by Chaudhuri in 1998, sampling methods should not be ignored in the quest for scalable data mining solutions.

One such sampling method, BOAT (Gehrke & Ganti et al., 1999), utilizes a bootstrapping approach where the dataset is partitioned into smaller subsets that are able to fit into main memory. A number of decision trees are created on each of these subsamples – from t_l to t_i where i is equal to the number of subsets created. Each of the trees $(t_l ... t_i)$ are analyzed and the final tree $(T`)$ constructed is usually a close approximation of the optimal tree.

Breiman and Friedman et al. (1998) discuss a number of sampling methods including *bootstrapping* and *one-shot sampling*. Many of these simple random sampling methods, as empirically tested by (Catlett, 1991), have significantly reduced accuracy rates. Windowing, developed by (Quinlan, 1983), is a sampling method designed to significantly decrease the time associated with decision tree induction by examining small samples from the training data (usually 10%-20%). The method will only add remaining records if the tree does not correctly classify. This method, in particular, is very susceptible to noisy data.

Catlett (1991) actually developed two methods – the first was a discretization method call D-2 that employed a static discretization process to speed up the induction of decision trees. The second method, called peepholing, is a sampling method that has two functions: (1) shortlisting and; (2) blinkering. The purpose of shortlisting is to eliminate attributes from the evaluation criterion (such as information gain). Once an attribute is scratched, it no longer needs to be considered at any of the lower levels of the tree induction process. *Blinkering* uses a sampling technique on the remaining attributes to reduce the search space through the use a pair of numbers that represent the left and right *blinkers*. These *blinkers* are initially set to infinitely large numbers to cover the entire range of the attribute but will be narrowed over time. The samples used in this process are referred to as *peeps* and this method is similar to windowing. Catlett's criticism of windowing (Quinlan, 1983) was that the performance decreases when data is "noisy." Although by the author's own admission, the *blinkering* method will only work on attributes that have one peak (i.e., well-behaved data).

Kamber and Winstone et al. (1997) proposed a heuristic-based 3-step approach to addressing scalability issues: (1) *attribute-oriented induction*; (2) *relevance analysis* and; (3) *multi-level mining*. With *attribute-oriented induction*, each continuous would be discretized prior to the decision tree induction through the use of *concept hierarchies*. These *concept hierarchies* must be supplied by domain experts, database administrators or using the database schema itself. *Relevance analysis*

involves removing irrelevant or redundant attributes prior to the decision tree induction using a normalized version of information gain called the uncertainty coefficient. This process will run into the same efficiency issue with attributes that have a large number of distinct values and as a result it is suggested by the authors to simply remove such attributes if no *concept hierarchy* can be determined. This indiscriminate removal of attributes could lead to a decision tree that is far from optimal. The third step, *multi-level* mining, does not necessarily relate to efficiency but allows for decision trees to be induced at different levels of abstraction based on the concept hierarchy.

From the statistics community, two related algorithms were developed to address scalability issues in CART. The first algorithm, FACT (Loh & Vanichsetakul,1988) calculates an ANOVA F-statistic for each attribute at each node and thereby choosing the attribute with the largest F-statistic. LDA (linear discriminant analysis) is then applied to find the actual split. In 1997, Loh and Shih presented QUEST which performs similarly to FACT except that it yields only binary splits.

METHODOLOGY

Our problem of finding the optimal split point is similar to that of the univariate parameter optimization problem (Hand et al., 2001) of finding the value of a parameter s so as to maximize the information gain function $\Psi(s)$. For continuous functions the local optima can be detected by applying differential calculus in a straight-forward manner. However, since we are dealing with a discrete set of points which is generated by an unknown function, optimization by taking derivatives is not possible. Our method for finding the optimal split point for continuous attributes is a two step process. The first step, which we call the Bisecting region Method (BRM), is based on the golden section search in one dimension (Press et al., 2007), and the second step is based on the gradient descent method applied to Newton-Raphson method for finding local optimum. In the first step we sort the parameter s and start with a bracket $[s_1, s_2]$ that contains the optimum of the function $\Psi(s)$, where s_1 and s_2 are the lower and upper bounds of s. We check the midpoint s_m such that $s_1 < s_m < s_2$. If $\Psi(s_m) > \Psi(s_1)$ and $\Psi(s_m) > \Psi(s_2)$ then a local maximum exists between s_1 and s_2. If that is not the case, then we create brackets $[s_m, s_2]$ and $[s_1, s_m]$ and repeat the above process. This step would find the maximum if the function $\Psi(s)$ is well-behaved and free from local fluctuations. However, most information gain functions may not have these properties, hence we need a second step to avoid stopping at a suboptimal point.

The second step in out methodology, called Hill Climbing Algorithm (HCA), works on the following principles based on Newton-Raphson method for gradient descent. The challenge is to find a close enough starting point so that the number of calculations can be minimized. We rely on the first step of our methodology (BRM) for identifying the starting point. Since we cannot derive the first and second derivative for the unknown functional form for an attribute with an unknown information gain function, we use the gradient descent approach to approximate the Newton-Raphson method. Instead of using the first derivative we can use the gradient information to determine the correct direction to move. Since we have applied our method to one attribute at a time, there are only two directions to choose from. In our methodology we choose the direction of positive ascent. If the information gain increases in both directions then both directions are traversed. The algorithm stops when the gradient becomes zero, which represents a summit. If the traversal was bidirectional, the higher summit point is returned as the maximum.

In the following section we first describe the algorithms for the two steps in our methodology, followed by some illustrative examples.

Algorithms

Let us assume that f is an attribute for which we are trying to determine the optimal split point for a given set of sorted values of f: $S = \{x_1, ... x_n\}$, where $x_i < x_{i+1}$. Our goal is to find out the point x^* that corresponds to the maximum information gain without exhaustively computing the information gain values for all points in S. Information gain is calculated as the difference in entropies before and after taking the attribute f into account, where entropy is calculated as $H(X) = -\sum_x p_x \log p_x$ (Liu et al., 2002). At the outset we do not know the information gain for any of the points in S. Our first algorithm, called Bisecting Region Method (BRM), computes the information gain for three points in set S: the mid-point (*mid*) between the lower and upper bounds of S, the mid-point of the right region, called *mid_right*, which is calculated by averaging *mid* and the upper bound (*max*), and that of the left region, called *mid_left*, which is calculated by averaging the lower bound (*min*) and *mid*. If *mid_right* is the point with the highest information gain the algorithm performs search on the region to the right of *mid*. Similarly, if *mid_left* has the highest information gain, the algorithm proceeds with a search to the left of *mid*. Otherwise the algorithm stops and returns *mid*. At this point, the second algorithm, hill climbing algorithm (HCA) is invoked with the return value of BRM as an input parameter. HCA starts by searching both to the left and right of the initial point (s_i) that as passed to it as a parameter by BRM. If the point to the left (and/or right) of s_i has a higher information gain than that of s_i, HCA continues its search. Otherwise it returns the point at which it has encountered the maximum information gain. The BRM and HCA algorithms are shown in Figures 1 and 2 respectively. The recursive function calls are shown for clarity and simplicity of presentation and can be implemented as iterations rather than recursions.

Figure 1. Bisecting region method

Algorithm 1: Bisecting Region Method

Input: S = *Sorted values of feature f, lower_bound, upper_bound* of S
Output: $s* \in S$, *where s* represents the point with the highest information gain found.*
{
mid $\leftarrow$ *(lower_bound+upper_bound)/2*
mid_left $\leftarrow$ *(lower_bound+mid)/2*
mid_right $\leftarrow$ *(mid+upper_bound)/2*
COMPUTE information gain *g()* for *mid, mid_left, mid_right*
IF *g(mid) > g(mid_left)* and *g(mid) > g(mid_right)*
  Return *mid(X)*
ELSE IF *g(mid_left > g(mid)*
   BRM ($(S_l \mid \forall s_i \in S_l, lower\_bound \leq s_i \leq mid)$, *lower_bound, mid)* // Shift to region on left
ELSE
   BRM ($(S_u \mid \forall s_j \in S_u, mid \leq s_j \leq upper\_bound)$, *mid, upper_bound)* // Shift to region on right
END IF

Exceptions:
IF *g(mid_left)=g(mid)=g_mid_right)* **Return** *mid*
IF *g(mid_left)=g(mid_right) > mid* **Return** *mid_left* or *mid_right* (random choice)
}

One of the features of the BRM algorithm is that it may cover only a small fraction of the points in *S*. While this reduces the computational time, it may not provide enough cover for *S*. We added a heuristic to force the BRM algorithm to go through more calculations by introducing two additional variables, *SUM1* and *SUM2*, where *SUM1* is the sum of the information gains of the *min* and *mid_left*, and *SUM2* is the sum of the information gains of the *mid_right* and *max*. This additional heuristic helps in identifying points of maximum information gains when they tend to appear on the left or right edges of the data. The methods are compared with detailed experimental results in Section *Results*.

Datasets Description

The data for these experiments consist of: (1) *Forest cover* dataset[1] and; (2) *Ionosphere* dataset[2]. *Forest cover* was obtained by the U.S. Forest Service (USFS) and contains 54 attributes to capture information such as soil type, elevation, horizontal and vertical distances to water sources and more. It is a classification dataset where the variable cover_type is the class label that designates the type of forest cover present – such as Spruce/Fir, Aspen, Douglas-Fir etc. *Forest cover* has a total of 581,012 records and for the purposes of these experiments we are using the 10 continuous attributes (the remainder of the attributes are binary variables). *Forest cover* was chosen not only due to the total number of records but also due to the high cardinality present in many of the attributes such as h_dist_roadways and h_dist_fire_points. This high cardinality was desired in order to test the efficacy of the BRM/HCA method against continuous attributes with a large number of distinct values. The number of distinct values and the ranges for both datasets are shown in Table 3.

Ionosphere is another classification dataset that contains 34 continuous attributes and one class label that classifies the ionosphere as either 'good' or 'bad.' The data was collected by radar

Figure 2. Hill climbing algorithm

Algorithm 2: Hill Climbing Algorithm

Input: $_i \in S$ s
Output: s_{max}, *where s_{max} is the point with the highest information gain.*
{
  COMPUTE information gain $g()$ for s_i
  $g(s_{max}) \leftarrow g(s_i)$
//Search to the right of s_i
  LOOP
      COMPUTE information gain $g()$ for s_{i+1}
    IF $g(s_i) < g(s_{i+1})$
      $s_i \leftarrow s_{i+1}$
      $s_{max} \leftarrow s_i$
      i++
    END IF
  UNTIL $g(s_i) > g(s_{i+1})$ **OR** $s_i = max$ // The upper bound has been reached

//Search to the left of s_i
  LOOP
      COMPUTE information gain $g()$ *for s_{i-1}*
    IF $g(s_i) < g(s_{i-1})$
      $s_i \leftarrow s_{i-1}$
      IF $g(s_{max}) < g(s_i)$ $s_{max} \leftarrow s_i$
      i- -
    END IF
  UNTIL $g(s_i) > g(s_{i+1})$ **OR** $s_i = min$ // The lower bound has been reached
  Return s_{max}
}

and consists of 'pulse numbers' which correspond "to the complex values returned by the function resulting from the complex electromagnetic signal (Asuncion & Newman, 2007)." The total number of records is 351 and the cardinality of each continuous attribute is in the range of 250. The predictability of the cardinality is due to the consistent range across each attribute since each pulse has a min of -1 and max of 1.

Illustrative Examples for the BRM/HCA Method

Two illustrations are presented to portray the process involved in discovering the global optimum using the BRM/HCA method[3]. We have chosen the following attributes to illustrate the BRM/HCA's capability of ascertaining the global optimum: (1) *slope* and (2) *hillshade_noon*, both from the dataset *forest cover*.

Table 3. Range and discrete values by attribute

DATASET	Attribute	Range	NBR of DISCRETE VALUES
Forest Cover	Aspect	360	361
Forest Cover	Elevation	1,999	1,978
Forest Cover	Slope	66	67
Forest Cover	H_dist_roadways	7,117	5,785
Forest Cover	H_dist_hydrology	1,397	551
Forest Cover	V_dist_hydrology	774	700
Forest Cover	H_dist_fire_points	7,173	5,827
Forest Cover	Hillshade_9am	254	207
Forest Cover	Hillshade_noon	254	185
Forest Cover	Hillshade_3pm	254	255
Ionosphere	Attr1	2	219
Ionosphere	Attr6	2	260
Ionosphere	Attr20	2	265
Ionosphere	Attr22	2	264
Ionosphere	Attr32	2	263

Figure 3 illustrates how the BRM/HCA method will determine the global optimum - this example utilizes the attribute *slope* from the *forest cover* dataset. The BRM will shift to the left after evaluating the three points: (1) *mid-point* (50); (2) *mid-left* (25) and; (3) *mid-right* (75). The BRM will then continue for another calculation as it calculates the information gain for the new *mid-left* and *mid-right* (denoted by 25(2) and 75(2) in Figure 3). At this point, since the stopping criterion has been met, the BRM stops and the high point is sent to the HCA to finish its ascent to the global optimum indicated by the star sign.

Figure 4 illustrates how the BRM/HCA method will determine the global optimum utilizing the attribute *hillshade_noon* from the forest cover dataset. The BRM will shift to the right after evaluating the three points: (1) *mid-point* (50); (2) *mid-left* (25) and; (3) *mid-right* (75). The BRM will then continue for one more calculation as it calculates the information gain for the new *mid-left* and *mid-right* (denoted by 25(2) and 75(2) in Figure 4). At this point, since the stopping

criterion has been met, the BRM stops and the high point is sent to the HCA to finish its ascent to the global optimum.

Illustrative Examples for the BRM/HCA Method Utilizing the SUM Extension

Figure 5 illustrates how the bisecting region method with the hill-climbing algorithm traverses a particular attribute to find the global optimum, in this case, *attr22* from the *ionosphere* dataset. There is an extra function as part of the SUM extension – called *firstpass*. The *firstpass* function is called once, prior to calling the BRM. Its main purpose is to attempt to *force* the BRM algorithm to iterate at least twice and aids in discovering global optima at the boundaries of an attribute.

The grey circles represent the initial calculation of the information gain for the *min, mid-left, mid-point, mid-right* and *max* data points. The information gain from the *min* and *mid-left* split points are then summed as depicted by *SUM1* in the

Figure 3. Example of finding global optimal

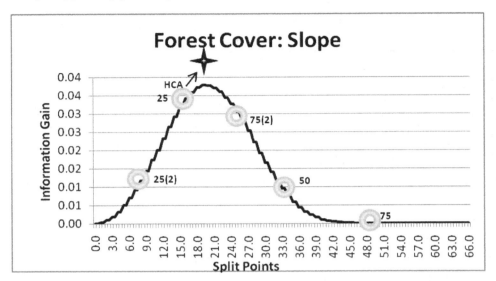

figure. Respectively, the information gain for the *mid-right* and *max* split points are summed, which is indicated by *SUM2*. At this point the *mid-point* is compared with *SUM1* and *SUM2*. In this particular case, *SUM1* is greater than *mid-point* and *SUM2* and therefore the stopping criteria have not been met for the bisecting region method.

The processing will continue by shifting to the left, whereby the new *mid-left* and *mid-right* points will be determined – this is analogous to the shifting logic in the BRM. The *mid-left* point will become the new *mid-point* and based on this the new *mid-left* and *mid-right* points (denoted in the figure with 25(2) and 75(2)) are established. The information gain from these points are compared

Figure 4. Example of finding global optimal

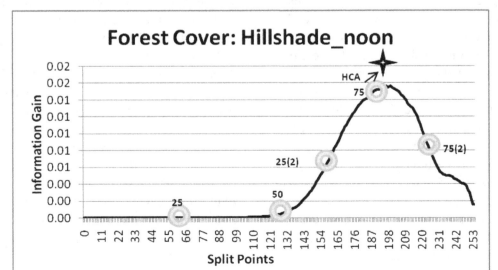

Figure 5. Example of finding global optimal with SUM extension

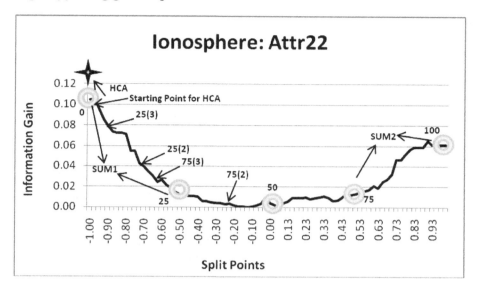

and as is visually obvious in the figure, the *mid-left* point (shown in the chart as 25(2)) is the highest.

This process consecutively continues shifting to the left as it ascends towards the global optimum (due to space constraints all calculated data points are not shown in the figure). The BRM, for this particular attribute, actually concludes when the information gains for all three split points (*mid-point*, *mid-left*, and *mid-right*) are equal.

The final split point, which will become the starting point for the HCA, is in this case the *mid-point* from the final round of processing of the BRM (indicated in Figure 5 as the starting point for the HCA). The HCA, will first search to the left and find that the information gain for the next data point is lower. It then proceeds to the right for two calculations until it begins its descent. At this time, the split point with the highest information gain, as returned by the BRM/HCA, is chosen as the final split point as denoted by the star in the figure.

Figure 6 illustrates another instance of how the BRM/HCA method will determine the global optimum. The example utilizes the attribute *Attr32*

from the *ionosphere* dataset. As denoted in the previous example, the grey circles represent the first pass. The BRM will shift to the right after evaluating the three points: (1) *mid-point*; (2) *SUM1* and; (3) *SUM2*. The BRM will then continue to the right for three more calculations as it calculates the information gain for the new *mid-left* and *mid-right* split points (not all split points are indicated on Figure 6 due to space constraints).

The last calculation of the BRM resulted in equivalent information gain values for the *mid-left*, *mid-point* and *mid-right* values therefore the stopping criterion has been met and the *mid-point* split point is selected as the starting point for the HCA. The HCA examines the splits to the left and right of the starting point and correctly determines that the starting point is the global optimum.

Experiments

The algorithms were implemented using PL/SQL on an Oracle 10g server.

Figure 6. Example of finding global optimal using SUM extension

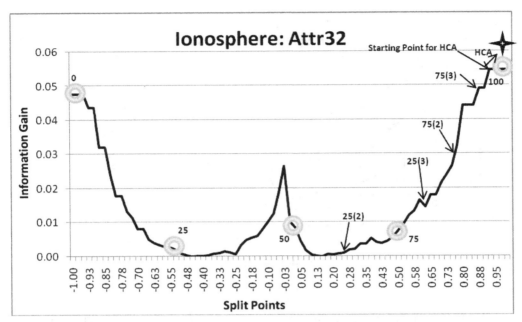

Figure 7. Accuracy comparison by method for forest cover

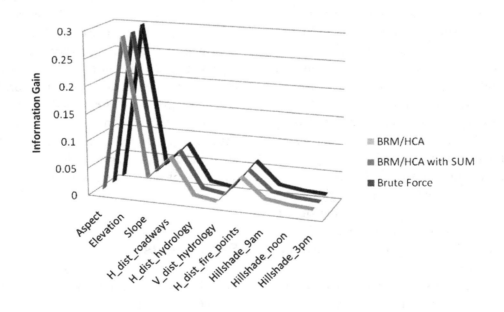

Figure 8. Accuracy comparison by method for ionosphere

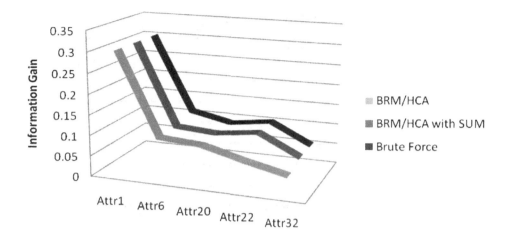

Brute Force Algorithm

Prior to comparing the results of the BRM/HCA with the *brute force* method, an explanation of the *brute force* algorithm will be briefly discussed. The *brute force* algorithm functions similarly to the discretization performed in Quinlan's C4.5 algorithm (Quinlan, 1993). In the *brute force* method, essentially the algorithm performs a sequential read of the sorted attribute. Each time the discrete value in the attribute record changes, a new split point is determined as the midpoint between the two values. If n is the number of discrete values for a particular attribute, then the number of calculations for the *brute force* method will be $n - 1$.

RESULTS

Figures 7-10 show the performance in terms of accuracy and efficiency for all three methods – *brute force*, *BRM/HCA* and *BRM/HCA* with the *SUM* extension – and their relative differences. Figures 7 and 8 specifically detail the accuracy of both the *BRM/HCA* and *BRM/HCA with SUM* methods when compared to the benchmark (brute force). It is obvious from these two charts that the information gain for each of these methods is comparable to the brute force. The BRM/HCA with SUM performs somewhat better in the *ionosphere* dataset. Overall, in i*onosphere*, the *BRM/HCA* method was able to discover the global optimum 80% of the time. For the *forest cover* dataset, the global optimum was discovered 60% of the time. However, it is important to note that the other (local) optima discovered in both *forest cover* and *ionosphere* had information gain values that were not significantly different from the global.

Figures 9 and 10 illustrate the dramatic differences in the number of information gain calculations for all the methods. It was necessary to stack these values in order to show the relative differences between the methods. For forest cover, it is palpable how the BRM/HCA and BRM/HCA with SUM methods are dramatically more efficient than the brute force method. The BRM/HCA method is most efficient in datasets where a large range and high cardinality are present.

For *forest cover*, processing time became an important factor to consider due to the large number of records combined with widespread ranges in some of the attributes. On average, the processing time for the brute force algorithm was over 7 minutes. The average process time for the BRM/HCA was just under 33 seconds (see Figure

Figure 9. Efficiency comparison by method for forest cover

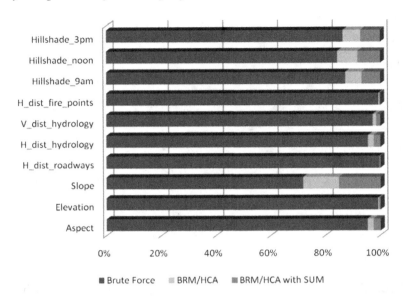

11 for processing time listings by attribute/method). The times collected were conducted using an Oracle 10g server – obviously if run in main memory the times would be significantly faster. However, large data sets might not fit into main memory, and hence we chose to use a database management system. Also, the purpose of reporting these times is to show the *relative* differences rather than absolute processing time. For each individual attribute in *forest cover*, there is a significant amount of variation, particularly with the brute force algorithm. This is due to three factors: (1) the number of records in the dataset; (2) the range associated with the individual attribute and; (3) the number of discrete values for each attribute. For reference, the information for

Figure 10. Efficiency comparison by method for ionosphere

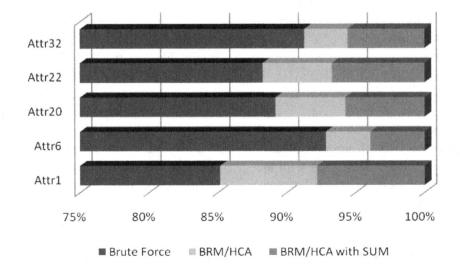

Figure 11. Processing time comparison (hours:minutes:seconds)

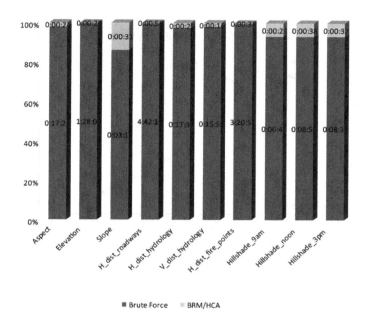

the range and number of discrete values for both *forest cover* and *ionosphere* can be found in the previous section in Table 3.

The results from the empirical tests comparing the *brute force* to the bisecting region method – *with the hill-climbing algorithm* - demonstrate that the BRM/HCA method and its SUM extension can find the (near) optimal split point and do so with noticeably less calculations. To report accuracy first, the average reduction (over both methods) in information gain was 4% with a 98% reduction in the number of calculations.

The Issue of Cost

The computational complexity of the brute force algorithm for discretization is O(n) where n is the number of distinct values per an attribute, which can be very large in applications such as the Sloan Digital Sky Survey data or the Baruch Options data warehouse discussed in the Introduction section of this paper. The brute force algorithm – albeit optimal – is not a feasible solution for such

datasets. The problem becomes worse in decision tree induction, where discretization is required at every node (i.e., local discretization as in C4.5) and this operation is therefore multiplied by the number of levels produced by the decision tree (though n is decreasing at each level).

The BRM/HCA discovers the global optimum in well-behaved datasets. However, when data is noisy the method may stop after discovering a local optimum. This is also true for other sampling methods such as Catlett's (1991) peepholing. However, for the empirical tests conducted, the local optima discovered were very close to the global. For example, the attribute v_dist_hydrology had an optimal split where the information gain was equal to .0079. The BRM/HCA method find a split point where the information gain was equal to .0078 – or 2% less than the (global) optimal split. Figure 12 shows the local optimum discovered for v_dist_hydrology by the BRM/HCA method in relation to the global optimum. The BRM/HCA method in this case, has in fact, stopped at a local optimum.

Figure 12. Example of BRM/HCA finding local optimum

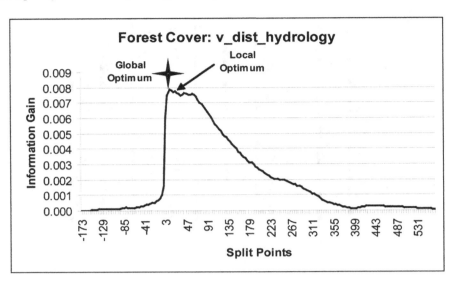

Figure 13. Comparison of class boundary changes with BRM/HCA

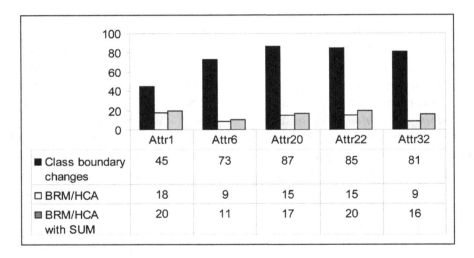

	Attr1	Attr6	Attr20	Attr22	Attr32
■ Class boundary changes	45	73	87	85	81
□ BRM/HCA	18	9	15	15	9
■ BRM/HCA with SUM	20	11	17	20	16

Comparison with Fayyad and Irani's Class Boundary Changes

Fayyad and Irani (1992) established that the optimal split point for any attribute will always occur where the class boundary label changes. Consequently, significantly less information gain calculations need to be performed since only where there is a change in the class label does the infor-

mation gain need to be examined. In regards to efficiency, the BRM/HCA method, for the datasets used in this empirical validation, outperforms the class label boundary changes. In Figure 13, we have compared our results from the BRM/HCA method as well as the SUM extension with Fayyad and Irani's theory using the *ionosphere* dataset. The comparison indicates that the BRM/HCA method is superior in terms of efficiency due to the fact that our method is examining approximately 75% fewer number of potential split points than the class boundary changes approach.

CONCLUSION

In this article we describe a new method (BRM/HCA) for finding optimal split points in continuous attributes. The BRM/HCA method has been empirically tested to find the global (or near-global) optima in a number of datasets although we have only presented a few of those results in this article. The necessity for the addition of the SUM extension was determined through empirical testing. However, finding global optima at the boundaries should be a rare occurrence and could indicate that the attribute has poor predictive power. Such an attribute should most likely not be included in a decision tree algorithm. Consequently, the SUM extension could be used to find such anomalies and exclude them from a decision tree algorithm. For general purposes, the SUM extension (as opposed to just the BRM/HCA) should be used for discretization procedures since it is able to more accurately identify the global optimum and it adds only a minimal number of calculations.

A limitation of the BRM/HCA method is that it does not guarantee the discovery of the global optimum due to the fact that it does not cover the entire range of attribute values. A possible improvement of this method could be to allow the user to specify a certain percentage of coverage of the attribute. One such method that is currently under development is to develop a functional form from a sample of the data points. This method would require an initial sampling of the attribute, from which a functional form for the information gain could be derived. We plan to investigate the effect of sample size on the accuracy of the functional form derived.

In closing, the purpose of this article was to present a novel entropy-based discretization method – the *bisecting region method with the hill-climbing algorithm*– and empirically validate its ability to find the (near) optimal split point with significantly fewer number of information gain calculations. This method could be a viable candidate for dynamic discretization especially for large datasets where computational efficiency becomes a critical factor to consider. The results from this empirical study show that the BRM/HCA can in fact find the optimal or near optimal split point when compared to the brute force method with only an average 4% reduction in information gain. In conclusion, on average, there was a 98% reduction in the number of information gain calculations when compared to the *brute force* method.

REFERENCES

Asuncion, A., & Newman, D. J. (2007). *UCI machine learning repository*. Retrieved from http://www.ics.uci.edu/~mlearn/MLRepository.html

Bagui, S. (2006). An approach to mining crime patterns. *International Journal of Data Warehousing and Mining, 2*(1), 50–80.

Baruch Options Data Warehouse. (2008). *Subotnik Financial Services Center*. Retrieved

Breiman, L., Friedman, J. H., Olshen, R. A., & Stone, C. J. (1998). *Megainduction: machine learning on very large databases*. Sydney, Australia: University of Sydney.

Catlett, J. (1991). *On changing continuous attributes into ordered discrete attributes*. Paper presented at the Proceedings of the European Working Session on Learning, Berlin, Germany.

Chan, C. C., Batur, C., & Srinivasan, A. (1991). *Determination of quantization intervals in rule based model for dynamic systems*. Paper presented at the Proceedings of the IEEE Conference on Systems, Man, and Cybernetics, Charlottesville, VA.

Chan, P. K., & Stolfo, S. J. (1993). *Experiments on multistrategy learning by metalearning.* Paper presented at the Proceedings of the Second International Conference on Information and Knowledge Management, Washington, D.C.

Chan, P. K., & Stolfo, S. J. (1993). *Metalearning for multistrategy and parallel learning.* Paper presented at the Proceedings of Second International Workshop on Multistrategy Learning.

Charles, F., & Cavazza, M. (2004). *Exploring the scalability of character-based storytelling.* Paper presented at the Third International Joint Conference on Autonomous Agents and Multiagent Systems.

Chaudhuri, S. (1998). Data mining and database systems: where is the intersection? *A Quarterly Bulletin of the Computer Society of the IEEE Technical Committee on Data Engineering, 21*(1), 4–8.

Chickering, D. M., Meek, C., & Rounthwaite, R. (2001). *Efficient Determination of Dynamic Split Points in a Decision Tree.* Paper presented at the First IEEE International Conference on Data Mining, San Jose, CA.

Chiu, D. K. Y., Cheung, B., & Wong, A. K. C. (1990). Information synthesis based on hierarchical entropy discretization. *Journal of Experimental & Theoretical Artificial Intelligence, 2*, 117–129. doi:10.1080/09528139008953718

Dougherty, J., Kohavi, R., & Sahami, M. (1995). *Supervised and unsupervised discretization of continuous features.* Paper presented at the Proceedings of the 12th International Conference on Machine Learning, Tahoe City, CA.

Fayyad, U. M., & Irani, K. B. (1992). On the handling of continuous-valued attributes in decision tree generation. *Machine Learning, 8*, 87–102.

Fayyad, U. M., & Irani, K. B. (1993). *Multi-interval discretization of continuous-valued attributes for classification learning.* Paper presented at the Proceedings of the 13th International Joint Conference on Artificial Intelligence.

Friedman, N., & Goldszmidt, M. (1996). *Discretizing continuous attributes whle learning Bayesian networks.* Paper presented at the Proceedings of the Thirteenth International Conference on Machine Learning, San Francisco, CA.

Ganti, V., Gehrke, J., & Ramakrishnan, R. (1999). Mining very large databases. *Computer, 32*(8), 38–45. doi:10.1109/2.781633

Gehrke, J., Ganti, V., Ramakrishnan, R., & Loh, W. Y. (1999). *BOAT - optimistic decision tree construction.* Paper presented at the 1999 ACM SIGMOD International Conference on Management of Data, Philadelphia, PA.

Gehrke, J., Ramakrishnan, R., & Ganti, V. (2000). Rainforest - A framework for fast decision tree construction of large datasets. *Data Mining and Knowledge Discovery, 4*, 127–162. doi:10.1023/A:1009839829793

Han, J., & Kamber, M. (2006). *Data Mining: Concepts and Techniques (2nd ed.).* Amsterdam: Morgan Kaufman.

Hand, D., Mannila, H., & Smyth, P. (2001). *Principles of Data Mining.* Cambridge, MA: MIT Press.

Ho, K. M., & Scott, P. D. (1997). *Zeta: A global method for discretization of continuous variables.* Paper presented at the KDD97: 3rd International Conference of Knowledge Discovery and Data Mining, Newport Beach, CA.

Holte, R. C. (1993). Very simple classification rules perform well on most commonly used datasets. *Machine Learning, 11*, 63–90. doi:10.1023/A:1022631118932

Hyafil, L., & Rivest, R. L. (1976). Constructing optimal binary decision trees is NP-complete. *Information Processing Letters*, *5*(1), 15–17. doi:10.1016/0020-0190(76)90095-8

June 20, 2008 from http://optionsdata.baruch.cuny.edu/

Kamber, M., Winstone, L., Gong, W., Cheng, S., & Han, J. (1997). *Generalization and decision tree induction: efficient classification in data mining.* Paper presented at the RIDE '97.

Kerber, R. (1992). *Chimerge: Discretization of numeric attributes.* Paper presented at the Proceedings of the Tenth National Conference on Artificial Intelligence.

Kohonen, T. (1989). *Self-Organization and Associative Memory.* Berlin, Germany: Springer-Verlag.

Liu, H., Hussain, F., Tan, C. L., & Dash, M. (2002). Discretization: An enabling technique. *Data Mining and Knowledge Discovery*, *6*, 393–423. doi:10.1023/A:1016304305535

Loh, W.-Y., & Shih, Y.-S. (1997). Split selection methods for classification trees. *Statistica Sinica*, *7*, 815–840.

Loh, W.-Y., & Vanichsetakul, N. (1988). Tree-structured classification via generalized discriminant analysis. *Journal of the American Statistical Association*, *83*(403), 715–725. doi:10.2307/2289295

Mehta, M., Agrawal, R., & Rissanen, J. (1996, 1996). *SLIQ: A Fast Scalable Classifier for Data Mining.* Paper presented at the EDBT, Avignon, France.

Ng, R. T., & Han, J. (2002). CLARANS: A Method for Clustering Objects for Spatial Data Mining. *IEEE Transactions on Knowledge and Data Engineering*, *14*(5), 1003–1016. doi:10.1109/TKDE.2002.1033770

Pfahringer, B. (1995). *Compression-based discretization of continuous attributes.* Paper presented at the Proceedings of the Twelfth International Conference on Machine Learning.

Press, W. H. (2007). *Numerical recipes: the art of scientific computing (3rd ed.).* New York: Cambridge University Press.

Quinlan, J. R. (1983). Learning efficient classification procedures and their application to chess endgames. In R. Michalski, T. Carbonell & T. Mitchell (Eds.), *Machine Learning: an AI approach.* Los Altos, CA: Morgan Kaufmann.

Quinlan, J. R. (1986). Induction of decision trees. *Machine Learning, 1*(81-106), 81-106.

Quinlan, J. R. (1993). *C4.5: Programs for Machine Learning.* Los Altos, CA: Morgan Kauffman.

Quinlan, J. R. (1996). Improved use of continuous attributes in C4.5. *Journal of Artificial Intelligence Research, 4*, 77–90.

Rastogi, R., & Shim, K. (2000). Public: A decision tree classifier that integrates building and pruning. *Data Mining and Knowledge Discovery*, *4*(4), 315–344. doi:10.1023/A:1009887311454

Richeldi, M., & Rossotto, M. (1995). Class-driven statistical discretization of continuous attributes. In N. Lavrac & S. Wrobel (Eds.), *Lecture notes in Artificial Intelligence (Vol. 914, pp. 335-338).* Berlin, Heidelberg, New York: Springer-Verlag.

Shafer, J., Agrawal, R., & Mehta, M. (1996). *SPRINT: A scalable parallel classifier for data mining.* Paper presented at the Proceedings of the 22nd International Conference of Very Large Databases, Mumbai (Bombay), India.

Sloan Digital Sky Survey. (2008). *The 5ᵗʰ data release of the Sloan digital sky survey.* Retrieved June 20, 2008 from http://cas.sdss.org/dr5/en

Tan, P.-N., et al. (2005) *Introduction to Data Mining*. Boston, MA: Addison-Wesley Longman Publishing Co., Inc.

Ting, K. M. (1994). Discretization *of continuous-valued attributes and instance-based learning* (Vol. 491) (Tech. Rep.). Australia: University of Sydney.

Tzanis, G., & Berberidis, C. (2007). Mining for Mutually Exclusive Items in Transaction Databases. *International Journal of Data Warehousing and Mining, 3*(3), 45–59.

Van de Merckt, T. (1993). *Decision trees in numerical attribute spaces*. Paper presented at the 13th International Joint Conference on Artificial Intelligence.

Vannucci, M., & Colla, V. (2004, April 28-30). *Meaningful discretization of continuous features for association rules mining by means of a SOM*. Paper presented at the European Symposium on Artificial Neural Networks, Bruges, Belgium.

Weiss, S. M., Galen, R. S., & Tadepalli, P. V. (1990). Maximizing the predicative value of production rules. *Artificial Intelligence, 45*, 47–71. doi:10.1016/0004-3702(90)90037-Z

Witten, I. H., & Frank, E. (2005). *Data Mining: Practical Machine Learning Tools and Techniques*. San Francisco: Elsevier, Inc.

Wong, A. K. C., & Chiu, D. K. Y. (1987). Synthesizing statistical knowledge from incomplete mixed-mode data. *IEEE Transactions on Pattern Analysis and Machine Intelligence, 9*, 796–805. doi:10.1109/TPAMI.1987.4767986

Zaki, M. J. (2000). Scalable Algorithms for Association Mining. *IEEE Transactions on Knowledge and Data Engineering, 12*(3), 372–390. doi:10.1109/69.846291

ENDNOTES

[1]   Forest cover dataset was obtained from UCI KDD Archive at http://kdd.ics.uci.edu/.

[2]   Ionosphere dataset was obtained from UCI Machine Learning Repository at http://mlearn.ics.uci.edu/MLRepository.html.

[3]   This method was implemented using PL/SQL on an Oracle 10g server.

This work was previously published in International Journal of Data Warehousing and Mining, Volume 6, Issue 2, edited by David Taniar, pp. 1-22, copyright 2010 by IGI Publishing (an imprint of IGI Global).

Chapter 6
Dimensionality Reduction with Unsupervised Feature Selection and Applying Non–Euclidean Norms for Classification Accuracy

Amit Saxena
G G University, India

John Wang
Montclair State University, USA

ABSTRACT

This paper presents a two-phase scheme to select reduced number of features from a dataset using Genetic Algorithm (GA) and testing the classification accuracy (CA) of the dataset with the reduced feature set. In the first phase of the proposed work, an unsupervised approach to select a subset of features is applied. GA is used to select stochastically reduced number of features with Sammon Error as the fitness function. Different subsets of features are obtained. In the second phase, each of the reduced features set is applied to test the CA of the dataset. The CA of a data set is validated using supervised k-nearest neighbor (k-nn) algorithm. The novelty of the proposed scheme is that each reduced feature set obtained in the first phase is investigated for CA using the k-nn classification with different Minkowski metric i.e. non-Euclidean norms instead of conventional Euclidean norm (L_2). Final results are presented in the paper with extensive simulations on seven real and one synthetic, data sets. It is revealed from the proposed investigation that taking different norms produces better CA and hence a scope for better feature subset selection.

DOI: 10.4018/978-1-61350-474-1.ch006

Copyright © 2012, IGI Global. Copying or distributing in print or electronic forms without written permission of IGI Global is prohibited.

INTRODUCTION

In most of the computer-based applications today, datasets are having a large number of patterns and relatively a smaller number of classes. Each pattern is characterized by a number of features and each pattern belongs to one of the total classes. Classification of these patterns is a major step in data mining (Han & Kamber, 2006). In majority of the data mining applications, patterns are required to be classified. As classification requires feature analysis, the latter becomes an important component of data mining. Feature analysis consists of feature selection and feature extraction. The function of a feature selection process is to select a subset of features from the entire set of features in a dataset. Feature extraction on the other hand, may combine or re-compute features among themselves to create a new feature. Curse of dimensionality caused due to redundancy of extra or derogatory features is a major issue of concern in data mining. Feature selection process can be useful to counter curse of dimensionality problem. Feature selection is applied to select most significant features in a dataset. By significant features here, we mean those features, which alone can predict the classes of the patterns in a dataset with maximum accuracy. If the feature selection makes use of information (such as class of a pattern) given before the process is applied, then the approach is called supervised. If no information is supplied a priory to grouping the patterns, the approach is called an unsupervised. In later case, the features are combined on the basis of some similarity (such as clustering). A number of supervised feature selection methods exist which use Neural Networks, Fuzzy logic, k-nearest neighbor search (k-nn) algorithms. On the contrary, the problem of unsupervised feature selection has been addressed rarely.

In most of the unsupervised feature selection approaches, grouping of features is based on the distance among individual features with each other. The computation of distance is central in the unsupervised approaches to decide the level of similarity among features. The decision of selecting significant features is heuristic. To select most effective features from a large number of features, evolutionary computing techniques can be applied. Genetic algorithm (GA) (Romero & Abelló, 2009; Goldberg, 1989), is a powerful evolutionary computing technique based on the principles of evolution. GA can be applied to select features in this manner.

With reduced number of feature selected through GA, next essential objective is to test the classification accuracy (CA) of the dataset due to this subset of features. The k-nn classification is a supervised method used to determine the CA of a data set. The distance between the test pattern and each pattern in the dataset is determined and the class is decided on the basis of the class of the pattern having minimum distance from the test pattern. In most cases, k=1, i.e. the pattern having minimum distance from the test pattern is marked as the class of the test pattern. A popularly known distance used for this purpose is a Euclidean distance, which is a special case of Minkowski metric or non-Euclidean norms. In this paper, we vary the Minkowski metric parameters for different values including the popular Euclidean distance to observe the effect of variation of Minkowski metric on CA of the dataset due to a particular feature set. The paper is organized as follows. Next section presents review of earlier work in the field. Section *Genetic Algorithm*, highlights brief description of GA. After that we outline Minkowski metric. The proposed method is explained in next. The brief summary of datasets is presented in Section *Datasets*. *Simulation studies* and *Result Analysis* are described separately in *Appendix*. Conclusions and future research scopes are presented in last section of main text.

REVIEW OF EARLIER WORK

Data mining is defined as a multidisciplinary joint effort from databases, machine learning, and statistics, which is championing in turning mountains of data into nuggets (Mitra, Murthy, & Pal, 2002). Feature selection (FS) is an important component of data mining as it helps in reducing dimensions of data set but still preserving the structure of the data set. Ho (1998) combined and constructed multiple classifiers using randomly selected features, which can achieve better performance in classification than using the complete set of features. As an option, the selection of an optimal feature vector can be made with an exhaustive search of all possible subsets of features (Zhang, 2005). FS methods can have two categories: the wrapper method; where the classification accuracy is employed to evaluate feature subsets and the second is filter approach in which, various measurements may be used as FS criteria. The wrapper methods may perform better, but huge computational effort is required (Chow, 2005). In case of extremely large feature sets, such as the gene (feature) set of a cDNA data, it can be enormously expensive to apply wrapper method. A hybrid method is suggested by Liu (2005), which attempts to take advantage of both the methods by exploiting their different evaluation criteria in different search stages.

An unsupervised algorithm (Mitra, 2002) uses feature dependency/similarity for redundancy reduction. The method involves partitioning of the original feature set into some distinct subsets or clusters so that the features within a cluster are highly similar while those in different clusters are dissimilar. A single feature from each such cluster is then selected to constitute the resulting reduced subset.

Use of soft computing methods like GA, fuzzy logic and Neural Networks for FS and Feature ranking is suggested in (Pal, 1999; Pal, 2002). Muni (2006) categorized FS method into five groups based on the evaluation function, distance,

information, dependence, consistency (all filter types), and classifier error rate (wrapper type). Further, Setiono and Liu (1997) state that the process of FS works opposite to ID3 (Quinlan, 1993). Instead of selecting one attribute at a time, it starts with taking whole set of attributes and removes irrelevant attribute one by one using a three layer feed forward neural network. Basak and Pal (2000) used neuro-fuzzy approach for unsupervised FS and compared with other supervised approaches. Further, Best Incremental Ranked Subset (BIRS) based algorithm (Roberto & Ruiz, 2006) presents a fast search through the attribute space and any classifier can be embedded into it as evaluator. BIRS chooses a small subset of genes from the original set (0.0018% on average) with similar predictive performance to others. For very high dimensional datasets, wrapper-based methods might be computationally unfeasible, so BIRS turns out a fast technique that provides good performance in prediction accuracy. Yan (2007) proposed a general formulation known as graph embedding to unify a large family of algorithms - supervised or unsupervised; stemming from statistics or geometry. They proposed a new supervised dimensionality reduction algorithm called marginal Fisher analysis MFA. Recently a new unsupervised forward orthogonal search (FOS) algorithm is introduced for feature selection and ranking (Wei, 2007) which uses a squared correlation function as the criterion to measure the dependency between the features.

The GA is biologically inspired and has many mechanisms mimicking natural evolution. Raymer (2000) used GA for dimensionality reduction. The pioneering work by Siedlecki (Siedlecki, 1989) demonstrated evidence for the superiority of the GA compared to representative classical algorithms. Few more papers can be found in (Pena, 2001; Dash, 1997; Kohavi, 1997; Yu, Shao, Luo, & Zeng, 2009).

Present paper is inspired from the work of Doherty (Doherty, 2007; Doherty, 2004). In these papers, the characteristics of non Euclidean norms within the unsupervised learning environment are examined. The performances of the k-means, self-organizing maps have been empirically assessed. It has been stated that the accuracy is improved by taking fractional norms (Aggarwal, 2001). In the present paper, we have first applied GA to find reduced feature subsets and then examined the effect of varying Minkowski metric norms by using its different values in the distance computation of k-nn classification algorithm.

GENETIC ALGORITHMS: AN OVERVIEW

First pioneered by John Holland in the 60s, Genetic Algorithms, GA, have been widely studied with interest, experimented and applied in many fields in science and engineering worlds. GA is an evolutionary algorithm, which optimizes a fitness function to find the solution of a problem. Different evolutionary algorithms have been used for FS. In a typical GA, each chromosome represents a prospective solution of the problem. The problem is associated with a fitness function – higher fitness refers to a better solution. The set of chromosomes is called a population. The population goes through a repeated set of iterations (or generations) with crossover and mutation operations to find better solutions. At a certain fitness level or after a certain number of iterations, the procedure is stopped and the chromosome giving the best solution is preserved as the solution of the problem. A detailed description of GA can be found in any book on evolutionary algorithms (Goldberg, 1989).

Minkowski Metric

A measurement of distance is a fundamental operation in the unsupervised learning process. Smaller is the distance between any two objects; closer these objects are assumed on the basis of similarity. A family of distance measures is the Minkowski metrics (Sneath, 1973), where the distance is measured by following equation

$$\|ij\|_r = \left\{ \sum_{k=1}^{d} \left| x_{ik} - x_{jk} \right|^r \right\}^{1/r} \qquad (1)$$

Where x_{ik} is the value of the k-th variable for entity $I x_{,jk}$ is the value of k-th variable for entity j.

The most popular and common distance measure is the Euclidean or L_2 norm ($r=2$). Due to our known or unknown use and experience of Euclidean distance, in most of the distance measurement framework, we stick to this form of Minkowski Metric. However, changing the values of r, will show different effects of this metric. Few illustrations have been provided in (Doherty, 2007). It is shown with these illustrations that the fractional norm can reduce the effect of large differences in individual attributes.

In this paper, we have demonstrated the effect of different norms on the classification accuracy obtained by various feature subsets in a dataset.

PROPOSED SCHEME

The proposed scheme is divided in two phases. In the first phase, GA is used to determine various subsets of reduced number of features in the data set. In the second phase, these features are tested for CA using k-nn method. The CA is resolved determined with different Minkowski Metric norms. Proposed two-Phase scheme is represented by Figure.1.

1. **Phase I: Feature Selection**: GA has been applied for majority of optimization problems, including shortest path distance, traveling salesman problem, training of neural networks etc. Here, we apply GA to select a reduced subset of entire set of features. The objective or the fitness function of the problem is Sammon's error (SE).

Figure 1. Proposed two- phase scheme

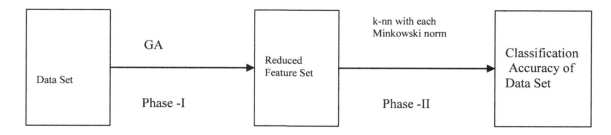

Smaller is SE, better fit is the solution. The complete process is described below (Saxena, 2007):

a. Let there be F features in the dataset. Suppose we want to select maximum m ($m < F$) number of features from the data set. Create a population consisting of N chromosomes. The number of cells (genes) in each chromosome consists of exactly the number of features in the dataset. Thus for iris dataset ($F = 4$), there will be four genes in a chromosome. Accordingly there will be N such chromosomes in the population. Initialize each chromosome with all zero values. We will use the convention that a 1 in the i-th position of a chromosome will indicate that i-th feature in the dataset will be present; whereas a 0 will mean that i-th feature in the dataset will remain absent.

b. Fill each chromosome randomly with minimum 1 and maximum m number of 1s at different positions. For generating different positions, in a chromosome, take some initial seed value to generate random numbers. Thus the population will consist of N chromosomes, some of them having a single 1 whereas some chromosomes will have m number of 1s.

c. Determine the fitness of each chromosome using SE function given by Equation (2).

Let $X = \{x_k \mid x_k = (x_{k1}, x_{k2}, ... x_{kp})^T, k = 1.2.....n\}$ be the set of n vectors in the original space and $Y = \{y_k \mid y_k = (y_{k1}, y_{k2}, ... y_{kq})^T, k = 1.2.....n\}$ be the unknown data vectors in the reduced space. Let $d^*_{ij} = d(x_i, x_j)$, $x_i, x_j \in X$ and $d_{ij} = d(y_i, y_j)$. $y_i, y_j \in Y$. where $d_{(xi, xj)}$ be the Euclidean distance between x_i and x_j. The Sammon Error E is given by (Sammon, 1969).

$$E = \frac{1}{\sum_{i<j} d^*_{ij}} \sum_{i<j} \frac{(d^*_{ij} - d_{ij})^2}{d^*_{ij}} \tag{2}$$

When all features are selected, SE will be 0. Usually more number of features selected will yield less SE. Our attempt is to seek small number of features with reasonably small SE.

d. Selection of chromosomes for crossover operation is done using Roulette Wheel (RW) Method on the basis of accumulated fitness of each chromosome. Form pairs of chromosomes selected using this method. Here we take first indexed chromosome obtained by RW method and pair it with immediate next indexed chromosome.

e. First, check for the suitability of each pair obtained using RW method. For this purpose, set a probability of crossover *PC*. Generate a random number between 0 and 1 corresponding to each pair. If this number is greater than or equal to *PC*, that particular pair will be selected for crossover operation. Apply simple crossover and mutation operations to pairs chosen suitable for crossover. For this, we use single point crossover. So in a suitable pair, generate a random index between *1* to *F* and mark this index. The right part of the index in the upper chromosome will be exchanged with the right part of the lower chromosome. Thus we get an entirely different pair, called *offspring*.

f. For each chromosome of the modified population, apply bit-by-bit mutation. Set a probability of mutation *PM* (usually 0.001-0.003). Generate a random value between 0 and 1 corresponding to each position (bit) in the chromosome. If the number generated is greater than or equal to *PM*, then flip the value of that position. Thus a 0 will be replaced by 1 and vice versa.

g. After crossover and mutation operation, the population is entirely different from the initial population created at step 1. Term this population as modified population.

h. Merge the initial and modified populations to obtain final population. Thus we have *2N* chromosomes in the final population. Sort the chromosomes according to ascending values of SE (descending values of fitness). Thus the fittest chromosome will be placed at the top and un-fittest at the bottom.

i. Select the first *N* chromosomes from the final population and put these into a new population which will be used as initial population for the next generation.

j. Repeat steps (b) through (i) for a given number of generations.

k. At the end of the procedure, from the final population, select the chromosome with minimum value of SE. Note the indexes of the positions of genes for which value is 1. These indexes will form the subset of features in the dataset.

l. For enhancing the chance of getting better feature subsets, we repeat steps (a) through (k) with different initial seed values. By doing so, we always get an initial fresh set of chromosomes in a population, it increases population diversity. We took 10 seed values and thus get 10 feature subsets though few feature subsets may repeat.

2. **Phase II**: In this phase we outline a k-nn classification method then apply it to check accuracy of each of the ten reduced feature subsets obtained in Phase-I with eight different values of Minkowski norms one by one.

K-NN Classification

Cluster analysis identifies unsupervised natural groupings within a data set. Generally, a metric distance between any two entities is called as a notion of proximity. If two entities are in the close proximity, then they are said to belong to the same class or group. The nearest neighbor search is a method to identify entities in the same proximity in a supervised manner and is defined as "Given a collection of data points and a query point in a d-dimensional metric space, find the data point that is closest to the query point"(Beyer, 1999).

For computing classification accuracy (CA) of a data set with the given number of features, we used k-nn classifier with k=1, as follows.

1. Given a data set consisting of say *P* patterns. Generate a random sequence of patterns with a given seed value fixed for this round.

2. Create five folds of patterns in this sequence such that each fold holds 1/5 of the patterns equally (last fold can have remaining patterns if *P* is not divisible by 5). First four folds *f1,f2,f3,f4* will be used for training and the last fold *f5* will be used for testing. Set the *CA* counter *c_a_c* to 0.

3. Compute the Minkowski distance of each pattern in *f1,f2,f3,f4* from first pattern in *f5*, considering only the reduced features of the patterns (excluding the class). In other words, in each pattern, only featured columns will be taken into account, rest columns will be set to zero while computing distance. We have applied k-nn for computing CA for selected number of features as well as for all features; and store the results separately.

4. Mark the pattern in training pattern for which its distance from first pattern of testing pattern in *f5* is minimum. Note the class of pattern in training set and compare with the class of first testing pattern. If both do not match, add the CA counter *c_a_c* by 1. Repeat the exercise for all patterns in the test fold *f5*.

Compute the average classification accuracy percentage by equation

$$avg\_c\_a = \frac{(100 * (100 - c\_a\_c))}{(P / 5)} \qquad (3)$$

6. Now create another sequence of patterns *P* starting with *f2,f3,f4,f5* as training and *f1* as test pattern.

7. Repeat steps (3) through (5).

8. Compute average value of *c_a_c* for 5 sets of folds. Note that the original sequence obtained in step (1) is not disturbed; we only slide training and testing folds sequentially.

9. Add 1 to round and set a new seed value for this round.

10. Repeat steps (1)-(9) for a given number of rounds (we used 10 rounds). Compute overall average percentage values of *c_a_c*.

The purpose of taking 10 rounds is to perturb the sequence of patterns in data set to validate the data set thoroughly with different sequences for training and testing. The k-nn procedure is applied for eight different values of Minkowski norms: ½, 1, 3/2, 2, 5/2, 3, 4 and 10 respectively.

Data Sets

For simulation purpose, we used seven real data sets obtained from UCI Machine learning repository (http://www.ics.uci.edu/$\sim$mlearn/MLRepository.html) and one synthetic data set. These datasets are displayed in Table-I.

1. **IRIS Data:** This is the well-known Anderson's Iris data set. It contains a set of 150 vectors in four dimensions each representing one of three different species or classes of Iris flowers. The four features are sepal length, sepal width, petal length and petal width. The data set contains 50 instances of each of the three classes.

2. **Thyroid:** Thyroid data set has 215 data patterns with five features distributed in three classes namely Euthyroidism, hypothyroidism and hyperthyroidism.

3. **Pima:** Pima data set has 768 instances of patients each with eight features distributed in two classes representing whether the patient is diabetic or not.

4. **Glass:** Glass data set has 214 points with nine features distributed in six classes.

5. **Wine:** Wine data set consist of 178 samples in 13-dimension distributed in three classes. These data represent the results of chemical analysis of wines grown in a particular region of Italy but derived from three differ-

ent cultivators. The analysis determined the quantities of 13 constituents found in each of the three types of wine.

6. **Synthetic:** The Synthetic data set has 588 data points each with five features distributed in two classes each representing two-isolated hyper sphere.

7. **Wisconsin Breast Cancer (WBC):** It has 699 samples distributed in two classes. Sixteen of the instances have missing values and. Hence, we removed them. All reported results are computed on the remaining 683 data points. Each data point is represented by nine attributes.

8. **Vehicle:** This data set has 846 points distributed in four classes. Each data point is represented by 18 attributes. The attribute values are normalized.

CONCLUSION AND FUTURE RESEARCH SCOPE

Dimensionality reduction is one of the major issues in data mining and knowledge discovery. Feature selection is an important component of dimensionality reduction. The focus in this paper is based on feature selection of a dataset but the reduced feature subset should be able to predict the class of that dataset in the best possible way i.e. with maximum classification accuracy (CA). The paper presented a two-phase scheme to select most significant features from the original set and then ensured that the CA produced by this feature subset should not be reasonable poor. Commonly used Euclidean distance is the conventional basis of computing CA using k-nn classification method. Euclidean distance is a special case of Minkowski norms with value of its parameter as 2. However it has been reported in other literature that varying parameter values of Minkowski norms can improve performance of various applications. The paper used genetic algorithm (GA) to se-

lect feature subsets in a dataset. For providing population diversity, the simulations were made with 10 different initial seed values to ensure a wide range of chromosomes in population. After phase-1, 10 feature subsets are obtained for each of the eight datasets considered in this paper. It is a natural question how to decide which of these subsets produces better CA. For this purpose, k-nn classification method was adopted. In Phase-2, k-nn method is used with eight different values of Minkowski norms including conventionally used Euclidean distance. This exercise helped us to provide a wide range of CA values pertaining to different feature subsets. The CA was computed with all features of the original dataset as well. It is concluded that in general a feature set produces different CA for different Minkowski norms values. Thus if we have a set of features and we want to find the best among them, one way is to apply each of them to k-nn classification with different Minkowski norms and can see which feature set produces maximum CA. There are other approaches also available to verify the strengths of this feature set. These approaches include correlation coefficient of the dataset by considering only the reduced features and ignoring rest; k-means clustering to see the structure topology of the reduced dataset. It is also concluded that GA with a wide diversity of population will produce a wide range of features so that we can have a wider choice to select a better combinations of features. In this paper, we simulated the proposed two-phase scheme on seven real and one synthetic data set. In general, the number of features is reduced to less than half of the original number of features in that data set. The CA with reduced feature subset under different Minkowski norms in some cases is found even higher than that with all features. Results produced by extensive simulation studies on different data sets, justify the strength of the proposed scheme. Thus the proposed scheme is capable to reduce the dimension of a data set and still able to predict a high CA of the dataset using k-nn classifier.

Although the investigation in the paper produces satisfactory empirical results yet it leaves certain points of discussions to researchers. There is no specific logic behind selecting the value of m, the maximum value of reduced number of features to initialize population in GA. An approximate idea of this value can be obtained from some of the established results available in literature for instance (Lim, 2000; Muni, 2006). Further, a lot more can be extended to this paper. How to select a particular feature set, the stopping criteria of a GA, other measures of selection of the feature set, how many values of Minkowski norms must be simulated, like in this paper we took eight values. More importantly, it is possible that a scheme which performs nicely for few data sets may behave differently with other datasets. The large datasets like micro array, image, satellite and multimedia will be a real test of any scheme proposed hereafter.

REFERENCES

Aggarwal, C. C., & Hinneburg, D. A. Keim. (2001). On the surprising behaviour of distance metrics in high dimensional space. In *Proceedings of the Eight International Conference on Data base Theory* (pp.420-434). London, UK.

Pal, S. K., De, R. K., & Basak, J., (2000, March). Unsupervised feature selection using a neuro-fuzzy approach. *IEEE Transactions on Neural Networks, 11*(2), 366–375. doi:10.1109/72.839007

Beyer, K., Goldstein, J., Ramakrishnan, R., & Shaft, U. (1999). When is nearest neighbor meaningful? In *Proceedings of the Seventh International Conference on Database theory* (pp. 217-235). Jerusalem, Israel.

Chow, T. W. S., & Huang, D. (2005, January). Estimating optimal feature subsets using efficient estimation of high-dimensional mutual information. *IEEE Transactions on Neural Networks, 16*(1), 213–224. doi:10.1109/TNN.2004.841414

Dash, M., Liu, H., & Yao, J. (1997). Dimensionality reduction for unsupervised data. In *Proceedings of 19th IEEE International Conference on Tools with (AI, ICTAI '97)*.

Doherty, K. A. J., Adams, R. G., & Davey, N. (2004). Non–Euclidean norms and data normalization. In *Proceedings of the 12h Euro. Symposium on Artificial Neural Networks* (pp. 181-186). Brugges, Belgium.

Doherty, K. A. J., Adams, R. G., & Davey, N. (2007). Unsupervised learning with normalized data and non –Euclidean norms. *Applied Soft Computing, 7*, 203–210. doi:10.1016/j.asoc.2005.05.005

Goldberg, D. (1989). *Genetic algorithms in search, optimization and machine learning.* Reading, MA: Addison-Wesley.

Han, J., & Kamber, M. (2006). *Data mining: Concepts and techniques, (2nd ed.)* San Francisco, CA: Morgan Kaufmann.

Ho, T. K. (1998). The random subspace method for constructing decision forests. *IEEE Transactions on Pattern Analysis and Machine Intelligence, 20*(8), 832–844. doi:10.1109/34.709601

Kohavi, R., & John, G. H. (1997). Wrappers for feature subset selection. *Artificial Intelligence, 97*, 273–324. doi:10.1016/S0004-3702(97)00043-X

Lim, L. (2000). A comparison of prediction accuracy, complexity, and training time of thirty-three old and new classification algorithms. *Machine Learning, 40*, 203–229. doi:10.1023/A:1007608224229

Liu, H., & Yu, L. (2005, April). Toward integrating feature selection algorithms for classification and clustering. *IEEE Transactions on Knowledge and Data Engineering, 17*(4), 491–502. doi:10.1109/TKDE.2005.66

Mitra, P., Murthy, C. A., & Pal, S. K. (2002). Unsupervised feature selection using feature similarity. *IEEE Transactions on Pattern Analysis and Machine Intelligence, 24*(3), 301–312. doi:10.1109/34.990133

Muni, D. P., Pal, N. R., & Das, J. (2006, February). Genetic programming for simultaneous feature selection and classifier design. *IEEE Transactions on Systems, Man, and Cybernetics- PART B, 36*(1), 106-117.

Pal, N. R. (1999). Soft computing for feature analysis. *Fuzzy Sets and Systems, 103*(2), 201–221. doi:10.1016/S0165-0114(98)00222-X

Pal, N. R., Eluri, V. K., & Mandal, G. K. (2002, June). Fuzzy logic approaches to structure preserving dimensionality reduction. *IEEE Transactions on Fuzzy Systems, 10*(3), 277–286. doi:10.1109/TFUZZ.2002.1006431

Pena, J. M., Lozano, J. A., Larranaga, P., & Iwza, I. (2001). Dimensionality reduction in unsupervised learning of conditional Gaussian networks. *IEEE Transactions on Pattern Analysis and Machine Intelligence, 23*(6), 590-603. doi:10.1109/34.927460

Quinlan, J. R. (1993). C4.5: *Programs for machine learning.* San Mateo, CA: Morgan Kaufmann.

Raymer, M. L., Punch, W. F., Goodman, E. D., Kuhn, L. A., & Jain, A. K. (2000, July). Dimensionality reduction using genetic algorithms. *IEEE Transactions on Evolutionary Computation, 4*(2), 164–171. doi:10.1109/4235.850656

Romero, O., & Abelló, A. (2009). A survey of multidimensional modeling methodologies. *International Journal of Data Warehousing and Mining, 5*(2), 1–23.

Ruiz, R., Riquelme, J., & Aguilar-Ruiz, J. (2006). Incremental wrapper- based gene selection from microarray data for cancer classification. *Pattern Recognition, 39*, 2383–2392. doi:10.1016/j.patcog.2005.11.001

Sammon, J. W. Jr. (1969). A nonlinear mapping for data structure analysis. *IEEE Transactions on Computers, c-18*, 401–409. doi:10.1109/T-C.1969.222678

Saxena, A., & Kothari, M. (2007). Unsupervised approach for structure preserving dimensionality reduction. In *Proceedings of the 6th International Conference on Advances in Pattern Recognition (ICAPR07)* (pp. 315-318). Singapore: World Scientific Publishing Co. Pte. Ltd.

Setiono, R., & Liu, H. (1997, May). Neural-network feature selector. *IEEE Transactions on Neural Networks, 8*(3), 654–662. doi:10.1109/72.572104

Siedlecki, W., & Sklansky, J. (1989). A note on genetic algorithms for large-scale feature selection. *Pattern Recognition Letters, 10*(5), 335–347. doi:10.1016/0167-8655(89)90037-8

Sneath, P. H., & Sokal, R. R. (1973). *Numerical taxonomy – The principles and practice of numerical classification.* San Francisco: W.H. Freeman and Company.

Wei, H. L., & Billings, S. A. (2007). Feature subset selection and ranking for data dimensionality reduction. *IEEE Transactions on Pattern Analysis and Machine Intelligence, 29*(1), 162–166. doi:10.1109/TPAMI.2007.250607

Yan, S. C., Xu, D., Zhang, B. H. J., Yang, Q., & Lin, S. (2007). Graph embedding and extensions: A general framework for dimensionality reduction. *IEEE Transactions on Pattern Analysis and Machine Intelligence, 29*(1), 40–51. doi:10.1109/TPAMI.2007.250598

Yu, G. Z., Shao, S. H., Luo, B., & Zeng, X. H. (2009). A hybrid method for high-utility itemsets mining in large high-dimensional data. *International Journal of Data Warehousing and Mining, 5*(1), 57–73.

Zhang, P., Verma, B., & Kumar, K. (2005, May). Neural vs. statistical classifier in conjunction with genetic algorithm based feature selection. *Pattern Recognition Letters, 26*(7), 909–919. doi:10.1016/j.patrec.2004.09.053

APPENDIX

A.1 Simulations and Results Analysis

Proposed scheme was implemented on a Pentium machine. In Phase-I, Genetic Algorithm (GA) was applied with parameters shown in Table 2.

Tables 3 (a-h), present lists of reduced feature sets, obtained after applying GA to given data sets. In these tables, first column indicates seed values, 1 to 10, for each set of generations. We have constantly taken a seed value of 22744 and its ten multiples for 1 to 10 values. The second column represents subset of features; the numbering of feature starts from 0 and the details of features are mentioned in Table 1. Third column shows Sammon Error (SE) and the last column shows the count of reduced number of features. The mean and standard deviation values of these 10 subsets obtained due to 10 different seed values are shown in this table.

Each of this reduced feature subset in the respective data set was tested using k-nn classifier. In the k-nn classier, the measure of distance was taken as Minkowski norms with values of r, as ½,1, 3/2, 2, 5/2,3,4 and 10. The classification accuracy (CA) of the k-nn classifier obtained after applying each reduced feature subset to data set with these eight values are shown in Tables 4 (a-h). In each of these tables, first column represents seed value 1...10. The second column to ninth column indicate the values of CA with different values of norms r as ½, 1, 3/2, 2, 5/2, 3, 4 and 10 respectively.

Table 1. Description of data sets used

Name of data set	#classes	# Features	Size of Data set
Iris	3	4	150(50+50+50)
Thyroid	3	5	215(150+35+30)
Pima	2	8	768(500+268)
Glass	6	9	214(70+76+17+13+9+29)
Wine	3	13	178(59+72+47)
Synthetic	2	5	588(252+336)
WBC	2	9	683(444+239)
Vehicle	4	18	846(212 + 217 + 218 +199)

Simulations and Results Analysis: please See Appendix

Table 2. Parameters used in GA

Number of random number generators (seed values)	Number of generations with each seed value	Probability of Cross-over Pc (Single point crossover)	Probability of Mutation Pm (bit by bit mutation)	Population size= (Number of chromosomes)
10	100	0.7	0.003	50

A.2 Results and Discussions

Results obtained after Phase-I are shown in Tables 3 (a…h). In each table, we display reduced feature subsets selected using GA. There are 10 seed values and at the start of first generation each time, initial population is randomized using these seed values one by one for maintaining population diversity. This will help in forming different chromosomes in a population. With a wider variety of chromosomes, different feature subsets are obtained which increases chances of selecting better and better feature subsets. After applying GA for a fixed number of generations, the feature subset with minimum SE is selected. The point to remember is that we initialize population with a desired number of features, $m < F$. The reduced feature subsets and respective SE are shown in Table 3. In the next phase, k-nn is applied with the value of Minkowski norms as 0.5 (1/2). We get 10 values of CA, corresponding to each reduced feature subset. Similarly, we also compute CA when all features in a dataset are taken, to see how much CA is affected due to presence of all features. We repeat the exercise with all eight norms (1/2,…,10) and the results obtained are shown in Table 4 (a,..,h). It is observed from Tables 3 that SE, which is a measure of fitness (similarity of features in unsupervised manner) vary when different combinations of features are selected. GA is a useful tool to form different combinations stochastically and it produces fitness value for each combination. It is also observed from these tables that it is not necessary that more number of features will compute smaller SE; as an example, in thyroid data, four features 0,1,2,4 produce SE as 0.023476 and three features 0, 3, 4 produce SE as 0.015818. Similarly, as an example, in Iris data, CA is 90.40 with three features 0,1 and 2 whereas CA is 91.73 when we take only one feature (feature # 2). It confirms that few features in a dataset may exist which are not only redundant but derogatory also and confuse classification. These features can be eliminated and the exercise done in Phase-I ensures this only.

In Phase-II, the CA obtained using k-nn classifier with different Minkowski norms are shown in Tables 4 (a…h). We observe an interesting fact from these tables, that for the same feature subset, we get different CA for different values of Minkowski norms. It shows that a feature subset will have different degrees of CA when computed with different Minkowski norms. When we compare CA of a dataset with conventional Euclidean distance (L_2) used in k-nn, with that when taking other norms values, we observe that there is a wide difference among various values of CA. As observed from Table 4 (e), CA is higher in case of $L_{1/2}$, than that in L_2. We can see that in the same data set, the maximum CA is 95.02 for norm = ½. Similar observations are noted with other datasets and norms. It is therefore noted that (i) Few features in a data set may be redundant and harmful in deciding the class of a pattern, GA can be applied to find a reduced set of features by taking Sammon Error as fitness function and (ii) the k-nn is an established tool of supervised classification of a dataset and mostly it is applied with only one form of Minkowski norms (Euclidean distance); we have shown the effect of Minkowski norms for its different eight values on the CA of the dataset with reduced features. We find that CA varies for different values of Minkowski norms. Precisely, we can select a better feature subset, smaller in size than the original set, when we have a wide range of CA obtained from different Minkowski norms. The selected reduced feature subset can better predict the class of a pattern than the entire feature set.

Table 3. Reduced feature sets obtained using GA

Synthetic				Iris			
seed	seed	Features (F)	SE	seed	Features (F)	SE	SE
1	1	0 1 2	0.0072	1	0 1 2	0.0072	0.0072
2	2	0 1 2	0.0072	2	0 1 2	0.0072	0.0072
3	3	0 2	0.0207	3	0 2	0.0207	0.0207
4	4	1 2	0.0419	4	1 2	0.0419	0.0419
5	5	0 2	0.0207	5	0 2	0.0207	0.0207
6	6	0 2	0.0207	6	0 2	0.0207	0.0207
7	7	0 1 2	0.0072	7	0 1 2	0.0072	0.0072
8	8	0 2 3	0.0074	8	0 2 3	0.0074	0.0074
9	9	0 1 2	0.0072	9	0 1 2	0.0072	0.0072
10	10	2	0.0778	10	2	0.0778	0.0778
Mean	Mean		0.0218	Mean		0.0218	0.0218
Std-Dev	StdDev		0.0226	StdDev		0.0226	0.0226
(a)				**(b)**			

Glass				Wine			
seed	Features (F)	SE	#F	seed	Features (F)	SE	#F
1	1 2 4 6 7	0.0122	5	1	0 3 4 9 10 12	0.0006	6
2	1 2 3 6	0.031	4	2	0 3 12	0.0009	3
3	1 2 5 6 7	0.0208	5	3	0 4 6 8 12	0.0035	5
4	2 4 6	0.0422	3	4	1 3 4 11 12	0.0076	5
5	2 5 6	0.075	3	5	1 4 9 12	0.0005	4
6	1 2 3 4 6	0.0099	5	6	0 4 6 9 12	0.0025	5
7	1 2 5 6 7	0.0208	5	7	1 4 12	0.0035	3
8	1 2 5 6 8	0.0256	5	8	0 4 5 12	0.0036	4
9	1 2 5 6 8	0.0256	5	9	3 4 9 12	0.0006	4
10	0 2 4 6 7	0.0348	5	10	0 4 8 9 12	0.0002	5
Mean		0.0298	4.5	Mean		0.0001	4.4
StdDev		0.0187		StdDev		0.0003	
(c)				(d)			

Thyroid				PIMA			
seed	Features (F)	SE	#F	seed	Features (F)	SE	#F
1	0 3 4	0.0158	3	1	1 3 4	0.0189	3
2	0 4	0.0461	2	2	1 4	0.0325	2
3	0 2 3 4	0.0138	4	3	1 2 3 4	0.003	4
4	0 3 4	0.0158	3	4	1 3 4	0.0189	3
5	0 3 4	0.0158	3	5	1 3 4 7	0.0127	4

continued on following page

Table 3. Continued

6	0 1 2 4	0.0235		4	6	1 3 4	0.0189	3
7	0 3 4	0.0158		3	7	1 3 4 7	0.0127	4
8	0 3 4	0.0158		3	8	1 3 4	0.0189	3
9	0 3 4	0.0158		3	9	1 3 4 7	0.0127	4
10	0 4	0.0461		2	10	1 3 4	0.0189	3
Mean			**0.0224**	3	Mean		**0.0168**	3.3
StdDev			**0.0127**		Stdev		**0.0075**	
(f)					(e)			
Vehicle					(h)			

seed	Features (F)	SE	#F		seed	Features (F)	SE	#F
1	2 3 4 6 7 10 11 12 15 17	0.0007	10		1	0 2 3 5 7	0.0491	5
2	3 5 8 9 10 11 12 15 17	0.0014	9		2	0 2 5 7	0.0886	4
3	2 3 6 9 10 11 12 14 15	0.0008	9		3	0 1 3 5 7	0.0486	5
4	3 4 6 9 10 11 12 13 17	0.0009	9		4	1 2 4 5 7	0.0954	5
5	1 2 6 10 11 12 13 15 17	0.0059	9		5	0 1 5 7	0.0863	4
6	2 3 4 6 7 10 11 12 15 17	0.0007	10		6	0 1 5	0.1507	3
7	3 5 8 9 10 11 12 15 17	0.0014	9		7	0 1 5 7	0.0863	4
8	2 3 6 9 10 11 12 14 15	0.0008	9		8	0 2 5 8	0.1301	4
9	3 4 6 9 10 11 12 13 17	0.0009	9		9	0 1 6 7	0.0528	4
10	1 2 6 10 11 12 13 15 17	0.0059	9		10	2 6 7	0.2315	3
Mean		**0.0019**	9.2		Mean		**0.1019**	4.1
StdDev		**0.0021**			StdDev		**0.0565**	
(g)					(h)			

Table 4. k-nn classification accuracies (CA) for different data sets

	(a)Synthetic data								
seed	k- nn CA $r(1/2)$	k- nn CA $r(1)$	k- nn CA $r(3/2)$	k- nn CA $r(2)$	k- nn CA $r(5/2)$	k- nn CA $r(3)$	k- nn CA $r(4)$	k- nn CA $r(10)$	
1	100	42.93	**100**	100	100	100	100	100	
2	100	42.93	100	100	100	100	100	100	
3	100	42.93	100	100	100	100	100	100	
4	100	42.93	100	100	100	100	100	100	
5	100	42.93	100	100	100	100	100	100	
6	100	42.93	100	100	100	100	100	100	
7	100	42.93	100	100	100	100	100	100	
8	100	42.93	100	100	100	100	100	100	
9	100	42.93	100	100	100	100	100	100	
10	100	42.93	100	100	100	100	100	100	
Mean	100	42.93	100	100	·100	100	100	100	
StdDev	0	0	0	0	0	0	0	0	
All	100	42.93	100	100	100	100	100	100	
	(b)Iris Data								
seed	k- nn CA $r(1/2)$	k- nn CA $r(1)$	k- nn CA $r(3/2)$	k- nn CA $r(2)$	k- nn CA $r(5/2)$	k- nn CA $r(3)$	k- nn CA $r(4)$	k- nn CA $r(10)$	
1	90.40	33.33	92.93	92.80	92.93	89.07	92.80	92.93	
2	90.40	33.33	92.93	92.80	92.93	91.73	91.73	91.73	
3	91.00	33.33	91.73	91.53	91.80	91.73	91.73	91.73	
4	91.20	33.33	91.20	91.27	91.20	92.93	95.13	95.13	
5	91.00	33.33	91.73	91.53	91.80	86.07	91.53	91.60	
6	91.00	33.33	91.73	91.53	91.80	59.67	59.73	59.73	
7	90.40	33.33	92.93	92.80	92.93	86.07	91.53	91.60	
8	93.67	33.33	95.13	95.07	95.13	96.60	95.67	95.67	
9	90.40	33.33	92.93	92.80	92.93	89.07	92.80	92.93	
10	91.73	33.33	91.73	91.73	91.73	91.87	95.20	95.20	
1	91.12	33.33	92.50	92.39	92.52	87.48	89.79	89.83	
StdDev	0.99	0	1.14	1.14	1.12	10.27	10.68	10.69	
All	92.80	33.33	94.87	95.53	96.13	92.40	95.80	95.87	
	(c) Glass Data								
seed	k- nn CA $r(1/2)$	k- nn CA $r(1)$	k- nn CA $r(3/2)$	k- nn CA $r(2)$	k- nn CA $r(5/2)$	k- nn CA $r(3)$	k- nn CA $r(4)$	k- nn CA $r(10)$	
1	69.02	6.09	70.47	69.77	69.86	60.84	69.58	67.86	
2	68.70	13.30	70.00	68.70	69.30	64.05	68.88	68.60	
3	66.88	13.53	68.19	67.91	68.98	65.12	65.02	67.58	

continued on following page

Table 4. Continued

4	63.40	6.09	66.28	66.09	64.60	58.84	63.81	64.09	
5	65.77	5.81	65.49	66.05	65.07	67.49	71.63	63.58	
6	70.37	6.14	72.70	72.05	71.40	60.28	68.88	70.14	
7	66.88	13.53	68.19	67.91	68.98	65.12	67.77	67.58	
8	65.49	13.53	68.60	67.77	68.74	62.88	67.77	65.63	
9	65.49	13.53	68.60	67.77	68.74	62.88	64.98	65.63	
10	63.35	6.09	65.53	65.49	63.72	55.95	66.02	64.09	
Mean	66.53	9.77	68.40	67.95	67.94	62.34	67.43	66.48	
StdDev	2.32	3.92	2.27	1.93	2.54	3.41	2.43	2.198	
All	72.28	12.23	71.81	71.91	71.63	60.00	71.77	70.09	

(d) Wine Data

seed	k-nn CA $r(1/2)$	k-nn CA $r(1)$	k-nn CA $r(3/2)$	k-nn CA $r(2)$	k-nn CA $r(5/2)$	k-nn CA $r(3)$	k-nn CA $r(4)$	k-nn CA $r(10)$	
1	76.00	40.06	72.89	72.17	71.44	69.22	70.78	71.06	
2	82.78	40.06	73.11	72.28	71.44	69.22	70.89	71.17	
3	79.67	40.06	74.83	75.11	74.22	72.56	74.06	74.00	
4	83.44	40.06	74.11	73.44	72.67	70.11	71.28	71.50	
5	82.00	40.06	73.72	73.00	71.83	69.17	70.78	71.06	
6	80.56	40.06	74.44	74.22	72.94	69.61	71.28	71.50	
7	70.50	40.06	70.39	71.67	70.72	69.17	70.33	70.39	
8	72.94	40.06	71.56	71.72	70.94	69.28	70.33	70.39	
9	81.72	40.06	73.72	73.44	72.61	70.11	71.28	71.50	
10	80.78	40.06	72.39	71.22	70.33	68.22	69.33	69.33	
Mean	79.04	40.06	73.12	72.83	71.92	69.67	71.03	71.19	
StdDev	4.40	0	1.36	1.24	1.19	1.145	1.21	1.19	
All	87.72	40.06	74.83	74.22	72.94	69.61	71.28	71.50	

(e)Thyroid Data

seed	k-nn CA $r(1/2)$	k-nn CA $r(1)$	k-nn CA $r(3/2)$	k-nn CA $r(2)$	k-nn CA $r(5/2)$	k-nn CA $r(3)$	k-nn CA $r(4)$	k-nn CA $r(10)$	
1	95.02	16.28	83.72	83.72	83.72	83.72	83.72	83.72	
2	84.88	16.28	83.72	83.72	83.72	83.72	83.72	83.72	
3	84.88	16.28	83.72	83.72	83.72	83.72	83.72	83.72	
4	84.88	16.28	83.72	83.72	83.72	83.72	83.72	83.72	
5	84.88	16.28	83.72	83.72	83.72	83.72	83.72	83.72	
6	82.28	16.28	83.72	83.72	83.72	83.72	83.72	83.72	
7	84.88	16.28	83.72	83.72	83.72	83.72	83.72	83.72	
8	84.88	16.28	83.72	83.72	83.72	83.72	83.72	83.72	
9	84.88	16.28	83.72	83.72	83.72	83.72	83.72	83.72	

continued on following page

Table 4. Continued

10	84.98	16.28	83.72	83.72	83.72	83.72	83.72	83.72
Mean	85.65	16.28	**83.72**	83.72	83.72	83.72	83.72	83.72
StdDev	3.39	16.28	0	0	**0**	0	0	0
All	95.67	16.28	**75.35**	94.56	93.81	86.60	93.72	93.58

(f) Pima Data

seed	k- nn CA r(1/2)	k- nn CA r(1)	k- nn CA r(3/2)	k- nn CA r(2)	k- nn CA r(5/2)	k- nn CA r(3)	k- nn CA r(4)	k- nn CA r(10)
1	66.09	59.69	66.90	66.88	66.44	65.30	66.83	66.96
2	64.12	54.23	64.09	63.65	64.01	58.55	63.64	63.62
3	66.18	65.09	66.18	66.3	66.00	63.60	65.58	65.34
4	66.09	59.69	66.90	66.88	66.44	65.30	66.83	66.96
5	66.92	64.60	68.84	68.66	68.71	63.95	69.40	69.25
6	66.09	59.69	66.90	66.88	66.44	65.30	66.83	66.96
7	66.92	64.60	68.84	68.66	68.71	63.95	69.40	69.25
8	66.09	59.69	66.90	66.88	66.44	65.30	66.83	66.96
9	66.92	64.60	68.84	68.66	68.71	63.95	69.40	69.25
10	66.09	59.69	66.90	66.88	66.44	65.30	66.83	66.96
Mean	66.15	61.16	67.13	67.04	66.84	64.05	67.16	67.15
Stdev	0.81	3.49	1.46	1.49	1.49	2.06	1.84	1.80
All	68.57	65.09	68.17	67.97	67.53	62.38	67.43	68.00

(g) Vehicle Data

seed	k- nn CA r(1/2)	k- nn CA r(1)	k- nn CA r(3/2)	k- nn CA r(2)	k- nn CA r(5/2)	k- nn CA r(3)	k- nn CA r(4)	k- nn CA r(10)
1	64.40	25.74	61.25	60.84	59.25	49.31	58.62	57.94
2	61.43	25.60	58.12	57.61	57.44	46.31	56.31	55.86
3	61.23	25.60	62.82	62.12	61.64	48.90	60.82	59.74
4	62.34	25.57	60.75	60.85	59.34	47.68	58.75	57.34
5	60.65	25.49	60.13	59.89	58.71	46.63	58.99	58.14
6	64.40	25.74	61.25	60.84	59.25	49.31	58.62	57.94
7	61.43	25.60	58.12	57.61	57.44	46.31	56.31	55.86
8	61.23	25.60	62.82	62.12	61.64	48.90	60.82	59.74
9	62.34	25.57	60.75	60.85	59.34	47.68	58.75	57.34
10	60.65	25.49	60.13	59.89	58.71	46.63	58.99	58.14
Mean	62.01	25.60	60.61	60.26	59.28	47.77	58.70	57.80
Stdev	1.38	0.08	1.62	1.58	1.44	1.26	1.51	1.32
All	67.79	25.60	64.13	64.17	62.28	48.04	60.86	59.81

continued on following page

Table 4. Continued

(h) WBC Data								
seed	k- nn CA r(1/2)	k- nn CA r(1)	k- nn CA r(3/2)	k- nn CA r(2)	k- nn CA r(5/2)	k- nn CA r(3)	k- nn CA r(4)	k- nn CA r(10)
1	96.53	64.99	96.18	95.96	95.93	94.95	95.88	95.88
2	96.42	64.99	96.12	96.09	95.94	95.17	96.00	96.00
3	96.67	64.99	96.16	96.13	96.07	95.05	96.00	96.00
4	95.65	64.99	95.82	96.12	95.91	94.36	95.99	95.99
5	96.28	64.99	96.19	96.01	96.13	95.37	96.01	96.01
6	95.71	64.99	96.01	95.91	96.01	95.80	95.91	95.91
7	96.28	64.99	96.19	96.01	96.13	95.37	96.01	96.01
8	94.80	64.99	94.42	94.7	94.34	94.92	94.70	94.70
9	94.69	64.99	94.89	94.92	94.89	93.97	94.93	94.93
10	93.77	64.99	93.75	93.72	93.74	93.15	93.72	93.72
Mean	95.68	64.99	95.57	95.56	95.51	94.81	95.52	95.52
Stdev	0.97	0.00	0.89	0.83	0.87	0.78	0.80	0.80
All	96.12	64.99	95.66	95.78	95.33	94.98	95.12	95.12

This work was previously published in International Journal of Data Warehousing and Mining, Volume 6, Issue 2, edited by David Taniar, pp. 23-40, copyright 2010 by IGI Publishing (an imprint of IGI Global).

Chapter 7
Graph–Based Modelling of Concurrent Sequential Patterns

Jing Lu
Southampton Solent University, UK

Weiru Chen
Shenyang Institute of Chemical Technology, China

Malcolm Keech
University of Bedfordshire, UK

ABSTRACT

Structural relation patterns have been introduced recently to extend the search for complex patterns often hidden behind large sequences of data. This has motivated a novel approach to sequential patterns post-processing and a corresponding data mining method was proposed for Concurrent Sequential Patterns (ConSP). This article refines the approach in the context of ConSP modelling, where a companion graph-based model is devised as an extension of previous work. Two new modelling methods are presented here together with a construction algorithm, to complete the transformation of concurrent sequential patterns to a ConSP-Graph representation. Customer orders data is used to demonstrate the effectiveness of ConSP mining while synthetic sample data highlights the strength of the modelling technique, illuminating the theories developed.

1. INTRODUCTION

The goal in patterns mining is to find useful patterns from very large databases. Frequent patterns mining is one of the most important knowledge discovery techniques, which includes frequent itemset mining (Agrawal et al., 1993), sequential patterns mining (Agrawal & Srikant, 1995; Pei et al., 2001; Zaki, 2001), graph mining (Cook & Holder, 2000; Huan et al., 2004) and tree mining (Asai et al., 2002; Zaki, 2005).

While frequent itemset mining aims to find frequent *itemsets* in a transaction database, sequential patterns mining aims to find *sub-sequences* that appear frequently (i.e. more than a given support threshold) in a sequence database. The problem

DOI: 10.4018/978-1-61350-474-1.ch007

Copyright © 2012, IGI Global. Copying or distributing in print or electronic forms without written permission of IGI Global is prohibited.

of discovering sequential patterns was first introduced by Agrawal and Srikant (1995) and their approach introduced some of the most important and basic definitions in sequential patterns mining. Since then, it has been studied extensively in the literature, resulting in algorithms such as GSP (*G*eneralized *S*equential *P*attern; Srikant & Agrawal, 1996), *FreeSpan* (*Fre*quent pattern-projected *S*equential *pa*tterns mi*ni*ng; Han et al., 2000), Prefix*Span* (*P*refix-projected *S*equential *pa*tterns mi*ni*ng; Pei et al., 2001) and SPADE (*S*equential *PA*ttern *D*iscovery using *E*quivalence classes; Zaki, 2001).

In traditional sequential patterns mining, as the support threshold decreases the number of sequential patterns can increase rapidly, and it is difficult to explore so many patterns or get an overall view of them. As a result, there are some trends to mine a more condensed or constrained set of sequential patterns such as *closed sequential patterns* (Yan et al., 2003), *compressed sequential patterns* (Chang et al., 2006) and *contiguous sequential patterns* (Chen & Cook, 2007).

With the successful implementation of efficient and scalable algorithms for mining sequential patterns and their variations, it is natural to extend the scope of previous study to structured data mining – the process of finding and extracting useful information from semi-structured databases – such as graph mining and tree mining.

Graph mining here means either graph-transaction mining or single-graph mining (Ivancsy & Vajk, 2005). In graph-transaction mining the database to be mined is a set of graphs and the purpose of this mining task is to search for sub-graphs which occur at least in a given number of graphs (Inokuchi et al., 2003; Huan et al., 2004). On the other hand, in the single-graph format, the input data of the mining process is a single large graph and reoccurring sub-graphs are searched in the single graph (Cook & Holder, 2000; Kuramochi & Karypis, 2004).

Tree mining, being another instance of frequent patterns mining, extracts frequent sub-trees from a database of labelled trees (Zaki, 2005). Mining frequent trees is useful in applications like bioinformatics, computer vision, text retrieval, web analysis and so on. For example, Asai et al. (2002) modelled semi-structured data by labelled ordered trees and studied the problem of discovering all frequent tree-like patterns in a given collection of datasets.

In the context of frequent patterns mining, the term *pattern* refers to itemset, sequence, graph and tree patterns. There are some questions in this area, for example: is it possible to summarise and represent these patterns? Can any other patterns be discovered beyond these to extend the scope of frequent patterns mining?

For the first question, Zaki et al. (2005) introduced the Data Mining Template Library and provided a description of the graphical representation of these frequent patterns. In particular, with respect to sequential patterns summary and analysis, Lu, Wang et al. (2004) proposed a Sequential Patterns Graph (SPG) as the minimal representation of a collection of sequential patterns. These research areas are discussed further in the Related Work section below.

For the second question, there is some research on mining more general structured patterns such as *partial orders*, by summarising sequential data (Garriga, 2005), and *structural relation patterns* from Post Sequential Patterns Mining (Lu & Adjei et al., 2004).

Garriga (2005) addressed the task of summarising sequences by means of local ordering relationships on items. Their work goes beyond the idea of closed sequential patterns in that they generalised sequential patterns into closed partial orders and modelled the patterns using the concept of a lattice. They showed that post-processing of the closed sequences leads to the generalisation of closed partial orders from sequential patterns.

Post Sequential Patterns Mining (PSPM) is a novel data mining approach that underpins the post-processing of sequential patterns (Lu et al., 2008). The aim of PSPM is to mine structural relation patterns – which include concurrent patterns, exclusive patterns and iterative patterns – motivated by the SPG model of representing the relations among sequential patterns. PSPM can be applied to all of the domains that involve sequential patterns mining and can discover other structured patterns beyond traditional sequences.

PSPM does not mine structures directly from the data, as it takes advantage of Prefix*Span* (Pei et al., 2001) to first generate sequential patterns and then these patterns are modelled using SPG. The graph-based *modelling* in PSPM is different from the graph *mining* referred to above: SPG is used to give a summary of all the sequential patterns and the method can be extended to the representation of structural relation patterns, as presented in this paper.

Related work is introduced next to provide relevant background on patterns modelling and graphical representation. Following the definition and properties of concurrency in patterns mining, including concurrent sequential and branch patterns, the Concurrent Sequential Patterns Graph (ConSP-Graph) model is proposed to represent concurrent sequential patterns graphically. The focus is on the outcome of ConSP mining and two associated modelling methods are presented in the following section, with worked examples to illustrate the approaches. The penultimate section gives an experimental evaluation using a real and a synthetic dataset, showing the results of ConSP mining and modelling. The paper draws to a close by making brief conclusions and indicating a potential application in workflow.

2. RELATED WORK

The aim of this research is the graphical representation of one of the new structural relation patterns, namely concurrent sequential patterns, to inform the analysis of mining results. This section will first describe two types of related work on patterns modelling to provide further motivation, where the latter is from the authors' previous research on sequential patterns modelling.

2.1 Graphical Representation of Frequent Patterns

The specific tasks encompassed by frequent patterns mining include the mining of increasingly informative patterns in complex structured and unstructured relational data, such as: itemset (transactional, unordered), sequential pattern (temporal or positional), tree pattern (semi-structured, e.g. XML) and graph pattern (complex relational). The various frequent patterns mining tasks have different input datasets and generate different forms of results. However, there are inherent relationships among these results such that every pattern can be modelled as a graph, as shown in Figure 1 (Zaki et al., 2005).

Each node is represented by a circle in the figure and node labels are shown inside the circle, with connecting lines (edges) as appropriate. An *itemset* is a simple basket of items where no two nodes have the same label. A *sequential pattern* is modelled as an ordered list of itemsets and thus the different nodes in a sequence can have the same label. Consider the graphical representation of the sequential pattern $<a\,(a,b)\,c>$ in the figure; two nodes are labelled as a but they are different because they correspond to two different items a in the sequential pattern $<a\,(a,b)\,c>$. The directed edges indicate the order in a sequence while the undirected edge is used to connect unordered items within the same itemset, e.g. (a,b).

Figure 1. Graphical representation of different types of patterns

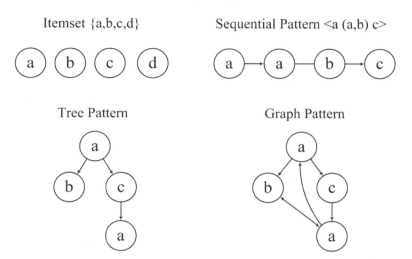

Rooted, ordered and labelled trees are considered more typically in tree mining. A *tree pattern* must satisfy all tree properties, namely i) the root has no parent, ii) edges are directed, iii) a node has only one parent, iv) the tree is connected, and v) the tree has no cycles. Finally, it is possible to model any *graph pattern* more generally as shown in the figure; for example connected graphs, induced sub-graphs or directed acyclic graphs.

2.2 Sequential Patterns Graph

In the field of data mining, using graphs is an expressive and versatile modelling technique that provides ways to reason about information implicit in the data. The previous sub-section shows that, as a general data structure, a graph can be used to model complex relations among data and this can be applied specifically to sequential patterns modelling.

In sequential patterns mining, given a customer sequence database and user-specified minimum support (*minsup*), a set of sequential patterns (i.e. frequently occurring sub-sequences within the database) can be discovered. All sequential patterns under the specified minimum support can be generated from the Maximal Sequence

Set (MSS). Thus, a directed acyclic graph called Sequential Patterns Graph (SPG) was defined to represent the maximal sequence set (Lu, Wang et al., 2004). Nodes (i.e. items or itemsets) of SPG corresponded to elements in a sequential pattern and directed edges were used to denote the sequence relation between two elements. Figure 2 shows two equivalent SPGs that model the same set of maximal sequences, $MSS=\{xab, xad, yad\}$.

SPG can be viewed as the visual embodiment of the relationship among sequential patterns. Two special types of nodes called a start node (represented by double circles) and a final node (represented by a bold circle) were defined to indicate the beginning and end of maximal sequences. Any path from a start node to a final node corresponds to one maximal sequence. SPG is also the minimal representation of a collection of discrete sequential patterns; for example Figure 2 represents all the sequential patterns *xa*, *xb*, *xd*, *ab*, *ad*, *ya*, *yd*, *xab*, *xad*, *yad*.

SPG is used to give a summary of all the sequential patterns as well as describing the inherent relationship among sequences – the method can be extended for the representation of structural relation patterns (e.g. concurrent sequential patterns) as presented in this paper.

Figure 2. Two equivalent SPGs

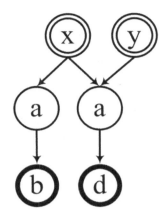 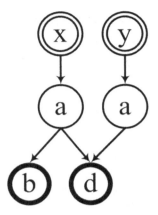

3. CONCURRENCY AND PATTERNS REPRESENTATION

Structural relation patterns have been defined in Lu et al. (2008), where a corresponding data mining method and algorithms have been presented. It was also indicated in the previous work that concurrent patterns could be refined further to provide more meaningful information. This section will focus on concurrent sequential patterns and their graphical representation.

3.1 Concurrent Patterns

The fundamental concepts related to sequential patterns are covered extensively in the literature (Agrawal & Srikant, 1995; Pei et al., 2001; Zaki, 2001). For the following definitions, it is assumed that $\{sp_1, sp_2, \ldots, sp_m\}$ is the set of m sequential patterns mined under minimum support *minsup* and they are *not* contained in each other.

Definition 1. The *concurrence* of sequential patterns $sp_1, sp_2, \ldots, sp_k$ $(1 \leq k \leq m)$ is defined as the fraction of data sequences that contains *all* of the sequential patterns. This is denoted by

$$concurrence(sp_1, sp_2, \ldots, sp_k) = |\{C : \forall i\ (i=1,2,\ldots,k)\ sp_i \angle C, C \in SDB\}| / |SDB|$$

where *SDB* is a *sequence database*, $sp_i \angle C$ represents sequential pattern sp_i *contained* in data sequence *C* and the symbol $|\ldots|$ denotes the number of data sequences.

Definition 2. Let *mincon* be the user-specified minimum concurrence. If

$$concurrence(sp_1, sp_2, \ldots, sp_k) \geq mincon$$

is satisfied, then $sp_1, sp_2, \ldots, sp_k$ are called *Concurrent Sequential Patterns*. This is represented by $ConSP_k = [sp_1 + sp_2 + \ldots + sp_k]$, where k is the number of sequential patterns which occur together and the notation '+' represents the concurrent relationship.

Example 1. Consider a *sequence database* $SDB = \{<a\ (a,b,c)\ (a,c)\ d\ (c,f)>, <(a,d)\ c\ (b,c)\ (a,c)>, <(e,f)\ (a,b)\ (d,f)\ c\ b>, <e\ g\ (a,f)\ c\ b\ c>\}$ and assume a *mincon* of 50%. Since both data sequences $<(e,f)\ (a,b)\ (d,f)\ c\ b>$ and $<e\ g\ (a,f)\ c\ b\ c>$ support sequential patterns *ebc*, *eacb*, *efcb* and *fbc* under a *minsup* of 50%, then:

$$concurrence(ebc, eacb, efcb, fbc) = 2/4 = 50\%.$$

Therefore, they constitute a concurrent sequential pattern given by $ConSP_4 = [ebc + eacb + efcb + fbc]$.

Using the above definitions, the problem of concurrent sequential patterns mining can be stated as follows: given a sequence database

SDB and sequential patterns mining results (i.e. sequential patterns which satisfy a minimum support threshold), *concurrent sequential patterns mining* aims to discover the set of all concurrent sequential patterns within a given user-specified minimum concurrence.

Given sequential patterns x, y and z, two features of concurrent sequential patterns and the '+' operator are stated in the following rules:

- **Commutative rule:** $[x+y]=[y+x]$
- **Associative rule:** $[x+y+z]=[[x+y]+z]=[x+[y+z]]$.

Taking a further look at the concurrent sequential pattern $ConSP_4$ from Example 1, it is clear that some sequential patterns have a common prefix and/or common postfix, e.g. *eacb* and *efcb* share *e* and *cb*. Factoring out the common prefix and/or postfix can lead to another type of pattern called a *Concurrent Branch Pattern* or *CBP*. The theorem below builds on concurrent sequential patterns and introduces CBP more formally.

Theorem 1. If n sequential patterns from a set *SP* make up a concurrent sequential pattern

$$ConSP_n=[x\alpha_1y+x\alpha_2y+\ldots+x\alpha_ny]$$

where $(x\alpha_iy\in SP, 1\leq i\leq n; \alpha_i\in SP; x,y\in SP$ or $x,y=\varnothing)$, then the following new pattern can be deduced:

$$x[\alpha_1+\alpha_2+\ldots+\alpha_n]y.$$

The above pattern is called a *Concurrent Branch Pattern* (CBP) and the notation $[\alpha_1+\alpha_2+\ldots+\alpha_n]$ represents n branches of a CBP.

Proof: For simplicity, let us first consider $n=2$. i.e. $ConSP_2=[x\alpha y+x\beta y]$ (where $x,y,\alpha,\beta\in$SP). Sequential patterns $x\alpha y$ and $x\beta y$ make up one concurrent sequential pattern that satisfies the concurrence condition (i.e. *concurrence*($x\alpha y,x\beta y$)$\geq$*mincon*). Therefore, for any data sequence C which supports patterns $x\alpha y$ and $x\beta y$, there is at least one α and one β occurring in C. There is at least one

x before α and one y after α; one x before β and one y after β. Thus it can be concluded that there is at least one x before α and β and at least one y after α and β. Hence, the sequence C supports $x[\alpha+\beta]y$ and the theorem is proven for $n=2$. That is, any sequence which supports the concurrent sequential pattern $[x\alpha y+x\beta y]$ must support the concurrent branch pattern $x[\alpha+\beta]y$.

Secondly, let us consider the case when $n=3$, i.e. $ConSP_3=[x\alpha y+x\beta y+x\gamma y]$ (where $x,y,\alpha,\beta,\gamma\in$SP). Sequential patterns $x\alpha y$, $x\beta y$ and $x\gamma y$ make up one concurrent sequential pattern that satisfies the concurrence condition (i.e. *concurrence*($x\alpha y,x\beta y,x\gamma y$)$\geq$*mincon*). According to the associative law of concurrent sequential patterns when $n=2$, $x[\alpha+\beta]y$ and $x\gamma y$ are concurrent. Therefore, from the above case for $n=2$, $x[\alpha+\beta+\gamma]y$ is also a concurrent branch pattern.

The rest may be deduced by analogy and induction. Hence, the theorem is proven.

As a corollary to the above, we state another rule:

Distributive rule: $[x\alpha+x\beta]=x[\alpha+\beta]$; $[\alpha y+\beta y]=[\alpha+\beta]y$; $[x\alpha y+x\beta y]=x[\alpha+\beta]y$.

Example 2. For $ConSP_4=[ebc+eacb+efcb+fbc]$ in Example 1, one can take out the common prefix e and postfix cb from sequential patterns *eacb* and *efcb* to yield a concurrent branch pattern $e[a+f]cb$; similarly, $[e+f]bc$ can be generated by taking out the common postfix bc from *ebc* and *fbc*.

Note that in a CBP such as $e[a+f]cb$, the order of branches a and f is indefinite. Therefore $e[a+f]cb$ can appear in a sequence database in the form of *eafcb* or *efacb* for example. Also, note that neither *eafcb* or *efacb* can be discovered from traditional sequential patterns mining with a *minsup* of 50%.

3.2 ConSP-Graph

The use of graphical models in data mining has led to the development of a sequential patterns model that explores the inherent relationship among sequential patterns. The idea is adapted here for modelling concurrent sequential patterns. The definition of SPG (Lu & Wang et al., 2004) is extended to define Concurrent Sequential Patterns Graph and followed by an example for illustration.

Definition 3. *Concurrent Sequential Patterns Graph* (ConSP-Graph) is a graphical representation of concurrent sequential patterns denoted by a 7-tuple expressed as: *ConSP-Graph*=(V, E, S, F, S', F', δ), where

1. V is a nonempty set of nodes. Each item (or itemset) in ConSP corresponds to one node in ConSP-Graph and each node in ConSP-Graph at least corresponds to one item in ConSP.

2. E is a set of directed edges. The sequential relation of any two adjacent items in a sequence of ConSP corresponds to the directed edge of two nodes in ConSP-Graph. Any one directed edge at least corresponds to the sequential relation of two adjacent items in a sequence of ConSP.

3. S is a set of start nodes, $S \subseteq V$, and $S \neq \varnothing$. There are no start nodes that have the same value in ConSP-Graph.

4. F is a set of final nodes, $F \subseteq V$, and $F \neq \varnothing$. There are no final nodes that have the same value in ConSP-Graph.

5. S' is a set of synchronizer nodes, $S' \subseteq V$, with two or more incoming sequential relations applied to concurrent paths to allow no more than one outgoing sequential relation.

6. F' is a set of fork nodes, $F' \subseteq V$, allowing independent execution between concurrent paths, modelled by connecting two or more outgoing sequential relations.

7. δ is a function from a set of directed edges to a set of pairs of nodes. δ can also be defined as a map function of $V \rightarrow V$, which indicates the relations between any two nodes.

For any node in ConSP-Graph, the subsequent paths of it cannot be the same, and the ancestor paths of it cannot be the same either. For each pair of different nodes in ConSP-Graph, if they have the same value, there must be different ancestor paths and subsequent paths for them. Graphical elements used in relation to ConSP-Graph are shown in Figure 3, where '+' represents the concurrent relationship across connected paths.

Example 3. The concurrent sequential pattern $ConSP_4$=[ebc+$eacb$+$efcb$+fbc] from Example 1 can be cast into its equivalent graphical representation in Figure 4.

Nodes e and f inside the double circles are the start nodes, while nodes b and c inside bold circles are the final nodes. Node e is also a *fork node* connecting three outgoing sequential relations acb, fcb and bc. Node c is a *synchronizer node* with two incoming sequential relations ea and ef; similarly for node b. The refinement of concurrent sequential patterns and construction of ConSP-Graph are discussed in the next section.

4. CONCURRENT SEQUENTIAL PATTERNS MODELLING

The natural way to approach transforming concurrent sequential patterns to a graphical representation, ConSP-Graph, is by identifying the inherent relationships through common prefix/postfix recognition. This section discusses two methods to model concurrent sequential patterns: one is refining and combining graphs successively, while the other is based on constructing graphs step-by-step.

Figure 3. ConSP-Graph elements

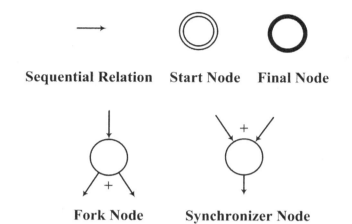

Sequential Relation　**Start Node**　**Final Node**

Fork Node　**Synchronizer Node**

4.1 From Concurrent Sequential Patterns to ConSP-Graph

Given a concurrent sequential pattern $ConSP_n=\{\beta_i|\beta_i\in SP,\ 1\leq i\leq n,\ n$ is the number of sequential patterns in $ConSP_n\}$, it tells you that all these sequential patterns will occur together within a *concurrence* threshold. However, this is not the minimal representation of these sequential patterns because any further relationships among them have not been explored. For example, some of them may share the same prefix and/or postfix and, in that case, we would want to use a model to predict what will happen concurrently after the prefix item(s) or what will cause the possibility of a postfix item(s).

There are five steps in the following method of modelling a concurrent sequential pattern $ConSP_n$.

1. **Initialisation:** Represent each sequential pattern in $ConSP_n$ by a directed graph $G(\beta_i)$ and specify the initial overall model as the union of these graphs – i.e. $G=G(\beta_1)\cup G(\beta_2)$ $\cup\ ...\cup G(\beta_n)$ – initialise a transitional graph model $G'=\varnothing$.

2. **Refinement:** For all pairs of $G(\beta_i)$ and $G(\beta_j)$ in G, where $i\neq j$, refine the overall model by finding each occurrence of a common

prefix and/or postfix – if a pair of graphs share a common prefix/postfix, then go to Step 3 – otherwise continue through each remaining pair of graphs in G until this cycle is complete, then go to Step 4.

3. **Combination:** Combine two graphs $G(\beta_i)$ and $G(\beta_j)$ which share a common prefix and/ or postfix and generate a new graph – accumulate this new graph in the transitional model G' – go back to Step 2.

4. **Deletion:** Delete all graphs from G which have been used successfully for combining as new graphs and include all the combined graphs from G' to form a new overall model G.

5. **Iteration:** Repeat Steps 2 to 4 until there are no further successful combinations of pairs of graphs – the final result G is the Concurrent Sequential Patterns Graph, *ConSP-Graph.*

Example 4. For the concurrent sequential pattern $ConSP_4=[ebc+eacb+efcb+fbc]$ from Example 1, Figure 5 is a graphical illustration of the procedure of modelling ConSP and highlights the above method.

Further explanation of steps (i) to (v) in Figure 5 is covered below:

Figure 4. ConSP-Graph example

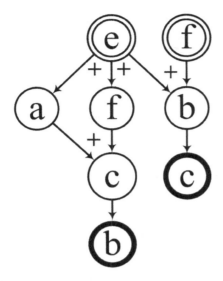

1. **Initialisation:** Represent each sequential pattern in *ConSP₄* by directed graphs G(1), G(2), G(3) and G(4), the overall initial model G being the union of these graphs, i.e. as shown in Figure 5(i).

2. **Refinement:** For all pairs of directed graphs in G, refine the overall model by finding each occurrence of a common prefix and/or postfix, e.g. G(1) and G(2) share a common prefix *e*; G(1) and G(3) share a common prefix *e* too; G(1) and G(4) share a common postfix *bc*; G(2) and G(3) share a common prefix *e* and postfix *cb*;

3. **Combination:** Combine G(1) and G(2) which share prefix *e* into G(12), and similarly generate new graphs G(13), G(14) and G(23), as shown in Figure 5(ii) – accumulate these new graphs in the transitional model *G'*.

4. **Deletion:** Delete all the graphs from G in Figure 5(i), as they have been used already in

Figure 5. Modelling concurrent sequential pattern [ebc+eacb+ efcb+fbc]

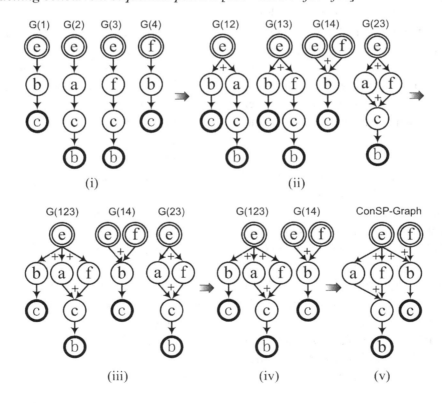

Step 3, and include all the combined graphs from G' to form the new overall model G in Figure 5(ii).

5. **Iteration:** Repeat Steps 2 to 4. G(12) and G(13) share a common prefix *e*, so that G(123) can be generated, and G(12) and G(13) can be deleted – see Figure 5(iii). Subsequently, G(23) can be deleted because it is contained by G(123), which leads to Figure 5(iv).

The final combination is then processed for this example and the result is shown in Figure 5(v) – it represents a graphical form of the concurrent sequential pattern $ConSP_4=[ebc+eacb+efcb+fbc]$.

4.2 An Alternative Approach Using SPG

The definition of ConSP-Graph is an extension of that for Sequential Patterns Graph and therefore the method to construct SPG could also be used for ConSP modelling, as described below.

1. **Initialisation:** Determine the longest length *m* of sequential patterns in $ConSP_n$ – represent one of the longest sequential patterns by a directed graph G – sort the remaining patterns in order of length.

2. **Construction:** For the next available sequential pattern *sp* in $ConSP_n$, find any common prefix and/or postfix with G – if they share a common prefix/postfix, then use the Algorithm below to construct the next transitional graph model G – otherwise represent *sp* by a separate graph G' and set G=G∪G'.

3. **Iteration:** For the remaining sequential patterns in $ConSP_n$, which have the same or shorter length – i.e. *m*, *m*-1, *m*-2, etc. – repeat Step 2 incrementally until there are no sequential patterns left in $ConSP_n$. The final result G is the ConSP-Graph.

The algorithm below shows the pseudo-code for the ConSP-Graph *construction* phase above by adapting the approach for SPG modelling (Lu, 2006).

ConSP-Graph Construction Algorithm

```
Input: A sequential pattern sp from
concurrent sequential pattern ConSP_n
and a transitional graph model G
Output: New directed graph G after
incremental construction
Procedure:
preS=common prefix of sp and G
postS=common postfix of sp and G
elemS=sp-preS-postS
Represent elemS by the directed graph
G'If preS is not empty
{The last node of preS in G is a fork
node;
  Add a directed edge from it to the
first node of G';
  Mark the connected paths with a
'+'}
If postS is not empty
{The first node of postS in G is a
synchronizer node;
  Add a directed edge to it from the
last node of G';
  Mark the connected paths with a
'+'}
```

This new directed graph includes a new pattern *sp* and is called G.

Example 5. Using the extension of the SPG method to model the concurrent sequential pattern $ConSP_4=[ebc+eacb+efcb+fbc]$.

1. **Initialisation:** Determine the longest sequential patterns in $ConSP_4$, i.e. *efcb* and *eacb*. Represent one of them by a directed graph G – e.g. *efcb* – see Figure 6(i).

2. **Construction:** For the next available sequential pattern, *eacb* in $ConSP_4$, find any

common prefix *preS* with G – this is *e*; and find any common postfix *postS* – this is *cb*. Taking out *preS* and *postS* from *eacb*, the remaining part *elemS=a* can be represented by a directed graph G '. Add a directed edge from the last node of *preS* in G (i.e. *e*) to the first node of G' (i.e. *a*) – *e* is a fork node – mark the connected paths with '+'. Also add a directed edge from the last node of G' (i.e. *a*) to the first node of *postS* (i.e. *c*) – *c* is a synchronizer node – mark the connected paths with '+'. The result of this step is the graph shown in Figure 6(ii), where the dotted line represents the new edges in the transitional model.

3.   **Iteration:** For the remaining sequential patterns in turn, i.e. *ebc* and *fbc*, construct new graphs in a similar manner. Figure 6(iii) shows the graph after adding sequential pattern *ebc* and Figure 6(iv) is the final result of this method, which is the same as the graph Figure 5(v).

The above example shows that extending the method of SPG modelling to ConSP-Graph construction is more straightforward in principle. It corresponds to incremental progression of the transitional graph model as opposed to the pairwise refinement and combination of directed graphs in the method of the previous sub-section.

5. EXPERIMENTAL EVALUATION

We study the effects of ConSP mining and the proposed modelling on both a real dataset and a synthetic sample. The method and algorithms are implemented using Microsoft Visual C++ where, to mine the sequential patterns, we use the Prefix*Span* algorithm. It is available from the *IlliMine system package*, a partially open-source data mining package: http://illimine.cs.uiuc.edu/, last accessed 12 May 2009.

5.1 Customers Orders Dataset

A real dataset pertaining to customer purchase data is obtainable from Blue Martini's Customer Interaction System in the public domain, http://cobweb.ecn.purdue.edu/KDDCUP/, last accessed: 12 May 2009. Three categories of data, i.e. Customer information, Orders information and Click-stream information are collected by the Blue Martini application server and further details about the data are provided in Kohavi et al. (2000).

The *Orders* dataset corresponds to customer purchase data made up of *customer IDs*, *order IDs* and *product IDs*. It contains data collected from 1,821 customers' behaviour between 28 January 2000 and 31 March 2000, and it includes 3,420 records (i.e. 3,420 purchases), 1,917 orders and

Figure 6. Modelling ConSP using SPG method

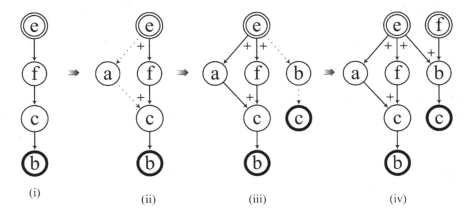

999 different kinds of product. Table 1 illustrates the format and contents of the *Orders* data.

Sequential Patterns Mining

Table 2 illustrates the relationship between *minsup* and the number of sequential patterns found in the *Orders* dataset, where sequential patterns mining has been performed using Prefix*Span* (Pei et al., 2001).

The Table shows that, when *minsup*=0.2%, there are 201 sequential patterns with a unique item and there are 17 sequential patterns with two items. Note that a sequence of length *k* is known

Table 1. Format/content of the orders dataset

Customer ID	Order ID	Product ID
...	...	...
62	3550	19155
62	30018	40393
96	100	13147
132	136	13147
168	832	14135
184	4124	40353
184	4124	44477
184	4124	45371
184	23126	35289
224	228	13143
224	228	14087
236	3412	44449
236	30078	37901
...	...	...
236	30078	51231
236	30090	39913
236	30090	39917
236	30090	37985
236	30090	38309
236	30090	39727
36	30090	40313
236	30090	40353
...	...	...

as a *k*-sequence; some of the 2-sequences among the 17 in Table 2 are (41929 41941), (38517 38533), (38537 38533) and (40141 40145). For example, (38517 38533) shows that 0.2% of customers who purchased product 38517 also bought product 38533.

Concurrent Sequential Patterns Mining

Using the method and algorithms described in Lu et al. (2008), Table 3 shows the extent of the concurrent sequential patterns mining results under various *minsup* and *mincon*.

It is shown from Table 3 that, for example when *minsup*=0.2% and *mincon*=0.1%, one hundred and nineteen $ConSP_2$, three $ConSP_3$ and two $ConSP_4$ are mined. The specific results for $ConSP_3$ and $ConSP_4$ here are:

[48005+39961+39969]

[38545+35273+45363]

[40013+39945+39953]

[40013+39945+40005+39941]

[45375+(35277,35265)+(35277,35273)+(35265,35273)]

For instance consider the first $ConSP_3$, [48005+39961+39969]; it shows that at least 0.2% of customers purchased products 48005, 39961 and 39969 concurrently (within a 0.1% concurrence degree). Comparing this $ConSP_3$ with the sequential patterns mining result in Table 2, for example when *minsup*=0.2%, there are no sequential patterns with length more than 2, i.e. no 3-sequence or 4-sequence either. Therefore, the concurrent sequential patterns $ConSP_3$ and $ConSP_4$ are new structured patterns which cannot be discovered by traditional sequential patterns mining.

The equivalent ConSP-Graphs for this real dataset show no connectivity or structure however, so we next use a more illustrative example to take the mining of concurrent sequential patterns to the modelling stage.

5.2 Synthetic Sample

This sub-section presents a complete synthetic example to highlight the concurrent sequential patterns mining and modelling method overall. The sequence database from Example 1 has been chosen as the sample dataset: $SDB=\{<a\ (a,b,c)\ (a,c)\ d\ (c,f)>, <(a,d)\ c\ (b,c)\ (a,c)>, <(e,f)\ (a,b)\ (d,f)\ c\ b>, <e\ g\ (a,f)\ c\ b\ c>\}$.

Sequential Patterns Mining

The *SDB* here has also been used as an example to explain sequential patterns mining when using the Prefix*span* algorithm (Pei et al., 2001). The output from this algorithm is listed in Table 4 when the user-specified minimum support (*minsup*) is set to 50%, where line number identifiers are shown for each of the 67 sequential patterns mined.

Concurrent Sequential Patterns Mining

Concurrent sequential patterns can be mined using the method in Lu et al. (2008) and, when *mincon* is set to 50%, the results comprise: [6+41+44],

Table 2. minsup and k-sequences on the orders dataset

minsup (%)	Number of *k*-sequences		
	1-sequence	2-sequence	3-sequence
0.4	74	1	-
0.35	90	4	-
0.3	112	11	-
0.25	163	11	-
0.2	201	17	-
0.15	261	39	1
0.1	444	113	9

Table 3. Concurrent sequential patterns mining on the orders dataset

mincon(%)	ConSP$_k$	minsup (%)						
		0.4	0.35	0.3	0.25	0.2	0.15	0.1
0.4	ConSP$_2$	36						
0.35	ConSP$_2$	37	44					
0.3	ConSP$_2$	38	45	54				
0.25	ConSP$_2$	40	47	56	80			
0.2	ConSP$_2$	43	53	60	86	100		
0.15	ConSP$_2$	48	59	65	91	106	122	
	ConSP$_3$	0	0	0	1	1	0	
0.1	ConSP$_2$	53	63	85	111	119	148	204
	ConSP$_3$	1	1	1	5	3	2	0
	ConSP$_4$	0	0	0	1	2	1	0

Table 4. Sequential patterns mining results (minsup=50%)

1 (*a*)	18 (*b*) (*f*)	35 (*a b*) (*d*)	52 (*e*) (*b*) (*c*)
2 (*b*)	19 (*c*) (*a*)	36 (*a b*) (*f*)	53 (*e*) (*c*) (*b*)
3 (*c*)	20 (*c*) (*b*)	37 (*b c*) (*a*)	54 (*e*) (*f*) (*b*)
4 (*d*)	21 (*c*) (*c*)	38 (*b c*) (*c*)	55 (*e*) (*f*) (*c*)
5 (*e*)	22 (*d*) (*b*)	39 (*b c*) (*a c*)	56 (*f*) (*b*) (*c*)
6 (*f*)	23 (*d*) (*c*)	40 (*a*) (*b*) (*a*)	57 (*f*) (*c*) (*b*)
7 (*a b*)	24 (*e*) (*a*)	41 (*a*) (*b*) (*c*)	58 (*a*) (*b*) (*a c*)
8 (*a c*)	25 (*e*) (*b*)	42 (*a*) (*c*) (*a*)	59 (*a*) (*c*) (*a c*)
9 (*b c*)	26 (*e*) (*c*)	43 (*a*) (*c*) (*b*)	60 (*a*) (*b c*) (*a*)
10 (*a*) (*a*)	27 (*e*) (*f*)	44 (*a*) (*c*) (*c*)	61 (*a*) (*b c*) (*c*)
11 (*a*) (*b*)	28 (*f*) (*b*)	45 (*a*) (*d*) (*c*)	62 (*a b*) (*d*) (*c*)
12 (*a*) (*c*)	29 (*f*) (*c*)	46 (*b*) (*d*) (*c*)	63 (*a*) (*b c*) (*a c*)
13 (*a*) (*d*)	30 (*a*) (*a c*)	47 (*c*) (*b*) (*c*)	64 (*a*) (*c*) (*b*) (*c*)
14 (*a*) (*f*)	31 (*a*) (*b c*)	48 (*c*) (*c*) (*c*)	65 (*a*) (*c*) (*c*) (*c*)
15 (*b*) (*a*)	32 (*b*) (*a c*)	49 (*d*) (*c*) (*b*)	66 (*e*) (*a*) (*c*) (*b*)
16 (*b*) (*c*)	33 (*c*) (*a c*)	50 (*e*) (*a*) (*b*)	67 (*e*) (*f*) (*c*) (*b*)
17 (*b*) (*d*)	34 (*a b*) (*c*)	51 (*e*) (*a*) (*c*)	

[11+36+62], [16+43+49], [23+63+65] and [52+56+66+67].

It can be seen that there are five concurrent sequential patterns and, by replacing the identifiers within the patterns by the corresponding sequential patterns in Table 4, the ConSP results at this stage are:

[*f*+*abc*+*acc*]

[*ab*+(*a*,*b*)*f*+(*a*,*b*)*dc*]

[*bc*+*acb*+*dcb*]

[*dc*+*a*(*b*,*c*)(*a*,*c*)+*accc*]

[*ebc*+*fbc*+*eacb*+*efcb*]

ConSP Modelling

ConSP-Graphs can be generated from these concurrent sequential patterns by using either of the modelling methods in this paper. Figure 7 gives the final ConSP modelling results.

ConSP modelling presents a useful visualisation here from which (e.g.) several concurrent branch patterns can be deduced. In Figure 7(i), associated with nodes *b* and *c*, the fork node *a* and synchronizer node *c* make up a *cycle* graph – a graph that consists of a single cycle – therefore a single concurrent branch pattern *a*[*b*+*c*]*c* can be identified alongside the freestanding node *f*.

The fork node (*a*,*b*) in Figure 7(ii) determines a new concurrent branch pattern (*a*,*b*)[*f*+*dc*]; similarly, [*a*+*d*]*cb* is another CBP linked through the synchronizer node *c* in Figure 7(iii). There is also one fork node *a* and one synchronizer node *c* in Figure 7(iv) and, as they are not part of a cycle graph, two CBPs pertain in this case, i.e. *a*[(*b*,*c*) (*a*,*c*)+*ccc*] and [*acc*+*d*]*c*.

Figure 7. Modelling of concurrent sequential patterns

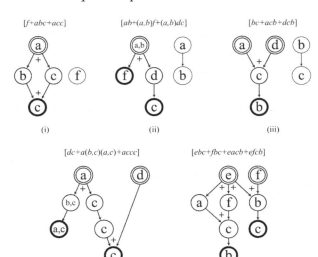

Finally, consider the ConSP-Graph in Figure 7(v), which represents greater complexity than the other four. The concurrent branch pattern $e[a+f]cb$ can be generated as an extension of a cycle graph, which contains the fork node e and synchronizer node c; the pattern $[e+f]bc$ is due to the synchronizer node b; and fork node e contributes to another two CBPs, namely $e[acb+bc]$ and $e[fcb+bc]$.

It can be seen that the models in Figure 7 bring together connectivity and structure, which opens up further pattern discovery through concurrent branch patterns. More generally, ConSP modelling can add value to the results of concurrent sequential patterns mining by providing a visualisation of otherwise intangible (algebraic) patterns.

In summary, the real dataset used in the previous sub-section aims to show the experimental results of mining from the application perspective, while the synthetic example here serves to demonstrate the strength of the graph-based modelling developed in the paper. The ConSP mining approach can indeed mine new patterns effectively, beyond sequential orders, and this new knowledge can be modelled in a meaningful way to represent the inherent structural relationships.

6. CONCLUSION

The refinement of concurrent sequential patterns and generation of graph-based models are the main challenges pursued in this article. It is shown that the expression and construction method of sequential patterns graph can be extended to concurrent sequential patterns modelling, where the features of ConSP-Graph make it straightforward to model the common prefix or postfix elements of concurrent sequential patterns. A construction algorithm is proposed which is based on SPG and instrumental in the transformation of concurrent sequential patterns to a ConSP-Graph representation.

A real dataset *Orders* from Blue Martini's website and synthetic sample data have been used in the experiments to present the results from ConSP mining and modelling, while contrasting with sequential patterns mining. This has shown that patterns otherwise hidden behind the data can be discovered through concurrent sequential patterns mining and represented by a graphical model. The synthetic sample in particular shows that new concurrent branch patterns can be deduced from

Figure 8. Graphical representation of workflow control patterns

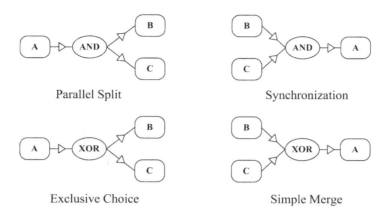

Parallel Split   Synchronization

Exclusive Choice   Simple Merge

graph-based modelling, adding value to the mining results and pointing a further way forward.

There are potentially related applications for ConSP mining and modelling, for example in the area of workflow induction, a technique to solve a problem in workflow model design (Herbst, 2000). Basic control patterns of workflow can be defined (van der Aalst et al., 2003) which, besides sequence, comprise *parallel split*, *synchronization*, *exclusive choice* and *simple merge*. Figure 8 shows these four constructs graphically.

The *parallel split* pattern allows a single thread of execution to be split into two (or more) branches which can execute tasks concurrently – it is equivalent to the fork node in ConSP-Graph. *Synchronization* comes into play once the control node receives input on one of its incoming branches, at a point in the workflow process where multiple parallel activities converge into one single thread of execution – it is equivalent to the synchronizer node in ConSP-Graph.

Taking workflow logs as source data, and following sequential patterns mining, one can apply ConSP mining and modelling to represent fundamental activities and events in order to provide a practical workflow scheme. And, with reference to structural relation patterns more generally (Lu et al., 2008), the concept of exclusive patterns would naturally extend to the *exclusive choice* and *simple merge* constructs in Figure 8 – the subject of future work.

REFERENCES

Aalst, W. M. P., van der Hofstede, A. H. M., ter Kiepuszewski, B., & Barros, A. P. (2003). Workflow patterns. *Distributed and Parallel Databases*, *14*(3), 5–51. doi:10.1023/A:1022883727209

Agrawal, R., Imielinski, T., & Swami, A. (1993). Mining association rules between sets of items in large databases. *Proceedings of the 1993 ACM (SIGMOD)* (pp.207-216).

Agrawal, R., & Srikant, R. (1995). Mining sequential patterns. In *Proceedings of 11th International Conference on Data Engineering* (pp. 3-14). Taipei, Taiwan: IEEE Computer Society Press.

Asai, T., Abe, K., Kawasoe, S., Arimura, H., Satamoto, H., & Arikawa, S. (2002). Efficient substructure discovery from large semi-structured data. In *Proceedings of the 2nd SIAM International Conference on Data Mining* (Vol.E87-D, No.12, pp. 2754-2763).

Chang, L., Yang, D. Q., Tang, S. W., & Wang, T. (2006). Mining compressed sequential patterns. In *Proceedings of the 2nd International Conference on Advanced Data Mining and Applications* (Vol.4093, pp.761-768). Xian, China.

Chen, J., & Cook, T. (2007). Mining contiguous sequential patterns from web logs. In *Proceedings of the 16th international conference on World Wide Web* (pp.1177-1178). Banff, Alberta, Canada.

Cook, D. J., & Holder, L. B. (2000). Graph-based data mining. *IEEE Intelligent Systems*, *15*(2), 32–41. doi:10.1109/5254.850825

Garriga, G. C. (2005). Summarizing sequential data with closed partial orders. In *Proceedings of the SIAM International Conference on Data Mining* (pp.380–391). California, USA.

Han, J. W., Pei, J., Mortazavi-Asl, B., Chen, Q., Dayal, U., & Hsu, M. C. (2000). Freespan: frequent pattern-projected sequential patterns mining. In *Proceedings of the 6th ACM SIGKDD International Conference on Knowledge Discovery and Data Mining* (pp.355-359). New York: ACM Press.

Herbst, J. (2000). Dealing with concurrency in workflow induction. In *Proceedings of the 7th European Concurrent Engineering Conference, Society for Computer Simulation* (pp.169-174).

Huan, J., Wang, W., Prins, J., & Yang, J. (2004). SPIN: Mining maximal frequent subgraphs from graph databases. *Proceedings of the 10th ACM (SIGKDD)* (pp. 581-586). Seattle, USA.

Inokuchi, A., Washio, T., & Motoda, H. (2003). Complete mining of frequent patterns from graphs: mining graph data. *Machine Learning*, *50*(3), 321–354. doi:10.1023/A:1021726221443

Ivancsy, R., & Vajk, I. (2005). A survey of discovering frequent patterns in graph. In *Proceedings of Databases and Applications* (pp. 60-72). Calgary, Canada: ACTA Press.

Kohavi, R., Brodley, C., Frasca, B., Mason, L., & Zheng, Z. J. (2000). KDD-Cup 2000 Organizers' Report: Peeling the onion. *SIGKDD Explorations*, *2*(2), 86–98. doi:10.1145/380995.381033

Kuramochi, M., & Karypis, G. (2004). GREW-A scalable frequent subgraph discovery algorithm. In *Proceedings of the 2004 IEEE International Conference on Mining* (pp. 439-442). Brighton, UK.

Lu, J. (2006). From Sequential Patterns to Concurrent Branch Patterns: A new post sequential patterns mining approach. Unpublished doctoral dissertation, University of Bedfordshire, UK.

Lu, J., Adjei, O., Chen, W. R., & Liu, J. (2004). Post Sequential Patterns Mining: A new method for discovering structural patterns. In *Proceedings of the Second International Conference on Intelligent Information Processing* (pp.239-250). Beijing, China: Springer-Verlag.

Lu, J., Chen, W. R., Adjei, O., & Keech, M. (2008). Sequential patterns post-processing for structural relation patterns mining. *International Journal of Data Warehousing and Mining*, *4*(3), 71–89.

Lu, J., Wang, X. F., Adjei, O., & Hussain, F. (2004). Sequential patterns graph and its construction algorithm. *Chinese Journal of Computers*, *27*(6), 782–788.

Pei, J., Han, J. W., Mortazavi-Asl, B., & Pinto, H. (2001). PrefixSpan: Mining sequential patterns efficiently by prefix-projected pattern growth. In *Proceedings of the Seventh International Conference on Data Engineering* (pp. 215-224). Heidelberg, Germany.

Srikant, R., & Agrawal, R. (1996). Mining Sequential Patterns: Generalizations and performance improvements. In *Proceedings of the Fifth International Conference on Extending Database Technology* (EDBT) (Vol.1057, pp. 3-17). Avignon, France.

Yan, X. F., Han, J. W., & Afshar, R. (2003). CloSpan: Mining closed sequential patterns in large datasets. In *Proceedings of SDM'03* (pp. 166-177). San Francisco, CA.

Zaki, M. J. (2001). SPADE: An efficient algorithm for mining frequent sequences. *Machine Learning, 42*(1/2), 31–60. doi:10.1023/A:1007652502315

Zaki, M. J. (2005). Efficiently Mining Frequent Trees in a Forest: Algorithms and applications. *IEEE Transactions on Knowledge and Data Engineering, 17*(8), 1021–1035. doi:10.1109/TKDE.2005.125

Zaki, M. J., Parimi, N., De, N., Gao, F., Phoophakdee, B., Urban, J., et al. (2005). Towards generic pattern mining. In *Proceedings of the ICFCA 2004* (LNCS 3403) (pp. 1-20). Berlin: Springer-Verlag.

This work was previously published in International Journal of Data Warehousing and Mining, Volume 6, Issue 2, edited by David Taniar, pp. 41-58, copyright 2010 by IGI Publishing (an imprint of IGI Global).

Chapter 8
User–Centric Similarity and Proximity Measures for Spatial Personalization

Yanwu Yang
Chinese Academy of Sciences, China

Christophe Claramunt
Naval Academy Research Institute, France

Marie-Aude Aufaure
Ecole Centrale Paris, France

Wensheng Zhang
Chinese Academy of Sciences, China

ABSTRACT

Spatial personalization can be defined as a novel way to fulfill user information needs when accessing spatial information services either on the web or in mobile environments. The research presented in this paper introduces a conceptual approach that models the spatial information offered to a given user into a user-centered conceptual map, and spatial proximity and similarity measures that considers her/his location, interests and preferences. This approach is based on the concepts of similarity in the semantic domain, and proximity in the spatial domain, but taking into account user's personal information. Accordingly, these spatial proximity and similarity measures could directly support derivation of personalization services and refinement of the way spatial information is accessible to the user in spatially related applications. These modeling approaches are illustrated by some experimental case studies.

DOI: 10.4018/978-1-61350-474-1.ch008

Copyright © 2012, IGI Global. Copying or distributing in print or electronic forms without written permission of IGI Global is prohibited.

INTRODUCTION

Personalization offers many opportunities to improve the way information is delivered to a given user. Web personalization should help to remove irrelevant information, to adapt web content and structure, and thus to improve the quality of web services and user's satisfaction. E-commerce and distance learning are some of domains where web personalization has been successfully applied, while personalization has been also applied to other domains, particularly where the information is complex and diverse per nature.

Spatial web personalization can be considered as an emerging research area of interest as the amount of geo-referenced data distributed either on the web or mobile environments grows exponentially. Let us consider that spatial data represents any item of information that is in one way or the other related to a given geographical location. Namely, geographical entities that appear on a map, or items that represent an information or an object located on Earth (e.g., a photograph, a given landmark).

The development of spatial Web services has been widely active over the past few years, together with significant progresses on spatial information retrieval and location-based services that open novel perspectives for real-time diffusion of geographical data (Harle & Hopper, 2008; Kwon & Shin, 2008). With respect to whether a given user is located in the virtual (such as the web) or in the physical environment, spatially related information services are closely related to the fields of spatial web information retrieval and location-based services.

In the past decade, the progressive integration of spatial information within web pages has been widely investigated to facilitate spatially related information retrieval on the web (Ding et al., 2000; Gravano et al., 2003). Two complementary strategies have been applied: a technique based on the spatial distribution of web links to a given page, and another based on the distribution of spatial references in a given web page. With consideration of user's location, (Gravano et al., 2003) identified whether a given query submitted to a search engine should be oriented towards either "local" or "global" pages. For example, a query oriented to some general biological information on "wildflowers" should consider global information, while a search for some "houses for sale" after local information, as this later case is locally oriented per definition.

More specifically, location-based spatial queries usually consider spatial queries that retrieve information based on the users' current locations which is likely to be mobile. When considering location-based spatial queries, a given user (and thus the entities of interest) is likely to be in displacement in the physical environment. Its movement can be represented as a sequence of time-stamped locations. Over the past few years, there has been several works oriented towards mobile spatial queries and sequential patterns (Jayaputera & Taniar, 2005), including nearest neighbor (NN), k nearest neighbor, continuous k nearest neighbor (Zhao et al., 2008; 2009), reverse nearest neighbor (Lee et al., 2008) and range search (Xuan et al., 2008). When considering road networks, (Zhang et al., 2004) studied spatial queries in the presence of obstacles, where the distance between two points is defined as the length of the shortest path that connects them without crossing any obstacles. (Zhang et al., 2003) considered a moving query as a query which is reevaluated only when the query exits the validity scope. Taking location dependency (Goh & Taniar, 2004a) into account, Goh and Taniar (2004b; 2005; 2007) built user profiles based on past mobile visiting data, filters and to mine mobile pattern and association rules from mobile users. (Wang et al., 2006; 2008) presented an approach that derives group patterns of mobile users based on their movement data, where a group pattern is defined as a group of users that are within a distance threshold from one another for at least a minimum duration.

Although spatial information is diverse and multiple, similarities in the semantic domain are likely to emerge as information is often delivered per domains of interest. Similarly, spatial entities of similar interest are often located at proximity as stated by the First Law of Geography (Tobler, 1970). The notion of similarity has been considered in web engineering as an important component for personalization (Baeza-Yates & Ribeiro-Neto, 1999; Mobasher et al., 2000; Kumar et al., 2007) and clustering (Zhang et al., 2008). Similarity measures have been used to identify the degree of similarity between two information entities. Similarity measures between trajectories on road networks are crucial to discover sequential patterns in moving trajectories and search for similar trajectories on road networks. Similarity between trajectories can be defined as non-metric distance functions based on trajectory properties such as longest common subsequence, or spatio-temporal functions.

To the best of our knowledge, the role of space when deriving similarities in an information space has been hardly (if any, not fully) considered (Mountrakis et al., 2005). On the one hand, the role of spatial proximity is a non-straightforward notion relatively distinct from the notion of similarity as developed in the semantic domain. One can say that the influence of the spatial distribution of the data is not fundamentally different from what arises in the semantic domain. However, space has the very specific property of being potentially the container of a human acting or planning to act in the environment (e.g., location-based services), this also leading to consider space from a cognitive point of view that influences the way information is perceived, and thus the way spatial information should be delivered to the user. Such influences and constraints imply to study the way human beings manipulate and interact with geographical data.

On the other hand, semantic similarity and especially spatial proximity is crucially influenced by different contexts such as location, time, user's interests and preferences, as which is a matter of human experience and judgment per nature. For example, A historian may consider she/he is "near" to a museum but "far" from a garden given other factors are either similar or equivalent, e.g., when considering distance.

The research presented in this paper introduces a conceptual approach that organizes the spatial information offered to a given user into a user-centered conceptual map, and a novel spatial proximity and similarity measure, with consideration of her/his location, interests and preferences. This approach is based on the concepts of similarity in the semantic domain, and proximity in the spatial domain, but taking into account user's personal information. The rationale behind is, to a specific user, her/his conceptual map is gradually formed while interacting with spatial entities in a given environment; meanwhile, based on this map comparing spatial entities, evaluating relationships among them, and making decisions on consequent activities. That is to say, information services based on user-centric conceptual map, spatial proximity and similarity measure is equivalent to the task that, the generation and delivery of personalized information on user's behalf.

This approach, grounded on a user-centric conceptual map, spatial proximity and similarity measure considers personalization at the level of data semantics, in order to generate personalized information services to the user. This method is based on the refinement of spatial proximity and similarity measures, by taking into account user interests and preferences as shown during interactions of the user on the web. Spatial proximities and similarities are modeled using the concept of user-centered conceptual map that reflects distortions in the information space. The modeling approach is illustrated by some experimental case studies.

The remainder of this paper is organized as follows. Section 2 introduces an approach for designing a user-centric conceptual map taking into account user's interests and preferences. Section 3 presents the spatial proximity and semantic similarity measures. Section 4 illustrates the potential of the approach by experimental case studies. Finally, section 5 concludes this paper and outlines future work.

Conceptualising Space

The Conceptual Map

A conceptual map is a cognitive abstraction that represents and organizes knowledge in a mental and spatial form that favors interpretation. For instance, a conceptual map can formalize a special image of the city space human beings have been interacting with. Cognitive maps are mostly qualitative where landmarks play a specific role, and most of the relations subjective and fuzzy per nature (Lynch, 1960). In fact, human beings perceive and interact with spatial entities in a given environment in an egocentric way (Franklin et al., 1992). Thus, a conceptual map is derived from an egocentric point of view where the user is generally the center of interest. Therefore, human make decisions on a given space partly based on their own conceptual map, and update it continuously according to their experiences and actions.

Distortions in the perception of a spatial environment have been largely recognized, even in the context of the Web where inference rules have been introduced to show that proximity relationships are distorted in a conceptual map. It has been also shown that the hierarchical arrangement of spatial entities in a given environment affects the construction of a conceptual map (Hirtle & Jonides, *1985*). User interests and preferences are amongst the most important factors of distortion in a conceptual map. Conceptual maps are influenced by social, cultural and knowledge criteria, but also by user experiences and interests. Proximity and similarity measures are sensitive to the contextual knowledge exhibited from a given representation (Roberts & Wedell, 1994; Goldstone et al., 1997; Aleksy et al., 2008). Semantic similarities are usually represented and judged by contextual fac-

tors such as the relative importance of the entities represented, interrelationships between entities, role of the neighboring environment.

When applied to space, these principles are illustrated by the concept of Cartogram, that is, a map in which the sizes of the enumeration units have been rescaled according to an attribute (e.g., population, Gross Domestic Product) that is distorted rather than their actual size (Gastner et al., 2005). Cartograms are effective ways of portraying geographic or social data. In this paper, we present a new conceptual map on which spatial relationships (e.g. proximity) are distorted according to user's location, preferences and interests.

An Approach for User-Centric Conceptual Map

The way the locations of some spatial entities are perceived by a given user should be considered in the light of spatial cognition principles (Klatzky, 1998). Let us consider the scenario of a given user located and interacting with some spatial entities distributed in a spatial environment. Let us also assume that an interest to a given entity increases when the distance to this entity decreases. The way these spatial entities are interpreted and represented directly influences the structure of a conceptual map. For instance, distances to things of interest are likely to decrease, and conversely.

Figure 1 illustrates a scenario of a user-centric conceptual map representing some spatial entities distributed in a given environment. Proximities to landmarks of interest are inversely proportional to the user distance to these landmarks, and proportional to the interest to the classes exhibited by these landmarks. This has a direct impact on the mental representation of the conceptual map, and the location of the entities represented and distances to the user. The case presented in Figure 1 illustrates the concept. Gray circles represent the original map of some spatial entities located in a given environment. Dark gray circles present a conceptual map as it might be conceptualized

Figure 1. User-centric conceptual map

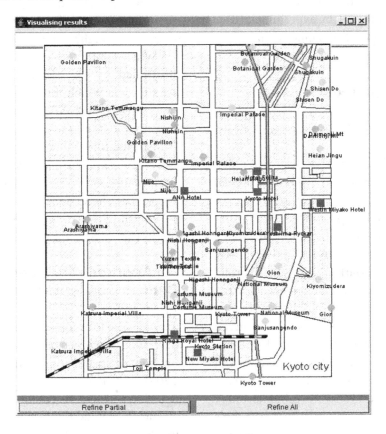

in the user mind. Distances in a conceptual map can be interpreted as a sort of contextual distance that takes into account the Euclidean distance and some semantic distortions.

In order to develop further the modeling approach we introduce some basic notations. Without loss of generality, a spatial entity is modeled by a pair of coordinates (x, y) to denote its location, and a set of membership degrees to denote its semantic content. The membership degrees of a spatial entity are given as a list of valued classes $\{w(C_1, e), w(C_2, e), ... w(C_n, e)\}$ where a membership degree $w(c_i, e)$ gives the relevance value of the spatial entity e associated to a semantic class C_i. A semantic class corresponds to a categorization of entities that share some semantic properties. A relevance value is given by the

unit interval [0,1] to reflect increasing membership degrees to corresponding classes.

User interests and preferences are represented with a preference pattern *prefPattern(pref_1,* $pref_2,..., pref_n)$, where $pref_i$ denotes a user preference index, that is, to which degree a given user is interested in properties related to a semantic class C_i. A user preference index $pref_i$ is bounded by the unit interval [0, 1] that denotes increasing degrees of interest. User preference indexes can be categorized into positive sets *like (pref_1,* $pref_2,..., pref_{like})$ and negative sets *disl (pref_1,* $pref_2,..., pref_{disl})$, where *like+disl=n*, *like* denotes the number of positive preference indexes, and *disl* the number of negative preference indexes in a given user preference pattern. Similarly, entity membership degrees of entities can be divided into user preferable set *like* $\{w(C_1, e), w(C_2, e),$

... $w(C_{like}, e)\}$, and user non-preferable set *disl* $\{w(C_1, e), w(C_2, e), ... w(C_{disl}, e)\}$.

When considering a user-centric conceptual map, the spatial proximity of a spatial entity is, to some degree, affected (or distorted) by user's preferences and interests with respect to her/his current location. A distorted degree describes to which degree the location of specific spatial entities is modified in the user conceptual map. These distortions are evaluated in positive and negative directions, and determined by preference indexes in positive (*like*) and negative sets (*disl*), respectively. The distorted degree is bounded by the interval [-1, 1], and represented as a function of user interests and preferences (e.g. *pref_i*), and membership degrees of a spatial entity. It is given as

$$distortDeg(e,u) =$$
$$\frac{1}{like} \sum_{i=1}^{like} [pref_i \times w(C_i, e)] + \frac{1}{disl} \sum_{j=1}^{dial} [(pref_j \times 1) w(C_j, e)]$$

The "distortion" of a spatial entity in terms of a given user's conceptual map, can be defined as

$$distortDeg(e,u) = d(e,u) \times distortDeg(e,u)$$

where $d(e,u)$ denotes the Euclidean distance between a spatial entity e and the user location u, and $distortDeg(e,u)$ the distorted degree.

As an example, let us consider the conceptual map of a given user illustrated in figure 1 is distorted with her/his preference pattern (0.9, 0.7, 0.1, 0.3). Concerning the Kyoto tower, the distorted degree is −0.55. That is, with such a preference pattern, the distance from user's location (the ANA hotel) to the Kyoto tower is distorted (specifically decreased) in her/his conceptual map.

SPATIAL PROXIMITY AND SEMANTIC SIMILARITY

From Semantic to Spatial Proximity

Geometric models and multidimensional scaling models can be considered as the most general approaches to analyze the similarity between two entities (Goldstone & Son, 2005). In a multidimensional approach, the semantic distance between two entities x_i and y_j is computed as follows

$$d(x_i, y_j) = [\sum_{k=1}^{n} | x_i^k - y_j^k |^r]^{(1/r)}$$

Where n is the number of dimensions, and x_i^k, y_j^k denotes membership degrees of entities x_i and y_j to a semantic class C_k, r an adjusting coefficient.

For instance, the Euclidean distance is a specialized form of multidimensional distance with r=2. One of the important factors that constrain human actions in the environment is the notion of spatial proximity. This should be modeled by a rule stating that the interest showed by a given user to a specific spatial entity increases when similar entities are located nearby. This is particularly important for a specific user acting or planning to act in a given urban space, as she/he will consider space as a recipient where her/his interests for a given spatial entity can be reinforced in the presence of similar entities nearby.

In the context of a Web interface, and at the design level, although spatial entities of interest and reference locations are geo-referenced, this information is often implicit as not directly accessible to the user. A Web interface encompasses information either explicitly (image schemata of the representative spatial entities) or implicitly (location of the spatial entities and the reference location in the city, proximity between them).

In the spatial domain, the distance between two spatial entities is influenced by the overall structure of a given spatial distribution. The proximity between two locations is usually approximated as an inverse of the distance factor. (Worboys, 1996) defined a "relativised distance" concept to evaluate the spatial proximity between two spatial entities. In a related work (Worboys, 2001), a relative form of spatial proximity has been introduced to take into account the qualitative component of the notion of distance and the fuzziness of boundaries. This reflects the fact, observed in qualitative studies that the distance from a region α to a distant region β should be magnified when the number of regions near α increases, and *vice versa* (Yang & Claramunt, 2004; Tversky, 1993). The relativised distance introduced by Worboys normalizes the conventional Euclidean distance between a region A and a region B by a dividing factor that gives a form of contextual value to that measure. This dividing factor is given by the average of the Euclidean distance between the region A and all the regions considered as part of the environment.

These approaches are valid when considering a homogenous set of spatial entities. However, when considering the semantic dimension, categories have an influence on the spatial proximity measures. Let us consider the case illustrated in Figure 2. First, the appearance of additional landmarks Figure 2b has an impact on the perception of the distance between the two entities represented in Figure 2a (ANA hotel and Nishi Honganji) as many entities that appear in Figure 2b are located in their neighboring environment. Secondly, many of the entities that appear in the neighborhood of the ANA hotel belong to the same class, which has effects on its semantic relationship with Nishi Honganji and thus its distance to it. This also reflects the fact that a contextual form of distance is per nature asymmetric (Worboys, 1996; Yang & Claramunt, 2004).

Figure 2. Spatial proximity scenario

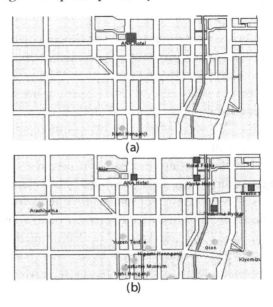

(a)

(b)

Towards an Integrated Form of Similarity and Proximity

We introduce a form "contextual proximity" to reflect an asymmetric form distance that takes into account the similarity factor. The contextual proximity encompasses two semantic properties that are modelled by the following rules (Krumhansl, 1978; Worboys, 1996; Yang & Claramunt, 2004; Sjberg, 1972):

- **Rule 1:** The spatial/semantic relationship between two entities is asymmetrical.
- **Rule 2:** The spatial/semantic relationship from one entity to another is weakened when the number of its nearby neighbours increases; magnified when the number of its distant neighbours increases; and vice versa.

In order to formalise these rules we make a distinction between proximities between entities from a same class (so-called intra- contextual proximity) and from a different class (so-called inter-contextual proximity).

Intra-Contextual Proximity

The contextual proximity between two spatial entities $x_i, x_j \in X = \{x_1, x_2, ..., x_p\}$, where p denotes the number of elements in set X, is given as

$$CP(x_i, x_j) = \frac{1}{1 + CD(x_i, x_j)^2}$$

Where $CD(x_i, x_j)$ denotes the contextual distance between x_i and x_j. The higher $CP(x_i, x_j)$, the closer x_i is to x_j, the lower $CP(x_i, x_j)$, the distant x_i is to x_j.

The intra- contextual proximity is relatively close to the "relativised distance" introduced by Worboys (Worboys, 1996). The difference is that a square factor in the denominator maximizes contextual proximities for small distances (vs. minimizing contextual proximities for large distances), and extends the amplitude of values within the unit interval.

The *contextual distance* normalizes the conventional Euclidean distance between a set of spatial entities A and a set of reference locations B by a dividing factor that gives a form of contextual value to that measure. The dividing factor is given by a function of two factors. The first is the average of all distances between the entities of one set A (in which α is located) with respect to the reference locations of a second set B (in which β is located). The second is the average of all distance between α and other entities in A. The *contextual distance* between a region α of set A and region β of set B magnifies when the number of regions of set B near the regions of set A increases, and *vice-versa*. The contextual distance between x_i and x_j is given as

$$CD(x_i, y_j) = \frac{d(x_i, y_j)}{d(x_i, X)}$$

Where $d(x_i, x_j)$ denotes the Euclidean distance between x_i and x_j, $d(x_i, X)$ the average distance between x_i and the entities in X.

The average distance between x_i and the other entities in X is computed as

$$d(x_i, X) = \frac{1}{p - 1} \sum_{j=1, j \neq i}^{p} d(x_i, x_j)$$

Intra-Contextual Proximity

The contextual proximity between two spatial entities $x_i \in X, y_j \in Y = \{y_1, y_2, ..., y_q\}$, *is* defined as follows,

$$CP(x_i, y_j) = \frac{1}{1 + CD(x_i, y_j)^2}$$

Where $CD(x_i, x_j)$ denotes the contextual distance between x_i and y_j. The higher $CP(x_i, x_j)$ the closer x_i to y_j, the lower $CP(x_i, x_j)$ the distant x_i to y_j.

The contextual distance between two entities from different sets is inversely proportional to two forms of distance: intra-distance and inter-distance. The former refers to the distance to entities in a same set, and the latter, the distance to entities in a different set with respect to entities under comparison. The inter-distance considers the first entity as the reference, reflecting an asymmetric characteristic of cognitive proximity measure. The contextual distance between x_i and y_j is given as,

$$CD(x_i, y_j) = \frac{d(x_i, y_j)}{\sqrt{d(x_i, Y)^2 + d(x_i, X)^2}}$$

Where $d(x_i, Y)$ denotes the distance between x_i and Y.

The inter-contextual proximity is a form of generalisation of Worboys's definition of "relativised distance" as the dividing factor is here the average of all distances between the regions of one set with respect to the regions of a second set. The distance between x_i and Y refers to the average distance between x_i and spatial entities in Y, it is given as,

$$d(x_i, Y) = \frac{1}{q} \sum_{j=1}^{q} d(x_i, y_j)$$

Semantic Distance

In order to extend the concept of to the semantic domain, at least two minor adaptations are required. The first consideration is that the semantic domain is essentially multidimensional. Unlike in the spatial domain, the semantic dimensions are not perpendicular to each other but are often intertwined. The second component to take into account is the respective and relative importance of these semantic dimensions with respect to the user interests. We make such distinctions as follows by introducing a semantic form of distance:

$$d(x_i, y_j) = \lambda [\sum_{k=1}^{like} | x_i^k - y_j^k |^2]^{(1/2)}$$
$$+ (1-\lambda)[\sum_{k=1}^{disl} | x_i^k - y_j^k |^2]^{(1/2)}$$

where k denotes the number semantic dimensions relevant a given application domain, λ is a constant valued by the unit interval that reflects the respective influences of the user preferences and preferable sets with respect to the semantic membership degrees of entities under consideration (a suggested value for λ is fixed to 0.8 in order to emphasize positive evidence on user interests).

Refinement of Semantic-Similarity Distance

Following the two rules previously introduced, we introduce a semantic-similarity form of distance

based on a domain ontology (See Figure 3). We first give an example of the hierarchical domain. An hierarchical domain ontology consists of a set of semantic classes N and links L. Classes are labelled with distinct labels. Links connect classes with different relationships e.g. is-a and part-whole. Let H be a hierarchical domain, Root (H) the root. The depth of a class is the number of links between Root (H) and the class. The least common ancestor of two classes is their deepest subsumer. The relationships between two semantic classes can be represented either by the number of links connecting them in the hierarchical structure, or by a function of the number of their common and distinctive super classes. The links and classes are also labeled by weights denoting different importance, based on depth and density of semantic classes in class hierarchy. Let us introduce the following variables:

- Let $sup(C_1)$ be the set of super classes of C1 in the hierarchical domain ontology,
- $deep(C_1)$ the depth of C_1,
- $sib(C_1)$ the number of siblings of C_1 with the most specific, common ancestor,
- $sup(C_1/C_2)$ the set of super classes of C_1 but not of C_2,
- $dis(C_1, C_2)$ the number of links between C_1 and C_2,
- $LCA(C_1, C_2)$ the least common ancestor of C_1 and C_2.

Following (Tversky, 1977), the similarity between two semantic nodes in a hierarchical structure can be modelled as a function of their common and distinct super classes, that is, the depth. The similarity between two semantic classes C1, C_2 in a given hierarchical domain ontology is given as follows:

$$sim(C_1, C_2) =$$
$$\frac{\lambda \, | \, sup(C_1) \cap sup(C_2) \, |}{| \, sup(C_1) \cup sup(C_2) \, | + \alpha \, | \, sup(C_1 / C_2) \, | - (1-\alpha) \, | \, sup(C_2 / C_1) \, |}$$

Figure 3. A terminological ontology extracted from WordNet

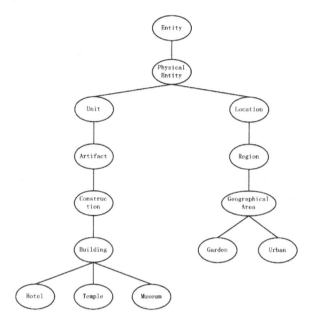

Where α is a parameter bounded by the unit interval [0, 1] that adjusts the weights of the distinct sets $sup(C_1/C_2)$ and $sup(C_2/C_1)$. λ denotes the depth parameter.

With consideration of the asymmetrical feature of similarity measure, the weight α is determined as a function of the distance between semantics C_1, C_2 and the least common ancestor of both classes, and the number of sibling C1, C2. It is given as

$$\alpha(C_1,C_2) = \frac{dis(C_1, LCA(C_1,C_2)) \times sib(C_1)}{dis(C_1, LCA(C_1,C_2)) \times sib(C_1) + dis(C_2, LCA(C_1,C_2)) \times sib(C_2)}$$

The depth parameter λ is given as

$$\lambda = \frac{2deep(LCA(C_1,C_2))}{deep(C_1) + deep(C_2)}$$

The similarity function yields values bounded by the unit interval [0,1]. The maximum value 1 occurs *iff* the two semantic classes under comparison are equivalent, that is, $C_1=C_2$. The similar-ity function reflects an asymmetric relationship between two semantic classes.

However, the semantic interrelationships given in a hierarchical structure of semantic classes are not sufficient to distinguish one class from another. An entity may pertain to more than one semantic class. Let *Oo(C)* denote the set of semantic classes to which the origin entity relates, *Ot(C)* the set of classes of the target entity. The semantic distance between two entities can be then computed as the averaged distance between semantic classes related to them. Given a class $C_i \in Oo(C)$, the semantic distance from C_i to the classes in *Ot(C)* is given as

$$sim_{C_i} = \frac{1}{|Ot(C)|-1} \sum_{j=1,j\neq i}^{|Ot(C)|} sim(C_i, C_j)$$

Finally, and in order to take intro account distances from the different dimensions, a final form of semantic-similarity distance derived from equation (10) is given as follows

$$d(x_i,y_j) = \alpha[\sum_{k=1}^{like} |\frac{x_{ik}-y_{jk}}{sim_{C_i}}|^2]^{(1/2)} + (1-\alpha)[\sum_{k=1}^{disl} |\frac{x_{ik}-y_{jk}}{sim_{C_i}}|^2]^{(1/2)}$$

EXPERIMENTATION

System Architecture

For implementation purposes, let us introduce a generic research framework for spatial web personalization (Figure 4), where the user modeling module interacts with the application systems using inter-process communications, e.g., "*tell*" and "*ask*" operations. A semantic user model can be considered as a formal representation of a given user background information, interests and preferences. Web application systems unobtrusively observe and record user's behaviors, then send such information to the user modeling component that allows the inference of domain-dependent user features. The application system then performs a matching between the user's query and her/his profile to provide services tailored to the user.

Case Study

Without loss of generality, let us consider an application scenario in the tourism domain, where an urban space represented on the Web. In a given city, there are diverse sightseeing places, distributed in space and that contain some semantic contents. Additionally, reference locations that are easy to find and where people can act from to visit the spatial entities are available. This application is intended to provide personalized information on a variety of spatial entities in order to assist the user to travel in an urban space, namely the city of Kyoto (Yang & Claramunt, 2004; 2005). Spatial entities of interest are modelled as places that might present an interest to a user who wants to visit the city of Kyoto, reference locations as hotels where the user will be able to act from in the city.

A Web-based prototype is developed to present a set of places of interest. These sightseeing places are characterized according to their memberships to some concepts in terminological ontology extracted from WordNet. We assume no prior – if any – little knowledge of the Web GIS environment presented by the Web interface, neither experiential nor survey knowledge[1]. Given a Web GIS environment of interest (i.e., the historical city of Kyoto in the prototype developed so far), the user is expected to plan a trip or to find valuable information in the city, and where she/he would like to find out some spatial entities of interest, and a reference location from which she/he will be able to act in the spatial environment.

The Web personalization system developed so far encodes two main levels of information inputs: places and hotels (Figure 5). These places are referenced by image schemata and encoded using fuzzy quantifiers according to predefined

semantic classes (e.g., urban, temple, garden and museum) and geo-referenced. Several places of interest in the city of Kyoto have been pre-selected to give a large range of preference opportunities to the user. Hotels are represented by a list of hotels also offered for selection.

The spatial web personalization system supports personalized search strategies, a hybrid personalization engine and a spatially enriched user interface. From user preference elicitation and personalization mechanisms, the personalized search strategies and the hybrid personalization engine are based on different principles. The former are based on static inferences, the latter, on dynamic inferences as the personalization engine takes into account user's current navigations. The former also allows for active interac-

Figure 4. A system architecture for web personalization systems

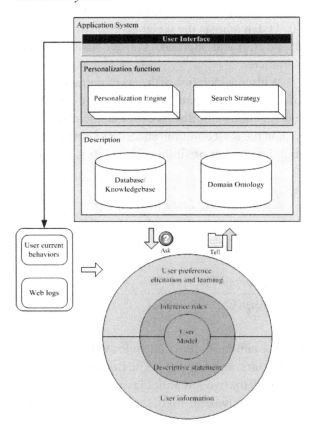

Figure 5. The initial user interface

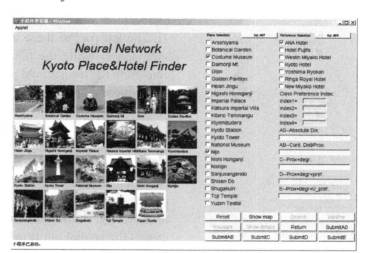

tions, while the latter performs in a passive mode. Integration of these personalized search strategies and the personalization engine give flexible mechanisms for supporting interactions between the user and spatial web applications. Personalization services also supports a Web-based interface enriched with image schemata and affordance concepts that facilitate interactions between the user and the spatial Web, and user preference elicitation process.

The whole personalized search strategy is implemented as an iterative process, namely an initial and a series of successive refinement steps based on the BNAM mechanism, taking into account user's interests and preferences as described previously, to search for the best reference location and top-n spatial entities recommended to the user. The direct result from initial personalized search process recalls the best reference location and a set of top-n ranked spatial entities, whose names are displayed at the interface.

We also introduced and implemented a hybrid personalization approach and reinforcement process that facilitate user's navigations and interactions with spatial entities embedded in web pages. It takes into account user current navigations to elicit user interests and preferences, and generates personalized results to the user. Markov chains implicitly monitors and records user's trails on the Web, and derives navigational patterns and knowledge in order to predict user's interactions on the web. A reinforcement process complements the approach by adapting the interactions between the user and the web, that is, a sequence of iterative negative/positive rewards evaluated on the basis of user's relevance feedbacks to personalized presentations (Yang & Claramunt, 2005).

We give a simple but illustrative case in the following about the personalization engine takes into account user's current navigations. Let us consider a set of web transactions as presented in Figure 4 (lower). The set of web transactions records user's navigational trails involving seven spatial entities that represent some historical and cultural interests. These entities include A (Kitano Temmangu), B (Nijo), C (Higashi Honnganji), D (Yuzen Textile), E (Arashiyama), F (Costume Museum) and G (Nishijin), represented as a labeled directed graph (the upper of Figure 6). We use a third-order Markov chain to model these transactions, i.e., k=3. Through some appropriate web usage mining processes, the set of user's

Figure 6. Navigation trails and transactions

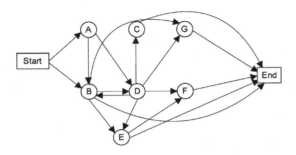

Transactions	Frequency
A, B, D, C	10
B, D, B, E	10
A, B, D, F	8
A, B, D, B	4
A, D, B	8
B, D, B, C	8
B, D, E, F	4
A, B, D,B, G	2

Figure 7. Transaction, frequency and transitional probability for 3-order Markov chains

Transactions			Frenquency	Transitional probability
A,	B,	D --> C	10	5/12
A,	B,	D --> F	8	1/3
A,	B,	D --> B	6	1/4
B,	D,	B --> E	10	5/12
B,	D,	B --> C	8	1/3
B,	D,	B --> G	2	1/12
B,	D,	B --> END	4	1/6
D,	E,	F --> END	8	1.0
B,	D,	E --> F	4	1.0
D,	B,	C --> END	8	1.0
A,	D,	B --> END	8	1.0
B,	D,	F --> END	8	1.0
D,	B,	E --> END	10	1.0
B,	D,	C --> END	10	1.0
D,	B,	G --> END	2	1.0

transactions is transformed to a set of transactions represented as a 3-order Markov chains (Figure 7). The left part of these transactions forms the state space, while the transitional probabilities constitute the transitional probability matrix.

Suppose a specific user is browsing entity D after visiting A and B successively. The web personalization component takes the transaction $A{\rightarrow}B{\rightarrow}D$, and the semantic and spatial criteria into account to predict users next visits. Possible candidate entities are C, F, B, and transitional probabilities from $A{\rightarrow}B{\rightarrow}D$ are 5/12, 1/3, 1/4 respectively. The Markov chain evaluation recommends the spatial entity which is most likely to be "visited", the entity F in the example above (Costume Museum). Personalization results are illustrated in Figure 8. The recommendation reflects the fact that most previous users with similar trails visit entity F, and F has relative strong relationship with previous three entities accessed by the user. Consequently the transitional probability from the sequence <A, B, D> to F, that is, $p(F\,|A,\,B,\,D)$ is positively reinforced if the user follows the personalized result, which shows user's feedback as *satisfied*; otherwise, as an example, if the user goes to visit the entity C, that is, in the case of *unsatisfied* feedback, then $p(F\,|A,\,B,\,D)$ is negatively reinforced and $p(C\,|A,\,B,\,D)$ positively.

Experimental Evaluation

Spatial proximity and similarity measures evaluate the "closeness" of spatial entities either from similar or different categories defined from the terminological ontology illustrated in Figure 3. User interests and preferences are modeled using preference indexes and a conceptual map (Figure 1). For example, Gion appears nearer to the user since it fits her/his interests, and Nijo, on the contrary. This is a result of the way contex-

Figure 8. Navigation on interactive maps

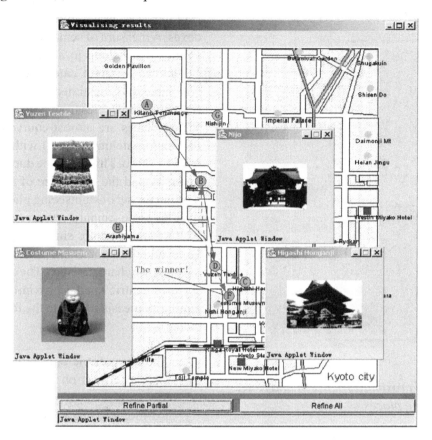

tual knowledge influences perception of spatial proximity measures.

Figure 9 illustrates some spatial proximities between Nijo and other sightseeing places: 9a illustrates the ones from Nijo to the other places, and 9b from the others to Nijo. The charts describe spatial proximities on the original map and those on the user-centric conceptual map. It appears that spatial proximities from Nijo to the other sightseeing places are more sensitive, than from others to Nijo, to user preference patterns. This also remains valid in the case of spatial proximities between the ANA Hotel (the user position) and the sightseeing places (Figure 10). These trends result from the fact that Nijo is nearer to the user location than the others. Comparing Figures 9 and

10, spatial proximities between the ANA Hotel and the sightseeing places are quite different from those between Nijo and the other sightseeing places. This can be explained by the fact that Nijo belongs to the category of Sightseeing places, but the ANA Hotel to a different category.

Semantic interrelationships between classes within hierarchical domain ontology can be used to refine semantic similarity measures. We extract a terminological ontology (Figure 3) from Word-Net. This ontology is mainly defined by the partial function of is-a relations between semantic classes. With the terminological ontology as a support, semantic interrelationships among semantic classes Hotel, Temple, Museum, Garden, Urban are computed using Equation 11 (Table 1),

Figure 9. Spatial proximities between Nijo and other sightseeing places

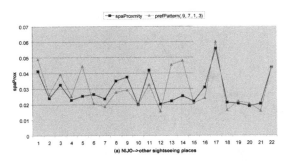

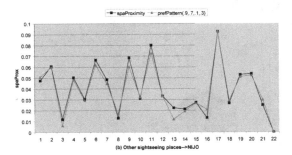

Figure 10. Spatial proximities between Ana Hotel and the sightseeing places

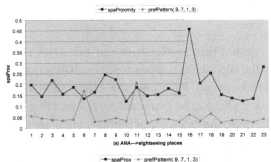

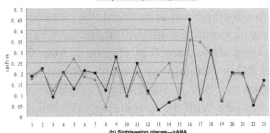

Semantic similarity measures can be specialized into user preferable and non-preferable indexes. A measure of semantic similarity between entities that belong to a same category (Figure 11) and to different categories (Figure 12) are computed and illustrated. Figure 11 shows that semantic similarities from Nijo to the other sightseeing places are almost equivalent (with only four non-matching values) with those from the others to Nijo. This might be due to less semantic diversity and the small size of the data set. Regarding the set of sightseeing places, three places have the same semantic representation as the place NIJO. But, semantic similarities between ANA Hotel and the sightseeing places show explicitly asymmetric characteristics. The experiment made for user-centric spatial proximity and semantic similarity measure leads to the following conclusions:

1. The user-centric conceptual map has substantial effects on spatial proximity measures, especially when spatial entities belong to different categories. It appears that spatial proximities from an entity located nearby a given user location are more sensitive to user preference pattern than distant spatial entities.
2. Spatial proximity and semantic similarity shows less asymmetric characteristics when those belong to same categories, than those of different categories. This illustrates our initial assumptions that category and level of abstraction are two influential factors when evaluating spatial proximity and similarity measures.

CONCLUSION

The research presented in this paper explores the role of semantic similarity and spatial proximity when applied to the development of personaliza-

Table 1. Semantic similarity between semantic classes in a hierarchical structure

	Hotel	Temple	Museum	Garden	Urban
Hotel	1	0.833	0.833	0.048	0.048
Temple	0.833	1	0.833	0.048	0.048
Museum	0.833	0.833	1	0.048	0.048
Garden	0.035	0.035	0.035	1	0.8
Urban	0.035	0.035	0.035	0.8	1

Figure 11. Semantic similarities with prefPattern(0.9, 0.7, 0.1, 0.3) (1)

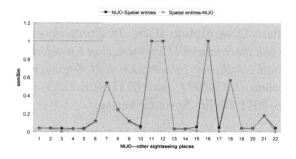

Figure 12. Semantic similarities with prefPattern(0.9, 0.7, 0.1, 0.3) (2)

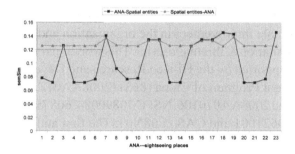

tion techniques related to spatial applications. The spatial proximity measure reflects and models a form of distance that takes into account to a certain degree the way a given user derived a personalized conceptual map on the Web. Similarities between spatial entities materialized in an information space are evaluated with a hierarchical and ontological support, and semantic commonalities and differences. Measures of similarity enrich the model by taking into account the overall structure of a given distribution of spatial entities, user interests and preferences. The semantic component of our approach is based on a terminological taxonomy derived from the WordNet. Similarities and distances in the spatial and thematic dimensions are thus confronted to user's interests and preferences, this providing a user-oriented perspective for these measures. Overall, the objective of these measures is to support the whole modeling approach and to reflect the role of these notions of spatial proximity and similarities in the semantic

and spatial domains. The work is illustrated by a demonstrative prototype applied to the historical city of Kyoto and some experimental results.

The contribution of the research presented in this paper can be summarized as follows. First, it presents a novel approach to the derivation of a conceptual map with user-centric styles where spatial entities are "distortedly" located in a given environment. Second, this approach provides a user-centric similarity measure that takes into account both semantic content and spatial proximity between spatial entities. Third, experimental studies are presented and validate the modeling approach.

This work opens several research perspectives. Alternative forms of measures are still left to further exploration and evaluation. In particular, we plan to extend the ontological component of the framework by enriching the extent of the information space represented, the nature of the relationships taken into account, and considering several levels of abstraction and user categories. Moreover, it's also valuable to extend these approaches to network-based environments and dynamic properties such as transportation and traffic patterns. Further validation and extension of the prototype to other application contexts is also another direction to explore.

ACKNOWLEDGMENT

We are thankful to anonymous reviewers who provided valuable suggestions that led to a considerable improvement in the organization and presentation of this manuscript. This work is partially supported by the Hi-tech Research and Development Program of China (863) (2008AA01Z121) and 2006AA010106, NSFC 70890084, 60875049, 60621001 and CAS 2F08N03. The first author's work is also supported by the Scientific Research Foundation for the Returned Overseas Chinese Scholars (State Education Ministry) and State Key Laboratory of Software Engineering (SKLSE).

REFERENCES

Aleksy, M., Butter, T., & Schader, M. (2008). Architecture for the development of context-sensitive mobile applications. *Mobile Information Systems*, *4*(2), 105–117.

Baeza-Yates, R., & Ribeiro-Neto, B. (1999). *Modern Information Retrieval*. New York: ACM Press.

Ding, J., Gravano, L., & Shivakumar, N. (2000). Computing Geographical Scopes of Web Resources. *VLDB*, 545-556.

Franklin, N., Tversky, B., & Coon, V. (1992). Switching points of view in spatial mental models. *Memory & Cognition*, *20*(5), 507–518.

Gastner, M. T., Shalizi, C. R., & Newman, M. E. J. (2005). Maps and cartograms of the 2004 US presidential election results. *Advances in Complex Systems*, *8*(1), 117–123. doi:10.1142/S0219525905000397

Goh, J., & Taniar, D. (2004a). Mobile Data Mining by Location Dependencies. In *Proceedings of the 5th International Conference on Intelligent Data Engineering and Automated Learning - IDEAL 2004* (LNCS 3177) (pp. 225-231). New York: Springer-Verlag.

Goh, J., & Taniar, D. (2004b). Mining Frequency Pattern from Mobile Users. In *Proceedings of the 8th International Conference on Knowledge-Based Intelligent Information and Engineering Systems, KES 2004, Part III* (LNCS 3215) (pp. 795-801). Berlin: Springer Verlag.

Goh, J., & Taniar, D. (2005). Mining Parallel Patterns from Mobile Users. *International Journal of Business Data Communications and Networking*, *1*(1), 50–76.

Goldstone, R. L., Medin, D. L., & Halberstadt, J. (1997). Similarity in Context. *Memory & Cognition*, *25*, 237–255.

Goldstone, R. L., & Son, J. (2005). Similarity. In K. Holyoak & R. Morrison (Eds.), *Cambridge Handbook of Thinking and Reasoning* (pp. 13-36). Cambridge, UK: Cambridge University Press.

Gravano, L., Hatzivassiloglou, V., & Lichtenstein, R. *Categorizing web queries according to geographical locality* (CIKM 2003) (pp. 325-333).

Harle, R. K., & Hopper, A. (2008). Towards autonomous updating of world models in location-aware spaces. *Personal and Ubiquitous Computing*, *12*(4), 317–330. doi:10.1007/s00779-006-0103-6

Hirtle, S. C., & Jonides, J. (1985). Evidence of Hierarchies in Cognitive Maps. *Memory & Cognition*, *13*(3), 208–217.

Jayaputera, J., & Taniar, D. (2005). Data retrieval for location-dependent queries in a multi-cell wireless environment. *Mobile Information Systems, 1*(2), 91–108.

Klatzky, R. L. (1998). Allocentric and egocentric spatial representations: Definitions, distinctions, and interconnections. In C. Freksa, C. Habel, & K. Wender (Eds.), *Spatial Cognition: An interdisciplinary approach to representing and processing spatial knowledge* (pp. 1-17). Berlin: Springer Verlag.

Kumar, P., Bapi, R. S., & Krishna, P. R. (2007). SeqPAM: a sequence clustering algorithm for Web personalization. *International Journal of Data Warehousing and Mining, 3*(1), 29–53.

Kwon, O., & Shin, M. K. (2008). LACO: A location-aware cooperative query system for securely personalized services. *Expert Systems with Applications: An International Journal, 34*(4), 2966–2975. doi:10.1016/j.eswa.2007.05.022

Lee, K. C. K., Zheng, B., & Lee, W. C. (2008). Ranked Reverse Nearest Neighbor Search. *IEEE Transactions on Knowledge and Data Engineering, 20*(7), 894–910. doi:10.1109/TKDE.2008.36

Lynch, K. (1960). *The Image of the City.* Cambridge, MA: MIT Press.

Mobasher, B., Cooley, R., & Srivastava, J. (2000). Automatic Personalization Based on Web Usage Mining. *Communications of the ACM, 43*(8), 142–151. doi:10.1145/345124.345169

Mountrakis, G., Agouris, P., & Stefanidis, A. (2005). Adaptable User Profiles for Intelligent Geospatial Queries. *Transactions in GIS, 9*(4), 561–583. doi:10.1111/j.1467-9671.2005.00235.x

Roberts, J. S., & Wedell, D. H. (1994). Context effects on similarity judgments of multidimensional stimuli: Inferring the structure of the emotion space. *Journal of Experimental Social Psychology, 30*(1), 1–38. doi:10.1006/jesp.1994.1001

Sjberg, L. (1972). A cognitive theory of similarity. *Gteborg Psychological Reports, 2*(10), 1–23.

Taniar, D., & Goh, J. (2007). On Mining Movement Pattern from Mobile Users. *International Journal of Distributed Sensor Networks, 3*(1), 69–86. doi:10.1080/15501320601069499

Tobler, W. R. (1970). A computer model simulating urban growth in the Detroit Region. *Economic Geography, 46*(2), 234–240. doi:10.2307/143141

Tversky, A. (1977). Features of similarity. *Psychological Review, 84*(4), 327–352. doi:10.1037/0033-295X.84.4.327

Tversky, B. (1993). Cognitive Maps, Cognitive Collages, and Spatial Mental Models. In A.U. Frank & I. Campari (Eds.), In *Proceedings of COSIT'93* (LNCS 716) (pp. 14-24). Berlin, Germany: Springer-Verlag.

Wang, Y., Lim, E. P., & Hwang, S. Y. (2006). Efficient mining of group patterns from user movement data. *Data & Knowledge Engineering, 57*(3), 240–282. doi:10.1016/j.datak.2005.04.006

Wang, Y., Lim, E. P., & Hwang, S. Y. (2008). Efficient algorithms for mining maximal valid groups, *The VLDB Journal — The International Journal on Very Large Data Bases, 17*(3), 515-535.

Worboys, M. (1996). Metrics and topologies for geographic space. In M. J. Kraak & M. Molenaar (Eds.), *Advances in GIS Research II* (pp. 365-375). London: Taylor and Francis.

Worboys, M. F. (2001). Nearness relations in environmental space. *International Journal of Geographical Information Science, 15*(7), 633–651. doi:10.1080/13658810110061162

Xuan, K. G., Taniar, D., & Srinivasan, B. (2008). Continuous Range Search Query Processing in Mobile Navigation. In *Proceedings of the 14th International Conference on Parallel and Distributed Systems (ICPADS 2008)* (pp. 361-368). Washington, DC: IEEE Computer Society.

Yang, Y., & Claramunt, C. (2004, August 23-25). A Flexible Competitive Neural Network for Eliciting User's Preferences in Web Urban Spaces. In P. Fisher (Ed.), *Proceedings of the 11th International Spatial Data Handling Conference* (pp. 41-57). Berlin: Springer-Verlag.

Yang, Y., & Claramunt, C. (2005, December). A hybrid approach for spatial web personalization. In K. J. Li & C. Vangenot (Eds.), *(LNCS 3833)* (pp. 206-221). Berlin: Springer Verlag.

Zhang, J., Manli, Z., Papadias, D., Tao, Y., & Lee, D. (2003). Location-based spatial queries. In *Proceedings of the ACM SIGMOD Conference* (pp. 443-454). New York: ACM.

Zhang, J., Papadias, D., Mouratidis, K., & Zhu, M. (2004). Spatial Queries in the Presence of Obstacles. In *Proceedings of the International Conference on Extending Database Technology (EDBT)* (pp. 366-384).

Zhang, X., Jing, L., Hu, X., Ng, M., Xia, J., & Zhou, X. (2008). Medical Document Clustering Using Ontology Based Term Similarity Measures. *International Journal of Data Warehousing and Mining*, *4*(1), 62–73.

Zhao, G., Xuan, K., Taniar, D., Safar, M., Gavrilova, M. L., & Srinivasan, B. (2009). Multiple Object Types KNN Search Using Network Voronoi Diagram. In *Proceedings of the International Conference on Computational Science and Its Applications - ICCSA 2009 Part II* (LNCS 5593) (pp. 819-834). Berlin: Springer Verlag.

Zhao, G., Xuan, K., Taniar, D., & Srinivasan, B. (2008). Incremental k-Nearest-Neighbor Search on Road Networks. [JOIN]. *Journal of Interconnection Networks*, *9*(4), 455–470. doi:10.1142/S0219265908002382

ENDNOTE

[1] Experiential knowledge is derived from direct navigation experience while survey knowledge reflects geographical properties of the environment.

This work was previously published in International Journal of Data Warehousing and Mining, Volume 6, Issue 2, edited by David Taniar, pp. 59-78, copyright 2010 by IGI Publishing (an imprint of IGI Global).

Chapter 9
Estimating Semi–Parametric Missing Values with Iterative Imputation

Shichao Zhang
Zhejiang Normal University and Zhongshan University, China

ABSTRACT

In this paper, the author designs an efficient method for imputing iteratively missing target values with semi-parametric kernel regression imputation, known as the semi-parametric iterative imputation algorithm (SIIA). While there is little prior knowledge on the datasets, the proposed iterative imputation method, which impute each missing value several times until the algorithms converges in each model, utilize a substantially useful amount of information. Additionally, this information includes occurrences involving missing values as well as capturing the real dataset distribution easier than the parametric or nonparametric imputation techniques. Experimental results show that the author's imputation methods outperform the existing methods in terms of imputation accuracy, in particular in the situation with high missing ratio.

INTRODUCTION

The real data usually are incomplete as some instances may have missing values. In fact, many reasons can result in missing values, for instance, malfunction of equipments, erroneous from human imputation, and so on. Missing values is an unavoidable problem in the real world, and various methods for dealing with such issues have been developed in data mining and in statistics. For example, case deletion, learning with no handling with missing data and missing values imputation.

DOI: 10.4018/978-1-61350-474-1.ch009

Copyright © 2012, IGI Global. Copying or distributing in print or electronic forms without written permission of IGI Global is prohibited.

In real application, the imputation method is a popular strategy comparing to other methods. Missing values imputation is to find an efficient way to "guess" the missing values (imputation) based on other information in datasets. One advantage of this approach is that missing values treatment is independent of the learning algorithm used. That allows users to select the most suitable imputation method for their applications.

Commonly used imputation methods for missing values include parametric regression imputation methods and non-parametric regression imputations. However, there are other relations within real world data, and both parametric imputation method and non-parametric imputation method are not adequate to capture the relations. That is, we know a part of relation between independent variables (condition attributes) and dependent variable (target attribute), e.g., we can regard this relation as parametric model, but we have no knowledge on the relation between other independent variables and dependent variable, e.g., we can take it as nonparametric model. However, combining these two parts, it is difficult for us to consider the compound relation with parametric model or nonparametric model. Moreover, the case is very general in real application. In this paper, we regard the relation containing two models as semi-parametric model or partial parametric model. In real application, semi-parametric model is natural than non-parametric model because users can always know some information but no all on the datasets, such some parameters in the datasets. To model this semi-parametric relation, in this paper, we design an efficient semi-parametric iterative imputation method (SIIA) that takes into account the advantages of parametric models and pure non-parametric models so as to overcome their certain shortcomings for each single model.

In the left parts, we will first review the existing literatures for dealing with missing values. And then we design the iterative imputation methods which can impute missing values with kernel method or even in the dataset with high missing ratio. After that, we will demonstrate our proposed methods with all kinds of experiments. Finally, we will conclusion our works and put forward our future work.

RELATED WORK

There are at least three different ways of dealing with missing data based on Little and Rubin (2002): single imputation, multiple imputation, and iterative procedure.

Single imputation strategies provide a single estimate for each missing data value. Many methods for imputing missing values are single imputation methods, such as, C4.5 algorithm, kNN method, and so on. We can partition single imputation methods into parametric methods and nonparametric ones. The parametric regression imputation methods are superior if a dataset can be adequately modeled parametrically, or if users can correctly specify the parametric forms for the dataset. Non-parametric imputation (Qin et al., 2007) offers a nice alternative if users have no idea on the actual distribution of a dataset because the method can provide superior fits by capturing structure in datasets. While much work focus on modeling data by parametric or nonparametric approaches, in Engle et al. (1986) have studied the semi-parametric model. They model the electricity demand y as the sum of a smooth function g of monthly temperature t, and a linear function of x_1 and x_2, as well as 11 monthly dummy variables $x_3, ..., x_{13}$, to build a semi-parametric model firstly. In fact, semi-parametric model is more ordinary in real application than nonparametric model or parametric model because we always contain a little but no all information on our datasets, however, there are a little literatures, such as, Nikulin (2008), focusing on this issue because of the analysis complexity, in this paper, we introduce SIIA algorithm to model the partial parametric model for filling up iteratively missing target values.

A disadvantage of single imputation strategies is that they tend to artificially reduce the variability of characterizations of the imputed dataset. The alternatives are to fill in the missing values with multiple imputation methods (e.g., Multiple Imputation (MI); Golfarelli & Rizzi, 2009) and iterative imputation methods (EM algorithm). In multivariate analysis, MI methods provide good estimations of the sample standard errors. However, data must be missing at random in order to generate a general-purpose imputation. In contrast, iterative approaches can be better developed for missing data since it can utilize all useful information including the instances with missing values (Pighin & Ieronutti, 2008). That can receive significant performance in the datasets with high missing ratio. The well-known of these methods is the Expectation-Maximization (EM) algorithm for parametric model. Articles (Caruana, 2001; Pighin & Ieronutti, 2008) present an EM-style nonparametric iterative imputation model embedded with kNN algorithm to impute missing attribute values.

In this paper, at first, we impute missing values with general methods (e.g., mean method) in order to utilize substantial all the useful information in the datasets, then we impute each missing values iteratively based on kernel regression imputation method until the algorithm converges. In this process, given part information between independent variables and dependent variable, we present semi-parametric iterative imputation algorithm (SIIA) to deal with missing target values since second imputation. Different from the existing parametric methods and nonparametric methods, the proposed method can be easily applied to real application because we usually have a little supplement knowledge on our datasets. Different from single imputation method and multiple imputation method, our iterative method can utilize substantial all useful information including the information in the instances with missing values for improving imputation performance.

SIIA ALGORITHM

SIIA method imputes each missing value several times until the algorithm converges. In the first iteration, all complete instances are used to estimate missing values. The information in instances with missing values is used from the second iteration. This method is of benefit to capture the distribution of a dataset much better and easier than parametric/nonparametric imputation or existing single imputation methods.

Existing imputation methods usually impute missing values with the instances without missing values, such as, C4.5, kNN algorithm, and so on. Indeed, the information in the instances with missing values can play an important role to estimate missing values. For example, it can be applied to identify the neighbors of an instance with missing values in nearest neighbor (NN) imputation algorithms, or the class of the instance in clustering-based imputation algorithms. On the other hand, the datasets do not enough complete instances to impute missing values even if the datasets contain low missing ratio. For example, the missing ratio in UCI datasets (Blake & Merz, 1998) Bridge only is 5.56% which is a low missing ratio in real application because most datasets in industrial reach to 50% or above. However, there are 38 complete instances in the dataset with 108 instances and 6 class labels. If we impute the missing values with only 38 complete instances with any imputation algorithms, the imputation performance will generate easily bias due to less complete instances because the size in large sample should be beyond 30 in statistics. On the other way, there are 6 classes in this dataset in which the maximal number of complete instances for one class only contains 11 complete instances, the classification accuracy won't be well even if the most excellent classification algorithm is employed. Furthermore, many datasets in UCI present the same case as Bridge. Hence, to utilize the information in the instances with missing values is useful for building our imputation model especially in the case with high missing ratio.

In SIIA, we employ some existing methods which fit for statistical proof (such as, mean/mode method) in the first imputation for all missing values in the dataset. After all missing values have been imputed once; we re-impute all the missing values till the algorithm converges. Since the second imputation, imputation is condition on all available information, that is, if the missing values have been imputed prior to being used as observed values for the other missing values. Generally speaking, we denote missing value as MV_i, $i = 1,...,n$ (n is the number of missing values) corresponding to the imputed missing values denoted as $\hat{MV}_i^j$, $i = 1,...,n$, $j = 1,...,t$ (j is the imputation time), all missing values MV_i are imputed as $\hat{MV}_i^1$ with the first imputation. Since the second imputation, the observed information will include $\hat{MV}_i^{j-1}$, $i = 1,...,k-1$, $k+1,...n$, $j=2,...,t-1$, while we want to impute a missing value $\hat{MV}_k^j$, $k \neq i$, $j=2,...,t$, the imputation process will continue till algorithms reach to approximate convergence. Meanwhile, since the second imputation, we will employ kernel regression method for imputing missing values under nonparametric model or semi-parametric model. The pseudo of algorithm SIIA is presented in Exhibit 1.

IMPUTATION AT FIRST ITERATION

There exist many methods to fill in missing values in the first iteration of imputation including any single imputation methods, such as, C4.5 algorithm, kNN algorithm, and so on. In Qin et al. (2007), the authors compute mean (or the mode if the attribute is categorical) to impute missing values in the first time. They think that the method is a popular and feasible imputation method in data mining and statistics. Meanwhile, they also believe to impute with the mean (or mode) is

valid if and only if the dataset is chosen from a population with a normal distribution. However, in real world application, we cannot know the real distribution of the dataset in advance. So running the extra iterations of imputation to improve imputation performance is reasonable based on the first iteration of imputation for dealing with the missing values. Caruana (2001) thinks the first step, which imputes each missing value with the mean/median values calculated from cases that are not missing that value, will cause cases missing many values to appear to be artificially close to each other. For example, if both cases being compared were missing values for attribute x, the distance along dimension x will be 0 since they will be imputed with the same value. The paper demonstrates this subtlety is not critical for the proper behavior of the method, but does speed convergence on datasets that have many missing values. However, the method in Caruana (2001) is designed to impute missing attribute values rather than missing target values. In our paper, we will employ mean/mode method to impute missing values in the first imputation.

SUCCESSIVE ALGORITHM

In real application, we can know partial relation between condition attributes and target attribute. For example, letting us consider the sales of ice-cream in summer, condition attributes can be weather, sale place, and so on. We could conclude easily that the relation between weather and the sale of ice cream is linear because the sale of ice-cream increases at hotter weather, hence, part condition attribute (such as, weather) is related linear to target attribute and we can explain the relation as parametric model (such as, linear model in this example). However, it is impossible for us to really know the relation between the other factors (such as, sale place, some unthinkable reasons, or the others condition attributes) and the sale of

Exhibit 1. Pseudo of algorithm SIIA

```
//The first iteration of imputation
 FOR each MV_i in Y
```

$\hat{MV}_i^1$ = mode $(S_r$ in Y); // if Y is discrete variable

$\hat{MV}_i^1$ = mean $(S_r$ in Y); // if Y is continuous ones

```
 END FOR
//t-th iteration of imputation (t>1)
t=1;
REPEAT
t++;
  FOR each missing value MV_i in Y
Get β^t based on Equation (7)
 If MV_i is current imputed missing value
```

$MV_i = \hat{MV}_i^t, \; p \in S_m, \; p = 1, \ldots, m, \; p \neq i$ // if Y is continuous variable

$MV_i = \begin{cases} 0 & if \; \hat{MV}_i^t < \chi, \\ 1 & if \; \hat{MV}_i^t < \chi, \end{cases} \; \hat{MV}_i^t, \quad p \in S_m, p=1,\ldots m, p \neq i$ // if Y is discrete variable

```
Else
```

$MV_i = \hat{MV}_i^{t-1}, \; p \in S_m, \; p = 1, \ldots, m, \; p \neq i$ **END FOR**

```
UNTIL //finishing iteration of imputation
```

$\dfrac{M_l}{M_{l+1}} \to 1$, and $\dfrac{V_l}{V_{l+1}} \leq \varepsilon$

```
3.0 //output the imputation iteration times and imputation results
OUTPUT
t; // t is the iterative times
Completed dataset;
```

ice cream but we know they must relate to the sale of ice-cream. Obviously, we can analyze the relation using non-parametric method under the assumption without any knowledge. Given combined these two relations, we can analyze them with single nonparametric mode or parametric model respectively, however, we cannot model the real relation between independent variables and dependent variable no matter that which one strategy is employed. So in this case, it is reasonable for us to build semi-parametric model to deal with this case.

In single semi-parametric imputation method (Nikulin, 2008), a general semi-parametric regression model is as follows:

$$Y_i = X_i^T \beta + g(T_i) \tag{1}$$

Where the Y_i's are i.i.d (independent identically distributed) scalar response variables, the X_i's are i.i.d d-dimensional random covariate vectors (parametric model), the T_i's are i.i.d d*- dimensional random covariate vectors, the function $g(T_i)$ is unknown (nonparametric model) on (Pearson, 2005; Pighin & Ieronutti, 2008; Qin et al., 2007).

In SIIA, for each iterative imputation, the value of β^t will be computed firstly, then compute the value of $g(T_i)$ based on the β^t based on Equation 3, we define:

$$Y_i^t = X_i^{T,t} \beta^t + g(T_i^t) \tag{2}$$

Where $Y_i^t = \begin{cases} Y_i, & \text{if } \delta_i = 0 \text{ or } i = 1, \ldots, r \\ \hat{Y}_i^{t-1}, & \text{if } \delta_i = 1 \text{ or } i = r+1, \ldots, n \end{cases}$

Where t is the number of iterative imputation, β^1 based on the first imputation. From (2), we have:

$$Y_i^t - X_i^{T,t}\beta^t = g(T_i^t). \quad i = 1, \cdots, r$$

Assuming β^t is known in advance, we have a kernel estimator $\hat{g}(T_i^t)$ for $g(T_i^t)$ based on the completely observed data:

$$\hat{g}(T_i^t) = \frac{\sum\limits_{j=1}^{n} \delta_j K(\frac{(T_i^t - T_j^t)}{h})(Y_j^t - X_j^t \beta^t)}{\sum\limits_{j=1}^{n} \delta_j K(\frac{(T_i^t - T_j^t)}{h}) + n^{-2}}. \quad i = 1, \cdots, r \tag{3}$$

Using $\hat{g}(T_i^t)$ to replace $g(T_i)$ in Equation. (3), we obtain:

$$Y_i^t - X_i^{T,t}\beta^t \approx \frac{\sum\limits_{j=1}^{n} \delta_j K(\frac{(T_i^t - T_j^t)}{h})(Y_j^t - X_j^t \beta^t)}{\sum\limits_{j=1}^{n} \delta_j K(\frac{(T_i^t - T_j^t)}{h}) + n^{-2}}, \quad i \in s_r. \tag{4}$$

Converting (4), we have

$$Z_i^t \approx U_i^{T,t}\beta^t, i \in s_r \tag{5}$$

Where

$$Z_i^t = Y_i^t - \frac{\sum\limits_{j=1}^{n} \delta_j Y_j^t K(\frac{(T_i^t - T_j^t)}{h})}{\sum\limits_{j=1}^{n} \delta_j K(\frac{(T_i^t - T_j^t)}{h}) + n^{-2}}, \quad i \in s_r$$

$$U_i^t = X_i - \frac{\sum\limits_{j=1}^{n} \delta_j X_j K(\frac{(T_i^t - T_j^t)}{h}))}{\sum\limits_{j=1}^{n} \delta_j K(\frac{(T_i^t - T_j^t)}{h}) + n^{-2}}, \quad i \in s_r.$$

$$\tag{6}$$

According to the theory of linear regression model, β^t is estimated by Equation (7):

$$\hat{\beta}_n^t = (\sum\limits_{i=1}^{n} \delta_i U_i^t U_i^{T,t})^{-1}(\sum\limits_{i=1}^{n} \delta_i U_i^t Z_i^t). \tag{7}$$

Where n is the sample size. Note that, for simplicity, the transform from Equation 4 to 5, we assume parametric model is linear for estimating the value of β^t, however, in real application, parametric model can be linear model, nonlinear model, and so on.

Combining with (3), the final estimator for $\hat{g}(T_i^t)$ is given by

$$\hat{g}(T_i^t) = \frac{\sum\limits_{j=1}^{n} \delta_j K(\frac{(T_i^t - T_j^t)}{h})(Y_j^t - X_j^t \widehat{\beta}_n^t)}{\sum\limits_{j=1}^{n} \delta_j K(\frac{(T_i^t - T_j^t)}{h}) + n^{-2}}. \tag{8}$$

Hence, in algorithm SIIA, since the second imputation, we use Equation 2 to impute missing target values till the algorithm converges.

In fact, the imputed values based on Equation 2 always is continuous values, and our SIIA algorithm can also impute discrete missing target attribute which is presented in pseudo of SIIA Algorithm 2.0. In our paper, we consider the case with two classes and the reader can extend our method to the case with multiple classes. In SIIA algorithm, instances are defined as belonging to class 0 if $\hat{MV}_i^t < \chi$, and class 1 otherwise. The actual value of the class for each incomplete instance x_i is denoted by MC_{x_i}. The new class assignment based on the imputed class is denoted by $\hat{MC}_{x_i}^t$ in t-th imputation to stress the dependence of the classification on. More specifically, the imputed value $\hat{m}_t(x) \in R$ is transformed into a (binary) class $MC_{x_i}^t \in \{0, 1\} \; \forall x_i \in D$ based on the rule specified in SIIA algorithm. χ is specified by the user of the technique and in many applications is set so that

$$| \{x_i \mid MC_{x_i}^t = 1\} | = | \{x_i \mid \hat{MC}_{x_i}^t = 1\} |$$

(i.e., the number of class 1 instances before and after the application of our technique is the same). This rule for class assignment is the most natural choice and is the one primarily considered in our case studies, although the user of the technique may explore different choices near this preferred cutoff point. Hence, our proposed algorithm SIIA can also be used to impute discrete missing target values.

Finally, we can output the final imputation result after algorithm converged. Note that, the imputation times is (t+1) rather than (t+2) times even if the procedure is performed (t+1) times and the first iteration is added. That is because the last imputation does not generate imputation result and only judge the fact whether the imputation reaches to convergence.

ALGORITHM CONVERGENCE AND COMPLEXITY

An important practical issue concerning iterative imputation method is to determine at which point additional iterations have no meaningful effect on

the imputed values, i.e., how to judge the convergence of the algorithm. Literatures Caruana (2001) and Pearson (2005) conclude that the average distance that the missing attribute values move in successive iterations drops to zero, that no missing values have changed and that the method has converged in nonparametric model. Here, we outline a strategy for the stopping criterion for our algorithms. With t imputation times, assuming mean and variance of three successive imputations are M_l, M_{l+1}, M_{l+2}, and $V_l, V_{l+1}, V_{l+2}, (1<l<t-2)$ respectively. If

$$\frac{M_l}{M_{l+1}} \to 1 \text{ , and } \frac{V_l}{V_{l+1}} \leq \varepsilon$$

That can be inferred that there is little change in imputations between the last and the former imputation, and the algorithm can be stopped for imputing without substantial impact on the resulting inferences. Different from the converged condition in existing algorithms, we summarize our stopping strategy using terminology such as 'satisfying a convergence diagnostic' rather than 'achieving convergence' to clarify that convergence is an elusive concept with iterative imputation.

While the complexity of the kernel method is $O(mn^2)$, where n is the number of instances of the dataset, m is the number of attributes, so the algorithm complexity of both NIIA and SIIA is $O(kmn^2)$ (k is the number of iteration times).

EXPERIMENTAL ANALYSIS

In order to show the effectiveness of the proposed methods, extensive experiments are done on real dataset with VC++ programming by using a DELL Workstation PWS650 with 2G main memory, 2.6G CPU, and WINDOWS 2000. We compare the performance of SIIA with the existing methods in Nikulin (2008), parametric method as well as nonparametric method.

At first, we design different algorithms to impute target missing values, such as, our proposed algorithm SIIA, we also design three single imputation methods (stochastic semi-parametric imputation method for single imputation in Nikulin (2008), Semi for shorted, nonparametric imputation method in Qin et al. (2007) and Qin, Zhang, and Zhang (2010), Non for shorted, linear imputation method, Linear for shorted). We use RMSE to assess the predictive ability after the algorithm has converged for iterative imputation methods or the missing values are imputed for single imputation methods:

$$RMSE = \sqrt{\frac{1}{m}\sum_{i=1}^{m}(e_i - \tilde{e}_i)^2}$$

Where e_i is the original attribute value; $\tilde{e}_i$ is the estimated attribute value, and m is the total number of predictions. The larger the value of the RMSE, the less accurate is the prediction.

We use the dataset in http://lib.stat.cmu.edu/DASL/Datafiles/USTemperatures.html to analyze the advantages of SIIA algorithm. The data give the normal average January minimum temperature in degrees Fahrenheit (Denoted as *JanTemp*) with the latitude (*Lat*) and longitude (*Long*) of 56 U.S. cities for each year from 1931 to 1960. Qin et al. in Nikulin (2008) presents there is an evident linear relationship between *JanTemp* and *Lat*, but the linear relationship between *JanTemp* and *Long* is not clearly. To apply our method to these real data, we denote the variables for *JanTemp*, *Lat* and *Long* to be Y, X and T respectively in the semi-parametric model. We suppose that Y, X and T satisfy the semi-parametric model. Because there exists linear relation as well nonparametric relation between independent variables and dependent variable in the real dataset, it is reasonable for us to design these algorithms to verify the advantages

of our proposed algorithm in our experiments. On the other hand, there exist little real dataset containing partial relation between independent variables and dependent variable, the experiment only utilizes one dataset for imputing continuous missing target attribute in this paper.

Note that the original data set is complete. We used all the 56 data and delete randomly 6, 14 or 23 Y values (Missing Rate is almost 10%, 20% or 40% respectively) and the repeated times are 1000.

Figures 1, 2 and 3 present the values of RMSE for our algorithm SIIA and single imputation method Linear, Non, and Semi at different missing ratio 10%, 20% and 40% respectively.

These results show SIIA can converge in semi-parametric model at any missing ratio. The higher missing ration, the more imputation times the algorithm SIIA is.

Comparing SIIA method with single imputation methods, in the first several imputation, the imputation results of SIIA are worse than single imputation methods at different missing ratio, for example, the results of RMSE in the first three times corresponding to algorithm Non, and the

Figure 1. Missing rate is at 10%

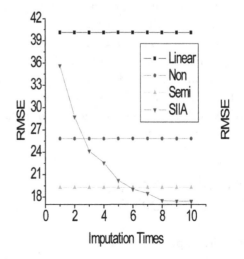

Figure 2. Missing rate is at 20%

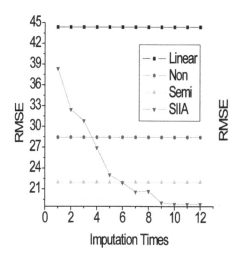

Figure 3. Missing rate is at 30%

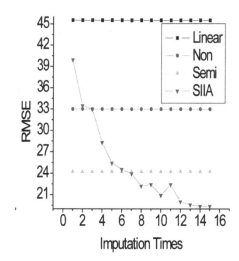

imputation times in the first 6 times, 6 times, and 7 times corresponding to algorithm Semi at missing ratio 10%, 20% and 40% respectively are better than SIIA. Since then, our method outperform single imputation methods, in particularly, in the high missing ratio case (such as, 40%), our method presents significant profit than single imputation methods. Moreover, in each imputation time, the performance of our proposed method outperforms the result of parametric method (such as, linear algorithm). At the same time, both semi-parametric single imputation and nonparametric method are better than parametric method. That presents, parametric model can not present good imputation performance if there is no priori knowledge or a little information on the datasets. To our surprised, there is a variation in Figure 3, that is, the RMSE of SIIA in 9th /11th imputation is worse than the result in 8th /10th one. The experimental results have a little fluctuate is because there are only 56 instances in the dataset. However, in left iterative imputations, the result of successive imputation will be better than the former one. That assures the algorithm converges. That shows our algorithm SIIA can tune the imputation performance because the situation does not occur again until algorithm converges.

CONCLUSION AND FUTURE WORK

In this paper, for dealing with missing values with high missing ratio, we present an iterative imputation method (SIIA) for imputing missing target values. That is, SIIA algorithm can deal with the case in which we have a little knowledge with our datasets by building semi-parametric model with kernel regression method to impute iterative missing target values. Experimental results show our methods outperform than the existing single imputation method in term of RMSE at different missing ratio in different cases. In our future work, we will focus on the study how to more effective estimate the value of β^t in semi-parametric model.

ACKNOWLEDGMENT

This work was supported in part by the Australian Research Council (ARC) under grant DP0985456, the Nature Science Foundation (NSF) of China under grant 90718020, the MOE Project of Key Research Institute of Humanities and Social Sciences at Universities (07JJD720044), the Guangxi NSF (Key) grants, and the Guangxi Colleges and Universities' Innovation Teams.

REFERENCES

Blake, C., & Merz, C. (1998). *UCI Repository of machine learning databases.*

Caruana, R. (2001, January). A Non-parametric EM-style algorithm for Imputing Missing Value. *Artificial Intelligence and Statistics.*

Engle, R. F. (1986). Semi-parametric Estimates of the relation between weather and electricity sales. *Journal of the American Statistical Association, 81*(394). doi:10.2307/2289218

Golfarelli, M., & Rizzi, S. (2009). A survey on temporal data warehousing. *International Journal of Data Warehousing and Mining, 5*(1), 1–17. doi:10.4018/jdwm.2009010101

Little, R., & Rubin, D. (2002). *Statistical Analysis with Missing Data* (2nd ed.). New York: John Wiley and Sons.

Nikulin, V. (2008). Classification of imbalanced data with random sets and mean-variance filtering. *International Journal of Data Warehousing and Mining, 4*(2), 63–78. doi:10.4018/jdwm.2008040108

Pearson, P. K. (2005). *Mining imperfect data: dealing with contamination and incomplete records.* SIAM.

Pighin, M., & Ieronutti, L. (2008). A methodology supporting the design and evaluating the final quality of data warehouses. *International Journal of Data Warehousing and Mining, 4*(3), 15–34. doi:10.4018/jdwm.2008070102

Qin, Y. S. (2007). Semi-parametric optimization for missing data imputation. *Applied Intelligence, 27*(1), 79–88. doi:10.1007/s10489-006-0032-0

Qin, Y. S., Zhang, S. C., & Zhang, C. Q. (2010). Combining kNN Imputation and Bootstrap Calibrated Empirical Likelihood for Incomplete Data Analysis. [DWM]. *International Journal of Data Warehousing and Mining, 6*(2).

Wang, Q., & Rao, J. N. K. (2002). Empirical likelihood-based inference under imputation for missing response data. *Annals of Statistics, 30,* 896–924. doi:10.1214/aos/1028674845

Yu, D., Shao, S., & Luo, B. (2009). A hybrid method for high-utility itemsets mining in large high-dimensional data. *International Journal of Data Warehousing and Mining, 5,* 57–73. doi:10.4018/jdwm.2009010104

Zhang, C. Q., et al. (2007). Efficient Imputation Method for Missing Values. In *Proceedings of PAKDD 2007* (LNAI 4426, pp. 1080-1087).

Zhang, S. C. (2008). Parimputation: From imputation and null-imputation to partially imputation. *IEEE Intelligent Informatics Bulletin, 9*(1), 32–38.

Zhang, S. C. (2010). *Shell-Neighbor Method And Its Application in Missing Data Imputation.* Applied Intelligence.

Zhang, S. C. (2009). POP Algorithm: Kernel-Based Imputation to Treat Missing Values in Knowledge Discovery from Databases. *Expert Systems with Applications, 36,* 2794–2804. doi:10.1016/j.eswa.2008.01.059

This work was previously published in International Journal of Data Warehousing and Mining, Volume 6, Issue 3, edited by David Taniar, pp. 1-11, copyright 2010 by IGI Publishing (an imprint of IGI Global).

Chapter 10

Exploring Disease Association from the NHANES Data:
Data Mining, Pattern Summarization, and Visual Analytics

Zhengzheng Xing
Simon Fraser University, Canada

Jian Pei
Simon Fraser University, Canada

ABSTRACT

Finding associations among different diseases is an important task in medical data mining. The NHANES data is a valuable source in exploring disease associations. However, existing studies analyzing the NHANES data focus on using statistical techniques to test a small number of hypotheses. This NHANES data has not been systematically explored for mining disease association patterns. In this regard, this paper proposes a direct disease pattern mining method and an interactive disease pattern mining method to explore the NHANES data. The results on the latest NHANES data demonstrate that these methods can mine meaningful disease associations consistent with the existing knowledge and literatures. Furthermore, this study provides summarization of the data set via a disease influence graph and a disease hierarchical tree.

INTRODUCTION

The National Health and Nutrition Examination Survey (NHANES) is a nationwide survey conducted by the National Center for Health Statistics and some other health agencies since 1971 (CDC,

n.d.). It aims at providing nationally representative information on the health and nutritional status of the population and tracking changes over time.

NHANES data has been used to evaluate the prevalence and risk factors of diseases in the population and to provide health guidelines. The prevalence of a disease is the percentage

DOI: 10.4018/978-1-61350-474-1.ch010

Copyright © 2012, IGI Global. Copying or distributing in print or electronic forms without written permission of IGI Global is prohibited.

of population having the disease. For example, in Beuther (2007) and Saydah et al. (2007), the NHANES data is used to study the prevalence of obesity and chronic kidney diseases over time and in different demographics groups (e.g., age, ethnicity and gender). A risk factor of a disease is a characteristic, condition or behavior that increases a person's chance of developing the disease. The NHANES data has been used to verify the hypotheses of risk factors of chronic kidney (Saydah et al., 2007), obesity (Gangwisch et al., 2005), congestive heart failure (He et al., 2001) and some other diseases. The analysis results from the NHANES data have been used in the development of health related guidelines and public policies. For example, the early NHANES data revealed that the blood levels of lead among Americans were too high. The findings led to the federal regulations on reducing the amount of lead in gasoline, paint and soldered cans (Pirkle et al., 1998).

The NAHNES data contains a questionnaire component in which selected people are interviewed for their medical conditions and disease histories. It is a valuable data source for discovering disease associations among dozens of diseases. Disease associations can provide useful information in disease prevention, diagnosis and treatment.

There are some studies on evaluating correlated diseases by using statistical methods (He et al., 2001; Manjunath et al., 2003; Spence et al., 2003). The statistical methods focus on evaluating a number of pre-defined hypotheses of a set of risk factors or some associated diseases with respect to a particular disease. In contrast to the statistical methods, data mining methods aim at discovering the knowledge of associated diseases among a large number of diseases without any hypotheses. However, to the best of our knowledge, the NHANES data has not been systematically explored for mining associations among extensive diseases.

Is mining disease association patterns straightforward? One may think that association rule mining or association pattern mining (Agrawal et al., 2003) can provide an immediate solution. In an association rule about diseases $A \Rightarrow B$, where A and B are two diseases, the probability that disease A appears in the population is called the *support* of the rule, and the probability that disease B appears in the condition of disease A appearing is called the *confidence* of the rule. Some other correlation measurements such as *lift* (Han et al., 2006), *all-confidence* (Omiecinski et al., 2003) and *cosine* (Han et al., 2006; Tan et al., 2002) are also proposed.

Since the number of people with diseases is usually much smaller than the number of healthy people, to mine association patterns of diseases, the support threshold often has to be set very low. Furthermore, diseases are very complex mechanisms. Different sub-types of a disease or people with different health conditions may have very different disease association patterns. Therefore, disease association patterns usually are not very strong. Consequently, a low confidence threshold has to be used in order to find many meaningful disease association patterns. Many other interestingness measures on association rules also meet some difficulties. For example, the lift for the patterns on high prevalence diseases is very different from the lift for patterns on low prevalence diseases.

Due to the complexity and diversity in disease association patterns, it is very difficult for a user to choose an appropriate threshold for a quality measure in the mining. If a user picks a low threshold in order to avoid missing some interesting patterns, the user may often be overwhelmed by a large number of rules and patterns which are hard to be analyzed and used.

To make disease association pattern mining practical and useful for health industry users, two problems need to be solved. First, to help users to understand the results, summarization of patterns and mining results should be provided. Second, a user should be able to interactively explore patterns interesting to the user.

In this paper, we tackle the problem of mining disease association patterns in the context of mining NHANES data. We develop a disease association pattern mining tool and present a detailed case study. The tool is publicly available at http://www.cs.sfu.ca/~zxing/personal/. We make the following contributions.

First, we give a direct pattern mining method to mine disease patterns and discuss the selection of measurements to rank the patterns. We propose a novel *disease influence graph* to summarize the top correlated patterns. The graph visualizes interactions among diseases and prevalence of diseases in the population.

Second, we develop an interactive disease pattern mining method by hierarchical clustering. It clusters the population based on disease similarities and generates candidate disease association patterns. It also comes with a cluster visualization module. The hierarchical clustering structure groups related disease patterns together. The interactive disease pattern mining method enables users to browse the hierarchical clustering structure and interactively explore interesting sub-trees for the related disease association patterns. The hierarchical clustering structure also provides interesting insights on the relationships among diseases and disease sub-groups/sub-types.

Third, we present a detailed case study on the latest NHANES data, which demonstrates that our methods can mine meaningful disease association patterns consistent with existing knowledge and literatures.

The rest of the paper is organized as follows. In the second section of, the direct pattern mining method is presented. In the third section, the interactive pattern mining method is described. An empirical study of the NHANES data is reported in the fourth section. The Fifth section reviews the related work. The paper is concluded in the last section.

DIRECT PATTERN MINING

The NHANES data contains four components, namely demographic data, examination data, laboratory data and questionnaire data. The demographic component contains information such as age, gender and ethnic group. The disease status data is contained in the questionnaire component. To find disease association patterns, we use the demographic component and the questionnaire. The details of data preprocessing and feature selection will be described in the Section of Experiments.

After the preprocessing of the raw data set, the population in the survey is presented as a relational table T. Each tuple in the table represents a person. Each column represents a disease. Using diseases as features, a person t is represented as a tuple $t = \langle t_1, t_2, ..., t_n \rangle$, where $t_i = 1$ if t had or has disease d_i, $t_i = 2$ if t never has the disease, and $t_i = 0$ if whether the person t has that disease is unknown.

To mine disease patterns, we do not consider patterns involving disease absence. A disease association pattern $D = \langle d_{i1}, d_{i2}, ..., d_{im} \rangle$ represents that diseases $d_{i1}, d_{i2}, ..., d_{im}$ occur together.

To evaluate a disease association pattern, we consider two aspects. One is the prevalence of the pattern in the population, and one is the correlations among diseases in the pattern.

Given a population T of size N, the prevalence of a pattern $D = \langle d_{i1}, d_{i2}, ..., d_{im} \rangle$, denoted by $P(\langle d_{i1}, d_{i2}, ..., d_{im} \rangle)$ is the percentage of people who have all the diseases in. Formally, we have $P(\langle d_{i1}, d_{i2}, ..., d_{im} \rangle) = |\{t \in T | t_{i1} = 1, t_{i2} = 1, ..., t_{im} = 1\}| / N$.

To evaluate the correlation among diseases in a disease association pattern, we need to choose a proper measurement. In Tan et al. (2002), they compared 21 interestingness measures for association patterns, including support, confidence, odds ratio, lift, cosine, mutual information and some others. The comparison shows that no single measurement is consistently better than the others in all application domains.

The number of people with diseases is much smaller than the number of healthy people.

Moreover, we consider disease co-presence more important than co-absence. Therefore, the disease data is sparse. Han et al. (2006) and Tan et al. (2002) suggest that the correlation measurements with the *null-invariance property* are suitable for applications with sparse data. In our application setting, a correlation measure is *null-invariant* means for a disease pattern D, that the value of the correlation measure is not affected by the number of people who do not have diseases in pattern D.

For example, measure *cosine* is null-invariant and measurement *lift* is not. The measurement cosine and lift (Han et al., 2006; Tan et al., 2002) for a disease pattern of two diseases are defined as follow,

$$cosine(<A,B>)= \frac{P\left(<A,B>\right)}{\sqrt{P\left(<A>\right)P\left(<B>\right)}}$$

$$lift(<A,B>)= \frac{P(<A,B>)}{P\left(<A>\right)P(<B>)}$$

Given a population, suppose disease A has prevalence 0.03, disease B has prevalence 0.02, and a pattern $<A, B>$ has prevalence 0.01. We have $cosine(<A,B>)= \frac{P(<A,B>)}{\sqrt{P\left(<A>\right)P(<B>)}} =$ 0.408 and $lift(<A,B>)= \frac{P(<A,B>)}{P\left(<A>\right)P(<B>)} =$ 16.67. Suppose we remove 90% of the population that do not have diseases A or B from consideration. Then, the prevalence of disease A increases to 0.3 and that of disease B becomes 0.2. The prevalence of pattern $<A, B>$ is upgraded to 0.1. We have $cosine(<A,B>)= \frac{(P(<A',B'>))}{\sqrt{P\left(<A'>\right)P(<B'>)}}$ =0.408, remained unchanged. This elaborates that cosine is null-invariant. On the other hand,

$$lift(<A,B>)= \frac{P(<A',B'>)}{P\left(<A'>\right)P(<B'>)} = 1.67. \text{ Thus,}$$

lift is not null-invariant.

As shown in this example, a measure which is not null-invariant may give a higher score to patterns involving low prevalent diseases. If a user picks the top-k patterns, those patterns may mainly involve diseases with low prevalence.

Two null-invariant correlation measures, cosine and Jaccard distance, are discussed in (Tan et al., 2002). However, they are not effective in guiding disease association pattern mining since they are only applicable to patterns involving two diseases. Therefore, we want to find a null-invariant correlation measure that can handle multiple diseases in a pattern.

One possible measure in the literature is all-confidence (Omiecinski, 2003). A disease association pattern D can induce a set $R(D)$ of $x^m - 2$ association rules in the form of $X \Rightarrow (D - X)$ such that $X \subset D$. The *all-confidence* of D is the lowest confidence among all the rules $r \in R(D)$.

Although all-confidence can measure the overall affiliation among all the diseases in a disease pattern, it captures the weakest correlation. For example, suppose we have a disease pattern $<A, B>$ where A is rare with prevalence 0.03, B is common with prevalence 0.3. If all people having A also have B, then $P(<A,B>) = 0.03$. Pattern $<A,B>$ induces two rules, $A \Rightarrow B$ with confidence 1 and $B \Rightarrow A$ with confidence 0.1. The all-confidence of pattern $<A,B>$ is 0.1. If a user sets the minimum all-confidence threshold to 0.4, the pattern, though interesting in disease association, is missed. In general, all-confidence may assign a low score to patterns involving the association between high prevalent diseases and low prevalent ones.

To serve our disease association pattern mining, we define a new null-invariant correlation measure. For a disease association pattern D, the *any-cosine* is the highest cosine score among all the rules induced by D. That is,

Figure 1. The disease influence graph of people of age at least 20

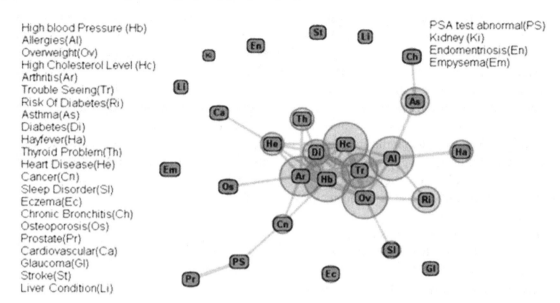

High blood Pressure (Hb)
Allergies(Al)
Overweight(Ov)
High Cholesterol Level (Hc)
Arthritis(Ar)
Trouble Seeing(Tr)
Risk Of Diabetes(Ri)
Asthma(As)
Diabetes(Di)
Hayfever(Ha)
Thyroid Problem(Th)
Heart Disease(He)
Cancer(Cn)
Sleep Disorder(Sl)
Eczema(Ec)
Chronic Bronchitis(Ch)
Osteoporosis(Os)
Prostate(Pr)
Cardiovascular(Ca)
Glaucoma(Gl)
Stroke(St)
Liver Condition(Li)

PSA test abnormal(PS)
Kidney (Ki)
Endomentriosis(En)
Empysema(Em)

$$any\text{–}cosine(D) = \max_{x \subset D} \left\{ cosine \left(X \Rightarrow \left(D - X \right) \right) \right\}$$

$$cosine \left(X \Rightarrow \left(D - X \right) \right) = \frac{P(D)}{\sqrt{P\left(X\right)P(D-X)}} .$$

Easily, we can show that *Any-cosine is a null-invariant correlation measure.*

Any-cosine captures the most interesting rule induced from *D*. We will compare the effectiveness of all-confidence and any-cosine in the experiments.

In our direct pattern mining, we use Apriori (Agrawal et al., 1993) to find all patterns passing a minimum prevalence threshold. Then, we rank those patterns by a correlation measure.

There may be many patterns passing the minimum support threshold. As discussed before, summarization of patterns is highly desirable. We summarize the top ranked patterns by a *disease influence graph.*

Figure 1 shows an example of the nodes in the graph being the diseases, and the size of each node is proportional to the prevalence of the corresponding disease. Two diseases are linked by an edge if they appear in a pattern. The thickness of the edge is proportional to the correlation score of the pattern. If two diseases appear in multiple top-ranked patterns, the thickness of the edge between them takes the highest correlation score in those patterns.

The visualization in a disease influence graph is intuitive. A disease influence graph provides an overview of the prevalence and the interactions among the diseases in a population. Moreover, in a disease influence graph, the hubs and the dense connected areas can be viewed as the influential diseases in association patterns. We will discuss more details in the Section of Experiments.

INTERACTIVE PATTERN MINING

More often than not, a user may only be interested in the disease patterns involving some certain diseases. For example, a clinical specialist may only be interested in the patterns involving diabetes. Can we provide an effective way to let the user interactively browse the disease patterns according to his/her own interests? In this section, we propose an interactive disease pattern mining method based on agglomerative hierarchical clustering (Murtagh, 1983).

Disease associations are sophisticated. People having different subtypes of a disease or people in different health conditions may have different disease co-occurrences. This motivates us to cluster people based on the similarity of their disease patterns. Intuitively, people in a cluster share some common diseases, such as a cluster of people with a kidney disease or a cluster of people with a heart disease.

There are many different clustering methods, such as partitioning based clustering and hierarchical clustering. In disease association pattern analysis, it is highly desirable to organize disease associations in a hierarchical structure. For example, people having diabetes form a big cluster. Among those people, some may only have diabetes, and the others may have diabetes and some other complications. Therefore, we employ hierarchical clustering instead of partitioning based clustering.

Clustering is useful beyond pattern exploration. A cluster can be used to generate hypotheses of disease associations by summarizing its semantic meaning. For example, if we find a cluster of people with the characteristics of high blood pressure and high blood cholesterol level, a hypothesis of disease associations, < High blood pressure, High blood cholesterol > can be generated.

Figure 2 demonstrates our interactive disease pattern mining system. Starting from the whole hierarchical clustering structure of the population, a user can click on a sub-cluster. The detailed distribution of the diseases in the selected sub-cluster will be visualized. Moreover, using the dominating diseases in the sub-cluster, a hypothesis disease association pattern is generated. If the user is interested in such a pattern, he/she can further test the pattern against the whole population using various statistical measures. The analysis can be conducted recursively in the hierarchical structure.

In order to obtain interesting clustering structures, a proper similarity measure between people is important. Recall that we represent a person p as a disease vector $<d_{i1},d_{i2},...,d_n>$, where $d_i = 1$ if p had or has disease d_i, $d_i = 2$ if p never has the disease, and $d_i = 0$ if whether the person has that disease is unknown. Given two persons $p_x=<d_{x1},d_{x2},...,d_{xn}>$ and $p_y=<d_{y1},d_{y2},...,d_{yn}>$ where $d_{x1},d_{x2},...,d_{xn}$ and $d_{y1},d_{y2},...,d_{yn}$ are the disease variable values of p_x and p_y, respectively, we define the similarity between disease values as

$$Sim\left(d_{xi},d_{yi}\right) = \begin{cases} 0 \text{ } if \text{ } d_{xi} \neq d_{yi} \text{ } and \text{ } d_{xi},d_{yi} \neq 0 \\ 1 \text{ } if \text{ } d_{xi} \neq d_{yi} \text{ } and \text{ } d_{xi},d_{yi} \neq 0 \\ 2 \text{ } if \text{ } d_{xi} = d_{yi} = 1 \end{cases}$$

Moreover, we define the similarity between p_x and p_y on the diseases known to them as

$$Sim1\left(d_{xi},d_{yi}\right) = \frac{\sum_{1 \leq i \leq n, d_{xi},d_{yi} \neq 0} sim(d_{xi},d_{yi})}{|\{i \mid d_{xi} \neq 0 \wedge d_{yi} \neq 0\}|}$$

$Sim1(p_x,p_y)$ is the normalized sum of weighted similarities on all diseases whose values are not missing. We use the sum of weighted similarities because we consider two persons more similar if they share some common diseases rather than they both do not have some diseases.

The NHANES survey data contains a significant amount of missing data. The questions on diseases are presented to different age groups. Some diseases are specific for some age groups. For example, disease Glaucoma is only applicable to people over 40 years old. For people under 40 years, the data on this disease is missing. Furthermore, even if a person is interviewed for the status of a certain disease, the data may still be missing since the person may refuse or cannot answer the interview question. In order to handle missing data, in $Sim1()$, the sum of weighted similarities

Figure 2. The interactive disease pattern mining system

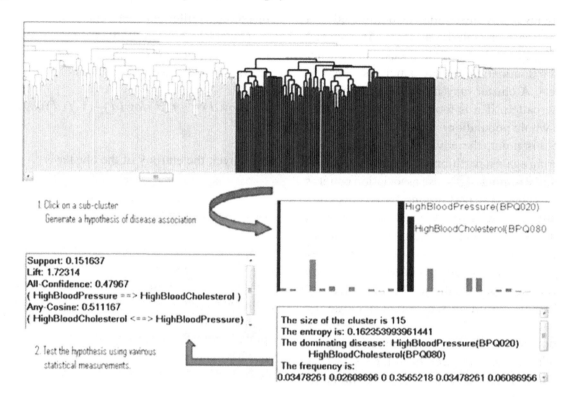

is normalized by the number of diseases without missing values.

The normalization may cause a bias of similarity on people with more missing data. In order to reduce the bias, we design $Sim2(p_x, p_y)$, which is defined as the similarity between p_x and p_y on the diseases common to them that is,

$$Sim2(p_x, p_y) = \frac{|\{i \mid d_{xi} = 1 \wedge d_{yi} = 1\}|}{n}$$

The distance between p_x and p_y is the combination of $Sim1()$ and $Sim2()$, which is defined as follow,

$$Dist(p_x, p_y) = \left(2 - Sim1(p_x, p_y)\right) + \left(1 - Sim2(p_x, p_y)\right).$$

The range of $Dis(p_x, p_y)$ is between 0 to 3. The smaller the distance is, the more similar the two persons are.

Hierarchical clustering builds a hierarchical clustering tree of clusters. We use the average pairwise distance of two clusters as the inter-cluster distance, since the average distance is more robust to noise data comparing to single link hierarchical clustering (Murtagh, 1983).

We visualize a cluster by a bar chart, which plots the prevalence of the diseases in the cluster. A cluster is summarized by its dominating disease pattern. A disease is a *dominating disease* of a cluster if the prevalence of the disease in the cluster passes a threshold. In this paper, we consider a disease in a cluster dominating if its prevalence in the cluster is higher than 75%. A *dominating disease pattern* is composed of all dominating diseases in the cluster. For example, in Figure 2, the dominating disease pattern of the picked cluster is < High blood pressure, High blood cholesterol level>. A cluster may be dominated by a single disease or multiple diseases. As a special case, if the prevalence of all diseases in a cluster is 0, the dominating disease pattern is <healthy people>. A cluster may not have a dominating disease pattern if it is too big, such as a cluster of the whole population.

At this point, the advantage of hierarchical clustering against partitioning based clustering in interactive mining of disease association patterns becomes clear. The partitioning-based clustering methods, such as k-mean, need the number of clusters as a parameter. Setting the number of clusters improperly may produce a messy clustering result. Hierarchical clustering does not require a user to specify the number of clusters. By summarizing the clusters, hierarchical clustering automatically provides a natural partitioning of the population. When a user browses down the hierarchical clustering tree from the root, at the top levels, the clusters may not have dominating disease patterns. The descendant clusters closest to the root which have dominating disease patterns form a natural partitioning of the population. We call those clusters the *natural clusters*. Importantly, in a natural cluster, most of the dominating disease patterns contained in its sub-clusters are the extended patterns of the dominating disease pattern in the natural cluster. When browsing the hierarchical clustering tree by clicking the sub-trees, a user can view how the related dominating disease patterns change in a hierarchical structure.

A user may also be interested in extracting all dominating disease patterns in a hierarchical cluster tree. We can output all patterns by recursively traversing the hierarchical cluster tree from the root. We use two parameters, a size threshold and an entropy threshold of a cluster, as the stopping conditions for the recursive traversing to select only significant dominating disease patterns.

A very small cluster is statistically insignificant. The dominating disease patterns extracted from such small clusters are not interesting in statistical analysis. Therefore, we can use a size threshold to filter out small clusters.

Consider a cluster C with m diseases, denoted by $Fre(C)=<f(d_1),f(d_2),...,f(d_m)>$. We define the entropy of a disease $d_i(1\leq i\leq m)$ as

$$Entropy(d_i) = -f(d_i) \, log \, (d_i) -(1-f(d_i))log(1-f(d_i))$$

Moreover, the entropy of the cluster is

$$Entropy(C) = \frac{\sum_{i=1}^{m} Entropy(d_i)}{m}$$

The entropy of a cluster measures how coherent the cluster is in terms of the disease pattern. The smaller the entropy is, the more coherent the cluster is. For examples, if in a cluster every disease has prevalence 0.5, the entropy is 1. The cluster does not have a dominating disease pattern and need to be further divided. In another cluster, if all the people do not have any disease, i.e., the cluster contains only healthy people, or all people share the exactly same disease(s), the entropy is 0. Using an entropy threshold, if a cluster is already very coherent, we do not further visit its sub-clusters.

Our interactive pattern mining tools is publicly available at http://cs.sfu.ca/~zxing/personal/. The tool is developed in C# using Microsoft Visual Studio 2005. As shown in Figure 1, the graphic user interface (GUI) contains the following functions.

1. Displaying the complete hierarchical clustering dendrogram;
2. Enabling clickable sub-clusters;
3. Visualizing the disease dominating pattern in a sub-cluster when the sub-cluster is clicked;
4. Computing the statistical measurements of a disease dominating pattern.

The graphic user interface is independent of particular hierarchical clustering methods. The GUI displays a dendrogram by taking an input file which represents the structure of a dendrogram. The GUI can easily be adopted for any applications which need the functions of dynamically exploring sub-clusters in a dendrogram and summarizing the dominating features in sub-clusters.

EXPERIMENTS

In this paper, we use the NHANES data of year 2005-2006. The data set contains in total 10,348 people. In the questionnaire component, interviewees are asked about the histories on a collection of diseases, such as allergies, cardiovascular diseases, kidney diseases, and diabetes. The disease statuses are obtained from the self reported answers in the following questions, "Has a doctor or other health professional ever told you/SP (for spouse) that you have/s/he/SP have... ?". We include the disease statuses obtained by the above questions. In total, the questionnaire covers 26 disease statuses/medical conditions. Some diseases such as heart disease are combined from several subtypes of appearing in the raw data such as congestive heart failure and coronary heart disease. We do not include any diseases about emotional health such as depression. The questions on diseases are presented to different age groups. For people of age 40 and older, all the 26 diseases are interviewed.

To people of age between 20 and 40, 23 diseases are presented. To people younger than 20, only 9 diseases are presented.

In this report, we analyze the data on the people of age 20 and older. There are in total 4,979 people in this age group.

The Result of Direct Pattern Mining

The direct data mining method obtains 1, 639 disease association patterns by setting the minimal support threshold to 0.5%.

To compare the effectiveness of various correlation measures, Table 1 lists the top-10 patterns in three measures, all-confidence, any-cosine and any-lift. For a disease pattern, Any-lift is the highest lift among all the rules induced from the patterns using all the item. From Table 1, we can see that the top-10 patterns ranked by all-confidence are similar to the top-10 patterns ranked by any-cosine: 7 out of the 10 patterns are in common, as highlighted in the table. Any-lift only finds one pattern common with the top-10 patterns in all-confidence and any-cosine. Each of the top 10 patterns in any-lift involves at least one disease of low prevalence, such as chronic bronchitis and kidney diseases. As analyzed in the Section of Background, this is because lift is not null-invariant.

Table 1. Top-10 patterns by various measures

All-con-fidence	*<High BP., High BC.>*	*<Over-weight, High BP.>*	*<Arthri-tis, High BP.>*	*<PSA, Pros-tate>*	*<Over-weight, High BC.>*	*<Ar-thritis, High BC.>*	*<Over-weight, Allergies>*	*<Over-weight, Arthri-tis>*	*<High BP., Allergies>*	*<High BC., Al-lergie>*
Any-cosine	*<PSA, Pros-tate>*	*<High BP., High BC.>*	*<Arthri-tis, High BP.>*	*<Over-weight, High BP.>*	*<Hay fever, Al-lergies>*	*<Over-weight, High BC.>*	*<Arthritis, High BC.>*	*<Over-weight, Arthri-tis>*	*<Asthma, Allergies>*	*<Arthri-tis, High BP., High BC.>*
Any-lift	*<PSA, Pros-tate>*	*<Em-physema, Chronic Bronchi-tis>*	*<Cancer, PSA, Prostate>*	*<Can-cer, PSA>*	*<Heart Disease, Diabetes, Kidney >*	*<Heart Disease, Stroke>*	*<Heart Disease, Cardiovas-cular>*	*<Heart Disease, Stroke, Diabe-tes>*	*<Heart Disease, Em-physema>*	*<Stroke, Cardio-vascu-lar>*
Rank	1	2	3	4	5	6	7	8	9	10

Among all the patterns in the top 10 lists in all-confidence and any-cosine, <*Arthritis, High BP., High BC.*> is the only long pattern involving 3 diseases which is ranked high by any-cosine, but low by all-confidence. By examining the ranked lists in any-cosine and all-confidence, we find that the major difference between the two measures is that any-cosine ranks some long patterns high, while all-confidence always ranks short patterns high. For example, among the top 50 patterns ranked by any-confidence, there are only 7 long patterns and there are 12 long patterns in the top-50 list of any-confidence. This clearly shows that any-cosine can promote long patterns which induce interesting rules, while all-confidence cannot.

The top-ranked disease association patterns in Table 1 can be well explained by the existing medical knowledge. For example, pattern < *High BP., High BC.* > is consistent with the well known fact that high blood pressure and high blood cholesterol level have a high chance to happen together. Pattern < *Arthritis, High BP.* > is supported by (Biomedical.Org, n.d.; Forman et al., 2007), which showed that some pain reliever drugs used frequently by people of arthritis increase the risk of high blood pressure. Pattern < *Arthritis, Overweight* > is consistent with the finding in (Gill et al., 2005), which showed that overweight and obesity are strongly related to arthritis.

In addition to viewing the top patterns one by one, a user may also see an overall picture of the disease interactions on the population. In Figure 1 (the graphics is generated by the TouchGraph Navigator package http://www.touchgraph.com/navigator.html), the top 50 patterns ranked by any-cosine are visualized using a disease influence graph defined in Section 2. From the graph we can see that Hb (High blood pressure), Al (Allergies), Ov (Overweight), Hc (High blood cholesterol), Ar (Arthritis), Tr (Trouble seeing even with glasses) are the top six high prevalent diseases, and they influence each other intensively by forming a clique in the graph. There are another 8 diseases which are directly connected with the clique through one or multiple edges. In other words, those diseases are 1 edge away from the clique. For example, Di (Diabetes) interacts with live diseases in the clique except for Al (Allergies). He (Heart disease) is linked with Di (Diabetes), Hb (High blood pressure), Ar (Arthritis), and Hc (High blood cholesterol) in the clique. There are several branches extending from the clique. For example, there is a branch of As (asthma) and Ch (Chronic bronchitis), which is a branch of allergy related diseases. There is also a branch of Cn (Cancer), Pr (Prostate diseases) and Ps (PSA test abnormal), which can be regarded as a cancer branch. Some diseases, such as Li (Liver condition) and Ki (Kidney diseases), are isolated in the graph. From this example, we can see that the disease influence graph provides an overview of the prevalence of diseases and their interactions measured by any-cosine.

The Result of Interactive Pattern Mining

Our interactive pattern mining method generates 23 natural clusters. In 22 of them, each is dominated by a single disease. The remaining natural cluster contains 905 healthy people who do not have histories on any diseases. There are in total 908 healthy people in the data set. 3 of them are merged into other clusters due to some missing data. This clearly shows that the hierarchical clustering method can naturally identify groups of people sharing similar disease patterns.

The largest natural cluster contains 1,392 people and is dominated by disease high blood pressure. The second largest cluster is the one of 905 healthy people.

Some diseases such as asthma do not dominate a natural cluster. The people with asthma are mainly within the cluster of high blood pressure and the cluster of allergies.

The sub-clusters as descendants of a natural cluster lead to disease dominating patterns closely related to the pattern of the natural cluster. For example, within the natural cluster of high blood pressure, the three biggest sub-clusters dominated by two diseases are the sub-cluster dominated by *<Overweight, High BP. >*, the sub-cluster dominated by *<High BP., High BC.>*, and the sub-cluster dominated by *<Arthritis, High BP.>*. The hierarchical clustering tree groups related disease association patterns together, and helps a user to browse the tree according to her interests.

Figure 3 shows more examples of interesting sub-clusters. Among those examples, some disease association patterns in the clusters are consistent with the existing medical knowledge or literatures. For example, the cluster dominated by pattern *< Arthritis, Allergies >* is supported by (Panush et al., 1990) that some cases of arthritis are triggered by food allergies. Moreover, a cluster of people dominated by overweight and sleep disorder verifies the association between sleeping disorder and overweight reported in (Gangwisch et al., 2001).

Furthermore, some disease patterns captured by the clusters reveal new findings. In Figure 3, we list four clusters with dominating disease patterns of <TroubleSeeing(MCQ140), LiverCondition(MCQ160L)>, <Arthritis(MCQ160A), HighBloodCholesterol(BPQ080)>, <TroubleSeeing(MCQ140), Arthritis(MCQ160A)> and <Cancer(MCQ220), HighBloodCholesterol(BPQ080)>. To the best of our awareness, those patterns are not well discussed by existing medical literatures. Interestingly, by searching those patterns on the internet, we found the associations of diseases in those patterns have already attracted attentions by people. For example, on an online discussion board (http://www.healthcentral.com/rheumatoid-arthritis/c/question/54342/29748), people asked "can RA(rheumatoid arthritis) cause high cholesterol? " On a MSN online discussion board (http://health.msn.com/health-topics/pain-management/arthritis/articlepage.aspx?cp-documentid=100200060), people asked "Are

there vision disorders associated with rheumatoid arthritis?" Those new findings from NHANES data invite further investigation and verifications.

The hierarchical clustering tree conveys interesting information about disease sub-groups and disease subtypes. For example, Figure 4 shows the sub-tree rooted at the natural cluster dominated by diabetes. The dominating diseases of some sub-clusters are tagged for easy understanding. The whole nature cluster, cluster 1, is composed of two sub-clusters, cluster 2 and cluster 3. Cluster 2 is dominated by heart disease and diabetes, while cluster 3 is dominated by diabetes.

Cluster 2 is furthered divided into clusters 4 and 5. Cluster 4 is dominated by heart disease, diabetes and stroke. This hierarchical cluster sub-tree suggests that many people with diabetes may also have heart disease. Among the people with diabetes and heart disease, stroke may appear. An article at the National Diabetes Information Clearinghouse website (NDIC, n.d.) suggests "people with diabetes are at least twice as likely as someone who does not have diabetes to have heart disease or a stroke".

In cluster 3, a part of people form sub-cluster 7, which is dominated by diabetes, overweight and thyroid problem. The other people in cluster 3 form cluster 7, which is a diabetes cluster. Further dividing cluster 6, we can get cluster 8 and cluster 9. For cluster 9, the dominating diseases are diabetes and vision problem. It is confirmed by (Klein et al., 1995), "diabetes is the leading cause of new cases of blindness in people age 20-74 years in the United States".

Diabetes and its treatments may cause many complications. The above hierarchical clustering sub-tree provides an insight on the sub-groups of patients with diabetes according to different situations of complications.

Comparisons

In addition to browsing the hierarchical clustering tree, our method can also output all disease

Figure 3. Examples of sub-clusters

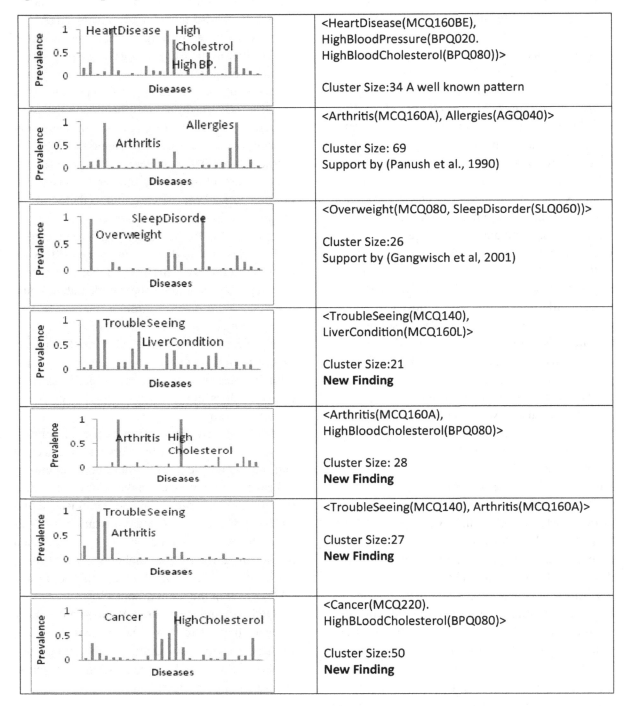

HeartDisease, High Cholestrol, High BP. (prevalence chart)	<HeartDisease(MCQ160BE), HighBloodPressure(BPQ020. HighBloodCholesterol(BPQ080))> Cluster Size:34 A well known pattern
Arthritis, Allergies (prevalence chart)	<Arthritis(MCQ160A), Allergies(AGQ040)> Cluster Size: 69 Support by (Panush et al., 1990)
SleepDisorde, Overweight (prevalence chart)	<Overweight(MCQ080, SleepDisorder(SLQ060))> Cluster Size:26 Support by (Gangwisch et al, 2001)
TroubleSeeing, LiverCondition (prevalence chart)	<TroubleSeeing(MCQ140), LiverCondition(MCQ160L)> Cluster Size:21 **New Finding**
Arthritis, High Cholesterol (prevalence chart)	<Arthritis(MCQ160A), HighBloodCholesterol(BPQ080)> Cluster Size: 28 **New Finding**
TroubleSeeing, Arthritis (prevalence chart)	<TroubleSeeing(MCQ140), Arthritis(MCQ160A)> Cluster Size:27 **New Finding**
Cancer, HighCholesterol (prevalence chart)	<Cancer(MCQ220). HighBLoodCholesterol(BPQ080)> Cluster Size:50 **New Finding**

Figure 4. The hierarchical structure of diabetes clusters

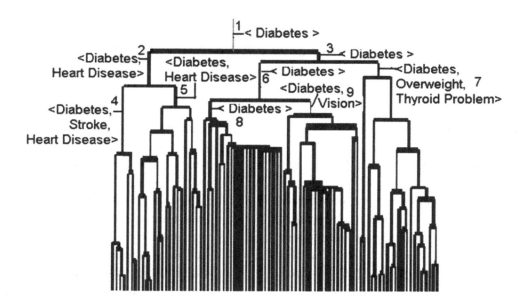

association patterns by setting a minimum size threshold and a minimum entropy threshold. When setting the minimum size threshold to 5 (i.e., a cluster should contain at least 5 people) and the minimum entropy threshold to 0.01 (i.e., we do not visit sub-clusters of a cluster of entropy less than 0.01), our method outputs 432 disease dominating patterns.

Can those patterns obtained from the hierarchical clustering tree cover the strong correlation patterns found by the direct mining methods? Table 2 makes a comparison. In the table, the value 10 in the cell of the row named "Support" and the column named "1~ 10" indicates that among the top 10 patterns ranked by measure support in the direct mining method, all of them are contained in the set of patterns generated by the hierarchical clustering tree. The other cells in the table can be explained similarly.

The top 10 patterns ranked by support, any-cosine and all-confidence are all among the patterns generated by the hierarchical clustering tree. 68 patterns of the top 70 in support can be generated by the hierarchical clustering tree, which can be translated into a recall of 97%. 63 of the top

70 patterns in any-cosine can be generated by the hierarchical clustering tree, that is, a recall of 90%. Among the top 70 patterns in all-confidence, 59 can be generated by the hierarchical clustering tree. The recall is 84.3%.

The number of patterns generated by the hierarchical clustering tree is smaller than the number of patterns generated by the direct mining method, however, a large percentage of the top patterns ranked in support, any-cosine and all-confidence can be generated by the hierarchical clustering tree.

For some highly ranked patterns which are not among the patterns generated by the hierarchical clustering tree, the descendants of those missing patterns can usually be found in the tree. For example, pattern D =<*Heart disease, Arthritis*> is ranked the 17-th in any-cosine. No cluster can be found in the hierarchical clustering tree having D as the dominating pattern. However, we find two clusters in the hierarchical clustering tree having dominating patterns < *Heart disease, Arthritis, High BP.* > and <*Heart disease, Arthritis, Diabetes* >, respectively. Those descendant patterns can be used to generate hypotheses about the associations between heart disease and arthritis.

Table 2. Comparison of the direct pattern mining and the interactive pattern mining method

Ranks	1~10	11~20	21~30	31~40	41~50	51~60	61~70
Support	10	10	10	10	9	10	9
Any-cos.	10	9	9	8	9	9	9
All-confi.	10	10	9	6	7	9	8

RELATED WORK

NHANES data has been used to find associated diseases using statistical methods. For example, by using statistical measurement population attributable risk, He et al. (2001) showed that diabetes and overweighting are two independent risk factors for congestive heart. By using the Chi-square test, Manjunath et al. (2003) showed that the level of kidney function is associated with atherosclerotic cardiovascular disease. Spence et al. (2003) studied the association between arthritis and high blood pressure.

Comparing to statistical methods, our data mining methods have the following advantages.

1. The existing statistical methods on analyzing the NHANES data mainly focus on testing a small number of hypotheses of disease associations or risk factors of diseases. While data mining methods aims to mine many disease patterns among dozens of diseases.
2. As we discussed above, different statistical methods are used to evaluate different pre-defined disease patterns. There is a lack of comparisons by using one measurement to evaluate the disease patterns on a given population. Our data mining methods enable the users to compare many disease patterns based on one population by ranking the patterns using a particular correlation measurement.
3. Although statistical methods are good at evaluating a particular disease pattern, they often have difficulties to provide an overview of the disease interactions on a population. Our disease influence graph can provide

a summarization and visualization of the overall structure of disease interaction on a population. If we have several different populations, such as people among different age ranges, we can easily compare the disease interactions structures in different population by using disease influence graph.
4. As shown before, our interactive disease pattern mining system can discover the hierarchical structure of diseases. The statistical methods cannot easily achieve that.

In summary, statistical methods focus on evaluating a particular disease pattern. Data mining methods are good at systematically generating many hypotheses of disease patterns, and providing different kinds of visualizations, comparisons and summarizations over the disease patterns. In our data mining system, we used several correlation measurements to evaluate disease patterns, such as all-confidence, all-cosine. Our system can also incorporate other statistical measurements to enhance our analysis.

Recently, some data mining methods have been applied to analyze the NHANES data. Walton et al. (2008) applied decision trees and linear regression to classify people into different categories of health conditions (e.g., excellent, fair or bad). Lee et al. (2008) used decision trees and association rules to find dependence among the laboratory and health condition variables in the latest NHANS data. Different from this study, the major findings in Lee et al. (2008) are on the dependence between the diet behaviors or medical conditions and disease absence. In this paper, we focus on the association among diseases.

Our direct pattern mining method uses null-invariant measures to rank disease patterns and summarize the top ranked patterns by a disease influence graph. The principles on choosing suitable measures to mine interesting patterns for different application domains are discussed in Tan et al. (2002). A method of mining risk patterns in medical data measured by relative risk is proposed in Li et al. (2005). Some methods of summarizing frequent patterns are proposed in Jin et al. (2008) and Yan et al. (2005).

In the interactively pattern mining method, hierarchical clustering is used. In bioinformatics, hierarchical clustering has been used in interactively exploring gene expression patterns, such as Saldanha et al. (2004) and Jiang et al. (2003).

DISCUSSIONS

In this paper, we tackled the problem of mining disease associations. We proposed the direct pattern mining method and the interactively pattern mining method. We applied the proposed methods on NHANES data. Our findings are consistent with the existing medical knowledge and literatures. In addition, interesting summarizations through a hierarchical disease tree and a disease influence graph provide insights into the relationships among diseases. Carrying the success on analyzing the NHANES data, our methods can be applied to analyze other data about disease association as well. We already made our software available for public use. In the future, we plan to enhance our mining tool through more statistical analysis and better visualization.

ACKNOWLEDGMENT

This work is based on a substantial extension of the author's winning entry in the 2008 American Medical Informatics Association (AMIA) Data Mining Competition: Discover Knowledge in NHANES data, sponsored by AMIA Knowledge Discovery and Data Mining Working Group. We would like to thank the organizers of the competition and the judge panelists for their suggestions. Although this winning entry was orally presented in an invited panel in the 2008 AMIA Annual Symposium, it is not published in any formats.

REFERENCES

Agrawal, R., Imielinsk, T., & Swami, A. (1993). Mining association rules between sets of items in large databases. In *Proceedings of the 1993 ACM SIGMOD international conference on management of data* (pp. 207-216). New York: ACM Press.

Beuther, D. A., & Sutherland, E. R. (2007). Overweight, obesity, and incident asthma, a meta-analysis of prospective epidemiologic studies. *American Journal of Respiratory and Critical Care Medicine, 175*(7), 661–666. doi:10.1164/rccm.200611-1717OC

Biomedical.Org. (n.d.). *Common pain relievers associated with high blood pressure.* Retrieved April 29, 2009, from http://news.bio-medicine.org/medicine-news-3/Use-of-common-pain-relievers-associated-with-increased-risk-of-blood-pressure-in-men-1642-1/

CDC. (n.d.). *National health and nutrition examination survey.* Retrieved April 29, 2009, from http://www. cdc.gov/nchs/nhanes.htm

Chen, C. S., Roberton, D., & Hammerton, M. E. (2004). Juvenile arthritis-associated uveitis: visual outcomes and prognosis. *Canadian Journal of Ophthalmology, 39*(6), 614–620.

Forman, J. P., Rimm, E. B., & Curhan, G. C. (2007). Frequency of analgesic use and risk of hypertension among men. *Archives of Internal Medicine, 167*(4), 394–399. doi:10.1001/archinte.167.4.394

Gangwisch, J. E., Malaspina, D., Boden-Albala, B., & Heymsfield, S. B. (2005). Inadequate sleep as risk factor for obesity: Analysis of the NHANES I. *Sleep, 28*(10), 1289–1296.

Gill, T., Taylor, A., Chittleborough, C., Grant, J., & Leach, G. (2002). *Overweight and obesity as risk factors for arthritis* (Tech. Rep.). Australia: The South Australian Monitoring and Surveillance System (SAMSS), Population Research and Outcome Studies Unit.

Han, J., & Kamber, M. (2006). From association analysis to correlation analysis. In *Data Mining: Concepts and Techniques* (pp. 261–264). San Francisco, CA: Morgan Kaufmann.

He, J., Ogden, L. G., Bazzano, L. A., Vupputuri, S., Loria, C., & Whelton, P. K. (2001). Risk factors for congestive heart failure in US men and women. *Archives of Internal Medicine, 161*(7), 996–1002. doi:10.1001/archinte.161.7.996

Jiang, D., Pei, J., & Zhang, A. (2003). Interactive exploration of coherent patterns in time-series gene expression data. In *Proceedings of the ninth ACM SIGKDD international conference on knowledge discovery and data mining (KDD'03)*, Washington, DC (pp. 565-570).

Jin, R., Abu-Ata, M., Xiang, Y., & Ruan, N. (2008). Effective and efficient itemset pattern summarization: regression-based approaches. In *Proceedings of the 14th ACM SIGKDD international conference on knowledge discovery in data mining (KDD '08)*, Las Vegas, NV (pp. 399-407).

Klein, R., & Klein, E. K. (1995). *Diabetes in America* (2nd ed., Chapter 14). Retrieved April 29, 2009, from http://diabetes.hiddk.nih.gov/dm/pubs/America/index.htm

Lee, J., Lin, Y., & Smith, M. (2008). *Dependency mining on the 2005-06 national health and nutrition examination survey data*. Paper presented in *American Medical Informatics Association 2008 annual symposium, knowledge discovery and data mining working group data mining competition*, Washington, DC.

Li, J., Fu, A., He, H., Chen, J., Jin, H., McAullay, D., et al. (2005). Mining risk patterns in medical data. In *Proceedings of the eleventh ACM SIGKDD international conference on Knowledge discovery in data mining*, Chicago (pp. 770-775).

Manjunath, G., Tighiouart, H., Ibrahim, H., MacLeod, B., Salem, D. N., & Griffith, J. L. (2003). Level of kidney function as a risk factor for atherosclerotic cardiovascular outcomes in the community. *Journal of the American College of Cardiology, 41*(1), 47–55. doi:10.1016/S0735-1097(02)02663-3

Murtagh, F. (1983). A survey of recent advances in hierarchical clustering algorithms. *The Computer Journal, 26*(4), 354–359.

Must, A., Spadano, J., Coakley, E. H., Field, A. E., Colditz, G., & Dietz, W. H. (1999). The disease burden associated with overweight and obesity. *Journal of the American Medical Informatics Association, 282*, 1523–1529.

Omiecinski, E. R. (2003). Alternative interest measures for mining associations in databases. *IEEE Transactions on Knowledge and Data Engineering, 15*(1), 57–69. doi:10.1109/TKDE.2003.1161582

Panush, R. S. (1990). Food induced ("allergic") arthritis: clinical and serologic studies. *The Journal of Rheumatology, 17*(3), 291–294.

Pirkle, J. L., Kaufmann, R. B., Hickman, D. J., Gunter, T. E. W., & Paschal, D. C. (1998). Exposure of the U.S. population to lead, 1991-1994. *Environmental Health Perspectives, 106*, 745–750. doi:10.2307/3434264

Saldanha, A. J. (2004). Java treeview-extensible visualization of microarray data. *Bioinformatics (Oxford, England)*, *20*(17), 3246–3248. doi:10.1093/bioinformatics/bth349

Saydah, S., Eberhardt, M., Rios-Burrows, N., Williams, D., & Geiss, L. (2007). Prevalence of chronic kidney disease and associated risk factors -United States, 1999-2004. *Journal of the American Medical Informatics Association*, *297*, 1767–1768.

Spence, J. D. (2003). Systolic blood pressure in patients with osteoarthritis and rheumatoid arthritis. *The Journal of Rheumatology*, *30*(4), 714–719.

Tan, P. N., Kumar, V., & Srivastava, J. (2002). Selecting the right interestingness measure for association patterns. In *Proceedings of the eighth ACM SIGKDD international conference on Knowledge discovery and data mining*, Edmond, Canada (pp. 32-41).

The National Diabetes Information Clearinghouse (NDIC). (n.d.). Retrieved April 29, 2009, from http://diabetes.niddk.nih.gov/dm/pubs/stroke/

Walton, N., Knight, S., Newman, M., & Poynton, M. R. (2008). *Predictions of self-reported health status using data mining techniques*. Paper presented at the American Medical Informatics Association 2008 annual symposium, knowledge discovery and data mining working group data mining competition, Washington, DC.

Yan, X., Cheng, H., Han, J., & Xin, D. (2005). Summarizing itemset patterns: a profile-based approach. In *Proceedings of the eleventh ACM SIGKDD international conference on knowledge discovery in data mining*, Chicago (pp. 314-323).

This work was previously published in International Journal of Data Warehousing and Mining, Volume 6, Issue 3, edited by David Taniar, pp. 12-28, copyright 2010 by IGI Publishing (an imprint of IGI Global).

Chapter 11
Classification of Peer-to-Peer Traffic Using a Two-Stage Window-Based Classifier with Fast Decision Tree and IP Layer Attributes

Bijan Raahemi
University of Ottawa, Canada

Ali Mumtaz
University of Ottawa, Canada

ABSTRACT

This paper presents a new approach using data mining techniques, and in particular a two-stage architecture, for classification of Peer-to-Peer (P2P) traffic in IP networks where in the first stage the traffic is filtered using standard port numbers and layer 4 port matching to label well-known P2P and NonP2P traffic. The labeled traffic produced in the first stage is used to train a Fast Decision Tree (FDT) classifier with high accuracy. The Unknown traffic is then applied to the FDT model which classifies the traffic into P2P and NonP2P with high accuracy. The two-stage architecture not only classifies well-known P2P applications, but also classifies applications that use random or non-standard port numbers and cannot be classified otherwise. The authors captured the internet traffic at a gateway router, performed pre-processing on the data, selected the most significant attributes, and prepared a training data set to which the new algorithm was applied. Finally, the authors built several models using a combination of various attribute sets for different ratios of P2P to NonP2P traffic in the training data.

DOI: 10.4018/978-1-61350-474-1.ch011

Copyright © 2012, IGI Global. Copying or distributing in print or electronic forms without written permission of IGI Global is prohibited.

1. INTRODUCTION

Peer-to-Peer(P2P) is a type of Internet application that allows a group of users to communicate with each other, directly access and download files from the peers' machine, and share computing resources (i.e., building a distributed computing environment). P2P traffic and its characteristics have changed the original assumptions under which the data networks were designed. P2P traffic is more symmetric (contrary to the assumption on which Asymmetric Digital Subscriber Line (ADSL) was designed); P2P traffic is less "bursty" which makes it difficult to take advantage of statistical multiplexing (under which the original data networks were designed). Also, P2P traffic lasts longer than typical web or email traffic, and packet lengths are mostly large, which keeps the queues in intermediate switches and routers more utilized, and consume more bandwidth and processing resources in the network devices. Various issues of traffic models associated with traffic in wireless networks are discussed in Doci et al. (2008) and Rohm et al. (2009).

Classification of Internet traffic is a fundamental requirement in areas such as network provisioning, network security, traffic engineering, and network management. Many efforts are made to classify the internet traffic for various applications including classification of P2P traffic by Internet Service Providers (ISPs) and corporate networks. P2P applications bypass central server control implemented by service providers and poses threats in terms of network congestion, and creating an environment for malicious attacks on networks. P2P applications may use randomly selected non-standard ports to communicate and consumes network resources (Shield, 2007). The volume and patterns of P2P traffic put pressure on service providers' networks in terms of congestion and business models. For example, maintaining Quality of Services (QoS) planned in the access network requires the provisioning of additional bandwidth sooner than expected.

One key challenge in this area is to adapt to the dynamic nature of Internet traffic. With the growth in Internet traffic, in terms of number and type of applications, traditional classification techniques such as port matching, protocol decoding or packet payload analysis are no longer effective. For instance, P2P applications may use randomly selected non-standard ports to communicate which makes it difficult to distinguish them from other types of traffic by inspecting only port numbers. As such, several data mining techniques are proposed to classify the internet traffic based on its statistical characteristics such as packet length, packet inter-arrival time, session duration, and source and destination IP addresses. These include both offline (for static data) and online (for stream data) data mining techniques. Stream data mining represents an important class of data-intensive applications where data flows dynamically in large volumes, often demanding fast and real-time responses. Many of the established data mining algorithms perform well on static data. However, unlike data processing techniques for stored datasets, methods for analyzing stream data require fast, memory efficient and computationally inexpensive algorithms producing results concurrent with the flow of the stream with acceptable accuracy.

Further efforts have been made to develop techniques utilizing window-based algorithms. In this paper, we present a widow-based approach to capture and classify internet traffic using a two-stage classifier with fast decision tree. We captured Internet traffic at various time intervals, preprocessed the data, and selected the most significant attributes for classification which include IP packet length, source IP address and destination IP address. We ran several experiments using different attribute sets and various ratios of P2P and NonP2P traffic and measured the performance of the classifier. The results demonstrated that we can classify the traffic with accuracy higher than 90%.

The rest of the paper is organized as follows. Section 2 gives an overview of research related to classification problems. Section 3 presents our proposed two stage window-based classifier. In this section, we also discuss our approach in attribute selection. Section 4 presents analyses of experimental results, and finally, section 5 concludes the paper.

2. RELATED WORKS

Classification of P2P traffic has gained much attention in both academic and industrial research communities, and various solutions have been developed for P2P traffic classification. A popular approach is the TCP port based analysis where tools such as Netflow (Cisco, 2006) and cflowd (Crovella et al., 2006) are configured to read the service port numbers in the TCP/UDP packet headers, and compare them with the known (default) port numbers of the P2P applications. The packets are then classified as P2P if a match occurs. Although P2P applications have default port numbers, newer versions allow the user to change the port numbers, or choose a random port number within a specified range. Hence, port-based analysis becomes inefficient and misleading.

Recently, researchers have considered the behavioral and statistical characteristics of the internet traffic to classify P2P applications. In Zander et al. (2005) a framework is proposed for IP traffic classification based on a flow's statistical properties using an unsupervised machine learning (ML) technique. In this approach, the authors first classified packets into flows according to IP (Src, Des) addresses, port numbers and protocol. Then they used the attributes: packet inter-arrival time, packet length mean and variance, flow size, and duration to build the ML classifier model using the autoclass classification system (Cheeseman et al., 1996).

Zuev and Moore (2005) proposed a supervised machine learning approach to classify network traffic. They started by allocating flows of traffic to one of several predefined categories: Bulk, DataBase, Interactive, Mail, WWW, P2P, Service,

Attack, Games and Multimedia. They then utilized 248 per-flow discriminators (characteristics) to build their model using Naive Bayes analysis.

Domingos and Hulten (2000) utilized Very Fast Decision Tree (VFDT) to mine the continuous web access data from the University of Washington main campus. VFDT is a decision tree learning system that utilizes Hoeffding trees. Accuracy achieved by applying VFDT was 72.7%. In 2001, VFDT-based mining was improved by extending it with Concept-Adapting Very Fast Decision Tree Learner (CVFDT) (Hulten et al., 2001). It contributed by addressing the issue of continuously changing data streams. While the initial research phase was focused on overcoming memory, time and computation issues, further efforts focused on selecting the best algorithm to apply on the stream data.

The training dataset may easily become imbalanced, meaning that the number of records in P2P class differs significantly from the number of records in NonP2P class. In Nikulin (2008) the author presents classification of imbalanced data with random sets and mean-variance filtering. The paper also introduces ensemble classifiers are learning algorithms that construct a set of several individual classifiers and combine them to classify test data points by sample average.

Oveissian et al. (2004) proposed a model based on applications of statistical inference techniques for identifying classes as well as deciding the likelihood that a particular flow belongs to a specific class. In Xu et al. (2005) an effort was done to profile Internet backbone traffic based on behavior models and applications. The concept of sliding window was adopted by Aggarwal et al. (2006) in their classification model (Aggarwal et al., 2006). In Chang and Lee (2005), the est-win method is proposed based on sliding windows. This method eliminates historical data packets and replaces it with new data items. A new method using application signatures was developed by Sen et al. (2004), noting the fact that P2P applications have a unique string (signature) located in the data portion of the packet (payload).

Other classification techniques are also discussed in the literature, including techniques based on fuzzy logic (Khabbaz et al., 2008), multi-label classification (Tsoumakas et al., 2007), and robust classification based on correlations between attributes (Nanopoulos, 2007).

3. TWO-STAGE CLASSIFIER WITH FAST DECISION TREE (FDT)

We present a two-stage architecture to classify P2P and NonP2P traffic. Relying on statistical analysis, data mining algorithms can determine the common characteristics of P2P traffic generated by different P2P applications. We apply the FDT classification technique to the Internet traffic captured at the campus gateway at the University of Ottawa. For this, we first clean the data, label, and prepare it for the modeling phase. In the first stage, traffic is filtered using well-known standard port numbers (layer 4 port matching). Here, based on the standard port numbers, the traffic is labeled as P2P, NonP2P, or Unknown. Then, the second stage is to build a classification model based on the labeled traffic produced in the first stage. In the second stage, the classifier is built using the Fast Decision Tree (FDT) algorithm. Fast Decision Tree (Witten & Frank, 2005) builds a decision tree using information gain/variance and prunes it using reduced-error pruning (with back fitting). It sorts values for numeric attributes once and missing values are dealt with by splitting the corresponding instances into pieces. It generates a confusion matrix as an output and a model is evaluated based on True Positive, True Negative, False Positive and False Negative rates. The accuracy of the model is calculated and "Unknown" traffic is introduced as an input to the classifier. The classifier then predicts which instance is most likely P2P or NonP2P. The model is kept in

memory. Its accuracy is periodically re-evaluated (with upcoming windows of traffic) and is only rebuilt if the accuracy drops below 90%. The two stage method is shown in Figure 1.

The architecture of Figure 1 performs four main tasks. First, it extracts the data and creates windows using a TCPdump script. Data streams generate continuous and high speed data items and therefore, there is not enough time to rescan the data or perform multiple scans. Data is extracted at different intervals using a Perl script and windows are processed using an application developed in our lab. This part solves the problem of extracting data on high speed links.

Second, the two stage architecture employs standard port filtering to label well-known P2P and NonP2P applications based on their port numbers, thus generating an accurate pool of training data that will be used in the second stage to train the FDT classifier.

Third, due to the high speed characteristics of online streams, each window needs to be processed and classified as fast as possible. This in turn requires a faster algorithm to classify traffic than the arriving window rate. It also trains the classifier based on examples generated as a result of port filtering. This makes sure that unknown traffic is classified on the most recent instances.

Fourth, due to the continuous change in the characteristics of data stream, the classifier has to be re-evaluated at periodic intervals. The requirement to re-evaluate is dictated based on accuracy of the classifier. We take the classified unknown traffic with the confidence level achieved during model analysis. If re-evaluation entails an accuracy of less than 90%, a new model is built based on most recent windows. Re-evaluation of the model solves the memory, storage and CPU limitation problems as it works within available resources without compromising the process time and accuracy. It optimizes the memory space by keeping most recent model in memory and constantly re-evaluating the model. The classifier is also updated

Figure 1. The two stage classifier

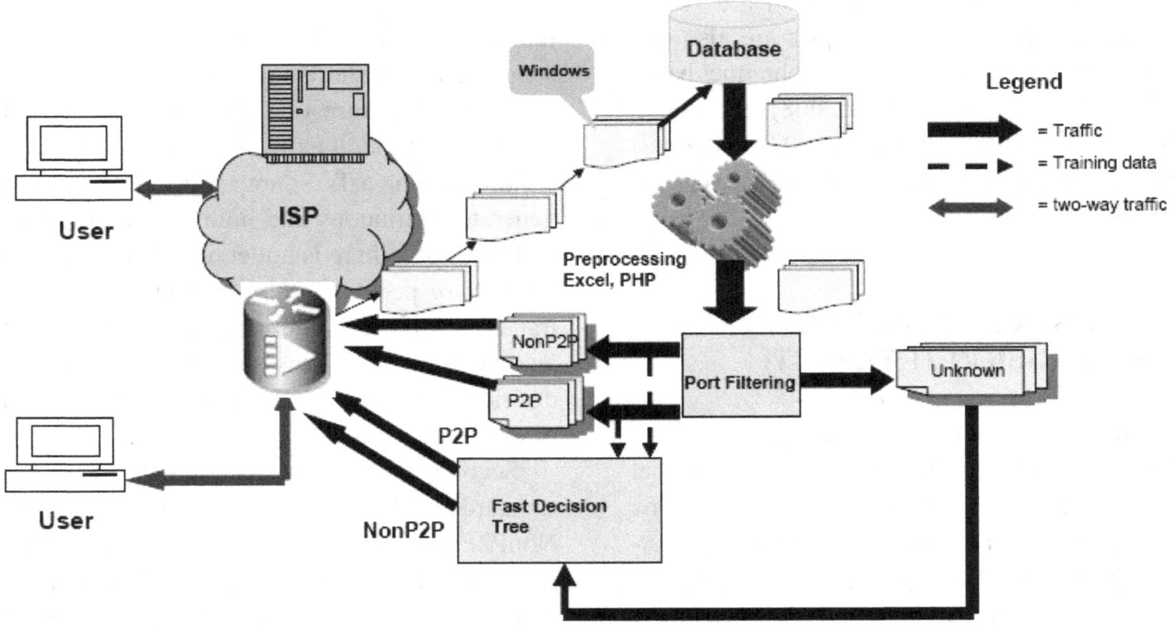

based on recently generated windows as it depicts most recent communication patterns. We now explain the details of the two-stage architecture in the following subsections.

3.1. Training Data Sets

Using Tcpdump, we captured the TCP/IP packet header of two-way internet traffic at the campus gateway over five days at different time periods in April 2006. Each record includes the full TCP/IP header, as shown in the following sample record:

11:39:54.370377 IP (tos 0x0, ttl 127, id 35953, offset 0, flags [DF], proto: TCP (6), length:603) 137.122.72.6.3688 > 137.122.14.100.80:P 1841279502:1841280065 (563) ack 548172814 win 16256

It was clear that the "tos", "flag" and "offset" fields have a single value for almost all records (unary attributes), and "ttl", "win", "cksum" and "Sequence number" contain no information to differentiate records (non-informative attributes). while the "Arrival time", "ID", "protocol", "Packet Length", "Source IP", "Destination IP", "Source Port" and "Destination Port" fields have discriminating values that can be utilized to distinguish records (informative attributes). Accordingly, we kept only the informative attributes, while discarding all other non-informative and unary fields.

3.2. Attribute Selection

All attributes were normalized, and 4 different data sets were considered with different number of attributes in each data set (Table 1).

A neural network model was built in Weka (Witten & Frank, 2005) using 5-fold validation, and the accuracy of the model was measured for each data set. As shown in Table 1, the time to build each model was between 1 to 2 minutes, depending on the number of attributes used.

Table 1. Four different sets considered in building the neural network models. Each attribute set includes 9 training sets with different rations of P2P/NonP2P records.

Attribute Set	Attributes	Time to Build the model (Sec)
Set 1	"Arrival Time", "ID", "Protocol", "Length", "Src. IP", "Des. IP"	119
Set 2	"Arrival Time", "Protocol", "Length", "Src. IP", "Des. IP"	92
Set 3	"Protocol", "Length", "Src. IP", "Des. IP"	76
Set 4	"Arrival Time", "Protocol", "Length"	55

We use the *Sensitivity, Specificity and correctness* metrics to measure the accuracy of the classifier. *Correctness* is the congruence of the classified P2P instances to the actual P2P instances, and it is measured by the percentage of the correctly classified number of instances to the total number of instances using the results from the confusion matrix. *Sensitivity* (also called True Positive Rate) is calculated as the ratio of P2P packets detected by the classifier divided by the total number of actual P2P packets:

$$\text{Sensitivity} = TP / (TP + FN). \qquad (1)$$

Specificity (also called True Negative Rate) is calculated as the ratio of Non_P2P packets detected by the classifier divided by the total number of actual Non_P2P packets:

$$\text{Specificity} = TN / (FP + TN). \qquad (2)$$

Correctness is calculated as:

$$\text{Correctness} = (TP+TN)/ (TP+TN+FP+FN). \qquad (3)$$

The higher the values of sensitivity, specificity and correctness, the more accurate the classifier.

Also, we compare different classifiers using Receiver Operating Characteristic (ROC) curves. An ROC curve depicts the TP rate vs. FP rate, where the TP rate is indeed the sensitivity calculated in (2), and the FP rate is:

$$\text{FP rate} = FP / (FP + TN) = 1 - \text{Specificity} \qquad (4)$$

The ROC curve demonstrates two important characteristics: the accuracy of the classifier, and the cost of mistakes (errors) in classifying the inputs. Figure 1, Figure 2, and Figure 3 show correctness, sensitivity, and specificity measures for 4 sets of attributes, and different mix of P2P/Non-P2P traffic. The simulation results and the corresponding charts demonstrate that the accuracy depends on two factors: the selected attribute set, and the ratio of P2P/NonP2P traffic. In particular, the higher the P2P/NonP2P ratio, the more accurate the classifier is. Also, removing the attributes "Src IP" and "Dst IP" degrades the accuracy of the classifier significantly.

As shown in Figure 2, Figure 3, and Figure 4, adding the two attributes "Src IP" and "Dst IP" increases the accuracy of the classifier significantly due to the fact that P2P applications tend to create a community of peers who are connected to each other and stay connected for a while. As such, incorporating the IP addresses will help to identify the P2P traffic more accurately.

Another important observation made from the simulation results of Figure 4 is that incorporating the "Time" attribute contributes significantly to building an accurate model. The "ID" attribute does contribute to building a good classifier, especially when the ration of P2P/NonP2P is moderate, and any additional information (attribute)

Figure 2. Sensitivity Vs. different ratios of P2P/Non-P2P records and various numbers of attributes

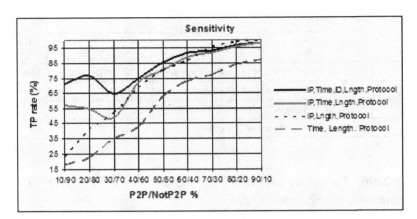

can help in training the classifier. However, for high values of P2P/Non-P2P ratios, where there were plenty of P2P records available in the training set, the information in the "time" attribute alone was enough to train the neural network classifier.

To plot the ROC curves, we select three curves representing three different values of P2P/Non-P2P ratios (Figure 5). The lower curve represents the dataset in which there are small number of P2P records available (4,318 records), the middle curve represents the data set with reasonable number of P2P records (10,797 records), and the top curve represents the data set with significant number of

P2P records (17,274 records). The closer the ROC curve is to the top-left corner, the more accurate and the less error costly (of wrong classification) the model will be. This is because the top-left corner of the ROC space represents the highest TP rate, (the maximum TP and the minimum FN), and the lowest FP rate (the minimum FP and the maximum TN). The maximum TP and TN means the best accuracy, while the minimum FN and FP means the least cost of error classified inputs. The ROC curve of Figure 5 confirms that as more P2P packets are included in the training set, the classifier becomes more accurate and less costly of erroneous classification.

Figure 3. Specificity Vs. different ratios of P2P/Non-P2P records and various numbers of attributes

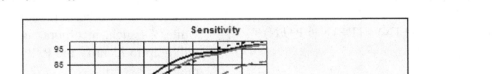

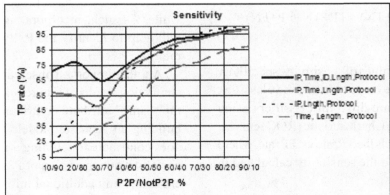

Figure 4. Correctness Vs. different ratios of P2P/Non-P2P records and various numbers of attributes

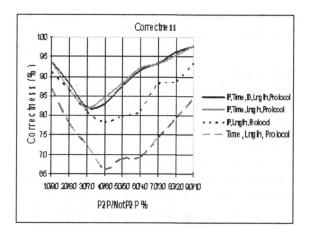

3.3. Port Filtering (First-Stage of the Two-Stage Classifier Model)

In this stage, we first process the data before applying to the filter. We prepared a training dataset through capturing and preprocessing traffic data as follows: we used Tcpdump to capture the IP packet header of two-way Internet traffic at the campus gateway over five days at different time periods in April 2006. In total 37 files were generated with different sizes. Using Windump, sample entries

were extracted from the captured files and transformed from binary format into a readable-text format. To make the IP headers suitable for data mining techniques, we consider each IP header as one example, and label all examples into two classes, namely "P2P", "NonP2P" based on their "source port" and "destination port".(Raahemi et al., 2007) The code below labels the traffic into P2P, NonP2P and Unknown traffic based on layer 4 port numbers. The criteria of filtering are based on the four assumptions: first, data instances having port numbers less than 1024 are classified as NonP2P as per well-known IANA port numbers. Second, some P2P applications use well-known standard and port numbers which are published by IANA. Third, the private port numbers are those in the range of 49152 to 65535. P2P applications randomly select port numbers out of this range as these ports are not permanently assigned to any publicly defined application. Fourth, if the port number in the data instance does not belong to first or second cases, then it is 'Unknown'. All instances, therefore, are labeled as being P2P, NonP2P and Unknown using the pseudo code in Algorithm 1.

The main objective of this stage is to generate a pool of accurate training data including P2P / NonP2P instances. The information gained from these instances will be used in the second stage

Algorithm 1. Pseudo code

```
If (Src. port number OR Des. port number) < 1024
    Type = "NonP2P"
Else
    If (Src. port number OR Des. port number) = {well-known standard port num-
bers including 1214, 6881, 6889, 6699, 6700, 6701, 4661, 4665, 4672, 4662,
6346, 6347, 6348, 6349, 6257, 1044, 1045, 1337, 2340, 2705, 4500, 4329, 5190,
5500, 5501, 5502, 5503, 6666, 6667, 7668, 7788, 8038, 8080, 28864, 8311, 8888,
8889, 41170, 3074, 3531}
 Type = "P2P"
Else
        Type = "UnKnown"
End
```

Figure 5. ROC curves for different mix of P2P traffic in the training data set

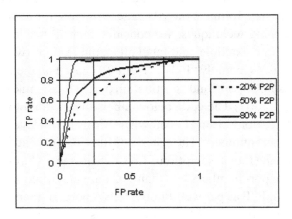

to build and train a classifier to classify the unknown instances in the data streams. The second purpose of introducing the filtering stage is to decrease processing time by eliminating traffic comprised of well-known and standard port numbers.

3.4. FDT Model Building (Second-Stage of the Two-Stage Classifier Model)

In this stage, a model is built based on P2P and NonP2P instances generated in stage-1. These instances are most current and exhibit the most recent communication patterns. IP addresses are first converted into numeric numbers. We build the model using 'REPTree' which is Fast Decision Tree implementation in Weka (Witten & Frank, 2005). The testing method to build the model is

10-fold cross validation. We then introduce Unknown traffic which is not labeled and has only three attributes; 'SrcIP', 'DesIP' and 'Len'. The Algorithm 2 trains the model based on P2P and NonP2P instances. It uses the FDT model and 10 folds cross validation method. It first invokes java classes for instances, evaluation and FDT algorithm. In the second block, it inputs the file containing P2P and NonP2P file 'win1'. It starts building a model by calling the method cls. buildClassifier(train). Once the model is build it evaluates the model.

Classification, being a supervised learning method, requires pre-defined classes and this condition was satisfied during the training stage. The classifier still expects a 'Type' field in order to run the Fast Decision Tree while unknown traffic does not contain any 'Type' information. We insert "? "in 'Type' for each instance in our window as shown in Table 2.

Algorithm 3 classifies the unknown traffic. First, it invokes 5 classes and then loads 'unknown' file and starts classifying the data instances based on training provided in the first stage. The output is 'predicted instances' which predicts the classes of all unknown traffic.

The classifier predicts the class of input instances based on the knowledge gained during training stage. The accuracy of the predicted output is based on the classifier's accuracy. It decides a class based on packet length and IP addresses, demonstrating that Peers on the network exhibit distinct behaviors and can be grouped together/detected based on these three attributes.

Table 2. Unknown traffic

Len	SrcIP	DesIP	Type
48	2306491956	1114520853	?
57	2306492148	1178900807	?
81	2306492148	1413907870	?
52	2306491336	1167863996	?
1480	2306492277	3386827531	?

Algorithm 2. Partial code

```
import weka.core.Instances;
import weka.classifiers.Evaluation;
import weka.classifiers.trees.REPTree; // FDT algorithm
...
Instances train = c:\internet\win1 // CSV file generated as a result of port
filtering
Instances test = c:\internet\win1
// we first train our classifier based on the P2P and NonP2P instances
Classifier cls = new REPTree();
cls.buildClassifier(train);
// evaluate classifier
Evaluation eval = new Evaluation(train);
eval.crossValidateModel(tree, newData, 10, new Random(1)); // 10 fold cross
validation
// Out put is printed
System.out.println(eval.toSummaryString("\nResults\n==\n", false)); // Print
on new line
```

3.5. Model Re-Evaluation

The classifier may lose accuracy over a period of time because of changes in communication patterns. Therefore, a constant re-evaluation is required to keep it accurate and up to date. We keep the model in memory and re-evaluate it using new instances. Model re-evaluation does not start model building from scratch and thus reduces overall process time. It assesses the accuracy of the classifier according to the recent observations. It is not necessary to re-evaluate the model with each upcoming window. We will rely on the model as long as it exhibits accuracy higher than a threshold (90% in our experiments) on periodically selected windows of traffic. When the accuracy drops below the threshold (90%), the FDT classifier is re-built using subsequent windows of instances.

Windowing technique is a scalable technique used in (Widmer, 1996; Orrego, 2004). The basic schema is that the examples in data streams are divided into disjoined windows with size *w*, and the model (classifier) is built on the first window.

Then, the trained model is kept in memory and its accuracy is periodically reevaluated with upcoming windows. The classifier model is rebuilt only if the accuracy significantly drops; that is, concept drift occurs. This method is easy to implement and avoids repetitive learning while providing stable performance for the trained model. The question is how to select proper window size as a compromise between fast adaptation and acceptable generalization when there is no concept drift. Fortunately, the rate of concept drifts (communities of peers leaving and joining) in P2P traffic is relatively slow. Therefore, it is not necessary to maintain a window with an adaptive size.

4. SIMULATION RESULTS

We conducted three experiments to measure the *accuracy, specificity* and *sensitivity* of the classifier. The experiments conducted on two IBM thinkCenter machine with 512MB RAM running Windows XP, Ubuntu Linux, and Weka. Performance of the proposed model is analyzed

Algorithm 3. Partial code

```
import java.io.BufferedReader;
import java.io.BufferedWriter;
import java.io.FileReader;
import java.io.FileWriter;
import weka.core.Instances;
...
// load Unknown data
Instances unlabeled = new Instances(
                    new BufferedReader(
                    new FileReader("/internet/unknown.arff"))); // loads
the unknown instances file
// set class attribute
unlabeled.setClassIndex(unlabeled.numAttributes() - 1);
// create copy
Instances labeled = new Instances(unlabeled);
// label predicted instances
for (int i = 0; i < unlabeled.numInstances(); i++) {
  clsLabel = tree.classifyInstance(unlabeled.instance(i));
  labeled.instance(i).setClassValue(clsLabel);
}
// save predicted labeled data
BufferedWriter writer = new BufferedWriter(
new FileWriter("/internet/unknownpredicted.arff"));
writer.write(labeled.toString());
writer.newLine();
writer.flush();
writer.close();
```

using three window sizes, each window includes a mixture of P2P and NonP2P packets. Table 3 shows the window size and distribution of P2P/NonP2P instances.

4.1. Accuracy and Model Building Time

Figure 6 shows accuracy/correctness of the classifier for the three different window size.

A window size of 1K shows an accuracy of 91.35%. As we increase the window size, accuracy starts increasing and reaches 94.78% with a window size of 5K. It further increases to 98% with a window size of 11K. During the experiments it was stipulated that memory constraints are addressed by using a window size less than 11K. The lab environment allowed experiments on computers having 512MB of RAM handling 11K window size without any problems. However, with the increase of window size above 11K significant deterioration was observed in system performance with respect to RAM. Although the accuracy of the classifier increases when the window size increases (because the classifier has more examples to build a model), in practice,

Table 3. Three window sizes with P2P/NonP2P Distribution

Experiment	Window Size	P2P	NonP2P
Window#1	1087	715	372
Window#2	5135	3723	1412
Window#3	11436	9329	2107

Figure 6. Accuracy/Correctness of FDT for various window sizes

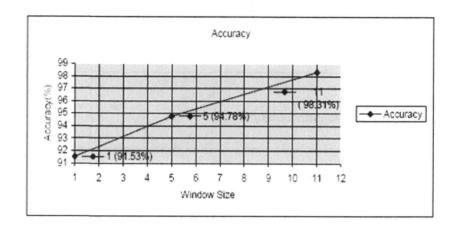

memory constraints and the time-to-build the model are critical factors in deciding the size of the windows. Figure 7, for instance, shows the time-to-build models in seconds for three different window sizes.

Window size of 1K exhibits model building time of .08 seconds which is higher than 5K window size. It is because 1K window size has not enough instances to build a model. If we move to higher window size of 5K and 11K accuracy of model increases without considerable increase in model building time. In order to optimize memory and increase accuracy, we recommended a window size between 5K and 11K records.

Figure 8 shows the specificity and Figure 9 shows the sensitivity of the classifier for three window sizes of 1K, 5K and 11K.

Specificity or True negative rate measures the percentage of instances correctly identified as NonP2P to the total number of NonP2P instances.

Window sizes with higher specificity depicts more suitable model as compared to the ones with low percentages.

5. CONCLUSION

We presented a two-stage window-based architecture for classification of Peer-to-Peer traffic where in the first stage we apply port filtering to label well-known P2P and NonP2P traffic leaving the rest of the traffic as Unknown. In the second stage, we train a Fast Decision Tree classifier using labeled records produced in the previous stage. The FDT classifier is then applied to the Unknown traffic to predict the classes of Unknown instances. We conducted experiments where the Internet traffic was captured at the campus gateway, preprocessed, and applied to the proposed two-stage architecture. To select

Figure 7. Model building time for three different window sizes

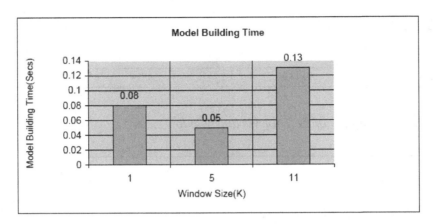

Figure 8. Specificity of fast decision tree classifier

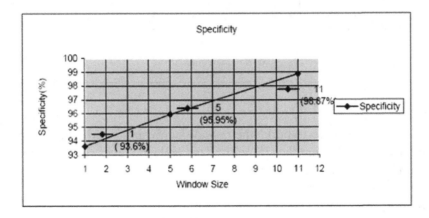

Figure 9. Sensitivity of the fast decision tree classifier

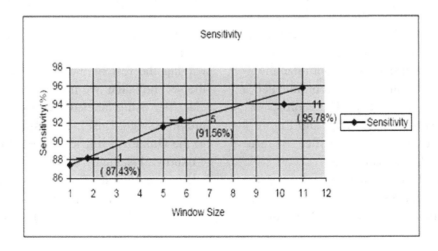

most significant attributes, we built several neural network models using a combination of different attributes for various ratios of P2P/Non-P2P in the training data set. We observed that the accuracy of the classification increases significantly when we take into account the source and destination IP addresses. This implies that the accuracy of the classifier increases when we add information about the community of peers.

The analysis shows that, utilizing the two-stage architecture, we can achieve an accuracy of higher than 90% in classification of Unknown traffic. The accuracy of the model is periodically re-evaluated on recent windows. When the accuracy falls below than 90%, a new FDT model is built using upcoming windows. This will keep the model up-to-date and accurate. The new classification technique only relies on three attributes, namely source IP address, destination IP address and packet length thus eliminating the need for deep packet inspection and the privacy issues associated with it.

6. ACKNOWLEDGMENT

This research was partially supported by the Ontario Research Networks for Electronic Commerce (ORNEC) and Natural Sciences and Engineering Research Council of Canada (NSERC).

7. REFERENCES

Aggarwal, C., Han, J., & Jianyong, W. (2006). A framework for on-demand classification of evolving data streams. *IEEE Transactions on Knowledge and Data Engineering*, *18*(5), 577–589. doi:10.1109/TKDE.2006.69

Chang, H., & Lee, W. (2005). estWin: Online data stream mining of recent frequent item sets by sliding window method. *Journal of Information Science*, *31*(2). doi:10.1177/0165551505050785

Cheeseman, P., & Stutz, J. (1996). Bayesian classification (Autoclass): theory and results. In *Proceedings of Advances in knowledge discovery and data mining, American Association for Artificial Intelligence*, Menlo Park, CA.

Cisco Inc. (2006). *Cisco IOS NetFlow Overview*. Retrieved from www.Cisco.com

Crovella, M., & Krishnamurthy, B. (2006). *Internet Measurement: Infrastructure, Traffic and Applications*. West Sussex, England: John Wiley and Sons Ltd.

Doci, A., & Xhafa, F. (2008). WIT: A wireless integrated traffic model. *Mobile Information Systems*, *4*(3), 219–235.

Domingos, P., & Hulten, G. (2000). Mining high-speed data streams. In *Proceedings of the Sixth ACM SIGKDD International Conference on Knowledge Discovery and Data Mining* (pp. 71-80).

Hulten, G., Spencer, L., & Domingos, P. (2001). Mining time-changing data streams. In *Proceedings of the Seventh ACM SIGKDD International Conference on Knowledge Discovery and Data Mining* (pp. 97-106).

Khabbaz, M., Kianmehr, K., Alshalalfa, M., & Alhajj, R. (2008). Effectiveness of Fuzzy Classifier Rules in Capturing Correlations between Genes. *International Journal of Data Warehousing and Mining*, *4*(4), 62–83.

Nanopoulos, A., Papadopoulos, A., Manolopoulos, Y., & Welzer-Druzovec, T. (2007). Robust Classification Based on Correlations Between Attributes. *International Journal of Data Warehousing and Mining*, *3*(3), 14–27.

Orrego, A. (2004). *SAWTOOTH: Learning from Huge Amounts of Data*. Unpublished master's thesis, West Virginia University, Morgantown, WV.

Oveissian, A., Salamatian, K., & Soule, A. (2004). Fast flow classification over internet. In *Proceedings of the Second Annual Conference on Communication Networks and Services Research (CNSR'04)*.

Raahemi, B., Hayajneh, A., & Rabinovitch, P. (2007). Classification of peer-to-peer traffic using neural networks. In *Proceedings of Artificial Intelligence and Pattern Recognition*, Orlando, FL (pp. 411-417).

Rohm, D., Goyal, M., Hosseini, H., Divjak, A., & Bashir, Y. (2009). A simulation based analysis of the impact of IEEE 802.15.4 MAC parameters on the performance under different traffic loads. *Mobile Information Systems*, *5*(1), 81–99.

Sen, S., Spatscheck, O., & Wang, D. (2004). Accurate, Scalable In-Network Identification of P2P Traffic using Application Signatures. In *Proceedings of the 13th International World Wide Web Conference*, NY (pp. 512-521).

Shield, C. (2007). *Peer-to-peer traffic control*. Retrieved from http://www.cloudshield.com/solutions/p2pcontrol.asp

Tsoumakas, G., & Katakis, I. (2007). Multi-Label Classification: An Overview. *International Journal of Data Warehousing and Mining*, *3*(3), 1–13.

Vladimir, N. (2008). Classification of Imbalanced Data with Random sets and Mean-Variance Filtering. *International Journal of Data Warehousing and Mining*, *4*(2), 63–78.

Widmer, G., & Kubat, M. (1996). Learning in the presence of concept drift and hidden contexts. *Machine Learning*, *23*(1), 69–101. doi:10.1007/BF00116900

Witten, I. H., & Frank, E. (2005). *Data Mining, Practical Machine Learning Tool and Techniques*. Amsterdam: Elsevier.

Xu, K., Zhang, Z., & Bhattacharyya, S. (2005). Profiling internet backbone traffic: Behavior models and applications. In *Proceedings of the 2005 Conference on Applications, Technologies, Architectures, and Protocols for Computer Communications*.

Zander, S., Nguyen, T., & Armitage, G. (2005). *Selflearning IP Traffic Classification based on Statistical Flow Characteristics* (LNCS 3431, pp. 325-328). Berlin: Springer.

Zuev, D., & Moore, A. (2005). *Traffic Classification using a Statistical Approach* (LNCS 3431, pp. 321-324). Berlin: Springer.

This work was previously published in International Journal of Data Warehousing and Mining, Volume 6, Issue 3, edited by David Taniar, pp. 29-42, copyright 2010 by IGI Publishing (an imprint of IGI Global).

Chapter 12
Constrained Cube Lattices for Multidimensional Database Mining

Alain Casali
Aix-Marseille Université, France

Sébastien Nedjar
Aix-Marseille Université, France

Rosine Cicchetti
Aix-Marseille Université, France

Lotfi Lakhal
Aix-Marseille Université, France

ABSTRACT

In multidimensional database mining, constrained multidimensional patterns differ from the well-known frequent patterns from both conceptual and logical points of view because of a common structure and the ability to support various types of constraints. Classical data mining techniques are based on the power set lattice of binary attribute values and, even adapted, are not suitable when addressing the discovery of constrained multidimensional patterns. In this chapter, the authors propose a foundation for various multidimensional database mining problems by introducing a new algebraic structure called cube lattice, which characterizes the search space to be explored. This chapter takes into consideration monotone and/or anti-monotone constraints enforced when mining multidimensional patterns. The authors propose condensed representations of the constrained cube lattice, which is a convex space, and present a generalized levelwise algorithm for computing them. Additionally, the authors consider the formalization of existing data cubes, and the discovery of frequent multidimensional patterns, while introducing a perfect concise representation from which any solution provided with its conjunction, disjunction and negation frequencies. Finally, emphasis on advantages of the cube lattice when compared to the power set lattice of binary attributes in multidimensional database mining are placed.

DOI: 10.4018/978-1-61350-474-1.ch012

Copyright © 2012, IGI Global. Copying or distributing in print or electronic forms without written permission of IGI Global is prohibited.

INTRODUCTION AND MOTIVATIONS

The extraction of constrained multidimensional patterns in the area of multidimensional database mining (OLAP database mining or data mining from categorical database relations) is achieved for solving various problems such as discovering multidimensional association rules (Lu, Feng, & Han, 2000), Roll-Up dependencies (Calders, Ng, & Wijsen, 2002), multidimensional constrained gradients (Dong et al., 2004), closed constrained gradients (Wang, Han, & Pei, 2006), classification rules (Liu, Hsu, & Ma, 1998; Li, Han, & Pei, 2001), correlation rules (Brin, Motwani, & Silverstein, 1997; Grahne, Lakshmanan, & Wang, 2000), datacube (Gray et al., 1997; Beyer & Ramakrishnan, 1999; Han, Pei, Dong, & Wang, 2001; Xin, Han, Li, & Wah, 2003), iceberg cube (Beyer & Ramakrishnan, 1999; Han et al., 2001), emerging cube (Nedjar, Casali, Cicchetti, & Lakhal, 2007; Casali, Nedjar, Cicchetti, & Lakhal, 2009b), quotient cube (Lakshmanan, Pei, & Han, 2002), and closed cube (Casali, Cicchetti, & Lakhal, 2003b; Li & Wang, 2005; Xin, Shao, Han, & Liu, 2006; Casali, Nedjar, Cicchetti, & Lakhal, 2009a). We believe that a precise semantics is required for characterizing the search space and solving these multidimensional data mining problems. Such semantics can be captured through an algebraic structure, the cube lattice, provided with a similar expression power than the power set lattice, which is used for binary database mining (transaction database mining (Agrawal, Mannila, Srikant, Toivonen, & Verkamo, 1996)).

Adapting to this new multidimensional context, approaches and algorithms successfully used when mining binary databases (and thus using the power set lattice as a search space) is possible but not relevant. However, such adaptations have been frequently proposed for the extraction of quantitative association rules (Srikant & Agrawal, 1996) and for classification (Liu et al., 1998; Li et al., 2001). Moreover, (Beyer & Ramakrishnan,

1999; Han et al., 2001) have extended Apriori (Agrawal et al., 1996) for computing iceberg cubes and observed that such extensions "perform terribly". Reasons behind these failures are the following. Firstly each multidimensional attribute must be replaced by a set of binary attributes, each of which representing a single value of the multidimensional attribute (Srikant & Agrawal, 1996). If the original attribute domains are large (which is the case in data warehouses (Beyer & Ramakrishnan, 1999)), the attribute substitution results in dealing with a great number of binary attributes (called items). On the other hand, the search space, considered when mining binary databases, is the lattice representing the power set of items. Nevertheless, this large search space encompasses a great number of solutions, which are known to be semantically erroneous in a multidimensional context. Let us suppose that in a relation the attribute A has k distinct values. It is replaced by k binary attributes $a_1,..., a_k$. In the powerset lattice, all the couples (a_i,a_j) with $1 \leq i, j \leq k$ and $i \neq j$ are considered and evaluating a constraint requires a costly memory space and a pass over the binary relation. But we know that the original data set does not contain any pattern (a_i,a_j), simply because the initial attribute A is atomic and thus its values a_i and a_j are exclusive.

If an anti-monotone constraint w.r.t. inclusion (e.g., Frequency() $\geq$ threshold) is enforced for mining frequent multidimensional patterns, the original complexity of levelwise algorithms is altered because the negative border (fundamental concept for the complexity analysis (Mannila & Toivonen, 1997)) used for pruning is enlarged with a possibly voluminous set of useless combinations. The problem worsens when a monotone constraint (e.g., Frequency() $\leq$ threshold) is considered because, although erroneous, the pattern (a_i,a_j) belongs to the yielded results.

In this chapter, we make the following contributions.

1. We introduce and characterize the search space to be considered for multidimensional database mining problems. Such a search space only encompasses semantically valid solutions. By introducing an order relation between elements of this space, and proposing two construction operators, we define a new algebraic structure, called cube lattice. In such groundwork, the extraction of multidimensional patterns can be achieved by using conjunctions of monotone and/or anti-monotone constraints according to our order relation.

2. We formalize condensed representations of constrained cube lattices. Condensed representations based on boundary sets (or borders) avoid to enumerate all the solutions (Mannila & Toivonen, 1996, 1997). Their practical advantage is that they limit the memory explosion problem especially critical when mining constrained multidimensional patterns. Moreover, condensed representations make it possible to build up the whole solution space or without performing such a construction to decide whether such or such multidimensional pattern is a solution or not. We show that the constrained cube lattice is a convex space and thus it can be represented through boundaries.

3. We show that the cube lattice is graded and describe a generalized levelwise algorithm without "backtracking" devised to mine borders of constrained cube lattices.

4. We use the constrained cube lattice structure to formalize different cubes: the datacube (Gray et al., 1997), the iceberg cube (Beyer & Ramakrishnan, 1999), the range cube, the differential cube (Casali, 2004) and the emerging cube (Nedjar et al., 2007; Casali et al., 2009b).

5. When considering frequent multidimensional patterns, an additional contribution is the proposal of a perfect concise representation of frequent multidimensional patterns.

It has two original features: on one hand it is not based on the power set lattice framework and on the other hand it differs from the representations using closed patterns (Pasquier, Bastide, Taouil, & Lakhal, 1999; Pei, Han, & Mao, 2000; Stumme, Taouil, Bastide, Pasquier, & Lakhal, 2002; Zaki & Hsiao, 2005) and non derivable patterns (Calders & Goethals, 2007). From such a representation, we show that any frequent multidimensional patterns (along with its conjunction, disjunction and negation frequencies) are obtained using an improved version of inclusion-exclusion identities. Experimental results are performed in order to compare the size of the essential frequent tuples, the size of iceberg cubes and the one of iceberg closed cubes.

6. According to our knowledge, it not exist a specific algebraic approach for extracting various kinds of multidimensional patterns; therefore we propose a comparison between our approach and extensions to the multidimensional context of approaches mining binary databases. We show in particular: (1) the relevance of our search and solution spaces when compared to the ones considered by the quoted extensions, and (2) the preservation of levelwise algorithm complexity in our approach and its alteration for the considered extensions.

Organization of the Chapter

In the second section, we detail the structure of the cube lattice. In the third section, we study its condensed representations for the various cases of constraint conjunctions. The algorithm computing such representations is given in the fourth section. In the fifth section, we use our framework for characterizing various types of cubes (datacube, iceberg cube...). Assuming that we are dealing with frequent multidimensional patterns, our perfect concise representation of the solution space is defined in the sixth section. We propose a comparison between the cube lattice and the power set lattice in the seventh section. As a conclusion, we underline the advantages of our proposal and evoke further work. Proofs are given in appendix.

This chapter consolidates research work presented in the conference papers (Casali, Cicchetti, & Lakhal, 2003a, 2005; Casali, Nejar, Cicchetti, & Lakhal, 2007).

THE CUBE LATTICE FRAMEWORK

In contrast with patterns considered when mining binary databases, multidimensional patterns are provided with a common structure and their characterization must exhibit such a structure. On another hand, links existing between patterns capture an important semantics. When addressing the former issue, we propose the concept of multidimensional space. Its elements represent multidimensional patterns. We soundly define links between such patterns through an order relation and propose two basis construction operators. Then the search space, for the various multidimensional database mining problems previously evoked, is characterized by defining the concept of cube lattice.

Multidimensional Spaces

Throughout the chapter, we make the following assumptions and use the introduced notations. Let r be a relation over the schema R. Attributes of R are divided in two sets *(1)* D the set of dimensions, also called categorical or nominal attributes, which correspond to analysis criteria for OLAP database, classification or concept learning (Mitchell, 1997) and *(2)* M the set of measures (for OLAP) or class attributes. Moreover, attributes of D are totally ordered (the underlying order is denoted by $<_d$) and $\forall A \in D$, r(A) stands for the projection of r over A.

The multidimensional space of the categorical database relation r groups all the valid combinations built up by considering the value sets of attributes in D, which are enriched with the symbolic value ALL (also denoted by '*'). The latter, introduced in (Gray et al., 1997) when defining the operator Cube-By, is a generalization of all the possible values for any dimension.

Definition 1: (Multidimensional Space). The multidimensional space of r is noted and defined as follows: Space(r) = $\{\times_{A \in D}(r(A) \cup ALL)\} \cup \{(\emptyset,...,\emptyset)\}$ where $\times$ symbolizes the Cartesian product, and $(\emptyset,...,\emptyset)$ stands for the combination of empty values. Any combination belonging to the multidimensional space is a tuple and represents a multidimensional pattern.

Example 1: Table 1 presents the categorical database relation used all along the chapter to illustrate the introduced concepts. In this relation, A, B, C are dimensions and M is a measure.

The following tuples $t_1 = (a_1, b_1, ALL)$, $t_2 = (a_1, b_1, c_1)$, $t_3 = (a_1, b_2, c_1)$, $t_4 = (a_1, ALL, c_1)$ and $t_5 = (ALL, b_1, ALL)$ are elements of Space(r).

Generalization Order

The tuples of the multidimensional space capture information at various granularity levels. In fact, any tuple of the original relation is generally involved in the construction of several tuples (at the first level of data synthesis, one of the dimensional attribute is provided with the value ALL); the latter tuples can in turn be synthesized and so on. At the most general level, the synthesis consists of a single tuple only encompassing ALL values. It provides the most compact summary of *r* but also the roughest. The multidimensional space of *r* is structured by the *generalization/specialization* order between tuples. This order is originally

Table 1. Relation example r

Row	A	B	C	M
1	a_1	b_1	c_1	3
2	a_1	b_1	c_2	2
3	a_1	b_2	c_1	2
4	a_1	b_2	c_2	2
5	a_2	b_1	c_1	1
6	a_2	b_1	c_1	1

introduced by Mitchell (1997) in the context of machine learning. In a data warehouse context, this order has the same semantic as the operator Rollup/Drilldown (Lakshmanan et al., 2002).

Definition 2: (Generalization relation). Let u, v be two tuples of the multidimensional space of r:

$$u \leq_g v \Leftrightarrow \begin{cases} \forall A \in D \ such \ that \ u[A] \neq \\ ALL \ and \ u[A] = v[A] \\ or \ v = (\varnothing, \ldots, \varnothing) \end{cases}$$

If $u \leq_g v$, we say that u is more general than v in Space(r).

The covering relation of $\leq_g$ is noted $\lessdot_g$ and defined as follows: $\forall$ t, t'$\in$ Space(r), t $\lessdot_g$ t' $\Leftrightarrow$ t $\leq_g$ t' and $\nexists$ t" $\in$ Space(r) such that t $<_g$ t" $<_g$ t'.

The direct lower bound of a tuple t, noted DLB(t), encompasses all the tuples which are covered by t (DLB(t)= {t' $\in$ Space(r) such that t' $\lessdot_g$ t}).

Example 2: In the multidimensional space of our relation example (cf. Table 1), we have: (ALL,b_1, ALL) $\leq_g$ (a_1,b_1,c_1), i.e., (ALL,b_1, ALL) is more general than (a_1,b_1,c_1) and (a_1,b_1,c_1) is more specific than (ALL,b_1, ALL) and (a_1, b_1, ALL) $\lessdot_g$ (a_1,b_1,c_1). Moreover any tuple generalizes the tuple ($\varnothing$, $\varnothing$, $\varnothing$) and specializes the tuple (ALL, ALL, ALL).

When applied to a set of tuples, the min and max operators yield the tuples that are the most general ones in the set or the most specific ones respectively.

Definition 3: (min/max operators). Let T $\subseteq$ Space(r) be a set of tuples:

$\min_{\leq_g}(T) = \{t \in T \ such \ that \ \nexists u \in T: u \leq_g t\}$.

$\max_{\leq_g}(T) = \{t \in T \ such \ that \ \nexists u \in T: t \leq_g u\}$.

Example 3: In our multidimensional space, let us consider T = {(a_1,b_1, ALL), (a_1,b_1,c_1), (a_1, ALL,c_1)}. Thus we have min(T)= {(a_1,b_1, ALL), (a_1, ALL,c_1)} and max(T)= {(a_1,b_1,c_1)}.

Basis Operators

The two basic operators provided for tuple construction are Sum (denoted by +) and Product (noted •). The Sum of two tuples yields the most specific tuple that generalizes the two operands.

Definition 4: (Sum operator). Let u and v be two tuples in Space(r).

$$t = u + v \Longleftrightarrow \forall A \in D, t[A] = \begin{cases} u[A] \ if \ u[A] = v[A] \\ ALL \ otherwise. \end{cases}$$

We say that t is the Sum of the tuples u and v.

Example 4: In our example of Space(r), we have (a_1,b_1,c_1)+(a_1,b_2,c_1)=(a_1,ALL,c_1). This means that (a_1,ALL,c_1) is built up from the tuples (a_1,b_1,c_1) and (a_1,b_2,c_1), and it generalizes both of them.

The Product of two tuples yields the most general tuple which specializes the two operands. If, for two tuples, there exists a dimension A having distinct and real world values (i.e. existing in the original relation), then the only tuple specializing them is the tuple $(\varnothing,...,\varnothing)$. Apart from it, the sets of tuples that can be used to retrieve them are disjoined.

Definition 5: (Product operator). Let u and v be two tuples in Space(r). Then,

$t = u \bullet v \Longleftrightarrow$
$$\begin{cases} t = (\varnothing,...,\varnothing) \text{ if } \exists A \in D \text{ such that } u[A] \neq v[A] \neq ALL, \\ \text{otherwise } \forall A \in D \begin{cases} t[A] = u[A] \text{ if } v[A] = ALL \\ t[A] = v[A] \text{ if } u[A] = ALL. \end{cases} \end{cases}$$

We say that t is the Product of the tuples u and v.

Example 5. In our example of Space(r), we have $(a_1,b_1,ALL) \bullet (a_1,ALL,c_1)=(a_1,b_1,c_1)$. This means that (a_1,b_1,ALL) and (a_1,ALL,c_1) generalize (a_1,b_1,c_1) and (a_1,b_1,c_1) participates to the construction of (a_1,b_1,ALL) and (a_1,ALL,c_1) (directly or not). The tuples (a_1,b_1,ALL) and (a_1,b_2,c_1) have no common point apart from the tuple of empty values.

In order to characterize a chief feature of our search space, we need to know the attributes for which the values associated with a tuple t are different from the value ALL. This is why the function Attribute is introduced.

Definition 6: (Attribute function). Let t be a tuple of Space(r), we have Attribute(t)= {A ∈ D such that t[A]= ALL}.

Example 6: In our example of Space(r), we have Attribute((a_1,b_1,ALL)) = {A, B}.

Characterization of the Cube Lattice

By providing the multidimensional space of r with the generalization order between tuples and using the above-defined operators Sum and Product, we define an algebraic structure which is called Cube Lattice. Such a structure provides a sound foundation for multidimensional database mining

issues. We give the fundamental properties of the cube lattice which are resumed in theorem 1. In this section, we make use of concepts well known when dealing with lattices, thus we adopt the conventional notations in the domain (Ganter & Wille, 1999), and state their equivalence with ours.

Lemma 1: The ordered set CL(r) = (Space(r), $\leq_g$) is a complete lattice and has the following properties:

$\forall T \subseteq CL(r), \wedge T = +_{t \in T} t$ where $\wedge$ stands for the infimum.

$\forall T \subseteq CL(r), \vee T = \cdot_{t \in T} t$ where $\vee$ symbolizes the supremum.

Through the following proposition, we characterize the order embedding from the cube lattice towards the power set lattice of the whole set of attribute values. To avoid ambiguities, each value is prefixed by the name of the concerned attribute.

Proposition 1: Let PL(r) be the power set lattice of attribute value set, *i.e.* the lattice

$$\langle P(\underset{A \in D}{\cup} A.a, \forall a \in r(A)), \subseteq \rangle .$$

Then it exists an order-embedding ϕ: CL(r) $\rightarrow$ PL(r)

$$t \mapsto \begin{cases} \underset{A \in D}{\cup} A.a, \forall a \in r(A) \text{ if } t = (\varnothing,...,\varnothing) \\ \{A.t[A], \forall A \in Attribute(t)\} \text{ otherwise.} \end{cases}$$

Consequently, if t $\leq_g$ t' then $\phi(t) \subseteq \phi(t')$.

The rank of a tuple t is the length of the minimal path which links it to the tuple (ALL,..., ALL).

Thus we have: *rank(t)* =
$$\begin{cases} |D| + 1 \text{ if } t = (\varnothing,...\varnothing) \\ |\Phi(t)| \text{ otherwise.} \end{cases}$$

Reminder: The coatoms (the atoms respectively) are the maximal elements, i.e. the most specific tuples (the minimal elements respectively, i.e., the most general tuples), of the lattice deprived of its universal upper bound: T (its lower bound respectively: ⊥). We denote by:

1. At(CL(r)) the atoms of the cube lattice (i.e. $\{t \in CL(r): |\Phi(t)| = 1\}$),
2. CAt(CL(r)) the coatoms of the cube lattice (i.e. $\{t \in CL(r): |\Phi(t)| = |D|\}$),
3. At(t)= $\{t' \in At(CL(r))$ such that $t' \leq_g t\}$ the atoms of a tuple t.

Lemma 2: CL(r) is a coatomistic lattice.

Lemma 3: CL(r) is an atomistic lattice.

Theorem 1: Let r be a categorical database relation over D ∪ M. The ordered set CL(r)=(Space(r), $\leq_g$) is a complete, atomistic and coatomistic lattice, called cube lattice in which Meet (∧), or GLB, and Join (∨), or LUB, operators are given by:

$$\forall\, T \subseteq CL(r),\ \wedge T = +_{t \in T}\, t$$

$$\forall\, T \subseteq CL(r),\ \vee T = \bullet_{t \in T}\, t$$

Example 7: Figure 1 exemplifies the cube lattice of the projection of our relation example (cf. Table 1) over the attributes A and B. In this diagram, the edges represent the generalization or specialization links between tuples.

Through the following proposition, we analyze the number of elements (for a given level or in general) of the cube lattice.

Proposition 2: The height (level number) of the cube lattice is $|D|+1$. The element number by level i (i ∈ 1..|D|) is:

$$\sum_{\substack{X \subseteq D \\ |X|=i}} (\prod_{A \in X} |\, r(A)\,|) \leq \binom{|\,D\,|}{i} \max_{A \in D} |\, r(A)\,|^i .$$

The total number of elements in the cube lattice is:

$$(\prod_{A \in |D|} (|\, r(A)\,| + 1)) + 1$$

Figure 1. Hass diagram of the cube lattice of r

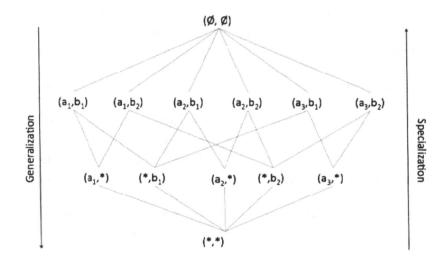

CONDENSED REPRESENTATIONS OF CONSTRAINED CUBE LATTICES

The cube lattice defines a graded search space for various multidimensional database mining problems. In this section, we study the structure of the cube lattice in presence of constraint conjunctions. Provided with such a structure, we propose condensed representations (or borders) of the constrained cube lattice with a twofold objective: defining in a compact way the solution space and deciding whether a tuple t belongs to the solution space or not. Finally, following from principles of levelwise approaches, we show that the cube lattice is graded and give an algorithm for computing condensed representations of constrained cube lattices. We take into account monotone and anti-monotone constraints frequently used in binary data mining (Ross, Srivastava, Stuckey, & Sudarshan, 1998; Raedt & Zimmermann, 2007; Pei, Han, & Lakshmanan, 2004). These constraints can be applied to:

1. Measures of interest (Bayardo & Agrawal, 1999) such as frequency of patterns, confidence, correlation, entropy... In these cases only the dimensional attributes of R are necessary;

2. Additive statistical functions (e.g., COUNT, SUM, MIN,...) which apply to measures of M for computing aggregates;

3. Class prediction measures for supervised classification approaches, in that case, apart from the dimensions of D, R encompasses class attributes (also noted M). We recall the definitions of monotone and anti-monotone constraints w.r.t $\leq_g$.

Definition 7: (Constraint).

1. A constraint Const is monotone if and only if: $\forall$ t, u $\in$ CL(r):
   a. [t $\leq_g$ u and Const(t)] $\Rightarrow$ Const(u).

2. A constraint Const is anti-monotone if and only if: $\forall$ t, u $\in$ CL(r):
   a. [t $\leq_g$ u and Const(u)] $\Rightarrow$ Const(t).

Example 8: In the multidimensional space example, we would like to know all the tuples for which the value of the sum for the attribute measure is greater or equal to 3. The constraint "$SUM_{val}(M) \geq 3$" is an anti-monotone constraint. In the same way, if we intend to mine all the tuples from which the sum of the values for the attribute M is less or equal to 5, the expressed constraint "$SUM_{val}(M) \leq 5$" is monotone.

Structure of the Constrained Cube Lattice

The cube lattice faced with monotone and/or anti-monotone constraints does not necessarily remain a lattice. We show in this section that such a partially ordered set is provided with a mathematical structure which is a convex space (Vel, 1993) and thus it can be represented by it boundary (Hirsh, 1991).

Notations: We note cmc (camc respectively) a conjunction of monotone constraints (anti-monotone respectively) and chc an hybrid conjunction of constraints (monotone and anti-monotone). According to the considered case, the introduced borders are indexed by the kind of the considered constraint. For example, U_{camc} symbolizes the upper border for the anti-monotone constraints (i.e. the set of the most specific tuples that satisfy the conjunction of anti-monotone constraints).

Remarks (extreme cases):

1. We suppose that the tuple (ALL,..., ALL) always satisfies the conjunction of an anti-monotone constraints and the tuple ($\emptyset$,...,$\emptyset$) always verifies the conjunction of monotone constraints. Under these assumptions, the solution space encompasses at least one element (possibly the tuple of empty values).

2. Moreover, we assume that the tuple (ALL,..., ALL) never verifies the conjunction of monotone constraints and the tuple $(\emptyset,...,\emptyset)$ never satisfies the conjunction of antimonotone constraints, because without making these assumptions, the solution space is CL(r).

Definition 8: (Convex Space). Let $(P, \leq)$ be a partially ordered set, $C \subseteq P$ is a convex space if $\forall x, y, z \in P$, $x \leq y \leq z$ and $x, z \in C \Rightarrow y \in C$. Thus C is bounded by two sets: an upper bound or "upper set" defined by $U = max_{\leq}(C)$ and a lower bound or "lower set" defined by $L = min_{\leq}(C)$.

Theorem 2: The constrained cube lattice CL(r)$_{const}$ is a convex space. Its upper set U$_{const}$ and lower set L$_{const}$ are:

- If const = cmc, $L_{cmc} = min (\{t \in CL(r) \mid cmc(t)\})$ and $U_{cmc} = (\emptyset,..., \emptyset)$.
- If const = camc, $L_{camc} = (ALL,..., ALL)$ and $U_{camc} = max (\{t \in CL(r) \mid camc(t)\})$.
- If const = chc, $L_{chc} = min (\{t \in CL(r) \mid chc(t)\})$ and $U_{chc} = max (\{t \in CL(r) \mid chc(t)\})$.

The generic upper bound Uconst represents the most specific tuples satisfying the constraint conjunction and the lower bound Lconst is the set of the most general tuples satisfying the constraint conjunction. Thus L$_{const}$ and U$_{const}$ are condensed representations of the constrained cube lattice with conjunction of monotone and/or anti-monotone constraints.

Corollary 1: Given U$_{camc}$ and cmc, the condensed representation of CL(r)$_{cch}$ is:

- $L_{chc} = min (\{t \in CL(r) \mid \exists t' \in U_{camc}: t \leq_g t'$ and $cmc(t)\})$
- $U_{chc} = \{t \in U_{camc} \mid \exists t' \in L_{chc}: t' \leq_g t\}$.
- Given L$_{cmc}$ and camc, the condensed representation of CL(r)$_{cch}$ is:

Table 2. Borders for the cube lattice constrained by "$3 \leq SUM_{va}l(M) \leq 5$"

U$_{camc}$	(a_1, b_1, c_1) (a_1, ALL, c_2)	(a_1, b_2, ALL)
U$_{chc}$	(a_1, b_1, c_1) (a_1, ALL, c_2)	(a_1, b_2, ALL)
L$_{cmc}$	(a_2, ALL, ALL) (ALL, b_2, ALL) (a_1, b_1, ALL) (ALL, b_1, c_1)	(a_3, ALL, ALL) (ALL, ALL, c_2) (a_1, ALL, c_1)
L$_{chc}$	(ALL, b_2, ALL) (a_1, b_1, ALL) (ALL, b_1, c_1)	(ALL, ALL, c_2) (a_1, ALL, c_1)

- $U_{chc} = max (\{t \in CL(r) \mid \exists t' \in L_{cmc}: t' \leq_g t$ and $camc(t)\})$
- $L_{chc} = \{t \in L_{cmc} \mid \exists t' \in U_{chc}: t \leq_g t'\}$.

  Example 9: Table 2 gives the borders U$_{camc}$, U$_{chc}$ L$_{cmc}$ and L$_{chc}$ of the cube lattice of the relation example by considering the hybrid constraint "$3 \leq SUM_{val}(M) \leq 5$".

The Algorithm GLA

Levelwise algorithms are proved to be efficient when dealing with very large data sets stored on disk and when the underlying search space is a graded lattice. Improvements of these algorithms have been proposed in order to minimize the number of database scans and optimize the candidate generation step (Bastide, Taouil, Pasquier, Stumme, & Lakhal, 2000; Geerts, Goethals, & Bussche, 2001; Stumme et al., 2002). This is why we adopt their principles when proposing an algorithm which computes borders of constrained cube lattices. More precisely, the algorithm GLA yields the borders U and L corresponding to the type of considered constraints and uses whether L⁻ (i.e., the negative border of CL(r)$_{camc}$) or L for the pruning step.

GLA follows from general principles of levelwise algorithms and introduces the following particular features:

1. The level construction step (or candidate generation) makes use of the operator Sub-Product, defined below using the operator Product,
2. The pruning step is performed without "back tracking" like in (Dehaspe & Toivonen, 1999), and
3. Monotone and anti-monotone constraints as well as their conjunction are taken into consideration.

Contrarily to a pattern language (Mannila & Toivonen, 1997; Raedt, Jaeger, Lee, & Mannila, 2002) which is a general model, the cube lattice is a specific pattern language for multidimensional database mining. The advantage is that the cube lattice is graded which is a fundamental property for convex spaces (cf., theorem 2) and for using levelwise algorithms. Obviously such a fundamental property is difficult to be proved in a general model.

Proposition 3: The cube lattice CL(r) is graded.

Definition 9: (Sub-product operator). Let u and v be two tuples of Space(r), X=Attribute(u) and Y=Attribute(v).

$$t = u \odot v \Leftrightarrow$$
$$\begin{cases} t = u \bullet v \ if \ X \setminus \max_{<_d}(X) = Y \setminus \\ \max_{<_d}(Y) \ and \ \max_{<_d}(X) <_d \max_{<_d}(Y) \\ (\varnothing, \ldots, \varnothing) \ otherwise. \end{cases}$$

where $<_d$ is a total order over D. Let us notice that $|\Phi(u)| = |\Phi(v)|$ is a necessary condition for the relevance of the Sub-Product operator.

The Sub-Product operator is a constrained product operator useful for candidate generation in a levelwise approach (Agrawal et al., 1996; Mannila & Toivonen, 1997). Provided with multidimensional patterns at the level i, the Sub-Product operator generates candidates of level i+1, if they exist (else the Sub-Product yields $(\varnothing,...,\varnothing)$). Moreover, each tuple is generated only once.

Example 10: In our example, we have (a_1,b_1,ALL) $\leq_g (a_1, ALL,c_1) = (a_1,b_1,c_1)$ but (a_1, ALL,c_1) $\leq_g (a_1,b_1,ALL) = (\varnothing,..., \varnothing)$.

Complexity of the GLA Algorithm

Mannila and Toivonen (1997) have studied complexity analysis for levelwise algorithms by using the positive and negative borders. The following complexity is given in (Gunopulos, Mannila, Khardon, & Toivonen, 1997): $O((|BD^-(Sol)| + |Sol|)\times$cost of camc test) where $BD^-(Sol)$ is the negative border (e.g., infrequent minimal elements in the context of frequent pattern discovery, L^- in our case) and Sol is the solution set of the problem. Such a complexity can be easily generalized for the levelwise algorithm GLA (Algorithm 1) which deals with monotone and/or anti-monotone constraint conjunctions. The complexity of GLA is: $O((|P| + |Q|) \times$ max(cost of camc test, cost of cmc test)) where:

- If camc = {}: $P = L_{cmc}$ and $Q = \{t \in CL(r)$ |cmc(t)\}.
- Else $P = L^-_{camc}$ and $Q = CL(r)_{camc}$.

FORMALIZATION OF EXISTING CUBES

In this section, we review different variants of datacubes and, by using the constrained cube lattice structure, propose a characterization both simple and well founded.

Algorithm 1. GLA Algorithm

```
Input: relation r over R, camc and cmc
Output: U, L
if cmc = {} then L:= {(ALL,..., ALL)}
else          L1:= At(CL(r))
         L:= {t ∈At(CL(r)) | cmc(t) and camc(t)}
         L₁:= L₁\L
end if
if camc = {} then U:= {(∅,..., ∅)}
else          L₁:= {t ∈At(CL(r)) | camc(t)}
         U:= L₁
              L⁻:= {t ∈At(CL(r)) |camc(t)}
end if
while (Lᵢ = ∅) do
         if (camc = {}) then
                 Cᵢ₊₁:= {v = t ⊙t' | t, t' ≠ Lᵢ,v ≠(∅,...,∅) and ∄u∈ L: u ≤_g v}
                 L:= {t ∈ Cᵢ₊₁ | cmc(t)}
                 Lᵢ₊₁:= Lᵢ\L
         else
                 Cᵢ₊₁:= {v = t ⊙ t' | t, t' ∈ Lᵢ,v ≠(∅,...,∅) and ∄u∈ L⁻: u ≤_g v}
                 L⁻:= {t ∈Lᵢ₊₁ |camc(t)}
                 Lᵢ₊₁:= Cᵢ₊₁\L⁻
                 U:= max_{≤g} (U ∪ Lᵢ₊₁)
                 if cmc = {} then L:= min_{≤g} (L ∪{t ∈ Lᵢ₊₁ | cmc(t)})
         end if
         i:= i + 1
end while
U:= {t ∈ U |∃ t' ∈ L: t' ≤_g t}
return U, L
```

Datacubes

Originally proposed by Gray et al. (1997), the datacube according to a set of dimensions is presented as the result of all the Group By which can be expressed using a combination of dimensions. The result of any Group By is called a cuboid, and the set of all the cuboids is structured within a relation noted Datacube(r). The schema of this relation remains similar to the one of r, i.e., D∪M and the very same schema is used for all the cuboids (in order to perform their union) by en- forcing a simple idea: any dimension which is not involved in the computation of a cuboid (i.e., not mentioned in the Group By) is provided with the value ALL. For any attribute set X ⊆ D, a cuboid of the datacube, noted Cuboid(X, f({M|*})), is yielded by the following Sql query:

1. Select [All,] X, f({M|*})
2. From r
3. Group By X;

Thus a datacube can be achieved by the one of two Sql queries:

1. By using the operator Cube By (or Group By Cube according to the DBMS):
    ○ Select D, f({M|*})
    ○ From r
    ○ Cube By D;
    ○ By performing the union of all the cuboids:

$$Datacube(r, f(\{M| *\})) = \bigcup_{X \subseteq D} Cuboid(X, f(\{M | *\}))$$

This union is expressed in Sql as follows:

1. Select f({M|*})
2. From r
3. Union
4. Select A, f({M|*})
5. From r
6. Group By A
7. Union
8. ...

Example 11: In our example, the set of all the aggregative queries can be expressed by using the operator Cube as follows:
    ○ Select A, B, C, Sum(M)
    ○ From r
    ○ Cube By A, B, C;

The previous query results in $2^3 = 8$ cuboids: according to ABC, AB, AC, BC, A, B, C and $\varnothing$. The cuboid according to ABC corresponds to the original relation itself.

A tuple t belongs to the datacube of r if and only if it exists a tuple t' in r which specializes t; else t cannot be built up. As a consequence, whatever the aggregative function is, the tuples of the datacube projected over the selected dimensions remain invariant, only the values computed by the aggregative function vary.

Proposition 4: Let r be a relation projected over D, the set of tuples (i.e. without the measure values) of the datacube of r is a convex cube for the constraint "$Count_{val}(t) \geq 1$":

$$Datacube(r) = \{t \in CL(r) \mid Count_{val}(t) \geq 1\}$$

Since the constraint "$Count_{val}(t) \geq 1$" is an antimonotone constraint (according to $\preceq_g$), a datacube is a convex cube. By applying theorem 2, we infer that any datacube can be represented by two borders: the relation r which is the upper set and the tuple (ALL,...,ALL) which is the lower set. Then we can easily assess the appurtenance of any tuple t to the datacube of r: we have just to find a tuple t' $\in$ r specializing t.

Example 12: Figure 2 exemplifies the datacube of our relation example (Cf. Table 1) using the function COUNT. The measure associated to a tuple is written after it (e.g., $(a_1, ALL, c_2)4$). For example, in this diagram, the tuples of the cuboid according to AC are in bold.

In this section, we have shown that we can characterize the datacube as a convex cube. In the similar way, in the following section we take advantage of the genericity of our structure to capture various types of cubes.

Others Cubes

Like the datacube, most of the existing cubes can achieved by Sql queries or by using our structure. Hereafter, we present the cubes the most used in practice.

*   Inspired from frequent patterns, Beyer et al. introduce the Iceberg cubes (Beyer & Ramakrishnan, 1999) which are presented as tuple subset of the datacube satisfying for the measure values a minimal threshold constraint. The proposal is motivated by the following objective: the decision mak-

Figure 2. Datacube of r w.r.t. COUNT ('' ⇔ ALL)*

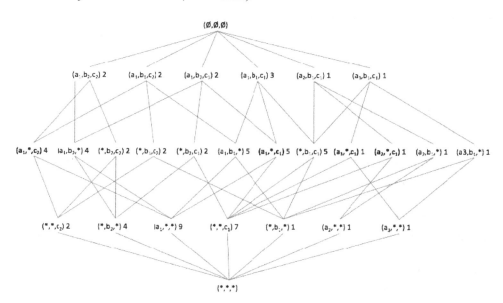

ers are interested in general tendencies, the relevant trends are trends sufficiently distinctive. Thus it is not necessary to compute and materialize the whole cube (the search space is pruned). This results in a significant gain for both execution time and required storage space.

- Windows cubes gather tuples having measure values which fit in a given range. Such cubes place emphasis on middle tendencies, not too general and not too specific.

- Differential cubes (Casali, 2004) result from the set difference between the datacubes of two relations r_1 and r_2. They capture tuples relevant in a relation and not existing in the other. In contrast with the previous ones, such cubes capture comparisons between two data sets. For instance in a distributed application, these data sets can be issued from two different sites and their differential cube highlights trends which are common here and unknown there. For OLAP applications as well as data stream analysis, trend comparisons along time are strongly required in order to exhibit trends, which are significant at a

moment and then disappear or on the contrary non-existent trends, which later appear in a clear-cut way. If we consider that the original relation r_1 is stored in a data warehouse and r2 is made of refreshment data, the differential cube shows what is new or dead.

- Emerging cubes (Nedjar et al., 2007; Casali et al., 2009b) capture trends, which are not relevant for the users (because under a threshold) but which grow significant or on the contrary general trends which soften but not necessarily disappear. Emergent cubes enlarge results of differential cubes and refine cube comparisons. They are of particular interest for data stream analysis because they exhibit trend reversals. For instance, in a web application where continuous flows of received data describe in a detailed way the user navigation, knowing the craze for (in contrast the disinterest in) such or such URL is specially important for the administrator in order to allow at best available resources according to real and fluctuating needs.

Concise Representations of Frequent Multidimensional Patterns

Lattice

In this section, we propose a perfect concise representation of the frequent cube lattices. From such a representation, any frequent multidimensional pattern along with its frequency is derived by using an improved version of inclusion-exclusion identities adapted to the cube framework.

Frequency Measures and Inclusion Exclusion Identities

Let us consider $t \in CL(r)$ (r is a relation over $D \cup M$), we define three weight measures, which are compatible with the weight functions defined in (Stumme et al., 2002), for t:(*i*) its frequency (noted (Freq(t)), (*ii*) the frequency of its disjunction (noted Freq($\vee t$)) and (*iii*) the frequency of its negation (noted Freq(t)).

$$\text{Freq}(t) = \frac{\sum\limits_{t' \in r} t'[M] \text{ such that } t \leq_g t'}{\sum\limits_{t' \in r} t'[M]} \quad (1)$$

$$\text{Freq}(\vee t) = \frac{\sum\limits_{t' \in r} t'[M] \text{ such that } t + t' \neq (ALL, \ldots, ALL)}{\sum\limits_{t' \in r} t'[M]} \quad (2)$$

$$\text{Freq}(\neg t) = \frac{\sum\limits_{t' \in r} t'[M] \text{ such that } t + t' = (ALL, \ldots, ALL)}{\sum\limits_{t' \in r} t'[M]} \quad (3)$$

Example 13: In the cube lattice of our relation example, we have:

- Freq((a_1,b_1, ALL)) = 5/11, Freq($\vee(a_1,b_1$, ALL)) = 1 and Freq((a_1,b_1, ALL)) = 0.
- The inclusion-exclusion identities make it possible to state, for a tuple t,

the relationship between its frequency, the frequency of its disjunction and the frequency of its negation, as follows:

$$\text{Freq}(\vee t) = \sum\limits_{\substack{t' \leq_g t \\ \perp \neq t'}} (-1)^{(|\Phi(t')|-1)} \text{Freq}(t') \quad (4)$$

$$\text{Freq}(t) = \sum\limits_{\substack{t' \leq_g t \\ \perp \neq t'}} (-1)^{(|\Phi(t')|-1)} \text{Freq}(\vee t') \quad (5)$$

$$\text{Freq}(\neg t) = - \text{Freq}(\vee t) \text{ (from De Morgan Law)} \quad (6)$$

Where Φ is the order-embedding (Cf. proposition 1) and $\perp$ stands for the tuple (ALL,..., ALL).

Example 14: In the cube lattice of our relation example, we have:

- Freq((a_1,b_1, ALL)) = Freq((a_1, ALL, ALL)) + Freq((ALL,b_1, ALL)) − Freq((a_1,b_1, ALL)) = 9/11 + 7/11 − 5/11 = 1
- Freq((a_1,b_1, ALL)) = Freq((a_1, ALL, ALL)) + Freq((ALL,b_1, ALL)) − Freq($\vee(a_1,b_1$, ALL)) = 9/11 + 7/11 − 1=5/11
- Freq((a_1,b_1, ALL)) = 1 − Freq($\vee(a_1,b_1$, ALL)) = 0.

Computing the frequency of the disjunction for a tuple can be performed along with computing its frequency and thus the execution time of levelwise algorithms is not altered.

Provided with the frequency of the disjunction for the tuples, a concise representation of frequent tuples can be defined and the computation of the negation frequency is straightforward.

Frequent Essential Tuples

Definition 10: (Essential tuple). Let $t \in CL(r)$ be a tuple, and *minfreq* a given threshold. We say that t is frequent if and only if $Freq(t) \geq$ *minfreq*. If $t = (ALL,..., ALL)$, then t is said essential if and only if:

$$Freq(\vee t) \neq \max_{DLB(t)}(Freq(\vee t')) \qquad (7)$$

where $DLB(t) = \{t' \in CL(r) \mid t' \prec g\ t\}$. Let us note Essential(r) the set of essential tuples.

Example 15: In the cube lattice of our relation example (Cf. Table 1), (a_1, b_1, ALL) is an essential tuple because $Freq(\vee(a_1, b_1, ALL)) \neq Freq(\vee(a_1, ALL, ALL))$ and $Freq(\vee(a_1, b_1, ALL)) \neq Freq(\vee(ALL, b_1, ALL))$.

Lemma 4: Let us consider the twofold constraint: "t is frequent" (C1) and "t is an essential tuple" (C2). Such a constraint conjunction is anti-monotone according to the order g (i.e., if t is either an essential or a frequent tuple and $t' \leq_g t$, then t' is also essential or frequent).

Frequency Inference Using Improved Inclusion Exclusion Identities

The following formulas show firstly how to compute the frequency of the disjunction from the set of essential tuples and secondly how to optimize the inclusion-exclusion identities for finding efficiently the frequency of a frequent tuple. A naive method for computing the frequency of a tuple t requires the knowledge of the disjunctive frequencies of all the tuples, which are more general than t. Formula 8, is an intuitive optimization based on the essential tuple concept while formula 9 is an original derivation of the frequency of t.

Lemma 5:

$$\forall t \in CL(r), Freq(\vee t) = \max_{t' \in Essential(r)}(\{Freq(\vee t') \mid t' \leq_g t\}).$$

Lemma 6: $\forall t \in CL(r)$, let $u = \text{Argmax}(\{Freq(\vee t') \mid t' \leq_g t$ and $t' \in Essential(r)\})$, then we have:

$$Freq(t) = \sum_{\substack{t' \leq_g t \\ \perp \neq t'}} (-1)^{|\Phi(t')|-1} \begin{cases} Freq(\vee u)\ if\ u \leq_g t' \\ Freq(\vee t')\ otherwise. \end{cases} \qquad (8)$$

Theorem 3: $\forall t \in CL(r), t \notin Essential(r)$, let $u = \text{Argmax}(\{Freq(\vee t') \mid t' \leq_g t$ and $t' \in Essential(r)\})$, then we have:

$$Freq(t) = \sum_{\substack{t' \leq_g t \\ \perp \neq t' \\ t' \leq_g u}} (-1)^{|\Phi(t')|-1} Freq(\vee t') \qquad (9)$$

Perfect Concise Representation of Frequent Multidimensional Patterns

Definition 11: (Perfect Concise Representation). CR(r) is a Concise Representation for the set of frequent tuples, noted FCL(r), if and only if (*i*) $CR(r) \subseteq FCL(r)$ and (*ii*) $\forall t \in FCL(r)$, its frequency can be derived from CR(r).

Unfortunately, the set Essential(r) cannot be a concise representation of FCL(r), this is why we add the set of maximal frequent tuples (U_{C1}) to obtain a perfect concise representation. Thus a tuple is frequent if and only if it generalizes a tuple of U_{C1}.

Algorithm 2. GLAE Algorithm

```
U_{C1}:= Max Set Algorithm(r, C1)
L1 = {t ∈ At(CL(r)) |∃u ∈ U_{C1}: t ≤_g u}
while L_i = ∅ do
        Ci+1:= {v = t⊙t | t, t' ∈ L_i, v ≠ (∅,...,∅),∃u ∈ U_{C1}: v ≤_g u and ∀w
∈DLB(v),w ∈ Li}
        Scan the database to find the frequencies of the disjunction ∀t ∈
Ci+1
        L_{i+1}:= C_{i+1}\{t ∈ C_{i+1} |∃t'∈ DLB(t): Freq(Vt) = Freq(Vt')}
        i:= i +1
 end while
return ∪_{j=1..i} L_j
```

Theorem 4: $U_{C1} \cup \{t \in CL(r) \mid t$ is a frequent essential tuple$\}$ is a perfect concise representation of the frequent cube lattice.

Claims:

1. In an OLAP database context, when the function *COUNT* is used, we have: Datacube(r)= $\{(t, freq(t)) \mid t \in CL(r)$ and $Freq(t) > 0\}$. Thus, frequent essential tuples and U_{C1} provide a perfect concise representation of datacubes.
2. The framework of frequent essential tuples can be used in the context of frequent pattern mining and the set of frequent essential patterns is a perfect concise representation of frequent patterns.

The Algorithm GLAE

In order to yield the frequent essential tuples, we propose a levelwise algorithm with maximal frequent pattern (U_{C1}) pruning. Our algorithm includes the function Max Set Algorithm which discovers maximal frequent multidimensional patterns. It could be enforced by modifying the algorithm Max-Miner (Bayardo, 1998) (See Algorithm 2).

Example 16: The concise representation of the relation illustrated in Table 1 for the anti-monotone constraint "$Freq(t) \geq 2/11$" is the following: the set of frequent essential tuples is exemplified in Table 3 and the set U_{C1} is given in Table 2.

We aim to know if (a_1, b_2, ALL) is frequent and if it is, what is the frequency of its disjunction and negation.

1. Since $(a_1, b_2, ALL) \leq_g (a_1, b_2, c_1)$, the former tuple is frequent. We use theorem 3 to retrieve its frequency: $Freq((a_1, b_2, ALL)) = Freq((a_1, ALL, ALL)) + Freq((ALL, b_2, ALL)) - Freq(\vee(a_1, b_2, ALL)) = Freq((ALL, b_2, ALL)) = 4/11$
2. In order to retrieve the frequency of the disjunction, we apply lemma 5: $Freq(\vee (a_1, b_2, ALL)) = Freq(\vee (a_1, ALL, ALL)) = 9/11$.
3. We use De Morgan law to retrieve the frequency of the negation: $Freq((a_1, b_2, ALL)) = 1 - Freq(\vee (a_1, b_2, ALL)) = 2/11$.

Let us retrieve the frequencies of the tuple (a_1, b_2, c_1).

1. Since $(a_1, b_2, c_1) \in U_{C1}$, it is frequent. We use theorem 3 to compute its frequency:

Table 3. Essential tuple for "Freq(t) ≥ 2/11"

rank	Tuple	Freq($\vee$t)
1	(a_1, ALL, ALL)	9/11
1	(ALL, b_1, ALL)	7/11
1	(ALL, b_2, ALL)	4/11
1	(ALL, ALL, c_1)	7/11
1	(ALL, ALL, c_2)	4/11
2	(a_1, b_1, ALL)	1
2	(a_1, ALL, c_1)	1
2	(ALL, b_1, c_1)	9/11
2	(ALL, b_2, c_1)	9/11
2	(ALL, b_2, c_2)	6/11

$Freq((a_1,b_2,c_1)) = Freq((a_1, ALL, ALL)) + Freq((ALL,b_2, ALL)) + Freq((ALL, ALL,c_1)) - (Freq(\vee (a_1,b_2, ALL)) + Freq(\vee (a_1, ALL,c_1)) + Freq(\vee (ALL,b_2,c_1))) + Freq(\vee (a_1,b_2,c_1)) = Freq((ALL,b_2, ALL)) + Freq((ALL,ALL,c_1)) - Freq(\vee (ALL,b_2,c_1)) = 4/11 + 7/11 - 9/11 = 2/11.$

2. We use lemma 5 to yield the frequency of the disjunction: $Freq(\vee (a_1,b_2,c_1)) = Freq(\vee (a_1, ALL,c_1))=1.$

3. We use De Morgan law to retrieve the frequency of the negation: $Freq((a_1,b_2,c_1)) = 1 - Freq(\vee (a_1,b_2,c_1)) = 0.$

We would like to know if (a_2,b_1,c_1) is frequent. Since $\nexists\ t \in U_{C1}\ |\ (a_2,b_1,c_1) \leq_g t$, (a_2,b_1,c_1) is not frequent.

Experimental Evaluations

By providing the disjunctive and the negative frequencies, the proposed approach enriches the results obtained with the two other perfect covers proposed in the literature. Our objective is now to show, through various experiments, that the size of this new cover is often smaller than the size of the cover based on the frequent closed patterns and this in the most critical cases: strongly correlated data. For meeting this objective, we evaluate the number of frequent essential tuples and compare it with the number of frequent closed tuples (iceberg closed cube (Casali et al., 2009a)) and the size of frequent tuples (iceberg cube) by using five datasets. Those datasets can be found at http://fimi.cs.helsinki.fi/. The characteristics of the datasets used for experiments are given in Table 4. They are:

- The dataset Chess,
- The dataset Connect,
- The dataset Mushrooms describing the characteristics of mushrooms,
- The datasets of census Pumsb and Pumsb*, extracted from "PUMS sample file". Pumsb* is the same dataset than Pumsb from which are removed all the patterns which have a threshold greater or equal to 80%, the synthetic datasets T10I4D100K and T20I6D100K, built from sale data.

Table 4. Dataset

Name	Number of transactions	Average size of each transaction	Number of items
Chess	3196	37	75
Connect	65557	43	129
Mushrooms	8124	23	119
Pumsb	49046	74	2113
Pumsb*	49046	50,5	2088

For all the experiments, we choose relevant minimum thresholds.

In these five datasets, only encompassing strongly correlated data, the ratio between frequent patterns and the total number of patterns is high. Thus we are in the most difficult cases. For finding the positive border we use Max-Miner (Bayardo, 1998).

In the dataset Pumsb*, using either the frequent closed patterns or the frequent essential patterns as a cover is advantageous: the gain compared to the set of frequent patterns for the dataset Pumsb* with the threshold *Minfreq* =20% is about 45. On the other hand, for this dataset, even if the approach by essential patterns is better than the one with closed patterns, the obtained gain is near to one. In the three remaining datasets, the approach by essential is very efficient.

With the dataset Chess, many of frequent patterns are closed patterns, but the number of essential patterns is relatively small. This results in a benefit, for the threshold *Minfreq* = 50%, of a factor 40 compared to the original approach and of a factor 20 compared to the approach using closed patterns. With the dataset Connect and a threshold *Minfreq* = 70%, the benefit compared to frequent patterns is approximately of a factor 2500 and compared to closed frequent pattern of a factor 20. We can see that with the dataset Pumsb, the benefit compared to the approach by frequent closed patterns is of a factor 20 for a threshold *Minfreq* = 60% and compared to the approach by frequent patterns is approximately 40.

For more readability in the figures, we have omitted ``frequent patterns'' in the legends. Thus "simple" means frequent tuples, "closed" stands

Figure 3. Experimental results for chess

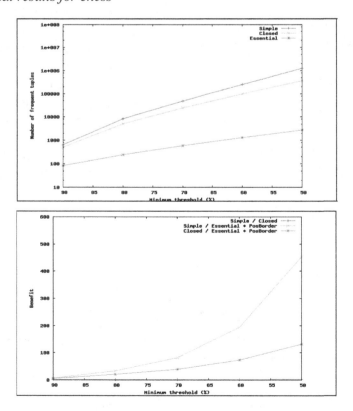

Figure 4. Expermiental results for connect

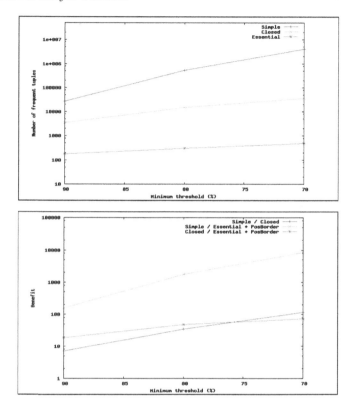

for frequent closed tuples and "essential" symbolizes frequent essential tuples (Figure 3, Figure 4, Figure 5, Figure 6, and Figure 7).

COMPARISON WITH RELATED WORK

According to our knowledge it does not exist a specific approach aiming to state an algebraic foundation for multidimensional or OLAP database mining. Several algorithms attempt to extend, to the multidimensional context, proposals successfully used for mining binary databases. They use the power set lattice as the search space. In (Mannila & Toivonen, 1997; Raedt et al., 2002; Raedt & Zimmermann, 2007), a pattern language approach is introduced as a general theoretical model for data mining. Unfortunately, this attempt

of formalization has a drawback: the property of graduation is not always preserved whereas it is fundamental for levelwise algorithms and to state a convex structure. This is why we believe that each mining context requires a specific approach: power set lattice for the binary databases and cube lattice for multidimensional databases.

We propose in this section a comparative analysis between binary data mining approaches, like quantitative association rules (Srikant & Agrawal, 1996) and classification rules, used in a multidimensional context and ours. We perform this comparison by studying search spaces to be traversed, solution spaces, and the behavior of levelwise algorithms. By considering the power set lattice $PL(r)$ and the cube lattice $CL(r)$ as search spaces for the discovery of constrained multidimensional patterns, our comparison focuses on four points: lattice and level sizes, lattice charac-

Figure 5. Expermental results for mushrooms

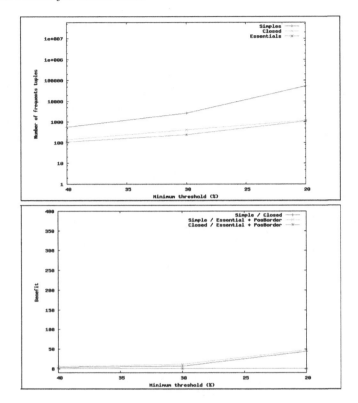

teristics, correctness of obtained solutions when faced with constraint conjunctions, and levelwise algorithm complexity. Table 5 summarizes the differences between the two lattices.

Lattice and Level Sizes

Let us examine the size of the compared lattices and their largest level. The following contributes to a more precise analysis of the computational complexity of multidimensional database mining algorithms. $| PL(r) |= 2^{\sum_{A \in D} |r(A)|}$, whereas $| CL(r) |= \Pi_{A \in D} (| r(A) | + 1) + 1$ (Cf. 2). An upper bound for the cube lattice cardinality is $O((\max_{A \in D} (| r(A) | + 1))^{|D|})$. Let us consider for instance a relation with 5 attributes, each of which having 10 possible values, we have $| PL(r) | = 2^{50}$, whereas $|CL(r)| = 11^5 + 1$.

We set $n = \sum_{A \in D} | r(A) |$. The size of the largest level in PL(r) is bounded by $\binom{n}{n/2}$, which is asymptotic to $\frac{2^n}{\sqrt{n}} \sqrt{\frac{2}{\pi}}$ whereas the maximal size of levels in the cube lattice is bounded by $\binom{|D|}{|D|/2} \max_{A \in D} (| r(A) |)^{|D|}$ which is asymptotic to $\frac{2^{|D|}}{\sqrt{|D|}} \sqrt{\frac{2}{\pi}} * \max_{A \in D} (| r(A) |)^{|D|}$.

Thus the size of the largest level in PL(r) is exponential in the value number of dimensional attributes of the relation (i.e., n). On the other hand, the size of CL(r) is exponential in the number of attributes (i.e., |D|).

Figure 6. Experimental results for Pumsb

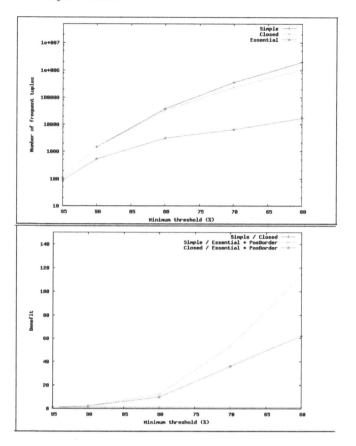

Lattice Characteristics

Since the order relation of the two considered lattices is different, we can deduce two consequences:

- $\wedge$ and $\vee$ operators are different in the two lattices: in the power set lattice $\wedge = \cap$ and $\vee = \cap$, whereas in the cube lattice $\wedge = +$ and $\vee = \bullet$.
- The power set lattice and the cube lattice are two complete, atomistic, co-atomistic and graded lattices but the cube lattice is not distributive.

Solution Correctness

The power set lattice PL(r) encompasses solutions semantically erroneous whereas the cube lattice is exactly the valid search space. More precisely, the embedded order ϕ (Cf. proposition 1) shows that for any tuple in the cube lattice it exists an equivalent combination in the power set lattice which is semantically valid whereas the converse equivalence does not hold because ϕ is not bijective. $\forall t \in CL(r)$, $\nexists a_i$, $a_j \in \phi(t)$ and $a_i, a_j \in r(A_k)$ according to definition 1. On the other hand $\forall A_k \in D$, $\forall$ ai, aj $\in r(A_k)$ with $i \neq j$, $(a_i, a_j) \in PL(r)$, nevertheless such combinations are proved to be erroneous because multidimensional patterns

Figure 7. Experimental results for Pumsb*

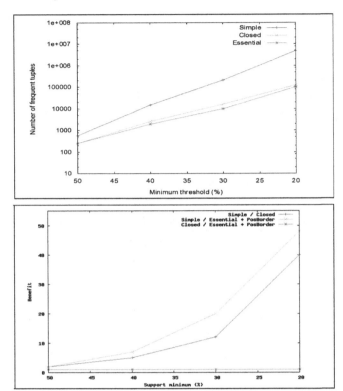

cannot encompass two values of the very same attribute. For instance, for the monotone constraint "Freq(∨) = 1", the set $\{b_1, b_2\}$ belongs to the set of solutions if we consider the power set lattice as the search space, but, as previously explained, this set is semantically erroneous. For the anti-monotone constraint "Freq(∨) ≤ 2/11", if we consider the power-set lattice as the search space, the set $\{a_2, a_3\}$ belongs to the set of solutions, but it is also erroneous. However, for the anti-monotone constraint "Freq(t) ≥ minfreq" (minfreq is a user threshold), the embedded order φ bijective, so we

Table 5. Differences between the cube lattice of r and the associated powerset lattice

	Cube Lattice CL(r)	**Power set Lattice PL(r)**
Order relation	Generalization($\leq_g$)	Inclusion ($\subseteq$)
Meet Operator	Sum (+)	Intersection ($\cap$)
Join Operator	Product (•)	Union ($\cup$)
Size of largest level	$O(\dfrac{2^{|D|}}{\sqrt{|D|}}\sqrt{\dfrac{2}{\pi}})$	$O(\dfrac{2^{n}}{\sqrt{n}}\sqrt{\dfrac{2}{\pi}})$

can use either algorithms based on the power set lattice, or algorithms based on the cube lattice in order to find the set of solutions.

Levelwise Algorithm Complexity

The generation of erroneous patterns obviously alters performances of the underlying algorithms. We study such an alteration through the comparison of size of borders relevant for monotone (Freq(t) $\leq$ threshold) and anti-monotone (Freq(t) $\geq$ threshold) constraints. Let us consider the most general solutions satisfying cmc for PL(r) and CL(r). We have $| L_{cmc}(PL(r)_{cmc}) | \geq | L_{cmc}(CL(r)_{cmc}) | + \sum_{A \in D} \frac{|r(A)|^2 - |r(A)|}{2}$. For anti-monotone constraints, the negative border for PL(r) also encompasses erroneous patterns (couples of values of a very same attribute), its size is greater than the size of L^{-}_{camc} for CL(r). In fact, the number of additional elements in the border L^{-}_{camc} for PL(r) is exactly the maximal number previously given (the very same couples are to be considered), $L^{-}_{camc}(PL(r)_{camc}) | \geq | L^{-}_{camc}(CL(r)_{camc}) | + \sum_{A \in D} \frac{|r(A)|^2 - |r(A)|}{2}$. The larger the attribute value sets are, the worse are the consequences of the negative border size. This is the reason behind the inefficiency, in a multidimensional context, of levelwise algorithms over PL(r).

CONCLUSION

In this chapter, we introduce a formal framework for solving various problems of multidimensional database mining. We propose a novel algebraic structure, the cube lattice as a graded search space. We also derived condensed representations of the cube lattice faced with monotone and/or anti-monotone constraints. Such a result is based on the particular structure of constrained cube lattice, which is a convex space structure.

Using this framework, we formalize various existing cubes. We propose an algorithm, which computes borders for the various conjunctions of constraints (w.r.t. generalization) while preserving the original complexity of levelwise algorithms. When considering the discovery of frequent multidimensional patterns, an additional contribution is the proposal of a perfect concise representation of frequent cube lattices. Then, we improve inclusion-exclusion identities for deriving frequencies. Finally, we compare the power set lattice of binary attributes and the cube lattice in order to show that our structure has several advantages: its size, the solution correctness, and the preservation of levelwise algorithm complexity. Defining set operations on constrained cube lattices (convex spaces) is an interesting future work. It could be a basis for providing convex space algebra in the cube lattice framework (with arbitrary monotone and/or anti-monotone constraints given in (Ross et al., 1998; Pei et al., 2004)).

REFERENCES

Agrawal, R., Mannila, H., Srikant, R., Toivonen, H., & Verkamo, A. I. (1996). Fast Discovery of Association Rules. In *Advances in Knowledge Discovery and Data Mining* (pp. 307-328).

Bastide, Y., Taouil, R., Pasquier, N., Stumme, G., & Lakhal, L. (2000). Mining Frequent Patterns with Counting Inference. *SIGKDD Explorations*, *2*(2), 66–75. doi:10.1145/380995.381017

Bayardo, R. (1998). Efficiently mining long patterns from databases. In *Proceedings of the international conference on management of data (sigmod)* (pp. 85-93).

Bayardo, R., & Agrawal, R. (1999). Mining the Most Interesting Rules. In *Proceedings of the 5th international conference on knowledge discovery and data mining (kdd)* (pp. 145-154).

Beyer, K., & Ramakrishnan, R. (1999). Bottom-Up Computation of Sparse and Iceberg CUBEs. In *Proceedings of the international conference on management of data (sigmod)* (pp. 359-370).

Brin, S., Motwani, R., & Silverstein, C. (1997). Beyond market baskets: generalizing association rules to correlations. In *Proceedings of the international conference on management of data (sigmod)* (pp. 265-276).

Calders, T., & Goethals, B. (2007). Non-derivable itemset mining. *Data Mining and Knowledge Discovery, 14*(1), 171–206. doi:10.1007/s10618-006-0054-6

Calders, T., Ng, R. T., & Wijsen, R. (2002). Searching for Dependencies at Multiple Abstraction Levels. In *Proceedings of the Acm transactions on database systems* (acm tods) (Vol. 27, No. 3, pp. 229-260).

Casali, A. (2004). Mining borders of the difference of two datacubes. In *Proceedings of the 6th international conference on data warehousing and knowledge discovery (dawak)* (pp. 391-400).

Casali, A., Cicchetti, R., & Lakhal, L. (2003a). Cube lattices: a framework for multidimensional data mining. In *Proceedings of the 3rd siam international conference on data mining (sdm)* (pp. 304-308).

Casali, A., Cicchetti, R., & Lakhal, L. (2003b). Extracting semantics from datacubes using cube transversals and closures. In *Proceedings of the 9th acm sigkdd international conference on knowledge discovery and data mining* (kdd) (pp. 69-78).

Casali, A., Cicchetti, R., & Lakhal, L. (2005). Essential patterns: A perfect cover of frequent patterns. In Tjoa, A. M., & Trujillo, J. (Eds.), *Dawak* (*Vol. 3589*, pp. 428–437). New York: Springer.

Casali, A., Nedjar, S., Cicchetti, R., & Lakhal, L. (2009a). Closed cubes lattices. *Annals of Information Systems, 3*, 145–165.

Casali, A., Nedjar, S., Cicchetti, R., & Lakhal, L. (2009b). Emerging cubes: Borders, size estimations and lossless reductions. *International Journal of Information Systems, Their Creation, Management and Utilization.*

Casali, A., Nejar, S., Cicchetti, R., & Lakhal, L. (2007). Convex cube: Towards a unified structure for multidimensional databases. In *Proceedings of the 18th international conference on database and expert systems applications (dexa)* (pp. 572-581).

Dehaspe, L., & Toivonen, H. (1999). Discovery of Frequent DATALOG Patterns. *Data Mining and Knowledge Discovery, 3*, 7–36. doi:10.1023/A:1009863704807

Dong, G., Han, J., Lam, J. M. W., Pei, J., Wang, K., & Zou, W. (2004). Mining constrained gradients in large databases. *IEEE Transactions on Knowledge and Data Engineering, 16*(8), 922–938. doi:10.1109/TKDE.2004.28

Ganter, B., & Wille, R. (1999). *Formal Concept Analysis: Mathematical Foundations.* New York: Springer.

Geerts, F., Goethals, B., & Bussche, J. (2001). A Tight Upper Bound on the Number of Candidate Patterns. In *Proceedings of the 1st IEEE international conference on data mining (icdm)* (pp. 155-162).

Grahne, G., Lakshmanan, L., & Wang, X. (2000). Efficient Mining of Constrained Correlated Sets. In *Proceedings of the 16th international conference on data engineering (icde)* (pp. 512-524).

Gray, J., Chaudhuri, S., Bosworth, A., Layman, A., Reichart, D., & Venkatrao, M. (1997). Data cube: A relational aggregation operator generalizing group-by, cross-tab, and sub-totals. *Data Mining and Knowledge Discovery, 1*(1), 29–53. doi:10.1023/A:1009726021843

Gunopulos, D., Mannila, H., Khardon, R., & Toivonen, H. (1997). Data mining, hypergraph transversals, and machine learning. In *Proceedings of the 16th symposium on principles of database systems (pods)* (pp. 209-216).

Han, J., Pei, J., Dong, G., & Wang, K. (2001). Efficient Computation of Iceberg Cubes with Complex Measures. In *Proceedings of the international conference on management of data (sigmod)* (pp. 441-448).

Hirsh, H. (1991). Theoretical Underpinnings of Version Spaces. In *Proceedings of the 12th international joint conference on artificial intelligence (ijcai)* (pp. 665-670).

Lakshmanan, L., Pei, J., & Han, J. (2002). Quotient cube: How to summarize the semantics of a data cube. In *Proceedings of the 28th international conference on very large databases (vldb)* (pp. 778-789).

Li, S.-E., & Wang, S. (2005). Semi-closed cube: An effective approach to trading off data cube size and query response time. *J. Comput. Sci. Technol.*, *20*(3), 367–372. doi:10.1007/s11390-005-0367-8

Li, W., Han, J., & Pei, J. (2001). CMAR: Accurate and Efficient Classification Based on Multiple Class-Association Rules. In *Proceedings of the 1st international conference on data mining (icdm)* (pp. 369-376).

Liu, B., Hsu, W., & Ma, Y. (1998). Integrating Classification and Association Rule Mining. In *Proceedings of the 4th international conference on knowledge discovery and data mining* (kdd) (pp. 80-86).

Lu, H., Feng, L., & Han, J. (2000). Beyond intra-transaction association analysis: mining multidimensional intertransaction association rules. *Acm tois, 18*(4), 423-454.

Mannila, H., & Toivonen, H. (1996). Multiple Uses of Frequent Sets and Condensed Representations: Extended Abstract. In *Proceedings of the 2nd International Conference on Knowledge Discovery and Data Mining (KDD)* (pp. 189-194).

Mannila, H., & Toivonen, H. (1997). Levelwise Search and Borders of Theories in Knowledge Discovery. *Data Mining and Knowledge Discovery*, *1*(3), 241–258. doi:10.1023/A:1009796218281

Mitchell, T. M. (1997). *Machine learning*. New York: MacGraw-Hill.

Nedjar, S., Casali, A., Cicchetti, R., & Lakhal, L. (2007). Emerging cubes for trends analysis in Olap databases. In *Proceedings of the 9th international conference on data warehousing and knowledge discovery (dawak)* (pp. 135-144).

Pasquier, N., Bastide, Y., Taouil, R., & Lakhal, L. (1999). Discovering frequent closed itemsets for association rules. In *Proceedings of the 7th international conference on database theory (icdt)* (pp. 398-416).

Pei, J., Han, J., & Lakshmanan, L. V. S. (2004). Pushing convertible constraints in frequent itemset mining. *Data Mining and Knowledge Discovery*, *8*(3), 227–252. doi:10.1023/B:DAMI.0000023674.74932.4c

Pei, J., Han, J., & Mao, R. (2000). CLOSET: An Efficient Algorithm for Mining Frequent Closed Itemsets. In *Proceedings of the Workshop on research issues in data mining and knowledge discovery (dmkd)* (pp. 21-30).

Raedt, L., Jaeger, M., Lee, S., & Mannila, H. (2002). A theory of inductive query answering. In *Proceedings of the 2002 ieee international conference on data mining (icdm)* (pp. 123-130).

Raedt, L. D., & Zimmermann, A. (2007). Constraint-based pattern set mining. In *Proceedings of the 7th siam international conference on data mining.*

Ross, K. A., Srivastava, D., Stuckey, P. J., & Sudarshan, S. (1998). Foundations of aggregation constraints. *Theoretical Computer Science, 193*(1-2), 149–179. doi:10.1016/S0304-3975(97)00011-X

Srikant, R., & Agrawal, R. (1996). Mining quantitative association rules in large relational tables. In *Proceedings of the international conference on management of data (sigmod)* (pp. 1-12).

Stumme, G., Taouil, R., Bastide, Y., Pasquier, N., & Lakhal, L. (2002). Computing Iceberg Concept Lattices with Titanic. *Data & Knowledge Engineering, 42*(2), 189–222. doi:10.1016/S0169-023X(02)00057-5

Vel, M. (1993). *Theory of Convex Structures*. Amsterdam: North-Holland.

Wang, J., Han, J., & Pei, J. (2006). Closed constrained gradient mining in retail databases. *IEEE Transactions on Knowledge and Data Engineering, 18*(6), 764–769. doi:10.1109/TKDE.2006.88

Xin, D., Han, J., Li, X., & Wah, B. W. (2003). Star-cubing: Computing iceberg cubes by top-down and bottom-up integration. In *Proceedings of the 29th international conference on very large data bases (vldb)* (pp. 476-487).

Xin, D., Shao, Z., Han, J., & Liu, H. (2006). *C-cubing: Efficient computation of closed cubes by aggregation-based checking* (p. 4). Icde.

Zaki, M. J., & Hsiao, C.-J. (2005). Efficient algorithms for mining closed itemsets and their lattice structure. *IEEE Transactions on Knowledge and Data Engineering, 17*(4), 462–478. doi:10.1109/TKDE.2005.60

APPENDIX

Proof of lemma 1: If CL(r) is a lattice then it is complete because it is finite. We show that any couple t,t' of CL(r) is provided with a lower bound (or infimum) and an upper bound (or supremum).

We show that CL(r) is a $\wedge$-semi lattice:

- ○ By definition of the operator +, $t+t' \leq_g t$ and $t+t' \leq_g t'$, thus $t+t'$ is a lower bound for t and t'.
- ○ Let us have $u \in Space(r) \mid u \leq_g t$ and $u \leq_g t'$, then $u + (t + t') = u + t + t' = u + t'$ (because $u \leq_g t$) = u (because $u \leq_g t'$).

• As a consequence, $u \leq_g t + t'$ and any couples of tuples in Space(r) has an infimum. Thus, CL(r) is a $\wedge$-semi lattice.

We show now that CL(r) is a $\vee$-semi lattice:

- ○ If t and t' are two tuples such that their product is different from $(\emptyset, \dots, \emptyset)$ then by definition of the operator •, $t \leq_g t \bullet t'$ and $t' \leq_g t \bullet t'$. As a consequence $t \bullet t'$ is an upper bound for t and t'.
- ○ Let us have $u \in Space(r) \mid t \leq_g u$ and $t' \leq_g u$ and $t \bullet t' \neq (\emptyset, \dots, \emptyset)$, then: $u \bullet (t \bullet t') = u \bullet t \bullet t' = u \bullet t'$ (because $t \leq_g u$) = u (because $t' \leq_g u$). Thus $t \bullet t' \leq_g u$ and couples of tuples in Space(r) has a supremum.

Consequently, CL(r) is a $\vee$-semi lattice.

Proof of proposition 1: Obvious because:

$$\{A.t[A] \mid \forall A \in Attribute(t)\} \subseteq P(\underset{A \in D}{\cup} A.a, \forall a \in r(A))$$

Proof of lemma 2: We look for a set T of CL(r) coatoms such that if $t \in CL(r)$, then $t = \wedge T$. Let us characterize the set of *CL(r)* coatoms: $Cat(CL(r)) = x_{A \in D} r(A)$. If $t \in Car(CL(r))$, then we have just to set T = {t}. Else, let us consider $t \in CL(r) \backslash Cat(CL(r))$. It exists a set of attributes $X \subseteq D \mid X = D \backslash Attribute(t)$.

Let us consider $t_1, t_2 \in x_{A \in D} r(A) \mid t \leq_g t_1, t \leq_g t_2$ and $\forall A \in X, t_1[A] \neq t_2[A]$.

By definition of the operator SUM, we have,

$$(t_1 + t_2)[A] = \begin{cases} t_1[A] \text{ if } A \notin X \\ ALL \text{ otherwise.} \end{cases}$$

Therefore $t_1 + t_2 = t$. Thus $T = \{t_1, t_2\}$, and any tuple is the infimum of the coatoms specializing it.

Proof of lemma 3: We look for a set T of CL(r) atoms such that if $t \in CL(r)$, then $t = \vee T$. If $t \in At(CL(r))$, then $T = \{t\}$. Otherwise, by definition of the operator Product, if $t \in CL(r) \backslash At(CL(r))$, then $t = \bullet_{t' \in At(CL(r))} t'$, thus we can set $T = \{t' \in At(CL(r)) \mid t' \leq_g t\}$. Moreover according to lemma 1, $\bullet$ is a supremum operator in the lattice CL(r), thus CL(r) is an atomistic lattice.

Proof of theorem 1: The proof of the theorem is directly derived from lemmas 1,2 and 3.

Proof of theorem 2: Let us consider $CL(r)_{cmc} = \{t \in CL(r) \mid \exists u \in U_{cmc}$ and $\exists v \in L_{cmc}$ such that $v \leq_g t \leq_g u\}$. We show that $CL(r)_{cmc}$ is the set of tuples satisfying the conjunction of monotone constraints. For the need of the demonstration, let us denote Sol_{cmc} this set of solutions. Let t be a tuple belonging to $CL(r)_{cmc}$.

○ By definition, it exists $v \in L_{cmc} \mid cmc(v)$ and $v \leq_g t$. Since cmc is a conjunction of monotone constraints, we have cmc(t). Therefore $t \in Sol_{cmc}$. Thus $CL(r)_{cmc} \subseteq Sol_{cmc}$.

○ Let be $t \in Sol_{cmc}$, thus it exists $v \in L_{cmc} \mid v \geq_g t$ because L_{cmc} represents the set of minimal tuples satisfying cmc. Moreover, the constraint $\exists u \in L_{cmc} \mid t \geq_g u$ is always satisfied. Thus $t \in CL(r)_{cmc}$ and $Sol_{cmc} \subseteq CL(r)_{cmc}$.

From the two above points, we have: $Sol_{cmc} = CL(r)_{cmc}$.

- True by application of the principle of duality (Ganter & Wille, 1999) over the cube lattice constrained by a conjunction of monotone constraints.
- True because if $Sol_{chc} = \{t \in CL(r) \mid chc(t)\}$, then $Sol_{chc} = Sol_{cmc} \cap Sol_{camc}$.

Proof of corollary 1: Obvious from definition of a convex space (Vel, 1993) and the characterization by borders of the constraint cube lattice (cf. Theorem 2).

Proof of proposition 3: CL(r) is graded if $\forall t, t' \in CL(r), t \leq_g t' \Rightarrow rank(t) + 1 = rank(t')$. $t \leq_g t' \Rightarrow \exists! A \in D \mid t[A] = ALL$ and $t'[A] \neq ALL$. Thus we have: $rank(t) + 1 = rank(t')$.

Proof of proposition 4: From the definition of a datacube: $t \in datacube(r) \Leftrightarrow \exists t' \in r \mid t \leq_g t' \Longleftrightarrow Count_{val}(t) \geq 1$.

Proof of lemma 4: It is well known that the frequency constraint (C_1) is an anti-monotone constraint. Let us focus on the second constraint. For helping us to prove the lemma, we need to introduce two concepts. The first one is the difference between two tuples:

$$t = u \backslash v \Leftrightarrow \forall A \in D, t[A] = \begin{cases} u[A] \ if \ u[A] \neq v[A] \\ ALL \ otherwise. \end{cases}$$

The second one is the function g which yields, from a cell t, the set of the identifiers of the tuple of the relation which have a common value with t (i.e. $g(t) = \{i' \in Tid(r)$ such that $t' \in r, t'[Tid] = I$ and $t + t' \neq (ALL, ..., ALL)\}$). Since the disjunctive frequency is a monotone increasing function, the function g is also a monotone increasing function (i.e. $t \leq_g t' \Rightarrow g(t) \subseteq g(t')$). Let t and u be two multidimensional tuples such that $t \leq_g u$. Let us suppose that t is not an essential tuple. We show that u is not an essential tuple too. Since t is not an essential tuple, it exists $t' \leq_g t$, which is an essential tuple. Moreover, we have g(t') = g(t). We show that g(u) = g(u\(t\t')).

We know that g(t\t') ⊆ g(t) = g(t'). However, g(u) = g((u\(t\t'))·(t\t')). By applying the increasing monotony of g over (u\(t\t')) and (t\t'), we obtain: g(u) = g((u\(t\t')))∪g(t\t').

*   Since g(t\t') ⊆ g(t'), we have: g(u) ⊆ g((u\(t\t')))∪g(t').
*   This expression is rewritten: g(u) ⊆ g((u\(t\t'))·t'). However $t' \leq_g u\backslash(t\backslash t')$, we deduce that g(u) ⊆ g(u\(t\t')).

Since $u\backslash(t\backslash t') \leq_g u$, by applying the increasing monotony of g over those two tuples, we obtain g(u\(t\t')) ⊆ g(u).

From the two above points, the tuple u is not an essential tuple since its disjunctive frequency is equal to the one of its generalized cells. As a consequence, the constraint t is not an essential tuple is a monotone constraint for the generalization order. By applying the principle of duality to this constraint over the cube lattice, we deduce that the constraint t is an essential tuple is an anti-monotone constraint for the generalization order.

Proof of lemma 5: If t∈Essential(r), then we know its disjunction frequency. Let us assume that t∉Essential(r), and u = Argmax({Freq(∨t) | $t' \leq_g t$ and t' ∈Essential(r)}) (i.e. Freq(∨u) = Max({Freq(∨t')| $t' \leq_g t$ and t'∈Essential(r)})). Therefore, we have $u \leq_g t$.

Moreover the function yielding the frequency of the disjunction is an increasing monotone function, and we have: ∀t_i, t_j∈CL(r), $t_i \leq_g t_j$ ⇒ Freq(∨t_i) ≤ Freq(∨t_j). Thus applying this formula with t_i = u and t_j = t results in: Freq(∨u) ≤ Freq(∨t).

If Freq(∨u) < Freq(∨t), then t is essential (Cf. formula 7), which is contradicting the initial assumption. Thus, Freq(∨u) = Freq(∨t).

Proof of lemma 6: The proof is based on inclusion-exclusion identities and the fact that ∀t'∈[u,t]: Freq(∨u) = Freq(∨t') (lemma 5).

Proof of theorem 3: Using lemma 6, we have:

$$Freq(t) = \sum_{\substack{t' \leq_g t \\ \bot \neq t' \\ t' \leq_g u}} (-1)^{|\Phi(t')|-1} Freq(\vee t') + \sum_{\substack{u \leq_g t' \leq_g t \\ \bot \neq t'}} (-1)^{|\Phi(t')|-1} Freq(\vee t')$$

There are $2^{|\Phi(t)|-|\Phi(u)|}$ tuples between u and t and the frequency of their disjunction is Freq($\vee$u). But, considering a power set lattice, the number of patterns which have an odd-numbered cardinality is equal to the number of patterns which have an even cardinality. Thus the second part of the equation is equal to zero.

Proof of theorem 4: The proof is based on theorem 2 and on lemmas 4, 5 and 6.

This work was previously published in International Journal of Data Warehousing and Mining, Volume 6, Issue 3, edited by David Taniar, pp. 43-72, copyright 2010 by IGI Publishing (an imprint of IGI Global).

Chapter 13
ASCCN:
Arbitrary Shaped Clustering Method with Compatible Nucleoids

Renxia Wan
North University for Nationalities, China & Donghua University, China

Lixin Wang
Anhui Institute of Architecture and Industry, China

Xiaoke Su
Donghua University, China

ABSTRACT

Special clustering algorithms are attractive for the task of grouping an arbitrary shaped database into several proper classes. Until now, a wide variety of clustering algorithms for this task have been proposed, although the majority of these algorithms are density-based. In this chapter, the authors extend the dissimilarity measure to compatible measure and propose a new algorithm (ASCCN) based on the results. ASCCN is an unambiguous partition method that groups objects to compatible nucleoids, and merges these nucleoids into different clusters. The application of cluster grids significantly reduces the computational cost of ASCCN, and experiments show that ASCCN can efficiently and effectively group arbitrary shaped data points into meaningful clusters.

1. INTRODUCTION

In data mining field, clustering pays a very important role. Clustering is the task of categorizing a set of objects into different clusters such that objects in the same cluster are more similar to each other than objects in different clusters according to some defined criteria (Huang, 1998). It is useful in a number of tasks, for example, by partitioning objects into clusters, interesting object groups may be discovered, such as the groups of clients in a banking database having a heavy investment in real estate, and clustering of data streams also can find some important applications in tracking evolution of various phenomena in

DOI: 10.4018/978-1-61350-474-1.ch013

Copyright © 2012, IGI Global. Copying or distributing in print or electronic forms without written permission of IGI Global is prohibited.

medical, meteorological, astrophysical, seismic studies (Bhatnagar et al., 2009).

Cluster analysis has become the subject of active research in several fields such as statistics, pattern recognition, machine learning and data mining. Up to now, a wide variety of clustering algorithms has been proposed, and also received a lot of attention in the last few years (c.f., section 2). In these algorithms, discovery of arbitrary shaped clusters is often to be a real obstacle for their applications. Ester (1996) and Halkidi (2001) imply that some typical clustering algorithms such as k-means, CURE, ClARANS and so on will get some poor results if there are some nonconvex shape data sets or some ball-shaped data sets of significantly differing sizes in the database. To get the arbitrary shaped clusters, algorithms based on density are designed (DBSCAN is a typical one), but these algorithms also face challenges from the efficiency and the affectivity such as the computation time may be intolerable or parameters input is not "user-friendly".

In this chapter, we present the new clustering algorithm ASCCN. It is a crisp partition method, and clusters objects with compatible nucleoids. The new algorithm requires only one input parameter, can discover arbitrary size and shaped clusters, is efficient even for large data sets especially data with high dimension. The rest of this chapter is organized as follows: In section 2, we survey related work. In section 3, we define the compatible relation. The new algorithm ASCCN is presented in section 4. The experimental results are reported to illustrate the new algorithm in section 5. Finally, we draw our conclusions in section 6.

2. RELATED WORK

There are many clustering algorithms proposed, these algorithms may be classified into partitioning, hierarchical, density and grid based methods (Han et al., 2001). Partitioning methods determine a partition of the points into clusters, such that the points in a cluster are more similar to each other than to points in different clusters. They start with some arbitrary initial clusters and iteratively reallocate points to clusters until a stopping criterion is met. They tend to find clusters with hyperspherical shapes. Examples of partitioning algorithms include k-means (MacQueen, 1967), k-prototypes (Huang, 1998), PAM (Kaufma et al., 1990), EM (Bradley et al., 1998), MaxEntEDA (Tan et al., 2005), and MeSH Graph (Zhang, H. et al., 2008). Hierarchical clustering methods can be either agglomerative or divisive, the agglomerative method starts with each point as a separate cluster, and successively performs merging until a stopping criterion is met, and the divisive method begins with all points in a single cluster and performs splitting until a stopping criterion is met. The result of a hierarchical clustering method is a tree of clusters called a dendogram. Examples of hierarchical clustering methods include BIRCH (Zhang et al., 1996), CURE (Guha et al., 1998), MeSH Ontology (Zhang, J. et al., 2008) and SM/DynGSC (Song et al., 2009). Density-based clustering methods try to find clusters based on the density of points in regions. Dense regions that are reachable from each other are merged to formed clusters. Density-based clustering methods excel at finding clusters of arbitrary shapes. Examples of density-based clustering methods include DBSCAN (Ester et al., 1996) and DENCLUE (Hinneburg et al., 1998). Grid-based clustering methods quantize the clustering space into a finite number of cells and then perform the required operations on the quantized space. Cells containing more than a certain number of points are considered to be dense. Contiguous dense cells are connected to form clusters. Examples of grid-based clustering methods include STING (Wang et al., 1997), PNMBG (Wan et al., 2009) and CLIQUE (Agrawa et al., 1998). Furthermore, some fuzzy methods are also introduced into the clustering task (Cannon et al., 1986; Hore et al., 2007; Kwok et al., 2002; Pal et al., 1995).

In our discussion, we will focus our interests on clustering algorithms which are reported to work reasonably on arbitrary shaped databases. ClARANS is introduced in (Ng et al., 1994), which is an improved k-medoids method. An experimental evaluation indicates that CLARANS runs efficiently on database of thousands of objects. Ester (1996) points out that CLARANS will get a poor clustering result if there are some nonconvex shape data sets or some ball-shaped data sets of significantly differing sizes in the database. Furthermore, CLARANS has a $O(n^2)$ computational complexity, where n is the number of objects. Thus for large databases, CLARANS is prohibitive due to its run time. The classical density-based spatial clustering algorithm is DBSCAN (Ester et al., 1996). To discover clusters, DBSCAN checks the ε-neighborhood of each point in the database. If the ε-neighborhood of a point P contains more than MinPts, a new cluster with P as a core object is created. Objects in the ε-neighborhood of P are then added to this new cluster. Then, DBSCAN iteratively aggregates points that are directly density-reachable from these core points. Merging clusters will happened when a core point belongs to these clusters. The process terminates when no new point can be added to any cluster. For spatial database, the average computational complexity of DBSCAN is $O(n\log n)$, otherwise, the average computational complexity is $O(n^2)$. OPTICS (Ankerst et al., 1999) is an extension of DBSCAN. Like DBSCAN, OPTICS requires the input of the two parameters, ε and MinPts. However, instead of producing the clustering result for one pair of parameter values, OPTICS produces an ordering of the data points such that clustering result for any lower value of ε and similar value of MinPts can be visualized and computed easily. Due to the structural equivalence, OPTICS has the same computational complexity of DBSCAN. DENCLUE (Hinneburg et al., 1998) is a clustering method based on a set of density distribution functions. Its basic idea is to model the overall point density analytically as

the sum of influence functions of the data points, clusters can be identified by determining density-attractors and clusters of arbitrary shape can be easily described by a simple equation based on the overall density function.

We summarize other algorithms that are reported to be feasible on clustering arbitrary shapes on some special data sets as follows:

Sun (2005) proposes an algorithm for clustering arbitrary shapes in data stream with an index structure CDS-tree, and data skew factor is used to adjust automatically the partition granularity according to the change of data streams. Cao (2006) presents a density-based cluster method which is designed to discover clusters in an evolving data stream. During the clustering process, the "dense" micro-cluster (named core-micro-cluster) is introduced to summarize the clusters with arbitrary shape, while the potential core-micro-cluster and outlier micro-cluster structures are proposed to maintain and distinguish the potential clusters and outliers. A pruning strategy is designed to guarantee the precision of the weights of the micro-clusters with limited memory. An approach for distributed density-based clustering is presented in (Le-Khac et al., 2007), the approach is based on two main concepts: the extension of local models created by DBSCAN at each node of the system and the aggregation of these local models by using tree based topologies to construct global models. Chen (2007) proposes an algorithm called as D-Stream. The algorithm is also a density-based approach, it uses an online component which maps each input data record into a grid and an offline component which computes the grid density and clusters the grids based on the density. A density decaying technique is adopted to capture the dynamic changes of a data stream. Biçici (2007) introduces the notion of local scaling in density based clustering, which determines the density threshold based on the local statistics of the data. The local maxima of density are discovered using a k-nearest-neighbor density estimation and used as centers of potential clusters. Each cluster is grown until the density falls below a pre-specified ratio of the center point's density. Li (2006) proposes a fully distributed clustering algorithm, called PENS (peer density-based clustering). PENS is hierarchical cluster assembly, which enables peers to collaborate in forming a global clustering model without requiring a central control or message flooding. In Chen et al. (2008), a similarity measure based on spatial overlapping relation is proposed, which calculates the similarity between a pair of data points by using the mutual overlapping relation between them in a multi-dimensional space, and a spatial overlapping based hierarchical clustering method is also developed and implemented to justify the effectiveness of the proposed similarity measure.

3. EXTENDED DISSIMILARITY ON OBJECT SET

- **Definition 1: (compatible relation)** Let S be a object set and D is a binary relation on S. $\delta (\geq 0)$ is a real number (which is usually viewed as a threshold), if it satisfies:
  1. D is reflexive (if and only if, for all objects $x \in S$, $D(x,x) \leq \delta$)
  2. D is symmetric (if and only if, for all objects $x,y \in S$, if $D(x,y) \leq \delta$ then $D(y,x) \leq \delta$

Then we call that D is a compatible relation, and S is a compatible set under D.

By the common intuition that the similarity between a pair of concepts may be assessed by "the extent to which they share information", the dissimilarity between concepts c_1 and c_2 can be defined as the information content of their lowest subsumer. In this opinion, for any object i and object j, they satisfy: $D(i, i)=0$, and $D(i, j)=D(j, i)$, so compatible relation measure is exactly an extended dissimilarity.

- **Definition 2: (compatible subset)** Let C be a subset of object set S, namely $C \subseteq S$, and suppose D is a relation measure on S, if C is a compatible set, then we call C a compatible subset of S under D

- **Definition 3: (maximal compatible subset)** Let C be one compatible subset of S under relation measure D, if there dos not exist another compatible subset C' of S, such that C is one proper subset of C', then we call C a maximal compatible subset of S.

- **Lemma1:** Suppose S is a finite object set, D is a relation measure on S, and C is a compatible subset of S under D, then there exists a maximal compatible subset C_D, such that $C \subseteq C_D$.

- **Proof:** Suppose $S = \{a_1, a_2, \ldots, a_n\}$, we construct a sequence of compatible subset of S under D as $C_0 \subset C_1 \subset C_2 \ldots$, where $C_0 = C$ and $C_{i+1} = C_i U\{a_j\}$, j is minimal subscript of a_j which satisfies $a_j \notin C_i$ and a_j is related to every object of C_i.

Since the number of objects in set S is $|S|=n$, hence structuring the aforementioned sequence can be finished after at most n-$|C|$ steps, and the last compatible subset in this sequence is the maximal.

- **Lemma 2:** Suppose S is a finite object set, D is a binary relation on S, then there exists and only exists a maximal compatible subset collection, such that the union of all subsets is equal to S.

- **Proof:** if under the relation D, every compatible subset of S is singleton, then these singletons are maximal; if there exists a common compatible subset, by lemma 1, then there must exist a maximal one that containing this subset. Suppose $\{S_1, S_2, \ldots S_m\}$ is the collection of all maximal compatible subsets of S under D, if there exists an object a_i, $a_i \in S$ while $a_i \notin \bigcup_{k=1}^{m} S_k$, if a_i is

Table 1. A compatible matrix of 7 objects {A, B, C, D, E, F, G}

	A	B	C	D	E	F
A	0	1	3	4	2	1
B	1	0	∞	∞	∞	∞
C	3	∞	0	1	2	1
D	4	∞	1	0	5	∞
E	2	∞	2	5	0	∞
F	1	∞	1	∞	∞	0

a singleton, then $\{a_i\}$ is a maximal compatible subset as the former mentioned, it conflicts with "$\{S_1,S_2,\ldots S_m\}$ is the collection of all maximal compatible subsets of S under D"; if there exists a maximal compatible subset S', then S' must belong to $\{S_1,S_2,\ldots S_m\}$, this also conflicts with $a_i \notin \bigcup_{k=1}^{m} S_k$, hence under D, there must exist a collection of maximal subsets, such that the union of all these subsets is equal to S.

If there exists another maximal compatible subset collection $\{S'_1,S'_2,\ldots,S'_1\}$, and $S = \bigcup_{k=1}^{m} S'_k$, we will show that $\{S_1,S_2,\ldots S_m\} = \{S'_1,S'_2,\ldots,S'_1\}$.

Suppose $S'_j (j \in \{1,2,\ldots,l\})$ is an arbitrary maximal compatible subset which is different from any S_i ($i=1,2,\ldots,m$), $S_{i1},S_{i2},\ldots,S_{im0}$ are the whole elements coming from $\{S_1,S_2,\ldots S_m\}$ and have a common part ΔS with S'_i, i.e. $\Delta S = S'_i \cap S_{i2} = S'_j \cap S_{j2} = \ldots = S'_i \cap S_{im0}$, and $S'_j - \Delta S = \{a_{j1},a_{j2},\ldots, a_{jr}\}$. Let $a_{j1} \in S_{i1}$, $a_{j2} \in S_{i2}$ (otherwise, there must exist another subset S'' of S that is different from $S_{i1},S_{i2},\ldots,S_{im0}$, which contains a_{j1} and ΔS. It conflicts with the hypothesis "$S_{i1},S_{i2},\ldots,S_{im0}$ are the whole elements that come from $\{S_1,S_2,\ldots,S_m\}$ and have a common part ΔS with S'_j"), because a_{j1}, a_{j2} belong to the same maximal compatible subset S'_j, hence $\{a_{i1}\} \cup \{a_{i2}\} \cup \Delta S$ is a compatible subset, due to S_{i2} being a maximal compatible subset that containing $\{a_{j1}\} \cup \Delta S$, hence $a_{j2} \in S_{i2}$, similarly $a_{j3} \in S_{i1},\ldots,a_{jr} \in S_{i1}$, namely $a_{j1},a_{j2},\ldots,a_{jr} \in S_{i1}$,

hence $\Delta S \cup \{a_{j1},a_{j2},\ldots,a_{jr} \subseteq S_{i1}$, namely $S'_j \subseteq S_{i1}$, because S'_j is a maximal compatible subset of S, hence $S'_j = S_{i1}$, this conflicts with the hypothesis "$S'_j (j \in \{1,2,\ldots,l\})$ is an arbitrary maximal compatible subset which is different from any S_i ($i=1,2,\ldots,m$)". Hence the uniqueness of the existent of maximal compatible subset is proved.

Instead, a given arbitrary compatible set can be described by an undirected and weighted graph $G=<V, E, W>$, where each node in V corresponds to an object in S, and each edge $e=<x, y>$ with weight w depicts the maximum of the relation measures $D(x, y)$ and $D(y, x)$ between the object x and object y. Then finding maximal compatible subset is equal to finding the fully connected subgraph of G.

If there are no relation between x and y, we denote $D(x, y)$ as ∞.

Then finding a maximal compatible subset in an object set is equal to finding a fully connected subgraph in the corresponding graph G.

- **Example:** as shows in Table 1, and Figure 1 shows the corresponding undirected weighted graph. Then the clustering results can be shown as Figure 2.

Definition 4: (measure between two sets) Suppose S_1 and S_2 are the given object sets, D is an object relation measure. The measure between S_1 and S_2 is defined as follows:

$$D(S_1, S_2)=\min\{D(x, y)|\forall x \in S_1, \forall y \in S_2\}$$

Figure 1. An undirected weighted graph corresponding to the dissimilarity matrix

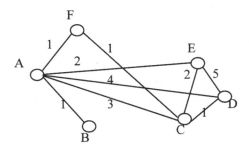

4 THE PROPOSED ALGORITHM

In this section, we present the algorithm ASCCN (Arbitrary Shape Clustering method with Compatible Nucleoids) based on the previous discussions.

4.1 ASCCN: Arbitrary Shaped Clustering Method with Compatible Nucleoids

The basic idea of the algorithm is to find out the maximal compatible subsets in an iterative way, and then merge the singletons and compatible subsets into clusters (Figure 3)

In ASCCN, MaxNucleoid (in line 2) is used to find the maximal compatible subsets (namely, nucleoids) of the object set S, and Merging is used to combine the singletons and compatible subsets into a bigger cluster. The Merging process is performed repeatedly until *ClusterSet* cannot be merged anymore. The final *ClusterSet* is the set of clusters we require. Algorithms MaxNucleoid and Merging are shown in Figure 4 and Figure 5.

- **MaxNucleoid:** is an application of lemma 2, it scans the object space S iteratively to get nucleoids, namely, maximal compatible subset of S.

The equation $D(C_x,C_y)==\min\{D(C_y,C_z)| C_z \neq C_y$ and $C_z \in CS\}$ in the line 6 of Merging ensures the object set C_x (compatible nucleoid or intermediate cluster) belonging to the nearest object set C_y, the inequation $D(C_x,C_y)\leq\delta'$ is used to confine the condition of emerging, we set $\delta'=\delta/2$, which is an experiential value.

- **Example:** as shows in Table 1, ABCDEFG forms sets of clusters with different threshold δ as $\{1, 2, 3, 4, 5\}$. The clustering results show as Table 2.

Since MaxNucleoid needs to scan the object space S, in the worst condition (namely, all objects in S are so dense that they almost can be included in one compatible nucleoid), the computational complexity is $O(n^2)$, and Merging takes a $O(n^2)$ computational complexity in the worst condition (namely, all compatible nucleoids are singletons). Thus the computational complexity of ASCCN is $O(n^2)$ in a total.

To decrease the computational cost of ASCCN, a region partition method is used for this goal, namely, cluster grids.

4.2 Improving ASSCN with Cluster Grids

We assume that the input data has d dimensions, and each input data record is defined within the space $S = S_1 \times S_2 \times \ldots \times S_d$, where S_i is the definition space for the ith dimension.

We partition the d-dimensional space S into grids. Suppose for each dimension, its space S_i, $I = 1,\ldots,d$ is divided into p_i partitions as $S_i = S_{i1} \cup S_{i2} \cup \ldots \cup S_{i,pi}$, then the data space S is partitioned into $N = \prod_{i=1}^{d} p_i$ grids, where each grid g is composed of $S_{1,j1} \times S_{2,j2} \times \ldots \times S_{d,jd}$, $j_i = 1,\ldots,p_i$, $1 <= j_i <= p_i$, denoted by $g = (j_1,j_2,\ldots,j_d)$.

A data record $x = (x_1,x_2,\ldots,x_d)$ can be mapped to a grid $g(x)$ as follows: $g(x) = (j_1,j_2,\ldots,j_d)$ where $x_i \in S_{i,ji}$.

Figure 2. Five undirected weighted graphs corresponding to the compatible matrix in Table 1. The black bold lines are the sharing edges, and the same color and line-type edge represents one cluster.

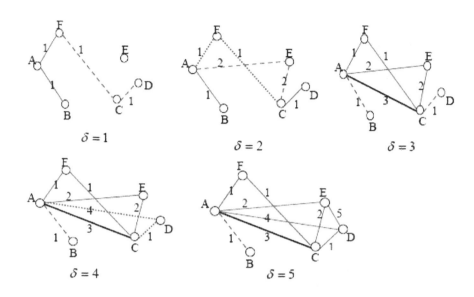

Figure 3. ASCCN: arbitrary shaped clustering method with compatible nucleoids

Algorithm: ASCCN(Object set: *S*, Relation measure: *D*, Threshold of *D*: δ)

1: *ClusterSet* = ϕ ;

2: *ClusterSet* = **MaxNucleoid** (*S, D,* δ);

3: repeat

4:    *previousCN*=| *ClusterSet* |;

5:    *ClusterSet* = **Merging**(*ClusterSet, D,* $\delta / 2$);

6: until | *ClusterSet* |= =*previousCN*

7: return *ClusterSet*

Table 2. Clusters with different threshold δ

δ	Clusters	Nucleoids
1	{A, B, F}, {C, D}, {E}	{A, B}, {C, D}, {E}
2	{A, B, F}, {C, D, E}	{A, B}, {C, D},
3	{A, C, E, B, D, F}	{A, C, F}
4	{A, C, F, B, D, E}	{A, C, F}
5	{A, C, D, E, B, F}	{A, C, D, E}

Figure 4. Algorithm MaxNucleoid

Algorithm: MaxNucleoid (Object set: S, Relation measure: D, Threshold of D: δ)

```
1: ClusterSet = φ
2: for each x in S do
3:      S=S-{x};
4:      let  Sₓ ={y| D(y,x)≤δ and D(x,y)≤δ, y∈S};
5:      for each z in Sₓ do
6:          Cₙₑw = {z, x},   Sₓ=Sx-{z};
7:          S`=Sₓ- Cₙₑw;
8:          for each w in S' do
9:              if ∀u ∈ Cₙₑw , D(w,u)≤δ  and D(u,w)≤δ  then
10:                 Cₙₑw = Cₙₑw + {w};
11:                 S'=S'-{w};
12:             end if
13:         end for
14:         if ClusterSet has no  C'⊇ Cₙₑw then
15:             ClusterSet = ClusterSet+{ Cₙₑw }
16:         end if
17:     end for
18: end for
19: return ClusterSet
```

Figure 5. Algorithm Merging

Algorithm: Merging(Clusters with compatible nucleoids: CN, Relation measure: D, Threshold of D: δ')

```
1: for each Cₓ in CN do
2:      if SC= =Φ then
3:          SC=SC+{Cₓ};
4:      end if
5:      for each C_y in SC do
6:          if D(Cₓ,C_y)= =min{D(C_y,C_z)|C_z≠C_y and  C_z∈ SC} and
             D(Cₓ,C_y)≤δ' then
7:                  C_y = Cₓ ∪ C_y ;
8:          else
9:              SC=SC+{Cₓ};
10:         end if
11:         CN=CN-{Cₓ};
12:     end for
13: end for
14: return SC;
```

Figure 6. Two clusters with arbitrary shapes

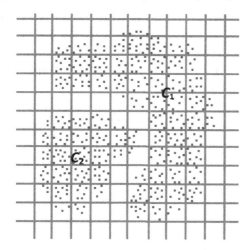

- **Definition 5: (neighboring grids)** Consider two grids $g_1 = (j^1_1, j^1_2, \ldots, j^1_d)$ and $g_2 = (j^2_1, j^2_2, \ldots, j^2_d)$, if there exists k, $1 \leq k \leq d$, such that:
  1. $|j^1_k - j^2_k| = 1$;
  2. $|j^1_l - j^2_l| = 1$ or $|j^1_l - j^2_l| = 0$, $1 \leq l \leq d$ and $l \neq k$.

Then g_1 and g_2 are called neighboring grids, denoted as $g_1 \sim g_2$.

- **Definition 6: (grid clique)** A set of grids $G = (g_1, \ldots, g_m)$ is a grid clique if for any two grids $g_i, g_j \in G$, there exist a sequence of grids $g_{k1}, \ldots, g_{kl}$ such that $g_{k1} = g_i$, $g_{kl} = g_j$, and $g_{k1} \sim g_{k2}$, $g_{k2} \sim g_{k3}, \ldots, g_{kl-1} \sim g_{kl}$.

- **Definition 7: (cluster grid cover)** Consider an object cluster C and a grid clique G, if each grid of G at least has one object of C, and each object of C is in a grid of G, then G is called the grid cover of the cluster C, and every grid in G is called cluster grid.

- **Definition 8: (internal and border grids)** Consider a cluster C and its grid cover gCov, For a grid g in G, if there exists a neighboring grid of g that is not in cluster C, then g is called a border grid of C. Otherwise g is called an internal grid of C.

Figure 7. The internal grids and the border grids of cluster

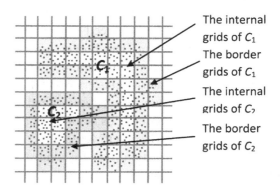

The internal grids of C_1
The border grids of C_1
The internal grids of C_2
The border grids of C_2

Figure 7 shows the internal grids and the border grids of cluster C_1 and C_2 which are described in Figure 6.

To decrease the merging computational consumption in ASCCN, we firstly partition the objects space S into grids with the dimensional unit metric e which satisfies $e \leq \dfrac{\delta}{k\sqrt{d}}$, where d is the number of the dimensions of S, k is a constant positive integer, namely, $k = 1, 2, \ldots$, in our discussion, we let it be 1. Then MaxNucleoid method (step 2 in ASCCN) is applied in every grid and the grid clique which surrounds the grid and totally has a no more than $\left\lceil \dfrac{\delta}{\sqrt{de}} \right\rceil \times \left\lceil \dfrac{\delta}{\sqrt{de}} \right\rceil$ grids in it, where $\left\lceil \dfrac{\delta}{\sqrt{de}} \right\rceil$ is the round up number of $\dfrac{\delta}{\sqrt{de}}$, and every two cliques have no intersection between them. In this time, the outputs of MaxNucleoid are the maximal compatible subsets in the given grid clique but not always the maximal ones of S. In the merging step (step 5 in ASCCN), ASCCN then merges every two subsets mentioned formerly into one object set (here, called interim cluster) according to definition 4. We only retrieve the objects in the border grids of the grid cover on these interim clusters with dictionary sort according by the subscript order. Merging will happen iteratively when the compatible relation measure value of the border grids of some interim clusters is not more than δ/2, and larger interim clusters will be produced till the final clusters come into being. The border grids of every new interim cluster is the union of border grids of its previous interim clusters which have been merged into the new one, it does not include the grids that being border grids before Merging while being internal grids after Merging.

In the extreme condition (namely, almost all objects are included densely in one grid), Due to the dimensional unit metric *e* satisfying:

$$e \leq \frac{\delta}{k\sqrt{d}},$$

we can affirm directly that objects in such grid belong to one compatible set. Then, in such situation, we just count objects in this grid while skipping the MaxNucleoid process, it will take a $O(n)$ computational consumption. Since merging only happens between the two object sets (compatible subsets or interim clusters) which have a no more than $2\sqrt{d}e + \dfrac{\delta}{2}$ compatible measure value between them, and every object set resides in a finite regional grid group, retrieving all these grid groups for merging is $O(lgn)$ computational cost. Thus, the average computational complexity of ASSCN with grids is $O(n)$.

Furthermore, due to the objects in internal grids are not computed in the merging step now, merging large interim clusters under this condition will cut down a dramatic computational consumption.

5. PERFORMANCE EVALUATION

In this section, we evaluate the performance of ASCCN. We compare it with the performance of DBSCAN because this is the first arbitrary shape clustering algorithm and original density based clustering algorithm. All the experiments are performed on a PC with 2.2GHz CPU and 512MB memory, running on Windows XP professional. We have implemented our algorithm in VC++6.0, which is hooked up with Matlab 7.0 to visualize the results.

Three synthetic sample databases SD1, SD2, SD3, which are depicted in Figure 8, were used in the effectivity (accuracy) test. SD1 has four ball-shaped clusters of significantly differing sizes. SD2 contains four clusters of nonconvex shape. SD3 has four clusters of different shape and size with additional noise.

To get ideal cluster results, we set different values of the parameter δ for SD1, SD2 and SD3. To show the results of both clustering algorithms, we visualize each cluster by a different color. In SD3, we use bright red asterisks to figure the outliers which are singletons or members of the clusters whose size is not more than 2 after the final merging has been done. The cluster results are presented in the Figure 8.

From Figure 8, one can see that ASCCN can detect correctly arbitrary shapes in the database. In this term, it has the same performance as DBSCAN (Ester et al., 1996).

In the efficiency test, a real data set and a synthetic data set were used. The real data set is from the Forest CoverType data set which is obtained from the UCI machine learning repository website (i.e., http://kdd.ics.uci.edu/databases/covertype/covertype.html). This data set contains totally 581012 observations and each observation consists of 54 attributes, including 10 quantitative variables, 4 binary wilderness areas and 40 binary soil type variables. In this set, there are 7 forest cover type classes. In our testing, we used all the 10 quantitative variables. Because the synthetic datasets can be generated by controlling the number of data points, the dimensionality, and the number of clusters, with different distribution, in a way similar to Aggarwal (2003), we produce one high dimensional synthetic data set hSD to test the abilities of these two algorithms in clustering

Figure 8. Clusters discovered by ASCCN

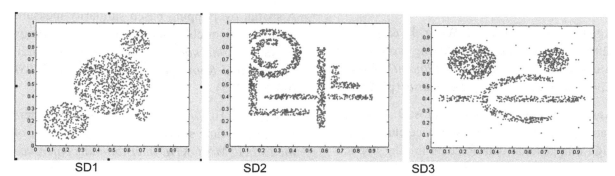

Table 3. Results of ASCCN and DBSCAN (ε is the radius parameter of DBSCAN, δ is the compatible threshold parameter of ASCCN)

			Forest CoverType	hSD
Parameters		ε	56.584	0.0154
		δ	89.652	0.0311
Run time(sec.)		**ASCCN**	456.767	392.815
		DBSCAN	1421.228	1055.426
Cluster purity		**ASCCN**	86.8%	91.2%
		DBSCAN	79.7%	69.4%

high dimensional data sets. The data set satisfies a series of Gaussian distributions, contains 10k data with 200 dimensions and belongs to 10 different classes. Like Ester (1996), we fix the parameter MinPts of DBSCAN to 4, and adopt cluster purity (c.f., appendix A) as the measure of the clustering quality. The comparison of ASCCN and DBSCAN on these data sets is shown in Table 3.

From this table, we can see that the run time of ASCCN is significantly shorter than that of DBSCAN. And the cluster purity of ASCCN is higher than that of DBSCAN, especially for high dimensional data sets. All the experimental results show that ASCCN has a better clustering quality than DBSCAN.

6. CONCLUSION

In this chapter, we present the algorithm ASCCN which is designed for arbitrary shaped clustering. ASCCN is a crisp partition method. It groups objects to compatible nucleoids first, and then classes these nucleoids into different clusters by merging method. The application of cluster grids will significantly reduce the computational time of ASCCN. Experiments also show that ASCCN has a good efficiency especially on the database with high dimensionality. In general, ASCCN outperforms DBSCAN in the terms of affectivity and efficiency.

REFERENCES

Aggarwal, C. C., Han, J., Wang, J., & Yu, P. S. (2003). A framework for clustering evolving data streams. In *Proceedings of 29th International Conference on Very Large Data Bases* (pp. 81-92).

Agrawa, R., Gehrke, J., Gunopulos, D., & Raghavan, P. (1998). Automatic subspace clustering of high dimensional data for data mining applications. In *Proceedings of the ACM SIGMOD conference on Management of Data (SIGMOD '98)* (pp. 94-105).

Ankerst, M., Breunig, M. M., Kriegel, H. P., & Sander, J. (1999). OPTICS: Ordering points to identify the clustering structure. In *Proceedings of the ACM SIGMOD Conference on Management of Data (SIGMOD '99)* (pp. 49-60).

Bhatnagar, V., Kaur, S., & Mignet, L. (2009). A parameterized framework for clustering streams. *International Journal of Data Warehousing and Mining, 5*(1), 36–56.

Biçici, E., & Yuret, D. (2007). Locally scaled density based clustering. In *Proceedings of the 8th International Conference on Adaptive and Natural Computing Algorithms (ICANNGA '07)* (pp. 739-748).

Bradley, P. S., Fayyad, U. M., & Reina, C. A. (1998). *Scaling EM (Expectation Maximization) clustering to large database* (Microsoft Research Rep. MSR-TR-98-35).

Cannon, R. L., Dave, J. V., & Bezdek, J. C. (1986). Efficient implementation of the fuzzy c-means clustering algorithms. *IEEE Transactions on Pattern Analysis and Machine Intelligence*, 248–255. doi:10.1109/TPAMI.1986.4767778

Cao, F., Ester, M., Qian, W., & Zhou, A. (2006). Density-based clustering over an evolving data stream with noise. In *Proceedings of the 2006 SIAM Conference on Data Mining (SDM '06)* (pp. 326-337).

Chen, H., Guo, G., Huang, Y., & Huang, T. (2008). A spatial overlapping based similarity measure applied to hierarchical clustering. In *Proceedings of the 5th International Conference on Fuzzy Systems and Knowledge Discovery (FSKD '08)* (pp. 371-375).

Chen, Y., & Tu, L. (2007). Density-based clustering for real-time stream data. In *Proceedings of the 13th ACM SIGKDD international conference on Knowledge discovery and data mining* (pp. 133-142).

Ester, M., Kriegel, H. P., Sander, J., & Xu, X. (1996). A density-based algorithm for discovering clusters in large spatial database with noise. In *Proceedings of 2nd International Conference on Knowledge Discovery and Data Mining (KDD '96)* (pp. 226-232).

Guha, S., Rastogi, R., & Shim, K. (1998). CURE: An efficient clustering algorithm for large databases. In *Proceedings of the ACM SIGMOD conference on Management of Data (SIGMOD '98)* (pp. 73-84).

Halkidi, M., & Vazirgiannis, M. (2001). Clustering validity assessment: Finding the optimal partitioning of a data set. In *Proceedings of International Conference on Data Mining*.

Han, J., Kanber, M., & Tung, A. K. H. (2001). *Spatial clustering methods in data mining: A survey. Geographic Data Mining and Knowledge Discovery*. New York: Taylor and Francis.

Hinneburg, A., & Keim, D. A. (1998). An efficient approach to clustering in large Multimedia Database with noise. In *Proceedings of 4th International Conference on Konwledge Discovery and Data Mining (KDD '98)* (pp. 58-65).

Hore, P., Hall, L. O., & Goldgof, D. B. (2007). Single pass fuzzy c-means. *IEEE International Fuzzy Systems Conference*, 1-7.

Huang, Z. (1998). Extensions to the k-Means algorithm for clustering large data sets with categorical values. *Data Mining and Knowledge Discovery*, 283–304. doi:10.1023/A:1009769707641

Kaufma, L., & Rousseeuw, P. J. (1990). *Finding groups in data: an introduction to cluster analysis*. New York: John Wiley & Sons.

Kwok, T., Smith, K. A., Lozano, S., & Taniar, D. (2002). Parallel Fuzzy c-Means Clustering for Large Data Sets. *Euro-Par, 365*-374.

Le-Khac, N., Aouad, L. M., & Kechadi, M. (2007). A new approach for distributed density based clustering on grid platform. In *Proceedings of the 24th British national conference on databases (BNCOD '07)* (pp. 247-258).

Li, M., Lee, G., Lee, W., & Sivasubramaniam, A. (2006). PENS: an algorithm for density-based clustering in peer-to-peer systems. In *Proceedings of the 1st international conference on scalable information systems*.

MacQueen, J. (1967). Some methods for classification and analysis of multivariate observations. In *Proceedings of the 5th Berkeley Symposium on Mathematical Statistics and Probability* (pp. 281-297).

Ng, R. T., & Han, J. (1994). Efficient and effective clustering methods for spatial data mining. In *Proceedings of the 20th International Conference on Very Large Data Bases (VLDB '94)* (pp. 144-155).

Pal, N. R., & Bezdek, J. C. (1995). On cluster validity for the fuzzy c-means model. *IEEE Transactions on Fuzzy Systems, 3*(3), 370–379. doi:10.1109/91.413225

Song, M., Hu, X., Yoo, I., & Koppel, E. (2009). A Dynamic and Semantically-Aware Technique for Document Clustering in Biomedical Literature. *International Journal of Data Warehousing and Mining, 5*(4), 44–57.

Sun, H., Yu, G., Bao, Y., Zhao, F., & Wang, D. (2005). CDS-Tree: An effective index for clustering arbitrary shapes in data streams. In *Proceedings of the 15th international workshop on research issues in data engineering: stream data mining and applications (RIDE-SDMA '05)*.

Tan, L., Taniar, D., & Smith, K. A. (2005). A clustering algorithm based on an estimated distribution model. *International Journal of Data Warehousing and Mining, 1*(2), 229–245.

Wan, R., Wang, L., & Su, X. (2009). PNMBG: Point neighborhood merging with border grids. *Journal of Information and Organizational Sciences, 33*(2), 297–305.

Wang, W., Yang, J., & Muntz, R. (1997). STING: A statistical information grid approach to spatial data mining. In *Proceedings of the 23rd International Conference on Very Large Data Bases (VLDB '97)* (pp. 186-195).

Zhang, T., Ramakrishnam, R., & Livny, M. (1996). BIRCH: an efficient data clustering method for very large databases. In *Proceedings of the 1996 ACM SIGMOD International Conference on Management of Data (SIGMOD '96)* (pp. 103-114).

Zhang, X., Hu, X., Xia, J., Zhou, X., & Achananuparp, P. (2008). A Graph-Based Biomedical Literature Clustering Approach Utilizing Term's Global and Local Importance Information. *International Journal of Data Warehousing and Mining, 4*(4), 84–101.

Zhang, X., Jing, L., Hu, X., Ng, M., Xia, J., & Zhou, X. (2008). Medical Document Clustering Using Ontology-Based Term Similarity Measures. *International Journal of Data Warehousing and Mining, 4*(1), 62–73.

APPENDIX A: PURITY

Cluster purity is one of the ways of measuring the quality of a clustering solution. Let there be k clusters of the dataset D and size of cluster C_j be $|C_j|$. Let $|C_j|_{class=i}$ denote number of items of class i assigned to cluster j. Purity of this cluster is given by

$$purity(C_j) = \frac{1}{|C_j|} \max_i (|C_j|_{class=i})$$

The overall purity of a clustering solution could be expressed as a weighted sum of individual cluster purities

$$purity = \sum_{j=1}^{k} \frac{C_j}{|D|} purity(C_j)$$

In general, the lager the value of purity is, the better the solution is.

This work was previously published in International Journal of Data Warehousing and Mining, Volume 6, Issue 4, edited by David Taniar, pp. 1-15, copyright 2010 by IGI Publishing (an imprint of IGI Global).

Chapter 14
A New Similarity Metric for Sequential Data

Pradeep Kumar
Indian Institute of Management, India

Bapi S. Raju
Infosys Technologies Limited, India

P. Radha Krishna
University of Hyderabad, India

ABSTRACT

In many data mining applications, both classification and clustering algorithms require a distance/similarity measure. The central problem in similarity based clustering/classification comprising sequential data is deciding an appropriate similarity metric. The existing metrics like Euclidean, Jaccard, Cosine, and so forth do not exploit the sequential nature of data explicitly. In this chapter, the authors propose a similarity preserving function called Sequence and Set Similarity Measure (S^3M) that captures both the order of occurrence of items in sequences and the constituent items of sequences. The authors demonstrate the usefulness of the proposed measure for classification and clustering tasks. Experiments were conducted on benchmark datasets, that is, DARPA'98 and msnbc, for classification task in intrusion detection and clustering task in web mining domains. Results show the usefulness of the proposed measure.

INTRODUCTION

Sequential data may arise from diverse application domains which may have time stamp associated with it or not (Salva & Chakravarthy, 2008). They may be music files, system calls, transaction records, web logs, genomic data and so on. In these data there are hidden relations that should be explored to find interesting information. For example, from web logs one can extract the information regarding the most frequent access path; from genomic data one can extract letter or motif (sequence of letters) frequencies; from music files one can discover harmonies etc. One can extract features from sequential data, represent them as vectors and cluster the data using exist-

DOI: 10.4018/978-1-61350-474-1.ch014

Copyright © 2012, IGI Global. Copying or distributing in print or electronic forms without written permission of IGI Global is prohibited.

ing clustering techniques. Similar to clustering, in classification task also a similarity measure is required to determine the class membership of test data or sequence. The central problem in similarity based classification/clustering problems is to come up with an appropriate similarity metric.

Usually when dealing with sequences, we first convert them into frequency vectors, treating all the events within the sequences as independent of one another. The resulting vectors corresponding to the data are then classified/clustered using existing classification/clustering techniques (Tan et al., 2006; Kumar et al., 2007). Treating sequences in this manner results in a loss of the sequential information embedded in them and leads to inaccurate classification or clustering.

A number of metrics have been proposed for sequences, many of them do not really qualify as metrics, as they do not satisfy one or more of the requirements of being a metric (Mitchell, 1997). Similarity has both a quantitative and a qualitative aspect. Some measures such as cosine similarity, hamming distance consider only the quantitative aspect whereas measures such as Longest Common Subsequence (LCS), feature distance consider only qualitative aspect. In this chapter, we introduce a new similarity measure that considers both sequence (qualitative or ordering aspect) and set similarity (quantitative aspect) among sequences while computing similarity. We tested the performance of our proposed similarity measure on both classification and clustering tasks. Standard algorithms like k-Nearest Neighbor (kNN) classification and Partitioning Around Mediod (PAM) clustering algorithms were used along with the cosine measure as well as the proposed similarity measure for comparative experimental analysis. In addition, in the case of classification task, the proposed measure was also compared with a recently proposed metric called, the Binary Weighted Cosine (BWC) similarity measure (Rawat et al., 2006). The effectiveness of the proposed measure is studied in both intrusion

detection (classification task) and in web usage mining (clustering task).

This chapter is organized as follows. In the next section, we discuss various aspects of sequence similarity. In the proposed measure, Longest Common Subsequence is one of the components therefore we provide study of longest common sub-sequence in the following section. A new similarity measure S^3M in is presented in the next followed section. Last but not the final section we present the results of the new measure for both classification and clustering tasks.

SEQUENCE SIMILARITY

A sequence is made of set of items that happen in time, or happen one after another, that is, in position but not necessarily in relation with time. We can say that a sequence is an ordered set of items. A sequence is denoted as follows:

$$S = <a_1, a_2, ..., a_n>$$

where $a_1, a_2, ..., a_n$ are the item sets in sequence S. Sequence S contains n elements or ordered item sets. Sequence length is defined as the count of number of item sets contained in the sequence. It is denoted as $|S|$ and here, $|S| = n$. Formally, *similarity* is a nonnegative real valued function S, defined on the Cartesian product $X \times X$ of a set X. It is called a *metric* on X if for every $x, y \in X$, the following properties are satisfied by S.

1. Non-negativity: $S(x, y) \geq 0$
2. Symmetry: $S(x, y) = S(y, x)$
3. Normalization: $S(x, y) \leq 1$

A set X along with a metric is called a *metric space*.

Sequence mining algorithms make use of either distance functions (Duda et al., 2001) or similarity functions (Bergroth et al., 2000) for comparing pairs of sequences. Sequence comparison finds important and interesting applications in the field of computer science both from the theoretical as well as practical points of view. A wide variety of applications of sequence similarity is seen in various interrelated disciplines such as computer science, molecular biology, speech and pattern recognition etc. Sankoff and Kruskal (1983) present the application of sequence comparison and various methodologies adopted in the literature. In computer science, sequence comparison finds application in various fields such as string matching, classification of imbalance data (Nikulin, 2008) and clustering. Mohamad et al (2006) proposes a similarity retrieval algorithm for time series data.

Given two sequences of equal length we can define a measure of similarity by considering distances between corresponding elements of the two sequences. The individual elements of the sequences may be vectors of real numbers (e.g., in applications involving speech or audio signals) or they may be symbolic data e.g., in applications involving gene sequences (Alshalalfa et al., 2008) or web data (Spiliopoulou & Brunzel, 2007). Symbolic data may be encoded into feature vectors in many ways such as encoding the absence or presence of feature (boolean vector), frequency count of the feature and encoding in a probabilistic way. When the sequence elements are feature vectors (with real components) standard metrics such as Euclidean distance, Cosine distance may be used for measuring similarity between two data elements. However, vector based distance measures are incapable of capturing subjective similarities effectively. For example, in speech or audio signals, similar sounding patterns may give feature vectors that have large euclidean distances and vice versa. When the sequences consist of symbolic data we have to define dissimilarity between every pair of symbols which in general is determined by the application. Below we describe some of the commonly used distance measures for sequences.

Feature distance is a simple and effective distance measure (Kohenen, 19985). A feature

is a short subsequence, usually referred to as N-gram, where N is the length of the subsequence. Feature distance is defined as the number of subsequences by which two sequences differ. This measure cannot qualify as a distance metric as two distinct sequences can have zero distance. For example, consider the sequences PQPQPP and PPQPQP. These sequences contain the same bi-grams (PQ, QP, and PP) and hence the feature distance will be zero with $N = 2$.

Another common distance measure for sequences is the *Levenshtein distance* (LD) (Levensthein, 1966). LD is also known as *edit distance*. It is also applicable for sequences of different lengths. LD measures the minimum cost associated with transforming one sequence into another using basic edit operations, namely, replacement, insertion and deletion of a subsequence. Each of these operations has a cost assigned with it. Consider two sequences s_1 = "test" and s_2 = "test". As no transformation operation is required to convert s_1 into s_2, the LD between s_1 and s_2, is denoted as $LD(s_1, s_2) = 0$. If s_3 = "test" and s_4 = "tent", then $LD(s_3, s_4) = 1$, as one edit operation is required to convert sequence s_3 into sequence s_4. The greater the LD, the more dissimilar the sequences are. Although LD can be computed directly for any two sequences, in cases where there are already devised scoring schemes as in computational molecular biology (Mount, 2004), it is desirable to compute a distance that is consistent with the similarity score of the sequences.

However, none of these methods captures both the quantitative as well as the order information embedded in the sequential data. Some of the metrics like N-gram captures both the quantitative as well as order information but the order information is limited to the size of N, where N is the size of the subsequence. Rawat et al. (2006) proposed a similarity measure, called *Binary Weigthed Cosine* similarity measure, which computes the cosine similarity considering the shared items of sequences. However, this measure does not capture the order information. Term reweighting of document vector is an important method to integrate domain ontology to clustering process (Zhang et al., 2008).

Based on these insights we felt the need for a technique that captures both sequential as well as content information while computing similarity between two sequences. In general, content information is captured using the well known *Jaccard* similarity measure. The order information can be captured using the sliding window concept, where local order information in contiguous subsequence is captured (Kumar et al., 2005). The above technique captures only the partial ordering information. In calculating similarity between sequences it is important to find an algorithm that computes a common subsequence between two given sequences as efficiently as possible (Simon, 1987). Intuitively, when two sequences are similar it is expected that the underlying sequences are also similar, in particular, then it is possible to find the LCS. In this chapter, we devise a new similarity measure which takes into account both the order of occurrence in-formation (with the help of LCS measure) and the content information (using Jaccard similarity measure) while comparing two data sequences. Firstly, we take a closer look at the LCS measure and then go on to devising the new measure.

LONGEST COMMON SUBSEQUENCE

The Longest Common Subsequence (LCS) problem can be defined as follows: Let A1 and A2 be two sequences of length n1 and n2, over alphabet $\sum = \{\sigma 1, \sigma 2, ...,\sigma N\}$. A subsequence of A1 can be obtained by removing zero or more symbols from A1. Similarly, a subsequence of A2 can be obtained by removing zero or more symbols from A2. The LCS problem for two sequences A1 and A2 is to find a sequence B such that B is a subsequence of both A1 and A2 and it has the largest length. For example, B = "ce" is the LCS

for A1 = "computer" and A2 = "science". Note that for a given set of sequences there can be more than one LCS.

The degree of similarity between two sequences can be measured by extracting the maximal number of identical symbols existing in both sequences in the same order and is known as (one of) the longest common subsequence(s). The length of this subsequence describes the similarity between the sequences.

Consider two sequences X[1...m] and Y[1...n] made up from D different symbols belonging to the alphabet $\sum$. A subsequence S[1...s] $(0 \le s \le m)$ of X can be obtained by deleting arbitrarily (m - s) symbols from X. Further, if S is also a subsequence of Y, then S is a common subsequence of X and Y, denoted by CS(X,Y). The longest common subsequence of X and Y, abbreviated by LCS(X,Y) is the CS(X,Y) having maximal length, whose length is denoted by LLCS. Between any pair of sequences the longest common subsequence need not be unique. That means there may be several subsequences satisfying the Longest Common Subsequence criterion. It is also possible that the same longest common subsequence occurs at multiple positions of the sequences.

In some applications, the length of the LCS is required, whereas in some applications the longest common subsequence itself is required. All algorithms calculating the length of longest common subsequence can be modified to obtain the longest common subsequence. Once the LLCS is known, the LCS can be constructed by backtracking the selections made during the computation of LLCS. Backtracking leads to time and space overhead, which means that the behavior of the LLCS of a LCS algorithm may considerably differ from its LCS-variant. This overhead can be diminished by having knowledge on the lower and the upper bound of LLCS. A large number of algorithms have been proposed for computing LCS in the literature (Bergorth et al., 2000).

LCS algorithms are implemented using dynamic programming approach. It is not hard to see that the straight-forward implementation of dynamic programming method for constructing the similarity score matrix would lead to $O(mn)$ time and space complexities, where m and n are the lengths of two sequences in consideration. Lot of research has been done in efficient implementation of LCS algorithm using dynamic programming approach. We have compiled various algorithms available in the literature with time complexities for computing LCS in Table 1. In the table, m and n are the lengths of two sequences such that n, m. S is the size of the alphabet from which two sequences are composed. K denotes the number of minimal mismatches in the two sequences and p is the length of LCS of two sequences.

S³M –SIMILARITY MEASURE FOR SEQUENCES

In this section, we propose a new similarity measure for computing similarity between sequences. In order to find patterns in sequences, it is necessary to not only look at the items contained in sequences but also the order of their occurrence. In order to account for both kinds of information, a new measure, called Sequence and Set Similarity Measure (S^3M), is proposed. S^3M consists of two parts: one that quantifies the composition of the sequence (set similarity) and the other that quantifies the sequential nature (sequence similarity). Sequence similarity is defined in terms of the order of occurrence of item sets within two sequences. Length of the longest common subsequence ($LLCS$) determines the sequence similarity aspect across two sequences. For two sequences A and B, sequence similarity is given by

$$SeqSim(A, B) = \frac{LLCS(A, B)}{\max(|A|, |B|)} \quad (1)$$

Set similarity (Jaccard similarity measure) is defined as ratio of the number of common item

Table 1. Compiled results for the LCS problem

Time Complexity	References
O(mn)	Wanger and Fischer (1974)
O(mn)	Hirschberg (1975)
O((n + S) log n)	Hunt and Szymanski (1977)
O(mn)	Hirschberg (1975)
O(mn)	Hirschberg (1975)
$O(\dfrac{n^2}{\log n})$	Masek and Paterson (1980)
O(n(m-p))	Nakatsu et al. (1982)
$O(pn \log \dfrac{n}{p} + pn)$	Hsu and Du (1984)
O(n(n-p))	Myers (1986)
O(n(n-p))	Apostolico and Guerra (1987)
O(nS+min(KS,pn))	Rick (1994)

sets and the number of unique item sets in two sequences. Thus, for two sequences A and B, set similarity is given by

$$SetSim(A, B) = \frac{|A \cap B|}{|A \cup B|} \quad (2)$$

Let us consider two sequences A and B, where $A = <a, b, c, d>$ and $B = <d, c, b, a>$. Now, the set similarity measure for these two sequences is *1*, indicating that their composition is alike. But we can see that they are not at all similar when considering the order of occurrence of item sets. This aspect is quantified by the sequence similarity component, which is *0.25* for these sequences. For two sequences, $C = <a, b, c, d>$ and $D = <b, a, k, c, t, p, d>$, $LLCS(C, D)$ works out to be *3* and after normalization, the sequence similarity component turns out to be *0.43*. The set similarity for these two sequences is *0.57*. The above two examples illustrate the need for combining set similarity and sequence similarity components into one function in order to take care of both the content as well as order based similarity aspects. Thus, S^3M is constituted as a linear combination of both set similarity and sequence similarity and is defined as below.

$$S^3M(A,B) = p \times \frac{LLCS(A,B)}{\max(|A|,|B|)} + q \times \frac{|A \cap B|}{|A \cup B|} \tag{3}$$

where *p + q = 1* and *p, q ≥ 0*.

Here, *p* and *q* determine the relative weights given for order of occurrence (sequence similarity) and to content (set similarity), respectively. In practical applications, user could specify these parameters.

Characteristics of S³M Similarity Measure

Given a set of finite and non-trivial sequences $s_i, s_j \in S$, a function $F(s_i, s_j) = Sim_{ij}$ from $S \times S \to R$ (set of real numbers) is called an index of similarity, if it satisfies the following properties.

1. Non-negativity: $Sim_{ij} \geq 0, \forall\ s_i, s_j \in S$
2. Symmetry: $Sim_{ij} = Sim_{ji}, \forall\ s_i, s_j \in S$
3. Normalization: $Sim_{ij} \leq 1, \forall\ s_i, s_j \in S$

Proposed similarity function has six parameters namely *p, q, LLCS(A, B), Max(|A|, |B|), |A∩B|* and *|A∪B|*. By the two conditions *p+q = 1* and *p,q ≥ 0*, we can infer that *p* and *q* can never be negative. Rest of the four parameters, being absolute values, cannot attain negative values. Hence, the parameters cannot be negative. Finally, the sum and division operations on non-negative values will always result in non-negative values. Thus, it is straightforward to see that the first condition of similarity holds. Since all the operations used in

computing the similarity score are symmetric, it is easy to see that the proposed similarity function also obeys the symmetry property. Further, the proposed measure is a convex combination of two parameters *p* and *q*. Also, the values of *p* and *q* lie between 0 and 1, hence the convex combination of *p* and *q* will lie between *0* and *1*. Thus, the third property of normalization also holds.

Theoretical Justification for Choosing 'p'

When the length of longest common subsequence is used as a measure of similarity between pair of sequences then it becomes important to have an idea of expected length of longest common subsequence between them. Equation 4 gives the expected length $EL_n^{(k)}$ of a longest common subsequence over an alphabet of size *k* over all pairs of sequences of length *n* (Paterson & Danick, 1994).

$$EL_h^{(k)} = \frac{1}{k^{2n}} \sum_{|u|=|v|=|n|} LLCS(u,v) \tag{4}$$

A bound γ_k on the expected length of the Longest Common Subsequence has been derived by Paterson and Danick (1994) (Table 2).

For every $k \geq 2$ there is some γ_k such that

$$Y_k = \lim_{n \to \infty} \frac{EL_n^{(k)}}{n} \tag{5}$$

Exact values of γ_k are not known. Upper bound on γ_k for *k* = 1, 2, …, 15 as calculated by Paterson and Danc'ik (1994) is 0.47620 for alphabet size 14 and 0.46462 for alphabet size of 15. The upper bound of γ_k can be used to specify the value of *p* (and hence *q*, as *q* = 1 – p) for S^3M similarity measure.

In this chapter, we used *p* = 0. 5 in the S^3M for the experiments conducted with *msnbc* web log dataset for clustering task. The alphabet size for the *msnbc* web log dataset is 17 and the value of *p*

Table 2. The Bounds on γ_k (Paterson & Danick, 1994)

Alphabet size	Lower Bound	Upper Bound	Alphabet size	Lower Bound	Upper Bound
2	0.77391	0.83763	9	0.40321	0.55394
3	0.61538	0.76581	10	0.38656	0.53486
4	0.54545	0.70824	11	0.37196	0.51785
5	0.50615	0.66443	12	0.35899	0.50260
6	0.47169	0.62932	13	0.34737	0.48880
7	0.44502	0.60019	14	0.33687	0.47620
8	0.42237	0.57541	15	0.32732	0.46462

= 0.5 seems reasonable. In the IDS classification experiments, we systematically varied the p value and investigated the sensitivity of classification performance.

EXPLOITING S³M

In this section, we describe the results of the experiments for classification and clustering tasks with the proposed metric, S^3M. kNN classification algorithm has been utilized and tested on benchmark dataset *IDS DARPA* '98 with the new measure and results are compared with those from cosine and BWC measures. *PAM* clustering algorithm on *msnbc* dataset, a benchmark dataset for web log mining, with the proposed measure S^3M has been experimented. The results are compared with the results of *cosine* measure. In this chapter we have used cosine and BWC similarity measures as a comparative similarity measure for S^3M. We briefly, define both the measures.

Cosine similarity is a common vector based similarity measure. This metric calculates the angle of difference in the direction of two vectors, irrespective of their lengths. Cosine similarity between two vectors, A and B is given by

$$C(\mid A \mid, \mid B \mid) = \frac{A \times B}{\mid A \mid\mid B \mid} \qquad (6)$$

Rawat et al. (2006) proposed binary weighted cosine (BWC) similarity measure for measuring similarity across sequences. This similarity measure considers both the number of shared elements between two sets as well as frequencies of those elements. The similarity measure between two sequences A and B is given by

$$BWC(A, B) = \frac{\mid A_b \cap B_b \mid}{\mid A_b \cup B_b \mid} \times \frac{A \times B}{\mid A \mid\mid B \mid} \qquad (7)$$

where, A_b, B_b denote binary values indicating the absence or presence of corresponding features. BWC measure captures the frequency and commonality of elements to calculate similarity. Cosine similarity measure is a contributing component in a BWC similarity measure. Hence, BWC similarity measure is also a vector based similarity measure. The effectiveness of the S³M is demonstrated with both the cosine as well as the BWC similarity measures for classification task and in the case of the clustering task, the effectiveness of S³M has been shown in comparison to the cosine similarity measure. All the experiments described in this chapter were implemented in Java 1.4 on 2.4 GHz, 256 MB RAM, Pentium-IV machine running Microsoft Windows XP 2002.

Classification Task

Formally, the intrusion detection problem on system calls or command sequences can be defined as follows: $\sum = \{s_1, s_2, s_3, ..., s_m\}$ be the set of system calls where m denotes the total number of system calls that occur in sequences. A training set D is defined as containing several sequences of normal behavior. The goal in this case, is to devise a binary classification scheme that maps the incoming sequence to either the class of normal sessions or to the class of intrusive sessions. In general, dealing with sequence data is difficult; hence each sequence is coded with vector notation. The coding could be binary indicating the presence or absence of a system call in the session or it may be the frequency of each system call in session. The other way of vector encoding could be in terms of time stamp associated with the system calls. However, all these techniques ignore the order information embedded within the session. In this work, we used the classical kNN classification algorithm with S^3M.

The algorithm consists of two phases namely, training and testing phases. Dataset D consists of m sessions. Each session is of variable length. Initially training set is built by extracting all the normal sequences from the dataset D. The model is trained with the dataset consisting of normal sessions. For an unlabelled session, the similarity metric is constructed using S^3M with all the sessions of the training set. If similarity between any session in training set and new session is equal to 1, we mark it as normal. In other case, we pick the k highest values of similarity between new sample P and training dataset. From this k maximum values, we calculate the average similarity. If the average similarity value is greater than user specified threshold value (τ) we mark the new session P as normal, else we mark P as abnormal.

Experimental Results

Experiments were conducted using k-Nearest Neighbor classifier with S^3M. The results of S^3M was compared to the results obtained using cosine and BWC similarity measures results with kNN classification algorithm. DARPA'98 IDS dataset (http://www.ll.mit.edu/IST/ideval/data/) was used for the experimental purpose.

DARPA'98 IDS dataset consists of TCPDUMP and BSM audit data. The network traffic of an Air Force Local Area Network was simulated to collect TCPDUMP and BSM audit data. The audit logs contain seven weeks of training data and two weeks of testing data. There were 38 types of attacks and several realistic intrusion scenarios conducted in the midst of normal background data. For experimental purpose, 605 unique processes were used as a training dataset, which were free from all types of attacks. Testing was conducted on 5285 normal processes. In order to test the detection capability of proposed approach, we incorporated 55 intrusive sessions into the test data.

To evaluate the efficiency and behavior of the classifier with different similarity measures Receiver Operating Characteristics (ROC) curve is used. It depicts the relationship between false positive rate (FPR) and detection rate (DR). Detection rate is the ratio of number of intrusive sessions (abnormal) detected correctly to the total number of intrusive sessions. False positive rate is defined as the number of normal sessions detected as abnormal divided by the total number of normal sessions. The threshold values determine how close the given session is to the training dataset containing all normal sessions. We performed both the parametric and comparative analysis (with cosine and BWC similarity measures) with the new measure called, S^3M.

Parametric Analysis

The parametric analysis was performed for two parameters namely p, parameter controlling the relative influence of sequential order on S^3M and k the number of neighbors of *kNN* classification algorithm. We performed the experiments with k = 5, and k = 10.

Figure 1 shows the ROC curve of kNN classification with S^3M measure for k = 5 and k = 10. Table 3 shows the FPR and DR values for threshold values for Figure 1. For both the k values the p value of S^3M was fixed at 0.5. A high DR of 1 at low FPR of 0.008 was recorded with *kNN* classifier for k = 5 which is comparatively far better than k =10, in which case DR value equal to 1 was recorded at FPR value of 0.013. Thus, a better results were observed for k = 5 than k = 10 with S^3M. A low k value means less comparison thus reducing time complexity. As a result, further experiments were carried out using k = 5. Table 4 shows the results for

k = 5 for different combinations of p and q values. Higher the p value, more is the sequential information considered. The low p value infers that more emphasis is given on the content infor-

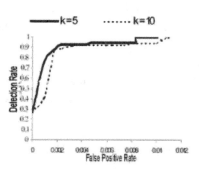

Figure 1. ROC Curves for k=5 and k=10 using S³M

mation than the sequential information. From Table 4, it can be observed that DR of 1 was recorded for low FPR value of 0.0053 for p value 1. The value of 1 for p means that only weightage is assigned to the sequential similarity and hence no weightage is given for content information. The second lowest FPR value of 0.007 was recorded for p = 0.6 and p = 0.7. This shows that the p value for *DARPA '98 IDS* dataset should be chosen between 0.5 and 0.7. These values of p will contain both sequential as well as content

Table 3. FPR vs DR for k =5 and k=10 at p = 0.5

	k=5		k=10	
Th	**FPR**	**DR**	**FPR**	**DR**
0.89	0.010028	1	0.010974	1
0.88	0.010028	1	0.010974	1
0.87	0.008325	1	0.010974	1
0.86	0.008325	0.94545	0.010785	1
0.84	0.00756	0.94545	0.009839	0.94545
0.8	0.00491	0.94545	0.008136	0.94545
0.78	0.004162	0.92727	0.00719	0.92727
0.75	0.00245	0.92727	0.00359	0.92727
0.7	0.00189	0.8909	0.00227	0.8909
0.65	0.000946	0.76363	0.0017	0.85454
0.6	0.000189	0.36363	0.00089	0.4
0.55	0	0.27272	0	0.2909

aspects of the dataset and lead to better classification accuracy. The effect of varying sequence weightage (p) on DR at various threshold values was also studied. With increase in p value, the DR value tends to approach the ideal value of 1 faster. That means that the order of occurrences of system calls plays significant role in determining the nature of a session, whether it is normal or abnormal.

Comparative Analysis

The comparative analysis of the S^3M measure was done with respect to *cosine* and *BWC* similarity measures. Figure 2 shows the comparative ROC curves for *DARPA '98 IDS* dataset with the three measures. The experiments were conducted for $k = 5$. The sequence controlling parameter, p, for the S^3M measure is taken as 0.5. As can be seen from Figure 2 ROC curve due to S^3M measure has high DR than cosine and BWC similarity measures at low FPR. As can be observed from the figure that the detection rate of 1 was achieved at FPR of 0.01 in the case of S^3M measure whereas in the case of cosine measure it is achieved at FPR of

0.12. With the BWC similarity measure the DR of 1 was achieved at 0.08 FPR value. These values indicate that with S^3MkNN classification algorithm performed well compared to cosine and BWC similarity measures. Both the cosine and BWC similarity measures use vector encoding of the sequences before feeding into the kNN classifier, thus losing the sequential information embedded in them. Whereas with the S^3M, the sequences are not encoded into the vector rather similarity is computed directly across two sequences taking both the sequential as well as content information into account.

Further unlike earlier cases (Liao & Vemuri, 2002; Rawat et al., 2006), where they achieved DR = 1 after removing two attacks from 55 attacks, DR of 1 was achieved with S^3M without removing any attacks. There were two attacks included in the testing data namely, 4:5it162228loadmodule and 5:5itfdformatchmod, which could not be detected by Rawat et al. (2006) whereas Liao and Vemuri (2002) scheme de-tected them at a lower threshold value. Rawat et al. (2006) quoted that though the attack 4:5it162228loadmodule was launched, it failed to compromise the system thus

Table 4. FPR vs DR for various combinations of p and q values (k=5)

Th	P=0.0, q=1.0		P=0.2, q=0.8		P=0.4, q=0.6		P=0.6, q=0.4		P=0.7, q=0.3		P=0.8, q=0.2		P=1.0, q=0.0	
	FPR	DR	FPR	DR	FPR	DR	FPR	DR	FPR	DR	FPR	DR	FPR	DR
0.89	0.0072	0.9455	0.0081	0.9455	0.01	1	0.0095	1	0.0108	1	0.01	1	0.0087	1
0.88	0.0072	0.9455	0.0081	0.9455	0.01	1	0.0095	1	0.0098	1	0.01	1	0.0072	1
0.87	0.0061	0.9455	0.0074	0.9455	0.0085	1	0.0089	1	0.0093	1	0.0083	1	0.0072	1
0.86	0.0059	0.9455	0.0074	0.9455	0.0083	1	0.0079	1	0.0089	1	0.0083	0.9455	0.0068	1
0.84	0.0057	0.9455	0.0064	0.9455	0.0076	0.9636	0.007	1	0.007	1	0.0076	0.9455	0.0053	1
0.8	0.0045	0.6182	0.0053	0.9455	0.0055	0.9455	0.0042	0.9455	0.0042	0.9273	0.0049	0.9455	0.0049	0.9455
0.78	0.0042	0.5455	0.0045	0.9455	0.0032	0.9273	0.0042	0.9273	0.004	0.9273	0.0042	0.9273	0.0042	0.9273
0.75	0.0021	0.4909	0.004	0.9091	0.0025	0.9091	0.0038	0.9091	0.0032	0.9091	0.0025	0.9273	0.004	0.8909
0.7	0.0004	0.4182	0.0011	0.4727	0.0019	0.8909	0.0021	0.8727	0.0021	0.8909	0.0019	0.8909	0.0015	0.8545
0.65	0.0002	0.2909	0.0002	0.4	0.0009	0.7818	0.0009	0.8	0.0011	0.8182	0.0009	0.7636	0.0008	0.7636
0.6	0	0.0545	0	0.2909	0.0002	0.4545	0.0002	0.6545	0.0002	0.6545	0.0002	0.3636	0.0002	0.6909
0.55	0	0.0182	0	0.0364	0	0.2545	0.0002	0.2545	0.0002	0.2545	0	0.2727	0.0002	0.1818

making the process seem normal. In case of the second one, 5:5*itfdformatchmod*, the attack was not launched in early stage. Hence, they argued that the attack has not manifested and thus may not be detected by their scheme as they are normal processes. Rawat et al. (2006) reported results on experiments after removing these two attacks from the testing data set. To compare with the Rawat et al. (2006) results we also removed these two attacks from our test set and conducted experiments. Figure 3 shows the comparative ROC curves with the full and reduced dataset of abnormal attacks. The curve shows that with the reduced abnormal test set S^3M performed better hence showing its effectiveness. The decrease in the performance on non-reduced dataset is minimal and of course on the reduced dataset the performance is superior.

For *DARPA'98 IDS* dataset we found that the order of occurrence of system calls plays a key role in determining the nature of the session. From the results presented in this section, we can conclude that the proposed similarity measure could form an integral part of an intrusion detection system that incorporates sequence classification. Experiments with *DARPA⁰98 IDS* dataset for $k = 10$ were also conducted. A similar trend and results were recorded.

Clustering Task

In this section, we used *PAM*, a standard clustering algorithm that represents data in a vectorial form and partitions the space into groups of items that are close to each other based on *cosine* similarity measure. *PAM* is also used here with S^3M, our new similarity measure that preserves sequence information within a session.

In the case of web transactions, each cluster represents a group of transactions that are similar, based on co occurrence patterns of page categories. Let $\sum = \{ p_1, p_2, p_3, ..., p_m \}$ be the set of page categories, t be a user session and $t \in \sum^*$, where $\sum^*$ represents the set of all sessions made up of sequences of page categories. Let D be the training dataset consisting of N user sessions, i.e., $D = \{ t_1, t_2, t_3, ..., t_N \}$. Each user session can be represented in two ways. In the vectorial representation, $t_i = < f(p_1), f(p_2), f(p_3), ... f(p_m) >$, where each $f(p_j)$ can be formulated in three different ways. $f(p_j) \in f\{0,1\}$ indicating the presence or absence of jth page category in the ith user session, t_i. Boolean representation has been used in the literature (Shahabi et al., 1997; Yan et al., 1996). If $f(p_j)$ could represent the duration of time user spends in the jth page category in the ith user session then user session can be vectorially formulated with respect to the time spent. It has been commented that time spent is not a good indicator of interest (Konstan et al., 1997). $f(p_j)$ can be used to repre-

Figure 2. Comparative ROC Curves for Cosine, BWC and S3M measures for k =5

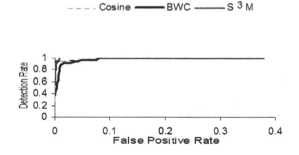

Figure 3. Comparative ROC graph with reduced and without reduced attacks

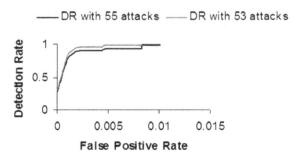

sent the frequencies of page categories for a user session. In this chapter, for experiments with PAM using cosine measure, we used the third approach (Kumar et al., 2007).

In the sequence representation scheme, the user session consisting of page categories, i.e., $t \in \sum^*$, is considered directly. We have used this formulation in all the experiments where S^3M similarity measure was considered.

Experimental Results

Experiments were conducted using *PAM* clustering algorithm with S^3M and cosine similarity measures. *msnbc weblogs* dataset was used for the experi-mental purpose. We collected *msnbc* data from the UCI dataset repository (http://kdd.ics.uci.edu/) that consists of Internet Information Server (IIS) logs for *msnbc.com* and news-related portions of *msn.com* for the entire day of September 28, 1999 (Pacific Standard Time). Each sequence in the dataset corresponds to page views of a user during that twenty-four hour period. Each event in the sequence corresponds to a user's request for a page. Requests are not recorded at the finest level of detail but at the level of page categories as determined by the site administrator. There are 17 page categories, namely, `frontpage', `news', `tech', `local', `opinion', `on-air', `misc', `weather', `health', `living', `business', `sports', `summary', `bbs' (bulletin board service), `travel', `msn-news' and `msn-sports'. Table 5 shows the characteristics of the dataset.

In the total dataset, the length of user sessions ranges from 1 to 500 and the average length of session is 5.7. In this chapter we build a proof of concept for performing the sequence classification and clustering tasks using new measure, S^3M. Hence, we randomly selected 200 sessions from the preprocessed dataset (consisting of 44,062 sessions) all of length 6 for our experimentation.

Experiments with PAM

For the experiments, value of k, the number of clusters is fixed at 4 since for *PAM* with cosine measure the optimal number of clusters achieved was 4. The sum of squared error is used to find the optimal number of clusters. Table 6 and Table 7 show the inter-cluster distance between clusters obtained with cosine and S^3M similarity measures, respectively. It is evident from the tables that the inter-cluster distances among the clusters resulting from PAM, either using the cosine metric or using the S^3M metric, are comparable. However, sum-of-squared error (SSE) measure does not adequately account for features of sequence similarity. We shall see that although SSE may be low, sequences may not be similar within a cluster.

Table 5. Description of the msnbc dataset

Total Dataset	
Number of users	989,818
Minimum session length	1
Maximum session length	500

Table 6. Sum of the squared error for PAM with cosine similarity measure

	C1	C2	C3	C4
C1	0	0.85	0.155	0.889
C2	0.85	0	0.749	0.25
C3	0.155	0.749	0	0.906
C4	0.889	0.25	0.906	0

Table 7. Sum of the squared error for PAM with S^3M similarity measure

	C1	C2	C3	C4
C1	0	0.723	0.162	0.123
C2	0.723	0	0.749	0.79
C3	0.162	0.749	0	0.044
C4	0.123	0.79	0.044	0

As these clusters are composed of sessions that are sequential in nature, the cost associated with converting the sequences within a cluster to the cluster representative must be minimum. At the same time, the cost of converting the sequences from two different clusters must be high. We computed a well known measure of the conversion cost of sequences, namely, the Levensthein distance for each cluster. The average Levensthein distance reflects the goodness of the clusters. Average Levenshtein distance (ALD) is expressed as,

$$ALD = \frac{1}{k}\sum_{j=1}^{k}\frac{\sum_{j_s=1}^{|C_j|}LD(t_j, \hat{t}_{js})}{|C_j|} \quad (8)$$

where, k is the number of clusters

- $|c_j|$ is the size of jth cluster
- $\hat{t}_j$ is the medoid of the jth cluster
- t_{js} is the sth element of the jth cluster
- $LD(\hat{t}_j, t_{js})$ is the Levensthein distance between the sth member of the jth cluster to its cluster mediod.

As can be seen from Table 8, the ALD for the clusters formed with the S^3M measure is less than that computed for clusters formed with the cosine measure. So, the user sessions within the clusters formed based on S^3M have retained more sequential information than those obtained by the cosine measure (Table 8).

So far, we have looked at the intra-cluster LD measure where S^3M performed better. The quality of a cluster is also measured by how well various clusters differ from each other and it is usually denoted as inter-cluster distance. Table 9 and Table 10 show the LD measure across cluster representatives formed using the two similarity measures. Since we considered only user sessions of length 6, the theoretical maximum and minimum

inter-cluster LD would be 6 and 0, respectively. In Table 9, we find that a minimum cost of 2 is required to convert a cluster representative to another cluster representative (shown in bold face in Table 9). Whereas, the minimum cost needed for conversion across clusters is 5 with the S^3M measure (see Table 10).

These results clearly point out the advantage of using a measure such as S³M that preserves order information for the dataset.

For *msnbc* web navigational dataset we found that the order of occurrence of page visits plays a key role in forming natural and understandable

Table 8. Comparison of clusters formed with the two similarity measures

	LD with cosine measure	LD with S^3M measure
C1	4.514	4.448
C2	4.938	4.62
C3	5.593	3.7
C4	4.92	3.908
ALD	4.9905	4.169

Table 9. LD between cluster representatives obtained using cosine measure

	C1	C2	C3	C4
C1	0	5	3	6
C2	5	0	5	**2**
C3	3	5	0	6
C4	6	**2**	6	0

Table 10. LD between cluster representatives obtained using S^3M measure

	C1	C2	C3	C4
C1	0	6	5	6
C2	6	0	5	5
C3	5	5	0	5
C4	6	5	5	0

groups. From the results presented in this section, we can conclude that the proposed similarity measure could form an integral part of a web personalization system that incorporates sequence clustering task (Kumar et al., 2007).

CONCLUSION

In many data mining applications, both classification as well as clustering algorithms requires a distance/similarity measure.

When two sequences are similar it is expected that the underlying sequences are similar. In this chapter, we devised a new similarity measure which takes into account both the order of occurrence information and the content information while comparing two sequences. The proposed measure is a linear weighted combination of *Jaccard* and *LCS* measures. The weights are assigned by the user based on experience or knowledge of the domain of application. However, we described an approach for choosing these parameters based on the theory of expected length of the longest common subsequence. We showed that the proposed measure qualifies to be a metric by satisfying properties of non-negativity, symmetry and normalization.

The new measure S^3M was used in conjunction with *kNN* classification algorithm and *PAM* clustering algorithms. Classification algorithm was tested on intrusion detection and clustering algorithm was experimented on web usage mining domains. The comparison in both cases was made with cosine similarity measure. Moreover, for classification task comparison was also made with an additional measure named *BWC* similarity measure. Results in both cases show the viability of the proposed measure in the two domains of sequence classification and clustering.

The proposed measure can be further tested in future for other domains where data exhibit sequentiality.

REFERENCES

Alshalalfa, M., Alhajj, R., Khabbaz, M., & Kianmehr, K. (2008). Effectiveness of fuzzy classifier rules in capturing correlations between genes. *International Journal of Data Warehousing and Mining, 4*(4), 62–83.

Apostolico, A., & Guerra, C. (1987). The longest common subsequence problem revisited. *Algorithmica, 2*, 315–336. doi:10.1007/BF01840365

Bergroth, L., Hakonen, H., & Raita, T. (2000). A survey of longest common subsequence algorithm. In *Proceedings of the Seventh International Symposium on String Processing and Information Retrieval SPIRE*, Atlanta (pp. 39-48). Washington, DC: IEEE Computer Society.

Duda, R. O., Hart, P. E., & Stork, D. G. (2001). *Pattern Classification* (2nd ed.). New York: John Wiley and Sons.

Hirschberg, D. S. (1975). A linear space algorithm for computing maximal common subsequences. *Communications of the ACM, 18*(6), 341–343. doi:10.1145/360825.360861

Hsu, W. J., & Du, M. W. (1984). Computing a longest common subsequence for a set of strings. *BIT, 24*, 45–59. doi:10.1007/BF01934514

Hunt, J. W., & Szymanski, T. G. (1977). A fast algorithm for computing longest common subsequences. *Communications of the ACM, 20*(5), 350–353. doi:10.1145/359581.359603

Kohonen, T. (1985). Median strings. *Pattern Recognition Letters, 3*, 309–313. doi:10.1016/0167-8655(85)90061-3

Konstan, J. A., Miller, B. N., Maltz, D., Herlocker, J. L., Gordon, L. R., & Riedl, G. L. (1997). Applying collaborative filtering to usenet news. *Communications of the ACM, 40*(3), 77–87. doi:10.1145/245108.245126

Kumar, P., Bapi, R. S., & Krishna, P. R. (2007). SeqPAM: A sequence clustering algorithm for web personalization. *International Journal of Data Warehousing and Mining, 3*(1), 29–53.

Kumar, P., Bapi, R. S., Krishna, P. R., & De, S. K. (2007). Rough clustering of sequential data. *Data & Knowledge Engineering, 63*(2), 183–199. doi:10.1016/j.datak.2007.01.003

Kumar, P., Rao, M. V., Krishna, P. R., & Bapi, R. S. (2005). Using sub-sequence information with kNN for classification of sequential data. In *International Conference on Distributed Computing and Internet Technology* (LNCS, pp. 536-546). New York: Springer.

Levenshtein, L. I. (1966). Binary codes capable of correcting deletions, insertions, and reversals. *Soviet Physics, Doklady, 10*(7), 707–710.

Liao, Y., & Vemuri, V. R. (2002). Using text categorization techniques for intrusion detection. In *Proceedings of the 11th USENIX Security Symposium*, Berkeley, CA (pp. 51-59). USENIX Association.

Masek, W. J., & Paterson, M. S. (1980). A faster algorithm computing string edit distances. *Journal of Computer Science and Systems, 20*(1), 18–31. doi:10.1016/0022-0000(80)90002-1

Mitchell, T. M. (1997). *Machine learning*. New York: McGraw Hill.

Mohamad, S. I. L., & Theodoulidis, B. (2006). Improving similarity search in time series using wavelets. *International Journal of Data Warehousing and Mining, 2*(2), 55–81.

Mount, D. W. (2004). *Bioinformatics: Sequence and Genome Analysis* (2nd ed.). Cold Spring Harbor, NY: Laboratory Press.

Myers, E. W. (1986). An O(nd) difference algorithm and its variations. *Algorithmica, 2*, 251–266. doi:10.1007/BF01840446

Nakatsu, N., Kambayashi, Y., & Yajima, S. (1982). A longest common subsequence algorithm suitable for similar text strings. *Acta Informatica, 18*(2), 171–179. doi:10.1007/BF00264437

Nikulin, V. (2008). Classification of imbalanced data with random sets and mean-variance filtering. *International Journal of Data Warehousing and Mining, 4*(2), 63–78.

Paterson, M., & Danc'ik, V. (1994). Longest common subsequences. In *Proceedings of the 19th International Symposium Mathematical Foundations of Computer Science*, Kosice, Slovakia (LNCS, pp. 127-142). Berlin: Springer Verlag.

Rawat, S., Gulati, V. P., Pujari, A. K., & Vemuri, V. R. (2006). Intrusion detection using processing techniques with a binary-weighted gosine metric. *Journal of Information Assurance and Security, 1*(1), 43–58.

Rick. (1994). *New algorithms for the longest common subsequence problem* (Tech. Rep. No. 85123-CS). Bonn, Germany: University of Bonn, Department of Computer Science.

Sankoff & Kruskal. J. B. (1983). *Time warps, string edits, and macromolecules: The theory and practice of sequence comparison*. Reading, MA: Addison-Wesley.

Savla, S., & Chakravarthy, S. (2007). A single pass algorithm for discovering significant intervals in time-series data. *International Journal of Data Warehousing and Mining, 3*(3), 28–44.

Shahabi, C., Zarkesh, A. M., Adibi, J., & Shah, V. (1997). Knowledge discovery from user's web-page navigation. In *Proceedings of the 7th International Workshop on Research Issues in Data Engineering, High Performance Database Management for Large-Scale Applications, Birmingham, England* (pp. 20-29). Washington, DC: IEEE Computer Society.

Simon, I. (1987). Sequence comparison: some theory and some practice. In Gross, M., & Perrin, D. (Eds.), *Electronic Dictionaries and Automata in Computational Linguistics, Saint Pierre d'Oleron* (pp. 79–92). Berlin: Springer Verlag.

Spiliopoulou, M., & Brunzel, M. (2007). Acquiring semantic sibling associations from web documents. *International Journal of Data Warehousing and Mining, 3*(4), 83–98.

Tan, L., Taniar, D., & Smith, K. A. (2006). Maximum-entropy estimated distribution model for classification problems. *International Journal Hybrid Intelligent System, 3*(1), 1–10.

Wagner, R. A., & Fischer, M. J. (1974). The string-to-string correction problem. *Journal of the ACM, 21*(1), 168–173. doi:10.1145/321796.321811

Yan, T. W., Jacobsen, M., Molina, H. G., & Dayal, U. (1996). From user access patterns to dynamic hypertext linking. In *Proceedings of the fifth international World Wide Web conference on Computer networks and ISDN systems* (pp. 1007-1014). Amsterdam: Elsevier.

Zhang, X., Hu, X., Xia, J., Zhou, X., & Achananuparp, P. (2008). A Graph-Based Biomedical Literature Clustering Approach Utilizing Term's Global and Local Importance Information. *International Journal of Data Warehousing and Mining, 4*(4), 84–10.

This work was previously published in International Journal of Data Warehousing and Mining, Volume 6, Issue 4, edited by David Taniar, pp. 16-32, copyright 2010 by IGI Publishing (an imprint of IGI Global).

Chapter 15
When Spatial Analysis Meets OLAP:
Multidimensional Model and Operators

Sandro Bimonte
Cemagref, France

Anne Tchounikine
INSA-Lyon, France

Maryvonne Miquel
INSA-Lyon, France

François Pinet
Cemagref, France

ABSTRACT

Introducing spatial data into multidimensional models leads to the concept of Spatial OLAP (SOLAP). Existing SOLAP models do not completely integrate the semantic component of geographic information (alphanumeric attributes and relationships) or the flexibility of spatial analysis into multidimensional analysis. In this chapter, the authors propose the GeoCube model and its associated operators to overcome these limitations. GeoCube enriches the SOLAP concepts of spatial measure and spatial dimension and take into account the semantic component of geographic information. The authors define geographic measures and dimensions as geographic and/or complex objects belonging to hierarchy schemas. GeoCube's algebra extends SOLAP operators with five new operators, i.e., Classify, Specialize, Permute, OLAP-Buffer and OLAP-Overlay. In addition to classical drill-and-slice OLAP operators, GeoCube provides two operators for navigating the hierarchy of the measures, and two spatial analysis operators that dynamically modify the structure of the geographic hypercube. Finally, to exploit the symmetrical representation of dimensions and measures, GeoCube provides an operator capable of permuting dimension and measure. In this chapter, GeoCube is presented using environmental data on the pollution of the Venetian Lagoon.

DOI: 10.4018/978-1-61350-474-1.ch015

Copyright © 2012, IGI Global. Copying or distributing in print or electronic forms without written permission of IGI Global is prohibited.

INTRODUCTION

Data warehousing and On-Line Analytical Processing (OLAP) systems are technologies designed to support business intelligence. OLAP models (hypercubes) are based on the concepts of dimensions and facts (Inmon, 1996). A fact is a concept that is relevant for the decision-making process, and it is described by a set of numerical indicators (measures). Dimensions, composed of hierarchies, allow for the analysis of facts along different analysis axes at different levels of detail.

New information and communication technologies make it possible to collect huge amounts of geographic data. These data are generated by remote sensing systems or other computer applications (Franklin, 1992). Geographic information is described by two components (Longley et al., 2001). The *spatial component* is the geometry and its position on the Earth's surface. The *semantic component* is a set of (1) descriptive attributes and (2) spatial, thematic and map generalization relationships. Geographic Information Systems (GIS) have been developed in order to store, organize, visualize and analyze geographic data, (Longley et al., 2001).

Spatial analysis aims to understand, estimate and predict real phenomena, showing recurrent spatial structures and shapes. Several spatial operators have been proposed (e.g., overlay, map join, etc.) but a "standard" model and allied algebra have not yet been defined (Voisard & David, 2002). Nevertheless, Longley et al. (2001) proposed a classification of spatial analysis operators, i.e., query and reasoning methods, measuring methods, transformation methods, and synthesis methods. *Transformation methods* modify geographic data (i.e., overlay, buffer, etc.) through logic and/or spatial rules. *Query and reasoning methods* exploit relationships between geographic objects to enable multigranular spatial analysis (Timpf & Frank, 1997; Camossi et al., 2008). Here, data are represented at different levels of detail (or 'granularity'), i.e., cities and regions, etc., to allow for

support spatial analysis by adding or downscaling details for particular datasets through zoom-out/zoom-in operations.

Therefore, a new kind of Decision Support Systems called Spatial OLAP (SOLAP) has been developed in order to effectively factor spatial data into multidimensional analysis. SOLAP tools integrate GIS functionalities (memorizing, analyzing and visualizing) into OLAP and data warehousing systems (Marketos et al., 2008; Rivest et al., 2005). SOLAP tools were recently successfully used to analyze agricultural, economic, seismological data (Marketos et al., 2008), etc.

These systems are based on spatio-multidimensional models composed of spatial dimensions, spatial measures, which are analyzed through spatio-multidimensional operators. Multidimensional models have been proposed for SOLAP (Ahmed & Miquel, 2005; Pourrubas, 2003; Jensen et al., 2004; Damiani & Spaccapietra, 2006; Gómez et al., 2009; Sampaio et al., 2006; Silva et al., 2008; Glorio & Trujillo, 2008) which formalize the concepts of spatial dimensions, spatial measures and spatio-multidimensional operators. In particular, they define spatial measures as geometric values and/or the result of spatial operators. Spatio-multidimensional operators are defined as extensions of OLAP operators for spatial dimensions.

However, in our opinion, the existing SOLAP models actually limit certain aspects of spatio-multidimensional capabilities, namely the *semantic component of geographic information* and *flexibility of spatial analysis*. When geographic information is used as measure, SOLAP models reduce it to geometry without taking into account its relationships. Consequently, they support multigranular analysis, but with some limitations.

Spatial and multidimensional analyses are different in terms of flexibility. SOLAP operators (spatial drill-down, spatial roll-up and spatial slice) only allow navigation in the hypercube, since multidimensional data structures (dimensions and measures) and instances (members and measures

Table 1. Case-study pollution data

Pollutant	Day	Unit	Value
Zinc	19-9-05	Mazzorbo	46.9
Sulfur Trioxide	19-9-05	Mazzorbo	45.2
…	…	…	…
Sulfur Trioxide	26-9-05	Coa di Latte	21.5

values) are fixed *a priori*. In contrast, spatial analysis requires changes and/or replacements to geographic data throughout the analysis process.

Therefore, in order to overcome these limitations, we extend the SOLAP concepts by introducing the concepts of *geographic measure* and *geographic multidimensional operators*. These concepts define new requirements that are not supported by existing spatio-multidimensional models. Therefore, the main contribution of the chapter is twofold. First, we enrich the set of SOLAP concepts, and secondly, we define a spatio-multidimensional model (GeoCube) extending (Bimonte et al., 2006) to support the requirements that our new SOLAP concepts entail. The implementation of our model into a SOLAP system is also described.

The chapter is organized as follows: the "Motivation" section presents the main existing SOLAP concepts and spatio-multidimensional models using an environmental case study on pollution in the Venetian Lagoon. Then, using this case study, we go on to describe the limits of existing SOLAP concepts and models. We define a new set of requirements for spatio-multidimensional models supporting our new SOLAP concepts. Finally, we detail how existing SOLAP fails to support these requirements. GeoCube is described in the section "GeoCube: A multidimensional model and its operators". The "Implementation" section provides a description of the system that implements the model, and presents the use of the system with simulated environmental data.

RESEARCH MOTIVATIONS

In this section, we present our new concepts of *geographic measure* and *geographic multidimensional operators*, and discuss the limits of the existing SOLAP models in terms of ability to handle the requirements associated with these new concepts.

Study Case

To present our work, we use simulated environmental data on pollution in Venice Lagoon generated through the CORILA[1] project. These data are analyzed according to time, lagoon units and zones, and pollutant. A "unit" is an environmental subdivision of the lagoon, described by geometry and certain descriptive attributes: name, salinity, list of plants, type and area. Units are grouped into zones, as illustrated in Figure 1c.

Table 1 gives a sample of this pollution data.

SOLAP models are based on the concepts of spatial dimension, spatial measure and spatio-multidimensional operators (a survey can be found in (Gomez et al., 2009).

Malinowski and Zimányi (2008) and Fidalgo et al. (2004) define a *spatial dimension* as a classical dimension where some levels have a spatial attribute. As an example of SOLAP application, in Figure 1a we present a conceptual model of our environmental application. It includes facts called "Pollution" which are described by a numerical measure "Value" that represents the pollution values of the lagoon's water. It is analyzed according to three dimensions: "Time", "Pollutants" and

Figure 1. Spatio-multidimensional model: a) spatial dimension and numerical measure, b) classical dimensions and spatial measure; c) Venice lagoon: units and zones

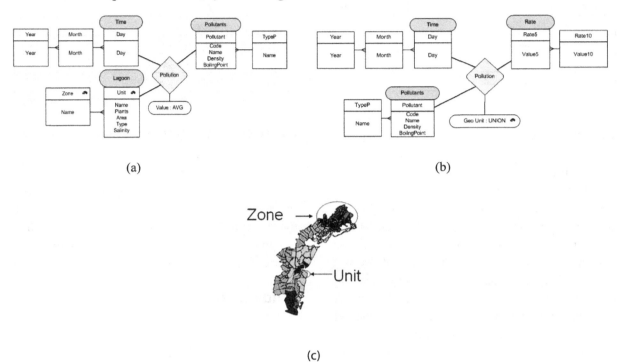

(a)

(b)

(c)

"Lagoon". The 'lagoon' dimension is described by a spatial hierarchy that organizes groups of units into zones. This model makes it possible to visualize pollution values on maps and to use spatial operators to perform slice operations.

A *spatial measure* is a collection of spatial objects (Stefanovic et al., 2000; Rivest et al., 2001; Malinowski & Zimányi, 2008; Gómez et al., 2009; Sampaio et al., 2006; Silva et al., 2008; Glorio & Trujillo, 2008) and/or the result of a spatial operator (i.e., the intersection, etc.) (Rivest et al., 2001; Malinowski & Zimányi, 2008) applied to spatial members. When the spatial measure is represented by geometric values, aggregation functions can become spatial, such as intersection, union, etc. Figure 1b illustrates an example of a SOLAP application using spatial measures, analyzed according to three dimensions: "Time", "Pollutants" and "Rate". The 'Rate' dimension represents 5 mg/l increments of pollution values,

e.g., 40-44 mg/l, 45-49 mg/l, etc. The spatial measure is "Geo Unit", which is the geometry of the geographic object "Unit". This geometry is represented as a polygon, and it is aggregated using topological union. The model moves the spatial component of Figure 1a model from dimension to measure. Here, geometries are used as subject of analysis (and not in a spatial dimension as in Figure 1a) making it possible to answer queries such as: "Which units have per month, per pollutant and pollution values of between 45 and 49 mg/l?" However, the alphanumeric attributes of the geographic object "Unit" are excluded by the spatio-multidimensional analysis.

SOLAP reformulates the OLAP operators to define: *spatial drill-down, spatial roll-up* and *spatial slice*. Spatial drill-down and spatial roll-up make it possible to navigate in spatial dimensions (Rivest et al., 2005; Sampaio et al., 2006) through straightforward interaction with the SOLAP client's interactive map; for instance, users can climb from "Unit" level to "Zone" level in the spatial dimension of Figure 1a model by clicking on a SOLAP client map. A spatial slice can be used to select a part of the hypercube using spatial and alphanumeric operators (Scotch & Parmanto, 2006). For example, a spatial slice operation could be used to formulate the query "What are the per-day pollution values for units located 1 km from Venice ?" on the Figure 1a model.

However, simply using spatial dimensions and spatial measures as defined by existing SOLAP models does not allow decision-makers to fully exploit the semantic component of geographic information and the flexibility of spatial analysis to carry out an effective OLAP-GIS analysis as described in the next section.

NEW SOLAP CONCEPTS

Semantic Component of Geographic Information: Geographic Measure

Alphanumeric attributes of geographic objects are at the base of spatial analysis operators. They are crucial to the spatial decision-making process as they can reveal hidden relationships between locations and alphanumeric values. Similarly, spatial and thematic relationships are also necessary to the spatial decision-making process, since they allow multigranular analysis (see 'Introduction' section).

Despite the high analytical power of the semantic component of geographic information (descriptive attributes, and spatial, thematic and map generalization relationships), spatial measure reduces geographic information to its spatial component and to numeric values calculated directly from the geometry. Let us consider the model of Figure 1b. Spatial analysts could need a less-detailed vision of the lagoon to analyze polluted zones through a zoom-out operator on the measure.

Therefore, there is the need for coupling spatial measure with all its alphanumeric attributes (numerical measures), and for extending it to spatial/thematic and map generalization relationships.

Based on these hypotheses, Bimonte et al. (2006) extend the concept of spatial measure by defining a *geographic measure* as a geographic object (a set of alphanumeric and spatial attributes) belonging to a hierarchy schema represented by spatial, thematic or map generalization relationships. Therefore, a measure is defined as a dimension level.

Figure 2a gives an example of a geographic measure. Measures are units of the lagoon. An example of a multidimensional query is "What regions (aggregated measures - their type, salinity, plants and area, or aggregation of units) are polluted per month, pollutant and pollution value?" In this application, we use we have chosen to apply the topological union for the geometry, the list of topological union for geometry, list for plants, average for salinity and a weighted all-area average for type. Therefore, the subject of analysis contains the spatial component of the units as well as their alphanumeric attributes. Moreover, the hierarchical relationships associated with the geographic measure enable multigranular analysis through new operators, as described in the next section.

This definition of measure entails several modelling requirements (Bimonte et al., 2006), such as *set of measures, multi-valued measures, user-defined aggregation functions, and derived measures.* Moreover, it also implies that the *aggregated measures can differ from the detailed measures* (an aggregated measure could present more or less attributes than the detailed measure (for example the geographic object representing aggregation of units has no name), and *many-to-many relationships between dimensions and facts* (i.e., a unit is an entity and could be polluted by several pollutants, and *vice versa*, a pollutant could be found in several units).

Figure 2. a) Geographic measure, "Unit", b) Complex measure, "Pollutant"

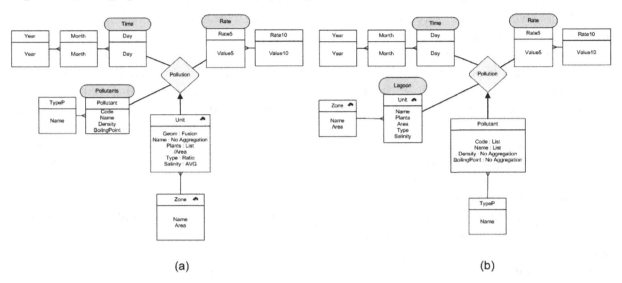

(a)   (b)

Flexibility of Spatial Analysis: Geographic Multidimensional Operators

The spatial analysis process is flexible and iterative (Mitchell, 2005), in the sense that the data and tools used cannot be defined a priori. The spatial decision-maker could run through all the steps in the process without necessarily finding a solution or further knowledge. She/he is therefore forced to revisit certain steps: changing visualization tools, adding data, transforming data, and/or replacing the subjects of analysis.

Conversely, spatio-multidimensional data and analysis paths are defined by the hypercube. Indeed, the SOLAP analysis process consists in the unpredictable exploration of unchangeable data through a set of predefined SOLAP queries defined using SOLAP operators. SOLAP operators only make it possible to navigate into dimensions and select a part of the hypercube; they do not make it possible to introduce new spatial members or to change measures on-the-fly. Thus, *when restricted to SOLAP operators, the spatio-multidimensional analysis is not flexible enough to effectively integrate spatial analysis transformation operators.*

Let us suppose that the analyst wants to analyze pollution values around the "Mazzorbo" unit. This spatial member should be calculated using the spatial buffer operator to the member "Mazzorbo" (see Figure 7a-b). Given a distance parameter, the buffer operator creates a zone inside or outside an input geometry, as illustrated in Figure 7d. Since it is not possible to pre-calculate all the possible buffer regions and integrate them into the spatial data warehouse, the buffer region cannot be used for spatio-multidimensional analysis.

Therefore, we advocate operators that dynamically modify spatial dimensions using spatial analysis transformation operators to create new spatial members using the original spatial members of the hypercube. The main modelling issue involved with these operators is the reformulation of the hypercube (i.e., add spatial members, calculate new measures, etc.).

Spatial measures (geometries) are defined differently from spatial dimensions (geographic objects with hierarchical relationships), which means the spatial analyst cannot replace spatial measures with other (geographic) objects limiting his/her analytical capabilities. Indeed, based on classical multidimensional models that propose the symmetry of dimensions and measures (Abello et al., 2006), we advocate an operator (called Permute) which dynamically permutes a measure with a dimension. We use a dimension level as a measure, and we introduce the hierarchy associated with the measure as a dimension, and *vice versa*. In this way, each dimension level can be a complex measure. We term *complex measure* an object that is described by a set of alphanumeric attributes and that belongs to a hierarchy schema.

For example, using this operator makes it possible to move from the spatio-multidimensional model of Figure 2a to the model of Figure 2b. The new SOLAP application allows decision-makers to answer queries such as "What are the pollutants in each zone of the lagoon per month?" In this way, it is possible to analyze the spatial evolution of pollutants in the lagoon. This could allow the discovery of possible trends and relationships between pollutants and their geo-localization.

Finally, multigranular analysis is pivotal to the spatial decision-making process (Timpf & Frank, 1997; Camossi et al., 2008). Indeed, in our case-study, the spatial analyst could be interested in polluted zones (i.e., "Which are the zones of the lagoon polluted by iron per day?") in order to have a less detailed vision of the phenomenon, which would allow him/her to focus on different spatial details or to discover a phenomenon that is not 'visible' at unit scale. Therefore, we advocate a *set of operators that enable changes in the measure of the spatio-multidimensional model using one if its hierarchy levels* in order to allow multigranular analysis in hypercubes.

In conclusion, SOLAP operators should be extended to provide the flexibility of spatial analysis. Consequently, we have identified three new types of SOLAP operators:

1. Operators that dynamically modify spatial dimensions
2. A permute operator that dynamically permutes a measure with a dimension

3. Operators to navigate into the hierarchy of measures

Related Work

The introduction of spatial data into data warehouses and OLAP systems raises several issues concerning performance, architectural and logical modelling.

Indeed some works provide ad-hoc indexes techniques for improve query performance (e.g., Tao & Papadias, 2005), or caching techniques such as Savari et al. (2007) that propose a semantic cache and a replacement policy for spatial data warehouses stored in GML in order to reduce memory used to store geographical queries.

Integration of GIS and OLAP systems is an important challenge as geovisualization (e.g., MultiMaps, Space-Time Cube, etc.) data mining (clustering, association rules, etc.) and spatial analysis (e.g., image compression and transformation, etc.) techniques should be adapted according to the spatio-multidimensional model and SOLAP operators (Marketos et al., 2008; Rivest et al., 2005).

In the same way, several authors address logical spatial data warehouse modelling taking into account particular features of the geographic information such as spatial data quality, temporal component, etc. Indeed some works investigate the integration of temporal data into spatial data warehouses (Gomez et al., 2009; Malinowsky & Zimanyi, 2008), which means evolving spatial data, multidimensional structures and ad-hoc query languages. In the same way, quality of spatio-multidimensional data is a hot topic that comprises of formal languages for integrity constraint definition such as OCL, and algorithms for detection of topo-semantic inconsistencies of groups of spatial objects as proposed in (Gadish, 2008).

Therefore, this section outlines how existing SOLAP conceptual and logical models only partially meet the requirements for modelling geographic measures and supporting the geographic multidimensional operators.

Ahmed and Miquel (2005) define a spatial dimension as a continuous space with a set of "infinite" members whose measures values are calculated through interpolation functions. Pourrubas (2003) provides a formal framework for integrating multidimensional and geographic databases. The model handles spatial dimensions where members of different levels are related by topological inclusion relationships. These two models only handle numerical measures.

Gómez et al. (2009) provide a model that integrates GIS, OLAP data and operators in an elegant way. The model answers OLAP queries using spatial predicates and viceversa, and defines the notion of geometric aggregation as the aggregation of numerical values using spatial dimensions. Since aggregations are handled by the OLAP component of the model, it does not support spatial measures and spatial aggregations.

Silva et al. (2008) present a SOLAP model that supports a set of aggregation functions for spatial measures defined as collections of geometries. These aggregation functions are classified according to whether numerical aggregation is scalar, distributive or holistic, and whether spatial aggregation is a unary or n-ary function.

Sampaio et al. (2006) propose an object-relation model, implemented in Oracle, which supports spatial dimensions and measures as collections of geometric objects.

Glorio and Trujillo, (2008) extend the powerful UML-based data warehouse model presented in (Mora et al., 2006) with stereotypes for spatial measures and spatial levels using their geometric attributes.

Malinowsky and Zimanyi (2008) provide a conceptual model for SOLAP applications based on the MADS model. The spatio-multidimensional model supports complex spatial dimensions and measures defined as geometries or results of spatial operators.

Excluding (Damiani & Spaccapietra, 2006; Jensen et al., 2004), all these models define different data structures for spatial dimensions and measures. Moreover, they reduce spatial measures to spatial and/or numerical attributes without taking into account spatial and thematic relationships.

Indeed, only Damiani and Spaccapietra (2006) define a model that aims to support measures as geographic objects, but it does not explicitly represent spatial and alphanumeric attributes, making a spatial measure (geographic object) a simple identifier. The model supports spatial measures organized into a hierarchy structure. An hypercube is defined for each spatial measure, and an operator is used to navigate between these hypercubes. Therefore, this model supports multigranular analysis in data cubes as it enables analysts to change measures on the fly.

The model proposed in (Jensen et al., 2004) handles imprecise hierarchical relationships in order to represent topological intersection relationships between spatial members of different levels. Hierarchical relationships are associated with a degree of precision of the containment relationship of a member into its father. For example, in a "Highway" < "French region" hierarchy, the member "A43" (i.e., a highway) is associated with the member "Ain" (i.e., a French region) with a 0.5 degree of precision, because highway A43 is not totally topologically contained into the region called "Ain". The model supports symmetry of measures and dimensions, but it does not allow the definition of derived measures (measures calculated using other measures) and dimension attributes (attributes that do not define hierarchies).

Let us now analyze all these spatio-multidimensional models according to the requirements defined in the previous section.

We focus solely on the data-modelling properties necessary to support measures as complex/geographic objects (Table 2), e.g., "What regions, i.e., aggregated measures (their type, salinity, plants and area) or aggregations of units, are polluted per month, with pollutant and

Table 2. Data modelling properties

Data-modelling properties	(Damiani & Spaccapietra)	(Jensen et al., 2004)	(Ahmed & Miquel, 2005)	(Pourabbas, 2003)	(Silva et al., 2008)	(Malinowsky & Zimanyi, 2008)	(Sampaio et al., 2006)	(Gómez et al., 2009)	(Glorio & Trujillo, 2008)
Set of measures	YES	YES	YES	YES	YES	YES	YES	YES	YES
Dimension attributes	NO	NO	NO	YES	YES	YES	YES	YES	YES
Multi-valued measures	YES	YES	YES	YES	YES	YES	YES	YES	YES
User-defined aggregation functions	YES	YES	NO	YES	YES	YES	YES	YES	YES
Derived measures (derived dimension attributes)	NO	NO	NO	NO	YES	YES	YES	NO	YES
Many-to-many relationships between dimensions and facts	YES	YES	NO	YES	YES	NO	NO	NO	YES
Complex hierarchies	YES	YES	NO	YES	YES	YES	YES	YES	YES

pollution value?" Therefore, we do not report other data-modelling properties that characterize multidimensional models for complex data (i.e., versioning of hierarchies, uncertain data, etc) (Abello et al., 2006) as they fall outside the scope of this work. Moreover, it is important to note that the property "symmetrical dimensions and measures" is represented in Table 3 by the operator "Permute" as dimensions and measures can only be permuted if they share equivalent data structures.

Table 2 shows that, contrary to classical multidimensional models (Abello et al., 2006), few models support derived measures/attributes and many-to-many relationships between dimensions and facts. On the other hand, the other modelling properties are supported by almost all models. Therefore, this evaluation reveals that SOLAP models, with the exception of (Glorio & Trujillo, 2008), support partially geographic measures as they provide only a subset of the necessary modelling properties.

We now present an evaluation of the geographic multidimensional operators in Table 3.

Note that no model extends the classical "insert members" operator (Rafanelli, 2003) taking geometries into account to calculate measures. Moreover, only Jensen et al. (2004) supports the *Permute* operator as it provides a symmetrical representation of measures and dimensions. Finally, only Damiani and Spaccapietra (2006) and Jensen et al. (2004) partially support the *navigation into measures hierarchy* because they do not let users choose how to replace detailed measures with coarser measures.

Table 3. Geographic multidimensional operators

Geographic multi-dimensional Operators	(Damiani & Spaccapietra)	(Jensen et al., 2004)	(Ahmed & Miquel, 2005)	(Pourabbas, 2003)	(Silva et al., 2008)	(Malinowsky & Zimanyi, 2008)	(Sampaio et al., 2006)	(Gómez et al., 2009)	(Glorio & Trujillo, 2008)
Operators that modify spatial dimensions	NO	NO	NO	NO	NO	NO	NO	NO	NO
Permute	NO	YES	NO	NO	NO	NO	NO	NO	NO
Navigation into measures hierarchy (Multigranular analysis)	Partially	Partially	NO	NO	NO	NO	NO	NO	NO

This evaluation shows that no SOLAP model fully integrates the semantics of geographic information together with the flexibility of spatial analysis.

Finally, Table 4 describes whether spatio-multidimensional models have been effectively implemented, and whether a visual interactive user interface has been developed. Note that this evaluation does not address technical features such as performances, visual techniques, etc., as they fall outside the scope of this chapter.

It is important to note that we do not introduce in this evaluation SOLAP tools, such as (Marketos et al., 2008; Rivest et al., 2005) that are based on classical multidimensional models enriched with simple spatial attributes.

GEOCUBE: A SPATIO-MULTIDIMENSIONAL MODEL AND ITS OPERATORS

In this section, we present the GeoCube data model and its operators. We show how GeoCube satisfies the requirements introduced in the previous section.

Spatio-Multidimensional Data Model

The main concepts of the data model are: *Entity*, *Hierarchy* and *Base Cube*.

Entity

GeoCube represents all data of the spatio-multidimensional application, dimensions members and measures, through the concepts of *Entity*

Table 4. Spatio-multidimensional model implementation

Implementation	(Damiani & Spaccapietra)	(Jensen et al., 2004)	(Ahmed & Miquel, 2005)	(Pourabbas, 2003)	(Silva et al., 2008)	(Malinowsky & Zimanyi, 2008)	(Sampaio et al., 2006)	(Gómez et al., 2009)	(Glorio & Trujillo, 2008)
Data model and operators	NO	YES	YES	YES	YES	YES	YES	YES	YES
Visual interactive interface	NO	NO	YES	NO	YES	NO	YES	YES	YES

Schema and *Entity Instance*. An Entity Schema defines the structure of a complex or geographic object through a set of attributes and functions. An Entity Instance is an instance of an object and is described by the values associated to the different attributes of the Entity Schema. Geographic and complex objects may possess some attributes which are calculated using other attributes. In this chapter, due to space constraints, we do not provide the formal definition of Entity, but give an example instead.

- **Definition:** An Entity Schema S_e is a Geographic Entity Schema if the domain of one of its attribute is the Euclidian space (R^2).

Example

The Geographic Entity Schema representing the units of Venice lagoon is S_{unit} = ⟨name_unit, geometry, salinity, listofplants, type, ⟨f^{area}⟩⟩ where geometry is the spatial attribute, and f^{area}: dom(geometry) → R is the function used to calculate the area of the geometry.

An example of instance of S_{unit} is t_1= ⟨'Canal Fondello', P1, 24, list('Spartima Marittima', 'Fullica'), 'Commercial', 245100⟩ where P1 is the geometry and $t_1.f^{area}$ = 245100.

The concept of Entity makes it possible to represent members and measures as complex/geographic objects described by (derived) alphanumeric and geometric attributes.

Hierarchy

Entities can be organized into hierarchies using the concepts of *Hierarchy Schema* and *Hierarchy Instance*. A level of a hierarchy is an Entity Schema, and a member is an Entity Instance. The Hierarchy Schema organizes levels into a lattice. The Hierarchy Instance makes it possible to organize members in a tree structure. The root is an instance of the Entity Schema which represents the top level of the lattice represented by the Hierarchy Schema. Leafs are the instances of the Entity Schema which represents the bottom level of the lattice.

- **Definition:** A Hierarchy Schema is a tuple H_h = ⟨L_h, $\lfloor_h$, $\lceil_h$, $\ddagger_h$⟩ where:
- L_h *is a set of Entity Schemas,*
- $\lfloor_h$ *and* $\lceil_h$ *are two Entity Schemas, and* $\lceil_h$ *contains one instance ('all'),*
- $\ddagger_h$ *is a partial order defined on the levels of the hierarchy (* $L_h \cup \lfloor_h \cup \lceil_h$ *) and* $\ddagger_h$ *is a lattice where* $\lfloor_h$ *and* $\lceil_h$ *are the bottom and the top levels of the order.*

We call *Entity Schema levels* (noted $L(H_h)$) entities belonging to the set {$L_h \cup \lfloor_h \cup \lceil_h$}, and we say that two Hierarchy Schemas are *disjoint* if the two sets of their Entity Schema levels are disjoint.

An Instance of a Hierarchy Schema H_h is a partial order $\uparrow_h$ defined on $I(L(H_h))$, such as:

- *if* $t_i \uparrow_h t_j$ *then* $S_i \ddagger_h S_j$, *where* $t_i \in I(S_j)$ *and* $t_j \in I(S_i)$
- $\forall t_i \in I(L(H_h)) \setminus I(\lceil_h)$, $\exists t_j \in I(L(H_h))$ *such as* $t_i \uparrow_h t_j$
- $\forall t_i \in I(L(H_h)) \setminus I(\lfloor_h)$, $\exists t_j \in I(L(H_h))$ *such as* $t_j \uparrow_h t_i$

Example

An example of a Hierarchy Schema representing the spatial hierarchy "Unit"<"Zone" of Venice lagoon is $H_{lagoon\_spatial}$ = ⟨{S_{zone}}, S_{unit}, S_{all_unit}, $\ddagger_{lagoon\_spatial}$⟩ where ($S_{unit} \ddagger_{lagoon\_spatial} S_{zone}$) and ($S_{zone} \ddagger_{lagoon\_spatial} S_{all\_unit}$) (Figure 3a).

The instance of $H_{lagoon\_spatial}$ is shown in Figure 3b.

We note as *leafs(H_h, t_i)* the set of leafs of the tree represented by $\uparrow_h$ with root t_i. In our example, leafs($H_{lagoon\_spatial}$, Bocca Lido)={Canal Fondello, Coa di Latte} (Figure 3b).

Figure 3. $H_{lagoon\_spatial}$ a) Schema, b) Instance

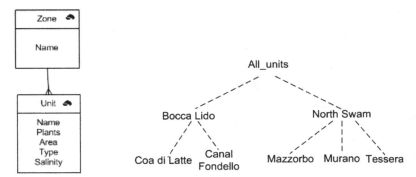

The concepts of Hierarchy Schema and Instance make it possible to model *complex hierarchies* (non-strict and non-covering) (Pedersen et al., 2001) which are compulsory in geographic multidimensional applications (Bimonte et al., 2006).

Base Cube

The hypercube can be represented as a hierarchical lattice of cuboids (Harinarayan et al., 1996). The most detailed cuboid contains detailed measures (basic cuboid). Other cuboids contain aggregated measures (see Figure 4).

Therefore, *Base Cube Schema* represents the conceptual schema of the application. The instance of the base cube represents the basic cuboid or the fact table where all dimensions are at the most detailed levels. In the previous section, we underlined the utility of a symmetrical representation of measures and dimensions for the decisional process. So, this symmetry is achieved by being able to represent members and measures in the same way (the measure is included into a hierarchy schema).

- **Definition:** A Base Cube Schema BC_{bc} is a tuple $\langle H_1, \ldots H_{m+1}, \delta \rangle$ where:

- $\forall\ i \in [1, \ldots m+1]$, H_i is a Hierarchy Schema, and all the Hierarchy Schemas are disjoints
- δ is a Boolean function defined on $I(L_1) \times \ldots \times I(L_{m+1})$ (δ is defined on the bottom levels of $H_1, \ldots H_{m+1}$)

We note as $H(BC_{bc}, S_e)$ the Hierarchy Schema of the Base Cube BC_{bc} that the Entity Schema S_e belongs to.

An Instance of a Base Cube Schema BC_{bc}, noted $I(BC_{bc})$, is a set of tuples such as $I(BC_{bc}) = \{\langle t_1, \ldots t_{m+1} \rangle\}$ where:

- $\forall\ i \in [1, \ldots m+1]\ t_i \in I(L_i)$
- $\delta(t_1, \ldots t_{m+1})$ is true.

A Base Cube Schema is a set of Hierarchy Schemas associated to a Boolean function. This function represents a multidimensional space where members of the most detailed dimension levels are projected onto the axes, and points are the values true and false. True means that data corresponding to this combination of Entity Instances are present in the multidimensional database.

The set of tuples representing an instance of a Base Cube Schema corresponds to tuples with the Boolean function on true. Since all members belong to the most detailed levels, an instance of

Figure 4. a) Hierarchy with levels "A" and "B" b) Hierarchy with levels "1" and "2" c) Cuboids lattice

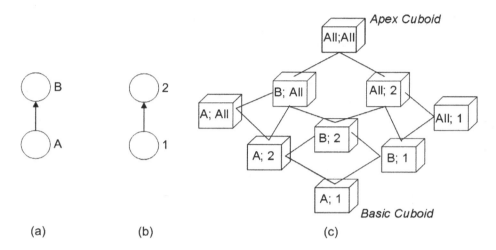

(a) (b) (c)

the Base Cube represents a fact table without facts. This particular organization of multidimensional data makes it possible to use an instance of a Base Cube to answer multidimensional queries using any of the most-detailed levels of the hierarchies as a measure, and the other hierarchies as axes of analysis.

Example

The Hierarchy Schemas of the Base Cube play all the roles of dimensions, and all the levels can be used as measures. The Base Cube Schema of the application concerning pollution in Venice lagoon is $BC_{corila} = \langle H_{pollutants}, H_{time}, H_{lagoon\_spatial}, H_{rate}, \delta \rangle$ where δ is defined on $I(S_{pollutant}) \times I(S_{day}) \times I(S_{unit}) \times I(S_{rate5})$.

Using the instance of BC_{corila} (Table 5), it is possible to answer queries with units as measures ("Which are the polluted units per pollutant and per day and pollution values?"), or using pollutants as measures ("What are the pollutants present in each unit per day and pollution values?").

This approach yields a symmetrical vision of measures and dimensions, and makes it possible to model many-to-many relationships between facts and dimensions and multi-valued measures,

which are some of the requirements defined for the geographic measure (see the "Geographic Measures" section).

Query Model

We define below the concepts of *View* and *Aggregation Mode* to represent a multidimensional query.

Aggregation Mode

The concept of *Aggregation Mode* represents the aggregation of complex and geographic objects. The idea is to consider an Entity Schema as the measure and another Entity Schema as the aggregated measure, and to link instances of the detailed measure to an instance of the aggregated measure through a set of spatial and/or alphanumeric *user-defined aggregation functions*. A function for each attribute of the aggregated measures is defined. Note that some attributes cannot be aggregated (i.e., names of units), and that the aggregated complex/geographic objects can have more or fewer attributes than detailed measures, and/or attributes of different types, which are some of the

Table 5. Instance of BC$_{corila}$

S$_{pollutant}$.name_pollutant	S$_{day}$.day	S$_{unit}$.name_unit	S$_{rate5}$.value5
Zinc	19-9-05	Mazzorbo	45-49
Sulfur Trioxide	19-9-05	Mazzorbo	30-34
Methane	19-9-05	Mazzorbo	30-34
Zinc	19-9-05	Canal Fondello	30-34
Methane	19-9-05	Murano	30-34
Zinc	19-9-05	Tessera	45-49
Methane	19-9-05	Coa di Latte	30-34
Zinc	19-9-05	Murano	45-49
Methane	26-9-05	Tessera	30-34
Sulfur Trioxide	26-9-05	Canal Fondello	20-24
Sulfur Trioxide	26-9-05	Coa di Latte	20-24

requirements defined by the geographic measure (see the "Geographic Measure" section).

- **Definition:** An Aggregation Mode Θ_k is a tuple $\langle S_a, S_b, \Phi \rangle$ where:
- S_a is an Entity Schema $\langle a_1,...a_m, [F_a] \rangle$ (detailed geographic/complex measure)
- S_b is an Entity Schema $\langle b_1,...b_p, [F_b] \rangle$ (aggregated geographic/complex measure)
- Φ a set of p ad-hoc aggregation functions φ_i

The aggregation of n instances $t_1,...$ t_n of S_a using the Aggregation Mode $\Theta_k = \langle S_a, S_b, \Phi \rangle$ is an instance t_b of $S_b = \langle val(b_1),...val(b_p), val(f_1),... val(f_l) \rangle$ such as:

$$\forall j \in [1,...p] \; val(b_j) = \underset{i=1}{\overset{n}{\varphi}}(t_i.a_1,...t_i.a_k) \; where \quad t_i \in I(S_a)$$

$$\forall t \in [1,... l], val(f_t) = f_t(val(b_r),...val(b_v))$$

We say that t_b is built from $t_1,...$ t_n

View

A *View* represents multidimensional query. Contrary to a Base Cube Schema, the *View Schema* defines the level used as measure, an Aggregation

Mode to aggregate this measure, and the dimensions levels used in the query. An instance of a View represents the cuboid with the levels defined by the View Schema (see Figure 4).

A View Schema is composed of a Base Cube Schema (the fact table), an Aggregation Mode, a set of Entity Schemas, and a Boolean function. The detailed measure of Aggregation Mode is the most detailed level of a hierarchy of the Base Cube Schema. Entity Schemas correspond to levels of the cuboid represented by the View. Each Entity Schema belongs to a Hierarchy Schema of the Base Cube that is different from the schema containing the measure. The Boolean function can be represented as a multidimensional space where all instances of members of the dimensions levels and the aggregated measure of Aggregation Mode are projected on the axes, and points are true or false values. True means that data corresponding to this combination of Entity Instances are present in the cuboid represented by the View.

Since the instance of a View where levels of dimensions are the most detailed levels corresponds to the basic cuboid, the Boolean function of the View is used to represent the cuboid that is not the basic cuboid. Cells of this cuboid contain aggregated measures. Conversely, the basic cuboid

Table 6. Instance of $V_{corila-unit-month}$

$S_{pollutant}$.name_pollutant	S_{day}.day	S_{unit_fusion}.name_unit_fusion	S_{rate5}.value5
Zinc	9-05	Mazzorbo+Tessera+Murano	45-49
Sulfur Trioxide	9-05	Mazzorbo	30-34
Methane	9-05	Mazzorbo+Tessera+Murano+Coa di Latte	30-34
Zinc	9-05	Canal Fondello	30-34
Benzo(b)fluoranthene	9-05	Murano	45-49
Methane	9-05	Coa di Latte	30-34
Sulfur Trioxide	9-05	Coa di Latte+ Canal fondello	20-24

is represented by an instance of the Base Cube and its cells contain instances of detailed measures.

- **Definition:** A View Schema V_v is a tuple $\langle BC_{bc}, L, \Theta_k, \gamma \rangle$ where:
- $BC_{bc} = \langle H_{b1}, ...H_{bm+1}, \delta \rangle$ *is a Base Cube Schema,*
- *L is a tuple of Entity Schemas* $\langle S_{L1}, ...S_{Lm} \rangle$ *such as* $\forall\ i, j \in [1, ...m]$ *with* $i \neq j$ *there exist two different Hierarchy Schemas* H_{bl} *and* H_{bp} *belonging to* BC_{bc} *such as:*
- $S_{Li} \in L(H_{bl})$ *and* $S_{Lj} \in L(H_{bp})$

(L represents the set of levels (S_{Li}) of the cuboid. All Entity Schemas (S_{Li}) of L belong to a different hierarchy of BC_{bc})

- Θ_k *is an Aggregation Mode* $\langle S_f, S_{af}, \Phi \rangle$ *such as:*
- *there exists one Hierarchy Schema belonging to* BC_{bc} *such as its bottom level is* S_f
- $\forall\ i \in [1, ...m]$ S_f *does not belong to the Hierarchy Schema containing* S_{Li}.
- γ *is a Boolean function defined on* $I(S_{L1}) \times ... \times I(S_{Lm}) \times I(S_{af})$

We call *Basic View* a View Schema V_v where all Entity Schemas of L are bottom levels, and *View Schema Levels* are the set of Entity Schemas of L.

An instance of a View Schema V_v, noted as $I(V_v)$, is a set of tuples such as:

- *if* V_v *is not the Basic View, then* $I(V_v) = \{\langle t_1, ...t_{m+1} \rangle\}$ *where* $\forall\ i \in [1, ...m]$, $t_i \in I(S_{Li})$, $t_{m+1} \in I(S_{af})$ *and* $\gamma(t_1, ...t_{m+1})$ *is true*
- *if* V_v *is a Basic View, then* $I(V_v) = I(BC_{bc})$

Examples

An example of a Basic View with units as measures is $V_{corila-unit} = \langle BC_{corila}, \langle S_{pollutant}, S_{day}, S_{rate5} \rangle, \Theta_{fusion-unit}, \gamma \rangle$. Its instance is equal to the instance of the Base Cube BC_{corila} because $V_{corila-unit}$ is a Basic View (Table 5).

An example of a Basic View with pollutants as measure is $V_{corila-pollutant} = \langle BC_{corila}, \langle S_{unit}, S_{day}, S_{rate5} \rangle, \Theta_{list-pollutant}, \gamma \rangle$. Its instance is shown in Table 5.

These examples show that even if $V_{corila-pollutant}$ and $V_{corila-unit}$ use two different measures, they share the same Base Cube because they use the same fact table. An example of a View Schema with units as measures and which is not the basic cuboid is $V_{corila-unit-month} = \langle BC_{corila}, \langle S_{pollutant}, S_{month}, S_{rate5} \rangle, \Theta_{fusion-unit}, \gamma \rangle$. Its instance is shown in Table 6.

It should be underlined that measures are instances of the aggregated measure of the Aggregation Mode because $V_{corila-unit-month}$ uses the month level (S_{month}) which is not its most detailed level.

Geographic Multidimensional Operators

GeoCube provides the following set of operators: *Roll-Up, Slice, Dice, Classify, Specialize,*

Permute, OLAP-Buffer and *OLAP-Overlay*. These operators are applied to a View and return another View.

In order to calculate the new View Instance, an algorithm has been defined for each operator. Due to space constraints, we do not detail the formal definitions of the *Roll-Up, Slice, Dice* (Bimonte et al., 2006; Bimonte, 2007), *Permute* and *OLAP-Overlay* operators, but instead we present some examples.

Classify and Specialize: Operators to Navigate in the Measure Hierarchy

Based on the concept of geographic measure, in order to introduce multigranular analysis into SOLAP analysis, we introduce two operators to navigate into the measure hierarchy, i.e., *Classify* and *Specialize*. These operators change the measure of the multidimensional application using a level of its hierarchy allowing multigranular multidimensional analysis (e.g., to climb from units to zones in the application of Figure 2a).

Classify and Specialize use two different rules to change the measure. Classify requires all the descendants of the new measure to be in the fact table. Specialize needs only one descendant. The choice of these two replacement predicates is based on the different kinds of OLAP hierarchies,

i.e., specialization and classification (Trujillo et al., 2001). In particular, classification hierarchies describe groups or classes of members (i.e., the spatial hierarchy "Unit" < "Zone" (Figure 1a and Figure 1c)). Specialization hierarchies define specialization/generalization (is-a) relationships among members (see Figure 5). At this juncture, the specialized member can be replaced by its father member, thus saving the semantic of the facts. For instance, replacing the measure's hierarchy in Figure 2a with the hierarchy in Figure 5a if "Murano" and "Mazzorbo" have been polluted, then, after the replacement, it is still correct to affirm that two "Industrial Units" have been polluted (Figure 5b).

Therefore, Specialize and Classification are the best-adapted operators for specialization and classification hierarchies, respectively, but this is not a restriction. Indeed, applying Classify and Specialize operators to the two kinds of hierarchies will result in different queries, as their replacement predicates correspond to the logic quantifiers "all" and "any", respectively. For example, in order to analyze lagoon zones such as all their units are polluted, the user applies the Classify operator. Alternatively, to analyze the zones such as at least one of their units is polluted, she/he applies Specialize.

Figure 5. Specialization hierarchy "Unit" < "Type", a) Schema b) Instance

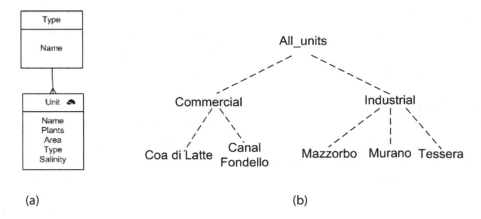

(a)   (b)

These operators are similar to the operator proposed in (Damiani & Spaccapietra, 2006). However, Damiani and Spaccapietra (2006) do not integrate a mechanism for choosing the replacement predicate ("all" and "any").

Before detailing Classify and Specialize, we present the concept of *Reduced Hierarchy*. A detailed measure is always the bottom level of the hierarchy. Following a Classify/Specialize operator, the definition of the Base Cube Schema of the View must remain consistent in the sense that the new measure has to be the bottom level of the hierarchy. The idea is then to replace the hierarchy containing the old measure with a new hierarchy having as bottom level the new measure. This hierarchy is called Reduced Hierarchy.

- **Definition:** Let H_h a be a Hierarchy Schema and S_t a an Entity Schema that belongs to the Entity Schema levels of H_h, then the Reduced Hierarchy is a hierarchy such as levels belong to the sub-tree of $\ddagger_h$ having as leafs S_t, and members belonging to the sub-tree of $\uparrow_h$ having as leafs the instances of S_t.

Example

An example of Reduced Hierarchy is shown in Figure 6.

The Classify operator, noted ω, makes it possible to change the granularity of the measure. It transforms a View into another View with a new measure.

- **Definition:** Let:
- V_v a Basic View $= \langle BC_{bc}, L, \Theta_k, \gamma \rangle$
- S_t an Entity Schema such as $S_f \ddagger_h S_t$ where S_f is the detailed measure of the Aggregation Mode Θ_k
- An Aggregation Mode $\Theta_t = \langle S'_t, S_{at}, \Phi \rangle$ where $S'_t = \lfloor_{h'}$ and $H_{h'}$ is the Reduced Hierarchy on S_t of the Hierarchy Schema of S_t

then $\omega(V_v)[S_t, \Theta_t] = V'_v = \langle BC'_{bc}, L, \Theta_t, \gamma' \rangle$ where:

- $BC'_{bc} = \langle H_{b1}, \dots H_{bm+1}, \delta' \rangle$ where:
- Without loss of generality, let $S_f \in L(H_{bt})$, then $\forall\ i \in [1 \dots t[\ \cup\ ]t \dots m+1]$, $H_{bi'} = H_{bi}$, and $H_{bt'}$ is the Reduced Hierarchy on S_t of H_{bt}
- $\delta': I(\lfloor_{b1}) \times \dots \times I(\lfloor_{bm+1})$ is calculated using Classification algorithm (Algorithm 1)
- $\gamma': I(S_{L1}) \times \dots \times I(S_{Lm}) \times I(S_{at})$

Figure 6. a) Hierarchy Schema H_a and its instance; b) Reduced Hierarchy of H_a on S_b (Schema and Instance)

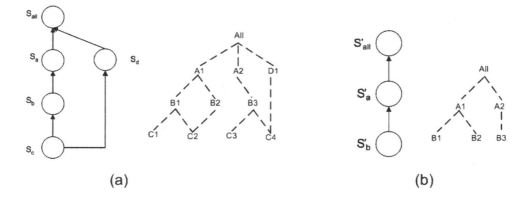

(a)　　　　　(b)

Algorithm 1. Classification algorithm

```
Inputs
V_v: Basic View, S_t: the new measure
Output
δ': Boolean function of the Basic View V'_v
Without loss of generality, let S_f ∈ L(H_bt) // The bottom level of the hierarchy
H_bt of the Base Cube is used as measure
Let list be a set of Entity Instances //list will contain the set of the de-
tailed measures which are the descendants of the new measure in the tuple ⟨t_1,…
t_m+1⟩ of V'_v
for each ⟨t_1,… t_m+1⟩ in dom(δ') { // List all possible tuple instances of
BC'_bc list:= ∅
for each ⟨t_b1,…t_bm+1⟩ in dom(δ) { //List all tuples as instances of BC_bc
if ((∀ i ∈ [1,…t-1] ∪ [t+1,...m+1] t_bi = t_i) and δ_f(t_b1,…t_bm+1) = true and t_bt ∈
leafs (H_bt, t_t) and t_bt ∉ list)
then add t_bt to list //Control that the tuple instance ⟨t_1,…t_m+1⟩ of BC'_bc has the
same instances of the tuple ⟨t_b1,… t_bm+1⟩ of BC_bc except for the measure t_bt which
has to be a descendant of the new measure t_t
}
if (list = leafs (H_bt, t_t)) //Control that all descendants of the new measure
are in the Base Cube BC_bc
then δ'(t_1,… t_m+1):= true else δ'(t_1,…t_m+1):= false
} return (δ')
```

Example

To answer the query "Which are the zones where all their units are polluted, per day and per pollutant?" the user applies the Classify operator. Let $\Theta_{fusion-zone} = \langle S'_{zone}, S'_{zone\_fusion}, \Phi \rangle$ then $\omega(V_{corila-unit})$ $[S_{zone}, \Theta_{fusion-zone}] = V_{corila-zone} = \langle BC_{corila-zone}, \langle S_{pollutant}, S_{day}, S_{rate5} \rangle, \Theta_{fusion-zone}, \gamma' \rangle$ where $BC_{corila-zone} = \langle H_{pollutants}, H_{time}, H'_{lagoon\_spatial}, H_{rate} \rangle, \delta' \rangle$ where δ' is defined on $I(S_{pollutant}) \times I(S_{day}) \times I(S'_{zone}) \times I(S_{rate5})$, and where $H'_{lagoon\_spatial}$ is the Reduced Hierarchy of $H_{lagoon\_spatial}$ on S_{zone}, and γ' is $I(S_{pollutant}) \times I(S_{day}) \times I(S_{rate5}) \times I(S'_{zone\_fusion})$.

The instance of $V_{corila-zone}$ is shown in Table 7. The Classification algorithm assigns true to the tuple ⟨Sulfur Trioxide, 26-9-05, Bocca Lido, 20-24⟩, because tuples ⟨Sulfur Trioxide, 26-9-05, Coa di Latte, 20-24⟩ and ⟨Sulfur Trioxide, 26-9-05,

Canal Fondello, 20-24⟩ are in the fact table (Table 2), and the descendants of Bocca Lido are Coa di Latte and Canal Fondello (Figure 3b).

- **Definition:** The Specialize operator is defined as the Classify operator, except for the statement of the algorithm "list = leafs(H_{bt}, t_t)" that is replace by "list ⊆ leafs(H_{bt}, t_t)". It checks that at least one descendant of the new measure is in the Base Cube BC_{bc}.

OLAP-Buffer and OLAP-Overlay: Operators that Dynamically Modify Spatial Dimensions

Since a set of "standard" GIS operators has not yet been defined (see the Introduction section),

Table 7. Instance of $V_{corila\text{-}zone}$

$S_{pollutant}$.name_pollutant	S_{day}.day	S'_{zone}.name_zone	S_{rate5}.value5
Zinc	19-9-05	*North Swam*	45-49
Methane	19-9-05	*North Swam*	30-34
Sulfur Trioxide	26-9-05	*Bocca Lido*	20-24

we focus on buffer and overlay operators among spatial analysis operators that can be used to modify the hypercube.

We introduce two multidimensional operators, *OLAP-Buffer* and *OLAP-Overlay*. Indeed, we keep the set of spatial analysis operators restricted to these two, because the buffer is representative of the spatial transformation operators which create *one* geographic object (i.e., fusion, etc.), and the overlay could be reformulated for handling spatial operators that create *n* new geographic objects (i.e., dissolve, etc.).

We do not therefore exclude the possibility of extending our model to other spatial transformation operators by modifying the input hierarchies containing new spatial members. In other words, even if these two operators do not cover the landscape of spatial transformation operators, they delve into two representative operators and lay the basis for a possible extension of the algebra.

OLAP-Buffer

OLAP-Buffer replaces the spatial dimension with another spatial dimension containing the geographic object resulting from the buffer operation.

The buffer operator creates a zone inside or outside an input geometry, as shown in Figure 7d. Thanks to a user-defined function which uses the geometric parts totally and/or partially covered by the buffer region, plus the original members and the associated measures values, OLAP-Buffer recalculates values of measures for the new spatial member.

- **Definition:** Let:
- V_v a Basic View $= \langle BC_{bc}, L, \Theta_k, \gamma \rangle$
- A Hierarchy Schema H_{buffer} which is the same as H_{bt} (without loss of generality) except for the bottom level which contains the members of $\llcorner_{bt}$ and the spatial member resulting from the buffer operator. This member is the child of 'All' member of H_{buffer}
- f_{buffer} is a function which takes as inputs a set of spatial members, their associated measure instances, and the new spatial member which is the result of the buffer. The result of the function is an instance of the detailed measure.

then $\beta(V_v)$ $[H_{buffer}, f_{buffer}] = V'_v = \langle BC'_{bc}, L', \Theta_k, \gamma' \rangle$ where:

- $BC'_{bc} = \langle H_{b1}, ...H_{bm+1}, \delta' \rangle$ where:
- $H_{bt'} = H_{buffer}$ and $\forall$ $i \in [1...t[\cup]t...m+1]$ $H_{bi'} = H_{bi}$
- δ': $I(\llcorner_{b1}) \times ... \times I(\llcorner_{bm+1})$ is calculated using the OLAP-Buffer algorithm (Algorithm 2)
- $L' = \langle S'_{L1}, ... S'_{Lm} \rangle$ such as if $S_{Lj} = \llcorner_{bt}$ then $S'_{Lj} = \llcorner_{buffer}$ and $\forall$ $i \in [1...j[\cup]j...m]$ $S'_{Li} = S_{Li}$
- γ': $I(S'_{L1}) \times ... \times I(S'_{Lm}) \times I(S_{af})$ where S_{af} is the aggregate measure of Θ_k

Example

Let $H_{lagoon\_spatialb}$ (Figure 7c) be a hierarchy equal to $H_{lagoon\_spatial}$ except for the bottom level S_{unitb} which contains the result of the buffer operator on the Mazzorbo unit (Mazzorbobuff). Mazzorbobuff

Figure 7. a) Cartographic representation of Mazzorbo; b) Cartographic representation of the result of the buffer on Mazzorbo; c) Instance of $H_{lagoon\_spatialb}$; d) GIS buffer operator

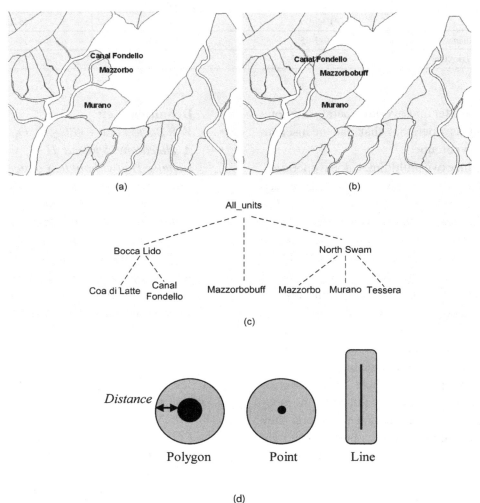

partially covers Canal Fondello and Murano (Figure 7a-b).

Let $V_{rate5}= \langle BC_{corila}, \langle S_{pollutant}, S_{day}, S_{unit}\rangle, \Theta_{avg\text{-}rate}, \gamma\rangle$, the View Schema that analyzes lagoon pollution according to zones, time and pollutants. Let $f_{avgbuffer}$ be the function recalculating the measure for Mazzorbobuff. $f_{avgbuffer}$ is a weighted average on the surface using geometries of geographic objects that totally or partially cover the geometry of Mazzorbobuff, together with measures associated to those members. Then $\beta(V_{rate5})$ $[H_{lagoon\_spatialb}, f_{avgbuffer}] = V_{rate5b} = \langle BC_{corilab}, \langle S_{pollutant}, S_{day}, S_{unitb}\rangle, \Theta_{avg\text{-}rate}, \gamma\rangle$ where $BC_{corilab} = \langle H_{pollutants}, H_{time}, H_{lagoon\_spatialb}, H_{rate}, \delta'\rangle$ where $\delta': I(S_{pollutant}) \times I(S_{day}) \times I(S_{unitb}) \times I(S_{rate5})$. The instance of V_{rate5b} is represented in Table 8. The OLAP-Buffer algorithm for the tuple $\langle zinc, 19\text{-}9\text{-}05, MazzorboBuff, 41\text{-}44\rangle$ searches in the fact table (Table 2) for tuples $\langle zinc, 19\text{-}9\text{-}05, Murano, 45\text{-}49\rangle$, $\langle zinc, 19\text{-}9\text{-}05, Canal Fondello, 30\text{-}34\rangle$ and $\langle zinc, 19\text{-}9\text{-}05, Mazzorbo, 45\text{-}49\rangle$, as the geometry of Mazzorbobuff covers the geometries of Canal Fondello and Murano.

Algorithm 2. OLAP-Buffer algorithm

```
Inputs
V_v: Basic View, H_buffer: Hierarchy that contains spatial members resulting from
the buffer operator, f_buffer: function used to recalculate the measure
Output
δ': Boolean function of the new Base Cube of the new View V'_v
Without loss of generality, let S_f ∈ L(H_bf) //The bottom level of the hierarchy
H_bf of the Base Cube is used as measure
Let t_buffer ∈ I(L_buffer) be the result of the buffer
Let listD be a set of Entity Instances //listD will contain a set of members
of the spatial dimension
Let listM be a set of Entity Instances //listM will contain the set of the de-
tailed measures associated to the spatial members of ListD
for each ⟨t_1,… t_m+1⟩ in dom(δ') { // List all possible tuples instances of V'_v
if((∀ i ∈ [1,…m+1] t_bi = t_i) and δ(t_b1,…t_bm+1) = true and
t_t ≠ t_buffer)
then δ'(t_1,…t_m+1):= true, else δ'(t_1,… t_m+1):= false
if (t_t = t_buffer) {
listD:= ∅
listM:= ∅
for each ⟨t_b1,…t_bm+1⟩ in dom(δ) { // List all tuple instances of the Base Cube BC_bc
if (∀ i ∈[1,… f-1] ∪ [f+1,…t-1] ∪ [t+1,…m+1] t_bi = t_i and δ(t_b1,…, t_bm+1) = true)
then add t_bt to listD and add t_bf to listM
}
if (t_f = f_buffer (t_buffer, listD, listM) //Control that all tuples instances used to
create the aggregated measure are tuples of the Base Cube
then δ'(t_1,…t_m+1):= true else δ'(t_1,…t_m+1):= false
}
}
return (δ')
```

As 41-44 is the result of the function $f_{avgbuffer}$ on (Murano, 45-49), (Canal Fondello, 30-34), (Mazzorbo, 45-49) and MazzorboBuff, then for tuple ⟨zinc, 19-9-05, MazzorboBuff, 41-44⟩, the new Boolean function δ' is true.

OLAP-Overlay

The GIS overlay operator creates a new layer whose features are obtained using the intersection operator on two input layers, as shown in Figure 8a.

GeoCube adapts this operator to create *n* new spatial members. The operator takes as its input a function used to calculate the measures for the new spatial members. The function uses the original spatial members, their associated measures and the spatial members intersecting them. The input hierarchy contains only one spatial level with spatial members resulting from the overlay.

Table 8. Instance of V_{rate5b}

$S_{pollutant}.$name_pollutant	$S_{day}.$day	$S_{unitb}.$name_unit	$S_{rate5}.$value5
Zinc	19-9-05	Mazzorbo	45-49
Sulfur Trioxide	19-9-05	Mazzorbo	30-34
Methane	19-9-05	Mazzorbo	30-34
Zinc	19-9-05	Canal Fondello	30-34
Methane	19-9-05	Murano	30-34
Zinc	19-9-05	Tessera	45-49
Methane	19-9-05	Coa di Latte	30-34
Zinc	19-9-05	Murano	45-49
Methane	26-9-05	Tessera	30-34
Sulfur Trioxide	26-9-05	Canal Fondello	20-24
Sulfur Trioxide	26-9-05	Coa di Latte	20-24
Zinc	19-9-05	Mazzorbobuff	41-44
Sulfur Trioxide	19-9-05	Mazzorbobuff	30-34
Methane	19-9-05	Mazzorbobuff	30-34

Due to space constraints, we do not provide the formal definition, but instead we give a usage example. OLAP-Overlay is noted as O.

Example

Let us consider that the spatial analyst is interested in pollution values for parts of units which have been depurated. Then, she/he applies the OLAP-Overlay operator: $O(V_{rate5})$ $[H_{lagoon\_spatialo}, f_{avgoverlay}]$ $= V_{rate5o} = \langle BC_{corilao}, \langle S_{pollutant}, S_{day}, S_{unito} \rangle, \Theta_{avg-rate} \gamma \rangle$ where $BC_{corilao} = \langle H_{pollutants}, H_{time}, H_{lagoon\_spatialo}, H_{rate}, \delta' \rangle$ with δ': $I(S_{pollutant}) \times I(S_{day}) \times I(S_{unito}) \times I(S_{rate5})$.

Here, $H_{lagoon\_spatialo}$ is a spatial hierarchy containing parts of units which are depurated (S_{unito}) (i.e., the result of overlaying units and depuration regions) and $f_{avgoverlay}$ is the weighted area average (see Figure 8b).

Permute

The *Permute* operator, noted as Π, makes it possible to permute dimension and measure. The bottom level of the hierarchy becomes the new measure, and the hierarchy associated to this new measure is used as the axis for analysis.

Figure 8. a) Overlay operator; b) OLAP-Overlay operator

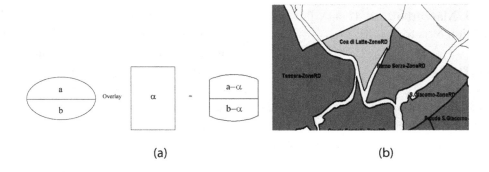

(a)　　　　　　　　　　(b)

Example

Let us suppose that the user wants to introduce pollutants as measures instead of the units. She/he applies the Permute operator $\Pi(V_{corila\text{-}unit})[\Theta_{list\text{-}pollutant}]$ $=V_{corila\text{-}pollutant}$. The instance of $V_{corila\text{-}pollutant}$ is the same as the instance of $V_{corila\text{-}unit}$ (Table 2).

Other Multidimensional Operators

Classical SOLAP operators are also supported by our model.

Roll-Up, noted as ρ, makes it possible to climb up into a hierarchy of the View.

Example

An example is $\rho(V_{corila\text{-}unit})[S_{month}] = V_{corila\text{-}unit\text{-}month}$. The Roll-up operator makes it possible to climb from days to months in the temporal dimension aggregating units using the Aggregation Mode.

Slice, noted σ, makes it possible to slice the hypercube using dimensions members and measures.

Example

$\sigma(V_{corila\text{-}unit})[S_{unit}.f^{area}>1000]=V_{corila\text{-}unit\text{-}1000}$ slices the hypercube using a spatial predicate on measures.

Dice, noted as η, eliminates a hierarchy from the View.

Example

$\eta\ (V_{corila\text{-}unit})\ [H_{time}]\ =V_{corila\text{-}unit/Time}\ =\ \langle BC_{corila/Time},$ $\langle S_{pollutant},\ S_{rate5}\rangle,\ \Theta_{fusion\text{-}unit},\ \gamma'\rangle$ where: $BC_{corila/Time} =$ $\langle H_{pollutants},\ H_{lagoon\_spatial},\ H_{rate},\ \delta'\rangle$ where δ': $I(S_{pollutant})\times I(S_{unit})\times I(S_{rate5})$. $V_{corila\text{-}unit/Time}$ makes it possible to analyze units according to pollutants and pollution values.

IMPLEMENTATION

GeoCube has been implemented in the Web-based prototype GeWOlap (Bimonte, 2010). GeWOlap is based on a three-tier architecture composed of the spatial data warehouse tier implemented using Oracle, the ROLAP Server Mondrian, and the Web-based SOLAP client integrating the OLAP client JPivot and an applet defined with MapXtreme Java for cartographic visualization and interaction functionalities. Thus, GeWOlap is an OLAP-GIS integrated solution that combines advanced functionalities of OLAP and GIS systems to grant an effective spatio-multidimensional analysis (Rivest et al., 2005; Marketos et al., 2008).

Logical Model

In order to support geographic/complex measures together with symmetrical measures and dimensions, we adopt a particular logical model composed of a fact table without measures (Kimball, 1996). Using this model, each level can be used as measure, and measures belong to hierarchies.

The logical model of our case-study application ($BC_{corila} = \langle H_{pollutants},\ H_{time},\ H_{lagoon\_spatial},\ H_{rate},$ $\delta\rangle$) is shown in Figure 9. Note that measures are defined as dimension levels (S_{unit}, $S_{pollutant}$, etc.). Aggregated measures are stored in specific tables ("unitagg" and "pollagg").

Note that the *Base Cube* is represented by the fact table and *complex and geographic measures* are the tables of the hierarchy levels.

The data cube model is represented in Mondrian by an XML file. As a multidimensional query is represented by a *View*, an XML file is defined for each used measure. These XML files differ only in measure tag. Thus, in order to aggregate geographic measures (*Aggregation Mode*), the SQL aggregation functions of Mondrian have been extended with a *user-defined aggregation function* which invokes ORACLE user-defined aggregation functions.

Figure 9. Logical model of the CORILA application

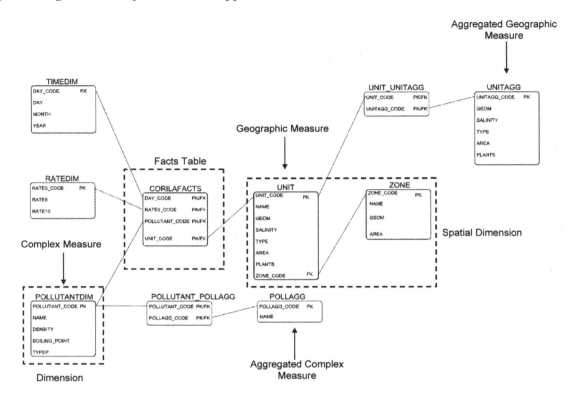

Operators

This particular logical model, combined with the extension of the aggregation functions of the OLAP Server and a set of geovisualisation techniques enables GeWOlap to implement the GeoCube operators as described below.

The *Permute* operator is implemented simply by changing the XML file.

The *Roll-up operator* uses user-defined aggregation functions defined in Oracle, making it possible to visualize alphanumeric identifiers of geographic or complex measures in the pivot table cells. For example, when using units as measures $(\rho(V_{corila-unit})[S_{month}] = V_{corila-unit-month})$, and the Roll-up operator is applied on the time dimension, then the result shown in Figure 10.

In our system, complex and/or geographic objects are aggregated through a two-step process:

1. Retrieve geographic/complex objects to aggregate,
2. Aggregate attributes of geographic/complex objects (Aggregation Mode functions).

Step 1 is specific to our model, and does not depend on the attributes of the geographic/complex objects used as measures, as our fact table only contains the identifiers of the dimensions members.

Step 1 is implemented as a user-defined aggregation function. It collects identifiers of measures and stores them into a temporary table during the iteration step (*ODCIAggregateIterate function*). It then checks whether the set of measures has already been aggregated (*ODCIAggregateTerminate function*). If so, it returns the identifier of the aggregated measures (table "unitaagg" for unit measures), otherwise it adds a tuple to the table representing the aggregated measures.

Figure 10. Aggregation of a geographic measures Unit

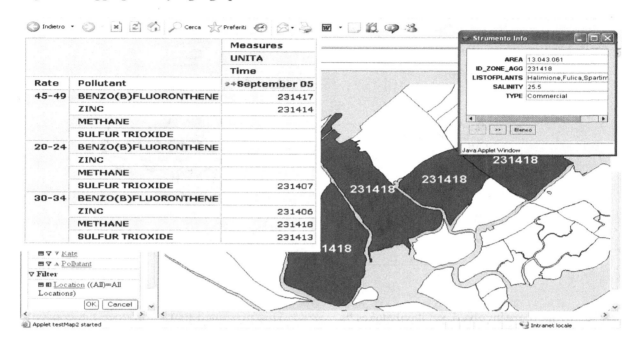

Then, Step 2 is performed when the user wants to visualize one aggregated geographic/complex object. This improves the performance of the overall aggregation process.

It is important to note that the first aggregation step is feasible for large data warehouses and does not compromise the overall performance of the system. Indeed, it does not depend on the number of tuples in the fact table (in the sense that the selection of all the tuples in the fact table has a constant time) but only on the number of measures to aggregate, and aggregation is not very time-intensive.

In fact, for step 1, using a spatial data warehouse with 5.140.097 tuples, the aggregation of 100 measures takes 9 s, 240 measures takes 22s, 1000 measures takes 25s and 8480 measures takes 29 s, on a PC with 512Mb RAM and an AMD Athlon processor.

Step 2 is the classical aggregation step, where spatial, numerical and user-defined aggregation functions are applied on measure values. Performance of Step 2 depends on the data. For example,

it takes a very long time to aggregate units as they are very complex polygons.

We have implemented the *Classify* and *Specialize* operators by associating a different fact table with each level of the geographic/complex measure's hierarchy. In order to calculate the fact table for the *Classify* operator, we use the same algorithm as for the Roll-up operator testing whether all detailed measures have to be aggregated, whereas the *Specialize* operator has been implemented using the SQL join and selection operators.

OLAP-Buffer and *OLAP-Overlay* have been implemented by exploiting the flexibility of the Mondrian XML file (Bimonte, 2009). The Spatial DBMS calculates the new geographic objects using a Spatial SQL query. These geographic objects are then added to the XML schema as calculated members. Their associated measures are calculated using an MDX formula and/or user-defined java functions. Figure 11 gives an example of OLAP-Overlay ($O(V_{rate5}) [H_{lagoon\_spatialo}, f_{avgoverlay}] = V_{rate5o}$). This query is highly complex as several

Figure 11. OLAP-Buffer Operator with units and depurated regions

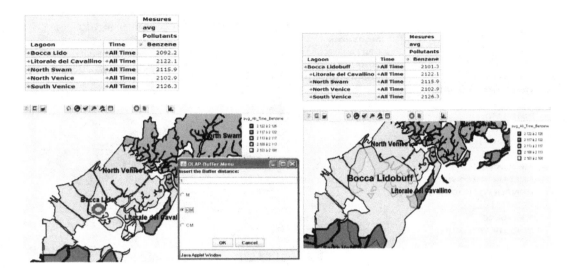

spatial members are involved, yet it only takes 9s to be executed. This demonstrates the feasibility of our operators which dynamically modify the spatial dimensions.

The *Dice* operator has been implemented using the SQL projection and selection operators on the fact table, by eliminating one dimension from the fact table, and removing all the tuples with the same values for the other dimensions.

Finally, the *Slice* operator has been implemented using the SQL selection operator. However, contrary to our formal model, the system does not use a selected part of the fact table for subsequent OLAP operations (Bimonte et al., 2006).

CONCLUSION

This chapter addresses the integration of geographic information and spatial analysis into multidimensional models. Existing spatio-multidimensional models reduce geographic information to its spatial component, and do not provide a dynamic representation of the hypercube, thereby limiting the capabilities of spatial analysis.

This prompted us to introduce the concepts of *geographic measures* and *geographic multidimensional operators*. These concepts have been formalized in a multidimensional model, called GeoCube.

GeoCube supports advanced multidimensional modelling properties such as derived measures, symmetry of dimensions and measures, complex hierarchies, etc. In order to integrate the semantic component of geographic information, GeoCube defines measures as geographic objects belonging to hierarchies (geographic measures). In this way, GeoCube makes it possible to dynamically change the granularity of measures and to use the alphanumeric attributes of geographic objects as measures.

Moreover, GeoCube introduces the flexibility of the spatial analysis process into multidimensional analysis through a new set of operators. These operators make it possible to permute dimensions and measures, and to adapt the buffer and the overlay spatial transformation operators to the multidimensional analysis paradigm.

The model has been implemented in a system called GeWOlap. However, there are implementation issues to contend with. Indexing (Tao &

Papadias, 2005) and spatial view materialization (Stefanovic et al., 2000) techniques have to be integrated into GeWOlap in order to speed-up the operators that dynamically change the structure of the hypercube and to improve the aggregation of geographic/complex measures. Moreover, the main limitation to the current implementation of the *Classify* and *Specialize* operators is that there is a trade-off in balancing time performance against storage performance. Materializing all possible hypercubes grants good response times, but in terms of data storage it is unfeasible with large data warehouses. On the other hand, calculating all possible hypercubes on the fly with the "all" and "any" SQL predicates only requires storage of one fact table, but has a knock-on effect on time performances.

At moment, we are working at the definition of integrity constraints using UML and OCL in order to grant quality of spatial data warehouse avoiding inconsistent spatial data (Gadish, 2008). We also investigate a logical implementation of GeoCube using GML as it is promising model for multidimensional geographical data mediating (Savary et al., 2007).

ACKNOWLEDGMENT

This work has been partially done by Sandro Bimonte during his Phd Thesis at INSA-Lyon, France. We would also like to acknowledge Pr. Michel Schneider who has spent valuable time reviewing this document to improve on its clarity and technical information.

REFERENCES

Abello, A., Samos, J., & Saltor, F. (2006). YAM²: A Multidimensional Conceptual Model Extending UML. *Information Systems*, *3*(6), 541–567. doi:10.1016/j.is.2004.12.002

Ahmed, T., & Miquel, M. (2006). Multidimensional Structures Dedicated to Continuous Spatiotemporal Phenomena. In *British National Conference on Databases* (pp. 29-40). Berlin: Springer.

Bimonte, S. (2007). *Intégration de l'information géographique dans les entrepôts de données et l'analyse en ligne: de la modélisation à la visualisation*. Unpublished doctoral dissertation, Lyon, France.

Bimonte, S. (2009). On Modelling and Analysis of Geographic Multidimensional Databases. In Bellatreche, L. (Ed.), *Data Warehousing Design and Advanced Engineering Applications: Methods for Complex Construction* (pp. 96–112). Hershey, PA: IGI Global.

Bimonte, S. (2010). A Web-based System for Multidimensional Analysis of Geographic and Complex Data. *International Journal of Agricultural and Environmental Information Systems*.

Bimonte, S., Tchounikine, A., & Miquel, M. (2006). GeoCube, a Multidimensional Model and Navigation Operators Handling Complex Measures: Application in Spatial OLAP. In *Proceedings of the International Conference in Advances in Information Systems* (pp. 100-109). Berlin: Springer.

Camossi, E., Bertolotto, M., & Bertino, E. (2008). Querying Multigranular Spatio-temporal Objects. In *Proceedings of the International Conference on Database and Expert Systems Applications* (pp. 390-403). Berlin: Springer.

Damiani, M., & Spaccapietra, S. (2006). Spatial Data Warehouse Modeling. In Darmont, J., & Boussaïd, O. (Eds.), *Processing and Managing Complex Data for Decision Support* (pp. 1–27). Hershey, PA: IGI Global.

Fidalgo, R. N., Times, V. C., Silva, J., & Souza, F. (2004). GeoDWFrame: A Framework for Guiding the Design of Geographical Dimensional Schemas. In *Proceedings of the International Conference on Data Warehousing and Knowledge Discovery* (pp. 26-37). Berlin: Springer.

Franklin, C. (1992). An Introduction to Geographic Information Systems: Linking Maps to databases. *Database, 15*(2), 13–21.

Gadish, D. A. (2008). Introducing the Elasticity of Spatial Data. *International Journal of Data Warehousing and Mining, 4*(3), 54–70.

Glorio, O., & Trujillo, J. (2008). An MDA Approach for the Development of Spatial Data Warehouses. In *Proceedings of the International Conference on Data Warehousing and Knowledge Discovery* (pp. 23-32). Berlin: Springer.

Gómez, L., Kuijpers, B., Moelans, B., & Vaisman, A. (2009). A Survey of Spatio-Temporal Data Warehousing. *International Journal of Data Warehousing and Mining, 5*(3), 28–55.

Harinarayan, V., Rajaraman, A., & Ullman, J. D. (1996). Implementing Data Cubes Efficiently. In *Proceedings of the ACM SIGMOD International Conference on Management of Data* (pp. 205-216). New York: ACM Press

Inmon, W. H. (1996). *Building the Data Warehouse* (2nd ed.). New York: Wiley.

Jensen, C., Kligys, A., Pedersen, T., & Timko, I. (2004). Multidimensional Data Modelling for location-based services. *International Journal on Very Large Data Bases, 13*(1), 1–21. doi:10.1007/s00778-003-0091-3

Kimball, R. (1996). *The Data Warehouse Toolkit: Practical Techniques for Building Dimensional Data Warehouses*. New York: Wiley.

Longley, P., Goodchild, M., Maguire, D., & Rhind, D. (Eds.). (2001). *Geographic Information Systems and Science*. New York: Wiley.

Lujan-Mora, S., Trujillo, J., & Song, I.-Y. (2006). A UML Profile for Multidimensional Modelling in Data Warehouses. *Journal of Data & Knowledge Engineering, 59*(3), 725–769. doi:10.1016/j.datak.2005.11.004

Malinowski, E., & Zimányi, E. (2008). *Advanced Data Warehouse Design From Conventional to Spatial and Temporal Applications*. Berlin: Springer.

Marketos, G., Theodoridis, Y., Ioannis, S., & Kalogeras, J. (2008). Seismological Data Warehousing and Mining: A Survey. *International Journal of Data Warehousing and Mining, 4*(1), 1–16.

Mitchell, A. (2005). The ESRI Guide to GIS Analysis: *Vol. 2. Spatial Measurements and Statistics*. Redlands, CA: ESRI Press.

Pedersen, T., Jensen, C., & Dyreson, C. (2001). A Foundation For Capturing And Querying Complex Multidimensional Data. *Information Systems, 26*(5), 383–423. doi:10.1016/S0306-4379(01)00023-0

Pourabbas, E. (2003). Cooperation with Geographic Databases. In Rafanelli, M. (Ed.), *Multidimensional Databases: problems and solutions* (pp. 393–432). Hershey, PA: IGI Global.

Rafanelli, M. (2003). Operators for Multidimensional Aggregate Data. In Rafanelli, M. (Ed.), *Multidimensional Databases: problems and solutions* (pp. 116–165). Hershey, PA: IGI Global.

Rivest, S., Bédard, Y., & Marchand, P. (2001). Towards Better Support For Spatial Decision-Making: Defining The Characteristics Of Spatial On-Line Analytical Processing. *Geomatica - Journal of the Canadian Institute of Geomatics, 55*(4), 539-555.

Rivest, S., Bédard, Y., Proulx, M., Nadeaum, M., Hubert, F., & Pastor, J. (2005). SOLAP: Merging Business Intelligence with Geospatial Technology for Interactive Spatio-Temporal Exploration and Analysis of Data. *Journal of International Society for Photogrammetry and Remote Sensing, 60*(1), 17–33. doi:10.1016/j.isprsjprs.2005.10.002

Sampaio, M., Sousa, A., & Baptista, C. (2006). Towards A Logical Multidimensional Model For Spatial Data Warehousing And OLAP. In *Proceedings of the ACM International Workshop on Data Warehousing and OLAP* (pp. 83-90). New York: ACM Press.

Savary, L., Gardarin, G., & Zeitouni, K. (2007). GeoCache: A Cache for GML Geographical Data. *International Journal of Data Warehousing and Mining, 3*(1), 67–88.

Scotch, M., & Parmanto, B. (2006). Development of SOVAT: A Numerical-Spatial Decision Support System For Community Health Assessment Research. *International Journal of Medical Informatics, 34*(10), 771–784. doi:10.1016/j.ijmedinf.2005.10.008

Silva, J., Times, V., Salgado, A., Souza, C., Fidalgo, R., & Oliveira, A. (2008). A Set of Aggregation Functions for Spatial Measures. In *Proceedings of the ACM 11th international workshop on Data warehousing and OLAP* (pp. 25-32). New York: ACM Press.

Stefanovic, N., Han, J., & Koperski, K. (2000). Object-Based Selective Materialization for Efficient Implementation of Spatial Data Cubes. *IEEE Transactions on Knowledge and Data Engineering, 12*(6), 938–958. doi:10.1109/69.895803

Tao, Y., & Papadias, D. (2005). Historical spatio-temporal aggregation. *ACM Transactions on Information Systems, 23*(1), 61–102. doi:10.1145/1055709.1055713

Timpf, S., & Frank, A. U. (1997). Using Hierarchical Spatial Data Structures For Hierarchical Spatial Reasoning. In *Spatial Information Theory - A Theoretical Basis for GIS* (pp. 69–83). Berlin: Springer Verlag. doi:10.1007/3-540-63623-4_43

Trujillo, J., Palomar, M., Gomez, J., & Song, I. (2001). Designing Data Warehouses with OO Conceptual Models. *Computer, 34*(12), 66–75. doi:10.1109/2.970579

Voisard, A., & David, B. (2002). A Database Perspective on Geospatial Data Modeling. *IEEE Transactions on Knowledge and Data Engineering, 14*(2), 226–243. doi:10.1109/69.991714

ENDNOTE

[1] Consortium for Coordination of Research Activities concerning the Venice Lagoon System

This work was previously published in International Journal of Data Warehousing and Mining, Volume 6, Issue 4, edited by David Taniar, pp. 33-60, copyright 2010 by IGI Publishing (an imprint of IGI Global).

Chapter 16
Combining *k*NN Imputation and Bootstrap Calibrated:
Empirical Likelihood for Incomplete Data Analysis

Yongsong Qin
Guangxi Normal University, China

Shichao Zhang
Zhejiang Normal University, China & University of Technology, Australia

Chengqi Zhang
University of Technology, Australia

ABSTRACT

The k-nearest neighbor (kNN) imputation, as one of the most important research topics in incomplete data discovery, has been developed with great successes on industrial data. However, it is difficult to obtain a mathematical valid and simple procedure to construct confidence intervals for evaluating the imputed data. This chapter studies a new estimation for missing (or incomplete) data that is a combination of the kNN imputation and bootstrap calibrated EL (Empirical Likelihood). The combination not only releases the burden of seeking a mathematical valid asymptotic theory for the kNN imputation, but also inherits the advantages of the EL method compared to the normal approximation method. Simulation results demonstrate that the bootstrap calibrated EL method performs quite well in estimating confidence intervals for the imputed data with kNN imputation method.

INTRODUCTION

Item non-response is usually handled by some form of imputation to fill in the missing item values. Imputation not only permits the creation of a general purpose complete public-use data file

that can be used for standard analyses, but also recoveries part of lost information. For example, we may intend to get (X_i, Y_i), $1 \leq i \leq n$, from n individuals. If X-values are observed completely and some of Y-values may be missing, we could use some ways to fill in the missing values of Y by the relationship between the variables X and

DOI: 10.4018/978-1-61350-474-1.ch016

Copyright © 2012, IGI Global. Copying or distributing in print or electronic forms without written permission of IGI Global is prohibited.

Y as each pair (X_i, Y_i) comes from one individual. It then would be better than to drop the *i*th pair (X_i, Y_i) if Y_i alone is missing. The *k*-nearest neighbor (*k*NN) imputation is one of the most important hot deck methods used to compensate for nonresponse in incomplete data mining. It is a nonparametric imputation method, which is simple but effective for many applications. With the method, a case is imputed using values from its *k* nearest neighbors (points). A thorough description of the *k*NN technique was presented by McRoberts et al. (2002).

The nearest neighbor (NN) imputation, a special case of *k*NN when *k* = 1, has widely been used in the data analysis applications, such as surveys conducted at Statistics Canada, the U.S. Bureau of Labor Statistics, and the U.S. Census Bureau (Chen & Shao, 2000). Although this happened, it is difficult to obtain a mathematical valid and simple procedure to construct confidence intervals for evaluating the imputed data. Instead of building a validation theory, the efficiency of *k*NN imputation is evaluated with few experiments in data mining and machine learning. This leaves open the confidence of the compensated values with the *k*NN imputation.

In this chapter, we propose a new estimation for missing (or incomplete) data, named *k*NN-BEL, that is a combination of the *k*NN imputation and bootstrap calibrated EL (Empirical Likelihood). The *k*NN-BEL first uses the Cross-validation method to choose *k*. And then missing values are estimated with their *k* nearest neighbors. Finally, a bootstrap calibrated empirical likelihood (EL) method is applied to construct confidence intervals for the mean of the dependent variable, i.e., evaluating the confidence of the compensated values with the *k*NN imputation.

In the complete data setting, the original idea of empirical (or nonparametric) likelihood (EL) dates back to Hartley and Rao (1968) in the context of sample surveys, and Owen (2001) made a systematic study of the EL method. The EL confidence intervals are range preserving and transformation respecting, and the shape and orientation of EL

intervals are determined entirely by the data, unlike the normal approximation based intervals.

In the incomplete data setting (Banek et al., 2008; Golfarelli & Rizzi, 2009; Gomez et al., 2009; Nikulin, 2008; Pighin & Ieronutti, 2008; Yu et al., 2009), the *k*NN imputation is used associated with the bootstrap calibrated EL. The use of the Cross-validation method can guarantee the smallest mean squared errors in the process of imputation, and the bootstrap calibrated EL method releases the burden of having a mathematical valid asymptotic theory for the estimators of parameters in interest, while this method also keeps the advantages of the EL method compared to the normal approximation method. Without loss of generality, we simulate the *k*NN-BEL and demonstrate that the combination of the *k*NN imputation and the bootstrap calibrated EL method perform quite well in data analysis with missing data.

The rest of the chapter is organized as follows. We first outline some commonly used imputation methods. And then, we propose the cross-validation method to choose *k* in *k*NN imputation, and propose a bootstrap calibrated EL method to construct confidence intervals. After that, some simulation results are reported on studying the performance of the proposed confidence intervals.

Finally, we conclude this chapter.

PRELIMINARY

In this section, we first list all symbols used in this chapter. Second, we briefly describe the missing mechanisms. Third, we review some imputation methods used in the literatures. Finally, some related work is briefly introduced.

Symbols

In this chapter, all symbols are defined as follows.

- *X*: A *d*-dimensional independent variable.
- *Y*: An univariate dependent variable.

- δ: Indicator variable to indicate if Y is missing or not.
- ε: Random error.
- $\mu = EY$: The mean of Y.
- $\hat{\mu}$: The estimator of μ.
- $\widehat{Y}_i$: A imputed value for Y_i when it is missing.
- $\left\{ \widehat{Y}_i^*, 1 \leq i \leq n \right\}$: Complete data of Y after imputation.
- $X \sim N(1,1)$: X is distributed as a normal distribution with mean 1 and variance 1.
- $\varepsilon \sim N(0,1)$: ε is distributed as a standard normal distribution.
- $\varepsilon \sim Y(-0.5,0.5)$: ε is uniformly distributed on the interval (-0.5,0.5).
- $Zi(_\mu)$: Score function used to define EL statistic.
- λn: A root of the EL equation.
- $l(\mu)$: EL statistic based on the kNN imputation.
- $l^*(\hat{\mu})$: Bootstrap EL statistic.
- $I(\alpha)$: Bootstrap calibrated EL confidence interval.

Types of Missing Data

Missing completely at random (MCAR) means that the probability of a value missing is independent of all values in the data set, observed and unobserved. Missing at random (MAR) is less restrictive, as it allows the mechanism that produces missing values to depend on observed values, but not on unobserved ones. The most severe form of missingness is missing not at random (MNAR), which allows missingness to depend on missing values. In this chapter, we mainly focus on the MAR case, which is a practical assumption in many cases.

Related Imputation Methods

Let X be a d-dimensional vector of factors and let Y be response variable influenced by X. In practice, one often obtains a random sample (sample size n) of incomplete data associated with a population (X,Y,δ),

$$(X_i, Y_i, \delta_i), i = 1,2,\ldots,n, \tag{1}$$

where all the X_i's are observed and $\delta_i = 0$ if Y_i is missing, otherwise $\delta_i = 1$. Suppose that (X_i, Y_i, δ_i)'s satisfy the following model:

$$Y_i = m(X_i) + \varepsilon_i, i = 1,2,\ldots,n,$$

where m is an unknown function, and the unobserved ε_i's are i.i.d. random errors with mean 0 and unknown finite variance, and independent of the i.i.d. random variables X_i's. In the situation of m is a linear function, i.e., Y and X fit a linear model, Wang and Rao (2002a) have compared the adjusted empirical likelihood methods and the normal approximation methods in terms of coverage accuracies and average lengths of the confidence intervals for the mean EY of Y. They indicate that the adjusted empirical likelihood methods perform competitively and the use of auxiliary information provides improved inferences and shows that the deterministic imputation method performance well in making inference for the mean of Y. Qin et al. (2008) have showed that one must use random imputation method in making inference for distribution functions and quantiles of Y. Yet in many complex practical situations, m (an unknown function) is not a linear function. When we do not know the form of m, i.e., the nonparametric situation, Wang and Rao (2002b) have considered empirical likelihood inference on the mean of response Y when Y is missing at random (MAR) by estimating m using kernel methods.

To avoid estimating *m*, NN imputation method replaces a missing value in a dataset with the value of the nearest neighbor in the dataset. In other words, NN imputation is a model free method. To improve the efficiency, *k*NN imputation method is proposed, which replaces a missing value in a dataset with the mean of *k* nearest neighbors in the process of imputation. NN or *k*NN imputation algorithms have experimentally been proved more efficient than other existing imputation methods. They have widely been used in applications. However, as mentioned before, (1) it must seek a proper *k* when using *k*NN imputation methods; and (2) the *k*NN imputation algorithms also suffer from low efficiency in some situations when using normal approximation methods. In this chapter, the first issue is tackled by using the Cross-validation method to choose *k*, and the second one is treated by using bootstrap calibrated empirical likelihood method in making inferences.

Related Work

The NN method was initially introduced by Skellam (1952). The NN imputation method has been a popular method in many survey agencies and it has a long history of applications in surveys such as the Census 2000 and the Current Population Survey conducted by the U.S. Census Bureau (Farber & Griffin, 1998; Fay, 1999), the Job Openings and Labor Turnover Survey and the Employee Benefits Survey conducted by the U.S. Bureau of Labor Statistics (Montaquila & Ponikowski, 1993). Theoretical studies of the NN imputation methodology started with Lee et al. (1994) and Rancourt (1999) who showed some properties of NN imputation estimators when *Y* and *X* are assumed to follow a simple linear regression model. The first theoretical work for NN imputation under a general nonparametric setting is given in Chen and Shao (2000) who established the consistency of NN imputation estimators such as the sample mean and sample quantile. Chen and Shao (2001)

investigated jackknife variance estimators for the sample mean. In practice, statistical inference such as setting an approximate confidence interval for a population parameter is often more important. Efficient method on confidence intervals with NN imputation is not available so far.

KNN-BEL: COMBINING *K*NN AND BOOTSTRAP CALIBRATED EL

Data Structures

Consider an i.i.d. sample of incomplete observations (X_i, Y_i, δ_i), $i = 1, 2, \ldots, n$ generated from (X, Y, δ) ($X \in R^d, Y \in R$ and $\delta \in R$), where all the X_i's are observed, and $\delta_i = 0$ if Y_i is missing and $\delta_i = 1$ otherwise. Let $r = \sum_{i=1}^{n} \delta_i$, $m = n - r$, and s_r and s_m be the sets of respondents and nonrespondents, respectively.

KNN Imputation

Before defining the *k*NN imputation, we present how to determine the value of *k*. Many methods have been designed for determining the value of *k*. This chapter seeks the value of *k* with the cross validation.

For $i \in s_r$, i.e., for non-missing Y_i, find *k* points in $\{X_j, j \in \{s_r - i\}\}$ nearest to X_i (measured in Euclidean distance in R^d). We denote the *k* points are $X_{i_j}, j = 1, \ldots, k$. Then use $\widehat{Y}_i = \frac{1}{k} \sum_{j=1}^{k} Y_{i_j}$ to impute the missing Y_i.

Choice of *k*

With the Cross-validation method, we can obtain $CV(k)$ for a *k* as follows.

$$CV(k) = \sum \left(Y_i - \widehat{Y}_{i,-i} \right)^2$$

where $\widehat{Y}_{i,-i}$ is the imputed value for Y_i after deleting the ith case.

Hence, we can choose k according to the following formula

$$K = \mathrm{arg}MIN^r_{k=1}\{CV(k)\}$$

It is possible that the size of dataset is very large. To scale up the above algorithm, one can seek the k in a sample of the dataset.

We now define the kNN imputation as follows.

Definition 1: For $i \in s_m$, i.e., for missing Y_i, let $NN(i,k)$ be a set of k points in $\{X_j, j \in s_r\}$ nearest to X_i (measured in Euclidean distance in R^d). The missing Y_i is imputed with the value $\widehat{Y}_i$ as follows.

$$\widehat{Y}_i = \frac{1}{k}\sum_{Y_j \in NN(i,k)} Y_j$$

EL Ratio Statistics for the Mean of Y

Based on the 'complete' data $\left\{Y_i^* = \delta_i Y_i + (1-\delta_i)\widehat{Y}_i, 1 \le i \le n\right\}$ after kNN imputation, we construct an EL statistic for $\mu = EY$ as follows.

Let $Z_i(\mu) = Y^*_i - \mu$. Then, the empirical log-likelihood ratio for μ is defined as

$$l(\mu) = -2\sum_{i=1}^{n} \log(np_i)$$

where $p_i, i = 1,\ldots,n$ maximize $\sum_{i=1}^{n}\log(np_i)$ subject to constraints

$$\sum_{i=1}^{n} p_i = 1, \sum_{i=1}^{n} p_i Z_i(\mu) = 0$$

It can be shown that

$$l(\mu) = 2\sum_{i=1}^{n}\left\{1 + \lambda_n Z_i(\mu)\right\} \tag{2}$$

where λ_n is the solution of the following equation:

$$\frac{1}{n}\sum_{i=1}^{n} \frac{Z_i(\mu)}{1 + \lambda_n Z_i(\mu)} = 0$$

As we do not know the asymptotic distribution of $l(\mu)$, we cannot obtain the confidence interval based on $l(\mu)$ alone. We will combine a bootstrap calibrated method to obtain confidence intervals on $\mu = EY$ in the next subsection.

KNN-BEL Algorithm

We now design the kNN-BEL algorithm that uses bootstrap method to approximate the asymptotic distribution of the EL Statistic $l(\mu)$, i.e., evaluating the confidence of the compensated values with the kNN imputation. Noting that the usual bootstrap method leads to invalid result (Shao & Sitter, 1996) with missing data, we employ the bootstrap procedure proposed in Shao and Sitter (1996) in which the bootstrap data set is imputed in the same way as

the original data set was imputed.

1. Draw a simple random sample S^*_n of size n with replacement from the extended sample $S_n = \{(X_i, Y^*_i), 1 \le i \le n\}$.

2. Let S^*_{nc} be the portion of S^*_n without imputed values and S^*_{nm} be the set of vectors in S^*_n with imputed values. Then replace all the imputed Y values in S^*_{nm} using the proposed kNN imputation method based on the bootstrap sample S^*_n.

3. Let $\widehat{\mu} = \frac{1}{n}\sum_{i=1}^{n} Y^*_i$ be the estimator of μ based on data $\{Y^*_i\}$. Let $l^*(\widehat{\mu})$ be the empirical likelihood ratio based on the re-imputed data set S^*_n.

4. Repeat the above steps B-times for a large integer B and obtain B bootstrap values $\left\{l_b^*(\hat{\mu})\right\}_{b=1}^B$. For given $0 < \alpha < 1$, let q^* be the $1 - \alpha$ sample quantile of the data $\left\{l_b^*(\hat{\mu})\right\}_{b=1}^B$.

Definition 2: An bootstrap calibrated empirical likelihood confidence interval for μ with nominal coverage level $1 - \alpha$ is:

$$I_\alpha = \{\mu \mid l(\mu) \leq q^*\} \qquad (3)$$

where $l(\mu)$ is defined in (2).

SIMULATION RESULTS

We conducted a set of simulations on the finite sample performance of the EL based confidence region on $\mu = EY$. For this purpose, we used the model $Y = 1.5X + g(X) + \varepsilon$, where $X \sim N(1,1)$ and $\varepsilon \sim N(0,1)$ or $\varepsilon \sim U(-0.5,0.5)$, and $g(x)$ was taken as:

- $g(x) = 0$,
- $g(x) = (3.2x^2 - 1)I(|x| \leq 1)$,
- $g(x) = x^2 + \sin(2\pi x)$,
- $g(x) = x^2 + \cos(2\pi x)$,
- $g(x) = x^3 + \exp(x)$.

We considered the following three cases of response probabilities under the MAR assumption:

- **Case 1:** $\pi_1(x) = P(\delta = 1|x) = 0.8 + 0.2|x - 1|$, if $|x - 1| \leq 1$, and 0.95 elsewhere.
- **Case 2:** $\pi_2(x) = P(\delta = 1|x) = 0.9 - 0.2|x - 1|$, if $|x - 1| \leq 4$, and 0.1 elsewhere.
- **Case 3:** $\pi_s(x) = 0.65$ for all x.

When $X \sim N(1,1)$, the average response rates corresponding to the preceding three cases are approximately 91%, 74% and 65%, respectively, which are designed to compare the performances of the proposed bootstrap calibrated EL confidence intervals under different response rates.

For each of the three cases, we generated a random sample of incomplete data $\{(X_i, Y_i, \delta_i), i = 1,2,\ldots,n\}$ for $n = 60, 100, 150, 200, 300$ and 400 from the model $Y = 1.5X + g(X) + \varepsilon$ and specified response probability function. In the bootstrap procedure, we took $B = 1000$. For nominal confidence level $1 - \alpha = 0.95$ and every data set (i.e., the simulated sample) $\{(X_i, Y_i, \delta_i), i = 1,2,\ldots,n\}$, we obtained an EL confidence interval $I_{\alpha,l}$ proposed in (3). Then repeat this procedure M = 1000 times, and obtained 1000 EL confidence intervals $I_{\alpha,1},\ldots,I_{\alpha,1000}$. Here we note that the data set would be different from one to another due to the randomization. We evaluated the coverage probability (CP) and average length (AL) of the empirical likelihood based (EL) confidence intervals to see the performance of the proposed method in this chapter, where

$$AL = \frac{1}{1000} \sum_{j=1}^{1000} \text{length of } I_{\alpha,j},$$

$$CP = \frac{1}{1000} \sum_{j=2}^{1000} I(\mu, I_{\alpha,j}) \text{ with}$$

$I(\mu, I_{\alpha,j}) = 1$ if the true

$\mu \in I(\mu, I_{\alpha,j})$, and 0 otherwise.

We conducted our simulations using a DELL Workstation PWS650 with 2G main memory, 2.6G CPU, and WINDOWS 2000. We used the Matlab software to implement simulations. The algorithm is simple. It took about 20 to 30 minutes to obtain CP and AL for one case. Our method as well as the NN imputation can be used to any model with two variables X and Y. The performance could be affected by different parameters and models chosen in the simulations. However, from the simulation results, we can see that the performance is quite robust with different models and parameters.

In our experiments, Table 1 reports the simulation results when $g(x) = 0$, $X \sim N(1,1)$ and $\varepsilon \sim N(0,1)$; Table 2 reports the simulation results when $g(x) =$

Table 1. Coverage probabilities (CP) and average lengthes (AL) of confidence intervals for μ when g(x) = 0, X ~ N(1,1) and ε ~ N(0,1) under different response probabilities and sample sizes

	CP			AL		
n	$\Pi_1(x)$	$\Pi_2(x)$	$\Pi_3(x)$	$\Pi_1(x)$	$\Pi_2(x)$	$\Pi_3(x)$
60	0.920	0.905	0.893	0.8924	1.1720	1.1462
100	0.935	0.915	0.908	0.7574	0.8071	0.8481
150	0.937	0.923	0.915	0.6183	0.6487	0.6960
200	0.942	0.931	0.922	0.5302	0.5553	0.5791
300	0.944	0.938	0.926	0.4342	0.4474	0.4745
400	0.948	0.942	0.935	0.3755	0.3906	0.4020

Table 2. Coverage probabilities (CP) and average lengthes (AL) of confidence intervals for μ when g(x) = 0, X ~ N(1,1) and ε ~ U(-0.5,0.5) under different response probabilities and sample sizes

	CP			AL		
n	$\Pi_1(x)$	$\Pi_2(x)$	$\Pi_3(x)$	$\Pi_1(x)$	$\Pi_2(x)$	$\Pi_3(x)$
60	0.895	0.885	0.865	2.2283	2.3806	2.8515
100	0.902	0.895	0.877	1.1535	1.6940	1.1754
150	0.914	0.913	0.896	0.8615	0.9610	0.6940
200	0.935	0.918	0.913	0.5247	0.4552	0.6940
300	0.935	0.924	0.915	0.3083	0.3068	0.3817
400	0.942	0.946	0.920	0.2285	0.2834	0.2964

Table 3. Coverage probabilities (CP) and average lengthes (AL) of confidence intervals for μ when g(x) = (3.2x² − 1)I(|x| ≤ 1), X ~ N(1,1) and ε ~ N(0,1) under different response probabilities and sample sizes

	CP			AL		
n	$\Pi_1(x)$	$\Pi_2(x)$	$\Pi_3(x)$	$\Pi_1(x)$	$\Pi_2(x)$	$\Pi_3(x)$
60	0.922	0.901	0.886	1.0615	1.1530	1.2688
100	0.927	0.915	0.905	0.8301	0.8599	0.9122
150	0.937	0.920	0.915	0.6728	0.7135	0.7395
200	0.937	0.925	0.917	0.5831	0.6058	0.6373
300	0.943	0.928	0.923	0.4762	0.4917	0.5155
400	0.944	0.935	0.924	0.4126	0.4222	0.4404

0, $X \sim N(1,1)$ and $\varepsilon \sim U(-0.5,0.5)$; Table 3 reports the simulation results when $g(x) = (3.2x^2 - 1)I(|x| \leq 1)$, $X \sim N(1,1)$ and $\varepsilon \sim N(0,1)$; Table 4 reports the simulation results when $g(x) = (3.2x^2 - 1)I(|x| \leq 1)$, $X \sim N(1,1)$ and $\varepsilon \sim U(-0.5,0.5)$; Table 5 reports the simulation results when $g(x) = x^2 + \sin$ (2πx), $X \sim N(1,1)$ and $\varepsilon \sim N(0,1)$; Table 6 reports the simulation results when $g(x) = x^2 + \sin(2\pi x)$, $X \sim N(1,1)$ and $\varepsilon \sim U(-0.5,0.5)$; Table 7 reports the simulation results when $g(x) = x^2 + \cos(2\pi x)$, $X \sim N(1,1)$ and $\varepsilon \sim N(0,1)$; Table 8 reports the simulation results when $g(x) = x^2 + \cos(2\pi x)$, X

Table 4. Coverage probabilities (CP) and average lengthes (AL) of confidence intervals for μ when g(x) = (3.2x² – 1)I(|x| ≤ 1), X ~ N(1,1) and ε ~ U(-0.5,0.5) under different response probabilities and sample sizes

n	CP			AL		
	$\Pi_1(x)$	$\Pi_2(x)$	$\Pi_3(x)$	$\Pi_1(x)$	$\Pi_2(x)$	$\Pi_3(x)$
60	0.936	0.870	0.870	1.2017	1.1631	1.2276
100	0.936	0.885	0.879	0.8401	0.8609	0.9135
150	0.940	0.902	0.902	0.6802	0.7251	0.7474
200	0.942	0.915	0.911	0.5956	0.6282	0.6408
300	0.943	0.920	0.914	0.4833	0.4967	0.5279
400	0.946	0.924	0.932	0.4326	0.4509	0.4772

Table 5. Coverage probabilities (CP) and average lengthes (AL) of confidence intervals for μ when g(x) = x² + sin(2πx), X ~ N(1,1) and ε ~ N(0,1) under different response probabilities and sample sizes

n	CP			AL		
	$\Pi_1(x)$	$\Pi_2(x)$	$\Pi_3(x)$	$\Pi_1(x)$	$\Pi_2(x)$	$\Pi_3(x)$
60	0.925	0. 917	0.907	1.9552	1.9986	1.9990
100	0.925	0.918	0.915	1.6725	1.8522	1.7361
150	0.935	0.920	0.915	1.3540	1.4034	1.4188
200	0.936	0.926	0.921	1.1782	1.1908	1.2135
300	0.938	0.932	0.922	0.9439	0.9620	0.9702
400	0.945	0.938	0.925	0.8247	0.8556	0.8365

Table 6. Coverage probabilities (CP) and average lengthes (AL) of confidence intervals for μ when g(x) = x² + sin (2πx), X ~ N(1,1) and ε ~ U(-0.5,0.5) under different response probabilities and sample sizes

n	CP			AL		
	$\Pi_1(x)$	$\Pi_2(x)$	$\Pi_3(x)$	$\Pi_1(x)$	$\Pi_2(x)$	$\Pi_3(x)$
60	0.890	0. 875	0.827	1.0836	1.2808	1.4514
100	0.905	0.882	0.842	0.6141	0.7606	0.8850
150	0.916	0.905	0.865	0.4775	0.5106	0.5500
200	0.933	0.913	0.905	0.3956	0.4226	0.4586
300	0.935	0.922	0.912	0.3216	0.3423	0.3746
400	0.949	0.924	0.912	0.2787	0.2983	0.3124

~ $N(1,1)$ and $ε \sim U(-0.5,0.5)$; Table 9 reports the simulation results when $g(x) = x^3 + \exp(x)$, $X \sim N(1,1)$ and $ε \sim N(0,1)$; and Table 10 reports the simulation results when $g(x) = x^3 + \exp(x)$, $X \sim N(1,1)$ and $ε \sim U(-0.5,0.5)$.

Tables 1-10 reveal the following facts:

1. For every response rate and sample size, the coverage probability (CP) of EL confidence

Table 7. Coverage probabilities (CP) and average lengthes (AL) of confidence intervals for μ when g(x) = x² +cos(2πx), X ~ N(1,1) and ε ~ N(0,1) under different response probabilities and sample sizes

n	CP			AL		
	$\Pi_1(x)$	$\Pi_2(x)$	$\Pi_3(x)$	$\Pi_1(x)$	$\Pi_2(x)$	$\Pi_3(x)$
60	0.908	0. 886	0.875	1.9718	1.9833	1.9934
100	0.915	0.891	0.976	1.6984	1.7906	1.8257
150	0.926	0.902	0.876	1.3538	1.6338	1.4244
200	0.934	0.915	0.895	1.1625	1.2432	1.2108
300	0.935	0.917	0.916	0.9345	0.9669	0.9707
400	0.955	0.926	0.918	0.8133	0.8264	0.8282

Table 8. Coverage probabilities (CP) and average lengthes (AL) of confidence intervals for μ when g(x) = x² + cos(2πx), X ~ N(1,1) and ε ~ U(-0.5, 0.5) under different response probabilities and sample sizes

n	CP			AL		
	$\Pi_1(x)$	$\Pi_2(x)$	$\Pi_3(x)$	$\Pi_1(x)$	$\Pi_2(x)$	$\Pi_3(x)$
60	0.925	0. 913	0.905	1.0611	1.2262	1.2747
100	0.936	0.925	0.917	0.7541	0.8081	0.8972
150	0.946	0.925	0.917	0.6321	0.6483	0.6849
200	0.951	0.931	0.927	0.5377	0.5586	0.5857
300	0.955	0.935	0.930	0.4380	0.4480	0.4725
400	0.951	0.945	0.935	0.3750	0.3868	0.4080

interval is close to the nominal level 95%, and the average lengths of intervals are small.

2. The coverage probability (CP) of intervals goes closer to the nominal level 95% as the sample size increases or the response rate becomes higher.

3. In almost all situations, the lengths of intervals also improve (become smaller) as the sample size increases or the response rate becomes higher.

CONCLUSION

We have proposed a new estimation for missing (or incomplete) data that is a combination of the kNN imputation and bootstrap calibrated EL. The simulations have demonstrated that the combina-

tion of the bootstrap calibrated EL method and kNN imputation is a good choice to make inference on the mean of the dependent variable. It is noted that the most important population parameter in surveys is the population mean (or a function of several population means).

Estimation or inference on population quantiles has become more and more important in modern survey statistics. For income variables, for example, the median (the 1/2 quantile) income or other quantiles are as important as the mean income. It would be interesting to combine the bootstrap calibrated EL method and kNN imputation to construct confidence intervals/regions on other parameters such as population quantiles. These will be left for the future study.

Simulations have shown that the method proposed in this article has very good performance,

Table 9. Coverage probabilities (CP) and average lengthes (AL) of confidence intervals for μ when g(x) = x³ + exp(x), X ~ N(1,1) and ε ~ N(0,1) under different response probabilities and sample sizes

n	CP			AL		
	$\Pi_1(x)$	$\Pi_2(x)$	$\Pi_3(x)$	$\Pi_1(x)$	$\Pi_2(x)$	$\Pi_3(x)$
60	0.909	0. 898	0.877	1.9990	1.9992	1.9993
100	0.915	0.899	0.977	0.9051	0.9993	0.9813
150	0.917	0.905	0.905	0.6530	0.7413	0.8901
200	0.926	0.913	0.909	0.3468	0.2769	0.8335
300	0.927	0.919	0.915	0.2571	0.3078	0.5758
400	0.936	0.927	0.927	0.1923	0.2707	0.3882

Table 10. Coverage probabilities (CP) and average lengthes (AL) of confidence intervals for μ when g(x) = x³ + exp(x), X ~ N(1,1) and ε ~ U(-0.5,0.5) under different response probabilities and sample sizes

n	CP			AL		
	$\Pi_1(x)$	$\Pi_2(x)$	$\Pi_3(x)$	$\Pi_1(x)$	$\Pi_2(x)$	$\Pi_3(x)$
60	0.925	0. 913	0.895	2.0943	2.0959	2.1732
100	0.935	0.916	0.905	1.6113	1.6171	1.6518
150	0.940	0.925	0.905	1.2908	1.3332	1.3595
200	0.940	0.928	0.914	1.1288	1.1430	1.1683
300	0.942	0.935	0.925	0.9223	0.9379	0.9523
400	0.951	0.935	0.930	0.7987	0.8026	0.8286

which would have better performance than that of the usual NN imputation method in a certain of cases. As we have seen from previous introduction that the NN imputation method has a long history of applications, we could hope that the method in this article could also be used for real data with good satisfactory. This will be left for the future study.

ACKNOWLEDGMENT

This work was supported in part by the Australian Research Council (ARC) under large grant DP0985456, the Nature Science Foundation (NSF) of China under grants 90718020 and 10971038, and the Guangxi NSF (Key) grants. The authors are thankful to the referees for constructive suggestions.

REFERENCES

Banek, M., Vrdoljak, B., Tjoa, A., & Skocir, Z. (2008). Automated integration of heterogeneous data warehouse schemas. *International Journal of Data Warehousing and Mining, 4*(4), 1–21. doi:10.4018/jdwm.2008100101

Chen, J., & Shao, J. (2000). Nearest neighbor imputation for survey data. *Journal of Official Statistics, 16*, 113–131.

Chen, J., & Shao, J. (2001). Jackknife variance estimation for nearest-neighbor imputation. *Journal of the American Statistical Association, 96*, 260–269. .doi:10.1198/016214501750332839

Farber, J. E., & Griffin, R. (1998). A comparison of alternative estimation methodologies for Census 2000. In *Proceedings of the Section on Survey Research Methods, American Statistical Association* (pp. 629-634).

Fay, R. E. (1999). Theory and application of nearest neighbor imputation in Census 2000. In *Proceedings of the Section on Survey Research Methods, American Statistical Association* (pp. 112-121).

Golfarelli, M., & Rizzi, S. (2009). A survey on temporal data warehousing. *International Journal of Data Warehousing and Mining, 5*(1), 1–17. doi:10.4018/jdwm.2009010101

Gomez, L., Kuijpers, B., Moelans, B., & Alejandro, V. A. (2009). A survey of spatio-temporal data warehousing. *International Journal of Data Warehousing and Mining, 5*(3), 28–55. doi:10.4018/jdwm.2009070102

Hartley, H. O., & Rao, J. N. K. (1968). A new estimation theory for sample surveys. *Biometrika, 55*, 547–557. .doi:10.1093/biomet/55.3.547

Lee, H., Rancourt, E., & Sarndal, C. E. (1994). Experiments with variance estimation from survey data with imputed values. *Journal of Official Statistics, 10*, 231–243.

McRoberts, R. E., Nelson, M. D., & Wendt, D. G. (2002). Stratified estimation of forest area using satellite imagery, inventory data, and the k-Nearest Neighbor technique. *Remote Sensing of Environment, 82*, 457–468. .doi:10.1016/S0034-4257(02)00064-0

Montaquila, J. M., & Ponikowski, C. H. (1993). Comparison of methods for imputing missing responses in an establishment survey. In *Proceedings of the Section on Survey Research Methods, American Statistical Association*, 446-451.

Nikulin, V. (2008). Classification of imbalanced data with random sets and mean-variance filtering. *International Journal of Data Warehousing and Mining, 4*(2), 63–78. doi:10.4018/jdwm.2008040108

Owen, A. B. (2001). *Empirical Likelihood*. New York: Chapman & Hall.

Owen, A. B. (2003). Data squashing by empirical likelihood. *Data Mining and Knowledge Discovery, 7*(1), 101–113. .doi:10.1023/A:1021568920107

Pighin, M., & Ieronutti, L. (2008). A methodology supporting the design and evaluating the final quality of data warehouses. *International Journal of Data Warehousing and Mining, 4*(3), 15–34. doi:10.4018/jdwm.2008070102

Qin, Y., Rao, J. N. K., & Ren, Q. (2008). Confidence intervals for marginal parameters under fractional linear regression imputation for missing data. *Journal of Multivariate Analysis, 99*, 1232–1259. .doi:10.1016/j.jmva.2007.08.005

Rancourt, E. (1999). Estimation with nearest neighbor imputation at Statistics Canada. In *Proceedings of the Section on Survey Research Methods, American Statistical Association* (pp. 131-138).

Shao, J., & Sitter, R. R. (1996). Bootstrap for imputed survey data. *Journal of the American Statistical Association, 91*, 1278–1288. .doi:10.2307/2291746

Skellam, J. G. (1952). Studies in statistical ecology: spatial pattern. *Biometrika, 39*, 346–362. .doi:10.2307/2334030

Wang, Q., & Rao, J. N. K. (2002a). Empirical likelihood-based inference in linear models with missing data. *Scandinavian Journal of Statistics, 29*, 563–576. .doi:10.1111/1467-9469.00306

Wang, Q., & Rao, J. N. K. (2002b). Empirical likelihood-based inference under imputation for missing response data. *Annals of Statistics, 30,* 896–924. .doi:10.1214/aos/1028674845

Yu, D., Shao, S., & Luo, B. (2009). A hybrid method for high-utility itemsets mining in large high-dimensional data. *International Journal of Data Warehousing and Mining, 5,* 57–73. doi:10.4018/jdwm.2009010104

Zhang, S. C. (2008). Parimputation: From imputation and null-imputation to partially imputation. *IEEE Intelligent Informatics Bulletin, 9*(1), 32–38.

Zhang, S. C. (in press). Shell-neighbor method and its application in missing data imputation. *Applied Intelligence.*

This work was previously published in International Journal of Data Warehousing and Mining, Volume 6, Issue 4, edited by David Taniar, pp. 61-73, copyright 2010 by IGI Publishing (an imprint of IGI Global).

Compilation of References

Aalst, W. M. P., van der Hofstede, A. H. M., ter Kiepusze-wski, B., & Barros, A. P. (2003). Workflow patterns. *Distributed and Parallel Databases*, *14*(3), 5–51. doi:10.1023/A:1022883727209

Abello, A., Samos, J., & Saltor, F. (2006). YAM²: A Multidimensional Conceptual Model Extending UML. *Information Systems*, *3*(6), 541–567. doi:10.1016/j.is.2004.12.002

Aggarwal, C. C., & Hinneburg, D. A. Keim. (2001). On the surprising behaviour of distance metrics in high dimensional space, in *Proceedings of the Eight International Conference on Data base Theory* (pp.420-434). London, UK.

Aggarwal, C. C., Han, J., Wang, J., & Yu, P. S. (2003). A framework for clustering evolving data streams. In *Proceedings of 29th International Conference on Very Large Data Bases* (pp. 81-92).

Agichtein, E., Castillo, C., Donato, D., Gionis, A., & Mishne, G. (2008, February 11-12). Finding high-quality content in social media. In *Proceedings of the international Conference on Web Search and Web Data Mining*, Palo Alto, California, USA, WSDM '08 (pp. 183-194). New York: ACM.

Agrawa, R., Gehrke, J., Gunopulos, D., & Raghavan, P. (1998). Automatic subspace clustering of high dimensional data for data mining applications. In *Proceedings of the ACM SIGMOD conference on Management of Data (SIGMOD '98)* (pp. 94-105).

Agrawal, R., & Srikant, R. (1994). Fast Algorithms for Mining Association Rules in Large Databases. In J. B. Bocca, M. Jarke, & C. Zaniolo (Eds), *Proceedings of the 20th International Conference on Very Large Data Bases*. San Francisco, CA: Morgan Kaufmann Publishers.

Agrawal, R., & Srikant, R. (1995). Mining sequential patterns. In *Proceedings of 11th International Conference on Data Engineering* (pp. 3-14). Taipei, Taiwan: IEEE Computer Society Press.

Agrawal, R., Imielinsk, T., & Swami, A. (1993). Mining association rules between sets of items in large databases. In *Proceedings of the 1993 ACM SIGMOD international conference on management of data* (pp. 207-216). New York: ACM Press.

Agrawal, R., Mannila, H., Srikant, R., Toivonen, H., & Verkamo, A. I. (1996). Fast Discovery of Association Rules. In *Advances in Knowledge Discovery and Data Mining* (pp. 307-328).

Ahmed, T., & Miquel, M. (2006). Multidimensional Structures Dedicated to Continuous Spatiotemporal Phenomena. In *British National Conference on Databases* (pp. 29-40). Berlin: Springer.

Ahn, Y.-Y., Han, S., Kwak, H., Moon, S., & Jeong, H. (2007). Analysis of topological characteristics of huge online social networking services. In *World Wide Web (WWW) Conference* (pp. 835–844), Banff, Alberta.

Aleksy, M., Butter, T., & Schader, M. (2008). Architecture for the development of context-sensitive mobile applications. *Mobile Information Systems*, *4*(2), 105–117.

Alshalalfa, M., Alhajj, R., Khabbaz, M., & Kianmehr, K. (2008). Effectiveness of fuzzy classifier rules in capturing correlations between genes. *International Journal of Data Warehousing and Mining*, *4*(4), 62–83.

Anagnostopoulos, A., Kumar, R., & Mahdian, M. (2008, August 24-27). Influence and Correlation in Social Networks. In *Proceedings of the 14th ACM SIGKDD international Conference on Knowledge Discovery and Data Mining*, Las Vegas, Nevada, USA (KDD '08) (pp. 7 – 15). New York: ACM.

Angelova, R., Lipczak, M., Milios, E., & Pralat, P. (2008). Characterizing a social bookmarking and tagging network. In A. Nanopoulos & G. Tsoumakas (Eds.), *Mining Social Data (MSoDa), a Workshop of the 18th European Conference on Artificial Intelligence (ECAI 2008)*, University of Patras, Greece.

Ankerst, M., Breunig, M. M., Kriegel, H. P., & Sander, J. (1999). OPTICS: Ordering points to identify the clustering structure. In *Proceedings of the ACM SIGMOD Conference on Management of Data (SIGMOD '99)* (pp. 49-60).

Antonellis, I., Bouras, C., & Poulopoulos, V. (2006). Personalized News Categorization Through Scalable Text Classification. In *Proceedings of the 8th Asia-Pacific Web Conference- Frontiers of WWW Research and Development, Lecture Notes in Computer Science: Vol. 3841*. New York: Springer-Verlag.

Apostolico, A., & Guerra, C. (1987). The longest common subsequence problem revisited. *Algorithmica*, *2*, 315–336. doi:10.1007/BF01840365

Asai, T., Abe, K., Kawasoe, S., Arimura, H., Satamoto, H., & Arikawa, S. (2002). Efficient substructure discovery from large semi-structured data. In *Proceedings of the 2nd SIAM International Conference on Data Mining* (Vol. []. Arlington, VA, USA.]. *E (Norwalk, Conn.)*, *87-D*(12), 2754–2763.

Asuncion, A., & Newman, D. J. (2007). *UCI machine learning repository*. Retrieved from http://www.ics.uci.edu/~mlearn/MLRepository.html

Baeza-Yates, R., & Ribeiro-Neto, B. (1999). *Modern Information Retrieval*. New York: ACM Press.

Bagui, S. (2006). An approach to mining crime patterns. *International Journal of Data Warehousing and Mining*, *2*(1), 50–80.

Banek, M., Vrdoljak, B., Tjoa, A., & Skocir, Z. (2008). Automated integration of heterogeneous data warehouse schemas. *International Journal of Data Warehousing and Mining*, *4*(4), 1–21.

Banos, E., Katakis, I., Bassiliades, N., Tsoumakas, G., & Vlahavas, I. (2006). *PersoNews: A Personalized News Reader Enhanced by Machine Learning and Semantic Filtering*. Paper presented at the 5th International Conference on Ontologies, DataBases, and Applications of Semantics (ODBASE 2006), Montpellier, France.

Barabási, A.-L., & Albert, R. (1999). Emergence of Scaling in Random Networks. [AAAS.]. *Science*, *286*(5439), 509–512. doi:10.1126/science.286.5439.509

Barabasi, A.-L. (2002). *Linked: The New Science of Networks*. Cambridge, MA: Perseus.

Baruch Options Data Warehouse. (2008). *Subotnik Financial Services Center*. Retrieved

Bass, F. (1969). A new product growth model for consumer durables. *Management Science*, *15*, 215–227. doi:10.1287/mnsc.15.5.215

Bastide, Y., Taouil, R., Pasquier, N., Stumme, G., & Lakhal, L. (2000). Mining Frequent Patterns with Counting Inference. *SIGKDD Explorations*, *2*(2), 66–75. doi:10.1145/380995.381017

Batagelj, C., & Zaveršnik, M. (2002). Generalized Cores. *ArXiv Computer Science e-prints*.

Bayardo, R. (1998). Efficiently mining long patterns from databases. In *Proceedings of the international conference on management of data (sigmod)* (pp. 85-93).

Bayardo, R., & Agrawal, R. (1999). Mining the Most Interesting Rules. In *Proceedings of the 5th international conference on knowledge discovery and data mining (kdd)* (pp. 145-154).

Bergroth, L., Hakonen, H., & Raita, T. (2000). A survey of longest common subsequence algorithm. In *Proceedings of the Seventh International Symposium on String Processing and Information Retrieval SPIRE*, Atlanta (pp. 39-48). Washington, DC: IEEE Computer Society.

Beuther, D. A., & Sutherland, E. R. (2007). Overweight, obesity, and incident asthma, a meta- analysis of prospective epidemiologic studies. *American Journal of Respiratory and Critical Care Medicine, 175*(7), 661–666. doi:10.1164/rccm.200611-1717OC

Beyer, K., & Ramakrishnan, R. (1999). Bottom-Up Computation of Sparse and Iceberg CUBEs. In *Proceedings of the international conference on management of data (sigmod)* (pp. 359-370).

Beyer, K., Goldstein, J., Ramakrishnan, R., & Shaft, U. (1999). When is nearest neighbor meaningful? In *Proceedings of the Seventh International Conference on Database theory* (pp. 217-235). Jerusalem, Israel.

Bhatnagar, V., Kaur, S., & Mignet, L. (2009). A parameterized framework for clustering streams. *International Journal of Data Warehousing and Mining, 5*(1), 36–56.

Biçici, E., & Yuret, D. (2007). Locally scaled density based clustering. In *Proceedings of the 8th International Conference on Adaptive and Natural Computing Algorithms (ICANNGA'07)* (pp. 739-748).

Bimonte, S. (2009). On Modelling and Analysis of Geographic Multidimensional Databases. In Bellatreche, L. (Ed.), *Data Warehousing Design and Advanced Engineering Applications: Methods for Complex Construction* (pp. 96–112). Hershey, PA: IGI Global.

Bimonte, S. (2007). *Intégration de l'information géographique dans les entrepôts de données et l'analyse en ligne: de la modélisation à la visualisation.* Unpublished doctoral dissertation, Lyon, France.

Bimonte, S. (2010). A Web-based System for Multidimensional Analysis of Geographic and Complex Data. *International Journal of Agricultural and Environmental Information Systems.*

Bimonte, S., Tchounikine, A., & Miquel, M. (2006). GeoCube, a Multidimensional Model and Navigation Operators Handling Complex Measures: Application in Spatial OLAP. In *Proceedings of the International Conference in Advances in Information Systems* (pp. 100-109). Berlin: Springer.

Biomedical.Org. (n.d.). *Common pain relievers associated with high blood pressure.* Retrieved April 29, 2009, from http://news.bio-medicine.org/medicine-news-3/Use-of-common-pain-relievers-associated-with-increased-risk-of-blood-pressure-in-men-1642-1/

Blake, C., & Merz, C. (1998). *UCI Repository of machine learning databases.*

Box, G. E. P., & Jenkins, G. M. (1994). *Time Series Analysis: Forecasting and Control.* New York: Prentice Hall PTR.

Bradley, P. S., Fayyad, U. M., & Reina, C. A. (1998). *Scaling EM (Expectation Maximization) clustering to large database* (Microsoft Research Rep. MSR-TR-98-35).

Breiman, L., Friedman, J. H., Olshen, R. A., & Stone, C. J. (1998). *Megainduction: machine learning on very large databases.* Sydney, Australia: University of Sydney.

Brin, S., Motwani, R., & Silverstein, C. (1997). Beyond market baskets: generalizing association rules to correlations. In *Proceedings of the international conference on management of data (sigmod)* (pp. 265-276).

Calders, T., & Goethals, B. (2007). Non-derivable itemset mining. *Data Mining and Knowledge Discovery, 14*(1), 171–206. doi:10.1007/s10618-006-0054-6

Calders, T., Ng, R. T., & Wijsen, R. (2002). Searching for Dependencies at Multiple Abstraction Levels. In *Proceedings of the Acm transactions on database systems* (acm tods) (Vol. 27, No. 3, pp. 229-260).

Camossi, E., Bertolotto, M., & Bertino, E. (2008). Querying Multigranular Spatio-temporal Objects. In *Proceedings of the International Conference on Database and Expert Systems Applications* (pp. 390-403). Berlin: Springer.

Cannon, R. L., Dave, J. V., & Bezdek, J. C. (1986). Efficient implementation of the fuzzy c-means clustering algorithms. *IEEE Transactions on Pattern Analysis and Machine Intelligence*, 248–255. doi:10.1109/TPAMI.1986.4767778

Cao, F., Ester, M., Qian, W., & Zhou, A. (2006). Density-based clustering over an evolving data stream with noise. In *Proceedings of the 2006 SIAM Conference on Data Mining (SDM'06)* (pp. 326-337).

Caruana, R. (2001, January). A Non-parametric EM-style algorithm for Imputing Missing Value. *Artificial Intelligence and Statistics*.

Casali, A., Nedjar, S., Cicchetti, R., & Lakhal, L. (2009a). Closed cubes lattices. *Annals of Information Systems, 3*, 145–165.

Casali, A., Cicchetti, R., & Lakhal, L. (2005). Essential patterns: A perfect cover of frequent patterns. In Tjoa, A. M., & Trujillo, J. (Eds.), *Dawak (Vol. 3589*, pp. 428–437). New York: Springer.

Casali, A. (2004). Mining borders of the difference of two datacubes. In *Proceedings of the 6th international conference on data warehousing and knowledge discovery (dawak)* (pp. 391-400).

Casali, A., Cicchetti, R., & Lakhal, L. (2003a). Cube lattices: a framework for multidimensional data mining. In *Proceedings of the 3rd siam international conference on data mining (sdm)* (pp. 304-308).

Casali, A., Cicchetti, R., & Lakhal, L. (2003b). Extracting semantics from datacubes using cube transversals and closures. In *Proceedings of the 9th acm sigkdd international conference on knowledge discovery and data mining* (kdd) (pp. 69-78).

Casali, A., Nedjar, S., Cicchetti, R., & Lakhal, L. (2009b). Emerging cubes: Borders, size estimations and lossless reductions. *International Journal of Information Systems, Their Creation, Management and Utilization*.

Casali, A., Nejar, S., Cicchetti, R., & Lakhal, L. (2007). Convex cube: Towards a unified structure for multidimensional databases. In *Proceedings of the 18th international conference on database and expert systems applications (dexa)* (pp. 572-581).

Catlett, J. (1991). *On changing continuous attributes into ordered discrete attributes*. Paper presented at the Proceedings of the European Working Session on Learning, Berlin, Germany.

Cattuto, C., Schmitz, C., Baldassarri, A., Servedio, V. D. P., Loreto, V., & Hotho, A. (2007). Network properties of folksonomies. []. IOS Press.]. *AI Communications Special Issue on Network Analysis in Natural Sciences and Engineering, 20*, 245–262.

CDC. (n.d.). *National health and nutrition examination survey*. Retrieved April 29, 2009, from http://www. cdc. gov/nchs/nhanes.htm

Cha, M., Kwak, H., Rodriguez, P., Ahn, Y., & Moon, S. (2007, October 24-26). I Tube, You Tube, Everybody Tubes: Analyzing the World's Largest User Generated Content Video System. In *Proceedings of the 7th ACM SIGCOMM Conference on internet Measurement*, San Diego, California, USA (IMC '07) (pp. 1-14). New York, NY: ACM.

Chan, C. C., Batur, C., & Srinivasan, A. (1991). *Determination of quantization intervals in rule based model for dynamic systems*. Paper presented at the Proceedings of the IEEE Conference on Systems, Man, and Cybernetics, Charlottesville, VA.

Chan, P. K., & Stolfo, S. J. (1993). *Experiments on multistrategy learning by metalearning*. Paper presented at the Proceedings of the Second International Conference on Information and Knowledge Management, Washington, D.C.

Chan, P. K., & Stolfo, S. J. (1993). *Metalearning for multistrategy and parallel learning*. Paper presented at the Proceedings of Second International Workshop on Multistrategy Learning.

Chang, L., Yang, D. Q., Tang, S. W., & Wang, T. (2006). Mining compressed sequential patterns. In *Proceedings of the 2nd International Conference on Advanced Data Mining and Applications* (Vol.4093, pp.761-768). Xian, China.

Charles, F., & Cavazza, M. (2004). *Exploring the scalability of character-based storytelling*. Paper presented at the Third International Joint Conference on Autonomous Agents and Multiagent Systems.

Chaudhuri, S. (1998). Data mining and database systems: where is the intersection? *A Quarterly Bulletin of the Computer Society of the IEEE Technical Committee on Data Engineering, 21*(1), 4–8.

Chen, C. S., Roberton, D., & Hammerton, M. E. (2004). Juvenile arthritis-associated uveitis: visual outcomes and prognosis. *Canadian Journal of Ophthalmology, 39*(6), 614–620.

Chen, H., Guo, G., Huang, Y., & Huang, T. (2008). A spatial overlapping based similarity measure applied to hierarchical clustering. In *Proceedings of the 5th International Conference on Fuzzy Systems and Knowledge Discovery (FSKD'08)* (pp. 371-375).

Chen, J., & Cook, T. (2007). Mining contiguous sequential patterns from web logs. In *Proceedings of the 16th international conference on World Wide Web* (pp.1177-1178). Banff, Alberta, Canada.

Chen, J., & Shao, J. (2000). Nearest neighbor imputation for survey data. *Journal of Official Statistics, 16*, 113–131.

Chen, J., & Shao, J. (2001). Jackknife variance estimation for nearest-neighbor imputation. *Journal of the American Statistical Association, 96*, 260–269. doi:10.1198/01621 4501750332839doi:10.1198/016214501750332839

Chen, S. F., & Goodman, J. (1996). An empirical study of smoothing techniques for language modeling. In *Proceedings of the 34th annual meeting on association for computational linguistics* (pp. 310–318). Morristown, NJ, USA: Association for Computational Linguistics.

Chen, Y., & Tu, L. (2007). Density-based clustering for real-time stream data. In *Proceedings of the 13th ACM SIGKDD international conference on Knowledge discovery and data mining* (pp. 133-142).

Chickering, D. M., Meek, C., & Rounthwaite, R. (2001). *Efficient Determination of Dynamic Split Points in a Decision Tree.* Paper presented at the First IEEE International Conference on Data Mining, San Jose, CA.

Chiu, D. K. Y., Cheung, B., & Wong, A. K. C. (1990). Information synthesis based on hierarchical entropy discretization. *Journal of Experimental & Theoretical Artificial Intelligence, 2*, 117–129. doi:10.1080/09528139008953718

Chow, T. W. S., & Huang, D. (2005, January). Estimating optimal feature subsets using efficient estimation of high-dimensional mutual information. *IEEE Transactions on Neural Networks, 16*(1), 213–224. doi:10.1109/TNN.2004.841414

Chung, F., & Lu, L. (2004). *Complex graphs and networks.* American Mathematical Society, U.S.A.

Clauset, A., Shalizi, C. R., & Newman, M. E. J. (2007). *Power-law distributions in empirical data.*

Cohen, R., Avraham, D., & Havlin, S. (2003). Structural properties of scale free networks. In S. Bornholdt & H. G. Schuster (Eds.), *Handbook of graphs and networks.* Wiley-VCH.

Cook, D. J., & Holder, L. B. (2000). Graph-based data mining. *IEEE Intelligent Systems, 15*(2), 32–41. doi:10.1109/5254.850825

Damiani, M., & Spaccapietra, S. (2006). Spatial Data Warehouse Modeling. In Darmont, J., & Boussaïd, O. (Eds.), *Processing and Managing Complex Data for Decision Support* (pp. 1–27). Hershey, PA: IGI Global.

Dash, M., Liu, H., & Yao, J. (1997). Dimensionality reduction for unsupervised data. In *Proceedings of 19th IEEE International Conference on Tools with (AI, ICTAI '97).*

Dehaspe, L., & Toivonen, H. (1999). Discovery of Frequent DATALOG Patterns. *Data Mining and Knowledge Discovery, 3*, 7–36. doi:10.1023/A:1009863704807

Ding, J., Gravano, L., & Shivakumar, N. (2000). Computing Geographical Scopes of Web Resources. *VLDB*, 545-556.

Doherty, K. A. J., Adams, R. G., & Davey, N. (2007). Unsupervised learning with normalized data and non – Euclidean norms. *Applied Soft Computing, 7*, 203–210. doi:10.1016/j.asoc.2005.05.005

Doherty, K. A. J., Adams, R. G., & Davey, N. (2004). Non–Euclidean norms and data normalization. In *Proceedings of the 12h Euro. Symposium on Artificial Neural Networks* (pp. 181-186). Brugges, Belgium.

Dong, G., Han, J., Lam, J. M. W., Pei, J., Wang, K., & Zou, W. (2004). Mining constrained gradients in large databases. *IEEE Transactions on Knowledge and Data Engineering, 16*(8), 922–938. doi:10.1109/TKDE.2004.28

Dougherty, J., Kohavi, R., & Sahami, M. (1995). *Supervised and unsupervised discretization of continuous features.* Paper presented at the Proceedings of the 12th International Conference on Machine Learning, Tahoe City, CA.

Dubinko, M., Kumar, R., Magnani, J., Novak, J., Raghavan, P., & Tomkins, A. (2006). Visualizing tags over time. In *Proceedings of the 15th international conference on World Wide Web* (pp. 193-202). New York: ACM.

Duda, R. O., Hart, P. E., & Stork, D. G. (2001). *Pattern Classification* (2nd ed.). New York: John Wiley and Sons.

Eirinaki, M., Vazirgiannis, M., & Varlamis, I. (2003). SEWeP: using site semantics and a taxonomy to enhance the Web personalization process. In *Proceedings of the 9th ACM SIGKDD International Conference on Knowledge Discovery and Data Mining* (pp. 99-108). New York: ACM Press.

Engle, R. F. (1986). Semi-parametric Estimates of the relation between weather and electricity sales. *Journal of the American Statistical Association, 81*(394). doi:10.2307/2289218

Ester, M., Kriegel, H. P., Sander, J., & Xu, X. (1996). A density-based algorithm for discovering clusters in large spatial database with noise. In *Proceedings of 2nd International Conference on Knowledge Discovery and Data Mining (KDD '96)* (pp. 226-232).

Falkowski, T., & Spiliopoulou, M. (2007). Users in volatile communities: Studying active participation and community evolution. *User Modeling, 2007,* 47–56. doi:10.1007/978-3-540-73078-1_8

Farber, J. E., & Griffin, R. (1998). A comparison of alternative estimation methodologies for Census 2000. In *Proceedings of the Section on Survey Research Methods, American Statistical Association* (pp. 629-634).

Fay, R. E. (1999). Theory and application of nearest neighbor imputation in Census 2000. In *Proceedings of the Section on Survey Research Methods, American Statistical Association* (pp. 112-121).

Fayyad, U. M., & Irani, K. B. (1992). On the handling of continuous-valued attributes in decision tree generation. *Machine Learning, 8,* 87–102.

Fayyad, U. M., & Irani, K. B. (1993). *Multi-interval discretization of continuous-valued attributes for classification learning.* Paper presented at the Proceedings of the 13th International Joint Conference on Artificial Intelligence.

Fidalgo, R. N., Times, V. C., Silva, J., & Souza, F. (2004). GeoDWFrame: A Framework for Guiding the Design of Geographical Dimensional Schemas. In *Proceedings of the International Conference on Data Warehousing and Knowledge Discovery* (pp. 26-37). Berlin: Springer.

Forman, J. P., Rimm, E. B., & Curhan, G. C. (2007). Frequency of analgesic use and risk of hypertension among men. *Archives of Internal Medicine, 167*(4), 394–399. doi:10.1001/archinte.167.4.394

Franklin, N., Tversky, B., & Coon, V. (1992). Switching points of view in spatial mental models. *Memory & Cognition, 20*(5), 507–518.

Franklin, C. (1992). An Introduction to Geographic Information Systems: Linking Maps to databases. *Database, 15*(2), 13–21.

Friedman, N., & Goldszmidt, M. (1996). *Discretizing continuous attributes whle learning Bayesian networks.* Paper presented at the Proceedings of the Thirteenth International Conference on Machine Learning, San Francisco, CA.

Gabrilovich, E., Dumais, S., & Horvitz, E. (2004). Newsjunkie: providing personalized newsfeeds via analysis of information novelty. In *Proceedings of the 13th International Conference on World Wide Web* (pp. 482-490). New York: ACM Press.

Gadish, D. A. (2008). Introducing the Elasticity of Spatial Data. *International Journal of Data Warehousing and Mining, 4*(3), 54–70.

Gangwisch, J. E., Malaspina, D., Boden-Albala, B., & Heymsfield, S. B. (2005). Inadequate sleep as risk factor for obesity: Analysis of the NHANES I. *Sleep, 28*(10), 1289–1296.

Ganter, B., & Wille, R. (1999). *Formal Concept Analysis: Mathematical Foundations.* New York: Springer.

Ganti, V., Gehrke, J., & Ramakrishnan, R. (1999). Mining very large databases. *Computer, 32*(8), 38–45. doi:10.1109/2.781633

Garriga, G. C. (2005). Summarizing sequential data with closed partial orders. In *Proceedings of the SIAM International Conference on Data Mining* (pp.380–391). California, USA.

Gastner, M. T., Shalizi, C. R., & Newman, M. E. J. (2005). Maps and cartograms of the 2004 US presidential election results. *Advances in Complex Systems, 8*(1), 117–123. doi:10.1142/S0219525905000397

Geerts, F., Goethals, B., & Bussche, J. (2001). A Tight Upper Bound on the Number of Candidate Patterns. In *Proceedings of the 1st IEEE international conference on data mining (icdm)* (pp. 155-162).

Gehrke, J., Ramakrishnan, R., & Ganti, V. (2000). Rainforest - A framework for fast decision tree construction of large datasets. *Data Mining and Knowledge Discovery, 4*, 127–162. doi:10.1023/A:1009839829793

Gehrke, J., Ganti, V., Ramakrishnan, R., & Loh, W. Y. (1999). *BOAT - optimistic decision tree construction.* Paper presented at the 1999 ACM SIGMOD International Conference on Management of Data, Philadelphia, PA.

Giannakidou, E., Koutsonikola, V., Vakali, A., & Kompatsiaris, I. (2008). *Co-clustering tags and social data sources.* Paper presented at the 9th International Conference on Web-Age Information Management (WAIM 2008), Beijing, China.

Gill, T., Taylor, A., Chittleborough, C., Grant, J., & Leach, G. (2002). *Overweight and obesity as risk factors for arthritis* (Tech. Rep.). Australia: The South Australian Monitoring and Surveillance System (SAMSS), Population Research and Outcome Studies Unit.

Gkanogiannis, A., & Kalamboukis, T. (2008). A novel supervised learning algorithm and its use for spam detection in social bookmarking systems. In *ECML PKDD discovery challenge 2008*.

Glorio, O., & Trujillo, J. (2008). An MDA Approach for the Development of Spatial Data Warehouses. In *Proceedings of the International Conference on Data Warehousing and Knowledge Discovery* (pp. 23-32). Berlin: Springer.

Goh, J., & Taniar, D. (2005). Mining Parallel Patterns from Mobile Users. *International Journal of Business Data Communications and Networking, 1*(1), 50–76.

Goh, J., & Taniar, D. (2004a). Mobile Data Mining by Location Dependencies. In *Proceedings of the 5th International Conference on Intelligent Data Engineering and Automated Learning - IDEAL 2004* (LNCS 3177) (pp. 225-231). New York: Springer-Verlag.

Goh, J., & Taniar, D. (2004b). Mining Frequency Pattern from Mobile Users. In *Proceedings of the 8th International Conference on Knowledge-Based Intelligent Information and Engineering Systems, KES 2004, Part III* (LNCS 3215) (pp. 795-801). Berlin: Springer Verlag.

Goldberg, D. (1989). *Genetic algorithms in search, optimization and machine learning.* Reading, MA: Addison-Wesley.

Golder, S., & Huberman, B. A. (2006). The Structure of Collaborative Tagging Systems. [Sage Publications, Inc.]. *Journal of Information Science, 32*(2), 198–208. doi:10.1177/0165551506062337

Golder, S. A., & Huberman, B. A. (2006). Usage patterns of collaborative tagging systems. *Journal of Information Science, 32*(2), 198–208. doi:10.1177/0165551506062337

Goldstone, R. L., Medin, D. L., & Halberstadt, J. (1997). Similarity in Context. *Memory & Cognition, 25*, 237–255.

Goldstone, R. L., & Son, J. (2005). Similarity. In K. Holyoak & R. Morrison (Eds.), *Cambridge Handbook of Thinking and Reasoning* (pp. 13-36). Cambridge, UK: Cambridge University Press.

Golfarelli, M., & Rizzi, S. (2009). A survey on temporal data warehousing. *International Journal of Data Warehousing and Mining, 5*(1), 1–17.

Gómez, L., Kuijpers, B., Moelans, B., & Vaisman, A. (2009). A Survey of Spatio-Temporal Data Warehousing. *International Journal of Data Warehousing and Mining, 5*(3), 28–55.

Gomez, L., Kuijpers, B., Moelans, B., & Alejandro, V. A. (2009). A survey of spatio-temporal data warehousing. *International Journal of Data Warehousing and Mining, 5*(3), 28–55.

Grahne, G., Lakshmanan, L., & Wang, X. (2000). Efficient Mining of Constrained Correlated Sets. In *Proceedings of the 16th international conference on data engineering (icde)* (pp. 512-524).

Gravano, L., Hatzivassiloglou, V., & Lichtenstein, R. *Categorizing web queries according to geographical locality* (CIKM 2003) (pp. 325-333).

Gray, J., Chaudhuri, S., Bosworth, A., Layman, A., Reichart, D., & Venkatrao, M. (1997). Data cube: A relational aggregation operator generalizing group-by, cross-tab, and sub-totals. *Data Mining and Knowledge Discovery, 1*(1), 29–53. doi:10.1023/A:1009726021843

Guha, S., Rastogi, R., & Shim, K. (1998). CURE: An efficient clustering algorithm for large databases. In *Proceedings of the ACM SIGMOD conference on Management of Data (SIGMOD'98)* (pp. 73-84).

Gunopulos, D., Mannila, H., Khardon, R., & Toivonen, H. (1997). Data mining, hypergraph transversals, and machine learning. In *Proceedings of the 16th symposium on principles of database systems (pods)* (pp. 209-216).

Halkidi, M., & Vazirgiannis, M. (2001). Clustering validity assessment: Finding the optimal partitioning of a data set. In *Proceedings of International Conference on Data Mining.*

Halpin, H., Robu, V., & Shepherd, H. (2007, May 8-12). The complex dynamics of collaborative tagging. In *Proceedings of the 16th international Conference on World Wide Web*, Banff, Alberta, Canada (WWW '07) (pp. 211-220). New York: ACM.

Han, J., Pei, J., Yin, Y., & Mao, R. (2004). Mining Frequent Patterns without Candidate Generation: A Frequent-Pattern Tree Approach. *Data Mining and Knowledge Discovery, 8*, 53–87. doi:10.1023/B:DAMI.0000005258.31418.83

Han, J., & Kamber, M. (2006). From association analysis to correlation analysis. In *Data Mining: Concepts and Techniques* (pp. 261–264). San Francisco, CA: Morgan Kaufmann.

Han, J., Kanber, M., & Tung, A. K. H. (2001). *Spatial clustering methods in data mining: A survey. Geographic Data Mining and Knowledge Discovery*. New York: Taylor and Francis.

Han, J. W., Pei, J., Mortazavi-Asl, B., Chen, Q., Dayal, U., & Hsu, M. C. (2000). Freespan: frequent pattern-projected sequential patterns mining. In *Proceedings of the 6th ACM SIGKDD International Conference on Knowledge Discovery and Data Mining* (pp.355-359). New York: ACM Press.

Han, J., & Kamber, M. (2006). *Data Mining: Concepts and Techniques (2nd ed.)*. Amsterdam: Morgan Kaufman.

Han, J., Pei, J., Dong, G., & Wang, K. (2001). Efficient Computation of Iceberg Cubes with Complex Measures. In *Proceedings of the international conference on management of data (sigmod)* (pp. 441-448).

Hand, D., Mannila, H., & Smyth, P. (2001). *Principles of Data Mining*. Cambridge, MA: MIT Press.

Harinarayan, V., Rajaraman, A., & Ullman, J. D. (1996). Implementing Data Cubes Efficiently. In *Proceedings of the ACM SIGMOD International Conference on Management of Data* (pp. 205-216). New York: ACM Press

Harle, R. K., & Hopper, A. (2008). Towards autonomous updating of world models in location-aware spaces. *Personal and Ubiquitous Computing, 12*(4), 317–330. doi:10.1007/s00779-006-0103-6

Hartley, H. O., & Rao, J. N. K. (1968). A new estimation theory for sample surveys. *Biometrika, 55*, 547–557. doi:10.1093/biomet/55.3.547

He, J., Ogden, L. G., Bazzano, L. A., Vupputuri, S., Loria, C., & Whelton, P. K. (2001). Risk factors for congestive heart failure in US men and women. *Archives of Internal Medicine, 161*(7), 996–1002. doi:10.1001/archinte.161.7.996

Healy, J., Janssen, J., Milios, E., & Aiello, W. (2008). Characterization of graphs using degree cores. In *Algorithms and Models for the Web-Graph: Fourth International Workshop, WAW 2006*, volume LNCS-4936 of *Lecture Notes in Computer Science*, Banff, Canada: Springer Verlag.

Herbst, J. (2000). Dealing with concurrency in workflow induction. In *Proceedings of the 7th European Concurrent Engineering Conference, Society for Computer Simulation* (pp.169-174).

Heymann, P., & Garcia-Molina, H. (2006). *Collaborative creation of communal hierarchical taxonomies in social tagging systems* (Preliminary Technical Report). InfoLab, Stanford, 2006. Retrieved September, 26, 2008, from: http://heymann.stanford.edu/taghierarchy.html.

Heymann, P., Koutrika, G., & Garcia-Molina, H. (2008). Can social bookmarking improve web search? In *Wsdm '08: Proceedings of the international conference on web search and web data mining* (pp. 195–206). New York: ACM.

Heymann, P., Ramage, D., & Garcia-Molina, H. (2008). Social tag prediction. *In Sigir '08: Proceedings of the 31st annual international acm sigir conference on research and development in information retrieval* (pp. 531–538). New York: ACM.

Hinneburg, A., & Keim, D. A. (1998). An efficient approach to clustering in large Multimedia Database with noise. In *Proceedings of 4th International Conference on Konwledge Discovery and Data Mining (KDD'98)* (pp. 58-65).

Hirschberg, D. S. (1975). A linear space algorithm for computing maximal common subsequences. *Communications of the ACM, 18*(6), 341–343. doi:10.1145/360825.360861

Hirsh, H. (1991). Theoretical Underpinnings of Version Spaces. In *Proceedings of the 12th international joint conference on artificial intelligence (ijcai)* (pp. 665-670).

Hirtle, S. C., & Jonides, J. (1985). Evidence of Hierarchies in Cognitive Maps. *Memory & Cognition, 13*(3), 208–217.

Ho, T. K. (1998). The random subspace method for constructing decision forests. *IEEE Transactions on Pattern Analysis and Machine Intelligence, 20*(8), 832–844. doi:10.1109/34.709601

Ho, K. M., & Scott, P. D. (1997). *Zeta: A global method for discretization of continuous variables.* Paper presented at the KDD97: 3rd International Conference of Knowledge Discovery and Data Mining, Newport Beach, CA.

Holte, R. C. (1993). Very simple classification rules perform well on most commonly used datasets. *Machine Learning, 11*, 63–90. doi:10.1023/A:1022631118932

Hore, P., Hall, L. O., & Goldgof, D. B. (2007). Single pass fuzzy c-means. *IEEE International Fuzzy Systems Conference*, 1-7.

Hotho, A., Jäschke, R., Schmitz, C., & Stumme, G. (2006). Trend detection in folksonomies. *In Lecture Notes in Computer Science* []. Springer.]. *Semantic Multimedia, 4306*, 56–70. doi:10.1007/11930334_5

Hotho, A., Jäschke, R., Schmitz, C., & Stumme, G. (2006). Information Retrieval in Folksonomies: Search and Ranking. In Y. Sure & J. Domingue (Eds.), *The Semantic Web: Research and Applications* (pp. 411-426). Springer.

Hotho, A., Jäschke, R., Schmitz, C., & Stumme, G. (2006). Trend Detection in Folksonomies. In *Lecture Notes in Computer Science 4306/2006, 56-70.* Springer Berlin / Heidelberg.

Hotho, A., Jäschke, R., Schmitz, C., & Stumme, G. (2006). Information retrieval in folksonomies: Search and ranking. In *Lecture Notes in Computer Science: The Semantic Web: Research and Applications* (Vol. 4011) (pp. 411-426). Springer.

Hsu, W. J., & Du, M. W. (1984). Computing a longest common subsequence for a set of strings. *BIT, 24*, 45–59. doi:10.1007/BF01934514

Huan, J., Wang, W., Prins, J., & Yang, J. (2004). SPIN: Mining maximal frequent subgraphs from graph databases. *Proceedings of the 10th ACM (SIGKDD)* (pp. 581-586). Seattle, USA.

Huang, Z. (1998). Extensions to the k-Means algorithm for clustering large data sets with categorical values. *Data Mining and Knowledge Discovery*, 283–304. doi:10.1023/A:1009769707641

Hunt, J. W., & Szymanski, T. G. (1977). A fast algorithm for computing longest common subsequences. *Communications of the ACM, 20*(5), 350–353. doi:10.1145/359581.359603

Hyafil, L., & Rivest, R. L. (1976). Constructing optimal binary decision trees is NP-complete. *Information Processing Letters, 5*(1), 15–17. doi:10.1016/0020-0190(76)90095-8

Inform Inc. (2008), *Inform's Essential Technology Platform.* Retrieved September, 26, 2008, from: http://www.inform.com/contents/pdf/informwhitepaper.pdf

Inmon, W. H. (1996). *Building the Data Warehouse* (2nd ed.). New York: Wiley.

Inokuchi, A., Washio, T., & Motoda, H. (2003). Complete mining of frequent patterns from graphs: mining graph data. *Machine Learning, 50*(3), 321–354. doi:10.1023/A:1021726221443

Ivancsy, R., & Vajk, I. (2005). A survey of discovering frequent patterns in graph. In *Proceedings of Databases and Applications* (pp. 60-72). Calgary, Canada: ACTA Press.

Janson, S., Łuczak, T., & Ruciński, A. (2000). *Random Graphs*. New York: Wiley.

Jäschke, R., Marinho, L., Hotho, A., Schmidt-Thieme, L., & Stumme, G. (2007). Tag recommendations in folksonomies. In *Proceedings of the 11th European conference on Principles and Practice of Knowledge Discovery in Databases* (pp. 506-514). Springer.

Jayaputera, J., & Taniar, D. (2005). Data retrieval for location-dependent queries in a multi-cell wireless environment. *Mobile Information Systems, 1*(2), 91–108.

Jensen, C., Kligys, A., Pedersen, T., & Timko, I. (2004). Multidimensional Data Modelling for location-based services. *International Journal on Very Large Data Bases, 13*(1), 1–21. doi:10.1007/s00778-003-0091-3

Jiang, T., & Wang, K. (2007). Mining Generalized Associations of Semantic Relations from Textual Web Content. *IEEE Transactions on Knowledge and Data Engineering, 19*(2), 164–179. doi:10.1109/TKDE.2007.36

Jiang, D., Pei, J., & Zhang, A. (2003). Interactive exploration of coherent patterns in time-series gene expression data. In *Proceedings of the ninth ACM SIGKDD international conference on knowledge discovery and data mining (KDD'03)*, Washington, DC (pp. 565-570).

Jiang, T., & Tan, A. H. (2006). Mining RDF Metadata for Generalized Association Rules: Knowledge Discovery in the Semantic Web era. In *Proceedings of the 15th International Conference on World Wide Web* (pp. 951-952). New York: ACM Press.

Jin, R., Abu-Ata, M., Xiang, Y., & Ruan, N. (2008). Effective and efficient itemset pattern summarization: regression-based approaches. In *Proceedings of the 14th ACM SIGKDD international conference on knowledge discovery in data mining (KDD '08)*, Las Vegas, NV (pp. 399-407).

Kaltenbrunner, A., Gómez, V., & López, V. (2007). *Description and Prediction of Slashdot Activity*. Paper presented at the LA-WEB 2007 5th Latin American Web Congress, Santiago, Chile.

Kaltenbrunner, A., Gómez, V., Moghnieh, A., Meza, R., Blat, J., & López, V. (2007). *Homogeneous temporal activity patterns in a large online communication space*. Paper presented at the 10th Int. Conf. on Business Information Systems. Workshop on Social Aspects of the Web (SAW 2007), Poznan, Poland.

Kamber, M., Winstone, L., Gong, W., Cheng, S., & Han, J. (1997). *Generalization and decision tree induction: efficient classification in data mining*. Paper presented at the RIDE '97.

Katakis, I., Tsoumakas, G., & Vlahavas, I. Multilabel Text Classification for Automated Tag Suggestion. *In ECML PKDD discovery challenge 2008*.

Katakis, I., Tsoumakas, G., Banos, E., Bassiliades, N., & Vlahavas, I. (2008). An adaptive personalized news dissemination system. *Journal of Intelligent Information Systems*. Springer. DOI - 10.1007/s10844-008-0053-8

Katakis, I., Tsoumakas, G., & Vlahavas, I. (2008). An Ensemble of Classifiers for coping with Recurring Contexts in Data Streams. In M. Ghallab, C. Spyropoulos, N. Fakotakis, & N. Avouris (Eds.), *Proceedings of the 18th Europeen Conference on Artificial Intelligence* (pp.763-764), Amsterdam: IOS Press.

Kaufma, L., & Rousseeuw, P. J. (1990). *Finding groups in data: an introduction to cluster analysis*. New York: John Wiley & Sons.

Kempe, D., Kleinberg, J., & Tardos, É. (2003). Maximizing the Spread of Influence through a Social Network. In *Proceedings of the 9th ACM SIGKDD international conference on Knowledge Discovery and Data Mining* (KDD '03), (pp. 137-146). New York: ACM.

Kerber, R. (1992). *Chimerge: Discretization of numeric attributes*. Paper presented at the Proceedings of the Tenth National Conference on Artificial Intelligence.

Kimball, R. (1996). *The Data Warehouse Toolkit: Practical Techniques for Building Dimensional Data Warehouses*. New York: Wiley.

Klatzky, R. L. (1998). Allocentric and egocentric spatial representations: Definitions, distinctions, and interconnections. In C. Freksa, C. Habel, & K. Wender (Eds.), *Spatial Cognition: An interdisciplinary approach to representing and processing spatial knowledge* (pp. 1-17). Berlin: Springer Verlag.

Klein, R., & Klein, E. K. (1995). *Diabetes in America* (2nd ed., Chapter 14). Retrieved April 29, 2009, from http://diabetes.hiddk.nih.gov/dm/pubs/America/index.htm

Kohavi, R., & John, G. H. (1997). Wrappers for feature subset selection. *Artificial Intelligence*, *97*, 273–324. doi:10.1016/S0004-3702(97)00043-X

Kohavi, R., Brodley, C., Frasca, B., Mason, L., & Zheng, Z. J. (2000). KDD-Cup 2000 Organizers' Report: Peeling the onion. *SIGKDD Explorations*, *2*(2), 86–98. doi:10.1145/380995.381033

Kohonen, T. (1985). Median strings. *Pattern Recognition Letters*, *3*, 309–313. doi:10.1016/0167-8655(85)90061-3

Kohonen, T. (1989). *Self-Organization and Associative Memory*. Berlin, Germany: Springer-Verlag.

Kolari, P., Finin, T., & Joshi, A. (2006). SVMs for the Blogosphere: Blog Identification and Splog Detection. *In AAAI spring symposium on computational approaches to analysing weblogs*. University of Maryland, Baltimore County.

Konstan, J. A., Miller, B. N., Maltz, D., Herlocker, J. L., Gordon, L. R., & Riedl, G. L. (1997). Applying collaborative filtering to usenet news. *Communications of the ACM*, *40*(3), 77–87. doi:10.1145/245108.245126

Koutrika, G. E_endi, F. A., Gy¨ongyi, Z., Heymann, P., & Garcia-Molina, H. (2007). Combating spam in tagging systems. *In Airweb '07: Proceedings of the 3rd int. workshop on adversarial information retrieval on the web* (pp. 57–64). New York: ACM.

Krause, B., Hotho, A., & Stumme, G. (2008). The antisocial tagger - detecting spam in social bookmarking systems. *In Airweb '08: Proceedings of the 4th int. workshop on adversarial information retrieval on the web* (pp. 61-68). New York: ACM.

Kumar, P., Bapi, R. S., & Krishna, P. R. (2007). SeqPAM: A sequence clustering algorithm for web personalization. *International Journal of Data Warehousing and Mining*, *3*(1), 29–53.

Kumar, P., Bapi, R. S., Krishna, P. R., & De, S. K. (2007). Rough clustering of sequential data. *Data & Knowledge Engineering*, *63*(2), 183–199. doi:10.1016/j.datak.2007.01.003

Kumar, P., Rao, M. V., Krishna, P. R., & Bapi, R. S. (2005). Using sub-sequence information with kNN for classification of sequential data. In *International Conference on Distributed Computing and Internet Technology* (LNCS, pp. 536-546). New York: Springer.

Kumar, R., Novak, J., & Tomkins, A. (2006). Structure and evolution of online social networks. In *Knowledge Discovery in Databases (KDD) Conference* (pp. 611–617), Philadelphia, PA: ACM.

Kuramochi, M., & Karypis, G. (2004). GREW-A scalable frequent subgraph discovery algorithm. In *Proceedings of the 2004 IEEE International Conference on Mining* (pp. 439-442). Brighton, UK.

Kwok, T., Smith, K. A., Lozano, S., & Taniar, D. (2002). Parallel Fuzzy c-Means Clustering for Large Data Sets. *Euro-Par*, 365-374.

Kwon, O., & Shin, M. K. (2008). LACO: A location-aware cooperative query system for securely personalized services. *Expert Systems with Applications: An International Journal*, *34*(4), 2966–2975. doi:10.1016/j.eswa.2007.05.022

Lakshmanan, L., Pei, J., & Han, J. (2002). Quotient cube: How to summarize the semantics of a data cube. In *Proceedings of the 28th international conference on very large databases (vldb)* (pp. 778-789).

Lam, X., Vu, T., Le, T., & Duong, A. (2008). *Addressing cold-start problem in recommendation systems*. In *Proceedings of the 2nd international Conference on Ubiquitous Information Management and Communication* (pp. 208-211). New York: ACM Press.

Lee, K. C. K., Zheng, B., & Lee, W. C. (2008). Ranked Reverse Nearest Neighbor Search. *IEEE Transactions on Knowledge and Data Engineering*, *20*(7), 894–910. doi:10.1109/TKDE.2008.36

Lee, H., Rancourt, E., & Sarndal, C. E. (1994). Experiments with variance estimation from survey data with imputed values. *Journal of Official Statistics, 10*, 231–243.

Lee, J., Lin, Y., & Smith, M. (2008). *Dependency mining on the 2005-06 national health and nutrition examination survey data*. Paper presented in *American Medical Informatics Association 2008 annual symposium, knowledge discovery and data mining working group data mining competition*, Washington, DC.

Le-Khac, N., Aouad, L. M., & Kechadi, M. (2007). A new approach for distributed density based clustering on grid platform. In *Proceedings of the 24th British national conference on databases (BNCOD '07)* (pp. 247-258).

Lerman, K. (2007). Social Information Processing in News Aggregation. In *IEEE Internet Computing special issue on Social Search 11*(6), 16-28. IEEE.

Levenshtein, L. I. (1966). Binary codes capable of correcting deletions, insertions, and reversals. *Soviet Physics, Doklady, 10*(7), 707–710.

Li, S.-E., & Wang, S. (2005). Semi-closed cube: An effective approach to trading off data cube size and query response time. *J. Comput. Sci. Technol., 20*(3), 367–372. doi:10.1007/s11390-005-0367-8

Li, J., Fu, A., He, H., Chen, J., Jin, H., McAullay, D., et al. (2005). Mining risk patterns in medical data. In *Proceedings of the eleventh ACM SIGKDD international conference on Knowledge discovery in data mining*, Chicago (pp. 770-775).

Li, M., Lee, G., Lee, W., & Sivasubramaniam, A. (2006). PENS: an algorithm for density-based clustering in peer-to-peer systems. In *Proceedings of the 1st international conference on scalable information systems*.

Li, W., Han, J., & Pei, J. (2001). CMAR: Accurate and Efficient Classification Based on Multiple Class-Association Rules. In *Proceedings of the 1st international conference on data mining (icdm)* (pp. 369-376).

Liao, Y., & Vemuri, V. R. (2002). Using text categorization techniques for intrusion detection. In *Proceedings of the 11th USENIX Security Symposium*, Berkeley, CA (pp. 51-59). USENIX Association.

Lim, L. (2000). A comparison of prediction accuracy, complexity, and training time of thirty-three old and new classification algorithms. *Machine Learning, 40*, 203–229. doi:10.1023/A:1007608224229

Lipczak, M. Tag Recommendation for Folksonomies Oriented towards Individual Users. In *ECML PKDD discovery challenge 2008*.

Little, R., & Rubin, D. (2002). *Statistical Analysis with Missing Data* (2nd ed.). New York: John Wiley and Sons.

Liu, H., Hussain, F., Tan, C. L., & Dash, M. (2002). Discretization: An enabling technique. *Data Mining and Knowledge Discovery, 6*, 393–423. doi:10.1023/A:1016304305535

Liu, H., & Yu, L. (2005, April). Toward integrating feature selection algorithms for classification and clustering. *IEEE Transactions on Knowledge and Data Engineering, 17*(4), 491–502. doi:10.1109/TKDE.2005.66

Liu, B., Hsu, W., & Ma, Y. (1998). Integrating Classification and Association Rule Mining. In *Proceedings of the 4th international conference on knowledge discovery and data mining* (kdd) (pp. 80-86).

Loh, W.-Y., & Shih, Y.-S. (1997). Split selection methods for classification trees. *Statistica Sinica, 7*, 815–840.

Loh, W.-Y., & Vanichsetakul, N. (1988). Tree-structured classification via generalized discriminant analysis. *Journal of the American Statistical Association, 83*(403), 715–725. doi:10.2307/2289295

Longley, P., Goodchild, M., Maguire, D., & Rhind, D. (Eds.). (2001). *Geographic Information Systems and Science*. New York: Wiley.

Lu, J., Chen, W. R., Adjei, O., & Keech, M. (2008). Sequential patterns post-processing for structural relation patterns mining. *International Journal of Data Warehousing and Mining, 4*(3), 71–89.

Lu, J., Wang, X. F., Adjei, O., & Hussain, F. (2004). Sequential patterns graph and its construction algorithm. *Chinese Journal of Computers, 27*(6), 782–788.

Lu, H., Feng, L., & Han, J. (2000). Beyond intratransaction association analysis: mining multidimensional intertransaction association rules. *Acm tois, 18*(4), 423-454.

Lu, J. (2006). From Sequential Patterns to Concurrent Branch Patterns: A new post sequential patterns mining approach. Unpublished doctoral dissertation, University of Bedfordshire, UK.

Lu, J., Adjei, O., Chen, W. R., & Liu, J. (2004). Post Sequential Patterns Mining: A new method for discovering structural patterns. In *Proceedings of the Second International Conference on Intelligent Information Processing* (pp.239-250). Beijing, China: Springer-Verlag.

Lujan-Mora, S., Trujillo, J., & Song, I.-Y. (2006). A UML Profile for Multidimensional Modelling in Data Warehouses. *Journal of Data & Knowledge Engineering, 59*(3), 725–769. doi:10.1016/j.datak.2005.11.004

Lynch, K. (1960). *The Image of the City*. Cambridge, MA: MIT Press.

MacQueen, J. (1967). Some methods for classification and analysis of multivariate observations. In *Proceedings of the 5th Berkeley Symposium on Mathematical Statistics and Probability* (pp. 281-297).

Malinowski, E., & Zimányi, E. (2008). *Advanced Data Warehouse Design From Conventional to Spatial and Temporal Applications*. Berlin: Springer.

Manjunath, G., Tighiouart, H., Ibrahim, H., MacLeod, B., Salem, D. N., & Griffith, J. L. (2003). Level of kidney function as a risk factor for atherosclerotic cardiovascular outcomes in the community. *Journal of the American College of Cardiology, 41*(1), 47–55. doi:10.1016/S0735-1097(02)02663-3

Mannila, H., & Toivonen, H. (1997). Levelwise Search and Borders of Theories in Knowledge Discovery. *Data Mining and Knowledge Discovery, 1*(3), 241–258. doi:10.1023/A:1009796218281

Mannila, H., & Toivonen, H. (1996). Multiple Uses of Frequent Sets and Condensed Representations: Extended Abstract. In *Proceedings of the 2nd International Conference on Knowledge Discovery and Data Mining (KDD)* (pp. 189-194).

Marketos, G., Theodoridis, Y., Ioannis, S., & Kalogeras, J. (2008). Seismological Data Warehousing and Mining: A Survey. *International Journal of Data Warehousing and Mining, 4*(1), 1–16.

Marlow, C., Naaman, M., Boyd, D., & Davis, M. (2006). Ht06, tagging paper, taxonomy, flickr, academic article, to read. In *Hypertext '06: Proceedings of the seventeenth conference on Hypertext and hypermedia* (pp. 31-40). New York: ACM.

Masek, W. J., & Paterson, M. S. (1980). A faster algorithm computing string edit distances. *Journal of Computer Science and Systems, 20*(1), 18–31. doi:10.1016/0022-0000(80)90002-1

McRoberts, R. E., Nelson, M. D., & Wendt, D. G. (2002). Stratified estimation of forest area using satellite imagery, inventory data, and the k-Nearest Neighbor technique. *Remote Sensing of Environment, 82*, 457–468. doi:10.1016/S0034-4257(02)00064-0

Mehta, M., Agrawal, R., & Rissanen, J. (1996, 1996). *SLIQ: A Fast Scalable Classifier for Data Mining*. Paper presented at the EDBT, Avignon, France.

Middleton, S., Shadbolt, N., & De Roure, D. (2004). Ontological User Profiling in Recommender Systems. *ACM Transactions on Information Systems, 22*(1), 54–88. doi:10.1145/963770.963773

Mika, P. (2005). Ontologies are us: A unified model of social networks and semantics. In *The Semantic Web (ISWC 2005)* (pp. 522-536). Springer Berlin / Heidelberg.

Mitchell, T. M. (1997). *Machine learning*. New York: MacGraw-Hill.

Mitchell, A. (2005). The ESRI Guide to GIS Analysis: *Vol. 2. Spatial Measurements and Statistics*. Redlands, CA: ESRI Press.

Mitra, P., Murthy, C. A., & Pal, S. K. (2002). Unsupervised feature selection using feature similarity. *IEEE Transactions on Pattern Analysis and Machine Intelligence, 24*(3), 301–312. doi:10.1109/34.990133

Mobasher, B., Cooley, R., & Srivastava, J. (2000). Automatic Personalization Based on Web Usage Mining. *Communications of the ACM, 43*(8), 142–151. doi:10.1145/345124.345169

Mobasher, B. (2007). Data Mining for Personalization. In P. Brusilovsky, A. Kobsa, & W. Nejdl, (Eds.), *Lecture Notes in Computer Science: Vol. 4321. The Adaptive Web: Methods and Strategies of Web Personalization* (pp. 90-135). Berlin-Heidelberg: Springer.

Mohamad, S. I. L., & Theodoulidis, B. (2006). Improving similarity search in time series using wavelets. *International Journal of Data Warehousing and Mining, 2*(2), 55–81.

Montaquila, J. M., & Ponikowski, C. H. (1993). Comparison of methods for imputing missing responses in an establishment survey. In *Proceedings of the Section on Survey Research Methods, American Statistical Association,* 446-451.

Moser, F., Ge, R., & Ester, M. (2007). Joint cluster analysis of attribute and relationship data without a-priori specification of the number of clusters. In *Knowledge Discovery in Databases (KDD) Conference* (pp. 510–519), San Jose, CA: ACM.

Mount, D. W. (2004). *Bioinformatics: Sequence and Genome Analysis* (2nd ed.). Cold Spring Harbor, NY: Laboratory Press.

Mountrakis, G., Agouris, P., & Stefanidis, A. (2005). Adaptable User Profiles for Intelligent Geospatial Queries. *Transactions in GIS, 9*(4), 561–583. doi:10.1111/j.1467-9671.2005.00235.x

Muni, D. P., Pal, N. R., & Das, J. (2006, February). Genetic programming for simultaneous feature selection and classifier design. *IEEE Transactions on Systems, Man, and Cybernetics- PART B, 36*(1), 106-117.

Murtagh, F. (1983). A survey of recent advances in hierarchical clustering algorithms. *The Computer Journal, 26*(4), 354–359.

Must, A., Spadano, J., Coakley, E. H., Field, A. E., Colditz, G., & Dietz, W. H. (1999). The disease burden associated with overweight and obesity. *Journal of the American Medical Informatics Association, 282,* 1523–1529.

Myers, E. W. (1986). An O(nd) difference algorithm and its variations. *Algorithmica, 2,* 251–266. doi:10.1007/BF01840446

Nakatsu, N., Kambayashi, Y., & Yajima, S. (1982). A longest common subsequence algorithm suitable for similar text strings. *Acta Informatica, 18*(2), 171–179. doi:10.1007/BF00264437

Nedjar, S., Casali, A., Cicchetti, R., & Lakhal, L. (2007). Emerging cubes for trends analysis in Olap databases. In *Proceedings of the 9th international conference on data warehousing and knowledge discovery (dawak)* (pp. 135-144).

Negoescu, R. (2007). An analysis of the social network of flickr. Technical report, Laboratory of nonlinear systems - LANOS, School of Computer and Communication Sciences, École Polytechnique Fédérale de Lausanne, Switzerland.

Newman, M. E. J. (2005). Power laws, Pareto distributions and Zipf's law. *Contemporary Physics, 46,* 323–351. doi:10.1080/00107510500052444

Ng, R. T., & Han, J. (2002). CLARANS: A Method for Clustering Objects for Spatial Data Mining. *IEEE Transactions on Knowledge and Data Engineering, 14*(5), 1003–1016. doi:10.1109/TKDE.2002.1033770

Ng, R. T., & Han, J. (1994). Efficient and effective clustering methods for spatial data mining. In *Proceedings of the 20th International Conference on Very Large Data Bases (VLDB'94)* (pp. 144-155).

Nikulin, V. (2008). Classification of imbalanced data with random sets and mean-variance filtering. *International Journal of Data Warehousing and Mining, 4*(2), 63–78.

Oberle, D., Berendt, B., Hotho, A., & Gonzalez, J. (2003). Conceptual User Tracking. In *Proceedings of the Atlantic Web Intelligence Conference, Lecture Notes in Computer Science: Vol. 2663.* Springer.

Omiecinski, E. R. (2003). Alternative interest measures for mining associations in databases. *IEEE Transactions on Knowledge and Data Engineering, 15*(1), 57–69. doi:10.1109/TKDE.2003.1161582

Owen, A. B. (2001). *Empirical Likelihood.* New York: Chapman & Hall.

Owen, A. B. (2003). Data squashing by empirical likelihood. *Data Mining and Knowledge Discovery, 7*(1), 101–113. doi:10.1023/A:1021568920107

Pal, S. K., De, R. K., & Basak, J., (2000, March). Unsupervised feature selection using a neuro-fuzzy approach. *IEEE Transactions on Neural Networks, 11*(2), 366–375. doi:10.1109/72.839007

Pal, N. R. (1999). Soft computing for feature analysis. *Fuzzy Sets and Systems*, *103*(2), 201–221. doi:10.1016/S0165-0114(98)00222-X

Pal, N. R., Eluri, V. K., & Mandal, G. K. (2002, June). Fuzzy logic approaches to structure preserving dimensionality reduction. *IEEE Transactions on Fuzzy Systems*, *10*(3), 277–286. doi:10.1109/TFUZZ.2002.1006431

Pal, N. R., & Bezdek, J. C. (1995). On cluster validity for the fuzzy c-means model. *IEEE Transactions on Fuzzy Systems*, *3*(3), 370–379. doi:10.1109/91.413225

Panush, R. S. (1990). Food induced ("allergic") arthritis: clinical and serologic studies. *The Journal of Rheumatology*, *17*(3), 291–294.

Papadopoulos, S., Vakali, A., & Kompatsiaris, I. (July, 2008). *Digg it Up! Analyzing Popularity Evolution in a Web 2.0 Setting.* Paper presented at MSoDa08 (Mining Social Data). *A satellite Workshop of the 18th European Conference on Artificial Intelligence*, Patras, Greece.

Pasquier, N., Bastide, Y., Taouil, R., & Lakhal, L. (1999). Discovering frequent closed itemsets for association rules. In *Proceedings of the 7th international conference on database theory (icdt)* (pp. 398-416).

Paterson, M., & Danc'ik, V. (1994). Longest common subsequences. In *Proceedings of the 19th International Symposium Mathematical Foundations of Computer Science*, Kosice, Slovakia (LNCS, pp. 127-142). Berlin: Springer Verlag.

Pearson, P. K. (2005). *Mining imperfect data: dealing with contamination and incomplete records.* SIAM.

Pedersen, T., Jensen, C., & Dyreson, C. (2001). A Foundation For Capturing And Querying Complex Multidimensional Data. *Information Systems*, *26*(5), 383–423. doi:10.1016/S0306-4379(01)00023-0

Pei, J., Han, J., & Lakshmanan, L. V. S. (2004). Pushing convertible constraints in frequent itemset mining. *Data Mining and Knowledge Discovery*, *8*(3), 227–252. doi:10.1023/B:DAMI.0000023674.74932.4c

Pei, J., Han, J. W., Mortazavi-Asl, B., & Pinto, H. (2001). PrefixSpan: Mining sequential patterns efficiently by prefix-projected pattern growth. In *Proceedings of the Seventh International Conference on Data Engineering* (pp. 215-224). Heidelberg, Germany.

Pei, J., Han, J., & Mao, R. (2000). CLOSET: An Efficient Algorithm for Mining Frequent Closed Itemsets. In *Proceedings of the Workshop on research issues in data mining and knowledge discovery (dmkd)* (pp. 21-30).

Pena, J. M., Lozano, J. A., Larranaga, P., & Iwza, I. (2001). Dimensionality reduction in unsupervised learning of conditional Gaussian networks. *IEEE Transactions on Pattern Analysis and Machine Intelligence*, *23*(6), 590-603. doi:10.1109/34.927460

Pfahringer, B. (1995). *Compression-based discretization of continuous attributes.* Paper presented at the Proceedings of the Twelfth International Conference on Machine Learning.

Pighin, M., & Ieronutti, L. (2008). A methodology supporting the design and evaluating the final quality of data warehouses. *International Journal of Data Warehousing and Mining*, *4*(3), 15–34.

Pirkle, J. L., Kaufmann, R. B., Hickman, D. J., Gunter, T. E. W., & Paschal, D. C. (1998). Exposure of the U.S. population to lead, 1991-1994. *Environmental Health Perspectives*, *106*, 745–750. doi:10.2307/3434264

Pourabbas, E. (2003). Cooperation with Geographic Databases. In Rafanelli, M. (Ed.), *Multidimensional Databases: problems and solutions* (pp. 393–432). Hershey, PA: IGI Global.

Press, W. H. (2007). *Numerical recipes: the art of scientific computing (3rd ed.).* New York: Cambridge University Press.

Qin, Y. S. (2007). Semi-parametric optimization for missing data imputation. *Applied Intelligence*, *27*(1), 79–88. doi:10.1007/s10489-006-0032-0

Qin, Y. S., Zhang, S. C., & Zhang, C. Q. (2010). Combining kNN Imputation and Bootstrap Calibrated Empirical Likelihood for Incomplete Data Analysis. [DWM]. *International Journal of Data Warehousing and Mining*, *6*(2).

Qin, Y., Rao, J. N. K., & Ren, Q. (2008). Confidence intervals for marginal parameters under fractional linear regression imputation for missing data. *Journal of Multivariate Analysis*, *99*, 1232–1259. doi:10.1016/j.jmva.2007.08.005

Quinlan, J. R. (1996). Improved use of continuous attributes in C4.5. *Journal of Artificial Intelligence Research, 4*, 77–90.

Quinlan, J. R. (1983). Learning efficient classification procedures and their application to chess endgames. In R. Michalski, T. Carbonell & T. Mitchell (Eds.), *Machine Learning: an AI approach*. Los Altos, CA: Morgan Kaufmann.

Quinlan, J. R. (1986). Induction of decision trees. *Machine Learning, 1*(81-106), 81-106.

Quinlan, J. R. (1993). *C4.5: Programs for Machine Learning*. Los Altos, CA: Morgan Kauffman.

Raedt, L. D., & Zimmermann, A. (2007). Constraint-based pattern set mining. In *Proceedings of the 7th siam international conference on data mining*.

Raedt, L., Jaeger, M., Lee, S., & Mannila, H. (2002). A theory of inductive query answering. In *Proceedings of the 2002 ieee international conference on data mining (icdm)* (pp. 123-130).

Rafanelli, M. (2003). Operators for Multidimensional Aggregate Data. In Rafanelli, M. (Ed.), *Multidimensional Databases: problems and solutions* (pp. 116–165). Hershey, PA: IGI Global.

Rancourt, E. (1999). Estimation with nearest neighbor imputation at Statistics Canada. In *Proceedings of the Section on Survey Research Methods, American Statistical Association* (pp. 131-138).

Rastogi, R., & Shim, K. (2000). Public: A decision tree classifier that integrates building and pruning. *Data Mining and Knowledge Discovery, 4*(4), 315–344. doi:10.1023/A:1009887311454

Rawat, S., Gulati, V. P., Pujari, A. K., & Vemuri, V. R. (2006). Intrusion detection using processing techniques with a binary-weighted gosine metric. *Journal of Information Assurance and Security, 1*(1), 43–58.

Raymer, M. L., Punch, W. F., Goodman, E. D., Kuhn, L. A., & Jain, A. K. (2000, July). Dimensionality reduction using genetic algorithms. *IEEE Transactions on Evolutionary Computation, 4*(2), 164–171. doi:10.1109/4235.850656

Richardson, M., & Domingos, P. (2002). Mining knowledge-sharing sites for viral marketing. In *Proceedings of the 14th ACM SIGKDD International Conference on Knowledge Discovery and Data Mining* (KDD '02), (pp. 61-70), Las Vegas, USA: ACM.

Richeldi, M., & Rossotto, M. (1995). Class-driven statistical discretization of continuous attributes. In N. Lavrac & S. Wrobel (Eds.), *Lecture notes in Artificial Intelligence (Vol. 914, pp. 335-338)*. Berlin, Heidelberg, New York: Springer-Verlag.

Rick. (1994). *New algorithms for the longest common subsequence problem* (Tech. Rep. No. 85123-CS). Bonn, Germany: University of Bonn, Department of Computer Science.

Rivest, S., Bédard, Y., Proulx, M., Nadeaum, M., Hubert, F., & Pastor, J. (2005). SOLAP: Merging Business Intelligence with Geospatial Technology for Interactive Spatio-Temporal Exploration and Analysis of Data. *Journal of International Society for Photogrammetry and Remote Sensing, 60*(1), 17–33. doi:10.1016/j.isprsjprs.2005.10.002

Rivest, S., Bédard, Y., & Marchand, P. (2001). Towards Better Support For Spatial Decision-Making: Defining The Characteristics Of Spatial On-Line Analytical Processing. *Geomatica - Journal of the Canadian Institute of Geomatics, 55*(4), 539-555.

Roberts, J. S., & Wedell, D. H. (1994). Context effects on similarity judgments of multidimensional stimuli: Inferring the structure of the emotion space. *Journal of Experimental Social Psychology, 30*(1), 1–38. doi:10.1006/jesp.1994.1001

Romero, O., & Abelló, A. (2009). A survey of multidimensional modeling methodologies. *International Journal of Data Warehousing and Mining, 5*(2), 1–23.

Ross, K. A., Srivastava, D., Stuckey, P. J., & Sudarshan, S. (1998). Foundations of aggregation constraints. *Theoretical Computer Science, 193*(1-2), 149–179. doi:10.1016/S0304-3975(97)00011-X

Ruiz, R., Riquelme, J., & Aguilar-Ruiz, J. (2006). Incremental wrapper- based gene selection from microarray data for cancer classification. *Pattern Recognition, 39*, 2383–2392. doi:10.1016/j.patcog.2005.11.001

Saldanha, A. J. (2004). Java treeview-extensible visualization of microarray data. *Bioinformatics (Oxford, England)*, *20*(17), 3246–3248. doi:10.1093/bioinformatics/bth349

Sammon, J. W. Jr. (1969). A nonlinear mapping for data structure analysis. *IEEE Transactions on Computers*, *c-18*, 401–409. doi:10.1109/T-C.1969.222678

Sampaio, M., Sousa, A., & Baptista, C. (2006). Towards A Logical Multidimensional Model For Spatial Data Warehousing And OLAP. In *Proceedings of the ACM International Workshop on Data Warehousing and OLAP* (pp. 83-90). New York: ACM Press.

Sankoff & Kruskal. J. B. (1983). *Time warps, string edits, and macromolecules: The theory and practice of sequence comparison*. Reading, MA: Addison-Wesley.

Savary, L., Gardarin, G., & Zeitouni, K. (2007). GeoCache: A Cache for GML Geographical Data. *International Journal of Data Warehousing and Mining*, *3*(1), 67–88.

Savla, S., & Chakravarthy, S. (2007). A single pass algorithm for discovering significant intervals in time-series data. *International Journal of Data Warehousing and Mining*, *3*(3), 28–44.

Saxena, A., & Kothari, M. (2007). Unsupervised approach for structure preserving dimensionality reduction. In *Proceedings of the 6th International Conference on Advances in Pattern Recognition* (ICAPR07) (pp. 315-318). Singapore: World Scientific Publishing Co. Pte. Ltd.

Saydah, S., Eberhardt, M., Rios-Burrows, N., Williams, D., & Geiss, L. (2007). Prevalence of chronic kidney disease and associated risk factors -United States, 1999-2004. *Journal of the American Medical Informatics Association*, *297*, 1767–1768.

Schein, A., Popescul, A., & Lyle, H. (2002). Methods and Metric for Cold-Start Recommendations. In *Proceedings of the 25th Annual International ACM SIGIR Conference on Research and Development in Information Retrieval* (pp. 253-260). ACM.

Schmitz, C., Grahl, M., Hotho, A., Stumme, G., Cattuto, C., Baldassarri, A., et al. (2007). Network properties of folksonomies. In *World Wide Web Conference (WWW)*, Banff, Canada.

Scotch, M., & Parmanto, B. (2006). Development of SOVAT: A Numerical-Spatial Decision Support System For Community Health Assessment Research. *International Journal of Medical Informatics*, *34*(10), 771–784. doi:10.1016/j.ijmedinf.2005.10.008

Seidman, S. B. (1983). Network structure and minimum degree. *Social Networks*, 269–287. doi:10.1016/0378-8733(83)90028-X

Setiono, R., & Liu, H. (1997, May). Neural-network feature selector. *IEEE Transactions on Neural Networks*, *8*(3), 654–662. doi:10.1109/72.572104

Shafer, J., Agrawal, R., & Mehta, M. (1996). *SPRINT: A scalable parallel classifier for data mining*. Paper presented at the Proceedings of the 22nd International Conference of Very Large Databases, Mumbai (Bombay), India.

Shahabi, C., Zarkesh, A. M., Adibi, J., & Shah, V. (1997). Knowledge discovery from user's web-page navigation. In *Proceedings of the 7th International Workshop on Research Issues in Data Engineering, High Performance Database Management for Large-Scale Applications, Birmingham, England* (pp. 20-29). Washington, DC: IEEE Computer Society.

Shao, J., & Sitter, R. R. (1996). Bootstrap for imputed survey data. *Journal of the American Statistical Association*, *91*, 1278–1288. doi:10.2307/2291746

Siedlecki, W., & Sklansky, J. (1989). A note on genetic algorithms for large-scale feature selection. *Pattern Recognition Letters*, *10*(5), 335–347. doi:10.1016/0167-8655(89)90037-8

Sigurbjörnsson, B., & van Zwol, R. (2008). Flickr tag recommendation based on collective knowledge. In *WWW '08: Proceeding of the 17th international conference on world wide web* (pp. 327–336). New York: ACM.

Silva, J., Times, V., Salgado, A., Souza, C., Fidalgo, R., & Oliveira, A. (2008). A Set of Aggregation Functions for Spatial Measures. In *Proceedings of the ACM 11th international workshop on Data warehousing and OLAP* (pp. 25-32). New York: ACM Press.

Simon, I. (1987). Sequence comparison: some theory and some practice. In Gross, M., & Perrin, D. (Eds.), *Electronic Dictionaries and Automata in Computational Linguistics, Saint Pierre d'Oleron* (pp. 79–92). Berlin: Springer Verlag.

Sjberg, L. (1972). A cognitive theory of similarity. *Gteborg Psychological Reports, 2*(10), 1–23.

Skellam, J. G. (1952). Studies in statistical ecology: spatial pattern. *Biometrika, 39*, 346–362. doi:10.2307/2334030

Sloan Digital Sky Survey. (2008). *The 5ᵗʰ data release of the Sloan digital sky survey.* Retrieved June 20, 2008 from http://cas.sdss.org/dr5/en

Sneath, P. H., & Sokal, R. R. (1973). *Numerical taxonomy – The principles and practice of numerical classification.* San Francisco: W.H. Freeman and Company.

Song, M., Hu, X., Yoo, I., & Koppel, E. (2009). A Dynamic and Semantically-Aware Technique for Document Clustering in Biomedical Literature. *International Journal of Data Warehousing and Mining, 5*(4), 44–57.

Song, X., Chi, Y., Hino, K., & Tseng, B. L. (2007, May 08-12). Information flow modeling based on diffusion rate for prediction and ranking. In *Proceedings of the 16th international Conference on World Wide Web*, Banff, Alberta, Canada (WWW '07) (pp. 191-200). New York, NY: ACM.

Specia, L., & Motta, E. (2007). Integrating folksonomies with the semantic web. *In Lecture Notes in Computer Science: The Semantic Web: Research and Applications* (Vol. 4519) (pp. 624-639). Springer.

Spence, J. D. (2003). Systolic blood pressure in patients with osteoarthritis and rheumatoid arthritis. *The Journal of Rheumatology, 30*(4), 714–719.

Spiliopoulou, M., & Brunzel, M. (2007). Acquiring semantic sibling associations from web documents. *International Journal of Data Warehousing and Mining, 3*(4), 83–98.

Srikant, R., & Agrawal, R. (1996). Mining Sequential Patterns: Generalizations and performance improvements. In *Proceedings of the Fifth International Conference on Extending Database Technology* (EDBT) (Vol.1057, pp. 3-17). Avignon, France.

Srikant, R., & Agrawal, R. (1996). Mining quantitative association rules in large relational tables. In *Proceedings of the international conference on management of data (sigmod)* (pp. 1-12).

Stefanovic, N., Han, J., & Koperski, K. (2000). Object-Based Selective Materialization for Efficient Implementation of Spatial Data Cubes. *IEEE Transactions on Knowledge and Data Engineering, 12*(6), 938–958. doi:10.1109/69.895803

Stumme, G., Taouil, R., Bastide, Y., Pasquier, N., & Lakhal, L. (2002). Computing Iceberg Concept Lattices with Titanic. *Data & Knowledge Engineering, 42*(2), 189–222. doi:10.1016/S0169-023X(02)00057-5

Sun, H., Yu, G., Bao, Y., Zhao, F., & Wang, D. (2005). CDS-Tree: An effective index for clustering arbitrary shapes in data streams. In *Proceedings of the 15th international workshop on research issues in data engineering: stream data mining and applications (RIDE-SDMA '05).*

Surowiecki, J. (2004). The *wisdom of crowds: Why the many are smarter than the few and how collective wisdom shapes business, economies, societies and nations.* Doubleday.

Tan, L., Taniar, D., & Smith, K. A. (2005). A clustering algorithm based on an estimated distribution model. *International Journal of Data Warehousing and Mining, 1*(2), 229–245.

Tan, L., Taniar, D., & Smith, K. A. (2006). Maximum-entropy estimated distribution model for classification problems. *International Journal Hybrid Intelligent System, 3*(1), 1–10.

Tan, P. N., Kumar, V., & Srivastava, J. (2002). Selecting the right interestingness measure for association patterns. In *Proceedings of the eighth ACM SIGKDD international conference on Knowledge discovery and data mining,* Edmond, Canada (pp. 32-41).

Tan, P.-N., et al. (2005) *Introduction to Data Mining.* Boston, MA: Addison-Wesley Longman Publishing Co., Inc.

Taniar, D., & Goh, J. (2007). On Mining Movement Pattern from Mobile Users. *International Journal of Distributed Sensor Networks, 3*(1), 69–86. doi:10.1080/15501320601069499

Tao, Y., & Papadias, D. (2005). Historical spatio-temporal aggregation. *ACM Transactions on Information Systems*, *23*(1), 61–102. doi:10.1145/1055709.1055713

Tatu, M., Srikanth, M., & D'Silva, T. RSDC'08: Tag Recommendations using Bookmark Content. *In ECML PKDD discovery challenge2008.*

The National Diabetes Information Clearinghouse (NDIC). (n.d.). Retrieved April 29, 2009, from http://diabetes.niddk.nih.gov/dm/pubs/stroke/

Timpf, S., & Frank, A. U. (1997). Using Hierarchical Spatial Data Structures For Hierarchical Spatial Reasoning. In *Spatial Information Theory - A Theoretical Basis for GIS* (pp. 69–83). Berlin: Springer Verlag. doi:10.1007/3-540-63623-4_43

Ting, K. M. (1994). Discretization *of continuous-valued attributes and instance-based learning* (Vol. 491) (Tech. Rep.). Australia: University of Sydney.

Tobler, W. R. (1970). A computer model simulating urban growth in the Detroit Region. *Economic Geography*, *46*(2), 234–240. doi:10.2307/143141

Trujillo, J., Palomar, M., Gomez, J., & Song, I. (2001). Designing Data Warehouses with OO Conceptual Models. *Computer*, *34*(12), 66–75. doi:10.1109/2.970579

Tsatsaronis, G., Varlamis, I., & Vazirgiannis, M. (2008). Word Sense Disambiguation with Semantic Networks. In *Proceedings of the 11th International Conference on Text, Speech and Dialogue*, Brno, Czech Republic.

Tsymbal, A. (2004). *The problem of concept drift: definitions and related work* (Technical Report). University of Dublin. Retrieved September 26, 2008, from https://www.cs.tcd.ie/publications/tech-reports/reports.04/TCD-CS-2004-15.pdf.

Tversky, A. (1977). Features of similarity. *Psychological Review*, *84*(4), 327–352. doi:10.1037/0033-295X.84.4.327

Tversky, B. (1993). Cognitive Maps, Cognitive Collages, and Spatial Mental Models. In A.U. Frank & I. Campari (Eds.), In *Proceedings of COSIT'93* (LNCS 716) (pp. 14-24). Berlin, Germany: Springer-Verlag.

Tzanis, G., & Berberidis, C. (2007). Mining for Mutually Exclusive Items in Transaction Databases. *International Journal of Data Warehousing and Mining*, *3*(3), 45–59.

Van de Merckt, T. (1993). *Decision trees in numerical attribute spaces.* Paper presented at the 13th International Joint Conference on Artificial Intelligence.

Vannucci, M., & Colla, V. (2004, April 28-30). *Meaningful discretization of continuous features for association rules mining by means of a SOM.* Paper presented at the European Symposium on Artificial Neural Networks, Bruges, Belgium.

Vel, M. (1993). *Theory of Convex Structures.* Amsterdam: North-Holland.

Voisard, A., & David, B. (2002). A Database Perspective on Geospatial Data Modeling. *IEEE Transactions on Knowledge and Data Engineering*, *14*(2), 226–243. doi:10.1109/69.991714

Voss, J. (2007). *Tagging, Folksonomy & Co - Renaissance of Manual Indexing?* In *Proceedings of the International Symposium of Information Science* (pp. 234–254).

Wagner, R. A., & Fischer, M. J. (1974). The string-to-string correction problem. *Journal of the ACM*, *21*(1), 168–173. doi:10.1145/321796.321811

Walton, N., Knight, S., Newman, M., & Poynton, M. R. (2008). *Predictions of self-reported health status using data mining techniques.* Paper presented at the American Medical Informatics Association 2008 annual symposium, knowledge discovery and data mining working group data mining competition, Washington, DC.

Wan, R., Wang, L., & Su, X. (2009). PNMBG: Point neighborhood merging with border grids. *Journal of Information and Organizational Sciences*, *33*(2), 297–305.

Wang, Y., Lim, E. P., & Hwang, S. Y. (2006). Efficient mining of group patterns from user movement data. *Data & Knowledge Engineering*, *57*(3), 240–282. doi:10.1016/j.datak.2005.04.006

Wang, Y., Lim, E. P., & Hwang, S. Y. (2008). Efficient algorithms for mining maximal valid groups, *The VLDB Journal — The International Journal on Very Large Data Bases*, *17*(3), 515-535.

Wang, Q., & Rao, J. N. K. (2002). Empirical likelihood-based inference under imputation for missing response data. *Annals of Statistics*, *30*, 896–924. doi:10.1214/aos/1028674845

Wang, J., Han, J., & Pei, J. (2006). Closed constrained gradient mining in retail databases. *IEEE Transactions on Knowledge and Data Engineering*, *18*(6), 764–769. doi:10.1109/TKDE.2006.88

Wang, Q., & Rao, J. N. K. (2002a). Empirical likelihood-based inference in linear models with missing data. *Scandinavian Journal of Statistics*, *29*, 563–576. doi:10.1111/1467-9469.00306

Wang, Q., & Rao, J. N. K. (2002b). Empirical likelihood-based inference under imputation for missing response data. *Annals of Statistics*, *30*, 896–924. doi:10.1214/aos/1028674845

Wang, W., Yang, J., & Muntz, R. (1997). STING: A statistical information grid approach to spatial data mining. In *Proceedings of the 23rd International Conference on Very Large Data Bases (VLDB'97)* (pp. 186-195).

Wasserman, S., & Faust, K. (1994). *Social network analysis: Methods and applications*. Cambridge: Cambridge University Press.

Wei, H. L., & Billings, S. A. (2007). Feature subset selection and ranking for data dimensionality reduction. *IEEE Transactions on Pattern Analysis and Machine Intelligence*, *29*(1), 162–166. doi:10.1109/TPAMI.2007.250607

Weiss, S. M., Galen, R. S., & Tadepalli, P. V. (1990). Maximizing the predicative value of production rules. *Artificial Intelligence*, *45*, 47–71. doi:10.1016/0004-3702(90)90037-Z

Witten, I. H., & Frank, E. (2005). *Data Mining: Practical Machine Learning Tools and Techniques*. San Francisco: Elsevier, Inc.

Wong, A. K. C., & Chiu, D. K. Y. (1987). Synthesizing statistical knowledge from incomplete mixed-mode data. *IEEE Transactions on Pattern Analysis and Machine Intelligence*, *9*, 796–805. doi:10.1109/TPAMI.1987.4767986

Worboys, M. F. (2001). Nearness relations in environmental space. *International Journal of Geographical Information Science*, *15*(7), 633–651. doi:10.1080/13658810110061162

Worboys, M. (1996). Metrics and topologies for geographic space. In M. J. Kraak & M. Molenaar (Eds.), *Advances in GIS Research II* (pp. 365-375). London: Taylor and Francis.

Wu, F., & Huberman, B. A. (2007). Novelty and collective attention. [PNAS.]. *Proceedings of the National Academy of Sciences of the United States of America*, *104*(45), 17599–17601. doi:10.1073/pnas.0704916104

Xin, D., Shao, Z., Han, J., & Liu, H. (2006). *C-cubing: Efficient computation of closed cubes by aggregation-based checking* (p. 4). Icde.

Xin, D., Han, J., Li, X., & Wah, B. W. (2003). Star-cubing: Computing iceberg cubes by top-down and bottom-up integration. In *Proceedings of the 29th international conference on very large data bases (vldb)* (pp. 476-487).

Xu, S., Bao, S., Fei, B., Su, Z., & Yu, Y. (2008). Exploring folksonomy for personalized search. In *SIGIR'08: Proceedings of the 31st annual international ACM SIGIR conference on Research and development in information retrieval* (pp. 155-162). New York: ACM.

Xuan, K. G., Taniar, D., & Srinivasan, B. (2008). Continuous Range Search Query Processing in Mobile Navigation. In *Proceedings of the 14th International Conference on Parallel and Distributed Systems (ICPADS 2008)* (pp. 361-368). Washington, DC: IEEE Computer Society.

Yan, S. C., Xu, D., Zhang, B. H. J., Yang, Q., & Lin, S. (2007). Graph embedding and extensions: A general framework for dimensionality reduction. *IEEE Transactions on Pattern Analysis and Machine Intelligence*, *29*(1), 40–51. doi:10.1109/TPAMI.2007.250598

Yan, T. W., Jacobsen, M., Molina, H. G., & Dayal, U. (1996). From user access patterns to dynamic hypertext linking. In *Proceedings of the fifth international World Wide Web conference on Computer networks and ISDN systems* (pp. 1007-1014). Amsterdam: Elsevier.

Yan, X. F., Han, J. W., & Afshar, R. (2003). CloSpan: Mining closed sequential patterns in large datasets. In *Proceedings of SDM'03* (pp. 166-177). San Francisco, CA.

Yan, X., Cheng, H., Han, J., & Xin, D. (2005). Summarizing itemset patterns: a profile-based approach. In *Proceedings of the eleventh ACM SIGKDD international conference on knowledge discovery in data mining*, Chicago (pp. 314-323).

Yang, Y., & Claramunt, C. (2004, August 23-25). A Flexible Competitive Neural Network for Eliciting User's Preferences in Web Urban Spaces. In P. Fisher (Ed.), *Proceedings of the 11th International Spatial Data Handling Conference* (pp. 41-57). Berlin: Springer-Verlag.

Yang, Y., & Claramunt, C. (2005, December). A hybrid approach for spatial web personalization. In K. J. Li & C. Vangenot (Eds.), *(LNCS 3833)* (pp. 206-221). Berlin: Springer Verlag.

Yu, G. Z., Shao, S. H., Luo, B., & Zeng, X. H. (2009). A hybrid method for high-utility itemsets mining in large high-dimensional data. *International Journal of Data Warehousing and Mining, 5*(1), 57–73.

Yu, D., Shao, S., & Luo, B. (2009). A hybrid method for high-utility itemsets mining in large high-dimensional data. *International Journal of Data Warehousing and Mining, 5*, 57–73.

Yu, D., Shao, S., & Luo, B. (2009). A hybrid method for high-utility itemsets mining in large high-dimensional data. *International Journal of Data Warehousing and Mining, 5*, 57–73.

Zaki, M. J. (2000). Scalable Algorithms for Association Mining. *IEEE Transactions on Knowledge and Data Engineering, 12*(3), 372–390. doi:10.1109/69.846291

Zaki, M. J. (2001). SPADE: An efficient algorithm for mining frequent sequences. *Machine Learning, 42*(1/2), 31–60. doi:10.1023/A:1007652502315

Zaki, M. J. (2005). Efficiently Mining Frequent Trees in a Forest: Algorithms and applications. *IEEE Transactions on Knowledge and Data Engineering, 17*(8), 1021–1035. doi:10.1109/TKDE.2005.125

Zaki, M. J., & Hsiao, C.-J. (2005). Efficient algorithms for mining closed itemsets and their lattice structure. *IEEE Transactions on Knowledge and Data Engineering, 17*(4), 462–478. doi:10.1109/TKDE.2005.60

Zaki, M. J., Parimi, N., De, N., Gao, F., Phoophakdee, B., Urban, J., et al. (2005). Towards generic pattern mining. In *Proceedings of the ICFCA 2004* (LNCS 3403) (pp. 1-20). Berlin: Springer-Verlag.

Zhang, P., Verma, B., & Kumar, K. (2005, May). Neural vs. statistical classifier in conjunction with genetic algorithm based feature selection. *Pattern Recognition Letters, 26*(7), 909–919. doi:10.1016/j.patrec.2004.09.053

Zhang, X., Jing, L., Hu, X., Ng, M., Xia, J., & Zhou, X. (2008). Medical Document Clustering Using Ontology Based Term Similarity Measures. *International Journal of Data Warehousing and Mining, 4*(1), 62–73.

Zhang, S. C. (2008). Parimputation: From imputation and null-imputation to partially imputation. *IEEE Intelligent Informatics Bulletin, 9*(1), 32–38.

Zhang, S. C. (2010). *Shell-Neighbor Method And Its Application in Missing Data Imputation*. Applied Intelligence.

Zhang, S. C. (2009). POP Algorithm: Kernel-Based Imputation to Treat Missing Values in Knowledge Discovery from Databases. *Expert Systems with Applications, 36*, 2794–2804. doi:10.1016/j.eswa.2008.01.059

Zhang, X., Hu, X., Xia, J., Zhou, X., & Achananuparp, P. (2008). A Graph-Based Biomedical Literature Clustering Approach Utilizing Term's Global and Local Importance Information. *International Journal of Data Warehousing and Mining, 4*(4), 84–101.

Zhang, X., Jing, L., Hu, X., Ng, M., Xia, J., & Zhou, X. (2008). Medical Document Clustering Using Ontology-Based Term Similarity Measures. *International Journal of Data Warehousing and Mining, 4*(1), 62–73.

Zhang, X., Hu, X., Xia, J., Zhou, X., & Achananuparp, P. (2008). A Graph-Based Biomedical Literature Clustering Approach Utilizing Term's Global and Local Importance Information. *International Journal of Data Warehousing and Mining, 4*(4), 84–10.

Zhang, C. Q., et al. (2007). Efficient Imputation Method for Missing Values. In *Proceedings of PAKDD 2007* (LNAI 4426, pp. 1080-1087).

Zhang, J., Ackerman, M. S., & Adamic, L. (2007, May 8-12). Expertise networks in online communities: structure and algorithms. In *Proceedings of the 16th international Conference on World Wide Web*, Banff, Alberta, Canada (WWW '07) (pp. 221-230). New York: ACM.

Zhang, J., Manli, Z., Papadias, D., Tao, Y., & Lee, D. (2003). Location-based spatial queries. In *Proceedings of the ACM SIGMOD Conference* (pp. 443-454). New York: ACM.

Zhang, J., Papadias, D., Mouratidis, K., & Zhu, M. (2004). Spatial Queries in the Presence of Obstacles. In *Proceedings of the International Conference on Extending Database Technology (EDBT)* (pp. 366-384).

Zhang, S. C. (2008). Parimputation: From imputation and null-imputation to partially imputation. *IEEE Intelligent Informatics Bulletin*, 9(1), 32–38.

Zhang, S. C. (in press). Shell-neighbor method and its application in missing data imputation. *Applied Intelligence*.

Zhang, T., Ramakrishnam, R., & Livny, M. (1996). BIRCH: an efficient data clustering method for very large databases. In *Proceedings of the 1996 ACM SIGMOD International Conference on Management of Data (SIGMOD '96)* (pp. 103-114).

Zhao, G., Xuan, K., Taniar, D., & Srinivasan, B. (2008). Incremental k-Nearest-Neighbor Search on Road Networks. [JOIN]. *Journal of Interconnection Networks*, 9(4), 455–470. doi:10.1142/S0219265908002382

Zhao, G., Xuan, K., Taniar, D., Safar, M., Gavrilova, M. L., & Srinivasan, B. (2009). Multiple Object Types KNN Search Using Network Voronoi Diagram. In *Proceedings of the International Conference on Computational Science and Its Applications - ICCSA 2009 Part II* (LNCS 5593) (pp. 819-834). Berlin: Springer Verlag.

About the Contributors

David Taniar received a PhD degree in databases from Victoria University (Australia, 1997). He is now a senior lecturer at Monash University (Australia). He has published more than 100 research articles and edited a number of books in the Web technology series. He is in the editorial board of a number of international journals, including *Data Warehousing and Mining, Business Intelligence and Data Mining, Mobile Information Systems, Mobile Multimedia, Web Information Systems* and *Web and Grid Services*. He has been elected as a Fellow of the Institute for Management of Information Systems (UK).

Lukman Hakim Iwan is a PhD student at the school of computer science and IT, RMIT University, Australia. He received a bachelor degree from Padjadjaran University, Indonesia and MCS degree from Monash University, Australia both in Computer Science. His research interests include data mining, pattern mining, information retrieval, and video processing.

* * *

Ralitsa Angelova is a researcher at the Databases and Information Systems Group at the Max-Planck Institute for Informatics (MPII), Germany. She graduated with honors from the Technical University, Sofia, Bulgaria and Saarland University, Saarbruecken, Germany where she obtained her B.C.Eng. and M.Sc. degrees. Her primary topics of interest are graph-based methods for clustering and classification, as well as heterogeneous graph analysis applied to social networks.

Marie-Aude Aufaure (PhD in computer science from the University of Paris 6) is full professor at Ecole Centrale Paris (MAS Laboratory) and head of the SAP Business Objects Chair on Business Intelligence. She is also scientific partner at INRIA in the Axis project. Her research interests deals with the analysis, retrieval and querying of unstructured data, and the combination of structured and unstructured data from a Business Intelligence perspective. She also works on ontology life-cycle (construction and evolution), semantic information retrieval and personalization/recommendation.

Christian Bauckhage is professor of media informatics at the University of Bonn and head of the multimedia pattern recognition group at Fraunhofer IAIS. He received the MSc and PhD degree in computer science from Bielefeld University in 1998 and 2002, respectively. He was a student fellow at INRIA in Grenoble and a postdoctoral fellow in the Applied Informatics group at Bielefeld University and in the Active and Attentive Vision Lab at York University in Toronto. Later, as a senior scientist at Deutsche Telekom Laboratories in Berlin, he conducted industrial ICT research. Christian has (co) authored more than 80 technical papers on computer vision, pattern recognition, and advanced human-machine interaction. His current work focuses on retrieval-based pattern recognition, Web X.0 services and interactive media, and applications of converging technologies in machine intelligence and user interfaces.

Sandro Bimonte is researcher at CEMAGREF, and more exactly he is at TSCF. He obtained his PhD at INSA-Lyon, France (2004-2007). From 2007-2008, he carried out researches at IMAG, France. He is Managing Editor de *Journal of Decision Systems*, Editorial Board member of *International Journal of Decision Support System Technology*, and *International Journal of Data Mining, Modelling and Management* and member of the *Commission on GeoVisualization of the International Cartographic Association*. His research activities concern Spatial Data Warehouses and Spatial OLAP, Visual Languages, Geographic Information Systems, Spatio-temporal Databases and GeoVisualization.

Alain Casali obtained the Phd degree in computer science from the University of Aix-Marseilles (France) in 2005. He is an assistant professor at the University of Aix-Marseille II - IUT of Aix en Provence and is a member of the LIF laboratory. He studies the lattice algorithmic and the multidimensional data mining.

Weiru Chen is the Dean of the Faculty of Computer Science and Technology at the Shenyang Institute of Chemical Technology (SYICT), China. He received his BSc in Computer Application (1985) from Dalian University of Technology, China, and MSc in Computer Science and Application (1988) from Northeastern University, China. He then joined SYICT as a Lecturer and has remained there ever since, becoming Dean of Faculty in 2004. His research interests include software architecture, software reliability engineering, biological information analysis, data mining and grid computing, and he is also a Director of the Liaoning Computer Federation in China. Professor Chen worked as an external supervisor for Jing Lu's PhD research from 2004 to 2006 and was invited to the University of Bedfordshire, UK in the summer of 2006.

Rosine Cicchetti is a full professor at the University of Aix-Marseilles (France) and responsible of the database and machine learning research team at the Laboratory of Fundamental Computer Science (LIF) of Marseilles. She obtained the PhD in 1990 (University of Nice, France) and the Habilitation for Research Direction in 1996 (University of Aix-Marseilles). Her research topics encompass Databases, Data Mining, Data Warehousing, Statistical databases and Multidimensional Skylines.

Christophe Claramunt is a Professor in Computer Science and Director of the Naval Academy Research Institute in North West France. He holds a PhD in Computer Science from the University of Burgundy. His current research interests are oriented towards the development of spatio-temporal models, semantic and cognitive-based model for GIS, and WEB, wireless and GIS. He has widely published in the domain of geographical information science and is regularly involved in major conferences in GIS.

Magdalini Eirinaki is an assistant professor at the Computer Engineering Department, San Jose State University, California. She received the PhD degree in Informatics from Athens University of Economics and Business. Her research interests cover the areas of web mining and recommender systems and, in particular, on personalization of web sites and search engines, interactive database exploration, and mining of social networks. She has published several papers in refereed journals and international conference proceedings in the above areas. More information is available at http://www.engr.sjsu.edu/meirinaki/

Kelley M. Engle received the master's degree in Information Systems from Pennsylvania State University in 2002. She is a PhD student in the Department of Information Systems at the University of Maryland Baltimore County (UMBC), Maryland. Her research interests center around the study of data mining and artificial intelligence, especially the area of healthcare informatics.

Aryya Gangopadhyay is a Professor of Information Systems at the University of Maryland Baltimore County (UMBC). He has a PhD in Computer Information Systems from Rutgers University. His research interests include privacy preserving data mining, data cube navigation, and core and applied research on data mining. He has co-authored and edited three books, many book chapters, and numerous papers in peer-reviewed journals. His research has been funded by the National Science Foundation, U.S. Department of Education, and various Government and commercial entities.

Panagiotis Giannikopoulos is a PhD candidate at the Department of Computer Science and Technology, University of Peloponnese, Greece, after receiving his BSc from the latter. His research interests focus on data mining, frequent-pattern mining (both centralized and distributed), generalized association rule mining, information retrieval, as well as information filtering.

Malcolm Keech is the Associate Dean of Creative Arts, Technologies & Science at the University of Bedfordshire, UK. Before joining the University in 1999, Malcolm Keech had worked extensively in computing and IT development and management, both in the academic and industrial sectors. While his original academic background lies in mathematics (BA Oxford, MSc/PhD Manchester), Malcolm's professional experience includes periods at the London School of Economics, the Universities of London and Manchester, Florida State University, British Telecom and British Aerospace. He was Head of Computing & Information Systems at the Luton campus in Bedfordshire for 5 years before taking up his present position. Malcolm is both a Fellow of the Institute of Mathematics & its Applications (Chartered Mathematician) and a Fellow of the British Computer Society (Chartered IT Professional).

Ioannis Kompatsiaris received the Diploma degree in electrical engineering and the PhD degree in 3-D model based image sequence coding from Aristotle University of Thessaloniki (AUTH), Thessaloniki, Greece in 1996 and 2001, respectively. He is a Senior Researcher with the Informatics and Telematics Institute, and currently he is leading the Multimedia Knowledge Laboratory. His research interests include semantic multimedia analysis, social media analysis, multimedia and the Semantic Web, multimedia ontologies, knowledge-based analysis, context aware inference for semantic multimedia analysis, personalization and retrieval. He is the co-author of 10 book chapters, 30 papers in refereed journals and more than 90 papers in international conferences. He has served as a regular reviewer for a number of international journals and conferences. He is a member of IEEE, ACM and IEE.

P. Radha Krishna received his Ph.D. in 1996 from the Osmania University, and M.Tech. in Computer Science from Jawaharlal Nehru Technological University, both in Hyderabad, India. Currently, he is working as Principal Researcher at SETLabs, Infosys Technologies Limited, Hyderbad. Prior to joining Infosys he has served Institute for Development and Research in Banking Technology (IDRBT), India as Associate Professor and National Informatics Centre (NIC), India as scientist. He has involved in various research and developmental projects, including implementation of data warehouse in banks, and standards and protocols for e-check clearing and settlement. He has to his credit two books and quite a few research papers in referred journals and conferences. His research interests include Data Mining, Data Warehousing, Electronic Contracts and Fuzzy Computing.

Pradeep Kumar currently Astt professor with Indian Institute of Management (IIM), Lucknow. Prior to joining IIM, he has served SET Labs, Infosys Technologies Limited, Bangalore and Institute for Development and Research in Banking Technology (IDRBT), Hyderabad, India as a Research Fellow and He received his Ph.D from Department of Computer and Information Sciences, Hyderabad University, India. He holds M.Tech in Computer Science from BIT, Mesra, and B.Sc(Engg) in Computer Sc and Engg from Magadh University, India. He receives his fellowship grant from Institute for development and research in Banking Technology (IDRBT), India. His research interest includes Data Mining, Web Mining, Soft Computing, Network Security and Image Processing.

Lotfi Lakhal received the Phd degree in computer science and the Habilitation for Research Direction from the University of Nice-Sophia-Antipolis (France) respectively in 1986 and in 1991. He is a full professor at the University of Aix-Marseille II - IUT of Aix en Provence and member of the laboratory LIF. His research interest includes Databases, Formal Concept Analysis, Data Mining, Data Warehousing and Multidimensional Skylines.

Marek Lipczak is a PhD student at the Faculty of Computer Science, Dalhousie University, Halifax, Canada. He obtained his M.Sc. degree at Warsaw University of Technology, Poland. Currently, Marek is a member of the Machine Learning and Networked Information Spaces group, and his work focuses on machine learning techniques applied to socially based data repositories.

Jing Lu is a Research Fellow in Computer Science at Southampton Solent University, UK. Her research focus lies in data mining and sequential patterns post-processing, with particular application to web access patterns mining and modelling. Jing Lu has been engaged in curriculum design, research and consultancy in knowledge management and intelligent systems at the University since the start of 2007. Jing was awarded her PhD in late 2006 from the University of Bedfordshire in the area of knowledge discovery and data mining. Prior to 2005, she had been working in China as an Associate Professor in the Faculty of Computer Science and Technology, Shenyang Institute of Chemical Technology. Jing was the academic leader for teaching and research in computer applications with a primary focus on the fields of artificial intelligence, data mining, database management and web-based systems.

Maryvonne Miquel is Associate Professor at the Department of IT and Computer Engineering- INSA (Institut National des Sciences Appliquées de Lyon) since 1989. She received PhD in Computer Sciences in 1987 (INSA Lyon) and habilitation to supervise research in 2005 (University Lyon 1 and INSA Lyon). She is a member of the LIRIS research laboratory (the Lyon Research Center for Images and Intelligent Information Systems,CNRS UMR 5205). Her research interests include data warehouse, advanced multi-dimensional models and OLAP systems and she takes part in several national and international projects.

Evangelos Milios received a diploma in Electrical Engineering from the National Technical University of Athens, Greece, in 1980 and Master's and PhD degrees in Electrical Engineering and Computer Science from the Massachusetts Institute of Technology, Cambridge, Massachusetts, from where he graduated in 1986. After working as a Research Scientist at the University of Toronto, and as an Associate Professor at York University, he joined the Faculty of Computer Science, Dalhousie University, Halifax, Nova Scotia, where he is Professor and Killam Chair in Computer Science. He served as Director of the Graduate Program (1999-2002) and he is currently Associate Dean, Research. He is a Senior Member of the IEEE. He was a member of the ACM Dissertation Award committee (1990-1992), a member of the AAAI/SIGART Doctoral Consortium Committee (1997-2001) and he is co-editor-in-chief of the journal Computational Intelligence. He has published on the processing, interpretation and use of visual and range signals for landmark-based navigation and map construction in single- and multi-agent robotics. His current research activity is centered on modelling and mining of content and link structure of Networked Information Spaces.

Ali Mumtaz received his MSc degree in E-Business Technologies from University of Ottawa. Prior to this, he graduated from the University of Peshawar with MSc degree in Electronics. Ali has over 8 years of industrial experience as a network architect, Unix Systems administrator. He worked for COMSATS, Islamabad as a Deputy Director and head of network operations and led a team to design and implement a VSAT based connectivity to link remote northern areas with the rest of the world. The project was funded by IDRC, Canada. Presently, he is working as an IT analyst with the Canada Revenue Agency in Ottawa, Canada.

Sébastien Nedjar obtained the Phd degree in computer science from the University of Aix-Marseille (France) in 2009. His research work concerns OLAP Mining and Data Warehousing and Multidimensional Skylines.

Symeon Papadopoulos received the Diploma degree in Electrical and Computer Engineering in the Aristotle University of Thessaloniki (AUTH), Greece in 2004. In 2006, he received the Professional Doctorate in Engineering (P.D.Eng.) from the Technical University of Eindhoven, the Netherlands. His P.D.Eng. thesis concerned the improvement of Digital Subtraction Angiography by means of real-time motion compensation. Since September 2006, he has been working as a researcher in the Multimedia Knowledge laboratory. His current research interests pertain to community detection in large networks and mining of social web data. He is currently a PhD candidate in the Informatics department of AUTH under the supervision of prof. Athena Vakali. He is also a holder of an MBA degree from the Blekinge Institute of Technology, Sweden.

Jian Pei is currently an Associate Professor of Computing Science and an Associate Director at the School of Computing Science at Simon Fraser University, Canada. He received a Ph.D. degree at the same school in 2002, under Dr. Jiawei Han's supervision. His research interests can be summarized as developing effective and efficient data analysis techniques for novel data intensive applications. Particularly, he is currently interested in various techniques of data mining, Web search, information retrieval, data warehousing, online analytical processing, and database systems, as well as their applications in social networks, health-informatics, business and bioinformatics. His research has been extensively supported by both government agencies and industry partners. Since 2000, he has published one monograph and over 140 research papers in refereed journals and conferences, has served in the organization committees and the program committees of over 130 international conferences and workshops, and has been a reviewer for the leading academic journals in his fields. He is an associate editor of ACM Transactions on Knowledge Discovery from Data (TKDD) and IEEE Transactions of Knowledge and Data Engineering (TKDE). He is a senior member of the Association for Computing Machinery (ACM) and the Institute of Electrical and Electronics Engineers (IEEE). He is the recipient of several prestigious awards including the British Columbia Innovation Council 2005 Young Innovator Award, an NSERC 2008 Discovery Accelerator Supplements Award, an IBM Faculty Award, a KDD Best Application Paper Award, and an IEEE Outstanding Paper Award.

François Pinet is researcher at the French Institute for Agricultural and Environmental Engineering (Clermont Ferrand, France). His field of research is in environmental information systems and geomatics. He belongs to several scientific committees of different conferences and journals in these fields. Also, he has been a co-organizer for several workshops on environmental systems.

Pawel Pralat is a Postdoctoral Fellow of the Department of Mathematics and Statistics at the Dalhousie University. His main research interests lie in graph theory with applications to real-world self-organizing networks such as the web graph or peer-to-peer networks. He also studies an adjacency propertiesof graphs, on-line Ramsey numbers, random graphs, edge-searching problems, and combinatorial games. His Erdos Number is 2, through Noga Alon, Hal Kierstead, Tomasz Luczak, or Nick Wormald. He received an M.Sc. in Mathematics in 2000, a M.Eng. and M.A.Sc. in Computer Science in 2001 from theTechnical University of Lodz, and a PhD in Mathematics and Computer Science from Adam Mickiewicz University, Poznan, Poland, 2004.

Yongsong Qin is a professor at Guangxi Normal University, China. He holds a PhD degree in Probability and Statistics from the University of Science and Technology of China, China. His research interests include nonparametric statistics and pattern discovery. He has published more than 30 international journal papers.

Bijan Raahemi is an associate professor at the Telfer School of Management, University of Ottawa, Canada, with cross-appointment with the School of Information Technology and Engineering. He received his Ph.D. in Electrical and Computer Engineering from the University of Waterloo, Canada, in 1997. Prior to joining the University of Ottawa, Dr. Raahemi held several research positions in Telecommunications industry, including Nortel and Alcatel, focusing on Computer Networks Architectures and Services, Dynamics of Internet Traffic, Systems Modeling, and Performance Analysis of Data Networks. His current research interests include Knowledge Discovery and Data Mining, Information Systems, and Data Communications Networks and Services. Dr. Raahemi's work has appeared in several peer-reviewed journals and conference proceedings. He also holds several patents in Data Communications. He is a senior Member of the Institute of Electrical and Electronics Engineering (IEEE), and a member of the Association for Computing Machinery (ACM).

Bapi S. Raju received BE (Electrical Eng) from Osmania University, India and MS and PhD from University of Texas at Arlington, USA. He worked for 3 years as a Research Fellow in University of Plymouth, UK and 2 years in the Kawato Dynamic Brain Project, ATR Labs in Kyoto, Japan. Since 1999 he has been working as a Professor in the Department of Computer and Information Sciences in University of Hyderabad, India. His research interest is in various areas of computatonal intelligence, including, Neural Networks and Applications, Neural and Cognitive Modeling, Computational Neuroscience, Brain imaging and Bioinformatics.

Amit Saxena is a Professor, of Computer Science and Information Technology at G G University, Bilaspur- India. He obtained his Ph.D. Degree in Computer Science in 1998 in India, on Efficient Computation of DSP Problems using ANN Techniques. He has been teaching in the University since 1990 and visited Malaysia, Kuwait, USA, Spain, Singapore on academic assignments. He published papers in National and International Journals and Conference proceedings. He presented his research at various conferences as invited speaker. He authored a book on C Programming Language.

Xiaoke Su received her BS from the School of Computer and Information Technology of Xinyang Normal University (2002). She has subsequently joined the Department of Information Engineering and Automation in Kunming University of Science and Technology (KMUST) to pursue her MS in computer software and theory (2007). During her graduate studies, Dr. Su has been involved in the research of computer science education. During her post-graduate studies, she has been a software designer. Since March 2007 she has been a post-doctoral researcher at the College of Information Science and Technology, Donghua University. Her research interests include data mining, clustering, pattern recognition and outlier detection.

Anne Tchounikine received a phD in computing science in 1993 from the University of Toulouse (France). Since 1996, she is associate professor at LIRIS, the Lyon Research Center for Images and Intelligent Information Systems (France) and at the Computer/ IT Department of the National Institute for Applied Sciences (INSA). Her current research is on advanced multidimensional models and OLAP systems.

Athena Vakali received a bachelor degree in Mathematics from the Aristotle University, Thessaloniki, an MSc degree in Computer Science from Purdue University, USA and a PhD degree in managing data storage from the Department of Informatics at the Aristotle University. Since 1997 she is a faculty member at the Department of Informatics at the Aristotle University (currently associate professor), where she is leading the research group of Web Data Management. Her current research interests include web usage mining, content delivery networks on the Web, Web and social Web data clustering and Web data caching/outsourcing. She has co-edited 3 books, co-authored 7 book chapters, 38 papers in refereed journals and more than 60 papers in international conferences. She is in the editorial board of "Computers &

Electrical Engineering" Journal and the International Journal of Grid and High Performance Computing. She has participated in more than 20 R&D projects.

Iraklis Varlamis is a lecturer at the Department of Informatics and Telematics of Harokopio University of Athens. He received his PhD in Computer Science from Athens University of Economics and Business, Greece. He collaborates with DB-NET (http://www.db-net.aueb.gr/) and WIM (http://wim.aueb.gr) research groups. His research interests focus in the area of data-mining and especially in the use of semantics in web mining. He has published several articles in international journals and conferences, concerning web document clustering, the use of semantics in web link analysis and web usage mining, word sense disambiguation using thesauruses etc. More information is available at: http://www.dit.hua.gr/~varlamis

Renxia Wan received his BS from the Mathematics Department of Jiangxi Normal University (1998), MS from the College of Mathematics and Computer of Fuzhou University (2005), and PHD from the College of Information Science and Technology of Donghua University (2009). Dr. Wan has published more than 30 papers in journals and refereed conferences. His current research interests include information systems, data mining, knowledge learning, and intelligent control systems.

John Wang is a professor in the Department of Management and Information Systems at Montclair State University, USA. Having received a scholarship award, he came to the USA and completed his Ph.D. in operations research from Temple University. He has published over 100 refereed papers and six books. He has also developed several computer software programs based on his research findings. He has served as a guest editor and referee for many highly prestigious journals. *He has served as track chair and/or session chairman numerous times on the most prestigious international and national conferences.* His long-term research goal is on the synergy of operations research, data mining and cybernetics.

Lixin Wang received his Master Diploma (2000) and now is a PhD candidate in College of Information Science and Technology, Donghua University, Shanghai, China. His research interests include data mining, theory of databases, development of information system, and software testing. He presided over and participated in development of some projects such as Water Management System and Universal Automatic Test System platform for industrial pipeline inspection, etc., and published more than 15 articles in scientific journals and conferences. He is a member of China Computer Federation.

Robert Wetzker, Dipl. Ing., is a PhD student in the Information Retrieval and Machine Learning research group at the Distributed Artificial Intelligence (DAI) Laboratory of the Technische Universität Berlin. His primary research interests and publications are in the area of social network analysis, trend detection and tracking in social communities as well as on recommender systems. He has also been working on the development of expert finding and collaborative knowledge sharing solutions. Robert has been a student fellow at the LUISS Guido Carli University in Rome. He received his diploma in Business Administration and Engineering from Technische Universität Berlin in 2005.

Zhengzheng Xing is currently a Ph.D. candidate in the School of Computing Science at Simon Fraser University, Canada. She has been working in the area of data mining and machine learning since 2007 under the supervision of Dr. Jian Pei. She received her M.Sc. in Computer Science from University of Windsor, Canada in 2006 and her B.Eng. in Computer Science from Beijing Institute of Technology, China in 2004. Her current research interests include data mining, machine learning, and their applications in health-informatics. Particularly, she has been conducting research in the area of temporal data analysis, classification, clustering and data visualization.

Yanwu Yang received a Ph.D degree in computer science from the doctoral school of the Ecole Nationale Superieure d'Arts et Metiers (ENSAM), France in 2006. He joined the lab of Complex Systems and Intelligence Sciences in 2007. His current research interests include user modeling, Human-Computer Interaction and data text mining.

Chengqi Zhang has been a Research Professor in Information Technology at The University of Technology, Sydney (UTS) since December 2001. He is currently the Director of the UTS Research Centre for Quantum Computation and Intelligent Systems. In addition, he is the Leader of the Data Mining program at the Australian Capital Market Cooperative Research Centre. Prof. Zhang obtained his PhD degree from Queensland University in 1991, followed by a Doctor of Science (DSc – Higher Doctorate) from Deakin University in 2002. Prof. Zhang's research interests mainly focus on Data Mining and its applications, especially domain driven data mining, negative association rule mining, and multi-database mining. He has published more than 200 research papers, including several in first-class international journals, such as Artificial Intelligence, IEEE and ACM Transactions. He has delivered 12 keynote/invited speeches at international conferences over the last six years.He has been Chairman of the Australian Computer Society National Committee for Artificial Intelligence since November 2005. He was also elected as the Chairman of the Steering Committee of KSEM (International Conference on Knowledge Science, Engineering, and Management) in August 2006, and as a member of the IEEE TCII (Technical Committee of Information Informatics), Steering Committee of PRICAI (Pacific Rim International Conference on Artificial Intelligence), and PAKDD (Pacific-Asia Conference on Knowledge Discovery and Data Mining). He has been serving as an Associate Editor for three international journals, including IEEE Transactions on Knowledge and Data Engineering, from 2005 to 2008; and he served as General Chair, PC Chair, or Organising Chair for five international Conferences including ICDM and WI/IAT. He is a Fellow of the Australian Computer Society (ACS) and a Senior Member of the IEEE Computer Society (IEEE). His personal web page can be found at: http://www-staff.it.uts.edu.au/~chengqi/.

Shichao Zhang is a distinguished professor and the director of Institute of Computer Software and Theory at Zhejiang Normal University, China. He holds a PhD degree in Computer Science from Deakin University, Australia. His research interests include data analysis and pattern discovery. He has published about 50 international journal papers and over 60 international conference papers. He is a CI for 10 competitive nation-level grants (China NSF, 863 Program, 973 Program grants, and Australia large ARC grants). He is served/ing as an associate editor for IEEE Transactions on Knowledge and Data Engineering, Knowledge and Information Systems, and IEEE Intelligent Informatics Bulletin.

Wensheng Zhang received a Ph.D. degree in Pattern Recognition and Intelligent Systems in 2000. He joined the Institute of Software, CAS, in 2001. His research interests are oriented towards Intelligent Information Processing, Pattern Recognition, Artificial Intelligence and Computer Human Interaction.

Carsten Zimmermann, PhD, is an assistant professor of Strategic Management at the University of San Diego, California. He is interested in questions that relate to the role of resources and capabilities in early-stage internationalization, as well as philosophical questions on the legitimacy of 'messiness' in building dynamic capabilities. Parts of this work have been awarded the Best PhD Paper Prize at the Judge Business School, University of Cambridge, for one of the two most outstanding papers combining intellectual excellence with persuasive argument. Zimmermann holds Master and PhD degrees from the University of Cambridge and has worked many years in the strategic management consultancies A.T. Kearney and Capgemini Consulting. There, Carsten was engaged in projects of strategic sourcing, revenue growth and operational effectiveness in Germany, Hungary, Czech Republic, Russia and the United States of America.

Index

A

adaptive quantizer 73
additive smoothing 46
aggregate level 52-54
Apriori algorithm 54
Arbitrary Shaped Clustering Method with Compatible Nucleoids (ASCCN) 219-220, 224-225, 227-229
attribute-oriented induction 75
Australian Research Council (ARC) 155, 287
AVC (attribute-value-count) 74
AVC-group 74
average computational complexity 221, 228
average length (AL) 244, 283-287

B

base cube schema 260-263, 265
Best Incremental Ranked Subset (BIRS) 93
binary equal width method 73
binomial random graphs 1-2, 11, 13, 15
Bisecting region Method (BRM) 69, 75-81, 83, 85-87
Blinkering 75
bookmark similarity graph 4, 9, 11
bootstrap calibrated method 282
bootstrapping 74, 156, 278-283, 286, 288
Bulk uploads 44-45

C

Child-Closure pruning 56, 63
classification accuracy (CA) 16, 66, 88-89, 91-94, 96-100, 102-103, 106, 126, 149, 172, 187, 242, 247, 276
closed sequential patterns 111, 126

closure enumeration tree (CET) 55, 59, 62-63
cluster grid cover 227
Clustering 2, 4-5, 11-15, 73, 89, 92, 98, 100, 130, 145-146, 157, 159, 162-164, 166-167, 169, 171-172, 219-225, 228-232, 234-236, 238-239, 243-244, 246-248, 255
clustering coefficient 2, 4-5, 11-15
Collaborative Tagging 1-3, 16, 31, 34-35, 48, 50, 53
Collaborative Technologies 17
collective attention 19, 32
common bookmark graph 3, 10
common tag graph 3
compatible relation 220, 222, 228
compatible subset 222-224
complex hierarchies 260, 274
compressed sequential patterns 111, 125
Concept-Adapting Very Fast Decision Tree (CVFDT) 176
concept hierarchies 75
Conceptual Map 128, 130-133, 140-143
Concurrent Branch Pattern (CBP) 115, 123-124
Concurrent Sequential Patterns (ConSP) 110, 112-125
confidence intervals 278-288
ConSP-Graph 110, 112, 115-120, 124-125
ConSP mining 110, 112, 120, 124-125
ConSP modelling 110, 119, 123-124
constrained cube lattices 189, 191, 196-197, 211
constrained multidimensional patterns 189-191, 207
contextual distance 132, 135
contiguous sequential patterns 111, 125
Continuous Attributes 69-70, 72-73, 75, 77, 87-89
coverage probability (CP) 135, 283-287
Cumulative Distribution Function (CDF) 21
cut points 70

K

k-core 5, 10-15

k-Nearest Neighbor (kNN) 91-92, 146, 148-150, 156, 234, 239-242, 246-247, 278-282, 286, 288

k-nearest neighbor algorithm 91-92, 94, 96-99, 102-103, 106

kNN imputation 156, 278-282, 286

Kolmogorov-Smirnov (KS) 21

K-tile method 73

L

language modeling 46, 49

lattices 189, 191, 194, 196-197, 202, 208-209, 211-212, 214

Levenshtein Distance (LD) 235, 245

Longest Common Subsequence (LCS) 130, 234, 236-238, 246-247

M

main memory 74, 84, 153, 283

maximal compatible subset 222-224

maximal marginal entropy 73

Maximal Sequence Set (MSS) 113

Maximum Likelihood Estimator (MLE) 21

Medical Informatics 157, 171-173, 277

merging 70, 220-221, 224, 226-229, 231, 277

Minimal Description Length (MDL) 72

Minkowski metric 91-92, 94

Missing at Random (MAR) 149, 280, 283

Missing Completely at Random (MCAR) 280

missing data 147-149, 156, 162-163, 166, 278-280, 282, 288-289

Missing not at Random (MNAR) 280

Missing Values 98, 147-150, 153-156, 163, 177, 278-280

Monothetic Contrast Criterions (MCC) 73

multidimensional database mining 189-192, 194, 196, 198, 208, 211

multidimensional model 249, 251, 274-275, 277

multi-level mining 75

N

National Health and Nutrition Examination Survey (NHANES) 157-159, 162, 165, 167, 170-172

Natural Sciences and Engineering Research Council of Canada (NSERC) 15, 187

nearest neighbor (NN) 96, 99, 129, 145, 149, 279, 281-283, 287-288

neural nets 73

Neural Networks 90, 92-94, 99-100, 188

News portals 53

Newton-Raphson method 70, 76

non-Euclidean norms 91-92

nucleoids 219-220, 224-225, 229

O

one-shot sampling 74

On-Line Analytical Processing (OLAP) 190, 192, 201, 204, 207, 213, 250, 252, 255-256, 264, 271-272, 274-277

Online Behavior 17

Online Community 17

Ontario Research Networks for Electronic Commerce (ORNEC) 187

opinion leaders 30

optimal split points 69-71, 75-76, 85-87

P

page-level navigation patterns 52-54

Partitioning Around Mediod (PAM) 220, 234, 239, 243-244, 246

partitioning methods 220

peer-to-peer (P2P) 174-177, 179-185, 187-188, 231

permute operator 255, 257, 270-272

Personomies 20, 25, 30

Post Sequential Patterns Mining (PSPM) 111-112, 126

power law graph 13-14

Predicative Value Maximization 72

Prune Children 57

Prune subtrees 57

pruning strategy 59, 221

Q

Quality of Services (QoS) 175

quantile binning 72

R

Really Simple Syndication (RSS) 36-37

Receiver Operating Characteristics (ROC) 179-180, 182, 240-243

relevance analysis 75

Resource Sharing 48

Roulette Wheel (RW) Method 95-96

S

Sammon's Error (SE) 91, 94-96, 102-103
sampling methods 6, 74-75, 85
SBS-based applications 17
scatter plots 11
search space 69, 75, 189-192, 194, 196-197, 201, 207, 209-211
semantic component 143, 249-250, 253, 274
semantic domain 128, 130, 136
Semi-Parametric Iterative Imputation Algorithm (SIIA) 147-155
sequence classification 233, 243-244, 246
sequence clustering 145, 233, 246-247
sequence data 233, 240
sequence mining algorithms 234
Sequential Patterns Graph (SPG) 111-113, 116-117, 119-120, 124, 126
sequential patterns mining 110-115, 121-126
Sequential Patterns Post-Processing 110, 126
session coverage (SC) 24, 30, 64-65
shared bookmarks 1
shortlisting 75
SIG distributions 30
SIG patterns 30
Similarity Measures 5, 128, 130-131, 137, 140-143, 146, 162, 222, 230-231, 233-240, 242-246
similarity metric 3, 233-234, 240
snowball sampling 6
Social Bookmarking 1-3, 14-15, 17, 30, 34-37, 42-43, 45, 47-50
social bookmarking data 48
Social Bookmarking Systems (SBS) 17-20, 24, 29-31, 34-36, 47-50
Social Correlation (SC) 24, 28, 30, 64
Social Influence Gain (SIG) 24, 30
social media 17-20, 29-31
social media systems 19
Social networks 1-3, 5, 16-17, 19-20, 22, 25, 31-32, 50
Social Susceptibility (SS) 24, 28-30
Social Tagging Systems (STS) 18, 48, 67
Social Web 19, 21, 47
Social web communities 47
SOM (self-organizing map) 73, 90
Spam Detection 34, 48-49
spamming 3, 34
spam users 35-37, 40, 44-45, 48
spatial analysis 249-251, 253-255, 258, 267, 274
spatial component 250, 252-253, 274
spatial data warehouse 249, 254-255, 271, 273, 275

spatial domain 128, 130, 134, 136
Spatial OLAP (SOLAP) 250-258, 264, 271, 275, 277
Spatial Personalization 128
spatial proximity 128, 130, 133-134, 140-143
SPRINT algorithm 74
stable tags 3
Static discretization 70-71, 75
stream data mining 174-175, 231
Structural Relation Patterns 110-114, 125-126
Subtree pruning 56, 60, 63
Supervised discretization 71

T

tag-based links 2
tag bundles 42, 45
Tagging Network 1, 15, 49
tagging systems 1, 3, 16, 18, 31, 35, 48-50, 67
tags clouds 1
tag similarity graph 4
taxonomy graph 61-62, 66
taxonomy tree 58, 61, 66
transaction identifier (TID) 56, 216
transformation methods 250
tree mining 110-111, 113
Trend Detection 32, 34-36, 42, 45, 49-50
tripartite structure 2
two-stage architecture 174, 177-178, 185, 187
two-stage classifier 174-175, 177, 181-182

U

Uniform approximation 73
Unsupervised Discretization 71-73, 88
User-Centric 128, 130-133, 141-143
User Generated Content systems 19

V

Vector Quantization 72
Very Fast Decision Tree (VFDT) 176
view schema 262-263, 268
Vote-history 20

W

Web 2.0 applications 17-18, 20, 52
Web personalization 52-53, 67-68, 129, 137-138, 140, 145-146, 246-247
WFP-Tree 54, 57-59, 61
windowing 75, 183